Secret Files

Naruto: The Official Fanbook

兵
の
書

Secret Files

Naruto: The Official Fanbook

Table of Contents

SHINOBI MILITARY PICTURE SCROLLS

Kishimoto-sensei poured his soul into these stunning drawings — a top secret pin-up that can only be found here! The map on the back comes in handy when scouting the village!

Countries and Hidden Shinobi Villages 11

Special report on the lands and customs of the countries where the warriors of the ninja world dwell! Top secret maps leading to Konoha!!

Analysis: Konoha Ninja 35

Weapons, equipment, basic styles and societal structures — we examine all aspects of the ninja of Konoha!!

Ninja Files 67

Data on the past and present of five of Konoha's finest!

Top Secret! Shinobi Missions 113

The furious battles of Team 7, as told by Kakashi!

Full Investigation: Ninja Academy 143

Academy principles and curriculum, ninja training and hand signs.

The Creator of *Naruto*: Masashi Kishimoto ... 175

All secrets revealed! Kishimoto-sensei tells everything about himself and the shinobi!

NARUTO 208

The original *Naruto* short story from *Akamaru Jump*! The very first Naruto adventure!!

Fan Pages!

Naruto fans are everywhere! In this Fanbook we show submissions from both U.S. and Japanese fans. These pages are noted with a small American or Japanese flag on the page, and Japanese readers' submissions show their names in Japanese.

Note: Italicized titles indicate Japanese fan pages.

Quiz Time!

Five tests of your ninja abilities...and the truth that awaits you at the end! Unless you can discover the truth, all the gates will not open!

Countries and Hidden Shinobi Villages

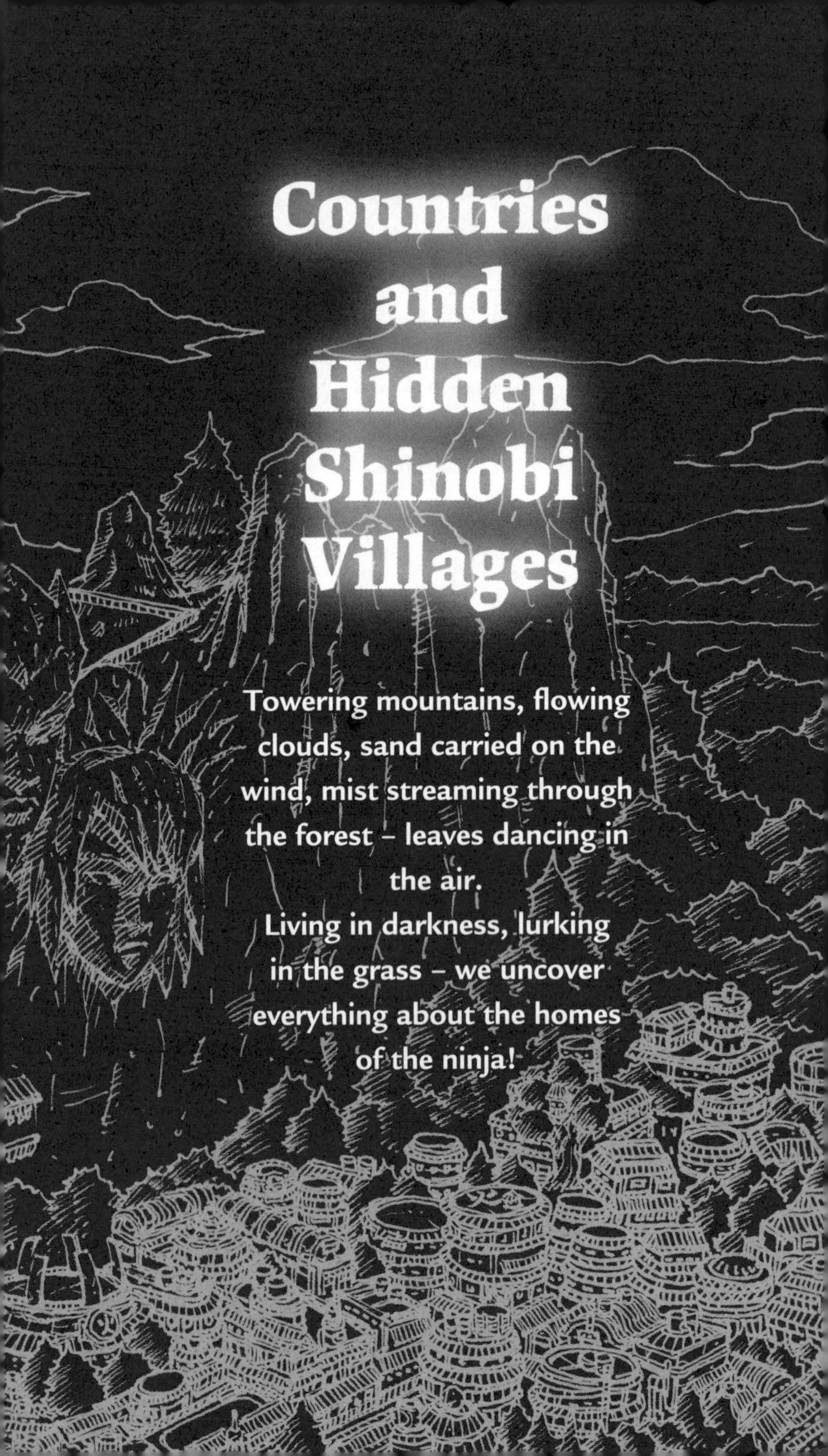

Towering mountains, flowing clouds, sand carried on the wind, mist streaming through the forest – leaves dancing in the air.
Living in darkness, lurking in the grass – we uncover everything about the homes of the ninja!

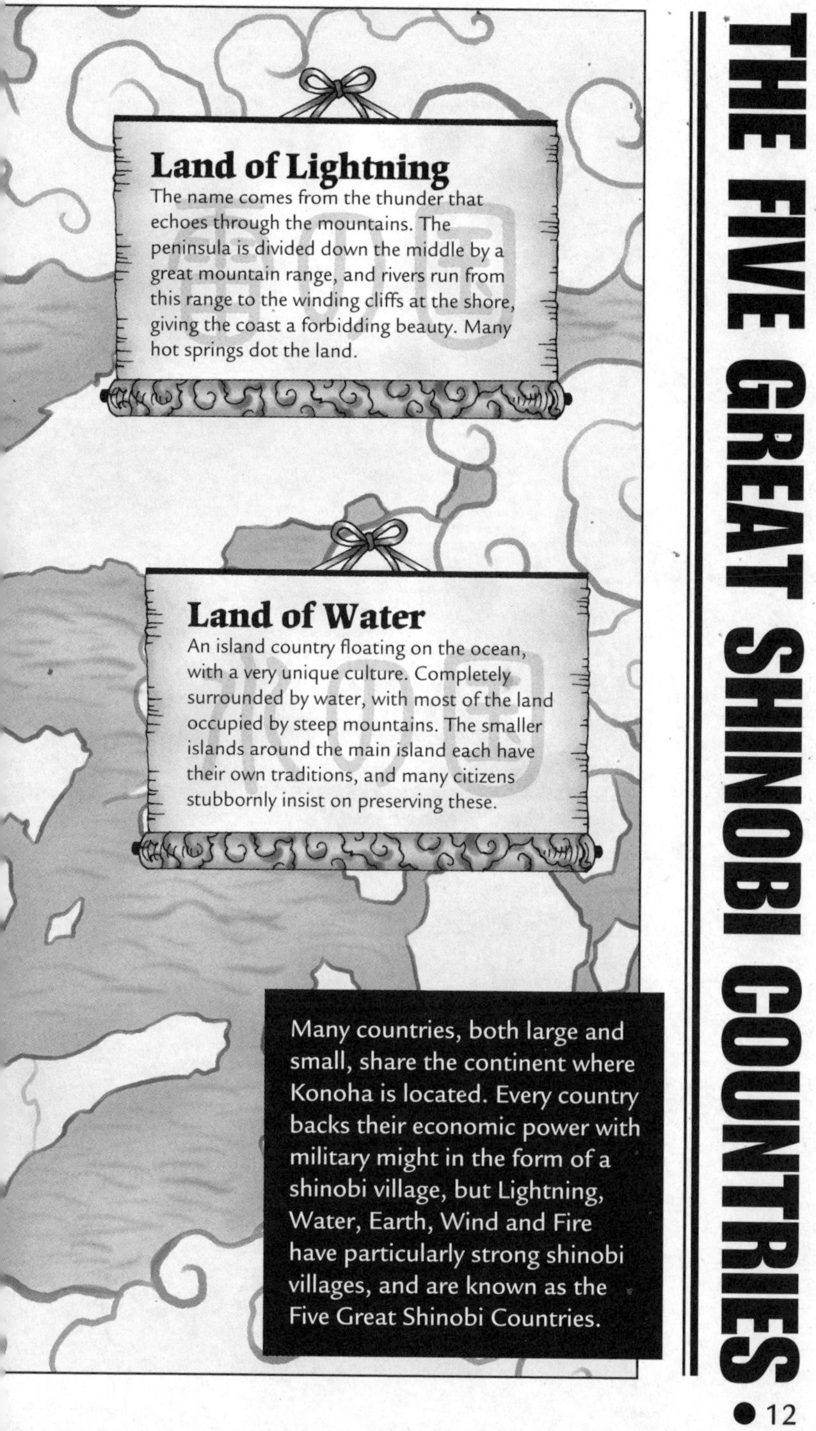

Land of Lightning

The name comes from the thunder that echoes through the mountains. The peninsula is divided down the middle by a great mountain range, and rivers run from this range to the winding cliffs at the shore, giving the coast a forbidding beauty. Many hot springs dot the land.

Land of Water

An island country floating on the ocean, with a very unique culture. Completely surrounded by water, with most of the land occupied by steep mountains. The smaller islands around the main island each have their own traditions, and many citizens stubbornly insist on preserving these.

Many countries, both large and small, share the continent where Konoha is located. Every country backs their economic power with military might in the form of a shinobi village, but Lightning, Water, Earth, Wind and Fire have particularly strong shinobi villages, and are known as the Five Great Shinobi Countries.

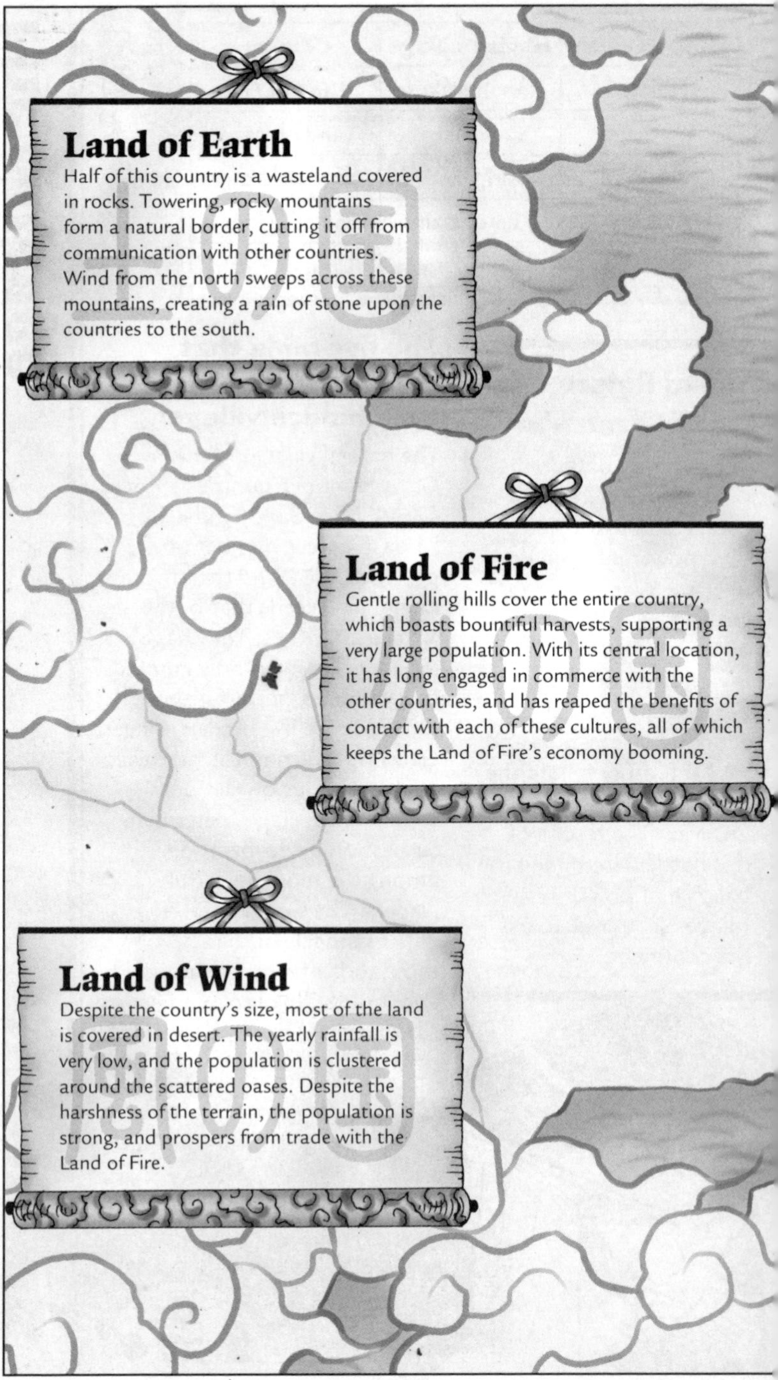

Land of Earth

Half of this country is a wasteland covered in rocks. Towering, rocky mountains form a natural border, cutting it off from communication with other countries. Wind from the north sweeps across these mountains, creating a rain of stone upon the countries to the south.

Land of Fire

Gentle rolling hills cover the entire country, which boasts bountiful harvests, supporting a very large population. With its central location, it has long engaged in commerce with the other countries, and has reaped the benefits of contact with each of these cultures, all of which keeps the Land of Fire's economy booming.

Land of Wind

Despite the country's size, most of the land is covered in desert. The yearly rainfall is very low, and the population is clustered around the scattered oases. Despite the harshness of the terrain, the population is strong, and prospers from trade with the Land of Fire.

The Extremely Powerful Village Leaders

The Gokage

The Five Great Countries and the Gokage

Village Leader	Hidden Village	Country
Hokage	Konohagakure	Land of Fire
Kazekage	Sunagakure	Land of Wind
Mizukage	Kirigakure	Land of Water
Raikage	Kumogakure	Land of Lightning
Tsuchikage	Iwagakure	Land of Earth

The five ninja that stand at the head of each hidden village!

The hidden villages in the Five Great Shinobi Countries - Rock, Cloud, Mist, Sand, and Leaf - boast a great number of powerful ninja, and their military might far exceeds that of the smaller countries. The "Kage" (Shadow) name is only granted to individuals powerful enough to lead those five hidden villages. Generally, the name is bestowed by the previous owner, but some of the villages determine succession by deliberation among the most powerful leaders. The Gogake stand at the pinnacle of the tens of thousands of ninja in the world, and it is not an overstatement to say that these five leaders keep the world peaceful.

Ninkai Daisen – The Era of Great War

The majority of hidden villages took part in these conflicts, throwing all their power into the Era of Great War!! The long battle gave rise to many heroes and resulted in the creation of many powerful jutsu. It also left countless victims and took a terrible toll on the resources of the countries involved. The results of this battle determined the balance of power in the villages scattered across the continent.

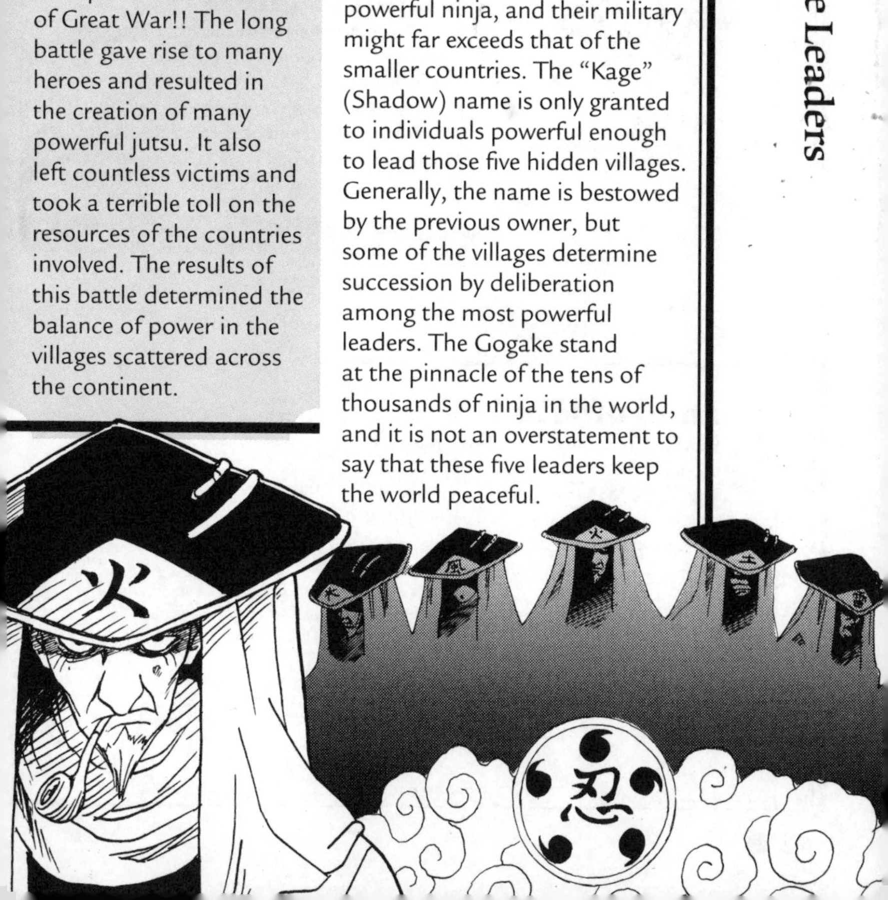

Hidden Shinobi Villages

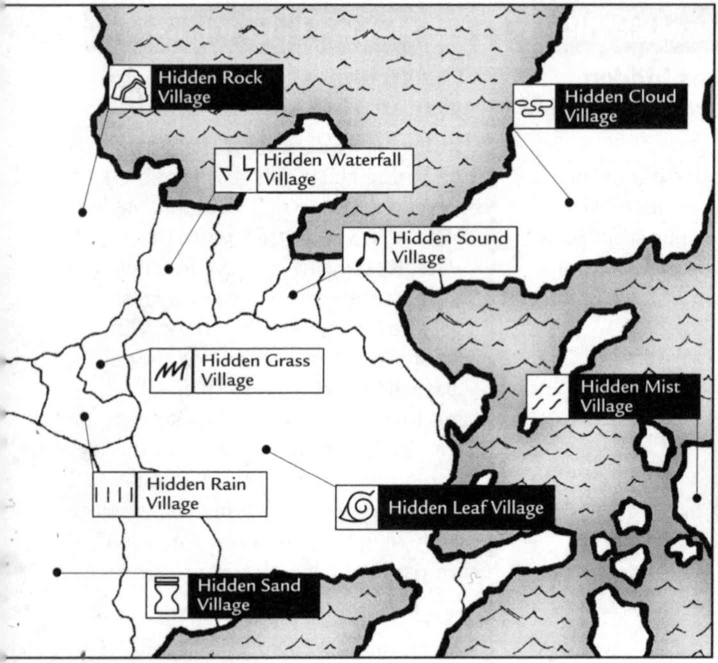
Hidden Rock Village
Hidden Cloud Village
Hidden Waterfall Village
Hidden Sound Village
Hidden Grass Village
Hidden Mist Village
Hidden Rain Village
Hidden Leaf Village
Hidden Sand Village

Relationship Between Country and Village

The *daimyo* in charge of a country protects the villages in their domain from enemy attacks and provides money and other supplies as well. While operating an independent government, the leader of a village also provides military support to the country he resides in. The country needs the villages, since their power can tip the balance in diplomatic relationships, and the villages rely on the country to provide a stable place of residence. The relationship remains equal.

What Is a Hidden Village?

The hidden villages were originally founded when a shinobi family left the city and formed a settlement in the mountains. Once villages demonstrated their strengths in battle, their economy stabilized and ordinary people began to move in, and the villages grew into the modern hidden villages.

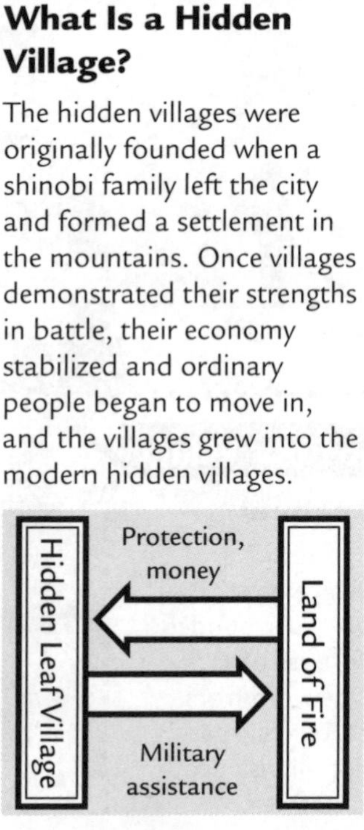
Hidden Leaf Village
Protection, money
Land of Fire
Military assistance

Hidden Mist Village

A mysterious hidden village entirely covered in fog....

Under the leadership of the Mizukage, the Hidden Mist Village ninja live by strict rules. Last year a group of shinobi staged a revolt, but it ended in failure.

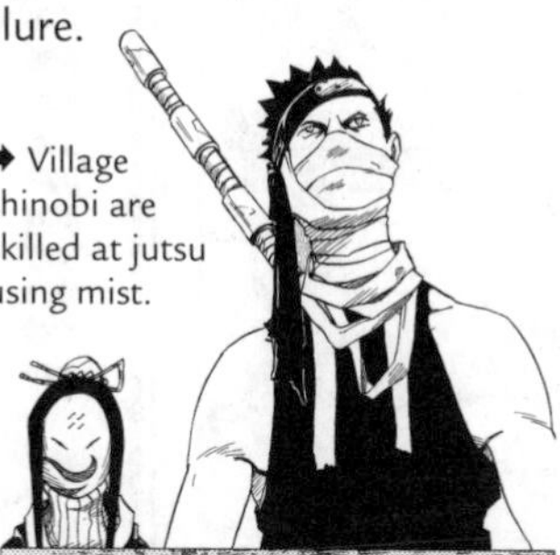

➡ Village shinobi are skilled at jutsu using mist.

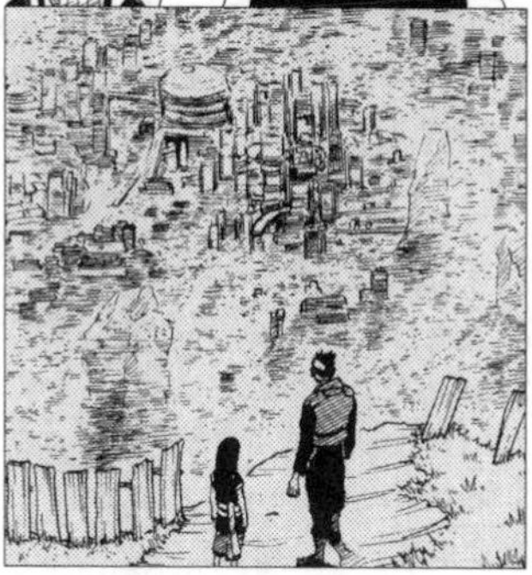

⬆ A mist-covered stronghold, deep in the mountains.

Hidden Rock Village

Rock-solid natural defenses!

This hidden village has the land in its favor - surrounded by a natural fortress of rocky mountains. One word from the leader, the Tsuchikage, and these ninja will risk death without a trace of fear.

Hidden Leaf Village

The strongest hidden village with an elite shinobi squad!!

Under the leadership of the Hokage, the Hidden Leaf Village is extremely successful, possessing great knowledge and skills, and a solid sense of unity. Key to this is a love for their home rarely seen in other villages. Despite living in the harsh world of the shinobi, the ninja of the Hidden Leaf Village are loyal to their village, and love and protect all its citizens like family. The persecution of those with unusual or unorthodox abilities that often occurs in other villages is rarely seen here. This open-minded atmosphere helps the village prosper.

⬇ Many of the Leaf ninja are known in other countries.

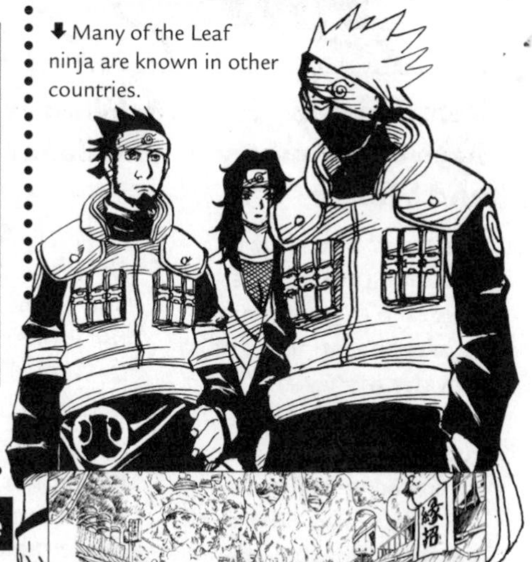

⬆ The village is closely built around the Hokage Rock.

Hidden Cloud Village

A powerful village beneath a sea of clouds.

This village is hidden high in the mountains, covered in clouds. Currently quite friendly with Konoha.

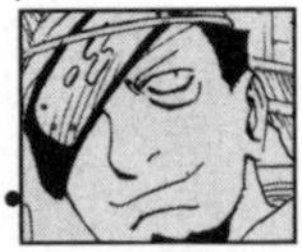

➡ Previous village head shinobi, now deceased.

Hidden Sand Village

The key to raising shinobi lies in the harsh desert that surround them.

The Hidden Sand Village fought Konoha during the Era of Great War, spilling much blood on both sides. The size of their force greatly reduced, they are now concentrating on raising a small number of extremely skilled shinobi.

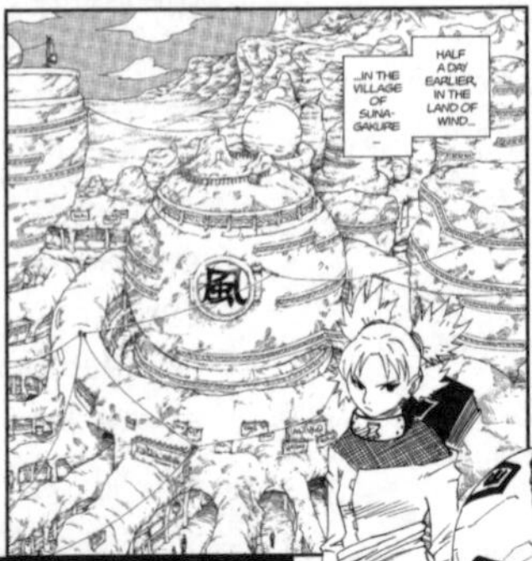
HALF A DAY EARLIER, IN THE LAND OF WIND...
...IN THE VILLAGE OF SUNA-GAKURE

⬇ The Kazekage's own children receive the toughest training.

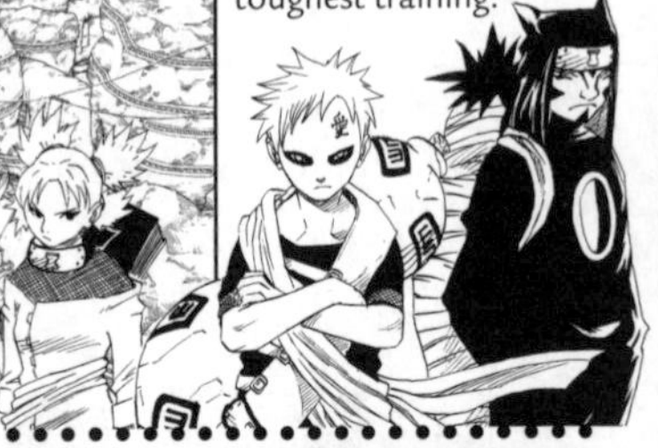

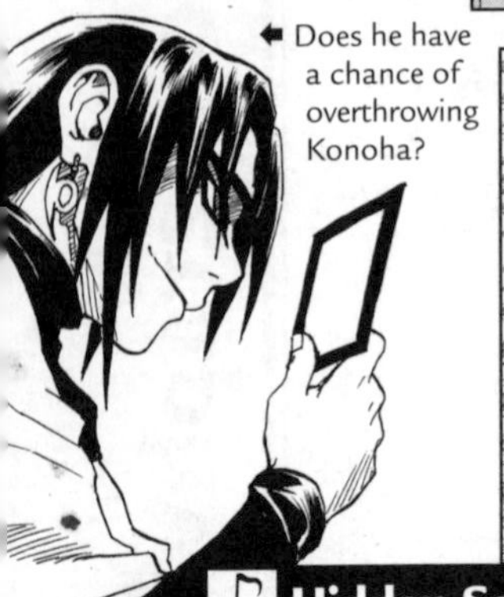

⬅ Does he have a chance of overthrowing Konoha?

Hidden Sound Village

This new force conceals a sinister ambition!!

Orochimaru, a rogue shinobi from the Hidden Leaf Village, recently founded this hidden village. Their numbers are small, but every one of them is powerful, and the strength of this village should not be underestimated.

Hidden Grass Village

Like the wind that plays across the grass, the true allegiance of these shinobi is never certain.

Using their diplomatic jutsu, they read the movements of the larger countries to stay one step ahead of events. They also love to analyze the jutsu of other countries.

Hidden Rain Village

Secluded village known for creating unusual jutsu.

This village pushes their shinobi to the limits of their abilities, creating many unique jutsu. Their assassination jutsu are in great demand by other countries.

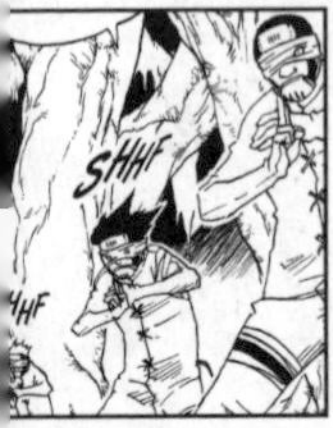
SHHF

⬅ Many shinobi skilled in genjutsu illusions live here.

Hidden Waterfall Village

The giant waterfall prevents invasion!

They are surrounded by four other countries, but take pride in never having been invaded! They are proud of their resilience.

Village Manners and Customs

Konoha Topography

Village Founding and Government

Konoha was founded about sixty years ago. A single highly skilled shinobi quietly gathered other shinobi together in the woods, forming his own unit. Ever since, the greatest ninja in the village has been called the Hokage, leading the ninja and running the village government. The current government is very democratic, and always listens to the voice of the people.

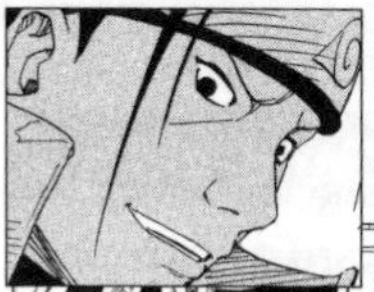

⬅ The First Hokage. Master of many powerful ninjutsu and a strong leader.

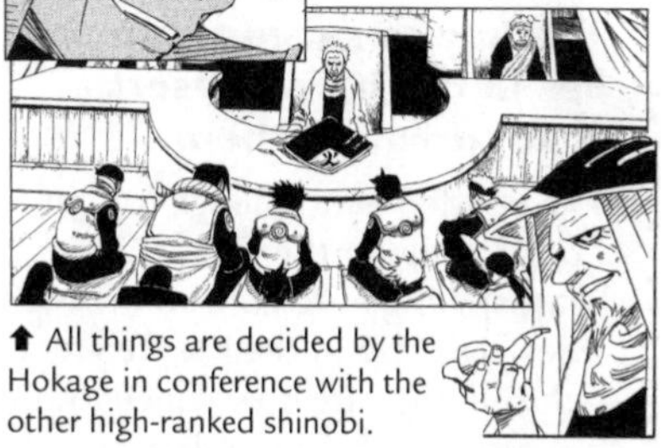

⬆ All things are decided by the Hokage in conference with the other high-ranked shinobi.

Village residents

When the village started, most citizens were shinobi, but to stay alive people gradually engaged in other occupations. Now, with the Era of Great War ended, more ordinary people have moved to the village.

⬇ Non-shinobi residents express themselves through fashion!

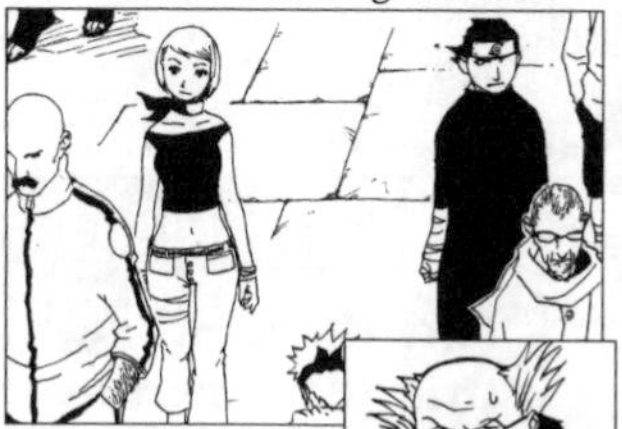

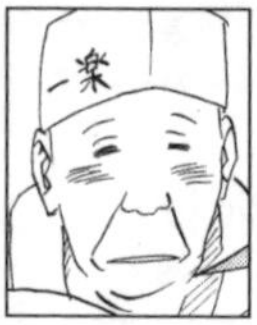

⬅ The owner of Ichiraku Ramen, the most famous ramen shop in Konoha.

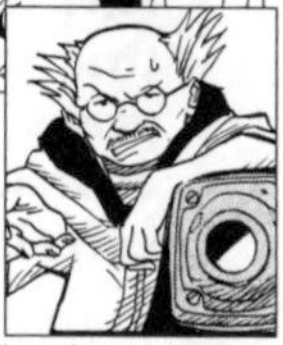

⬆ The photographer in charge of headshots for ninja ID cards.

The Streets of Konoha

Konoha was founded deep in the mountains and surrounded by forest. The buildings are made of wood and stone with an eye toward preserving harmony with the natural beauty around them.

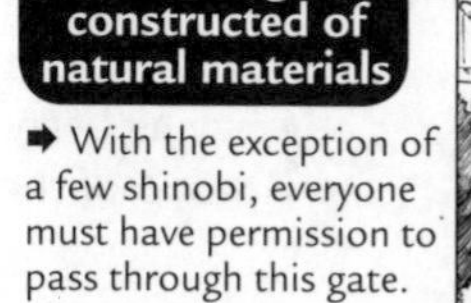

⬅ Lots of green creates a peaceful cityscape.

Buildings constructed of natural materials

➡ With the exception of a few shinobi, everyone must have permission to pass through this gate.

Walls and Gate

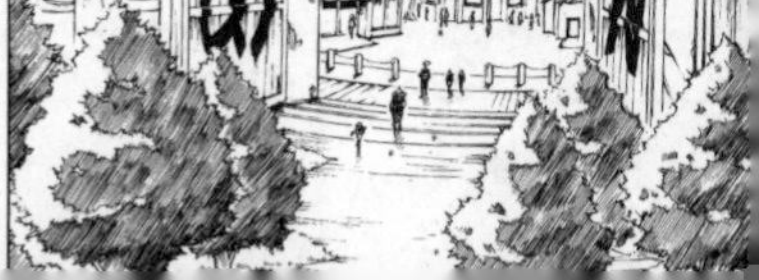

To defend against enemy attack, the entire village is surrounded by a sturdy wall, which is guarded at all times by shinobi. Even the strongest ninja would have trouble getting past these defenses!

The Greatest Tragedy in Village History

The Nine-Tailed Fox Spirit Attack

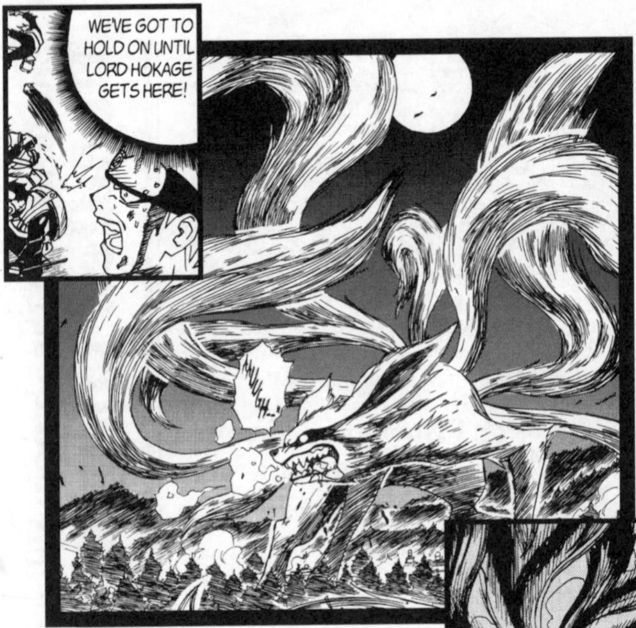
WE'VE GOT TO HOLD ON UNTIL LORD HOKAGE GETS HERE!

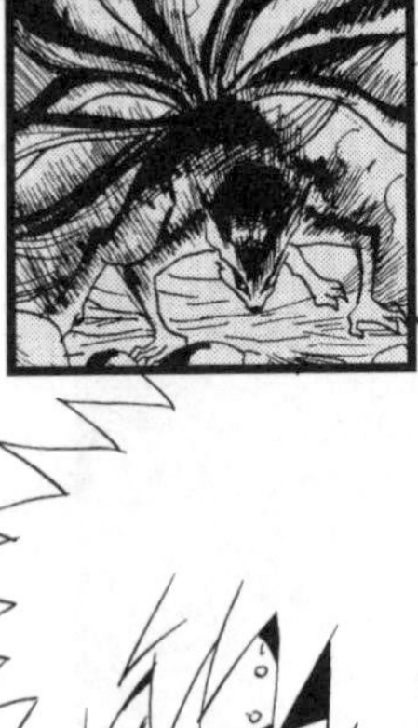

⬆ The tails of this giant appeared to reach the moon, and one swing could level mountains...

The hero who gave his life to defeat the fox

Twelve years ago, after the Era of Great War ended and peace returned at last to the village... tragedy struck. A monstrous fox, with nine tails and strength that could level mountains, attacked the village! It destroyed half of Konoha and claimed many lives but was at last defeated by the Fourth Hokage. In exchange for his life, he sealed the fox spirit inside the belly of a baby.

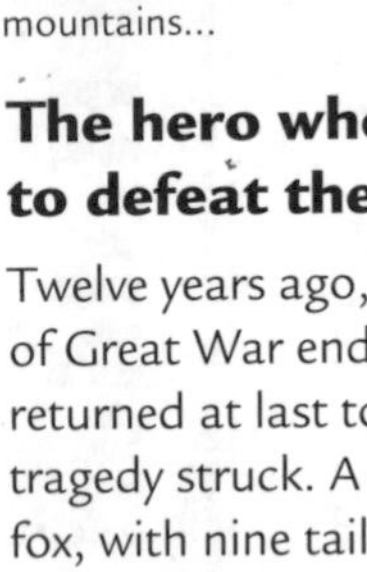

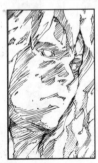

⬅ The Fourth Hokage, beloved savior of Konoha.

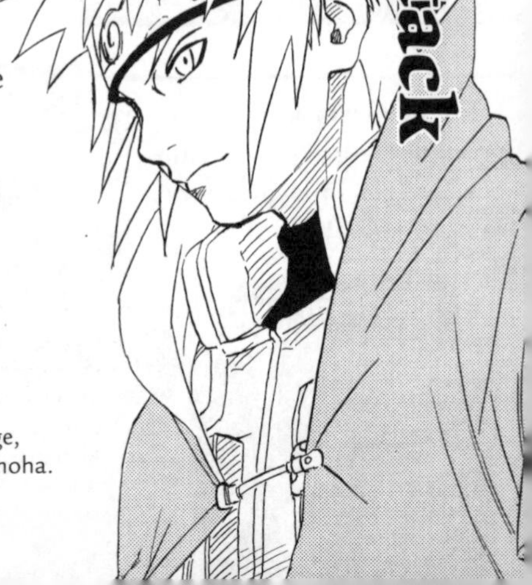

Sneaking into the Shinobi Village!!

Detailed Look at the Hidden Leaf Village!!

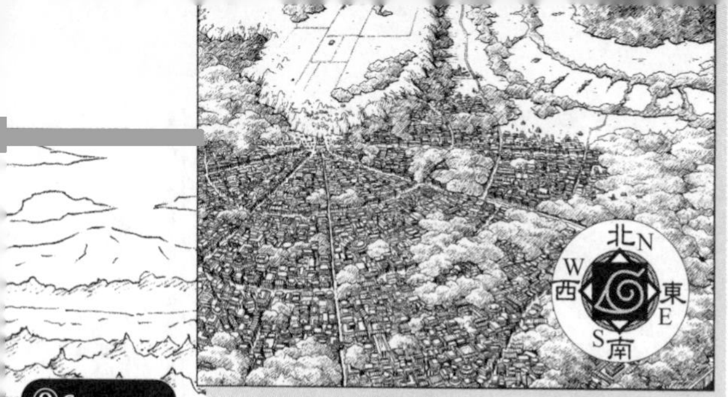

北N
W西
東E
S南

⬆ Long view of Konoha. Buildings are concentrated at the center, trees and earth spreading out around them.

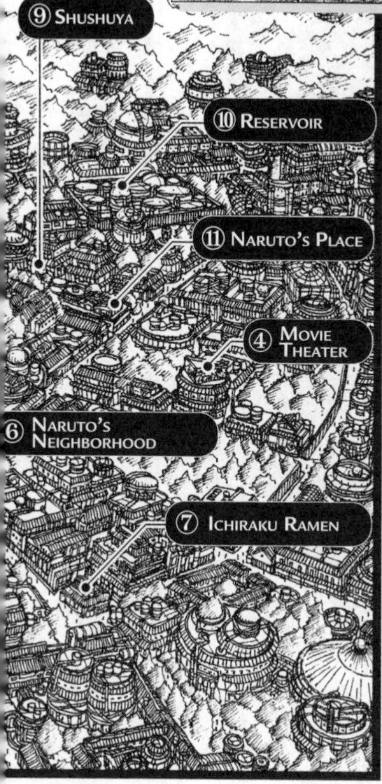

⑨ Shushuya
⑩ Reservoir
⑪ Naruto's Place
④ Movie Theater
⑥ Naruto's Neighborhood
⑦ Ichiraku Ramen

Prosperous shinobi village surrounding the Hokage Rock.

The Hidden Leaf Village is located near the center of the Land of Fire, and the tall mountains and dense forest around it provide natural defenses against enemy invasion. As part of one of the great shinobi nations, it is grand and imposing, far more majestic in appearance than other hidden villages. It boasts a healthy non-shinobi population, and both groups make Konoha more like a big city than a village.

Konoha covers a lot of ground. Here are the castles, practice grounds, and other famous shinobi spots!!

Konoha Hot Springs

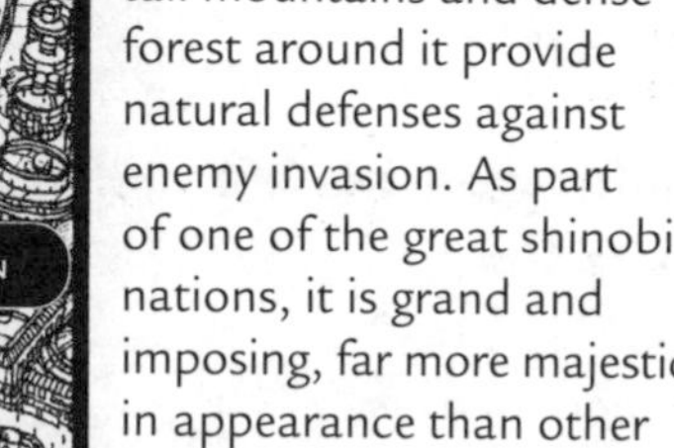

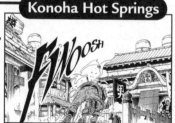

FWOOSH

⬆ Dozens of hot springs help the shinobi relax.

Kikyo Castle

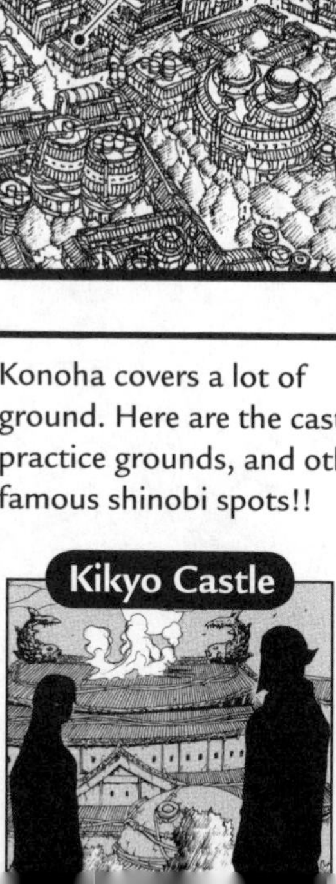

⬅ The castle near the village borders. Site of an epic battle...!!

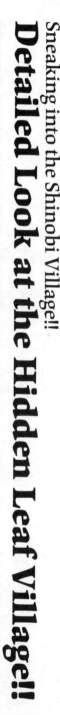

Map legend

The numbers and names on the map link to detailed articles on the following pages, allowing you to find the locations and their features instantly! A color version of the map is on the back of the fold-out poster, so once you know where everything is, you can find it again!

Full reports on central Konoha on the next page!

Complete guide to central Konoha

All the places where Kakashi's team met

Uzumaki Naruto's home!

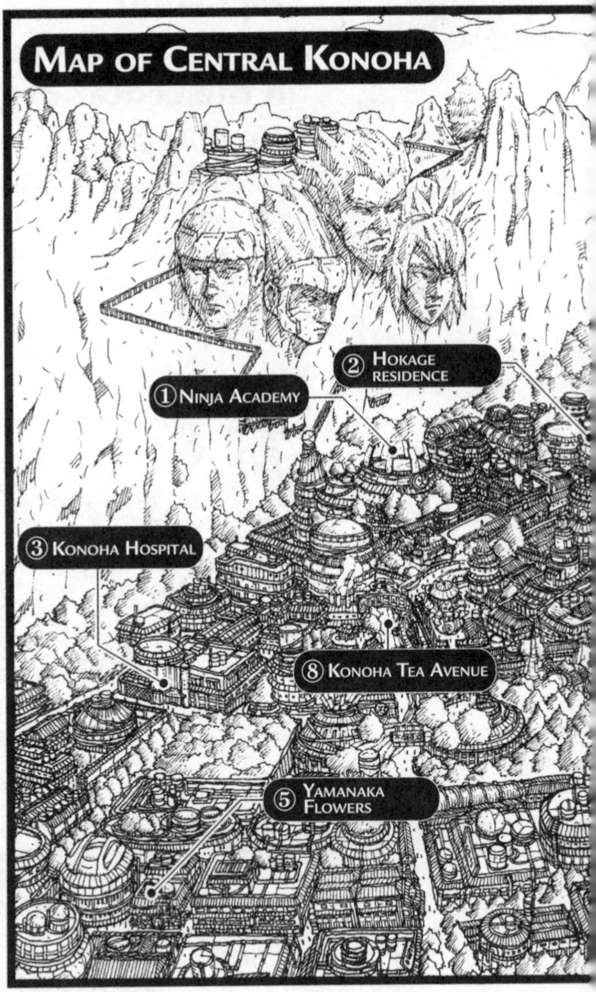

MAP OF CENTRAL KONOHA
① NINJA ACADEMY
② HOKAGE RESIDENCE
③ KONOHA HOSPITAL
⑧ KONOHA TEA AVENUE
⑤ YAMANAKA FLOWERS

—GUIDE TO VILLAGE ATTRACTIONS—

Third Exam main battleground

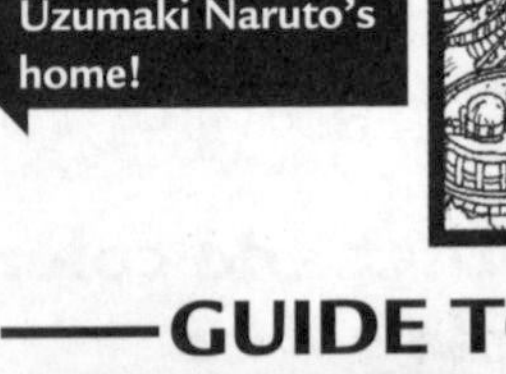

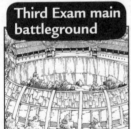

⬆ Battlefield stained with the blood and courage of warriors.

⬇➡ Used for shinobi training and skirmishes. More than fifty exist in different sizes and layouts.

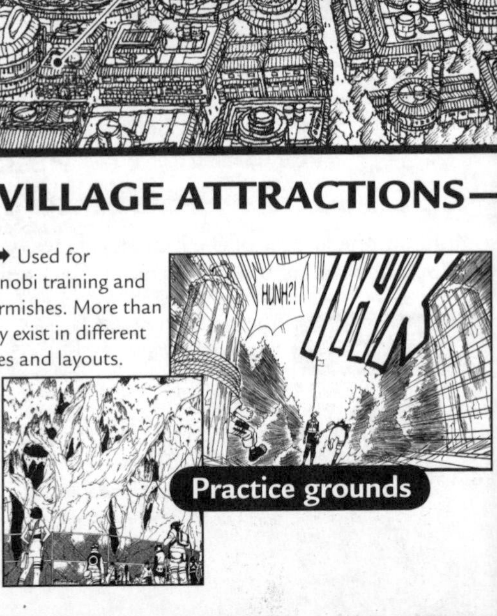

HUNH?!

Practice grounds

① Ninja Academy

Used heavily for both military and domestic affairs. Has been expanded many times to reach its current size.

Important shinobi locations in the center of the village

Many key shinobi facilities are located in the center of town, especially around the base of the Hokage Rock.

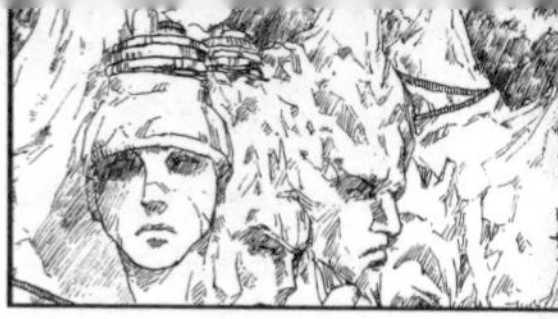

Hokage Rock

⬆Symbol of the village, with each Hokage's face carved into it. In emergencies, everyone assembles here.

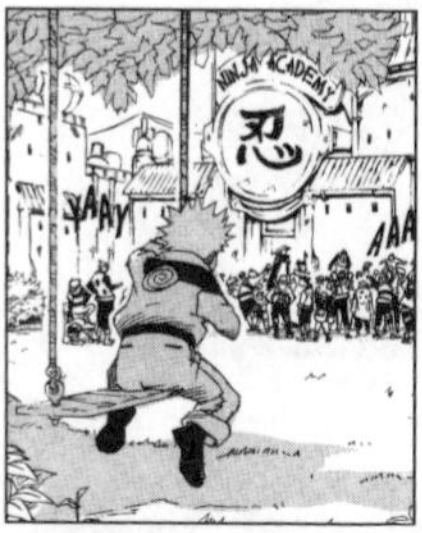
NINJA ACADEMY
YAAY

Swing ⬆ Near the entrance to the education facilities, covered in shade...

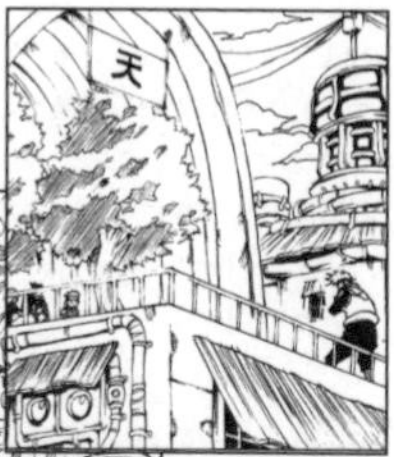

Terrace

⬆ Where Team Kakashi first told him their dreams.

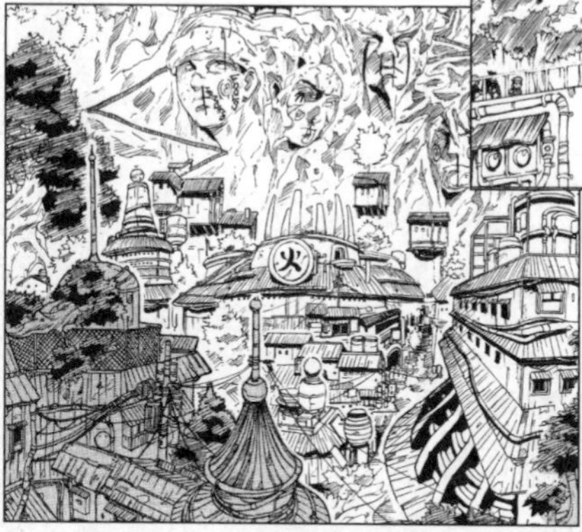

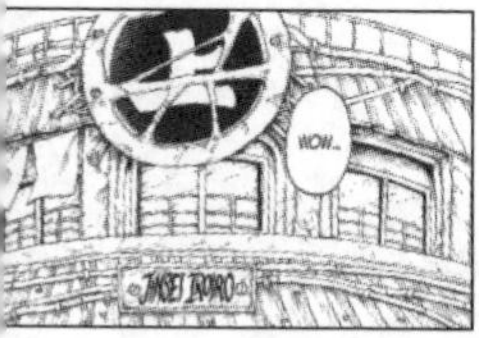
WOW...

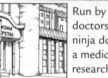

Jônin Station

⬆The heart of the village's power, the jônin stay here when not on duty, waiting for the Hokage's orders or emergencies.

② The Hokage's Residence

Passed down from the First Hokage. Filled with forbidden jutsu scrolls and other top secret documents.

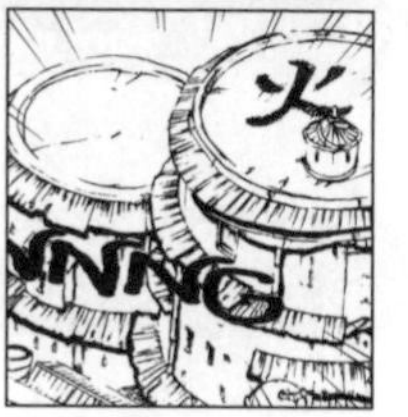

③ Konoha Hospital

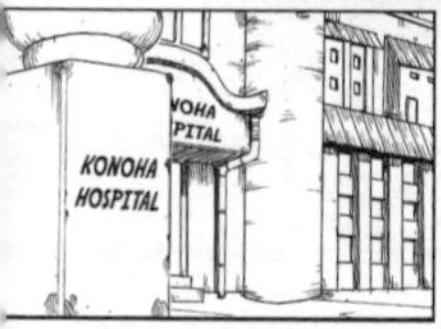
KONOHA HOSPITAL

Run by ordinary doctors as well as ninja doctors. Also a medical and jutsu research facility.

Places that add color to people's lives

Konoha, the largest of the hidden villages, is also a city with a large population and naturally has many places of entertainment.

⑤ Yamanaka Flowers

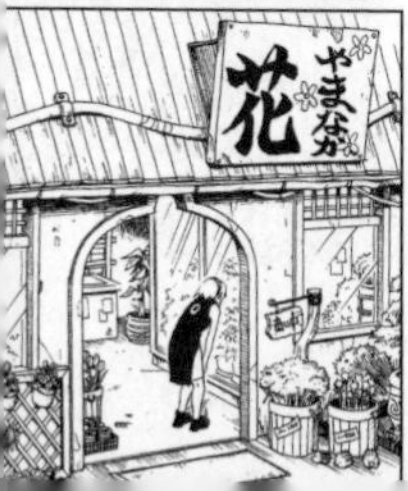

The flower shop run by the Yamanaka family. Like an invitation to the land of dreams, the shop is filled with beautiful colors and scents.

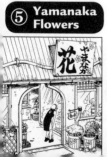

④ Movie Theater

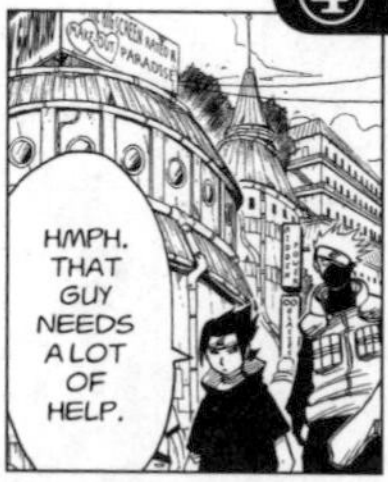
HMPH. THAT GUY NEEDS A LOT OF HELP.

Located on one of the largest roads, this is a popular site for grown-ups. *Make-Out Paradise* sold out for days on end!

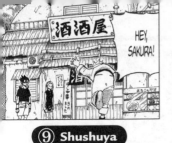

Famous, unique shops!

The best shops in Konoha keep people coming and going.

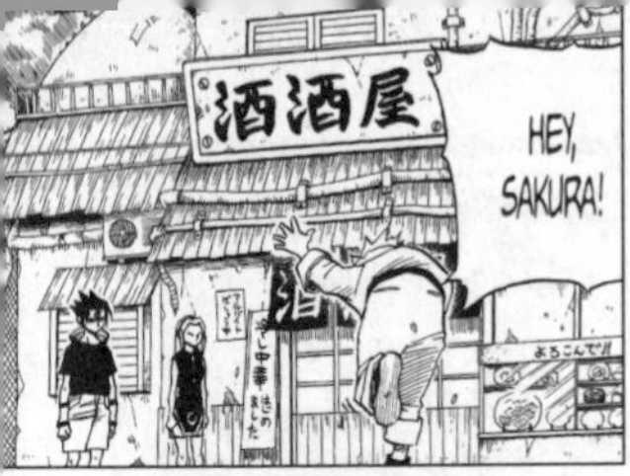
酒酒屋
HEY, SAKURA!

⑨ Shushuya

A Chinese restaurant selling huge plates of food and their own brand of *sake*.

⑧ Konoha Tea Avenue

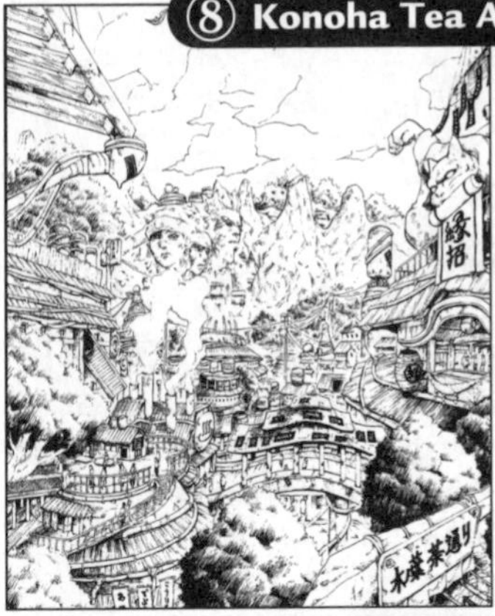

This row of tea and sweet shops has a great view of Hokage Rock!

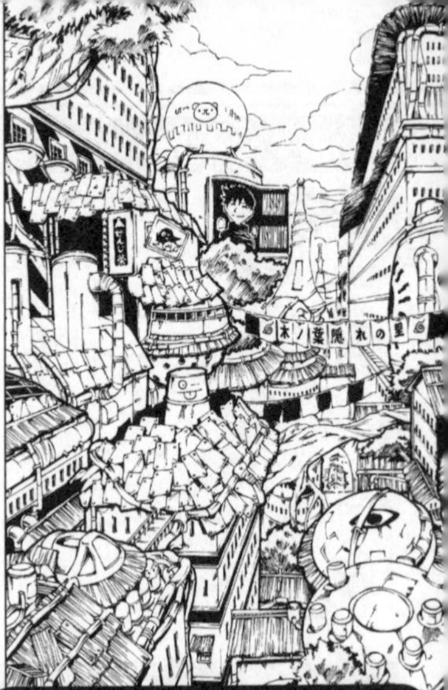

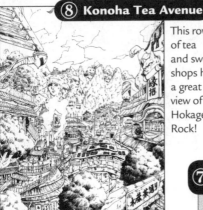

⑥ Naruto's Neighborhood

Near the Academy, always bustling. Many old shops keep it crowded!

⑦ Ichiraku Ramen

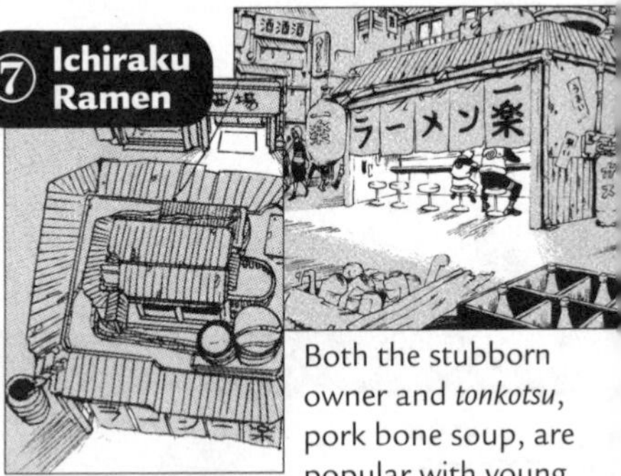
酒酒酒
ラーメン
一楽

Both the stubborn owner and *tonkotsu*, pork bone soup, are popular with young and old!

Amaguriama

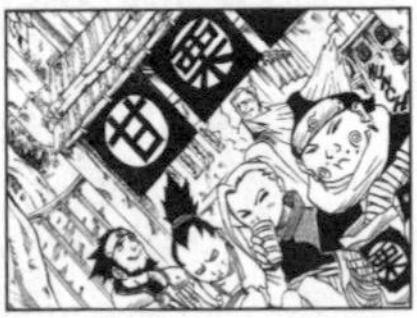

➡A sweet shop on Konoha Tea Avenue. *Kuriyoukan*, chestnuts and sweet bean jelly, and *kuri zenzai*, chestnuts and a sweet bean paste soup made from crushed red beans, and many other sweets!

Famous (?) signs of Konoha

On the streets of Konoha, the most famous or unusual signs make quite an impact!

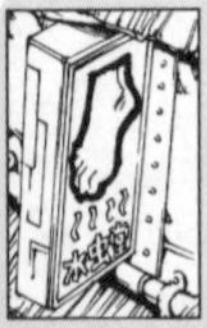

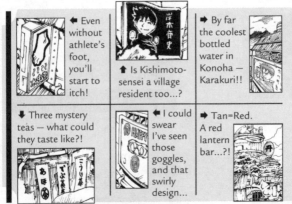

⬅ Even without athlete's foot, you'll start to itch!

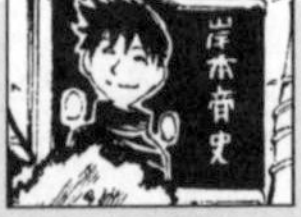
岸本斉史

⬆ Is Kishimoto-sensei a village resident too...?

➡ By far the coolest bottled water in Konoha — Karakuri!!

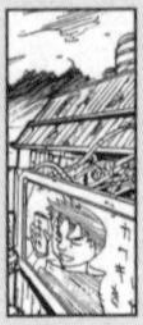

⬇ Three mystery teas — what could they taste like?!

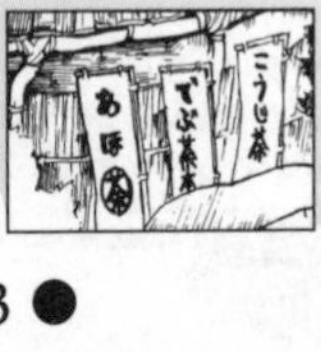

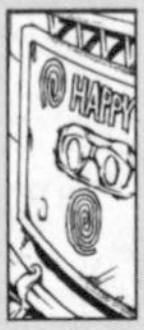
HAPPY

⬅ I could swear I've seen those goggles, and that swirly design...

➡ Tan=Red. A red lantern bar...?!

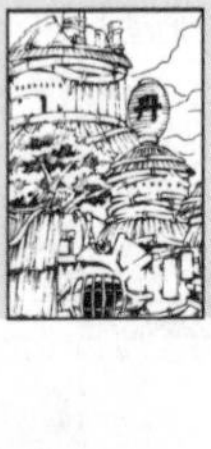

TEAM KAKASHI'S MEETING SPOTS Collection

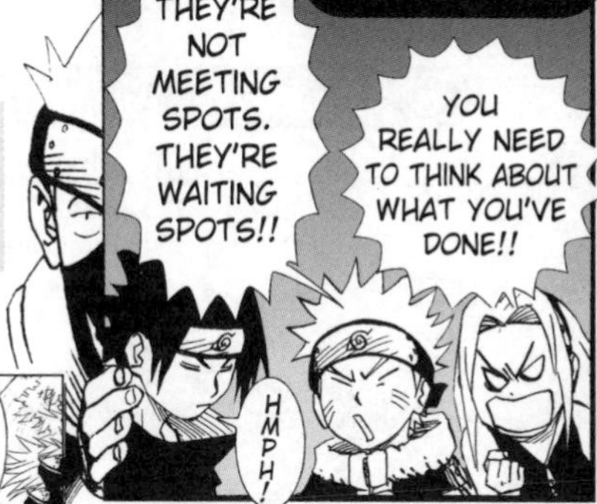
THEY'RE NOT MEETING SPOTS. THEY'RE WAITING SPOTS!!
YOU REALLY NEED TO THINK ABOUT WHAT YOU'VE DONE!!
HMPH!

These places are forever tainted with memories of anger and endurance! Kakashi's flawless excuses are also collected here.

Ninja Academy classroom

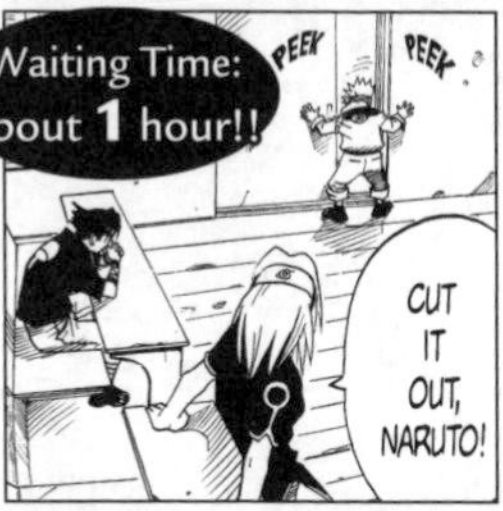
Waiting Time: about 1 hour!!
PEEK
PEEK
CUT IT OUT, NARUTO!

⬅ Where the team first met Kakashi. Naruto's trap was successful...

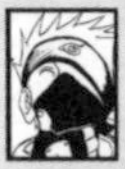

"Based on my first impression, I'd have to say... I hate you!" (Harsh words distract them from the truth!)

Off map: Practice grounds

➡ Survival practice. Had training already begun?

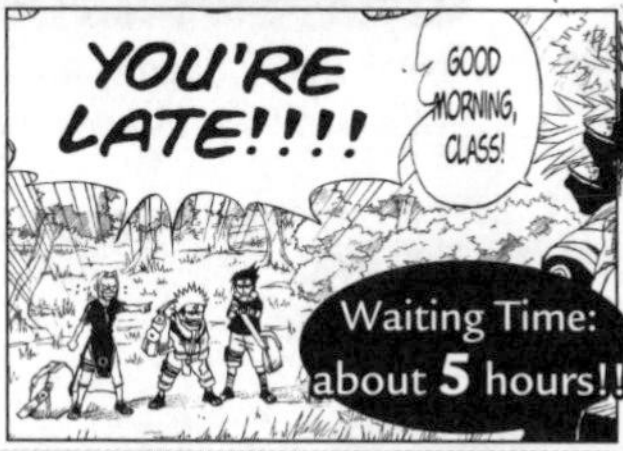
GOOD MORNING, CLASS!
YOU'RE LATE!!!!
Waiting Time: about 5 hours!!

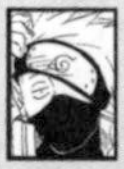

"My alarm clock wasn't working..." (And the alarm clock he showed them was working perfectly.)

Map ⑩ : Reservoir

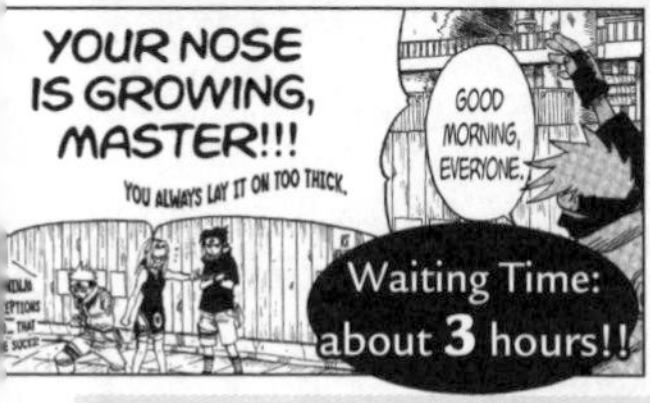
GOOD MORNING, EVERYONE.
YOUR NOSE IS GROWING, MASTER!!!
YOU ALWAYS LAY IT ON TOO THICK.
Waiting Time: about 3 hours!!

⬅ Three hours, just before their mission... the real reason their teamwork failed?

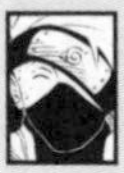

"I'm afraid I got lost on the way here..." (His Sharingan can't prevent his getting lost?)

Off map: Konoha Main Gate

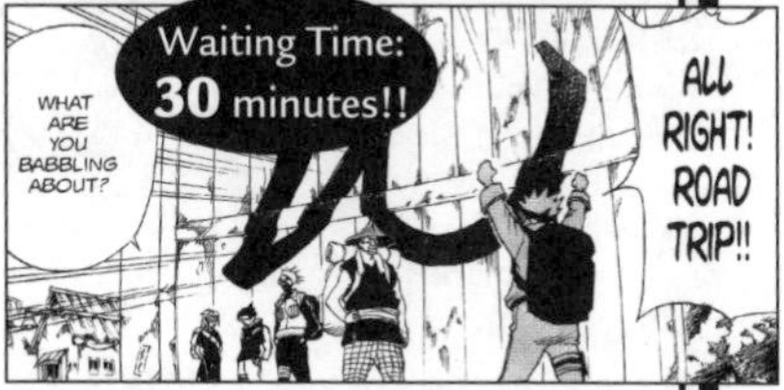
ALL RIGHT! ROAD TRIP!!
Waiting Time: 30 minutes!!
WHAT ARE YOU BABBLING ABOUT?

⬆ Heading to the Land of Waves. Is that why he arrived so quickly?

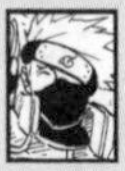

"It took so long to pack..." (Kakashi had the least baggage of anyone)

Off map: On the bridge

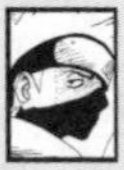

"Today, I wandered a bit from the path of life..." (*Life is a Rose-Colored Maze!* by Jiraiya)

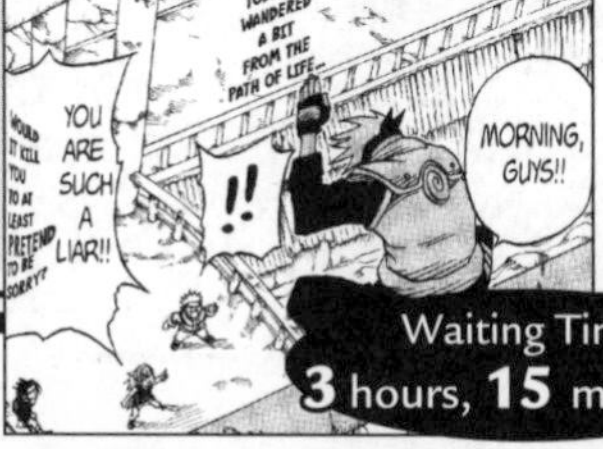
TODAY, I WANDERED A BIT FROM THE PATH OF LIFE...
MORNING, GUYS!!
YOU ARE SUCH A LIAR!!
!!
Waiting Time: 3 hours, 15 minutes!!

⬅ He informed them that he'd recommended them for the Chûnin Exam, and they were finished in a few minutes...

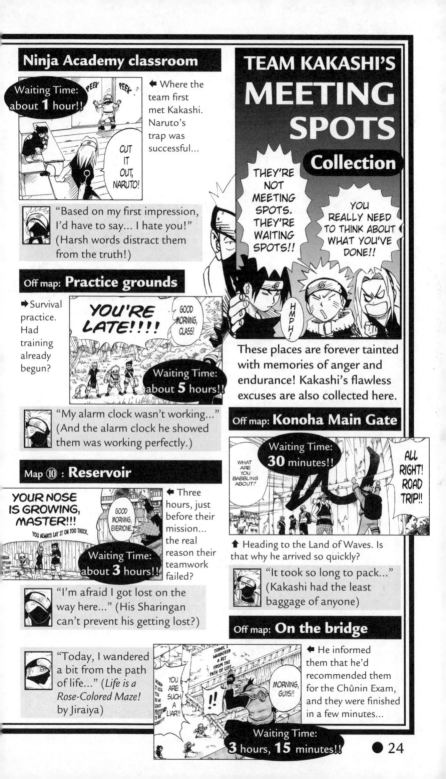

MUNCH
MUNCH

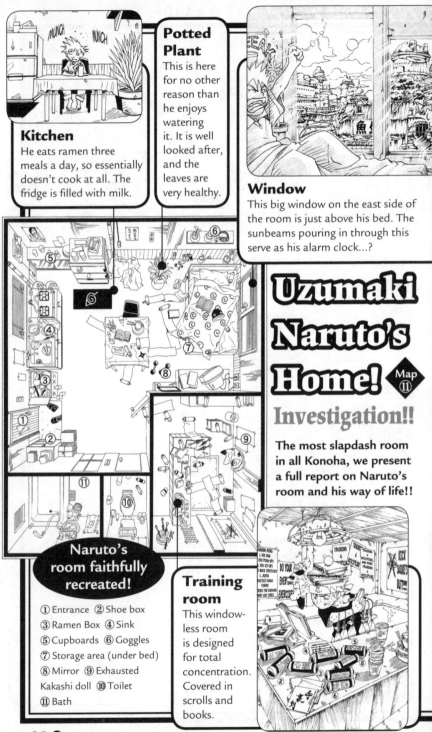

Kitchen
He eats ramen three meals a day, so essentially doesn't cook at all. The fridge is filled with milk.

Potted Plant
This is here for no other reason than he enjoys watering it. It is well looked after, and the leaves are very healthy.

Window
This big window on the east side of the room is just above his bed. The sunbeams pouring in through this serve as his alarm clock...?

Uzumaki Naruto's Home! Investigation!!

Map ⑪

The most slapdash room in all Konoha, we present a full report on Naruto's room and his way of life!!

①
②
③
④
⑤
⑥
⑦
⑧
⑨
⑩
⑪

Naruto's room faithfully recreated!

① Entrance ② Shoe box
③ Ramen Box ④ Sink
⑤ Cupboards ⑥ Goggles
⑦ Storage area (under bed)
⑧ Mirror ⑨ Exhausted Kakashi doll ⑩ Toilet
⑪ Bath

Training room
This windowless room is designed for total concentration. Covered in scrolls and books.

DO YOUR EVERYDAY EXERCISES
KICK SASUKE'S BUTT!!!!

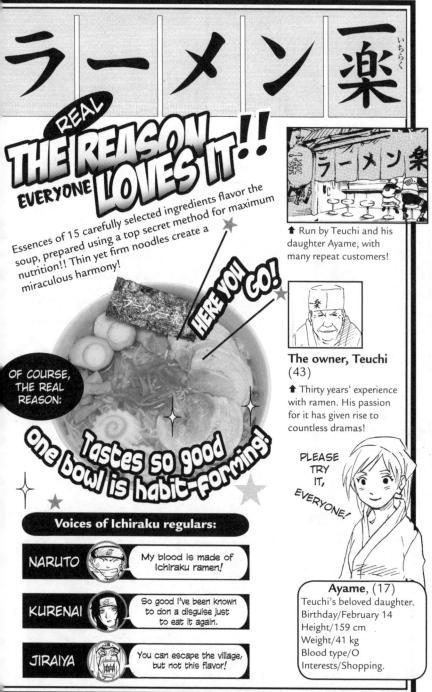

ラーメン一楽

いちらく

THE REAL REASON EVERYONE LOVES IT!!

Essences of 15 carefully selected ingredients flavor the soup, prepared using a top secret method for maximum nutrition!! Thin yet firm noodles create a miraculous harmony!

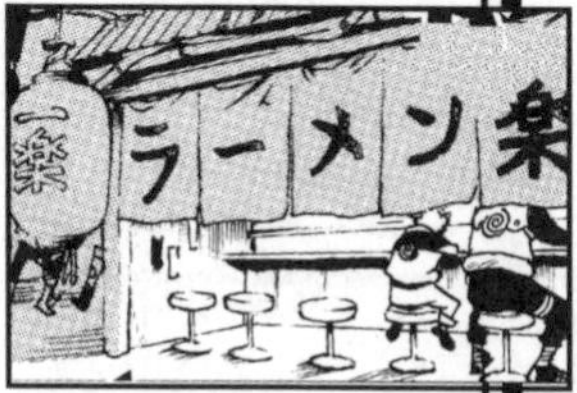
一楽
ラーメン一楽

⬆ Run by Teuchi and his daughter Ayame, with many repeat customers!

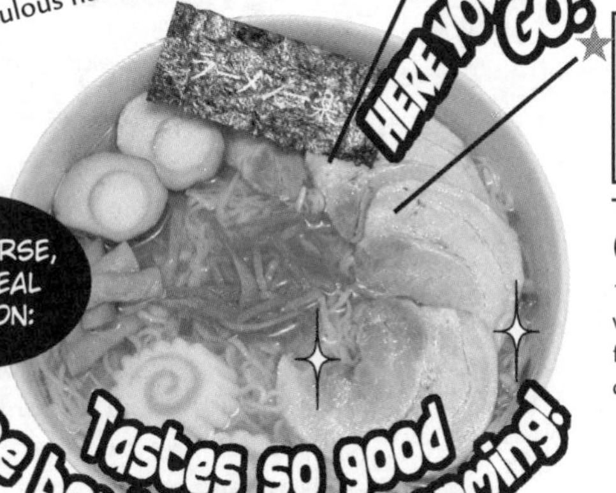
HERE YOU GO!

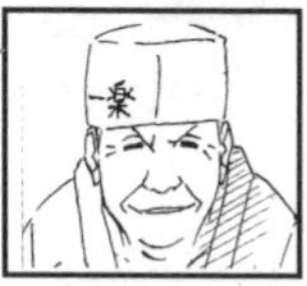

The owner, Teuchi (43)

⬆ Thirty years' experience with ramen. His passion for it has given rise to countless dramas!

OF COURSE, THE REAL REASON:

Tastes so good one bowl is habit-forming!

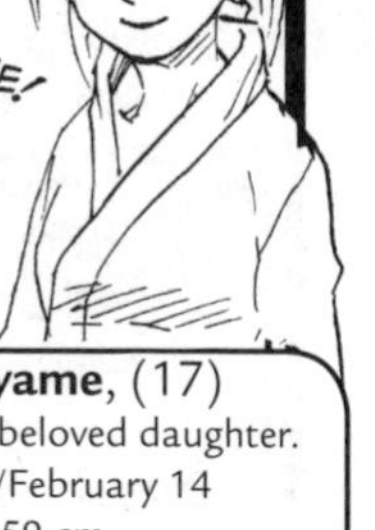
PLEASE TRY IT, EVERYONE!

Voices of Ichiraku regulars:

NARUTO 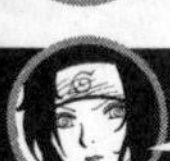 My blood is made of Ichiraku ramen!

KURENAI 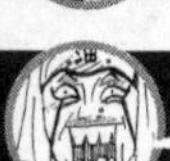 So good I've been known to don a disguise just to eat it again.

JIRAIYA 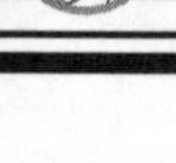 You can escape the village, but not this flavor!

Ayame, (17)
Teuchi's beloved daughter.
Birthday/February 14
Height/159 cm
Weight/41 kg
Blood type/O
Interests/Shopping.

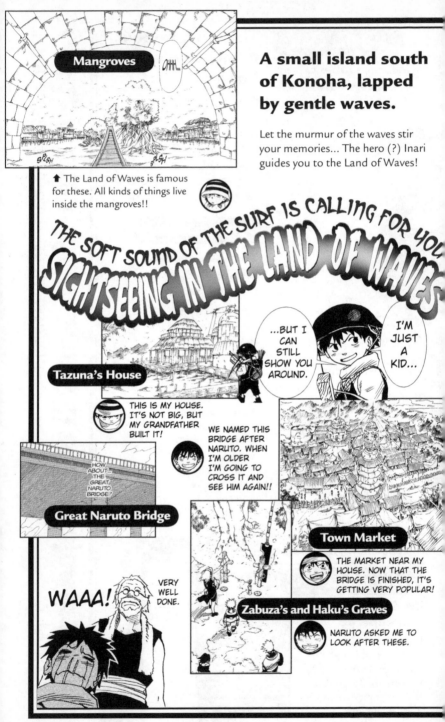

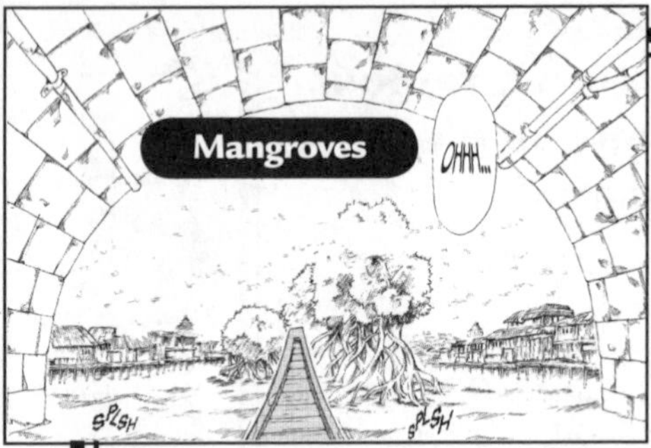
Mangroves
OHHH...
SPLSH
SPLSH

A small island south of Konoha, lapped by gentle waves.

Let the murmur of the waves stir your memories... The hero (?) Inari guides you to the Land of Waves!

⬆ The Land of Waves is famous for these. All kinds of things live inside the mangroves!!

THE SOFT SOUND OF THE SURF IS CALLING FOR YOU

SIGHTSEEING IN THE LAND OF WAVES

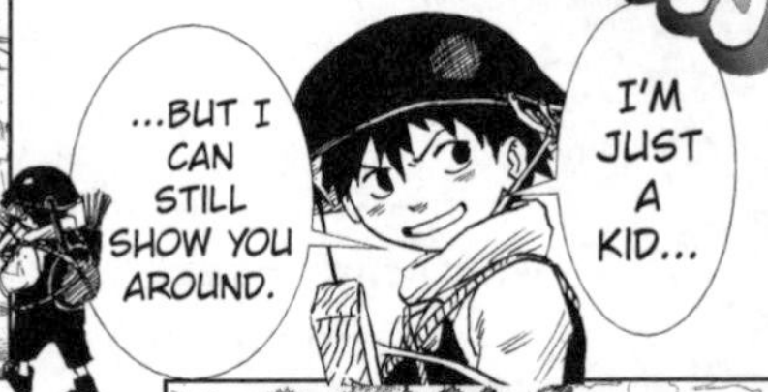
I'M JUST A KID...
...BUT I CAN STILL SHOW YOU AROUND.

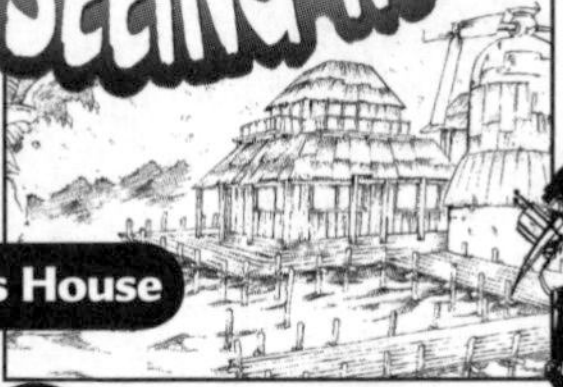
Tazuna's House

THIS IS MY HOUSE. IT'S NOT BIG, BUT MY GRANDFATHER BUILT IT!

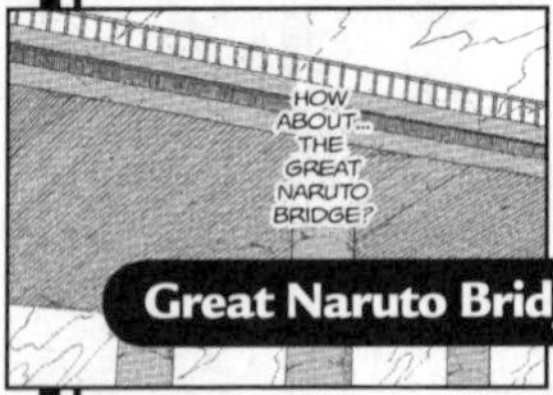
HOW ABOUT... THE GREAT NARUTO BRIDGE?
Great Naruto Bridge

WE NAMED THIS BRIDGE AFTER NARUTO. WHEN I'M OLDER I'M GOING TO CROSS IT AND SEE HIM AGAIN!!

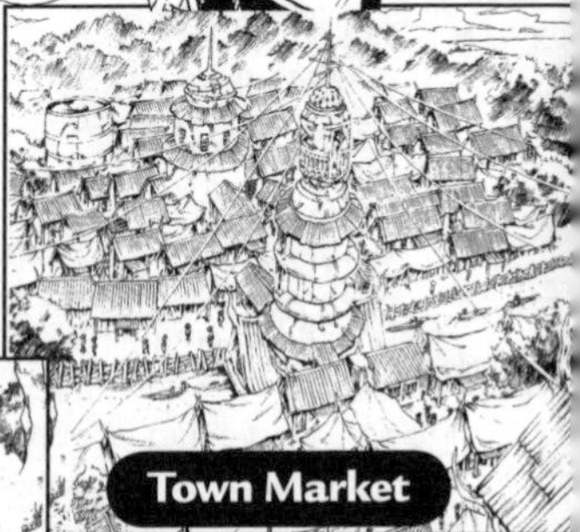
Town Market

THE MARKET NEAR MY HOUSE. NOW THAT THE BRIDGE IS FINISHED, IT'S GETTING VERY POPULAR!

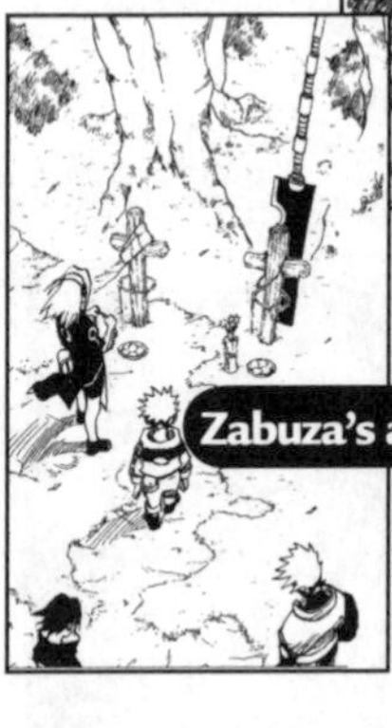
Zabuza's and Haku's Graves

NARUTO ASKED ME TO LOOK AFTER THESE.

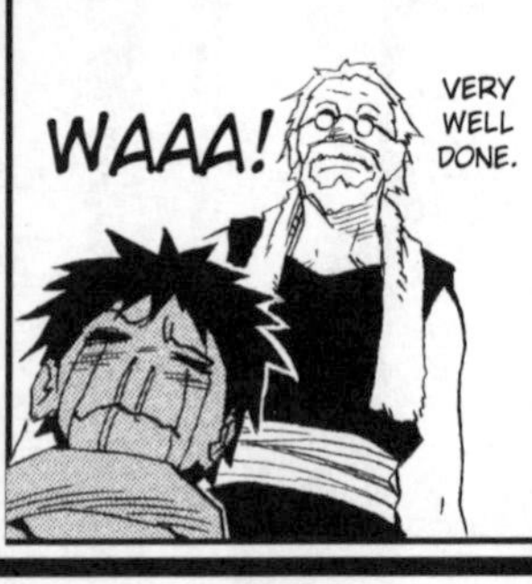
VERY WELL DONE.
WAAA!

Guide to the Hidden Leaf Village's Major Families!

Their name alone earns them respect!!

The most famous names in all Konoha!

Brilliance granted by the heavens, secrets honed on the earth – clans linked by blood and tradition. Their fame has spread for thousands of leagues, yet we are proud to call them home to Konoha...

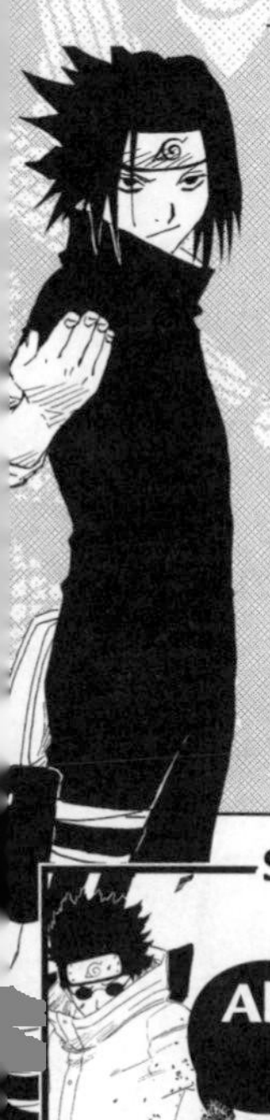

Uchiha Clan

Incomparable talent — blood-drenched tragedy

The Sharingan and their fearsome fighting ability once made them famous in and out of Konoha. But the entire family was slaughtered by one of their own, Itachi. Now the name is one of blood-soaked tragedy, with only Itachi and his brother Sasuke to carry it...

Hyuga Clan

Konoha's oldest family — Byakugan and iron rules

The Byakugan, the All-Seeing Eye, lies in the blood of this family. The Gentle Fist Technique created by the founder of the Hyuga clan is known to be the strongest taijutsu in the village. They have split into main and branch families, protecting their bloodline with strict regulations.

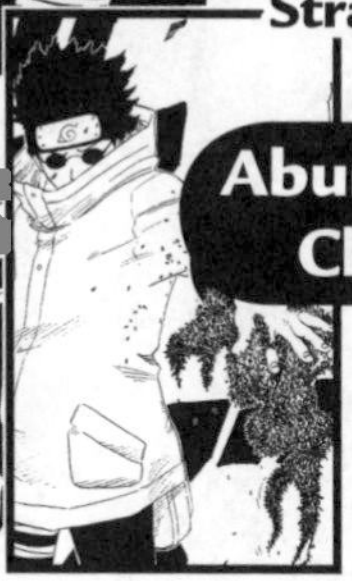

Aburame Clan

Strange insect masters

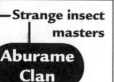

An uncanny family known for harboring countless insects inside their bodies, a technique known as the Kikaichu. They leave most of the fighting to these insects.

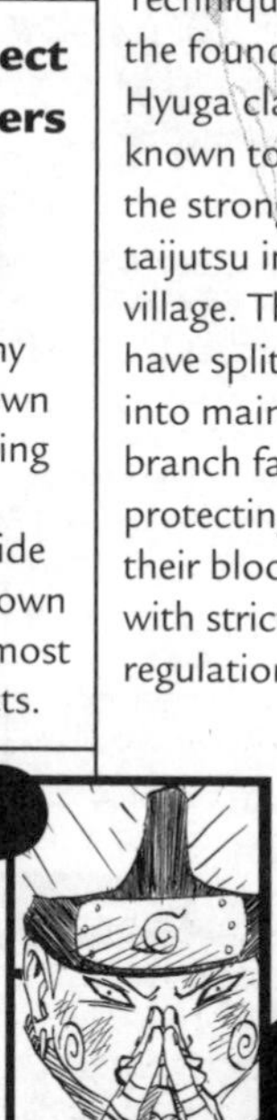

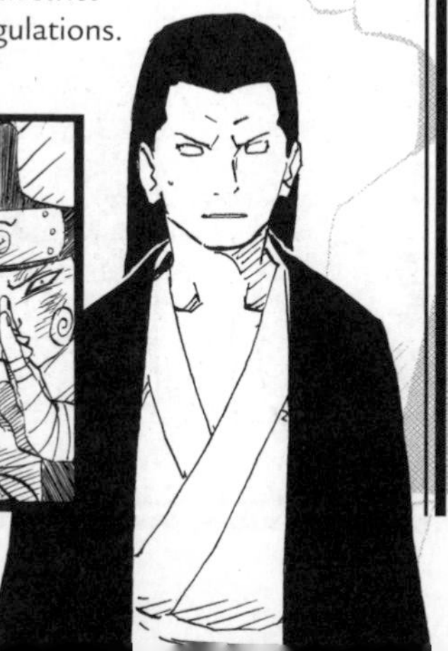

Akimichi Clan

Traditional figure and appetite

Blessed with plump physiques and insatiable appetites. Their digestive systems are designed to take in far more than any normal human's.

Secret Fighting Technique: Rotation
Hyuga Clan

⬆ The combination of the Byakugan with the clan fighting techniques creates an unbreakable defense.

Byakugan
Hyuga Clan

⬆ Hyuga's inherited trait, *kekkei genkai*, allows the user to see for great distances and read the flow of chakra inside the body.

The source of their fame — the secret abilities, passed down...

Honed by the founder of the clan, protected by blood and tradition. Acquired through great physical sacrifice, these techniques give their names luster.

➡ This technique allows them to enlarge their own bodies to attack. Uses a large amount of calories.

Baika no Jutsu: The Art of Expansion
Akimichi Clan

Kikaichu no Jutsu
Aburame Clan

⬆ Secret techniques allow them to control insects and make use of their special abilities. Skilled at reconnaissance and information gathering.

Sharingan
Uchiha Clan

⬆ Uchiha's inherited trait. Reads and reproduces any techniques.

Clan Sayings

Firm beliefs and mental strength far beyond what the knowledge of secret techniques can bestow...what can we learn from the words of the youth of the clans?

Hyuga Neji	"Each person's life consists only of being swept along in the inescapable current of his destiny..."

Neji saw the destiny of the branch family in his father's death and lost all hope. But ironically, it was his blood that carried the Hyuga's genius...

Hyuga Hinata	"The person I've admired for so long... is finally watching me, and... and in front of him... I can't bear to look uncool!!"

Born as the heir to the main Hyuga family, Hinata has struggled with her own lack of talent. It was Naruto's boundless self-confidence that gave her light.

Aburame Shino	"I am a member of Konoha's Aburame Clan...no matter how puny a bug our opponent is, we don't mock them... we face them full strength!"

You can see the clan's pride reflected in this young bug-master's words. More than anyone else, he knows the true strength of the most powerless insect.

Akimichi Choji	"I'm not fat! I'm pleasingly plump!"

The word "fat" sends him into a rage because his large stature is proof of his family's pride

Uchiha Sasuke	"On the path I walk, I have to do whatever it takes to gain power... even if it means selling my flesh to the devil."

His brother slaughtered his family, leaving only Sasuke alive. Sasuke's only goal is to kill his brother. The fate of his blood is too sad to call ambition...

FANTASTIC FAN ART

An amazing display of artistic skills came in from dedicated *Naruto* fans from around the country! There're so many, we've spread them throughout the Fanbook!

NARUTO 01 Fan

Jill, TX
⬅ Sasuke looks so relaxed.

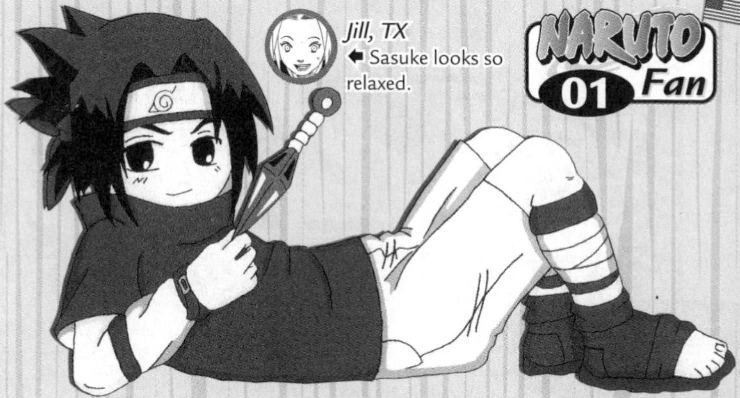

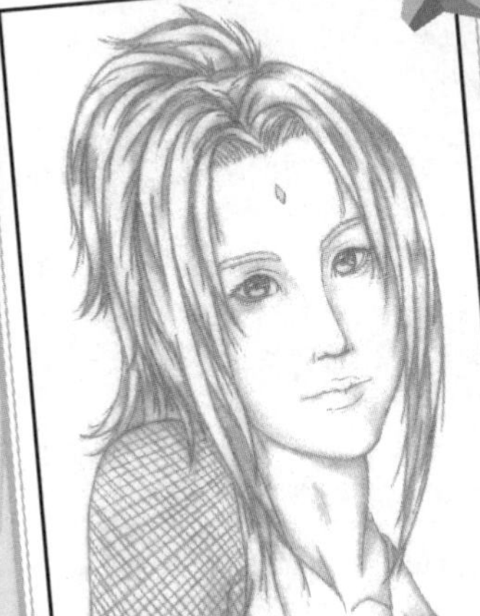

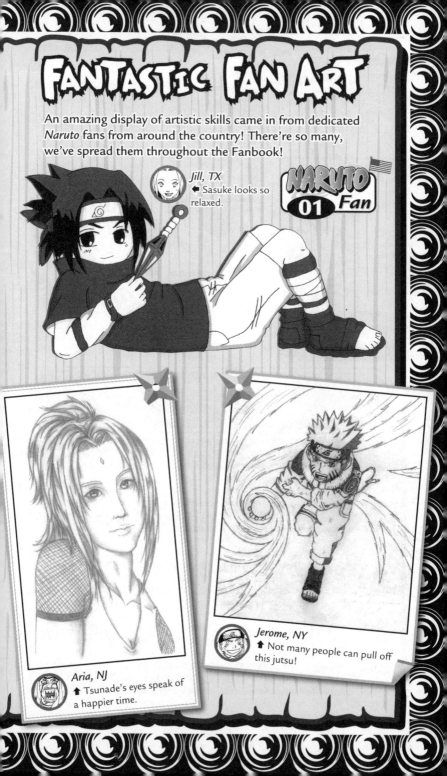

Aria, NJ
⬆ Tsunade's eyes speak of a happier time.

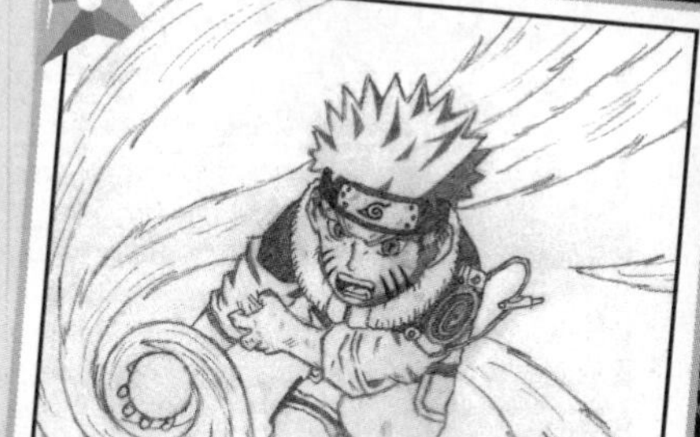

Jerome, NY
⬆ Not many people can pull off this jutsu!

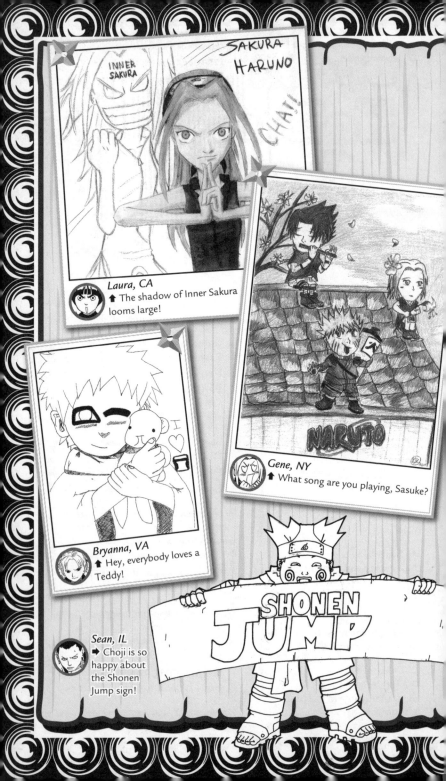

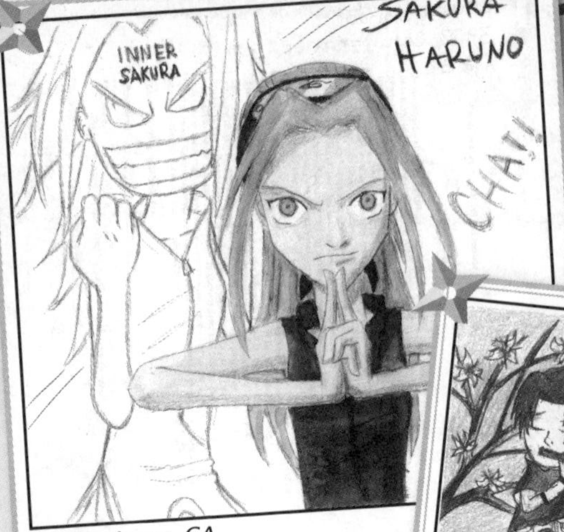
SAKURA HARUNO
INNER SAKURA
CHA!!

Laura, CA
⬆ The shadow of Inner Sakura looms large!

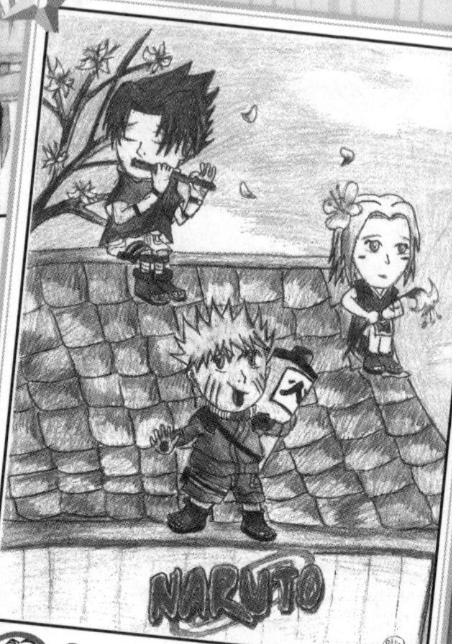
NARUTO

Gene, NY
⬆ What song are you playing, Sasuke?

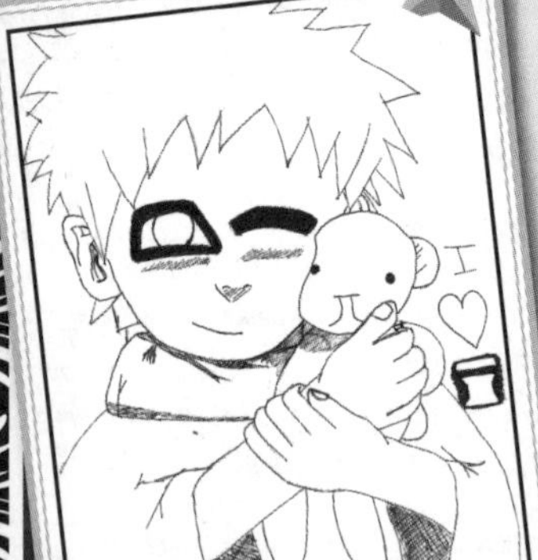
I ♥

Bryanna, VA
⬆ Hey, everybody loves a Teddy!

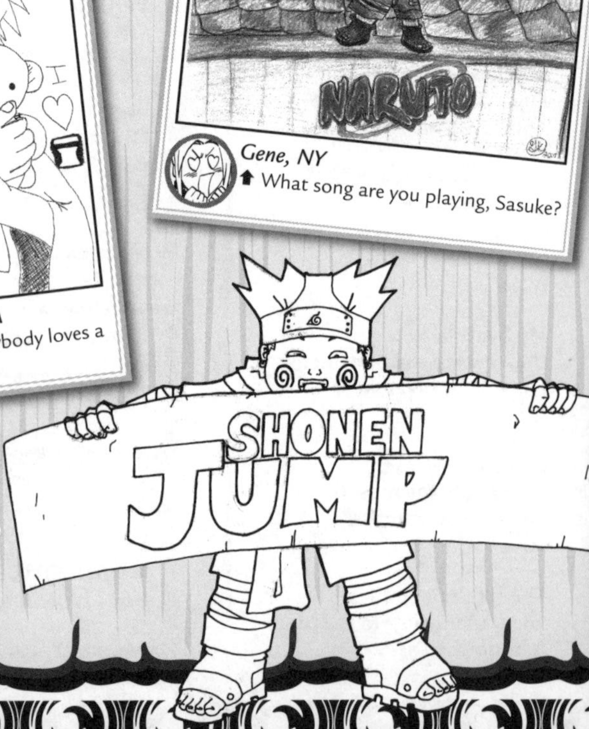
SHONEN JUMP

Sean, IL
➡ Choji is so happy about the Shonen Jump sign!

Konoha Haiku Festival

Naruto's Entry

I'm mega-awesome
I'm the best and you know it
I'll be Hokage!

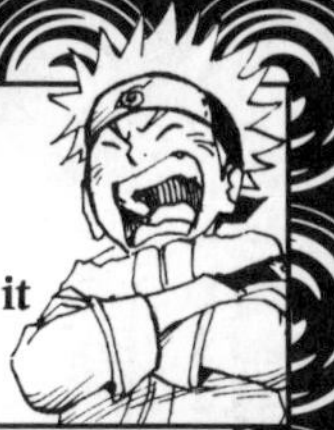

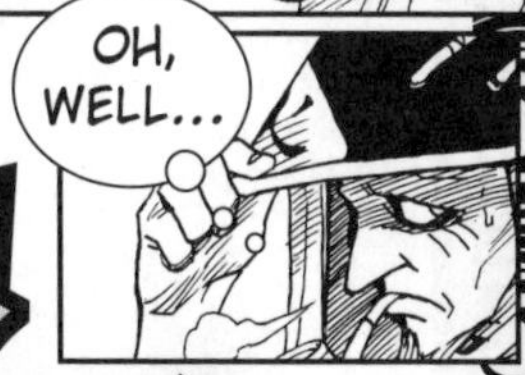
OH, WELL...

Unwavering heart
Protect those who are precious
His shinobi way
Gregory, MA

PERFECT!

⬅ Really captures the spirit of Naruto!

In the rising dawn
Enemies wait to attack
Among the bushes
Jennifer, CA

Love and enemies
Epic tales of brave ninja
This is *Naruto*
Greg, GA

I'm an avenger
My dark soul is relentless
My name – Sasuke
Waqar, IL

My heart lies hidden
Underneath my Sharingan
I just want revenge
Daisy, TN

Gaara of the sand
I fight only for myself
I don't need your love
Seana, CA

The soft hair ripples
Silent blade flies to the mark
A kunoichi's prey
Ida, NY

I am Konoha's
Uzumaki Naruto
Flowing with chakra
Chihiro, FL

⬆ He should shout this at his enemies.

Orochimaru
Evil is your bloody game
Power took your life
Autumn, IA

⬆ Orochimaru's motivation laid bare!

Konoha is great
Ninjas everywhere you look
I wish I was there
David, FL

⬆ Konoha has that effect on people.

People always say
What counts is what's inside you
But I have a fox
Sam, OR

⬆ The source of Naruto's inner power!

The scent of fresh blood
The eyes of a warrior
The real ninja way
Amy, CT

I train with my team
So we can become chûnin
Journeymen ninja
Marie, NH

Sharingan revealed
Yet it's still not perfected
I see through your moves
Salvador

Shadow Clone Jutsu
Makes the day fun! Clean my room
For me, understand?!
Matthew, IL

I'm a Leaf ninja
With my powerful techniques
You will surely die
Alex, GA

The great Zabuza
The feared demon of the mist
Lying in red snow
Cyndy, GA

Ah, man! Train! Train!
Is that the life of a ninja?
It sure seems that way
Terissa, TX

Seemingly carefree
Kakashi reads his novel
Secretly cautious
Patrick, GA

The citizens of Konoha are all interested in haiku, traditional Japanese poetry. The first line has five syllables, the second line has seven, and the third line has five. Writing haiku is easy and fun!

Hidden in plain view
We laugh in the face of death
Black Ops of the Leaf
Matthew, NJ

Dark eyes turning red
Power of the Sharingan
My eyes can see all
Victoria, MI

Sakura by name
Love of Sasuke by heart
Never will he know
Jaime, NY

Gaara stalks his prey
Hiding in the shifting sand
Thirsting for fresh blood
Richard, NJ

Fighting Neji-kun
Is like climbing mountains
Or stepping stones
Ediberto, Puerto Rico

Nine-Tailed kitsune
Messenger of Inari
Or bringer of death?
Ashlyn, MS

Spying on the girls
That Jiraiya the Toad Sage
A mega pervert
Lacy, LA

My name is Gaara
Shadows are my dwelling place
Rage is my tactic
Darren, MD

Jutsu and chakra
Those are my weapons of choice
I am a ninja
Adam, TX

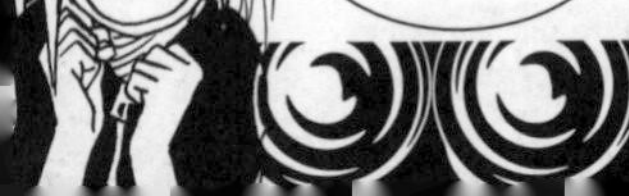
THEY'RE ALL FANTASTIC!

NARUTO 02 Fan

Unless you can discover the truth,
all the gates will not open!

1st GATE

Uzumaki Naruto Makes No Mistakes!

MULTIPLE SHADOW DOPPELGANGERS!

Find the original Naruto!

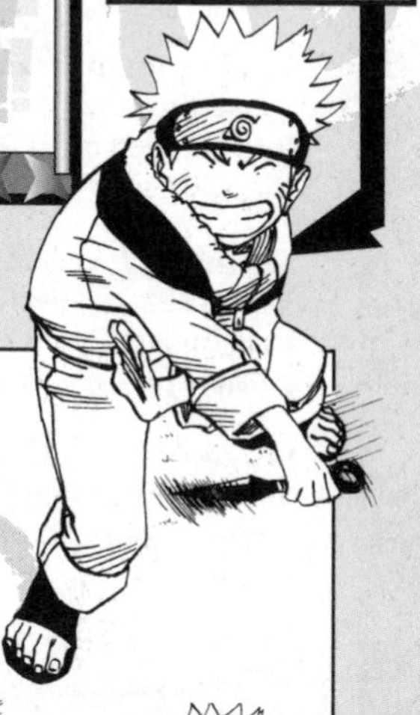

Naruto is demonstrating his favorite technique. All but one of the doppelgangers do not match...you have one minute to find the successful doppelganger!!

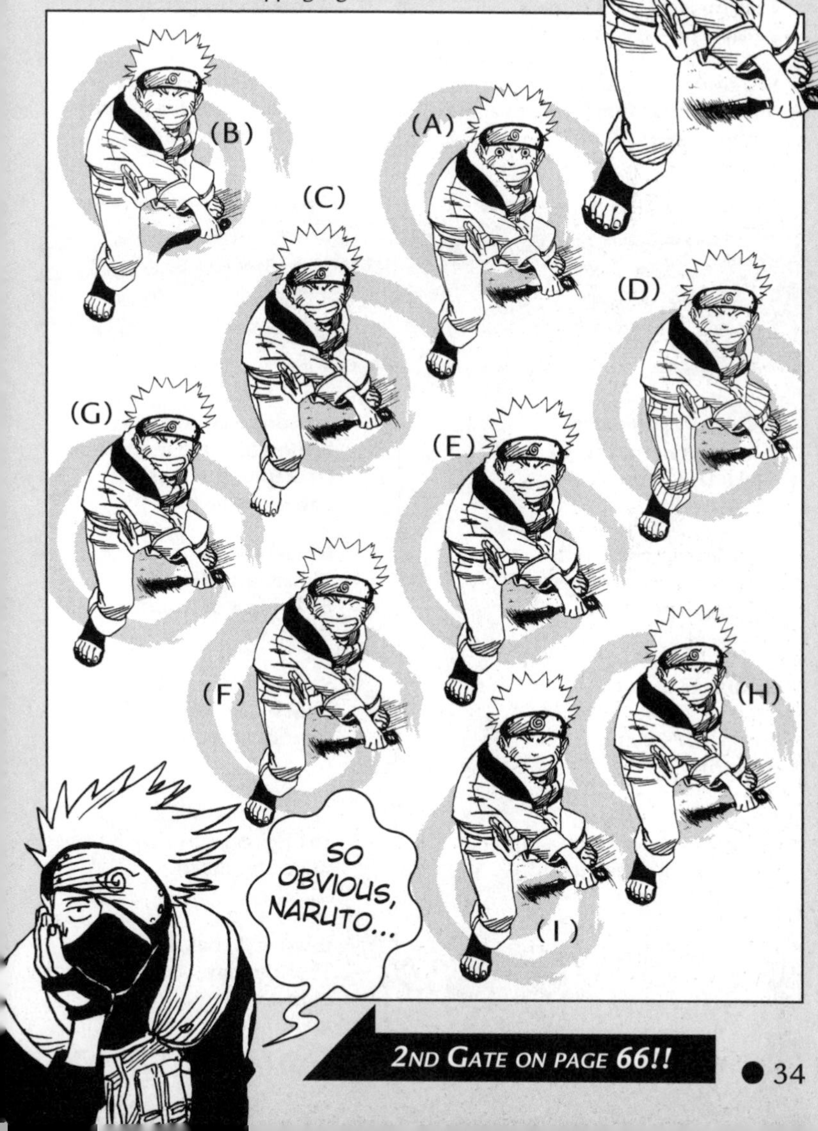
(B)
(A)
(C)
(D)
(G)
(E)
(F)
(H)
(I)
SO OBVIOUS, NARUTO...

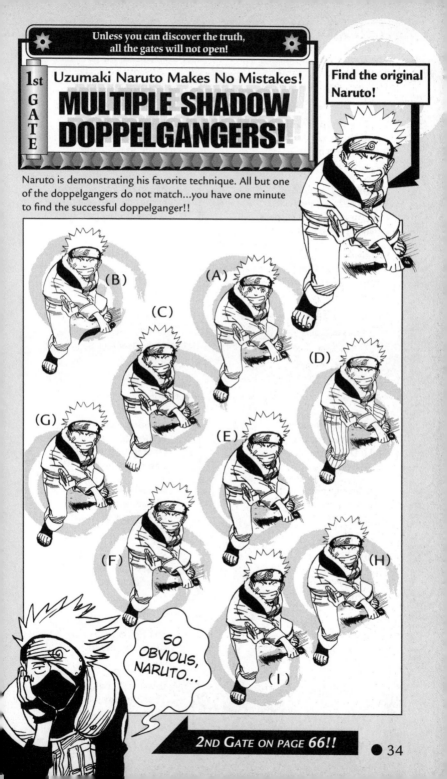

2ND GATE ON PAGE 66!!

Analysis: Konoha Ninja!

Unshakable bonds between unrivaled warriors!
Full report on the organization and style of Konoha's elite ninja forces!

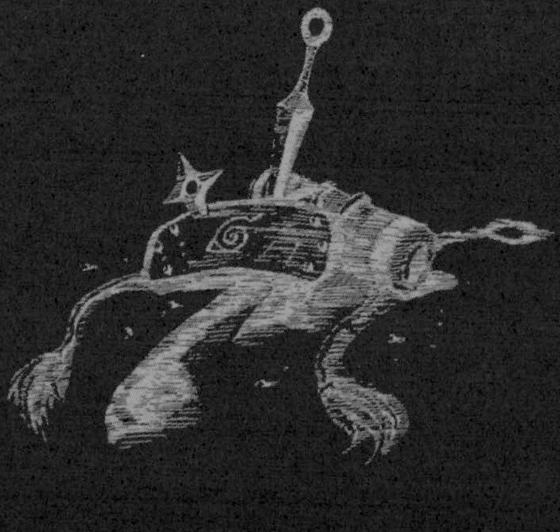

HIDDEN LEAF VILLAGE SHINOBI

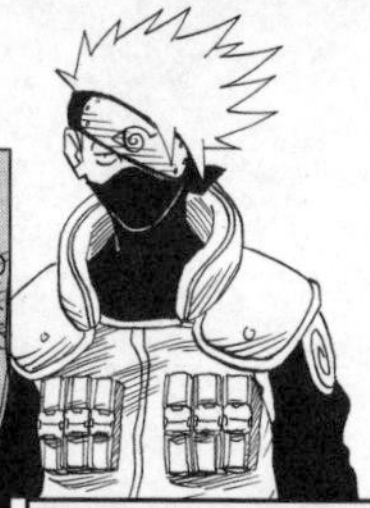

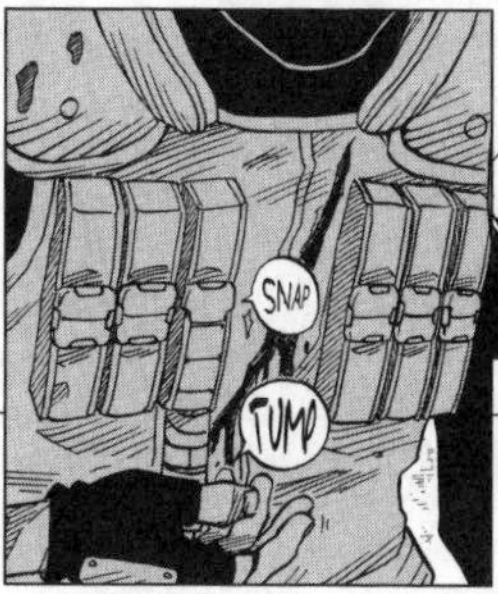
SNAP
TUMP

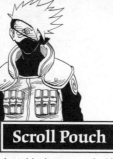

Scroll Pouch

⬅ Holds three on each side. Opens downward for easy use. Also capable of storing medicine or small weapons.

Basic style Detailed analysis!!

Lightweight, easy to move in, sturdy... the Hidden Leaf Village's clothes meet all these requirements. But the true value of this design can be seen in battle, where a moment's delay can cost a ninja his or her life.

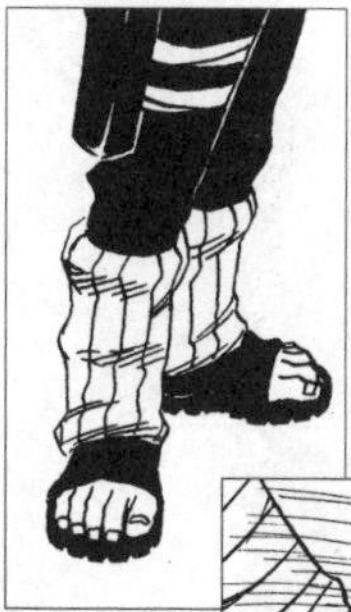

⬅ Lee wears training weights under these leg warmer-like covers.

Hand Guard

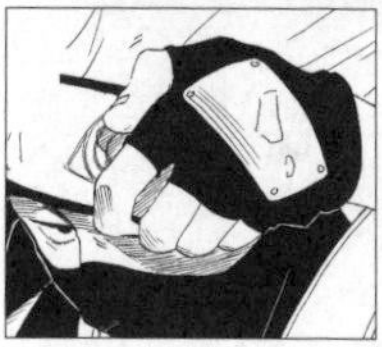

⬅ A metal plate is sewn onto the back of the glove to guard against injuries. Sturdy enough to block a Demon Wind Shuriken!

Leg Bandages

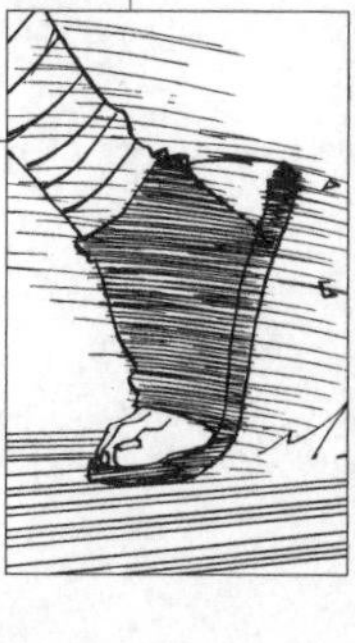

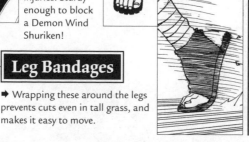

➡ Wrapping these around the legs prevents cuts even in tall grass, and makes it easy to move.

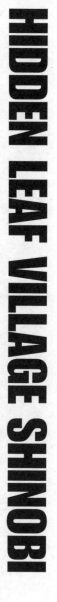

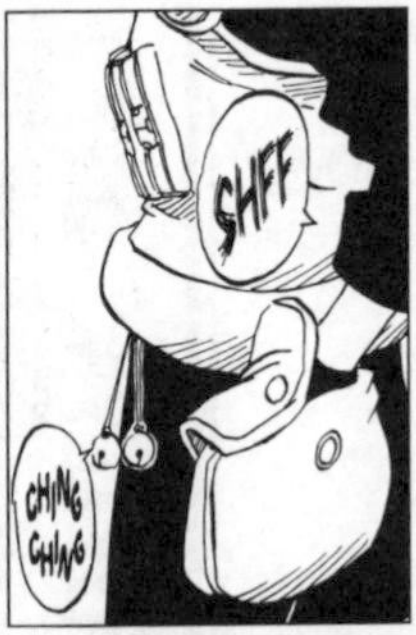
SHFF
CHING CHING

⬅ Sturdy pouches carry many kinds of ninja tools, which can be easily reached at all times.

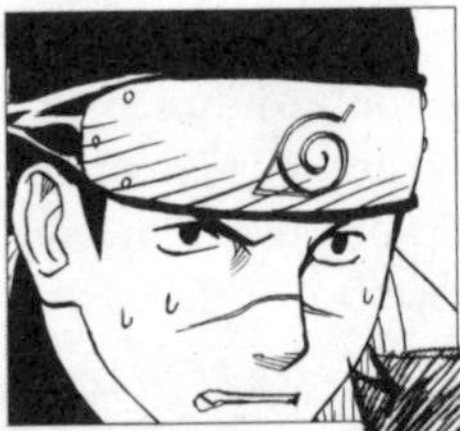

⬅ Protects against blows from the front. In the center is the mark of Konoha.

Headband

Waist Pouch

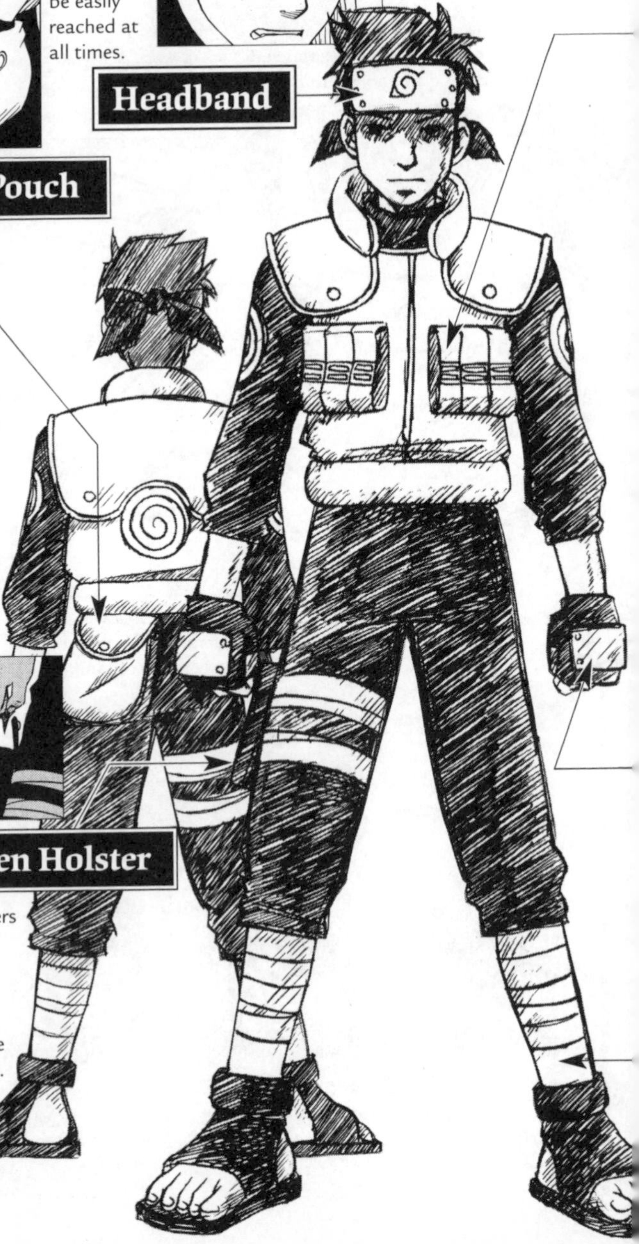

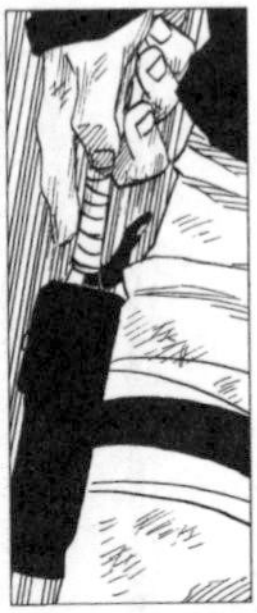

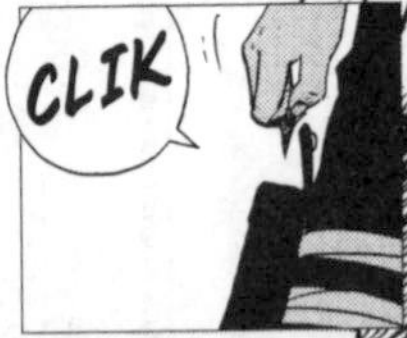
CLIK

Shuriken Holster

⬆ These holsters carry shuriken and kunai, and are worn strapped to the leg near the throwing hand.

The Ninja Badge
The Ninja Headband

The headband — symbol of shinobi pride!!

The headband is given only to those who have graduated from the academy and are recognized as being a full-fledged ninja. It is not only a protective item worn to guard the forehead, but also a symbol of the wearer's pride!!

⬇ Naruto wanted a headband even more than most people.

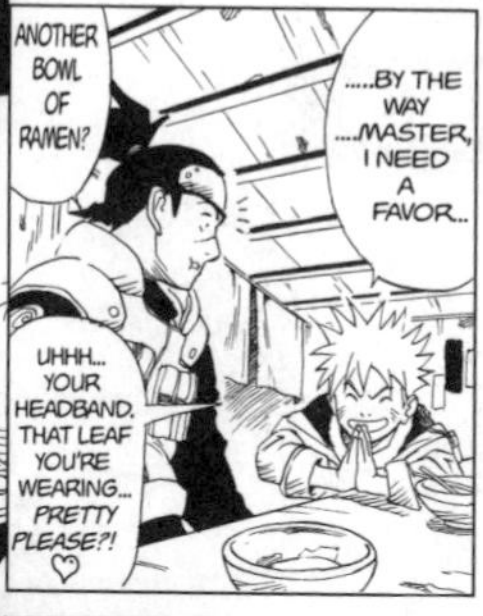

....BY THE WAY ....MASTER, I NEED A FAVOR..
ANOTHER BOWL OF RAMEN?
UHHH... YOUR HEADBAND. THAT LEAF YOU'RE WEARING... PRETTY PLEASE?! ♡

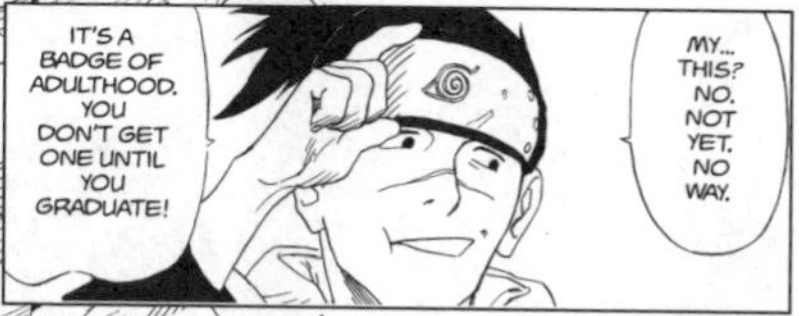

MY... THIS? NO. NOT YET. NO WAY.
IT'S A BADGE OF ADULTHOOD. YOU DON'T GET ONE UNTIL YOU GRADUATE!

⬆ Even Iruka wouldn't dream of lending someone his headband!

⬇ Naruto tying his headband on after he stole it back from Zabuza. His expression shows his pride as a shinobi returning!!

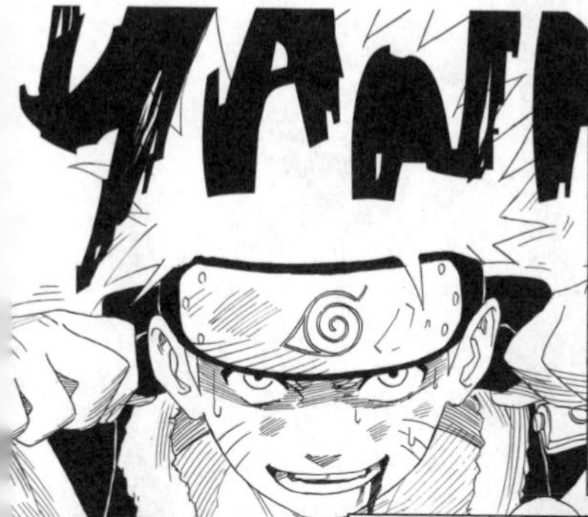

ONOHA- CHOOL NINJA!

Three basic ways to wear it!!

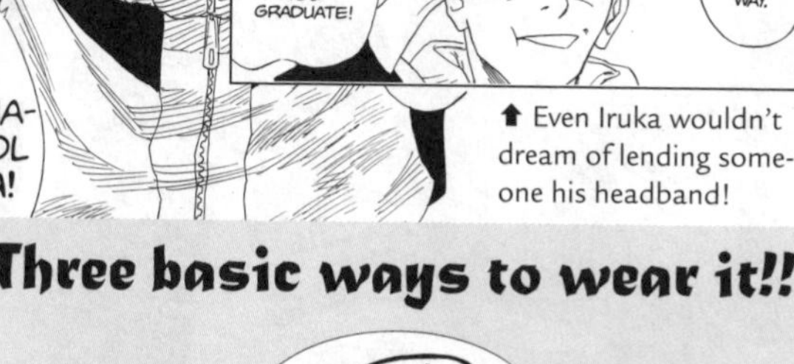

⬆ During missions, ninja often use a matching mask.

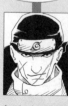

⬆ The bandana method, covering the entire head with it.

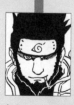

⬆ Tying it at the back of the head is the most common method.

WAYS TO MAKE A STATEMENT!

Some ninja choose to wear the headband in an unusual fashion, displaying their own unique character.

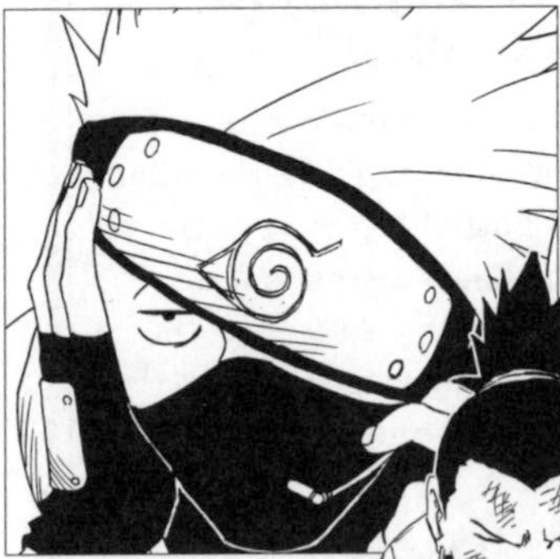

➡ Except when he's fighting, Kakashi wears his diagonally, to hide the Sharingan underneath!

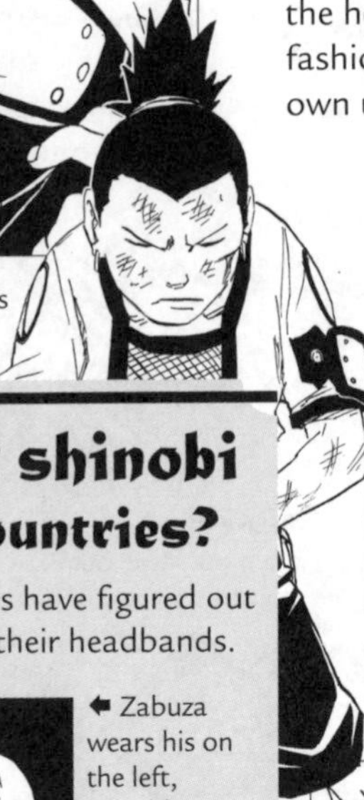

➡ The easygoing Shikamaru pins his to the left sleeve of his shirt.

⬇ Sakura wears hers on the back of her head, holding her hair in place.

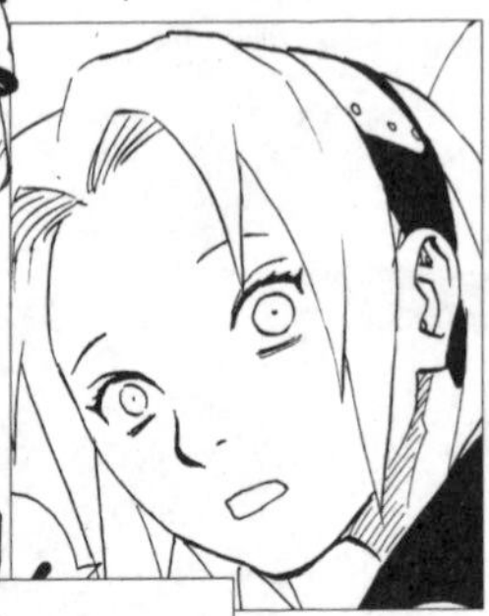

What about shinobi from other countries?

Ninja from other countries have figured out original ways to display their headbands.

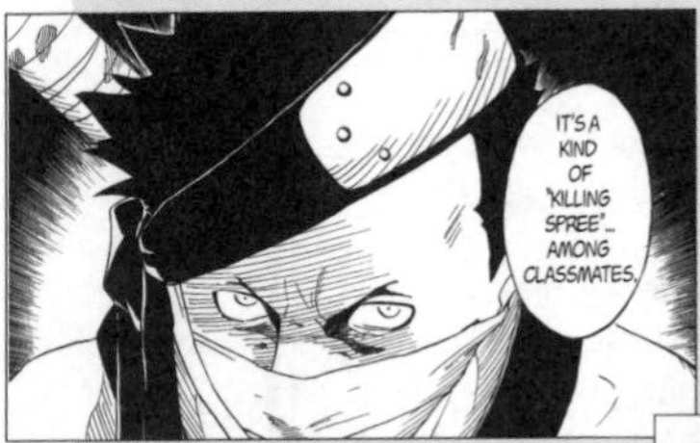
IT'S A KIND OF "KILLING SPREE"... AMONG CLASSMATES.

⬅ Zabuza wears his on the left, possibly protecting against attacks from that direction.

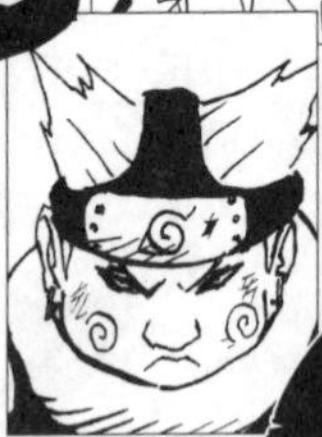

⬅ Choji has turned it into a kind of headgear, with three sections.

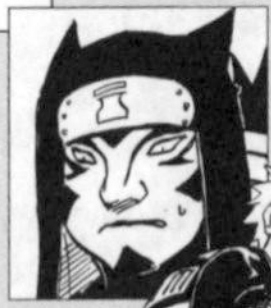

➡ Kankuro's headband looks like part of a hood.

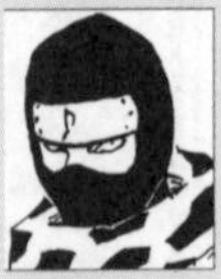

➡ Gaara's headband is tied to his trademark gourd.

⬆ The Sound ninja wear it under the cowl that completely covers their faces.

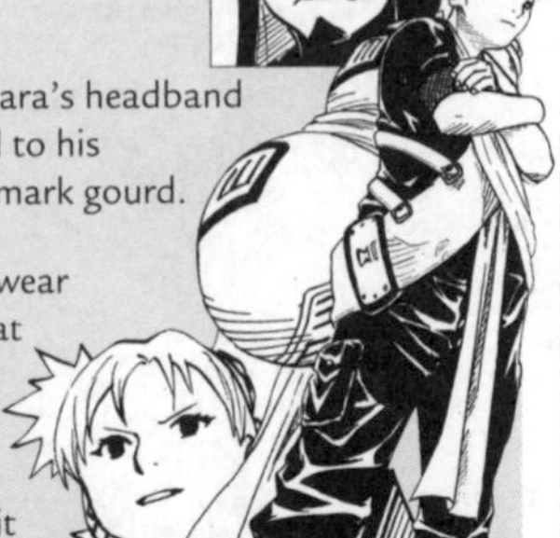

➡ Temari wears it around her neck, like jewelry.

⬇➡ Lee wears his at his waist, while Ino wears hers just below it.

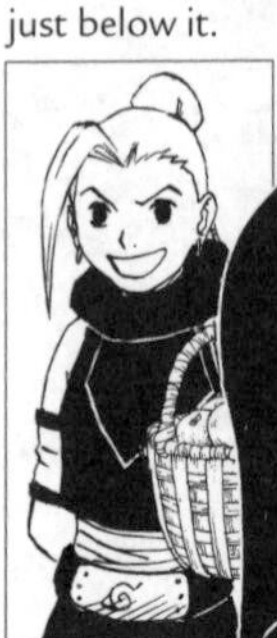

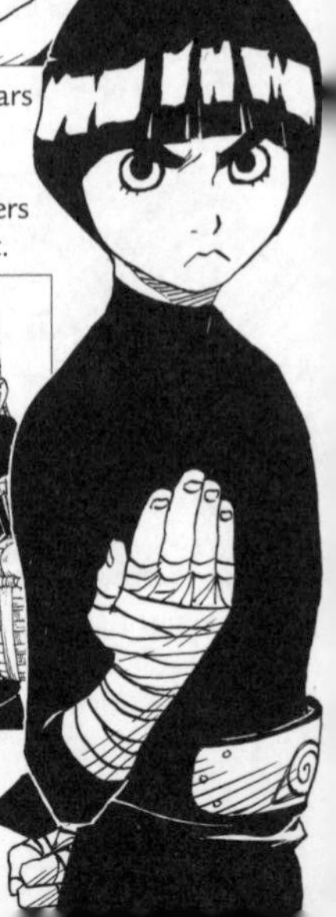

In Actual Fighting

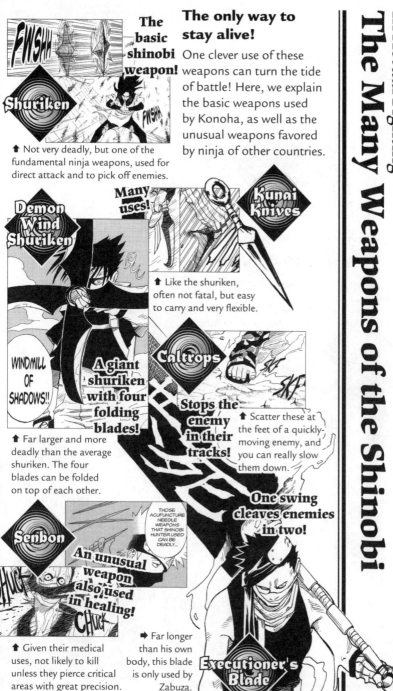

The Many Weapons of the Shinobi

The only way to stay alive!

One clever use of these weapons can turn the tide of battle! Here, we explain the basic weapons used by Konoha, as well as the unusual weapons favored by ninja of other countries.

Shuriken

The basic shinobi weapon!

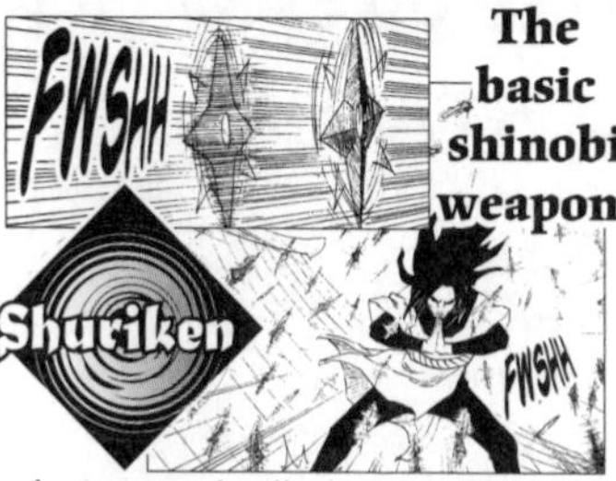
FWSHH
FWSHH

⬆ Not very deadly, but one of the fundamental ninja weapons, used for direct attack and to pick off enemies.

Kunai Knives

Many uses!

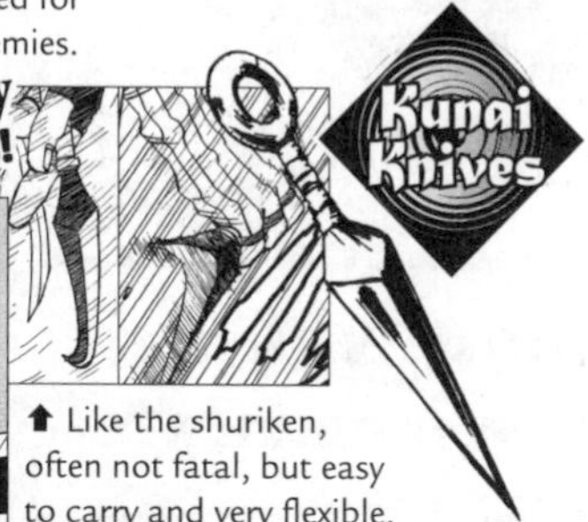

⬆ Like the shuriken, often not fatal, but easy to carry and very flexible.

Demon Wind Shuriken

A giant shuriken with four folding blades!

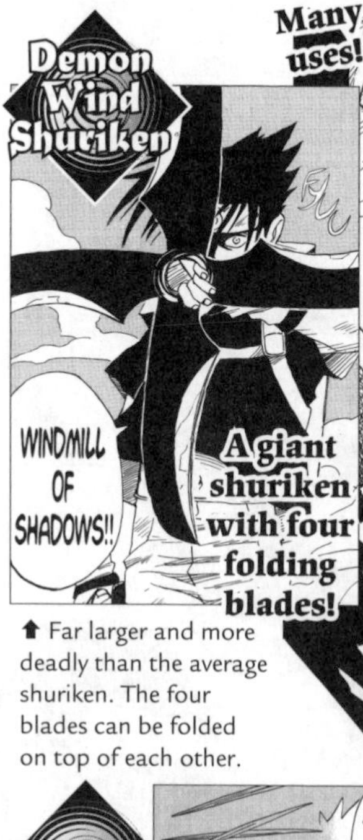
FUU
WINDMILL OF SHADOWS!!

⬆ Far larger and more deadly than the average shuriken. The four blades can be folded on top of each other.

Caltrops

Stops the enemy in their tracks!

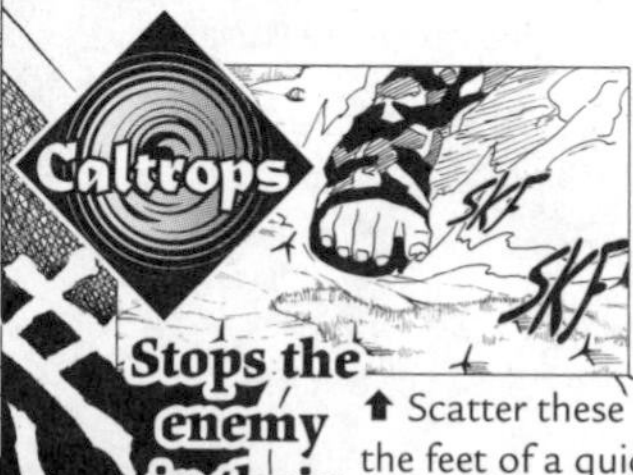
SKF
SKF

⬆ Scatter these at the feet of a quickly-moving enemy, and you can really slow them down.

Senbon

An unusual weapon also used in healing!

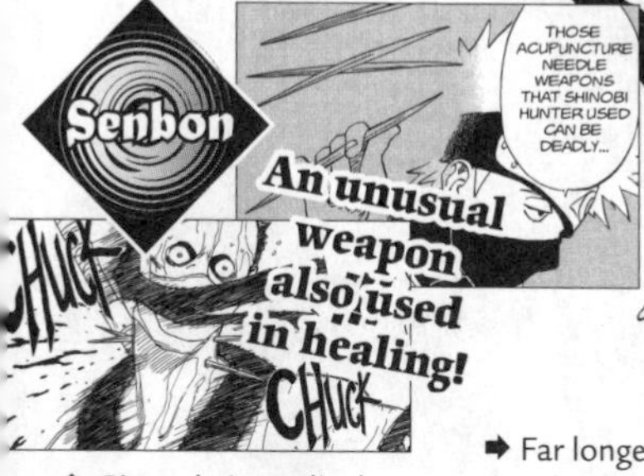
THOSE ACUPUNCTURE NEEDLE WEAPONS THAT SHINOBI HUNTER USED CAN BE DEADLY...
CHUCK
CHUCK

⬆ Given their medical uses, not likely to kill unless they pierce critical areas with great precision.

Executioner's Blade

One swing cleaves enemies in two!

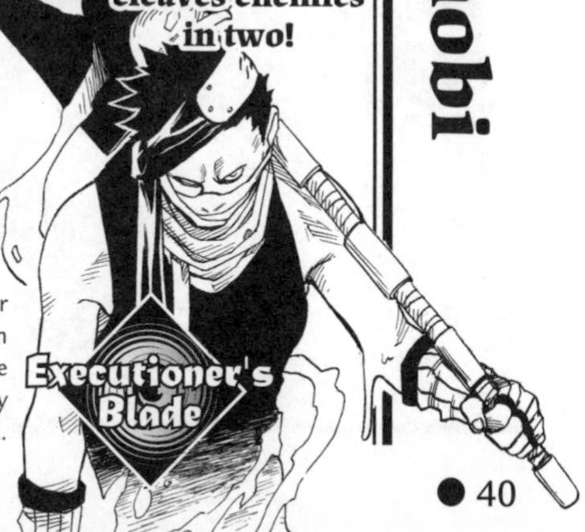

➡ Far longer than his own body, this blade is only used by Zabuza.

➡ Temari's personal weapon, creating razor sharp gusts of wind. Very sturdy, and equally useful as a shield!

Creates blades of wind!

Ultra-Giant Fan

A puppet filled with weapons!

The Crow

Compact but deadly!

⬆ Kankuro operates this puppet with his chakra. There are poisoned needles and other weapons hidden all over it!

A sword with a sinister gleam!

The Kusanagi Blade

Iron Knuckles

⬅ Very small, but they can punch and slice. Asuma's default weapon!

⬅ This uncanny katana appeared from inside Orochimaru's body. The very sight of it is terrifying!

The blade snakes out and back!

⬅ Specially designed for the Oni Brothers, this sharp blade on the end of a chain cuts their enemies to pieces!

Ultra-Amplifier

Total Noise!

Special Razor Chain

➡ Dosu's special weapon — the speaker on his arm creates a terrible noise, destroying his opponent's ear-drums.

Many Other Types of Ninja Tools!!

Poison smoke bomb	Smoke bomb	Explosive tags	Hyorogan
⬆ These blind your opponents and also force them to inhale poison gas.	⬆ Set them off in front of an enemy to block their vision, turning things to your advantage.	⬆ These explode a set time after being armed and can be used on animals or objects.	⬆ A medicine packed with stimulants that will let you fight three days and nights without resting.

A Key Shinobi Item
How to Use Scrolls

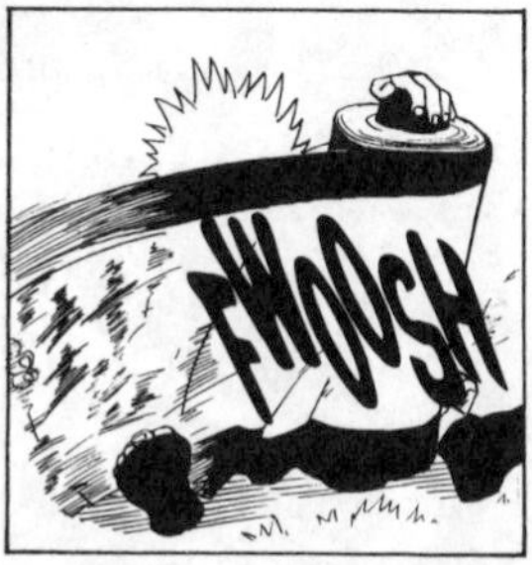
FWOOSH

Four basic uses for scrolls

Generally speaking, there are four basic actions performed with scrolls — read, write, activate, and make a contract. Let us look at each of these in turn.

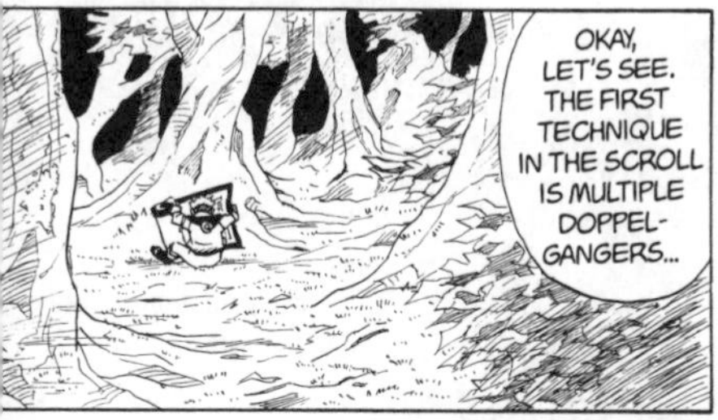
OKAY, LET'S SEE. THE FIRST TECHNIQUE IN THE SCROLL IS MULTIPLE DOPPEL-GANGERS...

READ 1

Reading scrolls can explain how to pull off a jutsu — these scrolls are basically textbooks.

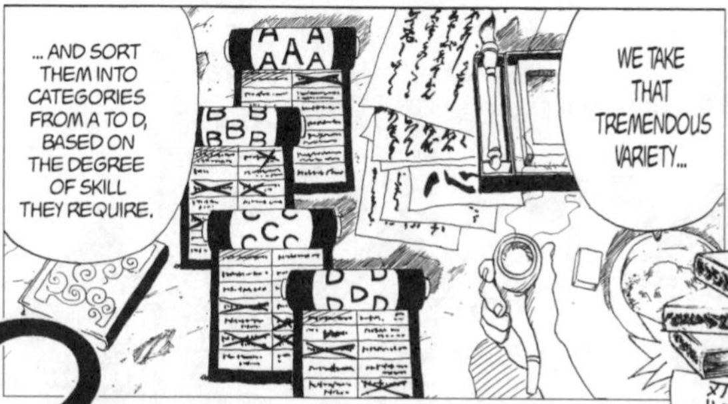
WE TAKE THAT TREMENDOUS VARIETY...
...AND SORT THEM INTO CATEGORIES FROM A TO D, BASED ON THE DEGREE OF SKILL THEY REQUIRE.
A A A A
B B B B
C C C
D D D

2 WRITE

Like notebooks. The Third Hokage's scrolls are filled with details of different ranked missions.

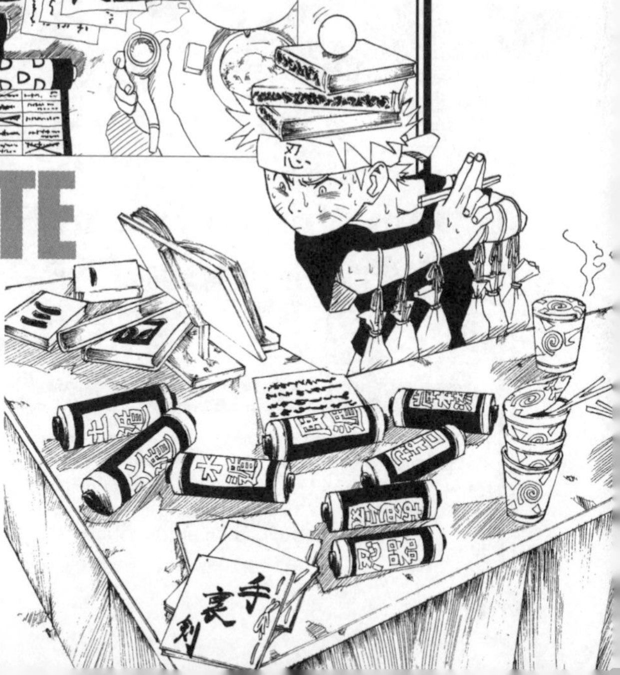
忍

3 ACTIVATE

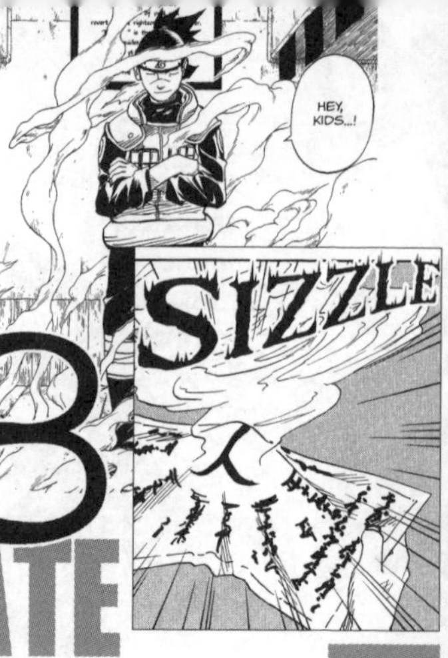
HEY, KIDS...!
SIZZLE

Complicated jutsu like Kuchiyose Summoning and Hypnotism can be placed on scrolls, arranged to activate the moment the scroll is opened.

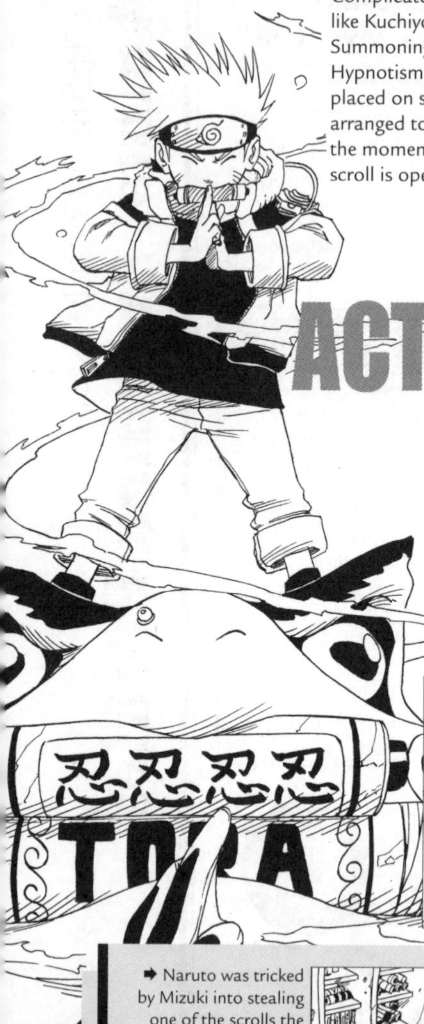
忍忍忍忍
TORA

4 MAKE A CONTRACT

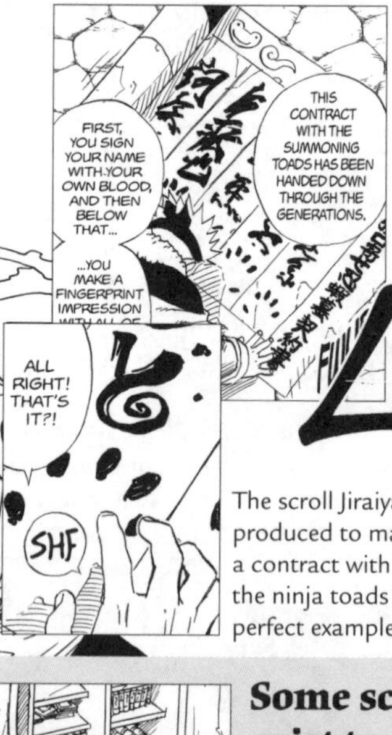
THIS CONTRACT WITH THE SUMMONING TOADS HAS BEEN HANDED DOWN THROUGH THE GENERATIONS.
FIRST, YOU SIGN YOUR NAME WITH YOUR OWN BLOOD, AND THEN BELOW THAT...
...YOU MAKE A FINGERPRINT IMPRESSION
ALL RIGHT! THAT'S IT?!
SHF

The scroll Jiraiya produced to make a contract with the ninja toads is a perfect example.

Some scrolls exist to seal away dangerous jutsu.

Scrolls with extremely dangerous jutsu on them are called sealed scrolls, and are carefully protected to keep them out of people's hands.

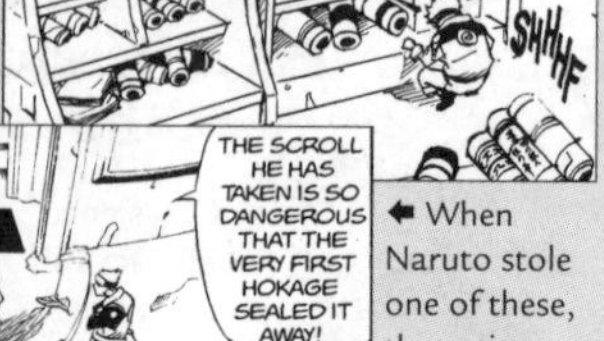
SHHHF

➡ Naruto was tricked by Mizuki into stealing one of the scrolls the First Hokage had sealed.

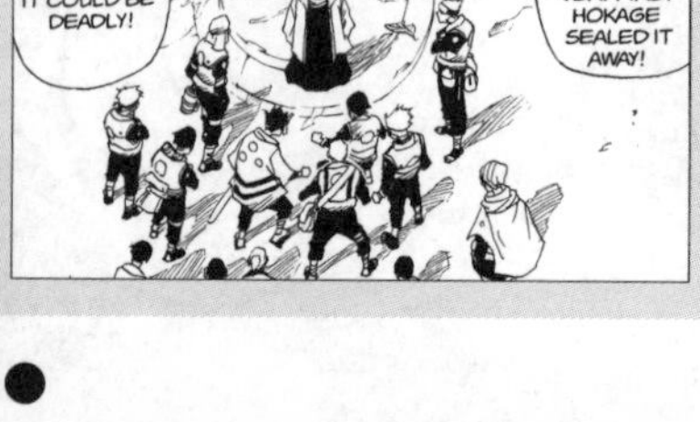
THE SCROLL HE HAS TAKEN IS SO DANGEROUS THAT THE VERY FIRST HOKAGE SEALED IT AWAY!
IF MISUSED, IN THE WRONG HANDS, IT COULD BE DEADLY!

⬅ When Naruto stole one of these, the entire village went on alert. That's how dangerous they are!

Faithful to Their Masters

Animal Summon Profiles

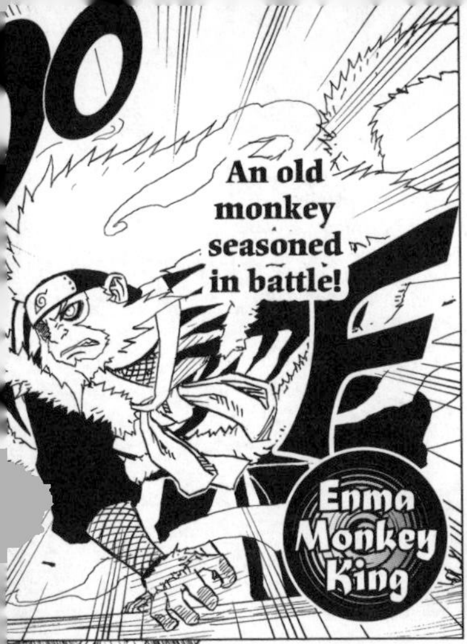
An old monkey seasoned in battle!
Enma Monkey King

⬆ An old monkey trusted by the Third Hokage. Many say he is the most powerful of all the creatures that can be summoned.

Their unusual abilities save their masters' lives!

These creatures risk their lives for the sake of their ninja masters. They come in many types and sizes, and each has unique powers.

Steps required to use a Kuchiyose Summoning Jutsu

1. Sign your name in your own blood on a contract with the animal you want to summon.
2. Place the fingerprints of all five digits of one hand in blood below the name.
3. When you wish to summon them, pour your chakra into the hand you used for the contract.
4. Make the following signs: Boar, Dog, Bird, Monkey, Sheep.

Magical Animals

If you sign a contract in your own blood, you can summon Kuchiyose animals with ninjutsu, regardless of time or place!

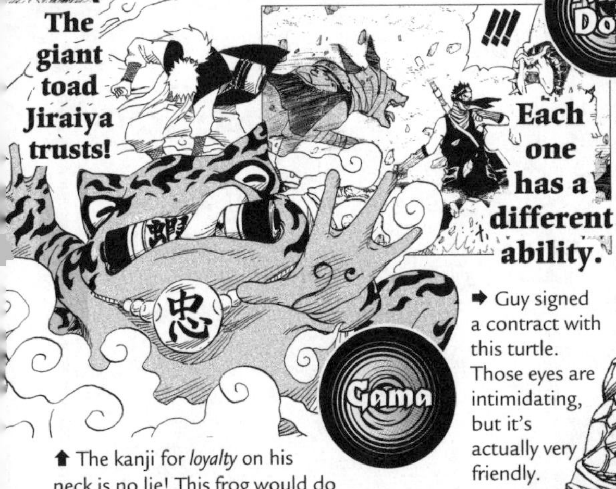
Ninja Dogs
!!!
Each one has a different ability.
The giant toad Jiraiya trusts!
忠
Gama

⬅ Kakashi's dogs are talented ninja — whether solo or in a pack!

⬆ The kanji for *loyalty* on his neck is no lie! This frog would do anything for Jiraiya.

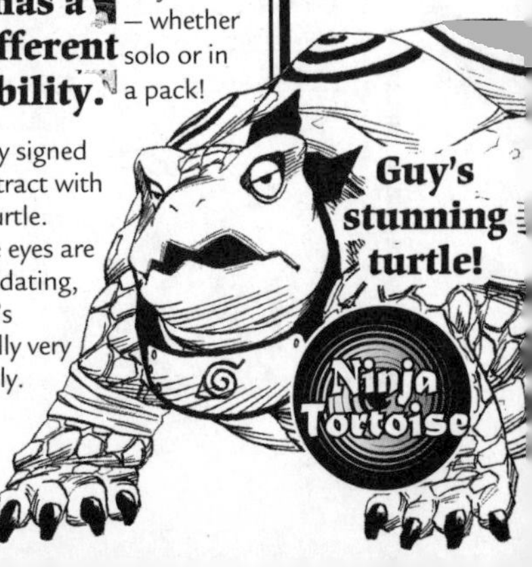
Guy's stunning turtle!
Ninja Tortoise

➡ Guy signed a contract with this turtle. Those eyes are intimidating, but it's actually very friendly.

Gamabunta

⬇ Naruto can summon this huge toad as a last resort!! One swing of his arm shakes the air like a mountain crumbling!

As big as a mountain!

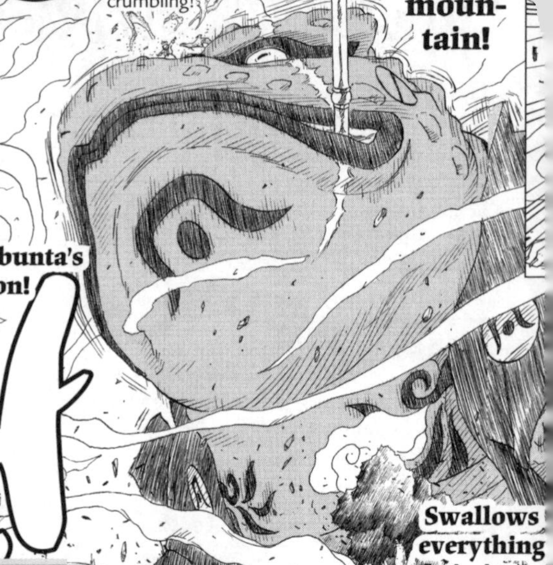

Gamakichi

⬇ This little frog is the apple of his father's eye! And his impertinent speech is just like his father's.

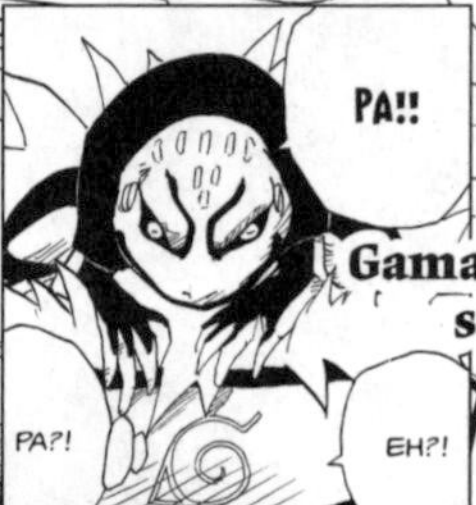

PA!!
PA?!
EH?!

Gamabunta's son!

Manda

Swallows everything in its massive jaws!

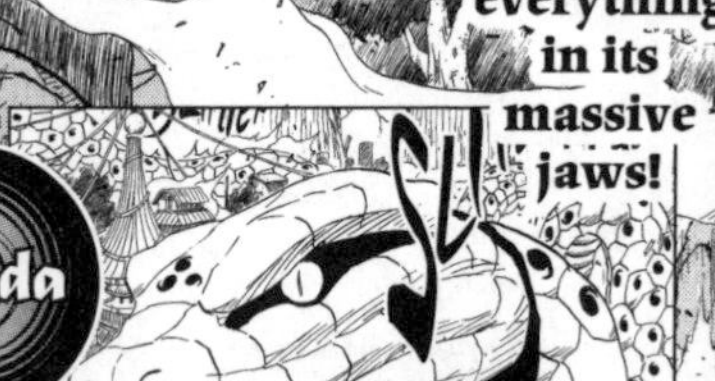

⬆ The giant snake Orochimaru summoned to attack the village. Terrifying icons appear on the surface of its skin.

Ninja Dogs

Extremely helpful to their masters on missions, these highly trained dogs have earned their name.

➡ Kiba's adorable Akamaru is still a puppy, but helps him constantly.

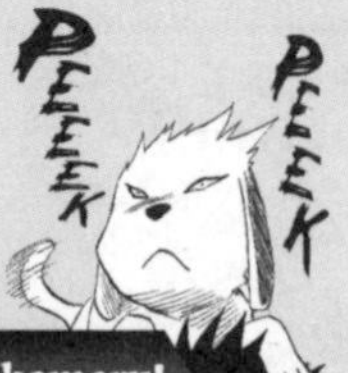

Kiba's dog: Akamaru!

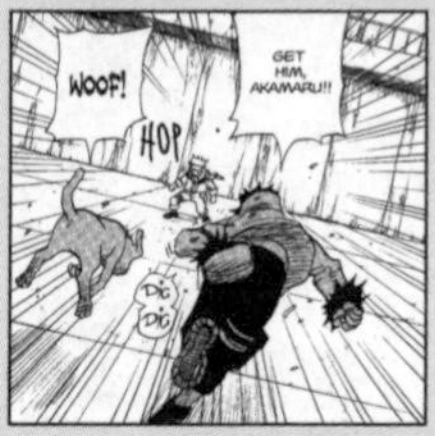

WOOF!
GET HIM, AKAMARU!!
HOP

⬅ During battles, they are as one, attacking in perfect unison.

Kikaichu

These Parasitic Destruction Beetles attack en masse and drain away their victims' chakra. The shinobi they serve feeds them his chakra in return for their service. They do nearly all his fighting!

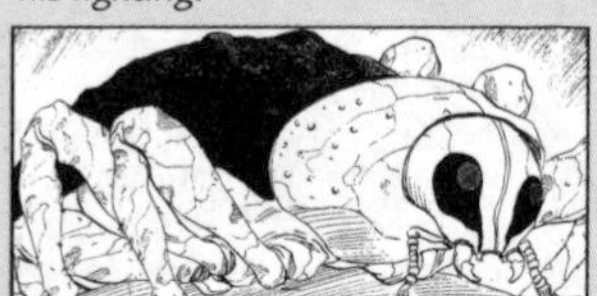

KIBA'S TIPS Make friends with puppies!!

ON HOW TO BE A TOP BREEDER!

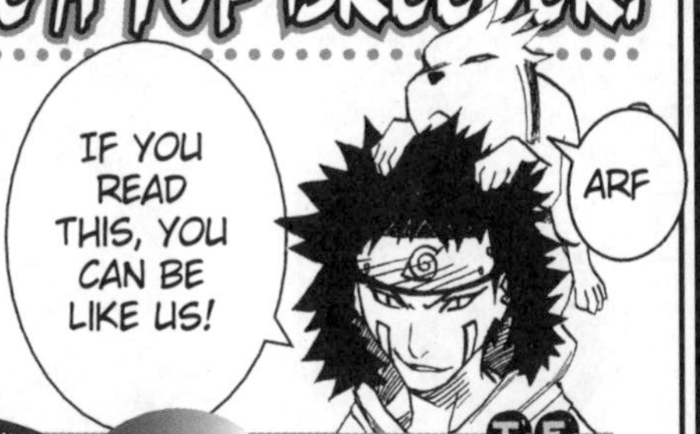

IF YOU READ THIS, YOU CAN BE LIKE US!
ARF

Be just like Kiba and Akamaru!

To all of you out there who want a puppy of your own, here are Kiba's tips! If you follow these, you too can be like them!!

STEP 1 Monitor your puppy's health constantly!!

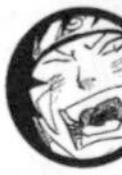

First, let me tell you how to know if your puppy is healthy!! Knowing their partner's health is only natural for any pet owner!

Key points TO CHECK ON THE PUPPY'S BODY

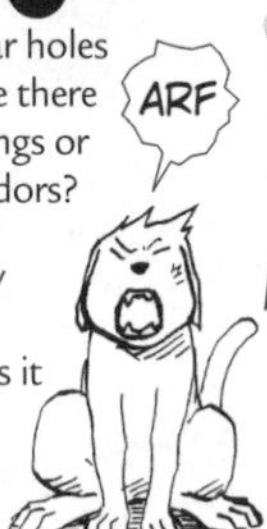

ARF

- **Ears** Are the ear holes clean? Are there red swellings or strange odors?
- **Nose** Is it glossy and cold, but dry? Is it running?
- **Butt** Is it clean? Or is it dirty?
- **Eyes** Are they shining and clear? Are the edges dirty?
- **Mouth** Are the gums pink? Do they smell bad? Is the bite normal?
- **Fur** Is it glossy and full? Is it shedding?

STEP 2 Make sure it knows that the human is in charge!!

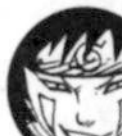

The first and most important thing a pet owner must do with a puppy is to establish dominance. You might feel sorry for it, but dogs are happier when their owners show leadership!

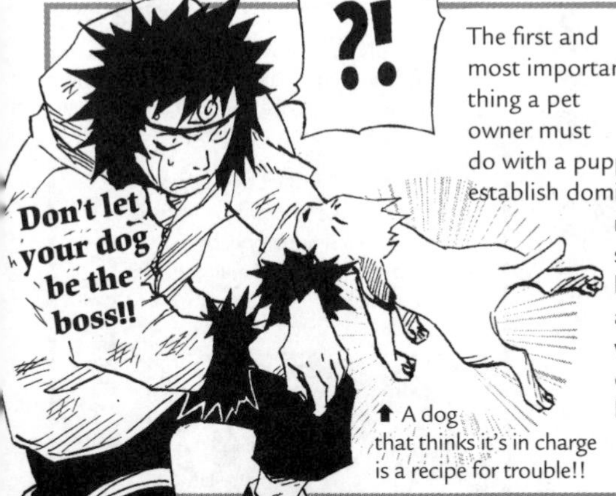

?!
Don't let your dog be the boss!!

⬆ A dog that thinks it's in charge is a recipe for trouble!!

STEP 3 Communication is critical!!

For a puppy, walking with its owner every day is vital for keeping it healthy. Not only does it improve the dog's athletic abilities, it also burns off stress!!

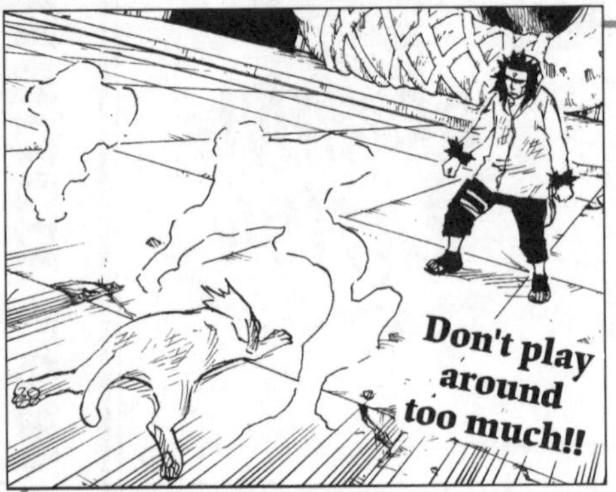

Don't play around too much!!

⬆ Different breeds have different skills and strengths, so don't force it to play games it doesn't like!

STEP 4 Pay attention to your dog's feelings!!

When a puppy is taken away from its parents and siblings, it does get lonely, and has a lot of mental stress. Make sure you figure out what is causing problems and adjust the environment it lives in!!

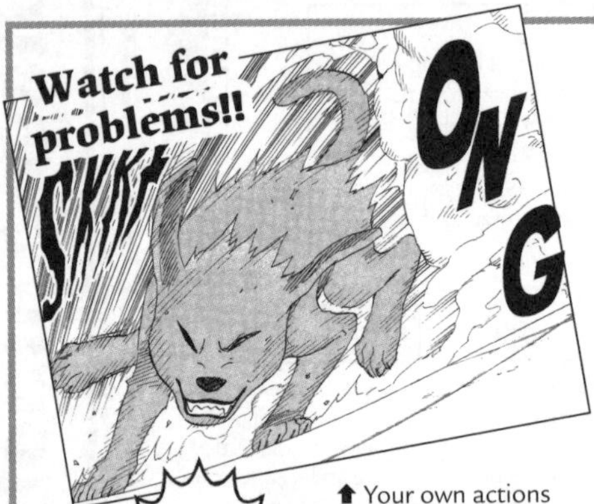

ONG
Watch for problems!!
SKK

⬆ Your own actions might be the cause!

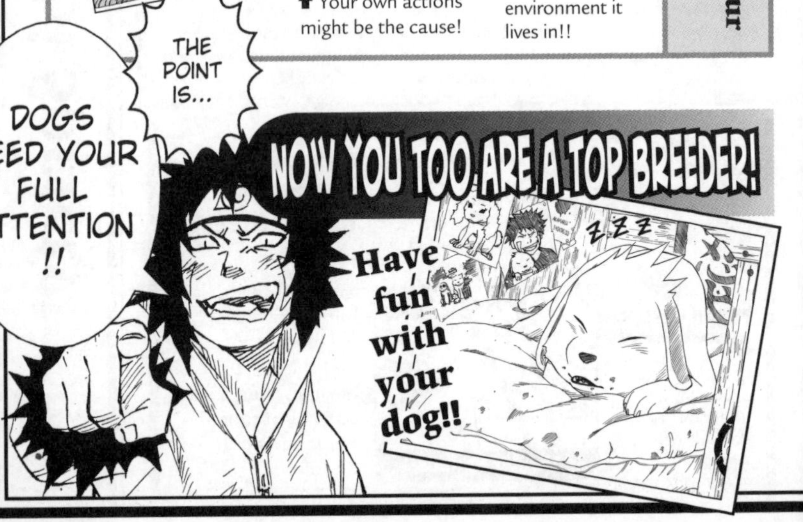

NOW YOU TOO ARE A TOP BREEDER!
THE POINT IS...
DOGS NEED YOUR FULL ATTENTION !!
ZZZ
Have fun with your dog!!

The Inner Ranks!!

Hidden Leaf Village Shinobi Society!

ORGANIZATION

A tightly bound society keeps the elite shinobi working as one unit.

The Konoha shinobi society is organized into several units placed under the control of the Hokage. Each unit has a jônin or a Special Jônin in charge of it, and they report to the Hokage and his advisors. Assignments to the different units are issued only after careful consideration.

Shinobi Organizational Chart

Hidden Leaf Village

Hokage

Advisors

The Hokage sits at the top of society, listening carefully to his advisors before making any decisions. There are other groups and units that are not known to the general public.

Operations Unit

Naruto and Kakashi, and indeed, most ninja, are in this division. Each team is given appropriate missions whose execution helps keep the village going.

Medical Corps

They remain on the back lines, supporting the warriors. They are divided into several groups by specialty — emergency staff, technical research, etc., healing all injuries swiftly and efficiently.

Anbu Black Ops

This shadowy unit is under the direct control of the Hokage. They specialize in torture and assassination. To ensure success, the makeup of the units varies according to the goals and difficulty of their missions.

Shinobi Society in other villages:

Each village organizes themselves differently depending on their customs and culture. There are many functions or types of squad not found in Konoha.

Shinobi Rulers

⬆ A rank found in the Hidden Clouds. Ranked above jônin, and given the authority to represent their village's interests.

Hunter Squads

⬇ A special unit of the Hidden Mist's Anbu. Also called the "corpse disposal unit," they possess medical and assassin training.

HOKAGE

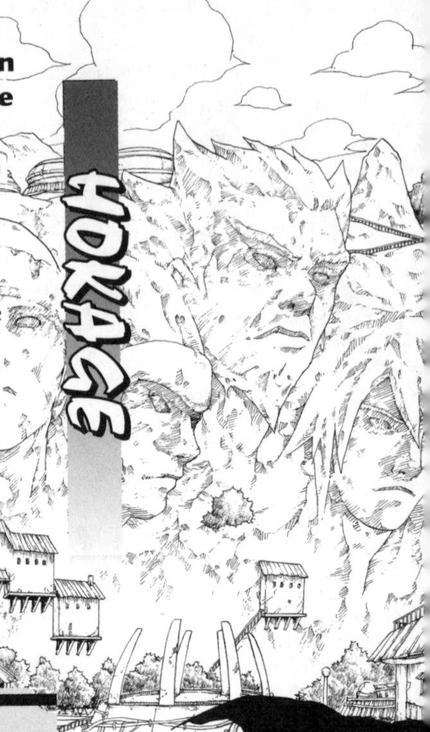

Wise in the ways of Heaven and Earth, he stands at the peak of Konoha!

The Hokage controls all the ninja in Konoha, by far the largest shinobi village. His wisdom and courage are godlike, and he stands at the pinnacle of not only Konoha, but the entire shinobi world. The village lives and dies with the Hokage, and the paths these four leaders walked form the history of the village itself.

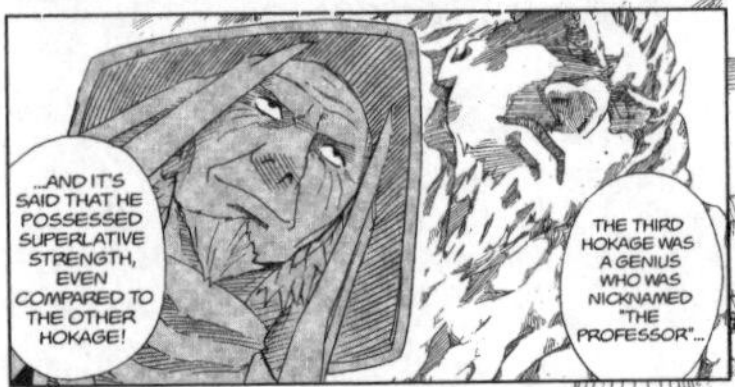
THE THIRD HOKAGE WAS A GENIUS WHO WAS NICKNAMED "THE PROFESSOR"...
...AND IT'S SAID THAT HE POSSESSED SUPERLATIVE STRENGTH, EVEN COMPARED TO THE OTHER HOKAGE!

⬆ The top of Konoha is the top of everything! None can compete with his wisdom!

Hokage History

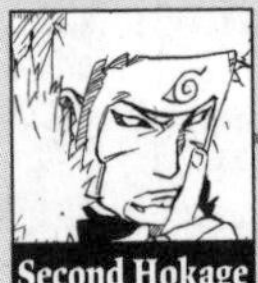
Second Hokage

Brother of the Founder, he organized the village's society, allowing it to develop.

Brothers

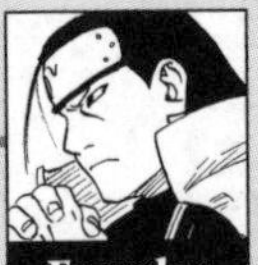
Founder

Sixty years ago he gathered together like-minded shinobi and founded Konoha.

Disciple

Disciple

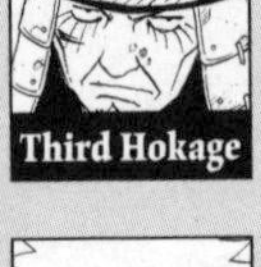
Third Hokage

This genius was trained by the First and Second. His reign has been the longest, and his entire life belongs to the village.

Jiraiya

Disciple

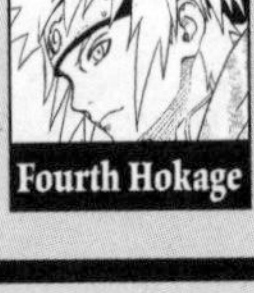
Fourth Hokage

Student of the Third Hokage's disciple. Earned the Hokage name at a very young age, but his reign ended when the Nine-Tailed Fox attacked.

Inherited Purpose!

It is not the secret arts and techniques that allow the Hokage to protect the village – "Those that believe in you and trust you are what truly support you." This pride and faith is what makes a man the true Hokage of Konoha.

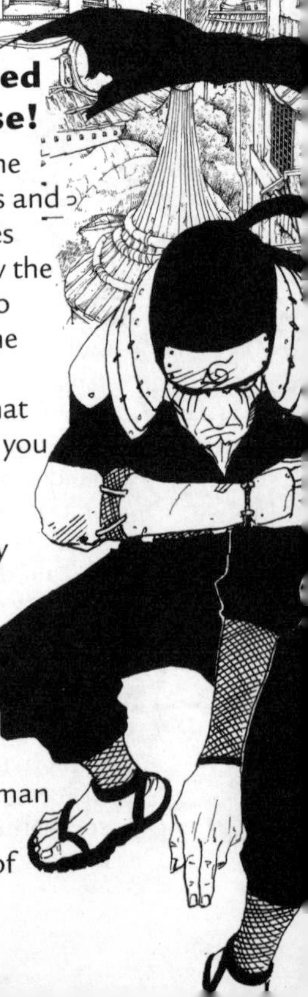

ANBU

Special operations for the Hokage!!

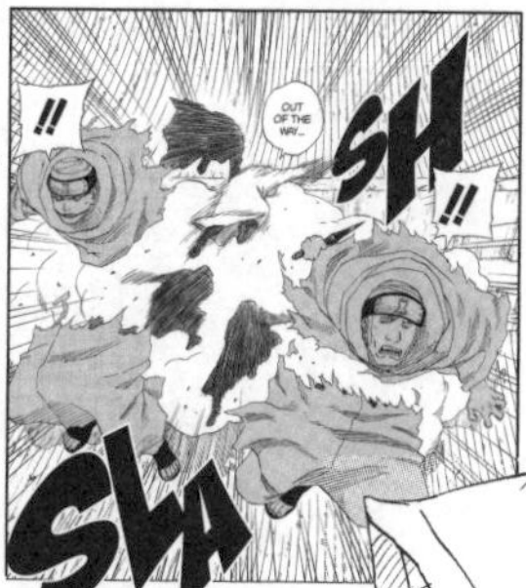
!!
OUT OF THE WAY...
SH
!!
SLA

⬅ Like a flash of light, their deadly techniques instantly break through enemy defenses!

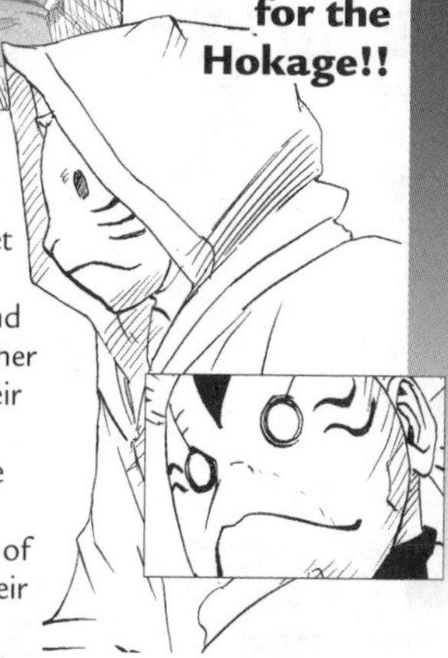

The Anbu are the Ninja Assassination Corps, the most secret and elite ninja. They specialize in spying and assassination, and other difficult missions. Their actions and faces are hidden in secrecy. The Hokage selects them personally, regardless of age or gender, and their orders come directly from him.

ADVISORS

The two advisors both lived through the war along with the Third Hokage. Their immense experience and expert knowledge help the Hokage rule well!

Help the Hokage to guide the village!!

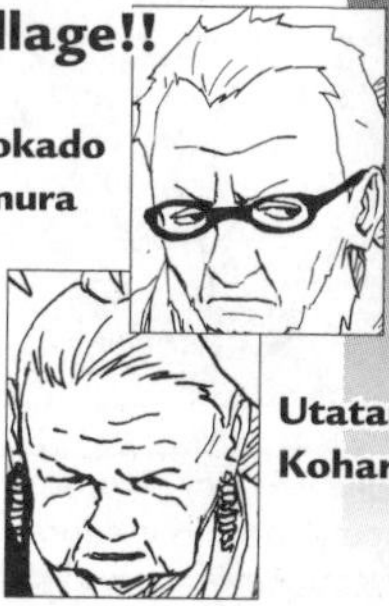

Mitokado Homura

Utatane Koharu

OPERATIONS UNITS

The backbone of Konoha!

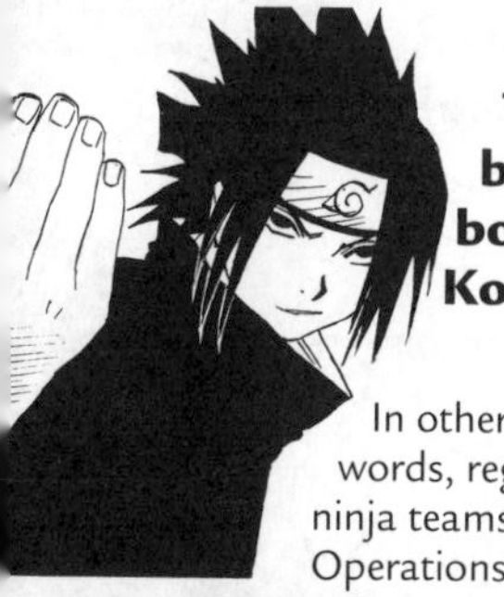

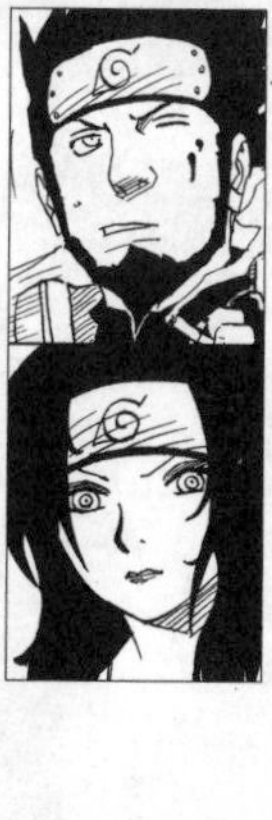

In other words, regular ninja teams. Operations teams or individuals handle the majority of missions the village receives, as well as education and other business. But when the world turns toward war, their knowledge and strength become weapons, and they concentrate on battle!

MEDICAL CORPS

Incomparable skills support those in battle!!

The medical team cooperates with ordinary doctors, learning knowledge and skills that allow them to provide emergency back-up in battle. They also develop new techniques and medicines, research diseases and the human body. By the time they reach the rank of jônin their healing skills are near godly.

⬇ They can make medical decisions from the smallest amount of information. Their care is precise and swift.

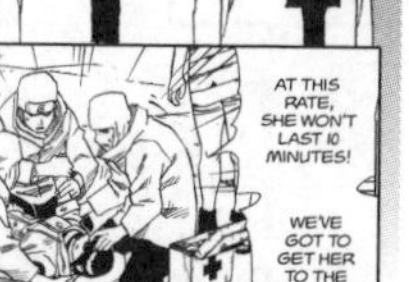

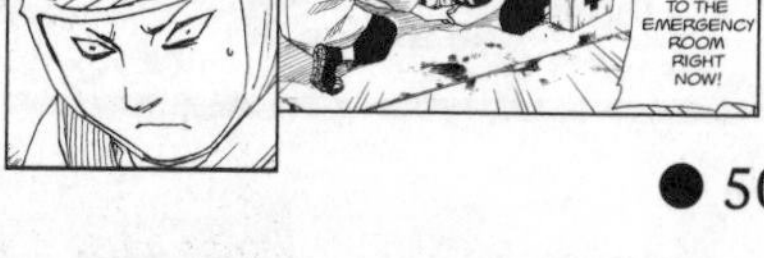
TAK
AT THIS RATE, SHE WON'T LAST 10 MINUTES!
WE'VE GOT TO GET HER TO THE EMERGENCY ROOM RIGHT NOW!

Ability and unique skills determine a shinobi's title!!

Konoha ninja are divided into five main ranks. These are given out based on raw strength and capability, and each rank has different duties and missions.

⬇ When a jônin activates a jutsu the air trembles and your blood will freeze!!

Konoha Ninja Ranks
Hokage
Jônin
Special Jônin
Chûnin
Genin
Academy Students

Academy Students are not technically shinobi, but in emergencies have been known to join the fight.

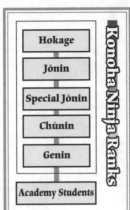

RANKS

Jônin

The heart of the village, with superhuman skills!!

These ninja have reached the peak of the shinobi forces through knowledge and courage. Their purpose — to demonstrate their incredible skills on the front lines, guiding and training young shinobi, and passing on their skills. As long as the jônin stand firm, Konoha will not fall.

⬆ Incredible speed and strength define taijutsu. Skills honed to perfection can knock enemy ninja right through walls!!

Special Jônin

Special Jônin are ranked between jônin and chûnin, and perform assigned missions according to their specialties. These missions are not limited to spying, torture/interrogation and the like, but extend to education or research, with each assignment matching their skills and knowledge.

BECAUSE THERE MAY BE CIRCUMSTANCES WHERE BEING CAUGHT IN AN ACT OF ESPIONAGE CAN COST YOU MORE THAN JUST YOUR LIFE.

YOU PAY IN WAYS THAT CAN BE TAKEN FROM YOU LITTLE BY LITTLE, TIME AND TIME AGAIN, WHEN MANY LIVES HANG IN THE BALANCE.

Specialists in their fields!!

⬆ Special Jônin Morino Ibiki. Those countless scars symbolize his resolve and dedication!

Chûnin

The elite squad commanders!

Chûnin are in the center of the rankings, but their abilities are far beyond those of genin. A chûnin is required to have the ability to command a small squad of shinobi. This means more than simple skill — they are also required to have leadership ability and good judgment.

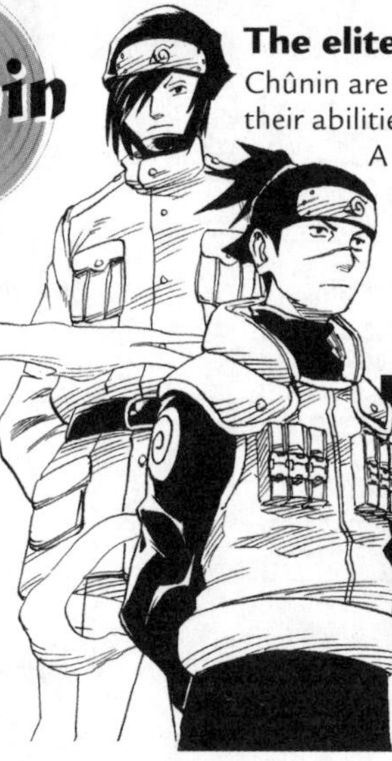

Particularly skilled chûnin might be asked to teach or monitor the Chûnin Selection Exams.

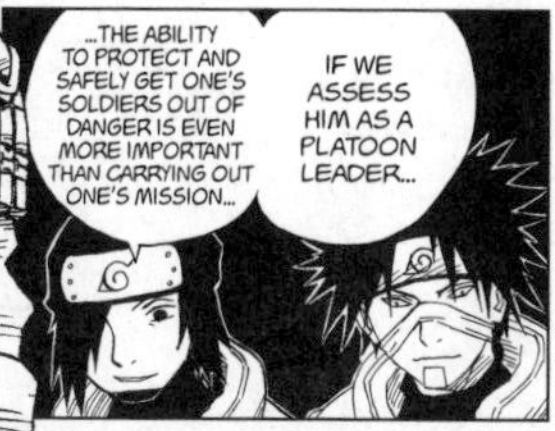
IF WE ASSESS HIM AS A PLATOON LEADER...
...THE ABILITY TO PROTECT AND SAFELY GET ONE'S SOLDIERS OUT OF DANGER IS EVEN MORE IMPORTANT THAN CARRYING OUT ONE'S MISSION...

⬆ Chûnin ninja monitored the third stage of the test, seeing themselves in the entrants' passion.

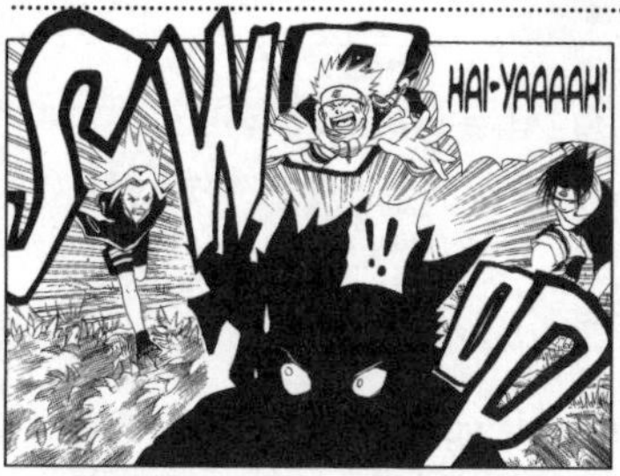
HAI-YAAAAH!
!!

Genin

Their abilities support the village!

For any shinobi village, the genin provide the foundation that determines the village's scale of operations. Without them, the countless missions, large and small, that constantly pour into the village would never be completed.

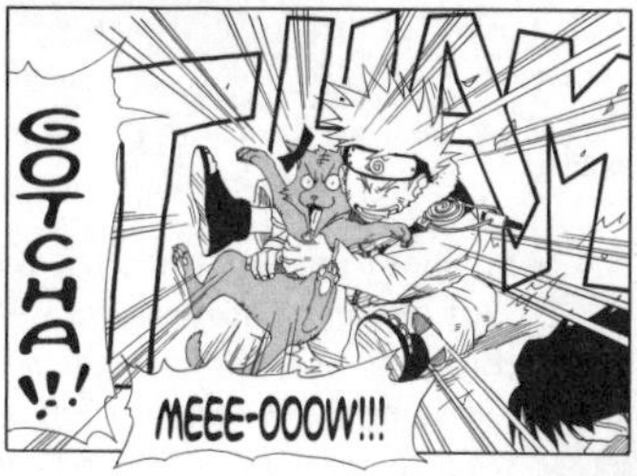
GOTCHA!!!
MEEE-OOOW!!!

New ⬆➡ genin are placed in three-man cells. As they carry out actual missions, their teamwork grows!

Their contributions to large-scale battles cannot be ignored either. They might be the lowest rank, but they are no mere soldiers. Each one is unique — they are the branches and the leaves that keep the great tree of Konoha alive, and the roots that support it in every battle.

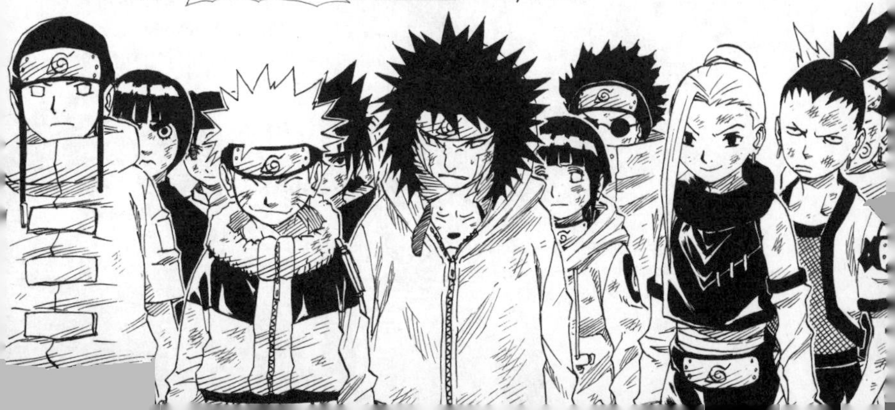

Academy Students

The next generation of ninja!
All members of the academy hope to be ninja one day. Whether from desire, admiration, or destiny...all of them practice furiously, their sights set on that single goal.

ALL RIGHT! THEN I'M GONNA BE THE FIFTH HOKAGE!
'CAUSE I'M SUPER-STRONG AND SUPER-COOL!

They hold infinite possibilities, with everything they learn, everything they think — they are the village's future.

⬅ Passionate, sincere eyes. Even as they enter the world of shinobi, their hearts are not clouded...

The Path to Hokage

Konoha Ninja Promotion System

- **Hokage**
  - Selection by the Hokage or a group of high-ranking ninja
- **Jônin**
  - Selection/Appointment
- **Special Jônin**
  - Selection/Appointment
- **Chûnin**
  - Chûnin Selection Exams
  - Selection/Appointment
- **Genin**
  - Genin Certification Exam
  - Final Exam
- **Academy Students**

The Hokage stands at the peak of Konoha — and the world. Just how long is the road to earning that name?

Chûnin Selection Exams

YOU'VE ALL PASSED THE SECOND EXAM.
CONGRATULATIONS.

⬆ Tests to see if you have the knowledge and character required to lead a squad. Occurs twice a year in Konoha, in conjunction with other villages.

Genin Certification Exam

THIS EXERCISE IS NOW CONCLUDED.
SNAP!
YOU ALL PASS!!
THAT'S ALL FOR TODAY, TEAM SEVEN. YOUR DUTIES WILL COMMENCE TOMORROW!!!

⬆ The team leader carries out the test directly after academy graduation, mercilessly testing the students' qualities as shinobi. Those that fail go directly back to the academy!

Final Exam

YOU FAIL!!!

⬆ The test subject is randomly selected from the basic ninjutsu. There is no limit to the number of people who can pass the test, so the bar doesn't seem to be set so high, but...

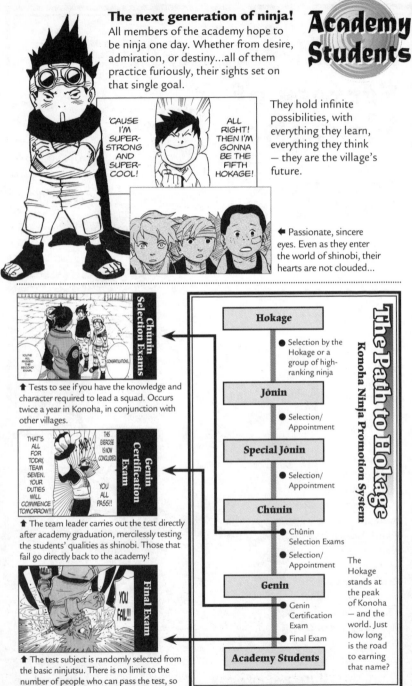

Heroic Tales

Secrets of Konoha:

The Three Great Shinobi

The Toad Sage, wandering and free!!

Three exceptional ninja in the village where flames burn the leaves. Their god-like skills shake the heavens.

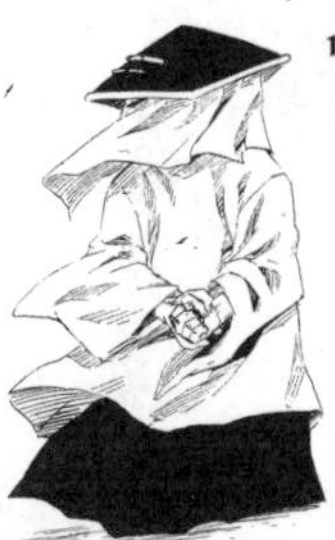

Their glory shall spread to the ends of the earth; all shall fear them, all shall praise them, spreading tales of the Konoha three.

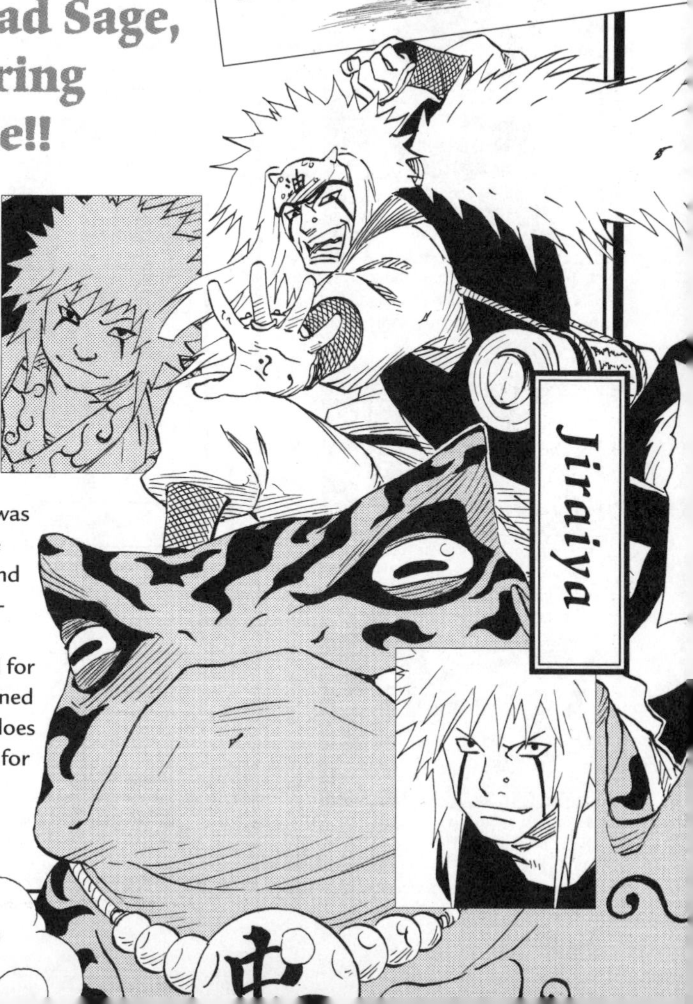
Jiraiya

With an expansive personality and a love of bright colors, Jiraiya endlessly boasts of his tales of heroism, along with his trusted partner, Gamabunta. He was the teacher of the Fourth Hokage and is a famous novelist. After chasing Orochimaru's tail for ten years he returned home, but what does fate have in store for him...?

Orochimaru

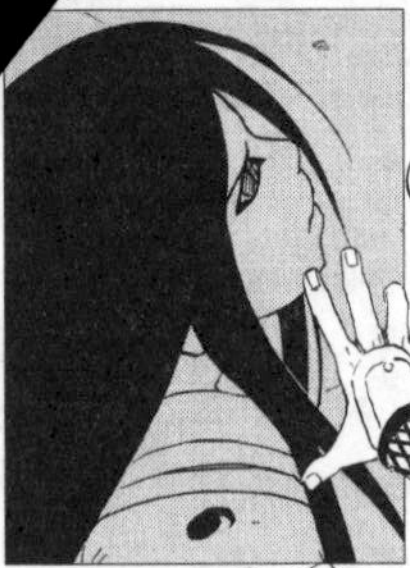

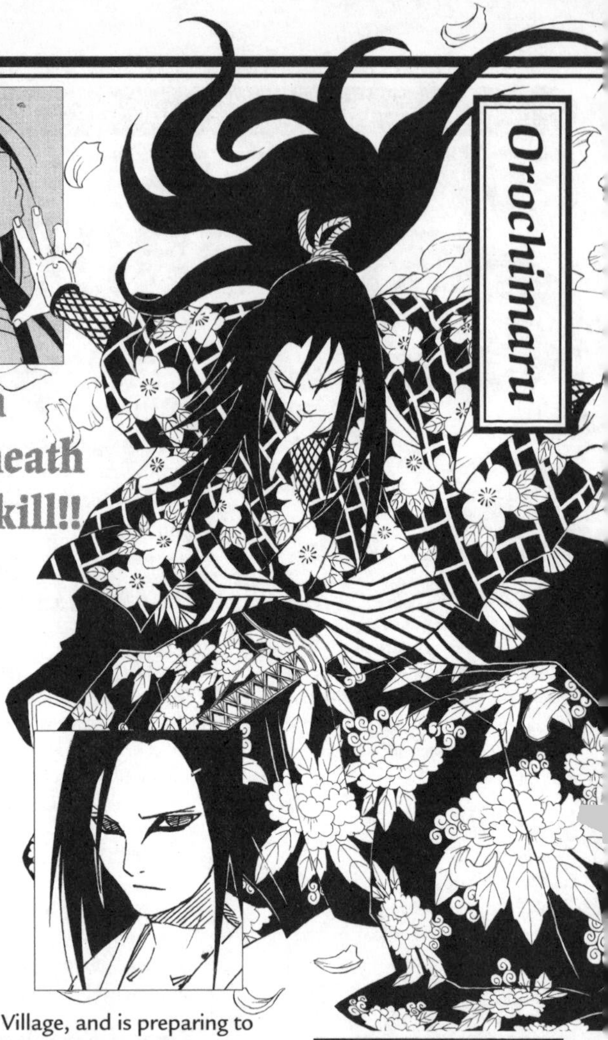

Ambition lurks beneath sinister skill!!

Even when young his name was known as a pre-eminent talent, and all feared the cold-hearted glint in his eyes — a sinister figure the likes of which had never been seen. Certain events forced him to leave Konoha and go into hiding. He secretly founded the Hidden Sound Village, and is preparing to attack Konoha. When he does, his homeland will burn in the black fires of his ambition!

Tsunade

A lonely blossom that flowered in Konoha!

Tsunade is the strongest kunoichi in Konoha history, every bit a match for Jiraiya and Orochimaru. Her whereabouts — indeed, her survival — are currently a mystery, but her name blossoms in the noble isolation of the shinobi.

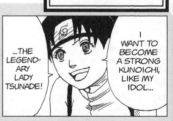

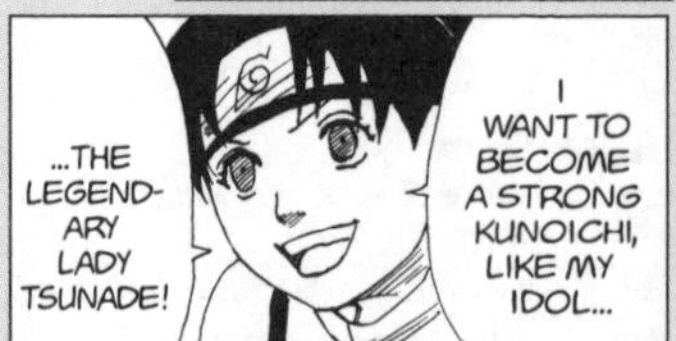
I WANT TO BECOME A STRONG KUNOICHI, LIKE MY IDOL...
...THE LEGENDARY LADY TSUNADE!

⬆ Her strength is the stuff of legends, and her very existence inspires young kunoichi.

Ebisu, Konoha's most elite tutor, has a lesso

HOW TO MAKE HYOROGAN!!

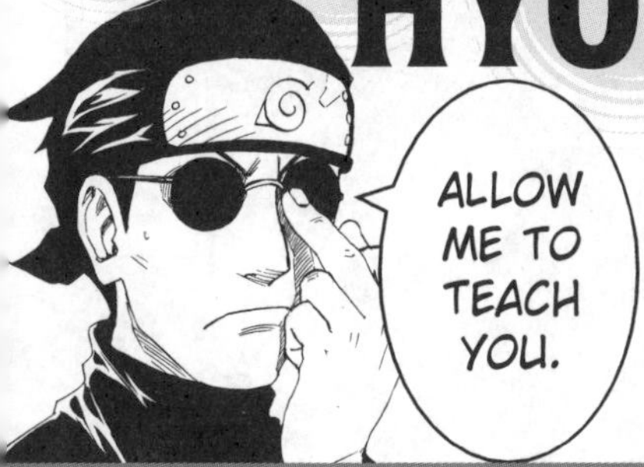
ALLOW ME TO TEACH YOU.

From ingredients at your local store!!

What are Hyorogan?

As I imagine you know, hyorogan, or military rations pellets, are dried ninja travel food, made with an eye on nutritional balance.

Ingredients: (For 25 Hyorogan)

Mixed Nuts

10 pieces (about 15 grams)

Almonds, walnuts, peanuts, and cashews are all important, but other nuts are okay too.

Almonds are especially nutritious, activating the brain and providing motivation. They also combat aging and fatigue.

Sesame Seeds

2 teaspoons

Said to prolong life since ancient times, even Cleopatra ate them regularly. Sesame seeds prevent loss of muscle strength and memory.

Shichimi Spice

dash (to taste)

The seven ingredients in this blend were all used in Chinese medicine. They strengthen the immune system, fighting cancer as well as colds.

Raisins - 25

can be replaced with varieties of mint, or plum mints

Raisins are extremely nutritious, encouraging growth, strengthening mucous membranes, heightening the immune system, preventing anemia, and many other things.

Powdered Cocoa

(sugar added) 1 tablespoon

Cocoa contains polyphenol, which prevents cancer, and a great deal of magnesium, which helps the body deal with stress and exercise.

Vegetable Juice

1 tablespoon

Contains many nutrients absolutely vital to healthy development and strong mucous membranes. Also contains rhodopsin, useful for seeing in the dark.

Green Snack

six pieces (about 10 grams)

**or other snack with string beans*

The protein in this snack is a fundamental requirement for good muscles and bones and healthy blood.

Vanilla Wafers

8 small ones (about 20 grams)

Like rice and bread, the carbohydrates in vanilla wafers are the only source of nutrition for the brain. They help with concentration and keep your academic abilities from slumping.

1

Put the biscuits in a plastic bag, and grind them to a fine flour!

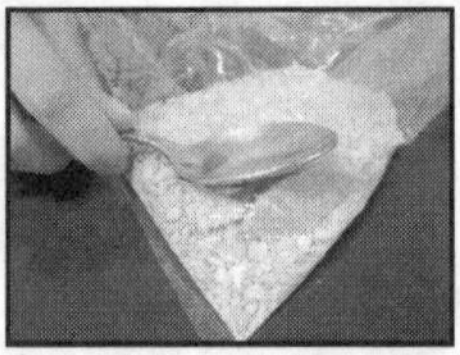

⬆ Do the same thing to the green snack and the mixed nuts.

2

Add the cocoa and shake, then add the vegetable juice and knead it from outside the bag.

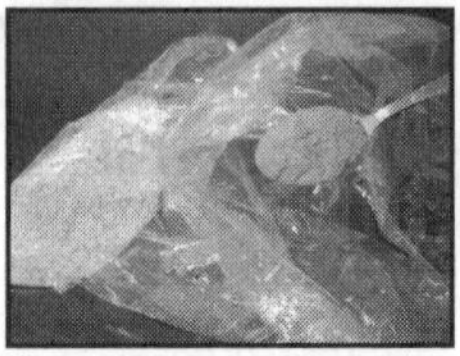

⬆ .....hunh?! Sorry, got distracted, right, knead it...

3

Add the green snack, mixed nuts, sesame seeds and shichimi, blending each of them in!

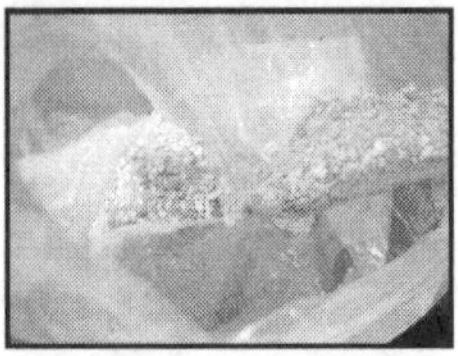

⬆ .....hunh?! Yes, just like that...blending it...yes...

4

When you're finished, place a raisin in the center, and roll it into a 2cm ball!

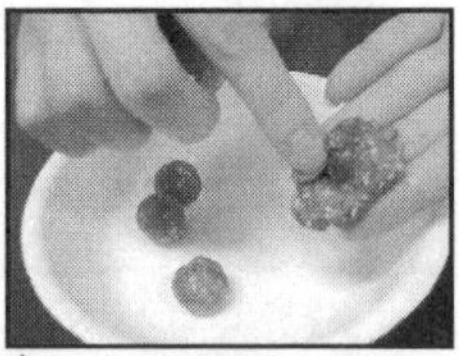

⬆ .....hunh?! Right, next...put a raisin inside, and roll it up...

5

Place them on a sheet of aluminum foil, and roast the balls in a toaster oven!
(Times will vary depending on type of toaster oven)

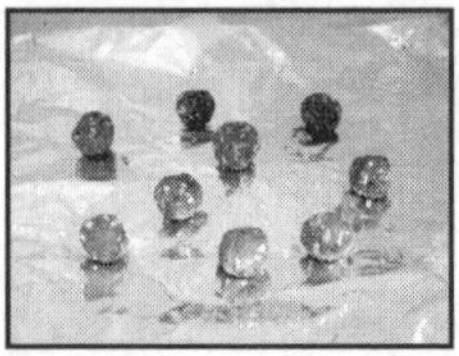

⬆ ....hunh?! So, roast them for about twelve minutes.

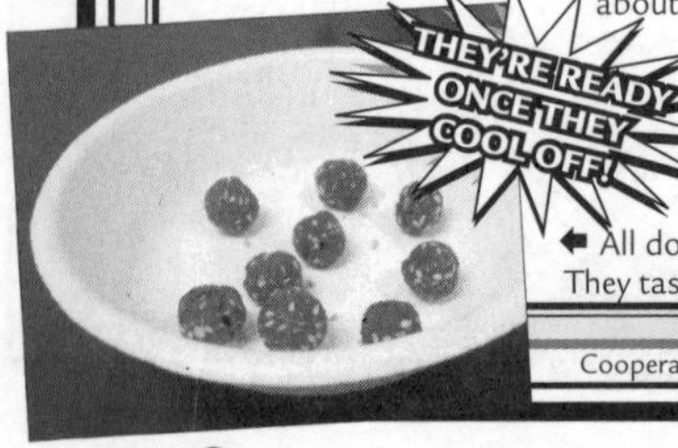
THEY'RE READY ONCE THEY COOL OFF!

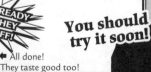

⬅ All done!
They taste good too!

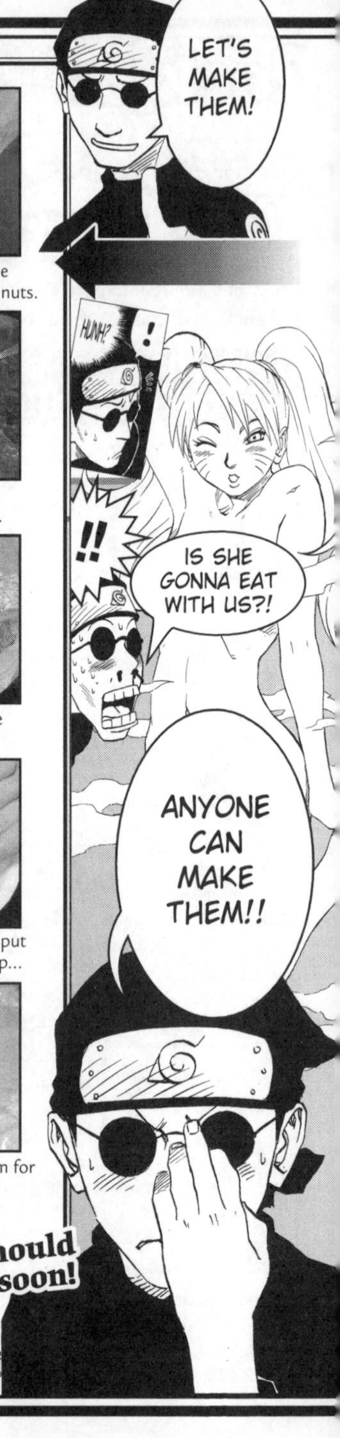
LET'S MAKE THEM!
HUNH?
!
!!
IS SHE GONNA EAT WITH US?!
ANYONE CAN MAKE THEM!!
You should try it soon!

Cooperation/Yoshie Watanabe

Rock Lee's Jutsu Seminar!

Detailed Analysis!!

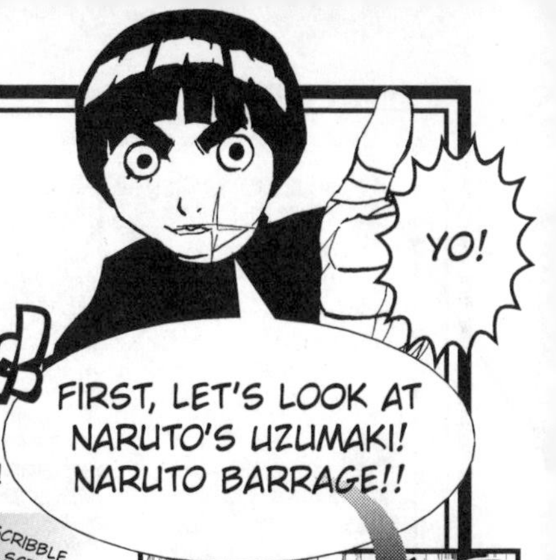
YO!
FIRST, LET'S LOOK AT NARUTO'S UZUMAKI! NARUTO BARRAGE!!

Konoha's Taijutsu Expert, Rock Lee, with a full analysis of the Uzumaki! Naruto Barrage!!

Let's check the KEY POINTS!

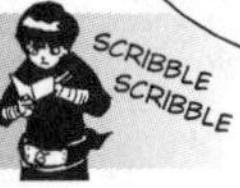
SCRIBBLE
SCRIBBLE

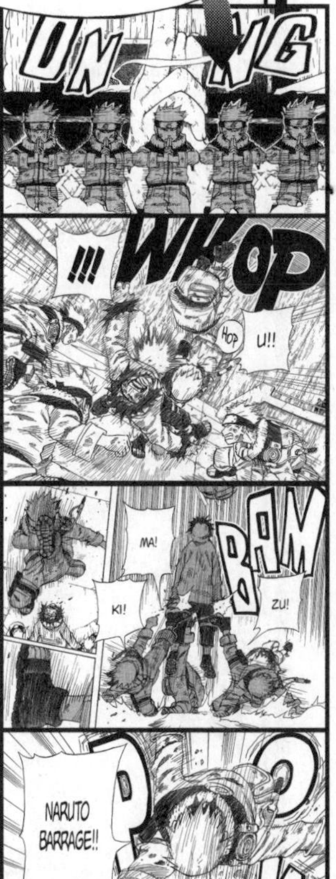
UN NG
WHOP
!!!
HOP
U!!
BAM
MA!
KI!
ZU!
NARUTO BARRAGE!!

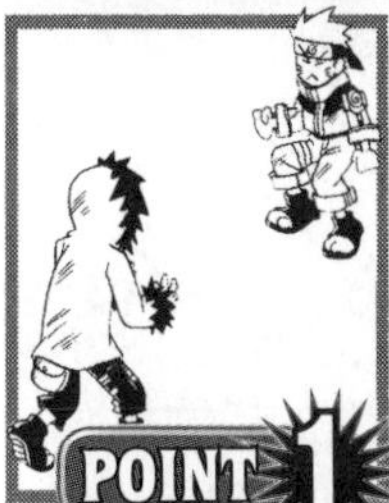

⬅⬇ First, Naruto stands facing Kiba, and makes five shadow doppelgangers! Why would he do this where his opponent could see...? To surprise and confuse him! Doppelganger techniques usually attempt to confuse the opponent, who will hesitate and fail to react quickly.

POINT 1 Shadow Doppelgangers

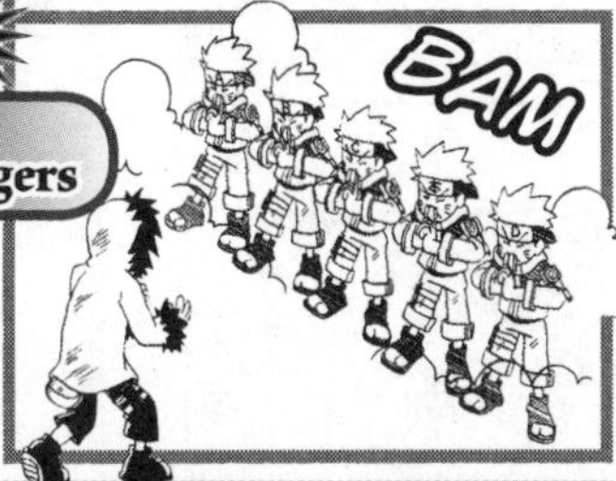
BAM

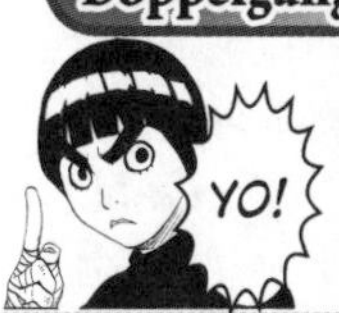
YO!

This technique requires multiple shadow doppelgangers to attack directly! This is not a technique just anyone can pull off.

POINT 2 Circle around into Blind Spot!

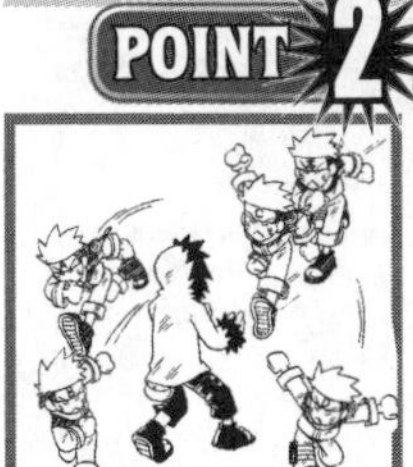

⬅ Without a moment's hesitation, the four doppelgangers rush at Kiba! At this point, Kiba is confused again, wondering where the fifth one went, causing yet another gap in his defenses! By this point, the technique is almost certain to succeed!

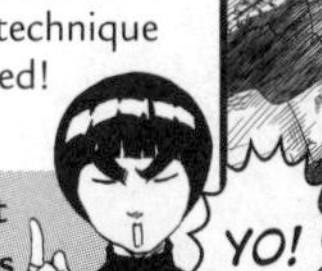
YO!

All of them act like they are going to attack, but three of them actually circle around behind! This leaves him with no way to escape!

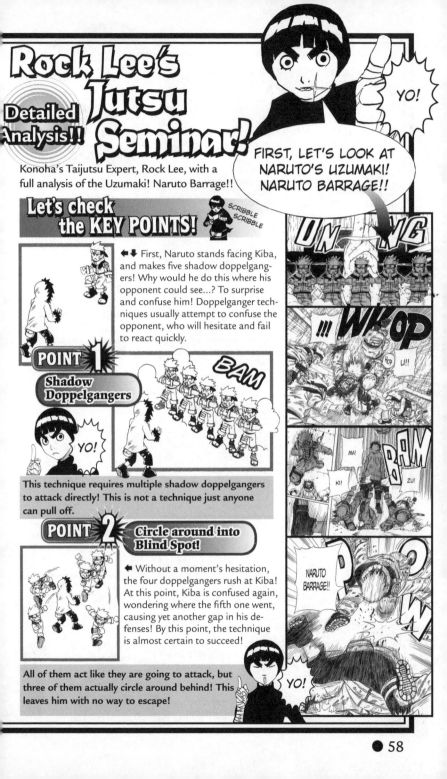

Use his back!

➡ Here's where it really starts! Doppelganger C, heading straight at Kiba, yells "U!" and puts his entire body weight behind a blow! On that signal, Doppelgangers A, B, and D, which have circled around behind him, move in closer, crouching low. Meanwhile, the real Naruto jumps into the air, spinning! Naruto and his doppelgangers all act in unison!

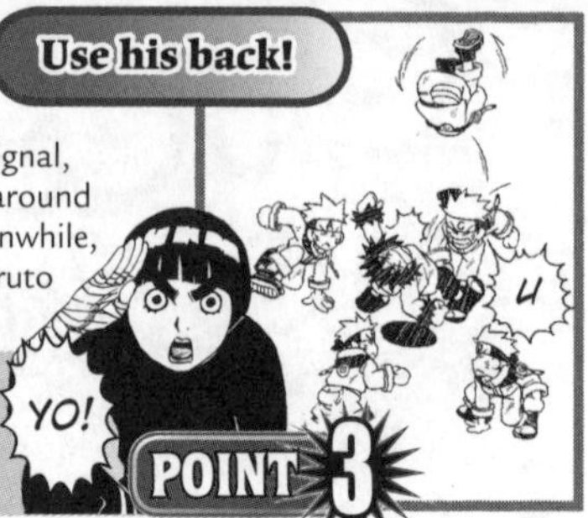
U
YO!

The key here is the height of the spinning jump! To gain height, he uses Doppelganger C's back as a springboard!

POINT 3

Shouting

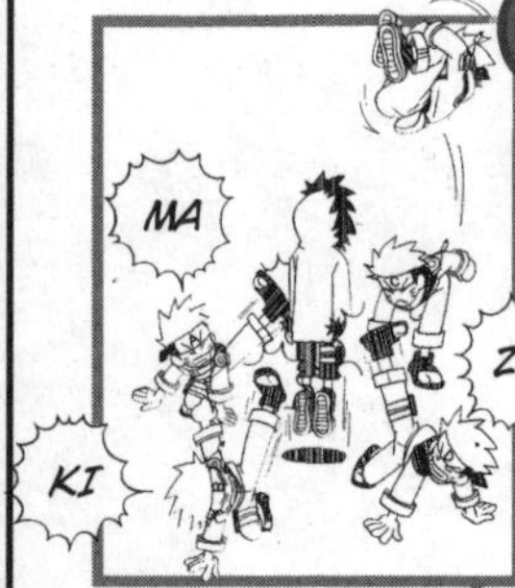
ZU
MA
KI

⬅ As Kiba falls, the three doppelgangers behind him kick him into the air! Exactly! This kick is exactly like my Lotus and Sasuke's Barrage of Lions! Naruto's own kick isn't strong enough, so he had to compensate by using three dopplegangers!

The key here is the rhythm and the shouting! This allows the spinning main body to match the timing of their attacks!!

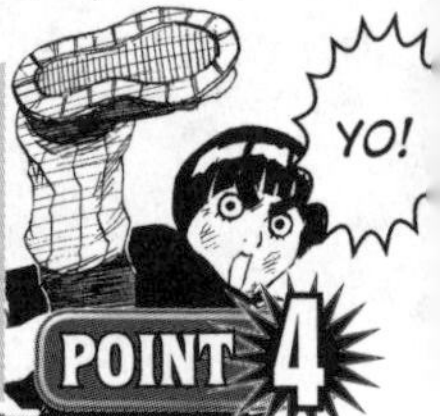
YO!

POINT 4

➡ While Kiba is flying high into the air, his head is completely defenseless...

Development points

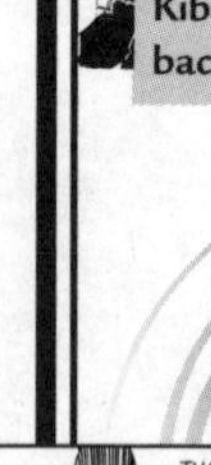
YO!

POINT 5

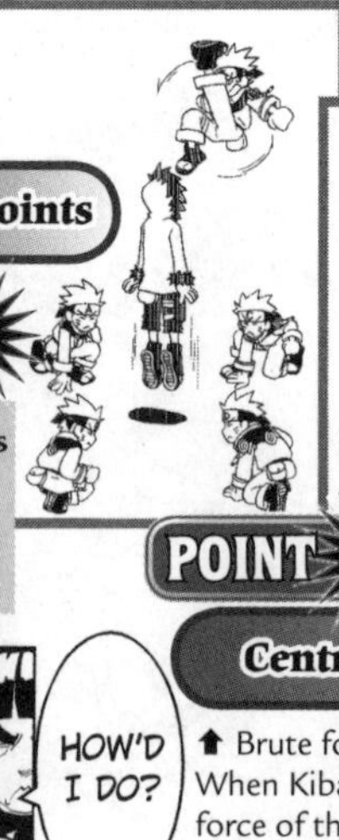

...The four doppelgangers spread out, waiting for Kiba to come slamming back down to earth!

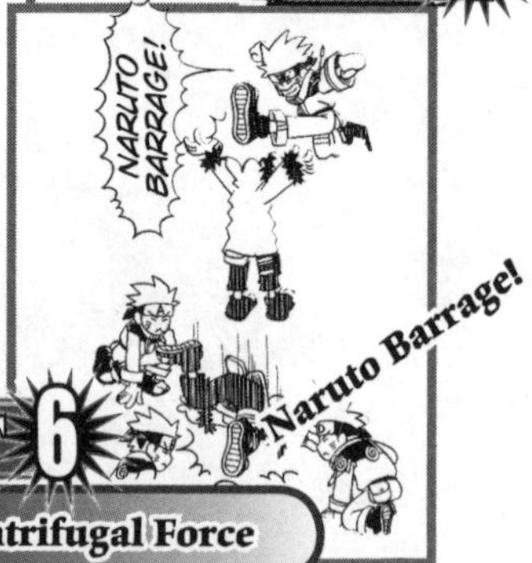
NARUTO BARRAGE!
Naruto Barrage!

POINT 6

Centrifugal Force

⬆ Brute force sends him back down! When Kiba hits the floor, the combined force of these six blows leaves him KO'd!

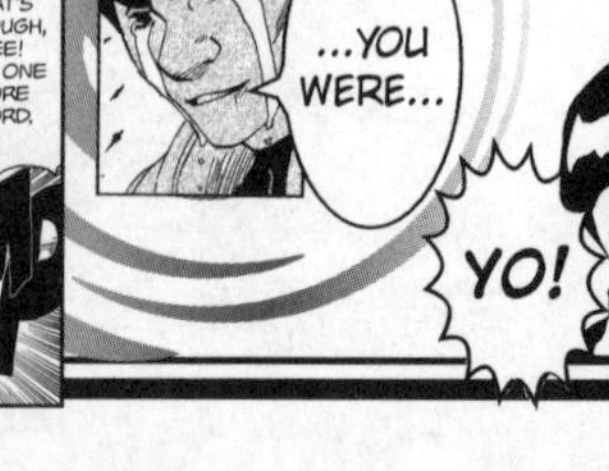
SO, SENSEI?
HOW'D I DO?
...YOU WERE...

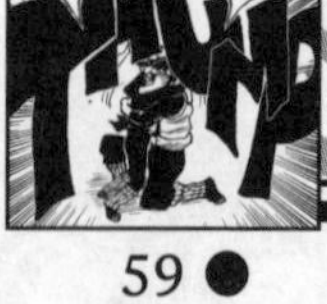
THAT'S ENOUGH, LEE! NOT ONE MORE WORD.
MASTER!!

The last step uses both the fall and the spin to strengthen the force behind the blow! The damage is several times that of a normal fall! Magnificent!!

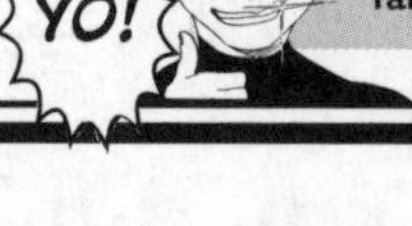
YO!

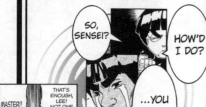

Pets! Gallery

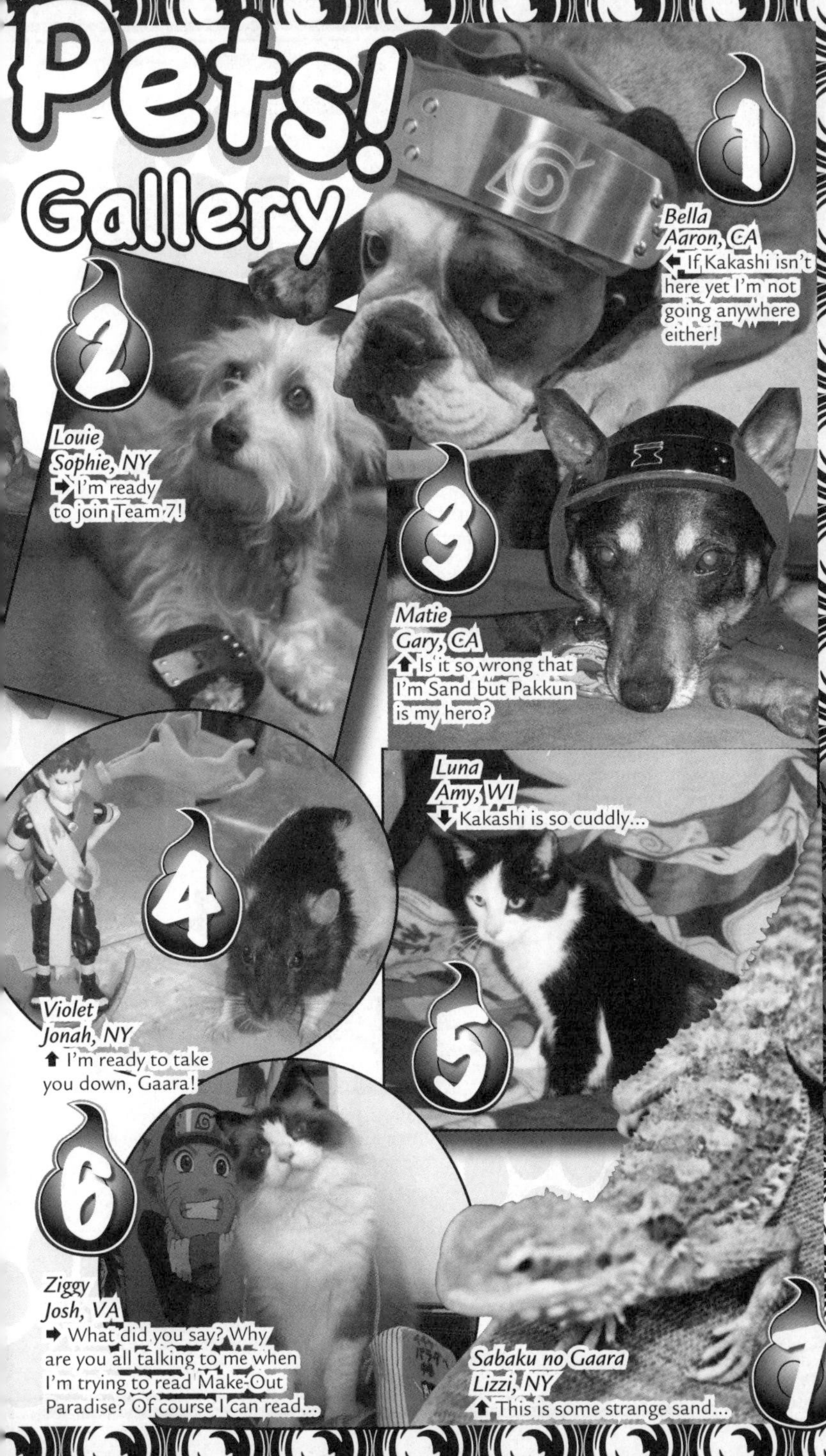

1 Bella
Aaron, CA
⬅ If Kakashi isn't here yet I'm not going anywhere either!

2 Louie
Sophie, NY
➡ I'm ready to join Team 7!

3 Matie
Gary, CA
⬆ Is it so wrong that I'm Sand but Pakkun is my hero?

4 Violet
Jonah, NY
⬆ I'm ready to take you down, Gaara!

5 Luna
Amy, WI
⬇ Kakashi is so cuddly...

6 Ziggy
Josh, VA
➡ What did you say? Why are you all talking to me when I'm trying to read Make-Out Paradise? Of course I can read...

7 Sabaku no Gaara
Lizzi, NY
⬆ This is some strange sand...

Ninja

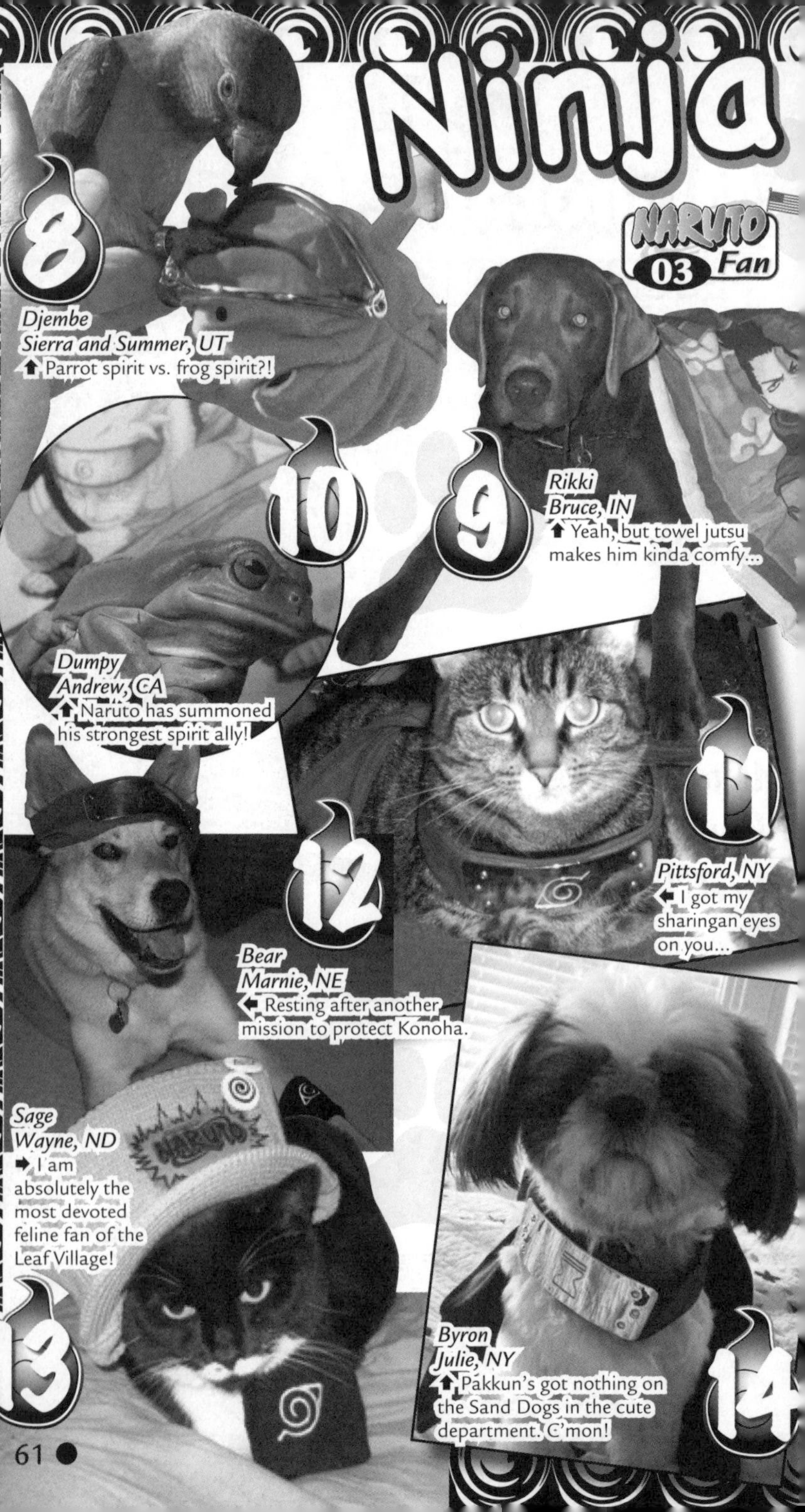

8
Djembe
Sierra and Summer, UT
⬆ Parrot spirit vs. frog spirit?!

9
Rikki
Bruce, IN
⬆ Yeah, but towel jutsu makes him kinda comfy...

10
Dumpy
Andrew, CA
⬆ Naruto has summoned his strongest spirit ally!

11
Pittsford, NY
⬅ I got my sharingan eyes on you...

12
Bear
Marnie, NE
⬅ Resting after another mission to protect Konoha.

13
Sage
Wayne, ND
➡ I am absolutely the most devoted feline fan of the Leaf Village!

14
Byron
Julie, NY
⬆ Pakkun's got nothing on the Sand Dogs in the cute department. C'mon!

The Top Ten Memorable Quotes!

Here we rank them...

NARUTO Fan 04

Out of countless great quotes, we polled readers to find the ones that made the biggest impact! Experience those feelings again!!

1

Volume 1, page 40

"I was so hard on you, yelling, scolding... It must have hurt."

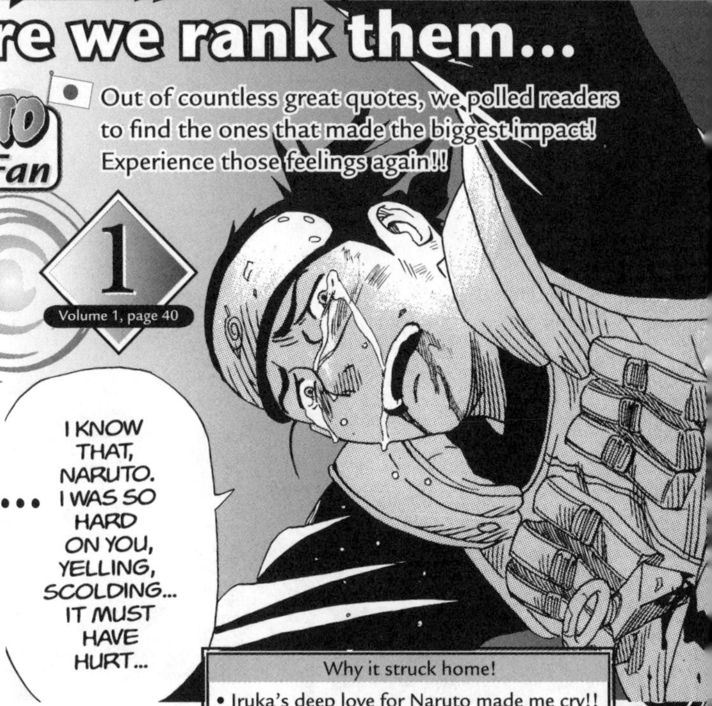
I KNOW THAT, NARUTO. I WAS SO HARD ON YOU, YELLING, SCOLDING... IT MUST HAVE HURT...

⬆ Using his body as a shield, Iruka barely managed to save Naruto. Tears of sympathy roll down his cheeks...

Why it struck home!

- Iruka's deep love for Naruto made me cry!!
- His words had me on the edge of my seat!!
- I can't put my feelings in words!!

2

Volume 2, page 102

I will never let my comrades die!!

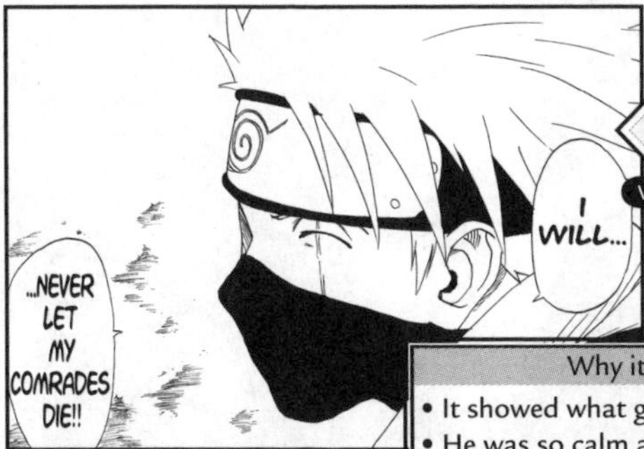
I WILL...
...NEVER LET MY COMRADES DIE!!

⬆ With this one line, Kakashi steadied his team, who had been bowled over by Zabuza's menace.

Why it struck home!

- It showed what great a man Kakashi was!!
- He was so calm and confident !!
- I was jealous of Naruto!!

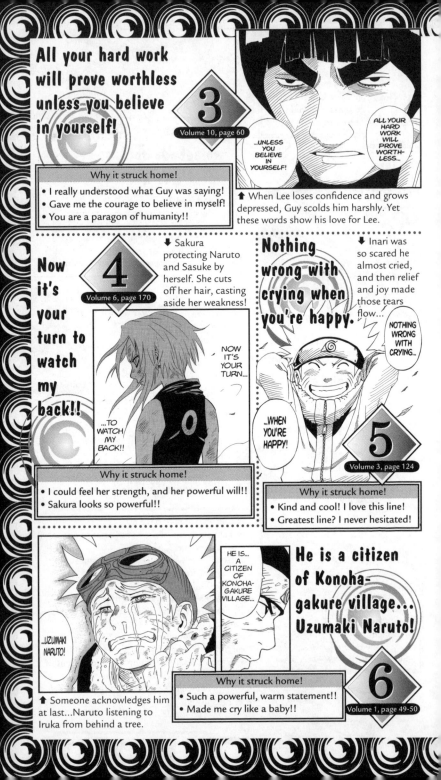

All your hard work will prove worthless unless you believe in yourself!

3

Volume 10, page 60

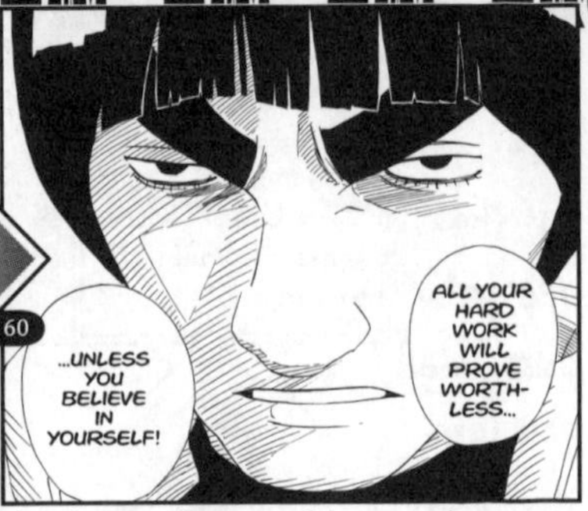
ALL YOUR HARD WORK WILL PROVE WORTH-LESS...
...UNLESS YOU BELIEVE IN YOURSELF!

⬆ When Lee loses confidence and grows depressed, Guy scolds him harshly. Yet these words show his love for Lee.

Why it struck home!

- I really understood what Guy was saying!
- Gave me the courage to believe in myself!
- You are a paragon of humanity!!

Now it's your turn to watch my back!!

4

Volume 6, page 170

⬇ Sakura protecting Naruto and Sasuke by herself. She cuts off her hair, casting aside her weakness!

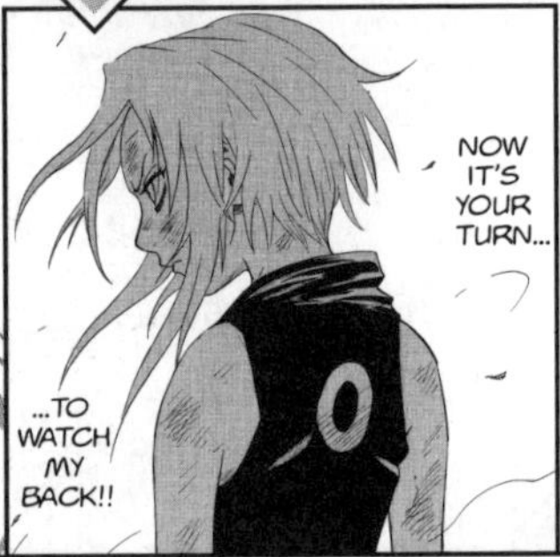
NOW IT'S YOUR TURN...
...TO WATCH MY BACK!!

Why it struck home!

- I could feel her strength, and her powerful will!!
- Sakura looks so powerful!!

Nothing wrong with crying when you're happy.

⬇ Inari was so scared he almost cried, and then relief and joy made those tears flow...

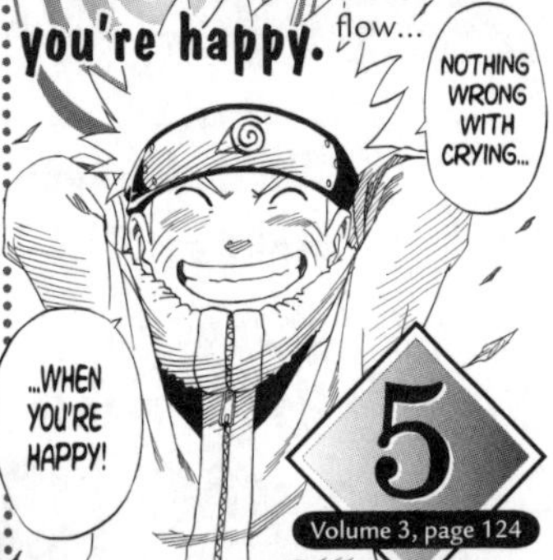
NOTHING WRONG WITH CRYING...
...WHEN YOU'RE HAPPY!

5

Volume 3, page 124

Why it struck home!

- Kind and cool! I love this line!
- Greatest line? I never hesitated!

He is a citizen of Konohagakure village... Uzumaki Naruto!

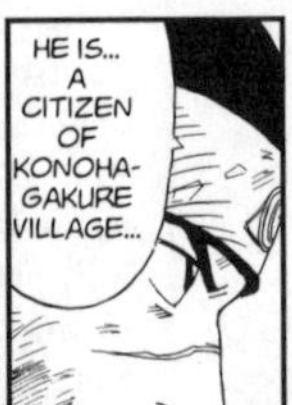
HE IS... A CITIZEN OF KONOHA-GAKURE VILLAGE...

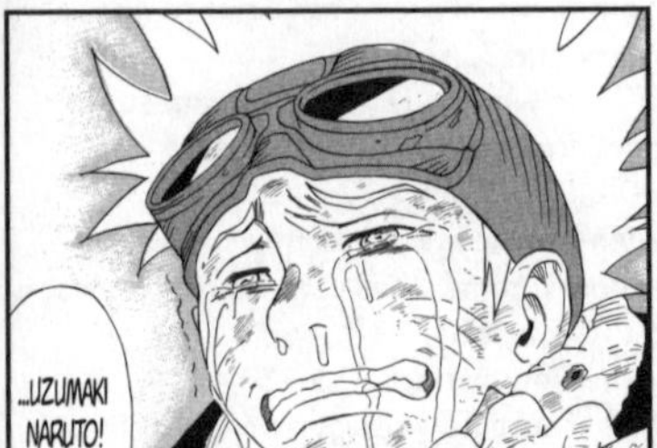
...UZUMAKI NARUTO!

⬆ Someone acknowledges him at last...Naruto listening to Iruka from behind a tree.

Why it struck home!

- Such a powerful, warm statement!!
- Made me cry like a baby!!

6

Volume 1, page 49-50

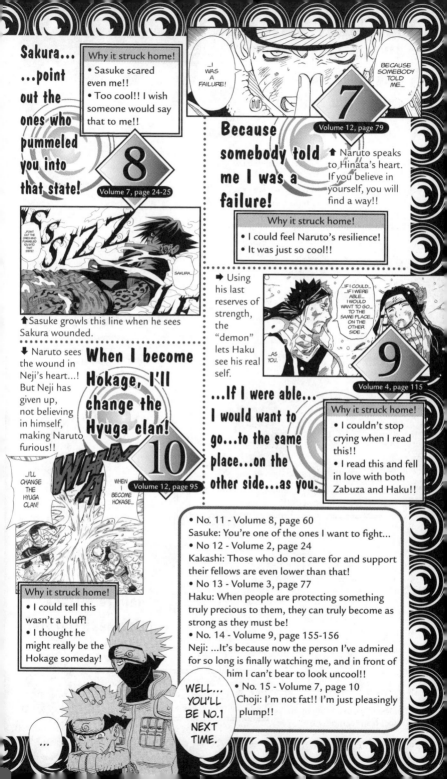

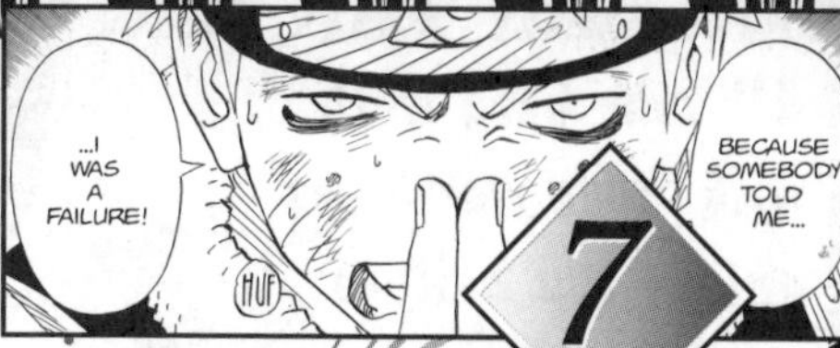
BECAUSE SOMEBODY TOLD ME...
...I WAS A FAILURE!
HUF

7

Volume 12, page 79

Because somebody told me I was a failure!

⬆ Naruto speaks to Hinata's heart. If you believe in yourself, you will find a way!!

Why it struck home!
- I could feel Naruto's resilience!
- It was just so cool!!

Sakura... ...point out the ones who pummeled you into that state!

Why it struck home!
- Sasuke scared even me!!
- Too cool!! I wish someone would say that to me!!

8

Volume 7, page 24-25

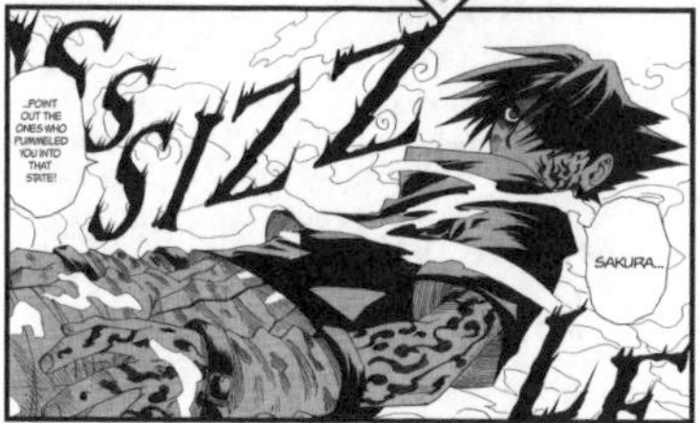
SAKURA...
...POINT OUT THE ONES WHO PUMMELED YOU INTO THAT STATE!
SSIZZ

⬆Sasuke growls this line when he sees Sakura wounded.

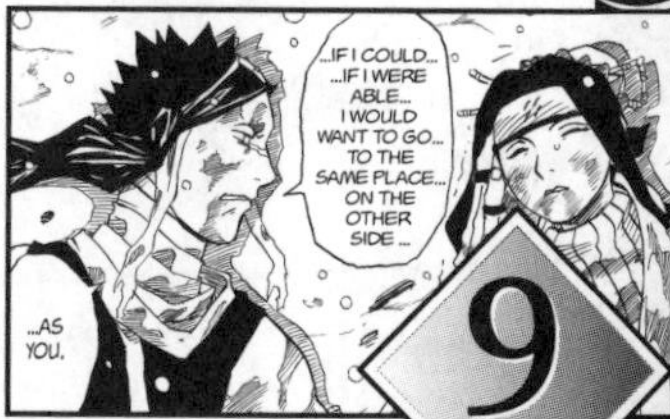
...IF I COULD... ...IF I WERE ABLE... I WOULD WANT TO GO... TO THE SAME PLACE... ON THE OTHER SIDE ...
...AS YOU.

➡ Using his last reserves of strength, the "demon" lets Haku see his real self.

9

Volume 4, page 115

...If I were able... I would want to go...to the same place...on the other side...as you.

Why it struck home!
- I couldn't stop crying when I read this!!
- I read this and fell in love with both Zabuza and Haku!!

⬇ Naruto sees the wound in Neji's heart...! But Neji has given up, not believing in himself, making Naruto furious!!

When I become Hokage, I'll change the Hyuga clan!

10

Volume 12, page 95

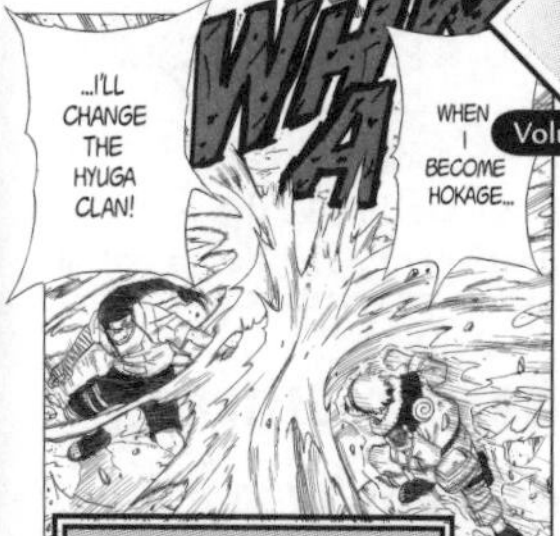
WHEN I BECOME HOKAGE...
...I'LL CHANGE THE HYUGA CLAN!
WHA

Why it struck home!
- I could tell this wasn't a bluff!
- I thought he might really be the Hokage someday!

- No. 11 - Volume 8, page 60
Sasuke: You're one of the ones I want to fight...
- No 12 - Volume 2, page 24
Kakashi: Those who do not care for and support their fellows are even lower than that!
- No 13 - Volume 3, page 77
Haku: When people are protecting something truly precious to them, they can truly become as strong as they must be!
- No. 14 - Volume 9, page 155-156
Neji: ...It's because now the person I've admired for so long is finally watching me, and in front of him I can't bear to look uncool!!
- No. 15 - Volume 7, page 10
Choji: I'm not fat!! I'm just pleasingly plump!!

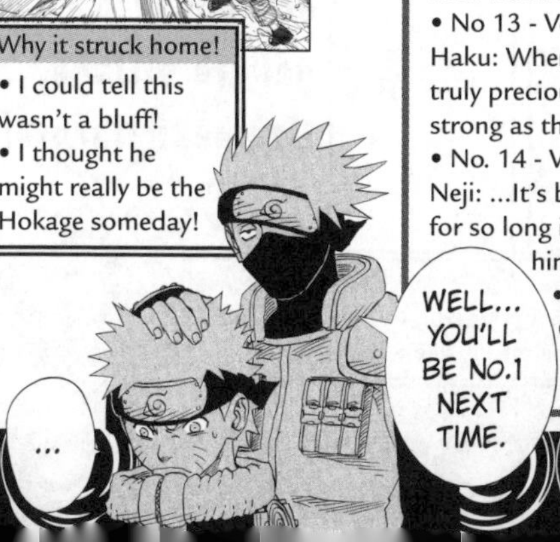
WELL... YOU'LL BE NO.1 NEXT TIME.
...

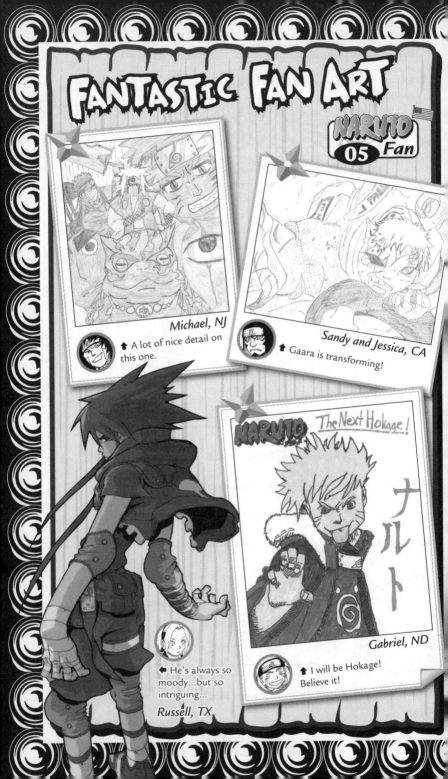

FANTASTIC FAN ART

NARUTO 05 Fan

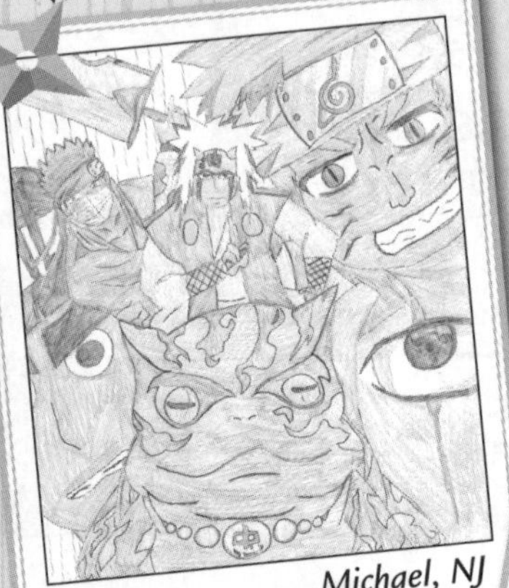

Michael, NJ

⬆ A lot of nice detail on this one.

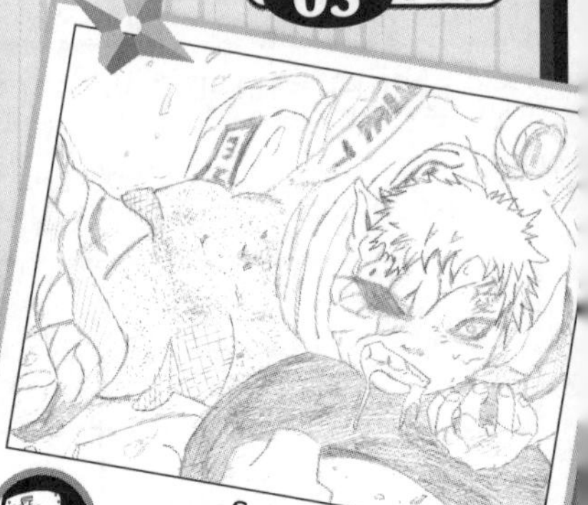

Sandy and Jessica, CA

⬆ Gaara is transforming!

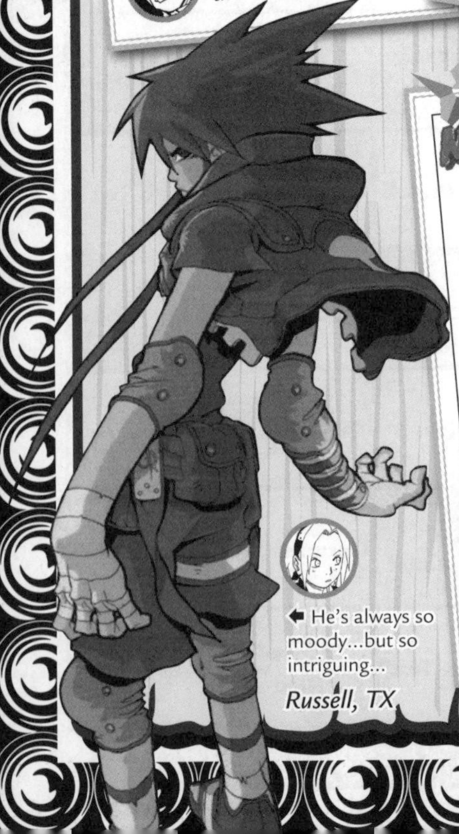

⬅ He's always so moody...but so intriguing...

Russell, TX

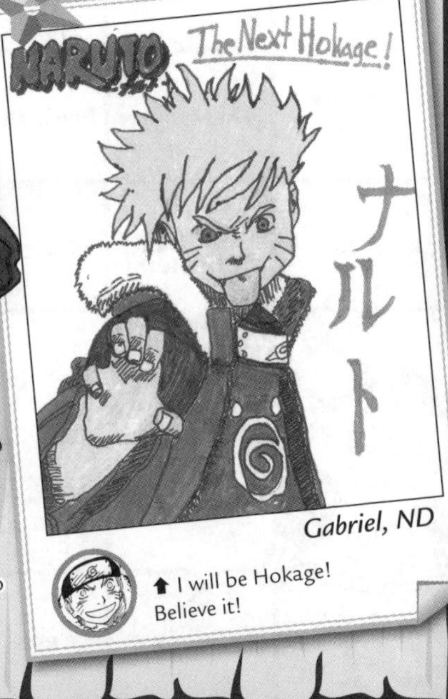
NARUTO
The Next Hokage!
ナルト

Gabriel, ND

⬆ I will be Hokage! Believe it!

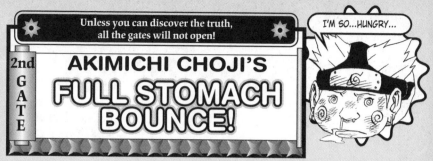

Unless you can discover the truth, all the gates will not open!

2nd GATE

AKIMICHI CHOJI'S FULL STOMACH BOUNCE!

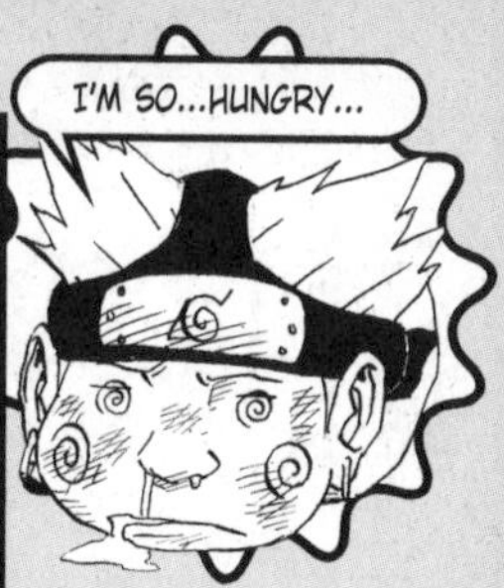
I'M SO...HUNGRY...

Help Choji eat as many things as possible to fill his stomach so he can pull off the Baika no Jutsu!! How many things can you make him eat?

* You can only move vertically and horizontally, not diagonally. Always alternate drinks and food! You can't eat the same thing twice!

Tomato Juice	Lemon Tea	Katsudon	Milk	Start! Hyorogan
Lemonade	Yakisoba	Sushi	Mac & Cheese	Coffee
Takoyaki	Ramen	Mineral Water	Cafe au Lait	Pudding
Orange Juice	Hamburger	Fruit Punch	Yogurt Drink	Herb Tea
Beef Stew	Fried Chicken	Spaghetti	Cocoa	Dumplings
	Yakiniku! Goal!	Aojiru	Fried Rice	Oolong Tea
	Cola	Meat Dumplings	Genmai Tea	Apple Juice
	Fried Egg	Green Tea	Curried Rice	Mapo Tofu

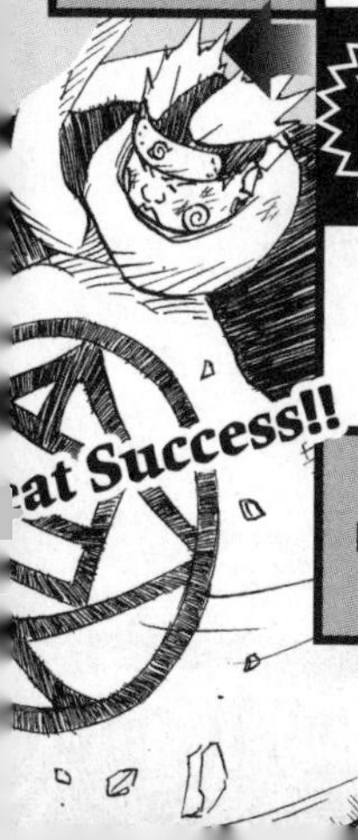
at Success!!

GATE 3 IS ON PAGE 142!!

Ninja Files

As a ninja...

As a person...

Secret files on five people
Konoha is most proud of!!

Uzumaki Naruto

Uchiha Sasuke

Haruno Sakura

Hatake Kakashi

Iruka

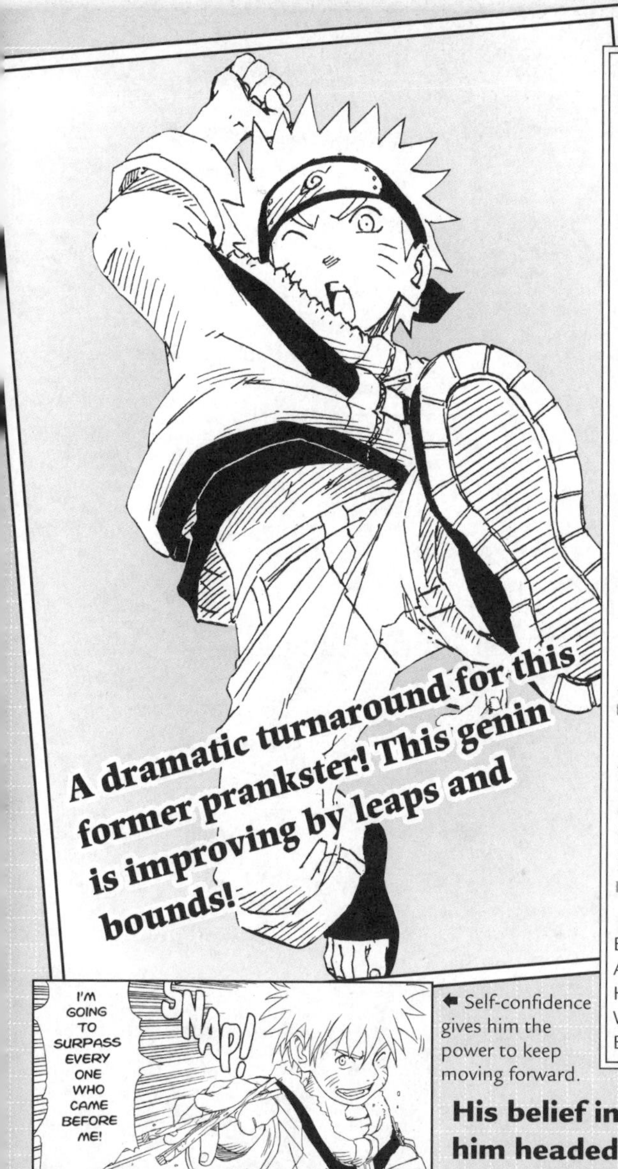

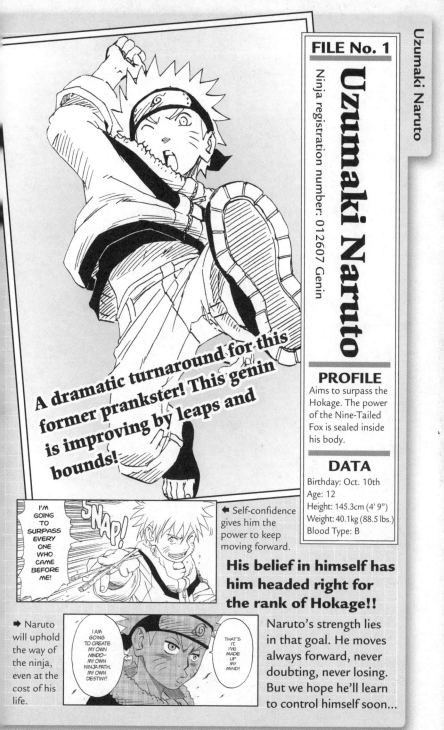

A dramatic turnaround for this former prankster! This genin is improving by leaps and bounds!

FILE No. 1

Uzumaki Naruto

Ninja registration number: 012607 Genin

PROFILE

Aims to surpass the Hokage. The power of the Nine-Tailed Fox is sealed inside his body.

DATA

Birthday: Oct. 10th
Age: 12
Height: 145.3cm (4' 9")
Weight: 40.1kg (88.5 lbs.)
Blood Type: B

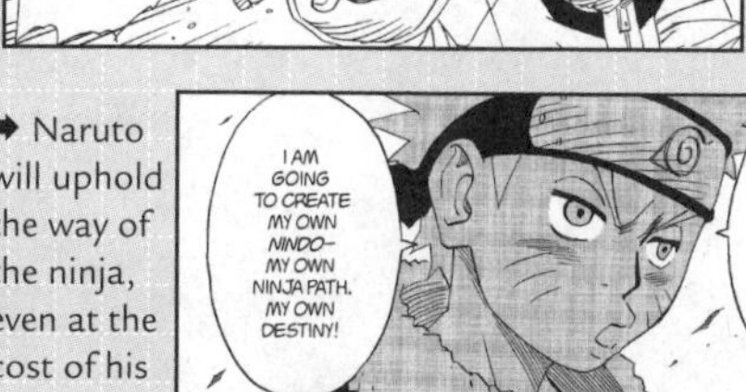
SNAP!
I'M GOING TO SURPASS EVERY ONE WHO CAME BEFORE ME!

⬅ Self-confidence gives him the power to keep moving forward.

His belief in himself has him headed right for the rank of Hokage!!

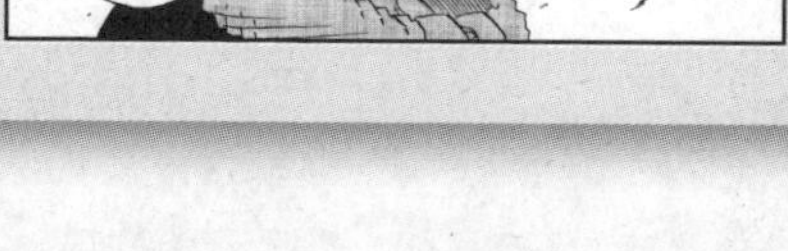
THAT'S IT. I'VE MADE UP MY MIND!
I AM GOING TO CREATE MY OWN NINDO– MY OWN NINJA PATH. MY OWN DESTINY!

➡ Naruto will uphold the way of the ninja, even at the cost of his life.

Naruto's strength lies in that goal. He moves always forward, never doubting, never losing. But we hope he'll learn to control himself soon...

Uzumaki Naruto's Past

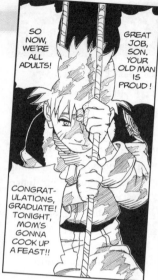

Using his orphaned isolation as a springboard to strength!

Because the Nine-Tailed Fox Spirit that attacked Konoha lives inside Naruto's body, most villagers resented him as a child. He had no idea what he really was, but he remained positive, building resilience and fighting spirit!

GREAT JOB, SON. YOUR OLD MAN IS PROUD!
SO NOW, WE'RE ALL ADULTS!
CONGRATULATIONS, GRADUATE! TONIGHT, MOM'S GONNA COOK UP A FEAST!!

⬆ He failed the test over and over again, but his will never wavered, and he kept going back to try again.

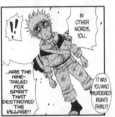

IN OTHER WORDS, YOU...
!!
...ARE THE NINE-TAILED FOX SPIRIT THAT DESTROYED THE VILLAGE!!
IT WAS YOU WHO MURDERED IRUKA'S FAMILY!!

⬅ His childhood was filled with despair.

The true strength of the Nine-Tailed Fox Spirit!

SPOT LIGHT!

The origins and goals of the demon fox sealed inside Naruto are a mystery, but we know it killed the Fourth Hokage, which testifies to its immense power!

HE SELECTED A NEWBORN CHILD, THE UMBILICAL CORD FRESHLY CUT, AND BOUND UP ALL NINE TAILS OF THE FOX WITHIN THE INFANT'S NAVEL.
NARUTO WAS SACRIFICED, FOR THE SAFETY OF US ALL, TO BECOME A LIVING VESSEL FOR THE IMPRISONMENT OF THE FOX.

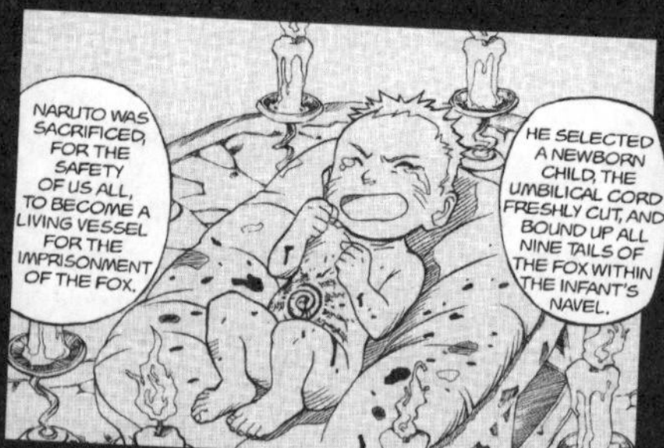

⬅ Just after his birth, Naruto was chosen to bear the demon fox inside his body!

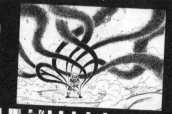

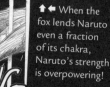

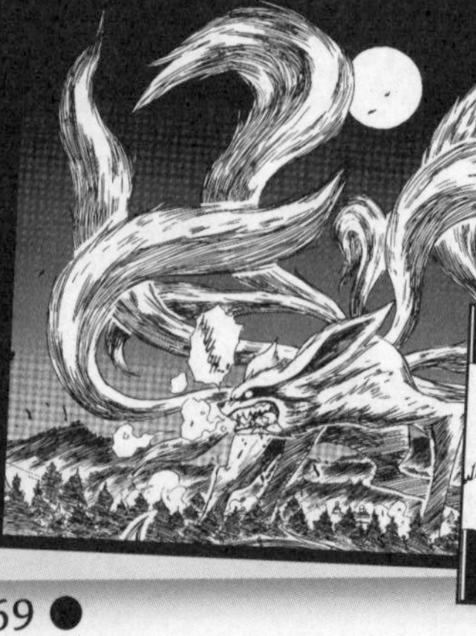

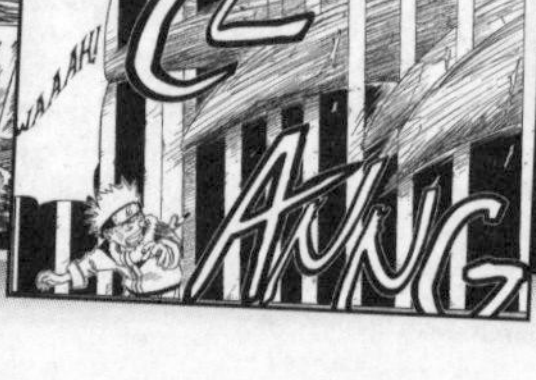

CL
ANNG

⬆⬅ When the fox lends Naruto even a fraction of its chakra, Naruto's strength is overpowering!

Uzumaki Naruto's Present

Days of Battle – How powerful will he become?!

Naruto is currently taking part in the Chûnin Selection Exams. His experiences as a ninja are blossoming at this stage. He is beginning to learn to control the Nine-Tailed Fox Spirit's chakra, and we have great hopes for him.

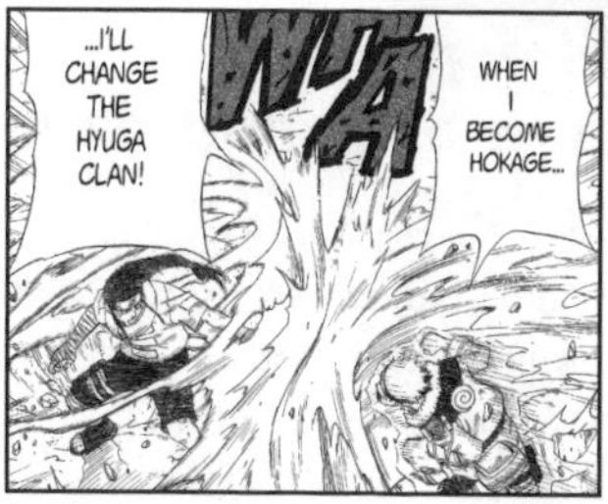
WHEN I BECOME HOKAGE...
...I'LL CHANGE THE HYUGA CLAN!
⬆ All Naruto's actions are motivated by his primary goal – to become the greatest Hokage.

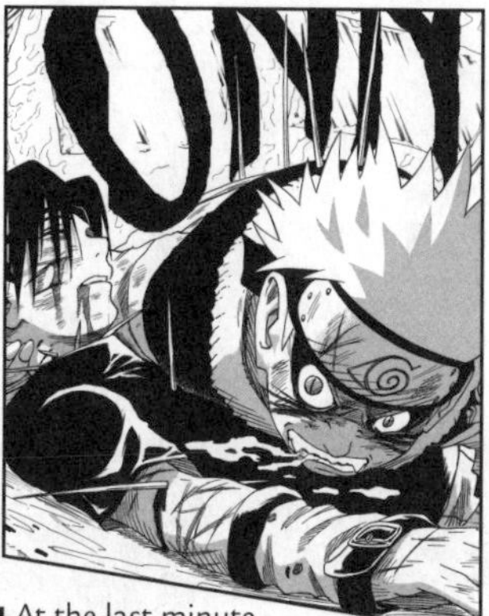
⬅ Now that Naruto understands the importance of friends, he will become a good ninja.

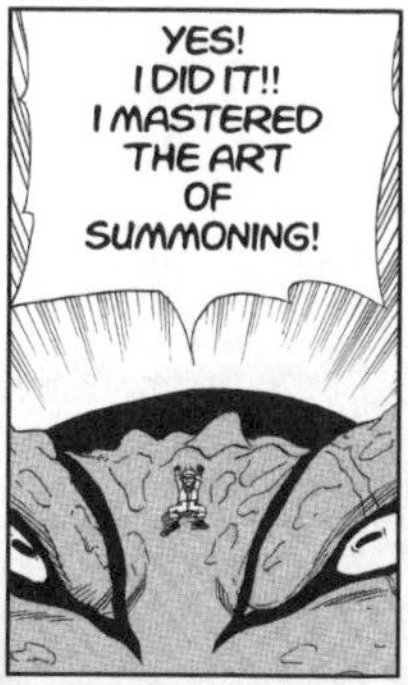
YES! I DID IT!! I MASTERED THE ART OF SUMMONING!
⬅ At the last minute, he managed to summon Gamabunta. But who was really in charge?

SPOT LIGHT!

Naruto's Greatest Battles!

Recognized by Konoha?! Naruto's three greatest battles!

1 vs. Orochimaru

Faced off against *the* Orochimaru! No one beats his nerve!

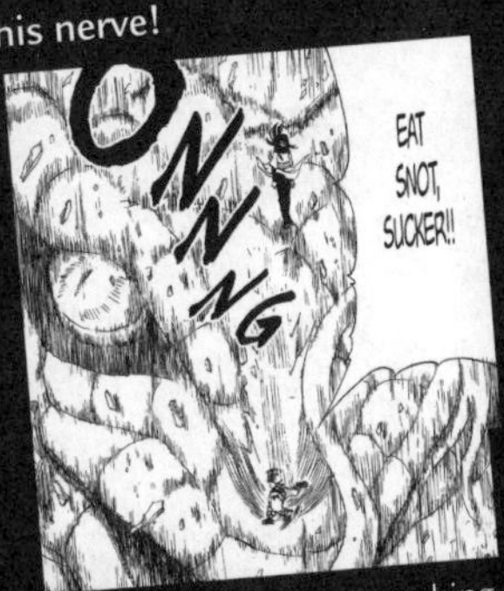
EAT SNOT, SUCKER!!
⬆ Naruto delivers a crushing blow to the giant snake Orochimaru summoned!

2 vs. Hyuga Neji

Tearing through Neji's fatalism with his bare fists! This battle held deep meaning!

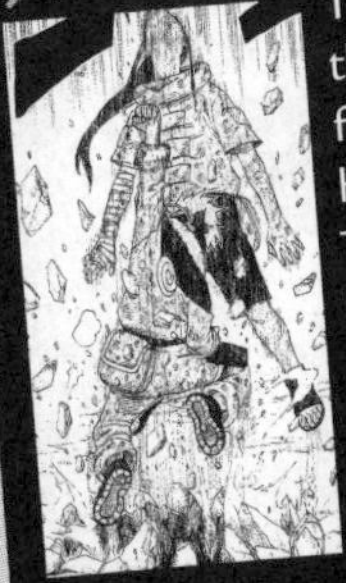
⬅ Naruto took Neji down with his clever strategy!!

3 vs. Inuzuka Kiba

Creating openings by passing gas...a technique only Naruto would use!

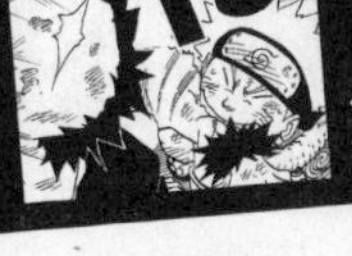
⬅ Victory by always staying two steps ahead!

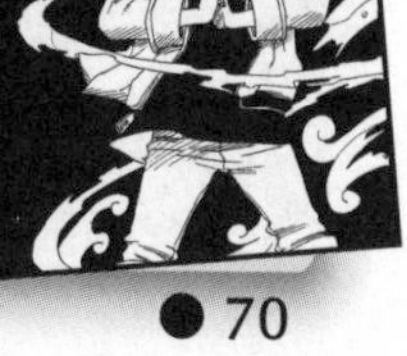

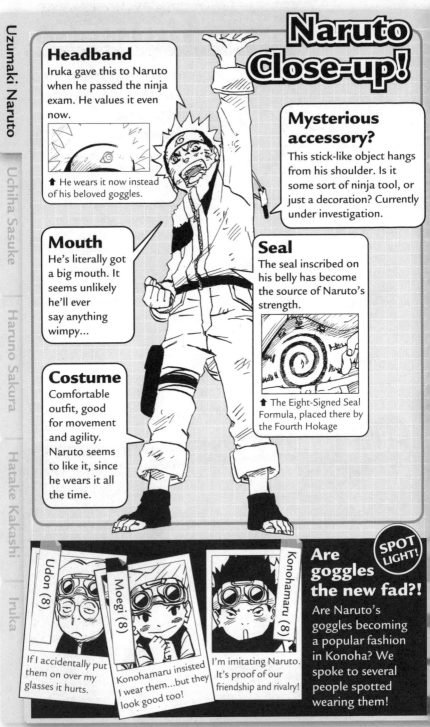

Naruto Close-up!

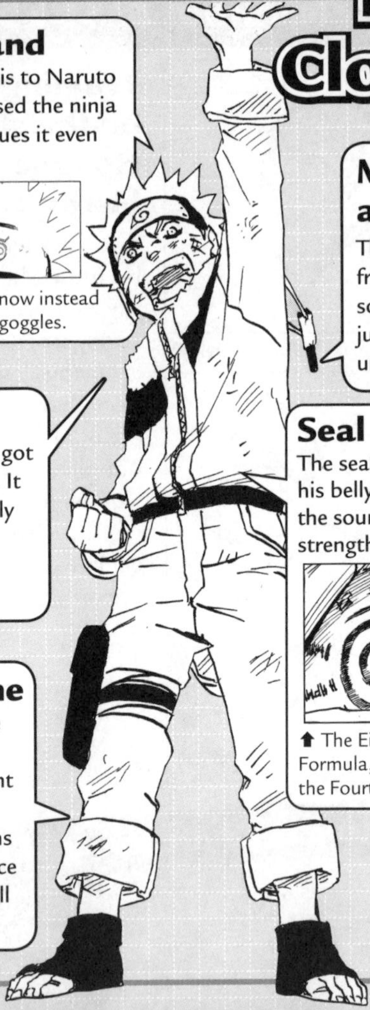

Headband
Iruka gave this to Naruto when he passed the ninja exam. He values it even now.

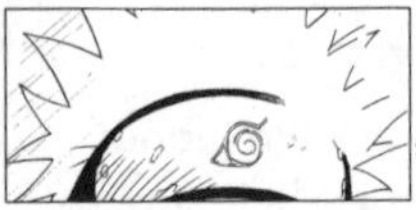

⬆ He wears it now instead of his beloved goggles.

Mysterious accessory?
This stick-like object hangs from his shoulder. Is it some sort of ninja tool, or just a decoration? Currently under investigation.

Mouth
He's literally got a big mouth. It seems unlikely he'll ever say anything wimpy...

Seal
The seal inscribed on his belly has become the source of Naruto's strength.

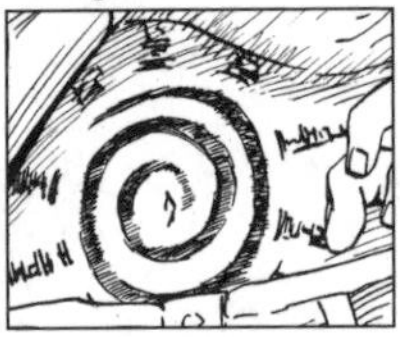

⬆ The Eight-Signed Seal Formula, placed there by the Fourth Hokage

Costume
Comfortable outfit, good for movement and agility. Naruto seems to like it, since he wears it all the time.

SPOTLIGHT! Are goggles the new fad?!

Are Naruto's goggles becoming a popular fashion in Konoha? We spoke to several people spotted wearing them!

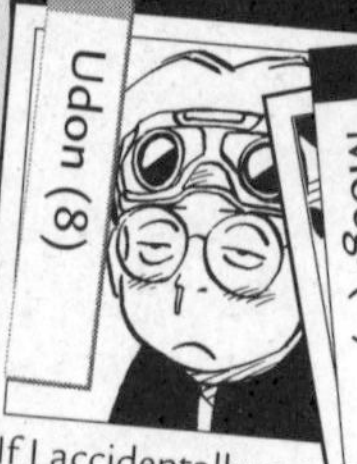
Udon (8)

If I accidentally put them on over my glasses it hurts.

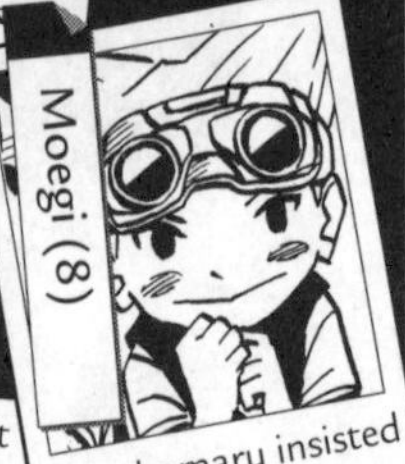
Moegi (8)

Konohamaru insisted I wear them...but they look good too!

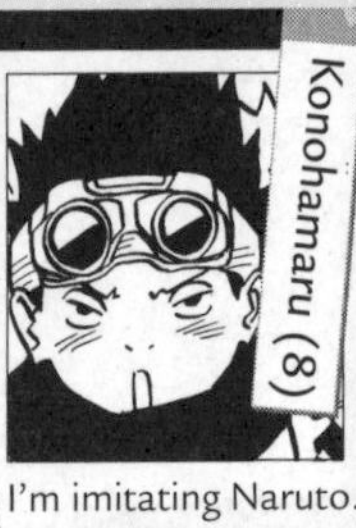
Konohamaru (8)

I'm imitating Naruto. It's proof of our friendship and rivalry!

Uzumaki Naruto's Future

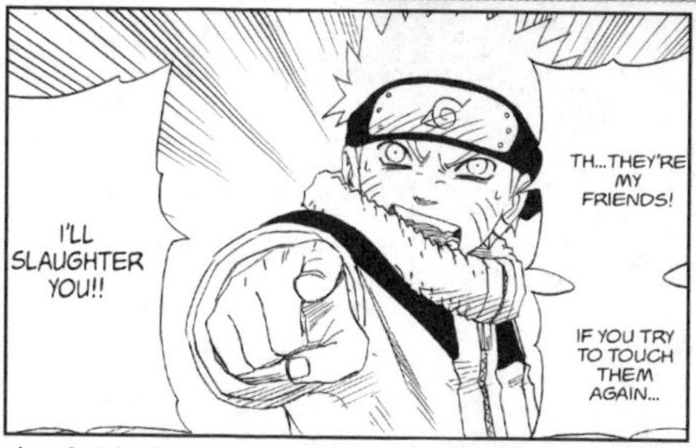
TH...THEY'RE MY FRIENDS!
IF YOU TRY TO TOUCH THEM AGAIN...
I'LL SLAUGHTER YOU!!

⬆ Afraid of no one, can he make his dream reality?

Training hard to be the strongest Hokage in history!!

If you ask him about his future, he's sure to say, "I'll become the strongest Hokage." He is obviously still very far from that goal. But there are occasionally flashes of brilliance where you wonder if he just might do it...? Certainly, he is a genin worth keeping an eye on.

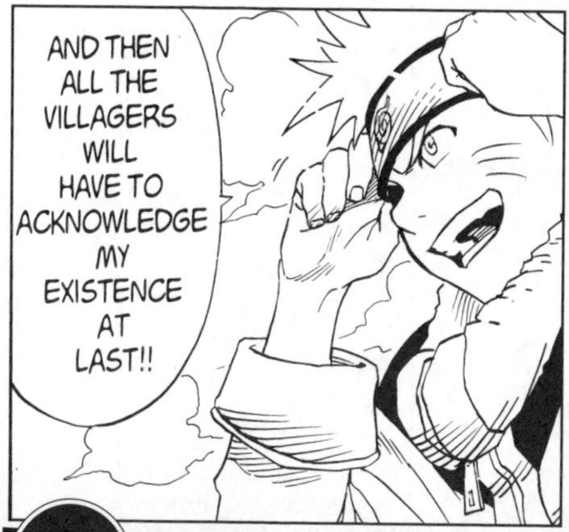
AND THEN ALL THE VILLAGERS WILL HAVE TO ACKNOWLEDGE MY EXISTENCE AT LAST!!

⬅ He is improving on a daily basis. We look forward to his continued progress!

SPOT LIGHT! Is Naruto a seed dreaming of flowers?

⬇ But this "Ukki-kun" next to Kakashi's pillow might be a present from Naruto.

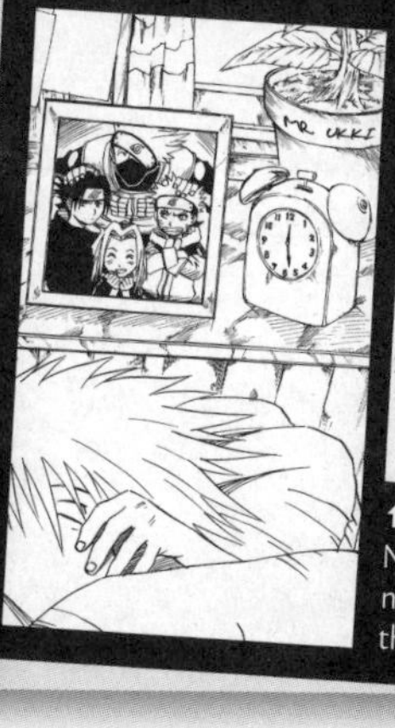
MR. UKKI

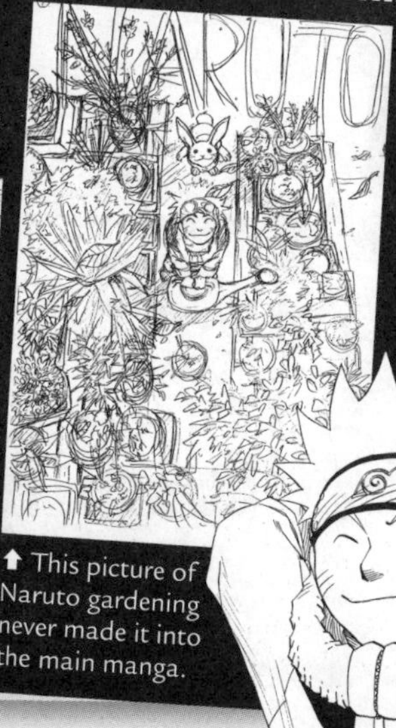
NARUTO

⬆ This picture of Naruto gardening never made it into the main manga.

His mysterious interest in gardening!

According to the neighborhood records, Naruto's hobby is gardening. A little surprising, but possibly he sees himself as a seed that would be a flower...

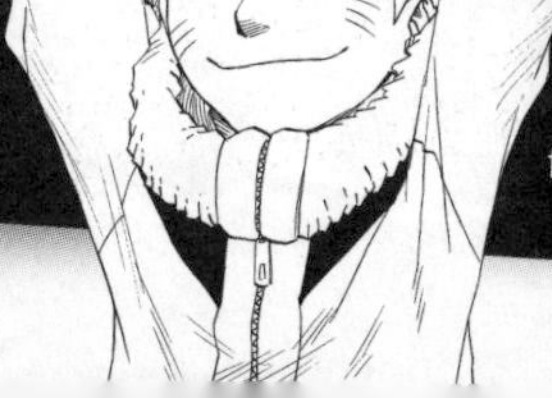

NARUTO 06 Fan

Naruto Special

THE FUTURE HOKAGE ANSWERS ALL QUESTIONS!

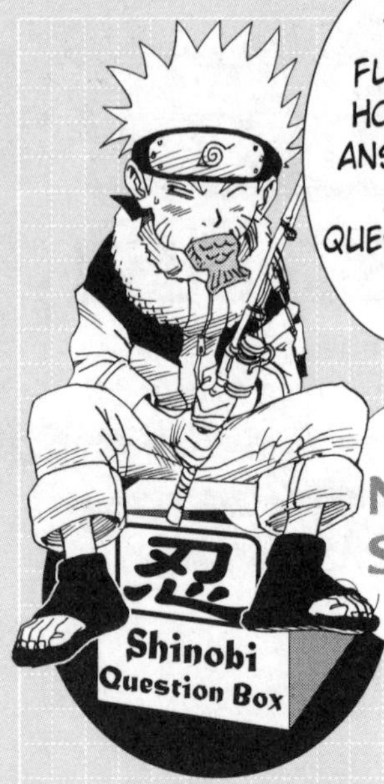
忍
Shinobi
Question Box

Small body, big dreams!
How does he stay so positive?
What do his answers tell us?

How much longer till you become Hokage?

<千葉県> 横山綾可さん

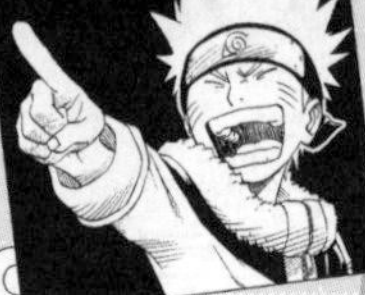

I'd love to say "Soon!" but there are no short-cuts to being Hokage! Just look forward to it!

Who do you admire most?

<千葉県> よっすぃ〜さん

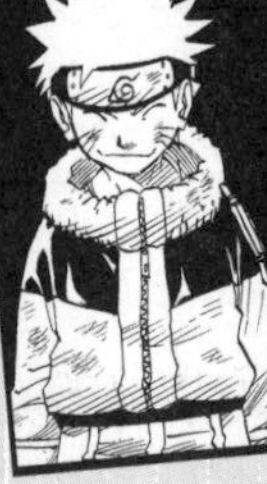

Admire...? I love Iruka-sensei, and I think the Hokage's amazing, but is that really admiration?

I know Naruto likes ramen, but what kind?

<福島県> すーちゃんさん

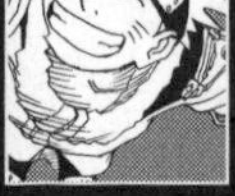

I like all kinds of ramen, but my favorite is miso ramen! Especially with extra chashu (sliced pork placed on top of ramen)!

If you can't be Hokage, what will you do?

<三重県> 牛丼タロウさん

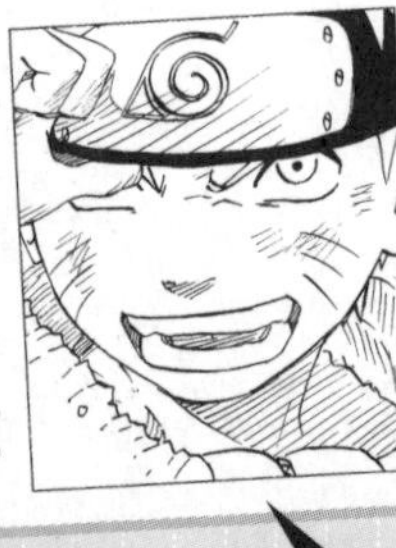

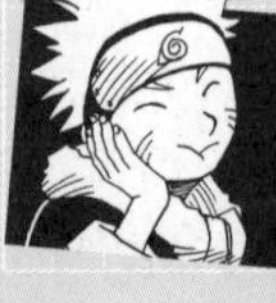

I'm not much good at thinking about ifs. I mean, I am gonna be Hokage, so why worry about it?

What do you think of Hinata?

<東京都> 木名瀬圭さん

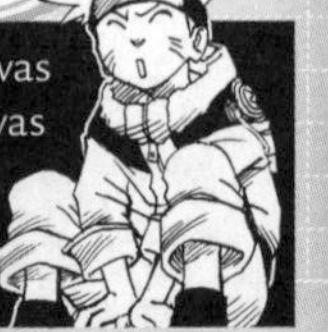

I dunno. First she was a wimp, then she was really tough...but I know she's got a good heart!

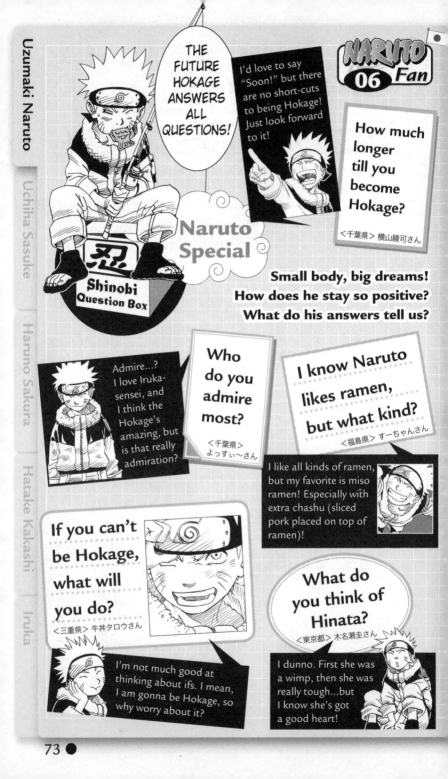

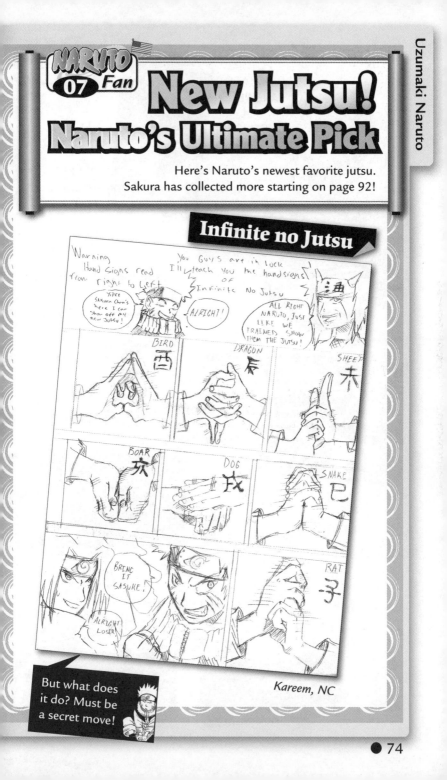

NARUTO 07 Fan

New Jutsu! Naruto's Ultimate Pick

Here's Naruto's newest favorite jutsu.
Sakura has collected more starting on page 92!

Infinite no Jutsu

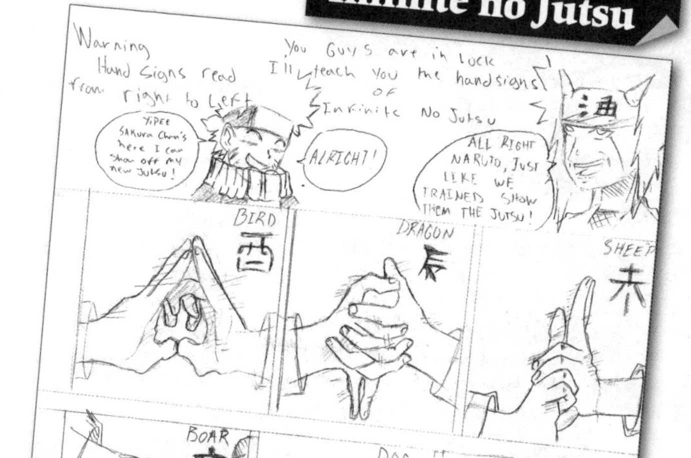
Warning Hand Signs read from right to left
YIPEE SAKURA Chan's here I can show off my new Jutsu!
You Guys are in luck I'll teach you the handsigns of Infinite No Jutsu
ALRIGHT!
ALL RIGHT NARUTO, JUST LIKE WE TRAINED SHOW THEM THE JUTSU!
BIRD 酉
DRAGON 辰
SHEEP 未
BOAR 亥
DOG 戌
SNAKE 巳
BRING IT SASUKE!
ALRIGHT LOSER!
RAT 子

Kareem, NC

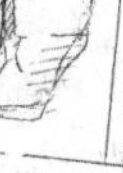

But what does it do? Must be a secret move!

Don't Let Naruto Win!

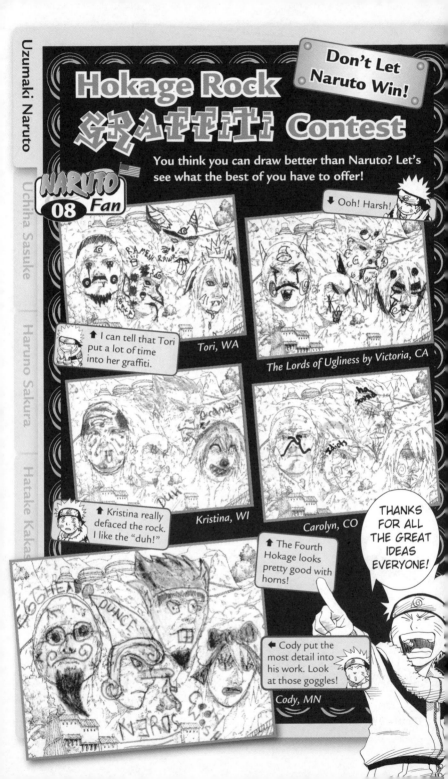

Hokage Rock GRAFFITI Contest

NARUTO Fan 08

You think you can draw better than Naruto? Let's see what the best of you have to offer!

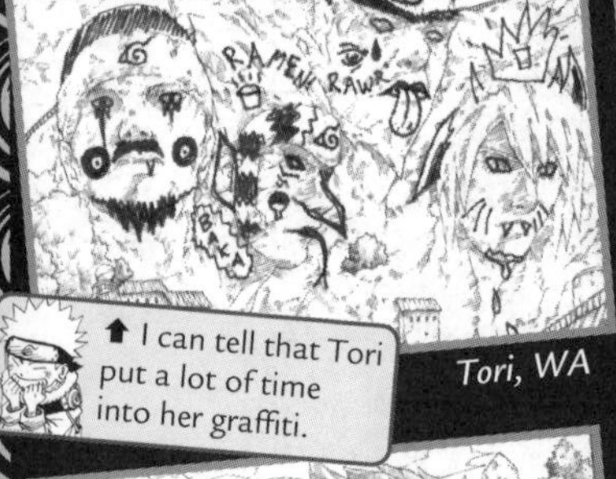
RAMEN
RAWR
Tori, WA

⬆ I can tell that Tori put a lot of time into her graffiti.

⬇ Ooh! Harsh!

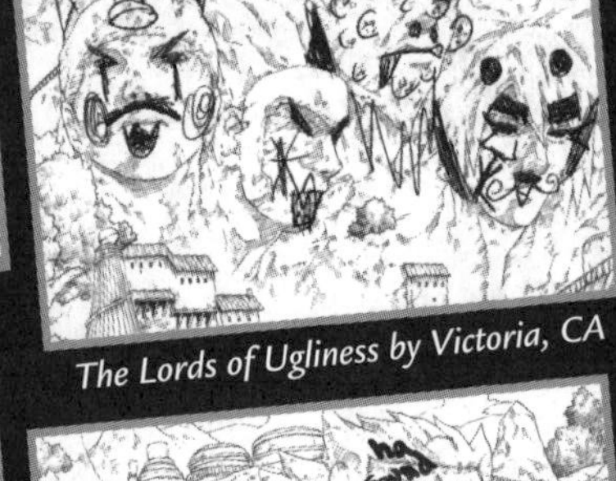
The Lords of Ugliness by Victoria, CA

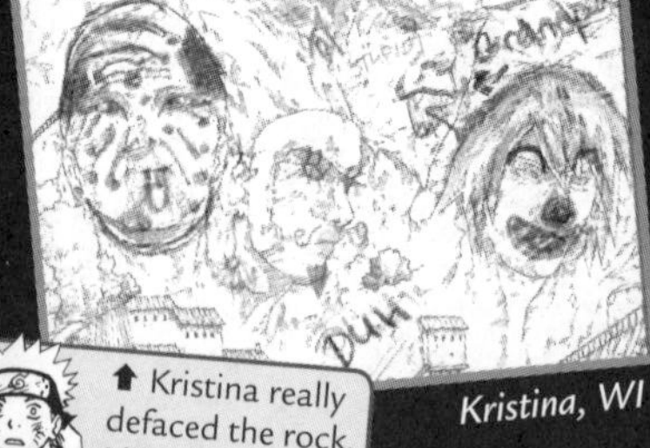
DUH
Kristina, WI

⬆ Kristina really defaced the rock. I like the "duh!"

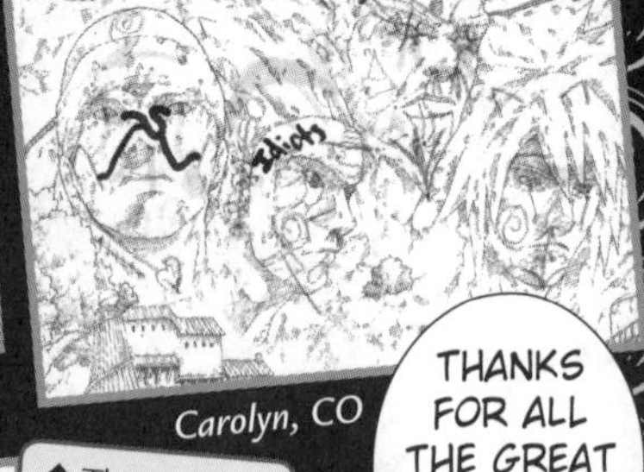
Idiots
Carolyn, CO

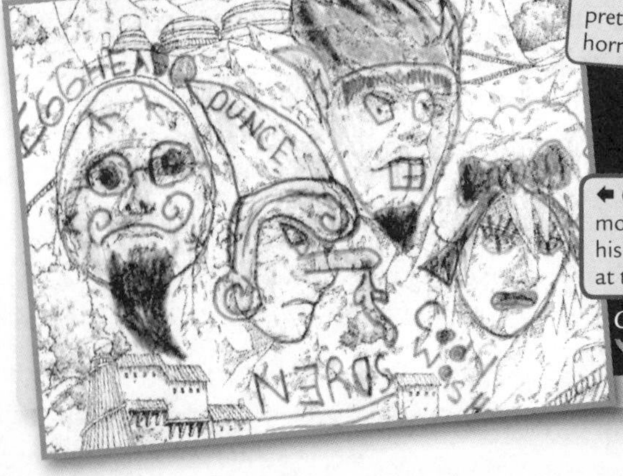
DUNCE
NERDS
Cody, MN

⬆ The Fourth Hokage looks pretty good with horns!

⬅ Cody put the most detail into his work. Look at those goggles!

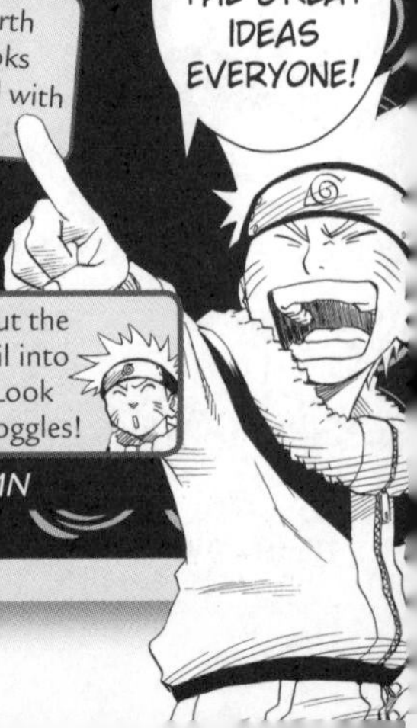
THANKS FOR ALL THE GREAT IDEAS EVERYONE!

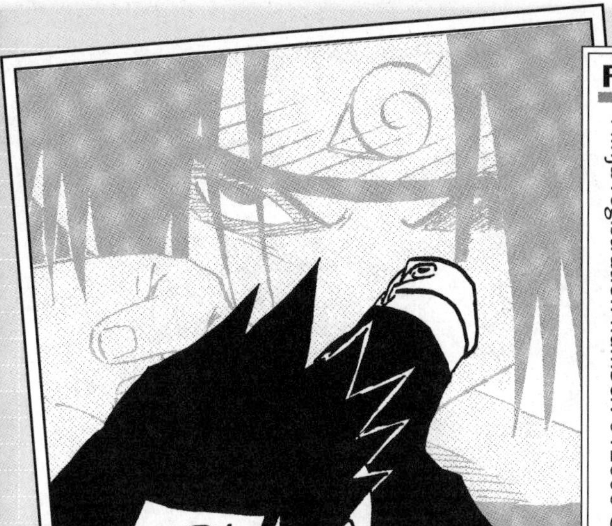

Heir to the Uchiha—the blood of Konoha's best!!

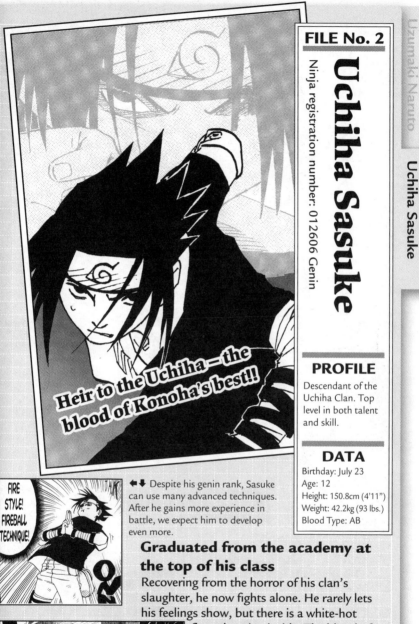

FILE No. 2

Uchiha Sasuke

Ninja registration number: 012606 Genin

PROFILE

Descendant of the Uchiha Clan. Top level in both talent and skill.

DATA

Birthday: July 23
Age: 12
Height: 150.8cm (4'11")
Weight: 42.2kg (93 lbs.)
Blood Type: AB

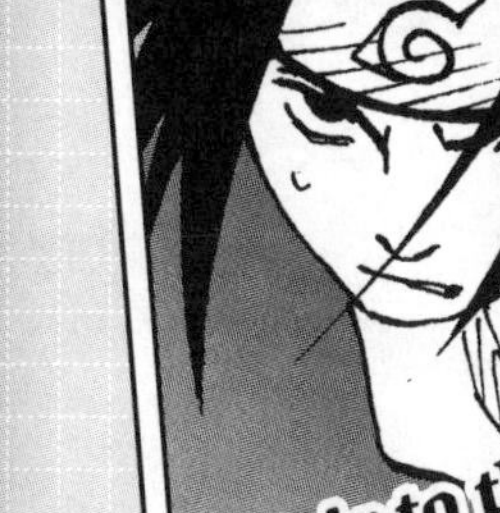
FIRE STYLE! FIREBALL TECHNIQUE!

⬅⬇ Despite his genin rank, Sasuke can use many advanced techniques. After he gains more experience in battle, we expect him to develop even more.

Graduated from the academy at the top of his class

Recovering from the horror of his clan's slaughter, he now fights alone. He rarely lets his feelings show, but there is a white-hot flame burning inside. The blood of the famed Uchiha Clan runs in his veins, giving him the Kekkei Genkai ability – Sharingan...

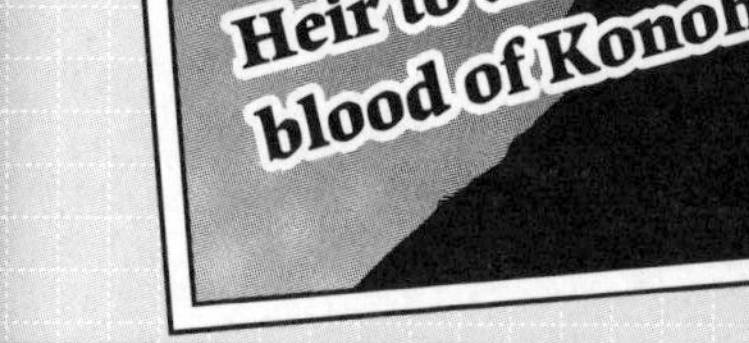

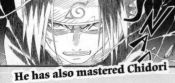

He has also mastered Chidori

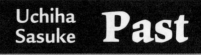

Uchiha Sasuke Past

His single-minded ambition: to live for his dream!

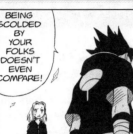

BEING SCOLDED BY YOUR FOLKS DOESN'T EVEN COMPARE!

When he was young, he lost his entire family at his brother's hands, but this also made him strong. This is a response to his fears and longing for power, but it feeds him even now.

⬆ Sasuke always keeps his distance between himself and others. But is that what he truly desires?

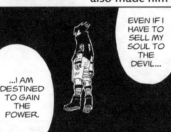

EVEN IF I HAVE TO SELL MY SOUL TO THE DEVIL...
...I AM DESTINED TO GAIN THE POWER.

⬅ He longs for the power to face his destiny. What future lies in store?

The mystery of the Uchiha Clan's destruction!

SPOTLIGHT

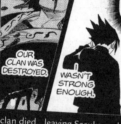

EVERYONE WAS KILLED...
OUR CLAN WAS DESTROYED.
I WASN'T STRONG ENOUGH.
THE ME... OF LONG AGO?!
ULTIMATELY, WITHOUT STRENGTH, THERE'S NOTHING YOU CAN DO.

The famous Uchiha Clan were massacred in a single night...and Sasuke saw it all happen. The images that come into his mind in flashbacks... are they fragments of the truth, or...?

⬆ That night, the clan died...leaving Sasuke and his brother Itachi behind.

BECAUSE YOU'RE NOTHING BUT A WEAKLING!
YOU JUST... STOOD THERE AND WATCHED!
PEEL
...LET THEM DIE!

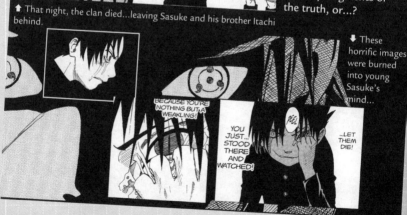

⬇ These horrific images were burned into young Sasuke's mind...

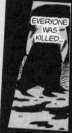

Uchiha Sasuke Present

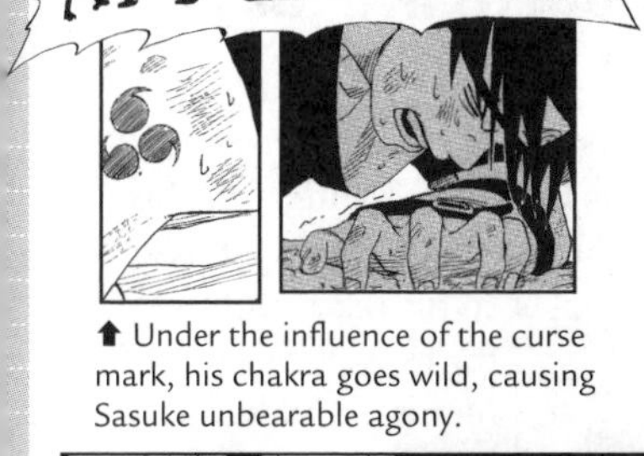
AIIIEEE!!

⬆ Under the influence of the curse mark, his chakra goes wild, causing Sasuke unbearable agony.

Orochimaru's curse mark restrains him

Orochimaru placed a curse mark on Sasuke, much like the one placed on Special Jônin Anko. Kakashi performed a binding ritual which has kept it suppressed, but there's no telling what will happen when Sasuke unleashes his full power...

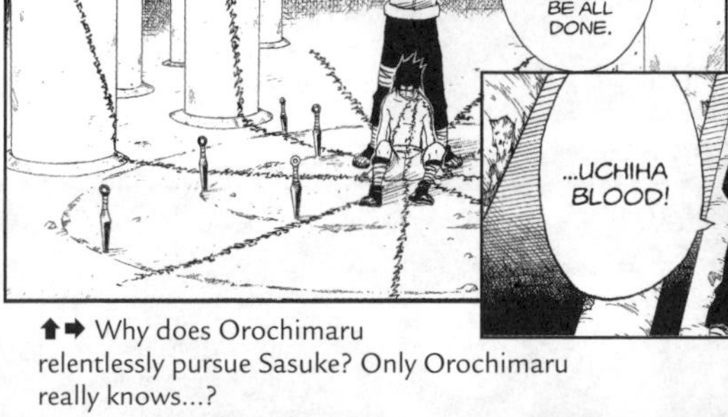
JUST A LITTLE LONGER AND IT'LL BE ALL DONE.

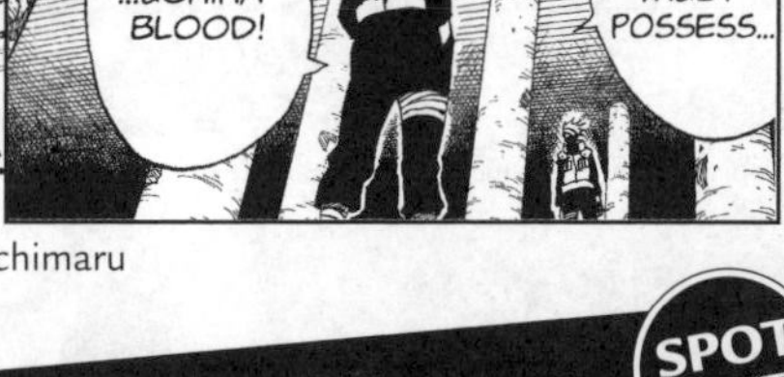
I MUST POSSESS...
...UCHIHA BLOOD!

⬆➡ Why does Orochimaru relentlessly pursue Sasuke? Only Orochimaru really knows...?

SPOT LIGHT!

Top 5 Sasuke Heartthrob Photos!

Sakura, Ino, and many other girls find Sasuke's cool demeanor very attractive. Here are some images that were considered most appealing! I'm sure all female readers will want to hang on to these forever!

Number 1

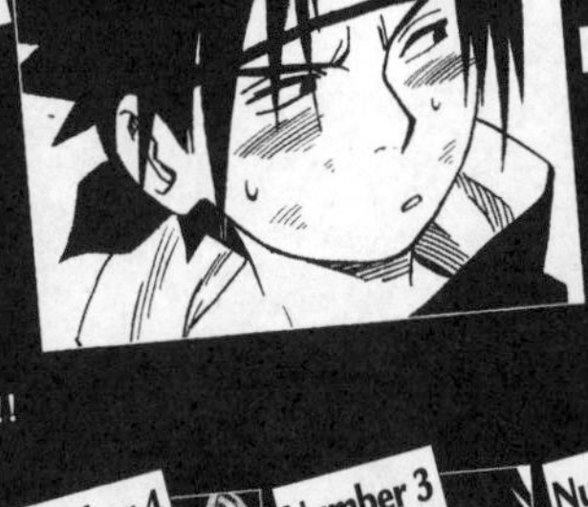

➡ A very rare glimpse of Sasuke looking bashful. His usual cool, hostile expression is great, but red-faced Sasuke is every bit as good!!

Number 5

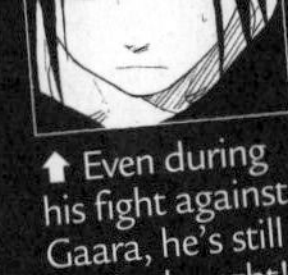

⬆ Even during his fight against Gaara, he's still lost in thought!

Number 4

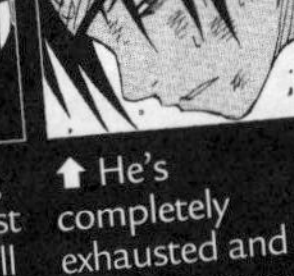

⬆ He's completely exhausted and moments away from falling into a dream.

Number 3

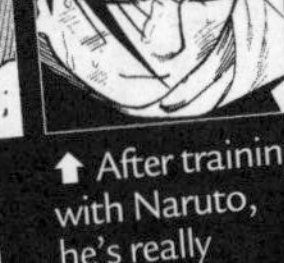

⬆ After training with Naruto, he's really worked up a sweat!

Number 2

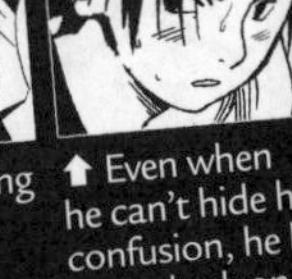

⬆ Even when he can't hide his confusion, he has a sexy look on his face.

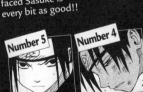

Sasuke Close-up!

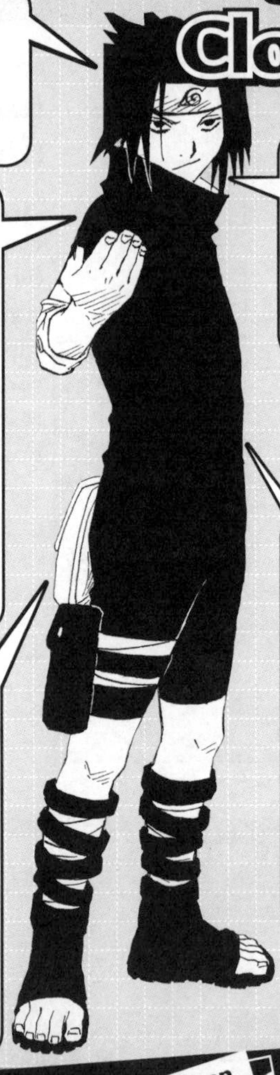

Sharingan
When he uses his Kekkei Genkai, his eyes take on an odd pattern.

Lips
Sasuke's smile shows his invincibility, never joking or admitting weakness.

Curse Mark
This mark releases the darkness that lies dormant within him and allows his chakra to run wild.

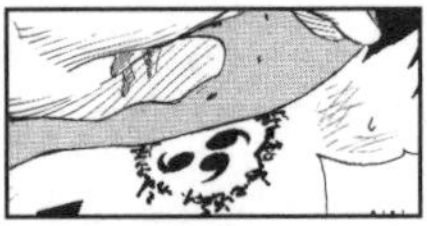

⬆The sinister icon and the seal controlling it are on his left shoulder.

Strap
The strap wrapped around his right arm supports his arm when attacking.

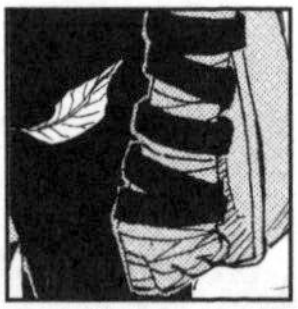

⬆Or is it just a fashion statement?

Uchiha
The Uchiha mark on his back is believed to come from the Uchiha name.

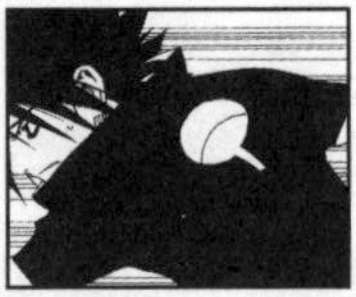

⬆The symbol is a typical manga touch, a little too cute for Sasuke.

Fashion check!! SPOT LIGHT!

Sasuke's costume changed during the Chûnin Selection Exams. Now he wears all black and looks sharper and more aggressive. What changed?

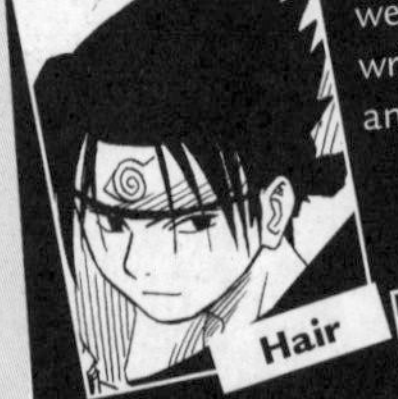
Hair

⬆ After training with Kakashi, his hair was noticeably longer.

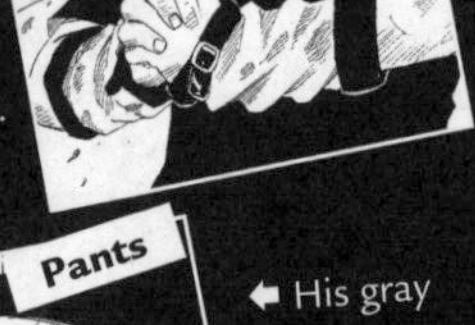
Strap

➡ He used to wear a cloth wrist-cover with an attached belt.

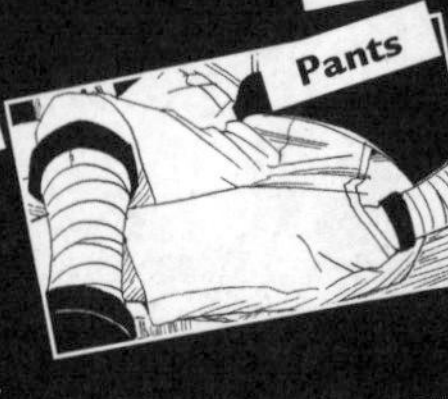
Pants

⬅ His gray pants were also very athletic.

Uchiha Sasuke Future

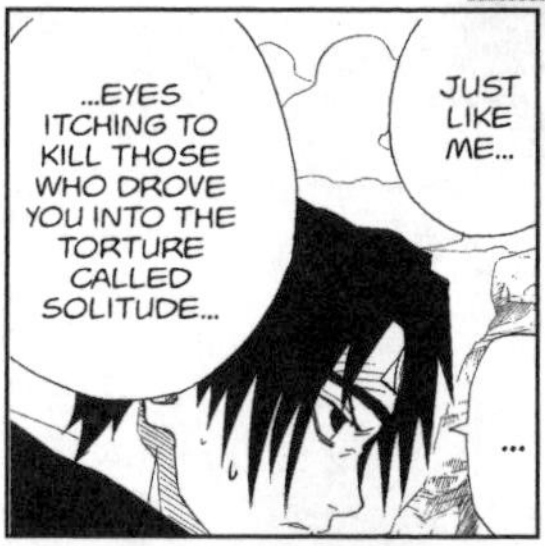
JUST LIKE ME...
...EYES ITCHING TO KILL THOSE WHO DROVE YOU INTO THE TORTURE CALLED SOLITUDE...
...

⬅ The darkness lurking in his heart was born the day he swore revenge on Itachi.

Defeat his brother Itachi and rebuild the Uchiha Clan

His desire to restore his clan drives him, allowing him to endure agonizing training and improve rapidly. Someday he will surpass his brother and restore his family...Will he finally be able to rest?

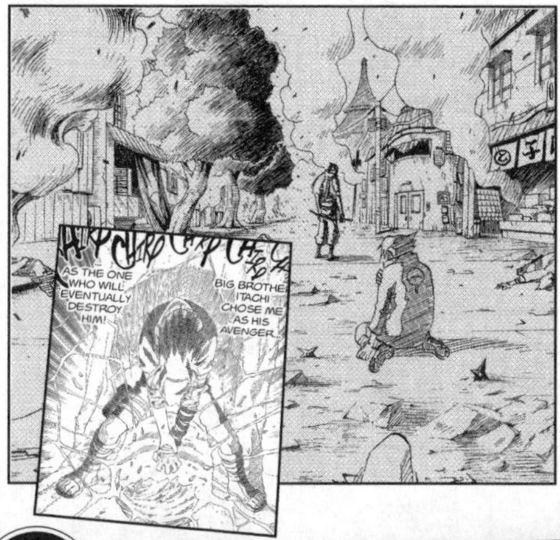
BIG BROTHER ITACHI CHOSE ME AS HIS AVENGER...
AS THE ONE WHO WILL EVENTUALLY DESTROY HIM!

⬅ Does Itachi want Sasuke to make amends for the crimes he commits?

SPOT LIGHT! Sasuke's Food: A Hunger for Strength!

Sasuke's every move is designed to make him stronger, and he approaches his diet with equal intensity. He never selects his meals based on what he actually likes. Here we analyze his favorite foods, according to the neighborhood records...

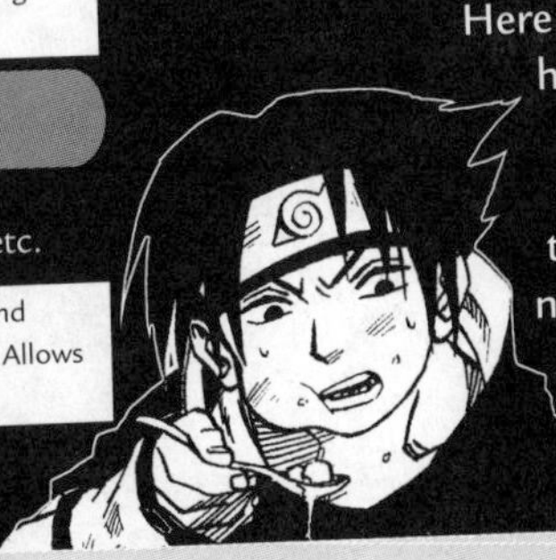

Nutritious Omusubi with Okaka

Starch, calcium, phosphorus, iron, natrium, kalium, vitamin B1 and 2, etc.

Effect Increases stamina and endurance, making it harder to wear yourself out during long periods of intense activity.

Tomatoes

Lycopene, beta carotene, vitamin U, quercetin, chlorogenic acid, calcium, etc.

Effect Keeps your body running smoothly, and makes it easy to recover from fatigue. Allows even for harder training.

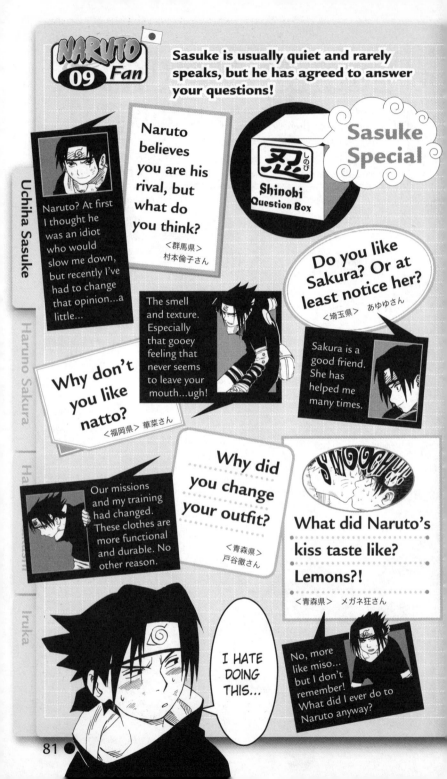

NARUTO 09 Fan

Sasuke is usually quiet and rarely speaks, but he has agreed to answer your questions!

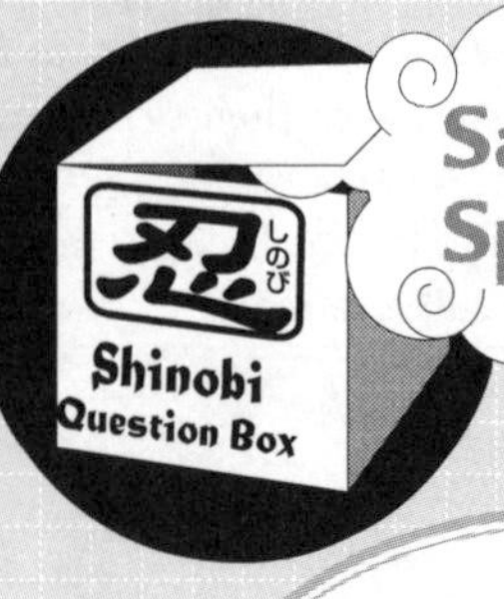
忍 しのび
Shinobi
Question Box

Sasuke Special

Naruto believes you are his rival, but what do you think?

<群馬県>
村本倫子さん

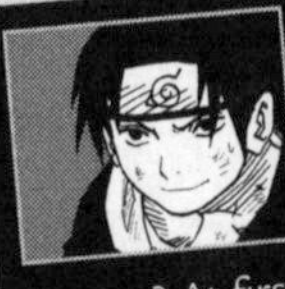

Naruto? At first I thought he was an idiot who would slow me down, but recently I've had to change that opinion...a little...

Do you like Sakura? Or at least notice her?

<埼玉県> あゆゆさん

Sakura is a good friend. She has helped me many times.

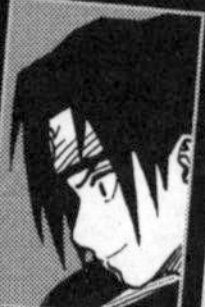

Why don't you like natto?

<福岡県> 華菜さん

The smell and texture. Especially that gooey feeling that never seems to leave your mouth...ugh!

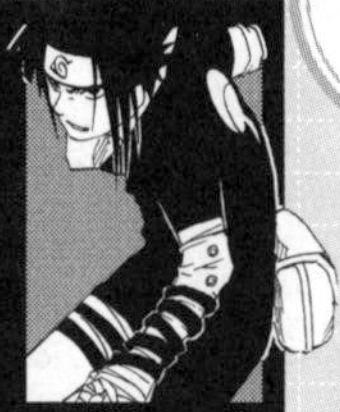

Why did you change your outfit?

<青森県>
戸谷徹さん

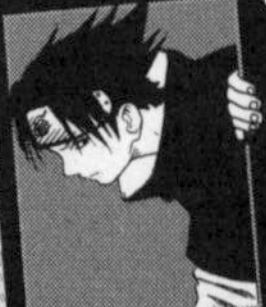

Our missions and my training had changed. These clothes are more functional and durable. No other reason.

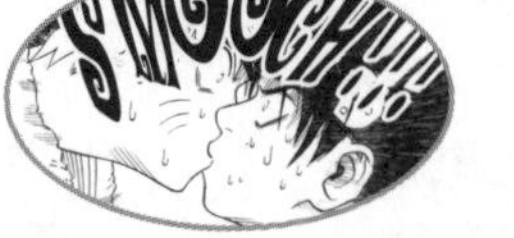

What did Naruto's kiss taste like? Lemons?!

<青森県> メガネ狂さん

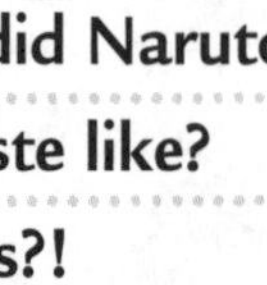

No, more like miso... but I don't remember! What did I ever do to Naruto anyway?

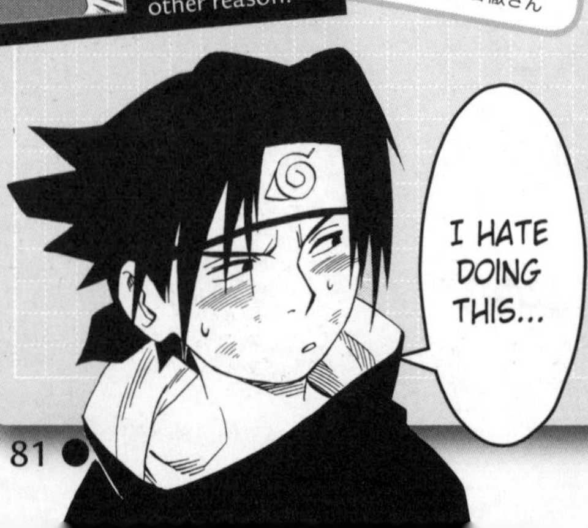
I HATE DOING THIS...

Young Sasuke Gallery

Is it any surprise that Naruto fans flooded us with their drawings of Sasuke? Sasuke seems to be especially popular with the ladies. He's a real heartbreaker already!

NARUTO 10 Fan

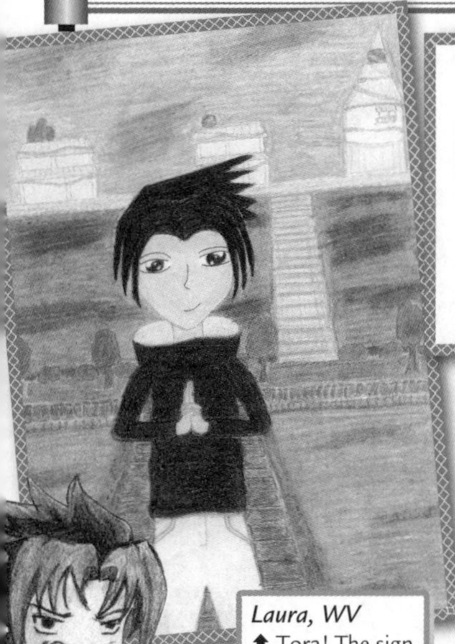

Laura, WV
⬆ Tora! The sign of the Tiger!

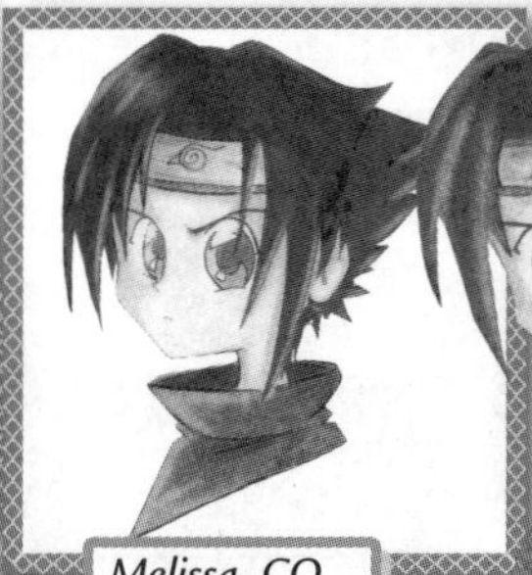

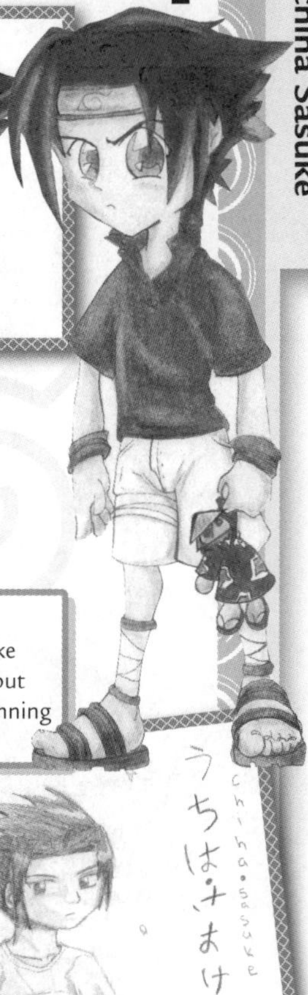

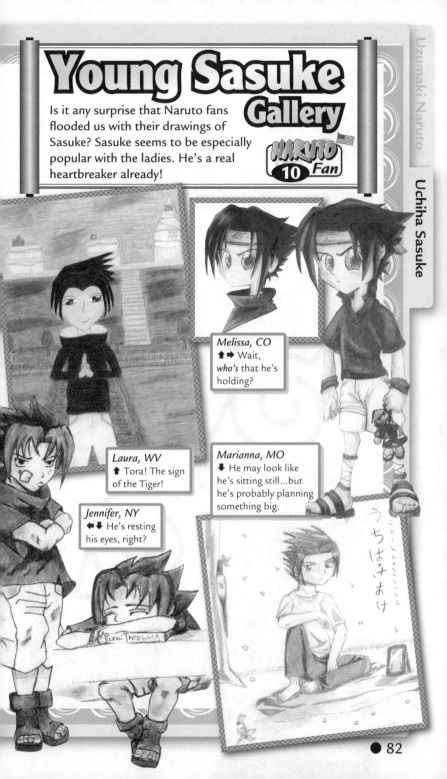

Melissa, CO
⬆➡ Wait, *who's* that he's holding?

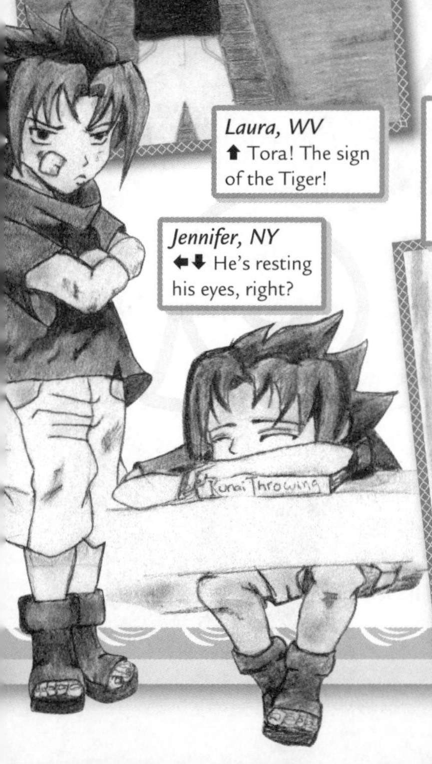
Kunai Throwing

Jennifer, NY
⬅⬇ He's resting his eyes, right?

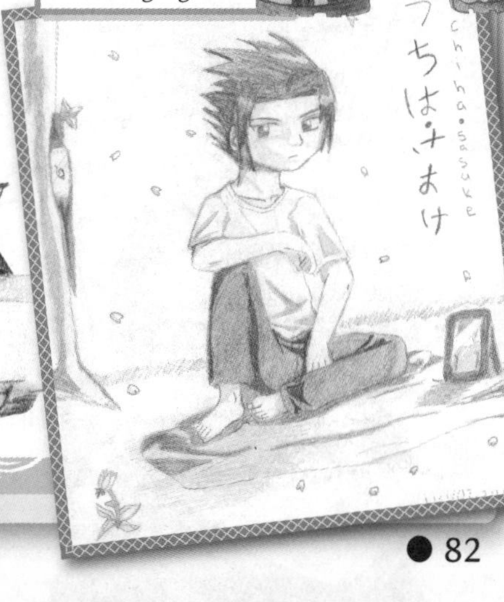

Marianna, MO
⬇ He may look like he's sitting still...but he's probably planning something big.

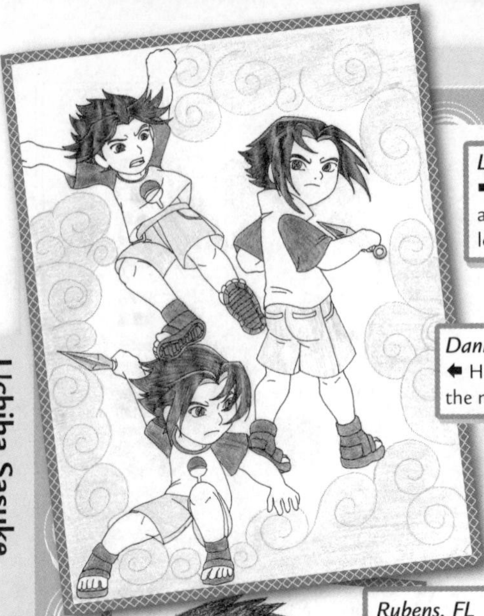

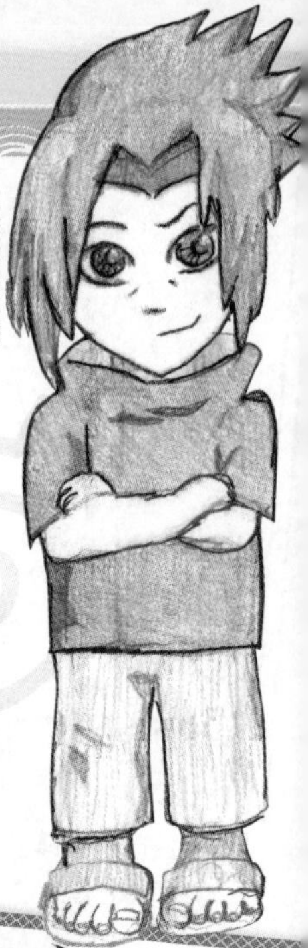

Lauren, NJ
➡ Now that's a skeptical look.

Danielle, GA
⬅ He's got the moves!

Uchiha Sasuke

Haruno Sakura

Hatake Kakashi

Iruka

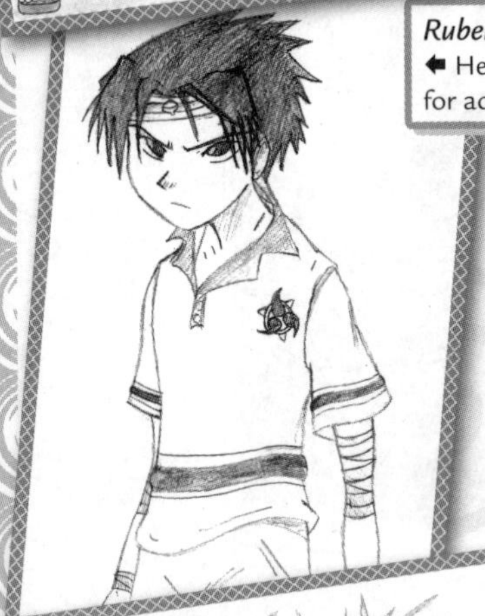

Rubens, FL
⬅ He looks ready for action!

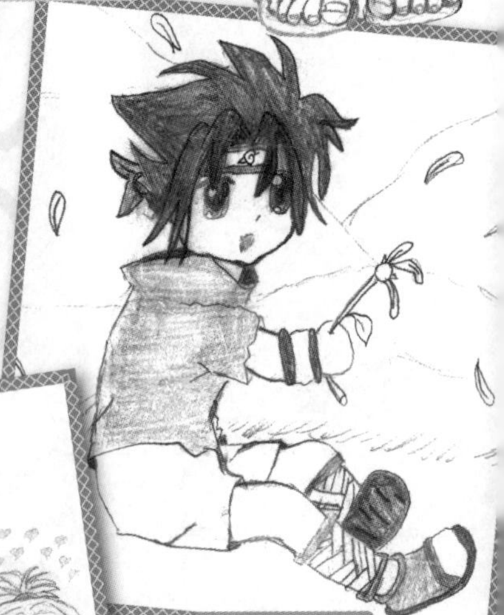

Amanda, CA
⬆ Now that's just cute.

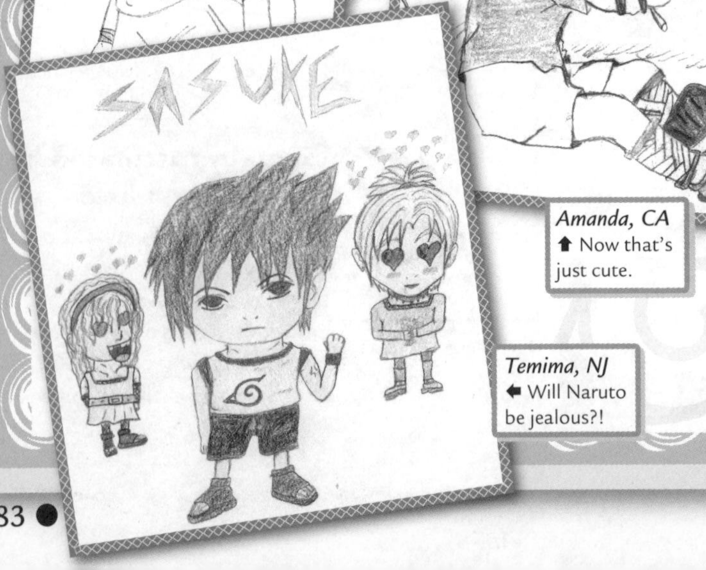
SASUKE

Temima, NJ
⬅ Will Naruto be jealous?!

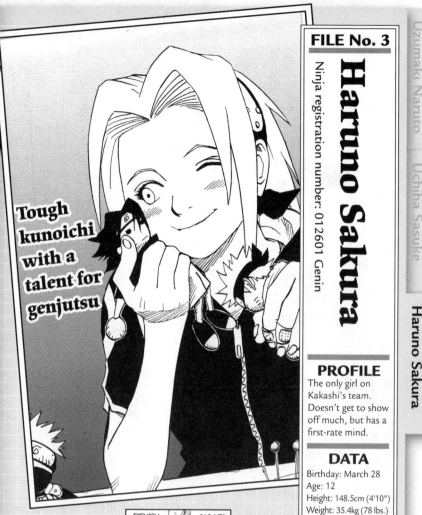

Tough kunoichi with a talent for genjutsu

FILE No. 3

Haruno Sakura

Ninja registration number: 012601 Genin

PROFILE

The only girl on Kakashi's team. Doesn't get to show off much, but has a first-rate mind.

DATA

Birthday: March 28
Age: 12
Height: 148.5cm (4'10")
Weight: 35.4kg (78 lbs.)
Blood Type: O

⬇ She has a strong sense of responsibility, and the brains to back it up.

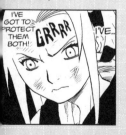

I'VE...
GRRRR
I'VE GOT TO PROTECT THEM BOTH!

SASUKE! MY SWEET, OLD-FASHIONED BOY! ♡
DID YOU SUMMON UP YOUR NERVE?! I'M RIGHT HERE, READY AND WAITING!!

⬆ Her intense focus on love is common in girls her age...

Equally fascinated by shinobi and love

At first glance Sakura appears to favor romance over practice, chatting over missions, but in fact has a much deeper understanding of nindo than most. She's easily one of the most intelligent genin.

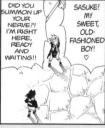

When they met, Ino was like an older sister, guiding the shy Sakura.

THIS STUFF'S A BREEZE, ONCE YOU GET THE HANG OF IT.

OH, COME ON SAKURA, THAT'S PATHETIC! HOW CAN YOU BE BAD WITH FLOWERS WHEN YOUR NAME MEANS "CHERRY BLOSSOM"?

REALLY?

A close friendship with Ino

When she was very small, Sakura would not talk to anyone but

IF YOU'RE A COSMOS, INO...

...THEN I GUESS I'M LIKE THE PURPLE TROUSERS.

Yamanaka Ino. Their relationship has become competitive, and this rivalry may turn out to be a sign that fortune favors Sakura...

SO, INO...

I'LL ER AT

She struggled with an inferiority complex as a child, and the root of her strength has always been Ino.

Complete Comparision!! Sakura and Ino! (SPOT LIGHT!)

Haruno Sakura

VS

Yamanaka Ino

Let's look closely at Konoha's greatest rivalry! Which kunoichi is better?

GUTS
Ino is a little selfish, and lacks patience. Sakura doesn't yield to difficulty.

Sakura Wins!

INITIATIVE
As their attempts to capture Sasuke's favor indicate, Ino takes a much more aggressive approach.

Ino Wins!

PHYSICAL ABILITY
Their battle in the Chûnin Selection Exams was evenly matched. Their physical strength is identical!

It's a tie!

It's a tie!

The result – 1 to 1, yep – a tie!!

Haruno Sakura

Hatake Kakashi

Iruka

Haruno Sakura Present

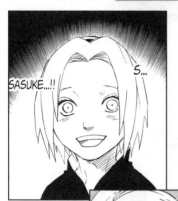

Chasing Sasuke, battling fiercely to become chûnin!

Her split decision with Ino in the Chûnin Selection Exams has left her watching Naruto and Sasuke from the stands. Between trying to make Sasuke notice her, and trying to become a great shinobi, she's got a full schedule every day!!

S...
SASUKE...!!

🡅 Cheering Sasuke on from the stands.

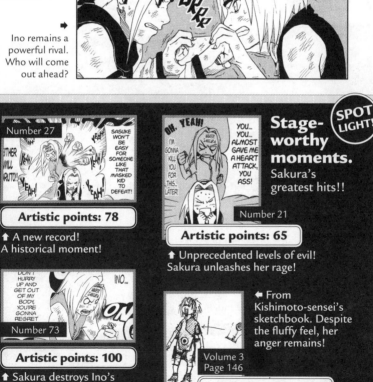

GRRR

🡆 Ino remains a powerful rival. Who will come out ahead?

Stage-worthy moments. SPOT LIGHT!

Sakura's greatest hits!!

SASUKE WON'T BE EASY FOR SOMEONE LIKE THAT MASKED KID TO DEFEAT!
YEAH!
YEAH!
YEAH!
YEAH!
YEAH!

Number 27

Artistic points: 78

🡅 A new record! A historical moment!

OH, YEAH!
YOU... YOU... ALMOST GAVE ME A HEART ATTACK, YOU ASS!
INNER SAKURA
I'M GONNA KILL YOU FOR THIS... LATER!

Number 21

Artistic points: 65

🡅 Unprecedented levels of evil! Sakura unleashes her rage!

INO...
DON'T HURRY UP AND GET OUT OF MY BODY, YOU'RE GONNA REGRET
INNER SAKURA

Number 73

Artistic points: 100

🡅 Sakura destroys Ino's Shintenshin no Jutsu!

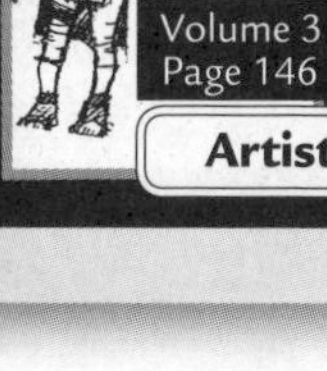

Volume 3 Page 146

Artistic points: 80

🡄 From Kishimoto-sensei's sketchbook. Despite the fluffy feel, her anger remains!

Sakura Close-up!

Headband

A symbol of Sakura's resolve, she normally wears it across the top of her hair, like a little girl.

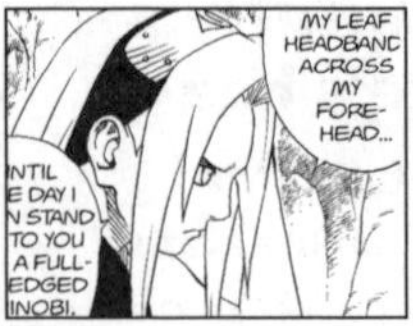
MY LEAF HEADBAND ACROSS MY FORE-HEAD...
NTIL E DAY I N STAND TO YOU A FULL-EDGED INOBI.

⬅ She only put it on her forehead during her grim battle with Ino.

Forehead

Sakura was bullied for having a large forehead as a child, but no longer seems to care so much?

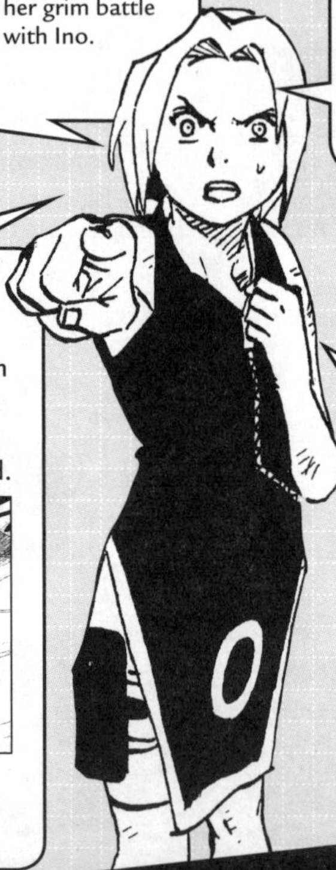

Hair

Sakura cut her own hair during the Chûnin Selection Exams. Her current style makes it easier to move around.

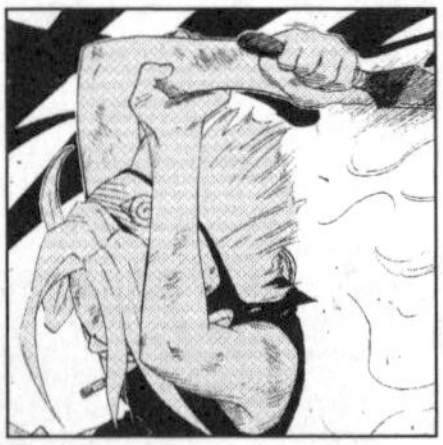

⬆ When she cut her hair with a kunai, she seemed so graceful...

Fists

She's exchanged fearsome blows with Ino with these fists. We had her down as an intellectual, but she might be more physical than we suspected...

SPOT LIGHT!

How long will it take Sakura's hair to grow back!??!

Many of you have said, "I want to see Sakura with long hair again!" OK, let's figure out how many days that would take. If we assume she cut about 15 cm, then the result is...to the left!

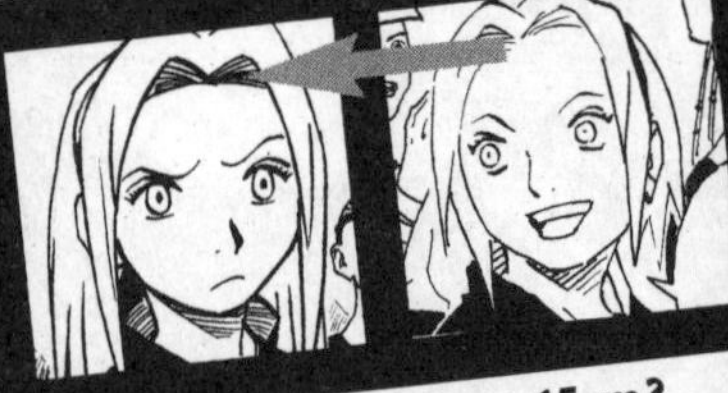

Length cut = about 15cm?
Speed hair grows= 1 day, .35mm

Total: 14 months and 3 days!

Haruno Sakura Future

Wants to be a great kunoichi and capture Sasuke's heart!

With her talent for genjutsu, Sakura should become a good kunoichi with a little hard work. But will romance with Sasuke bloom...?!

NOW IT'S YOUR TURN...
...TO WATCH MY BACK!!

⬆ Her resolve to walk on her own should help her develop...

WHAT IS GOING ON?!
KAI! ELEASE!

⬅ Kakashi has already noticed her aptitude for genjutsu.

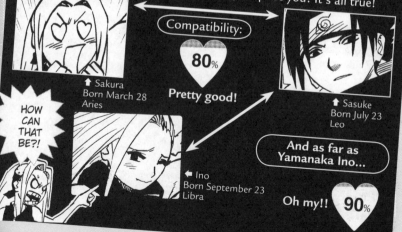

SPOT LIGHT!

What does astrology say about Sakura and Sasuke's future?

Sakura is obsessed with Sasuke, so we took their info to an astrologer...but the results may surprise you! It's all true!

⬆ Sakura
Born March 28
Aries

Compatibility:

80%

Pretty good!

⬆ Sasuke
Born July 23
Leo

HOW CAN THAT BE?!

⬅ Ino
Born September 23
Libra

And as far as Yamanaka Ino...

Oh my!! 90%

NARUTO Fan 11

No one can explain the inner workings of the female heart better than her! We asked the sole female on Team 7 all sorts of questions.

You're a cute girl, so are you ever afraid to fight a big strong man?

<群馬県>
ラッコくちびるさん

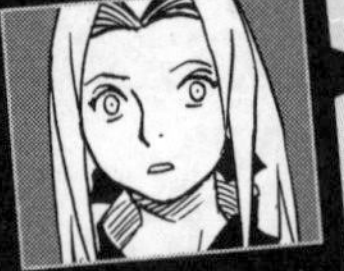

Eh...I never really thought about it. Even if you are scared, once the fight starts your body naturally begins moving...

Sakura Special

忍 しのび

Shinobi Question Box

What kind of kunoichi do you want to be?

<北海道>カントリーMAIさん

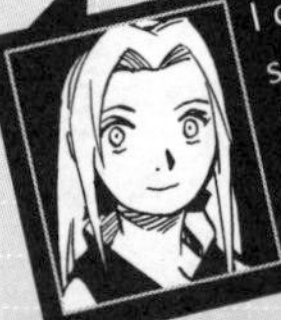

I don't think I'll ever be as strong as Tsunade...I guess I'd prefer to balance beauty and brains, working as a strategist!

You always say "Oh Yeah!" but what does it mean?

<東京都> ユリさん

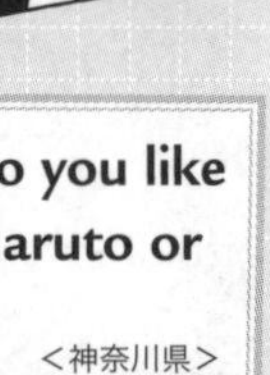

People always shout when they get worked up, right? This phrase just seemed a little more cool.

You really like Ino, don't you?

<埼玉県>
野菊さん

That pig? We used to be friends, but now we're rivals! I guess it'd be a bit dull without her around...

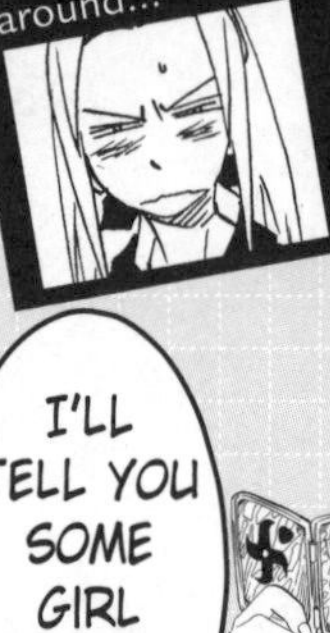

Whom do you like better, Naruto or Sasuke?

<神奈川県>
藤原敬司さん

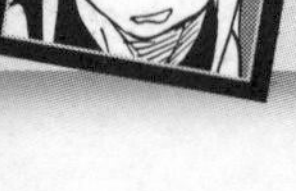

Don't get any weird ideas! I am all about Sasuke! Naruto's just... I mean, he's impressive lately, but still...

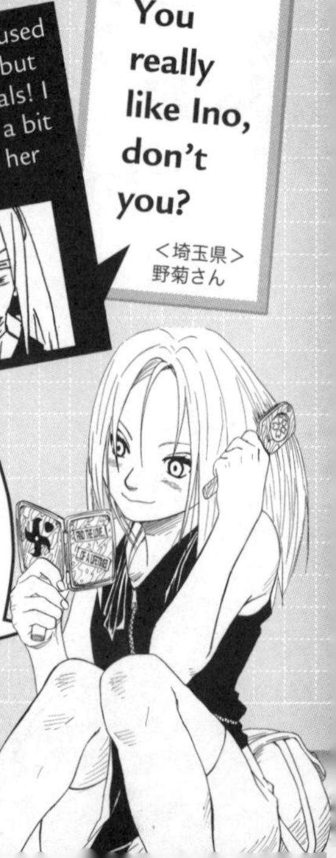
I'LL TELL YOU SOME GIRL SECRETS ♥
FIND THE LOVE OF A LIFETIME

NARUTO Fan 12

New Jutsu!
Sakura's Ultimate Picks

It seems Konoha's ninja aren't the only keepers of secret techniques! Fans have plenty as well! Sakura has collected a few of them from you here.

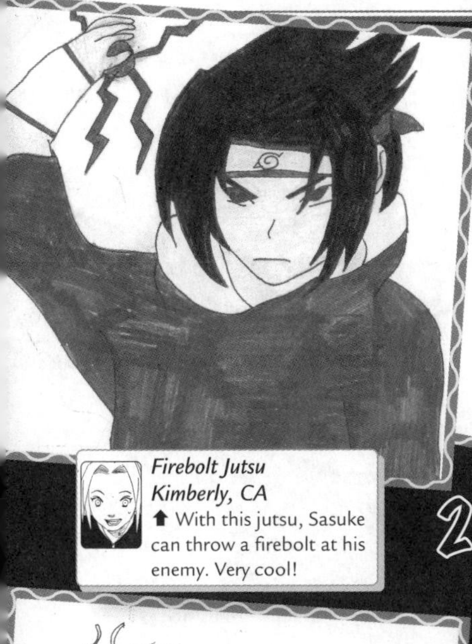

Firebolt Jutsu
Kimberly, CA
⬆ With this jutsu, Sasuke can throw a firebolt at his enemy. Very cool!

Summoning Jutsu: Firebred Sala
Dustin, GA
⬇ Summoning a Salamander seems similar to summoning a Toad.

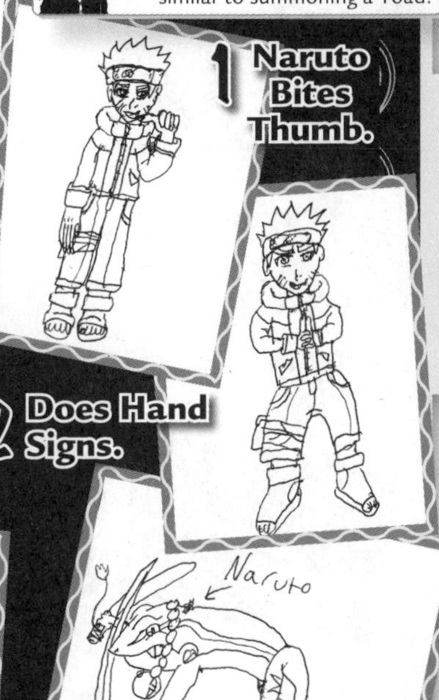
1 Naruto Bites Thumb.
2 Does Hand Signs.
Naruto
3 Summons Salamander

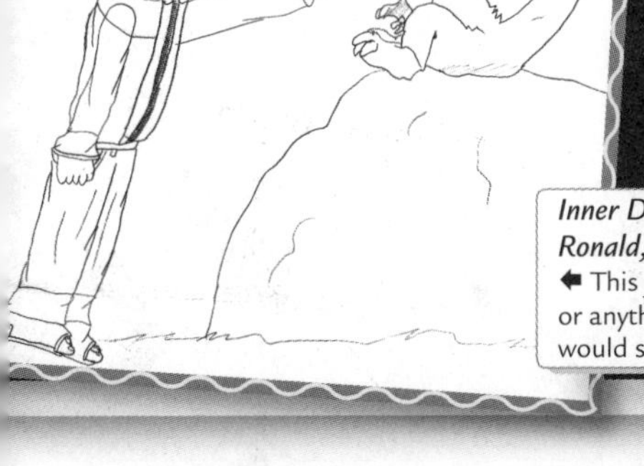
YAAAWN

Inner Dragon Jutsu
Ronald, FL
⬅ This jutsu puts anyone or anything to sleep! That would stop the battle quick.

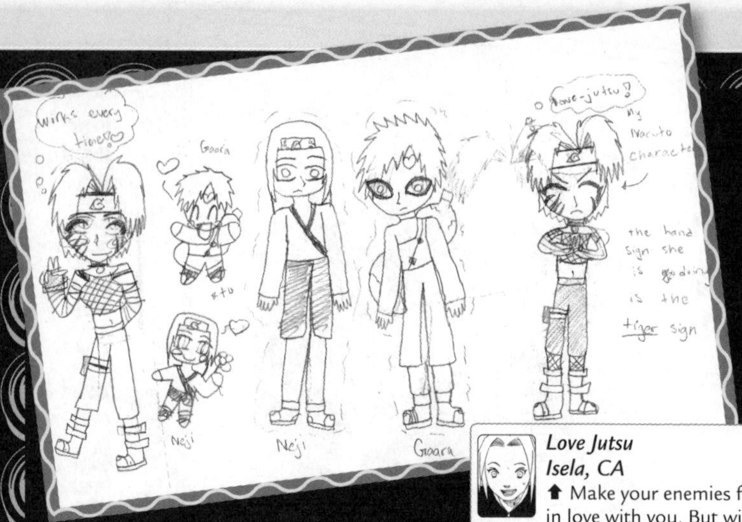
works every time!
Gaara
Love-jutsu!
My Naruto Character
the hand sign she is doing is the tiger sign
Neji
Neji
Gaara

Love Jutsu
Isela, CA
⬆ Make your enemies fall in love with you. But will it work on Orochimaru?

Element Sword Jutsu
Tre, CA
➡ A sword with the power of water, earth, fire & wind makes the wielder one with the elements. Sounds powerful!

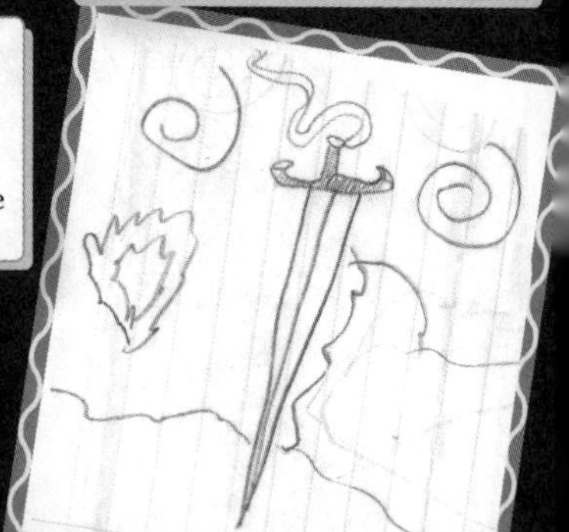

Hikari Booru no Ki!
Debbie, OH
⬇ This one summons a shiny, powerful ball. That is very useful!

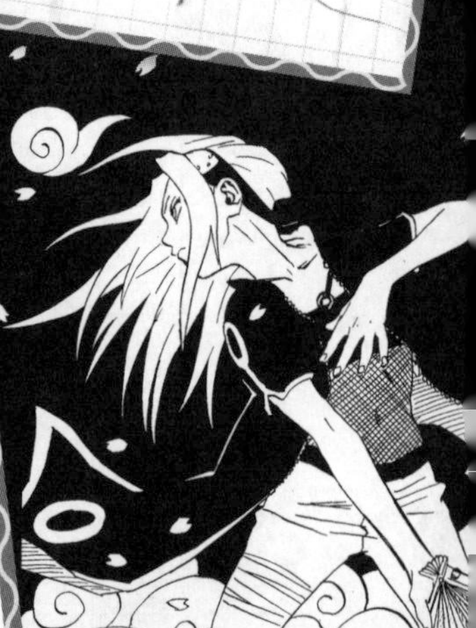

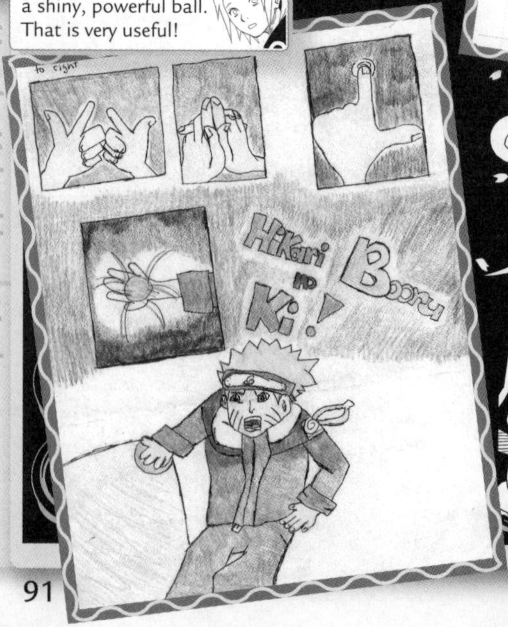
to fight
Hikari Booru no Ki!

FILE No. 4

Hatake Kakashi

Ninja registration number: 009720 Jônin

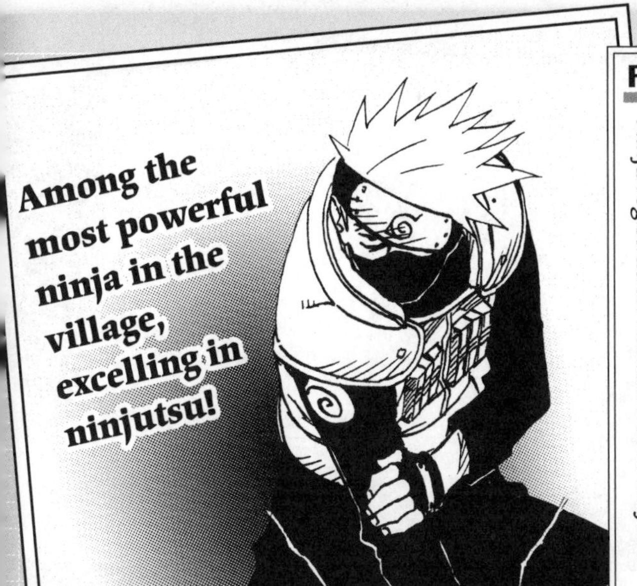

Among the most powerful ninja in the village, excelling in ninjutsu!

PROFILE

Also known as Kakashi of the Sharingan or The Mirror Ninja

DATA

Birthday: Sept. 15
Age: 26
Height: 181cm (5'11")
Weight: 67.5kg (149 lbs)
Blood Type: O

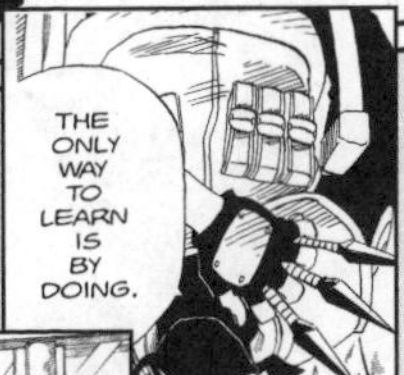
THE ONLY WAY TO LEARN IS BY DOING.

➡ Thanks to his accurate
structions, the genin are
nproving rapidly.

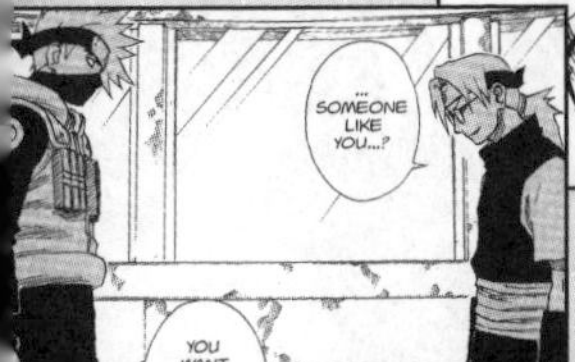
...SOMEONE LIKE YOU...?
YOU WANT TO TEST "SOMEONE LIKE ME"...?

⬅ He never drops his guard, swiftly noticing and dealing with any disturbances in the village.

Leading a genin team on their daily duties in the village

Kakashi's talent was respected from a very early age, and his abilities developed accordingly; now the village could not survive without him. While carrying out missions as a jônin, he also leads the 7th genin team.

Hatake Kakashi Past

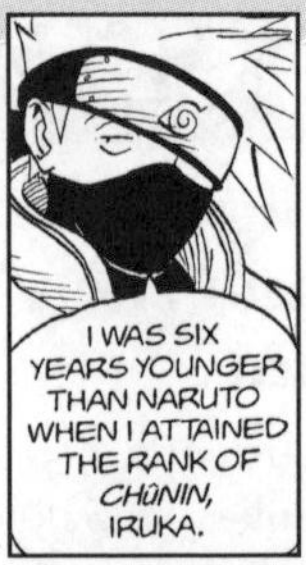
I WAS SIX YEARS YOUNGER THAN NARUTO WHEN I ATTAINED THE RANK OF CHŪNIN, IRUKA.

➡ Kakashi has fought through many harrowing battles.

Chûnin at six. Assigned to the Anbu, faced certain death countless times.

After becoming chûnin at the shocking age of six, Kakashi went on to great heroics, using his Sharingan ability, and his name is now known in many countries. His swift, precise handling of every mission led to his assignment to the Anbu. He seems to have carried out many missions for them, but there are no records containing any details.

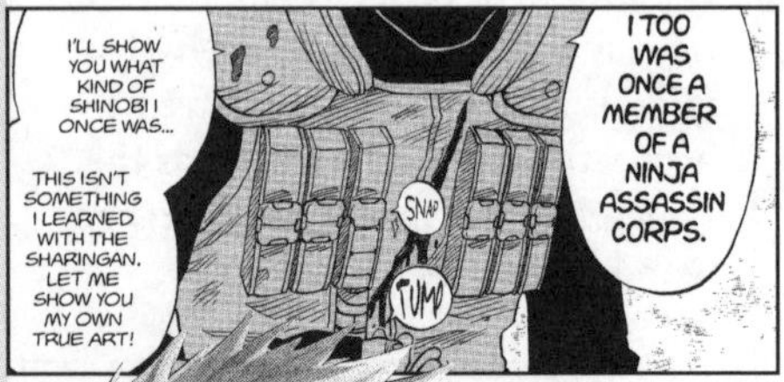
I TOO WAS ONCE A MEMBER OF A NINJA ASSASSIN CORPS.
SNAP
TUMP
I'LL SHOW YOU WHAT KIND OF SHINOBI I ONCE WAS...
THIS ISN'T SOMETHING I LEARNED WITH THE SHARINGAN. LET ME SHOW YOU MY OWN TRUE ART!

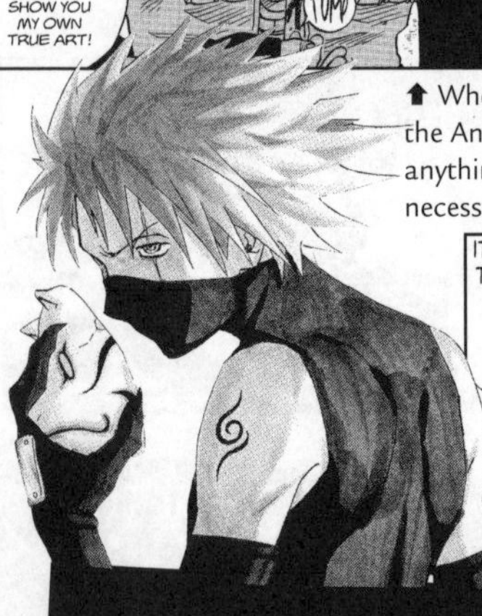

⬆ When he was in the Anbu, he did anything that was necessary...?

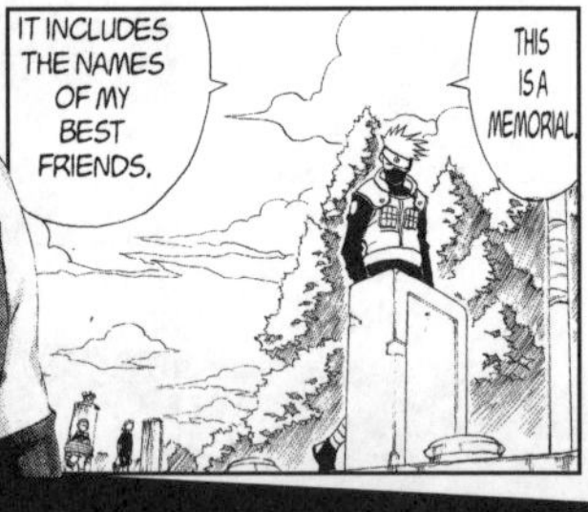
THIS IS A MEMORIAL.
IT INCLUDES THE NAMES OF MY BEST FRIENDS.

⬅ Looking at the stone, with his friend's names carved on it...what is he thinking?

The Sharingan hints at a secret past?

SPOT LIGHT!

Kakashi is famed for his Sharingan, but there are many mysteries relating to his unusual ability. Kakashi is not of the Uchiha Clan, so how can he have their Kekkei Genkai? And why is it only in his left eye? The truth is not yet known...

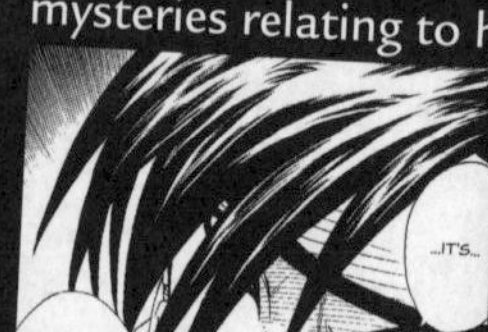
...IT'S...
...THE SHARINGAN!!

⬆ It seems like Orochimaru knows how Kakashi got the eye...

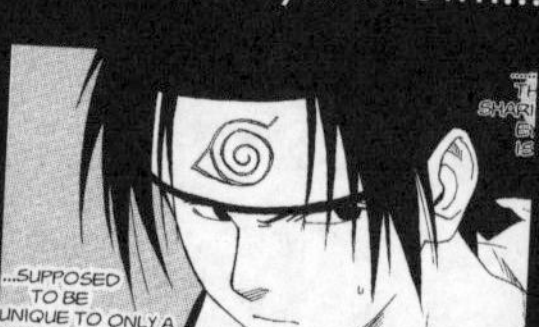
...SUPPOSED TO BE UNIQUE TO ONLY A SMALL NUMBER OF THE UCHIHA

⬅ What links Uchiha, Kakashi, and the Sharingan?

Hatake Kakashi Present

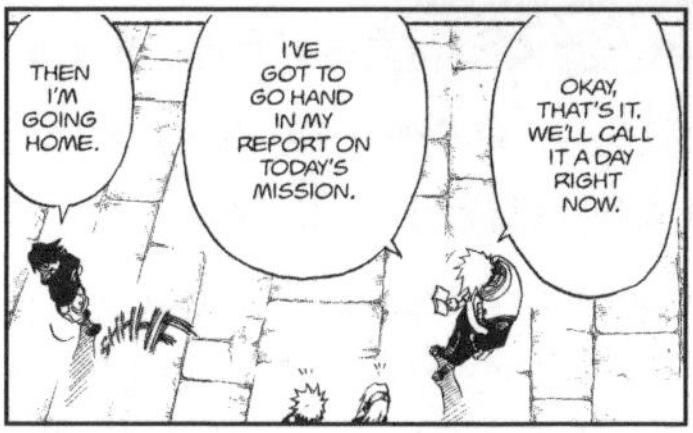
OKAY, THAT'S IT. WE'LL CALL IT A DAY RIGHT NOW.
I'VE GOT TO GO HAND IN MY REPORT ON TODAY'S MISSION.
THEN I'M GOING HOME.
SHHF

🠅 Whenever a mission is completed, the team leader must write a full report. Kakashi does this too.

Balancing two roles: sensei and the village's top jônin!

Kakashi is currently instructing Naruto, Sasuke and Sakura. Using his powers of observation, Kakashi quickly picked out their strengths, and his advice is proving extremely accurate. Meanwhile, he leads the fight when the village is threatened, working hard as a jônin.

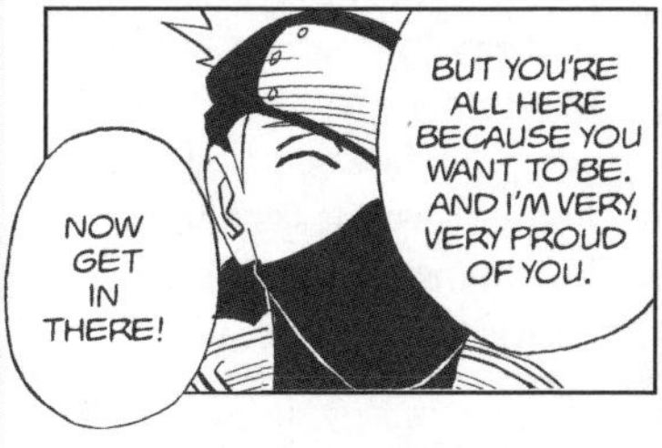
BUT YOU'RE ALL HERE BECAUSE YOU WANT TO BE. AND I'M VERY, VERY PROUD OF YOU.
NOW GET IN THERE!

🠅 More than anything, he wants his team to trust each other and be independent.

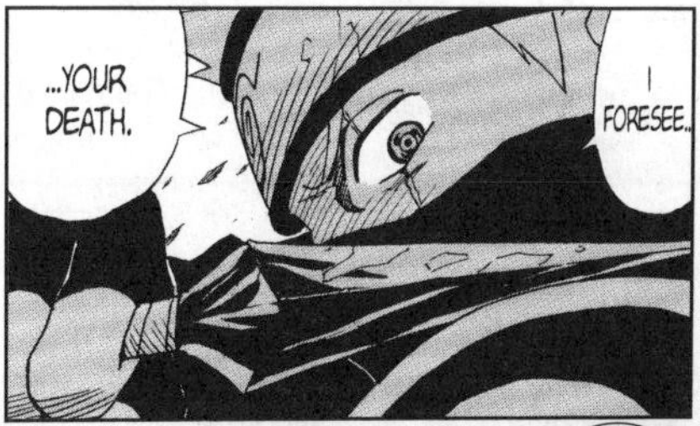
I FORESEE...
...YOUR DEATH.

➡ He never hesitates to show his power in battle, and anyone going up against him risks death.

SPOT LIGHT!

Kakashi's personality and interests...

His abilities are without comparison, but he has a few qualities not desirable in a shinobi...

World's most dedicated *Make-Out Paradise* fan!

Kakashi's passion for the adults-only novel series *Make-Out Paradise* is legendary! But jônin are supposed to be role models for other shinobi...will he ever reform?!

Loose with time?!

Punctuality would seem a prerequisite in a shinobi, but Kakashi is always late for meetings. This has yet to cause any serious problems, but can nothing be done?

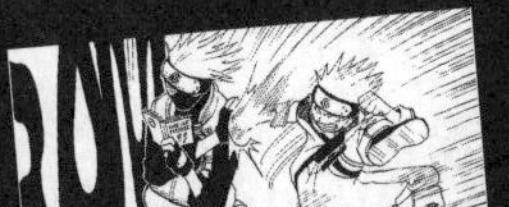

🠅 Reading while instructing genin...we worry it will have a negative effect on them!

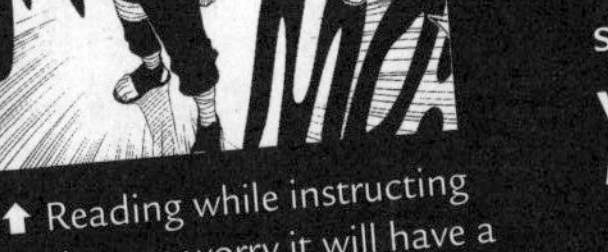
GOOD MORNING, CLASS!
YOU'RE LATE!!!!

🠅 Even his subordinates complain, harming his credibility as a jônin.

Kakashi Close-up!

Mask

A mask covers half his face. Is his reluctance to let others see him a habit learned from his days spent living in darkness?

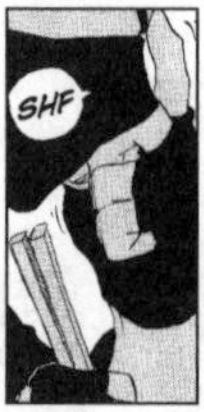
SHF

The staff at Ichiraku Ramen are among the few who have ever seen his face.

Headband and Sharingan

He normally wears his headband diagonally to hide his Sharingan. When the Sharingan is exposed, it automatically activates and expends chakra?!

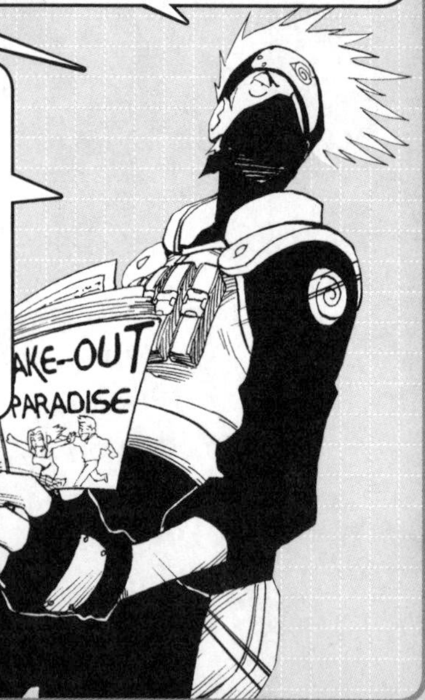
AKE-OUT
PARADISE

Vest (with scroll pouches)

A number of different scrolls fill the pouches on his vest. The Kuchiyose scrolls have seen a great deal of use since his time in the Anbu. Those scrolls came in handy during his battle with Zabuza.

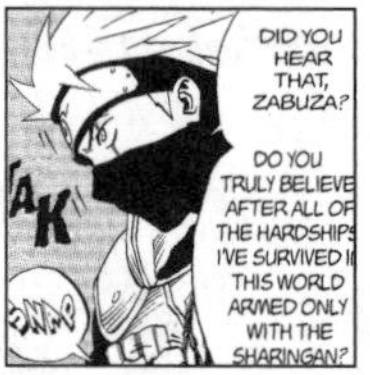
DID YOU HEAR THAT, ZABUZA?
DO YOU TRULY BELIEVE AFTER ALL OF THE HARDSHIPS I'VE SURVIVED I THIS WORLD ARMED ONLY WITH THE SHARINGAN?

Handguards

Some shinobi wear them, some don't; Kakashi does. They bring peace of mind!

Hatake Kakashi

Iruka

Hatake Kakashi Future

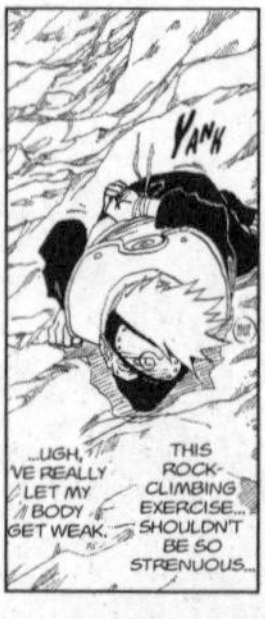
YANK
...UGH, I'VE REALLY LET MY BODY GET WEAK.
THIS ROCK-CLIMBING EXERCISE... SHOULDN'T BE SO STRENUOUS...

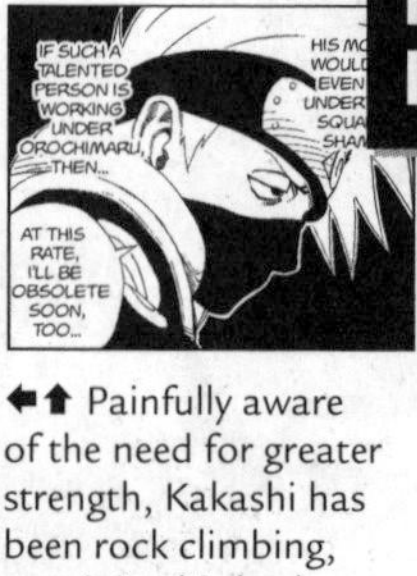
IF SUCH A TALENTED PERSON IS WORKING UNDER OROCHIMARU, THEN...
AT THIS RATE, I'LL BE OBSOLETE SOON, TOO...

⬅⬆ Painfully aware of the need for greater strength, Kakashi has been rock climbing, retraining his body.

Devoting himself to reaching even greater heights!!

Since he learned of Orochimaru's actions, Kakashi seems to have set his sights even higher. Is this solely a product of his jônin duty to protect the village and the people in it?

NARUTO Fan 13

Uzumaki Naruto | Uchiha Sasuke | Haruno Sakura | **Hatake Kakashi**

Shinobi Question Box — Kakashi Special

Survivor of countless battlegrounds, master of countless techniques...there's so much we want to ask Kakashi!

You're famous for being late. But are you always late?

<大阪府> 別城あきこさん

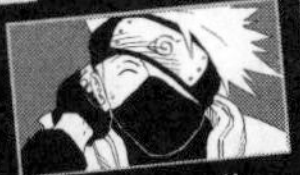

Eh...not really. Ah, Naruto! He's been spreading these stories around, I'm sure.

You always wear a mask, but isn't it uncomfortable?

<静岡県> 村松伊久美さん

Oh, this? It's made of fabric that breathes well, so it's very comfortable.

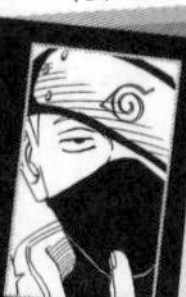

Did you name the Ninja Dogs? Tell me all their names!

<東京都> こたろうさん

Yes, I named them. You want to know them all? I'd like to tell you, but we just don't have the space...some other time!

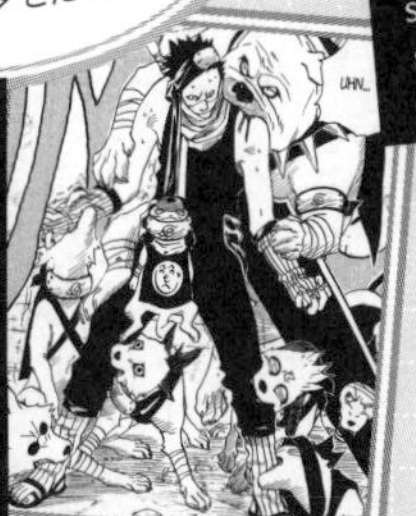

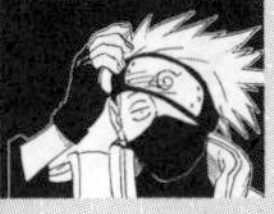

On your missions, did you ever really think you were going to die?

<長崎県> 峰祐一郎さん

If you live in the world I do, that happens a few times. But if you talk about it, everyone gets spooked...

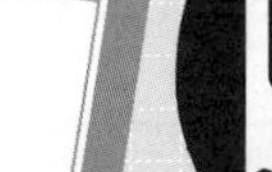

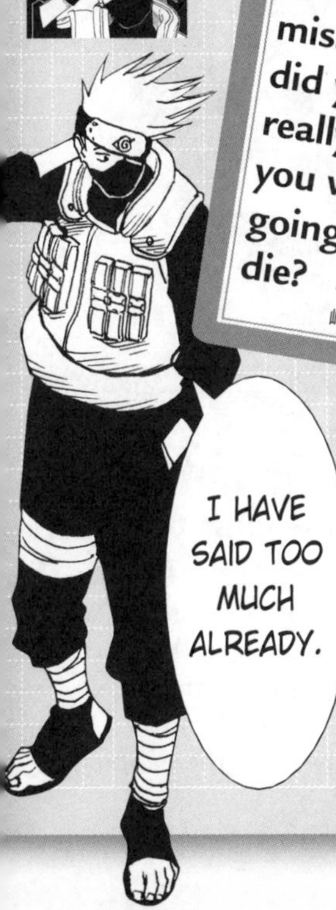
I HAVE SAID TOO MUCH ALREADY.

Who taught you the One Thousand Years of Death? Is it your original technique?

<東京都> 加藤千笑さん

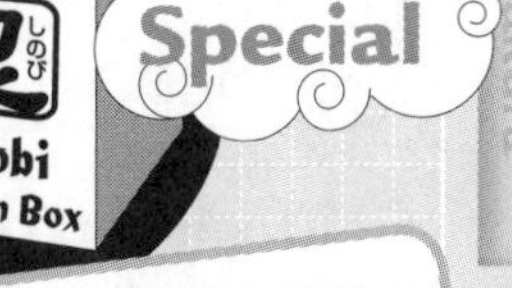
KONOHAGAKURE VILLAGE'S MOST SECRET AND MOST SACRED TECHNIQUE!!!
ONE THOUSAND YEARS OF DEATH!
KABOOOOM

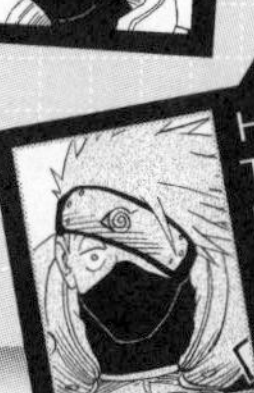

Hunh? The One Thousand Years of Death? Oh, that! That technique is, well, top secret, so I couldn't possibly tell you. Sorry.

NARUTO Fan 14

KAKASHI IN TWO PANELS

WHAT DO YOU WANT, SENSEI?!
LET ME COPY THE NINJA CENTER-FOLD...
URG
GRUNT

We had everyone think up what should go in the balloons! Kakashi chose the best suggestions!

<福岡県> 野中辰弥さん

SHARINGAN PRIZE

KAKASHI'S COMMENTS Ah ha, I could have done...wait! If I use that jutsu myself, I won't be able to see myself transformed! I mean, I'm gonna copy it anyway...

MAKE-OUT PARADISE PRIZE

I ONLY SPILLED A DROP OF THE RAMEN BROTH!!
CRIMES AGAINST MAKE-OUT PARADISE... ARE SERIOUS!!!
URG
GRUNT

<佐賀県> 夏夜ホタルさん

KAKASHI'S COMMENTS Naruto is clearly to blame! Obviously, I bought a second copy in case this happened...

LIGHTNING BLADE PRIZE

AUGH! WHAT'S GOING ON!
FINALLY... FOR THE FIRST TIME IN THREE DAYS, I CAN EAT.
URG
GRUNT

<北海道> PRIESTさん

KAKASHI'S COMMENTS Nicely done! Matches my sinister expression.

GENIN

PASS!!

KAKASHI'S COMMENTS All of you seem to understand what a two-panel manga is, so you pass!!

Wheee! This is so much fun!

My head hurts...blood rushing to it...

<宮崎県> MIROKUさん

You can't bungee jump with packing tape!!

One jump, 500 yen...thrilling, isn't it?

<北海道> かずやさん

Why is this rope so springy?!

.... Because this is a manga!!

<静岡県> 後藤浩太さん

Hatake Kakashi

A passionate teacher who hides his abilities in order to stand behind the Academy podium.

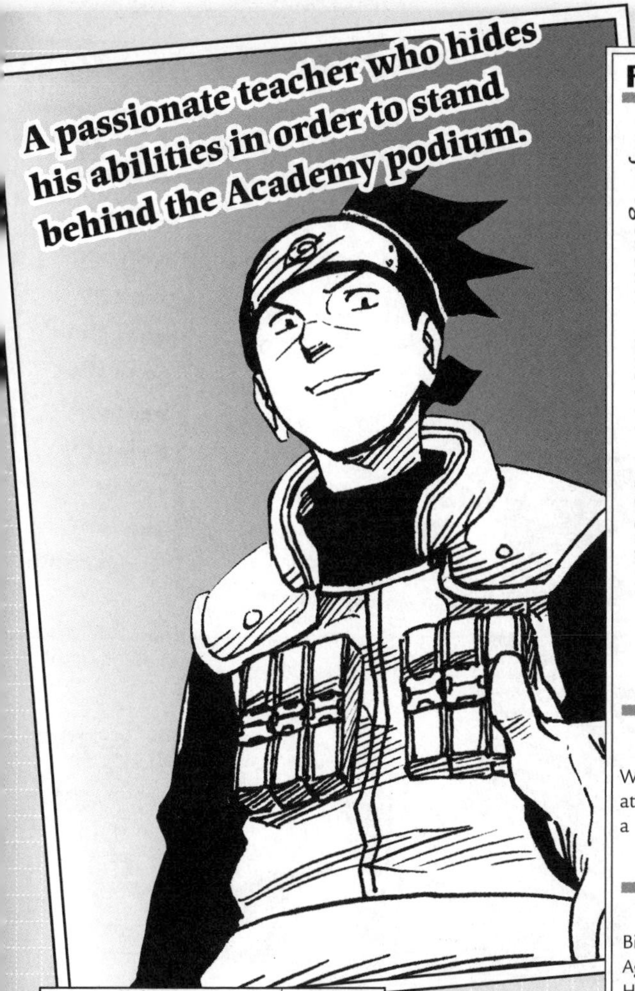

FILE No. 5

Iruka

Ninja registration number: 011450 Chûnin

PROFILE

Working as a teacher at the Academy. Has a big heart.

DATA

Birthday: May 26
Age: 25
Height: 178cm (5'10")
Weight: 66.2kg (146 lbs)
Blood Type: O

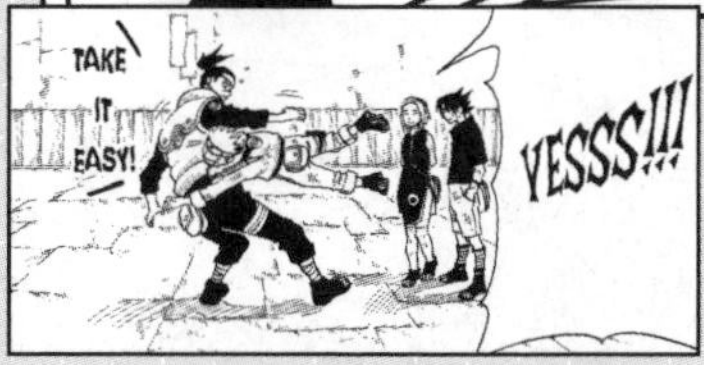
TAKE IT EASY!
YESSS!!!

⬅ Naruto was especially fond of Iruka.

⬇ The Third Hokage was evidently pleased with Iruka's instruction.

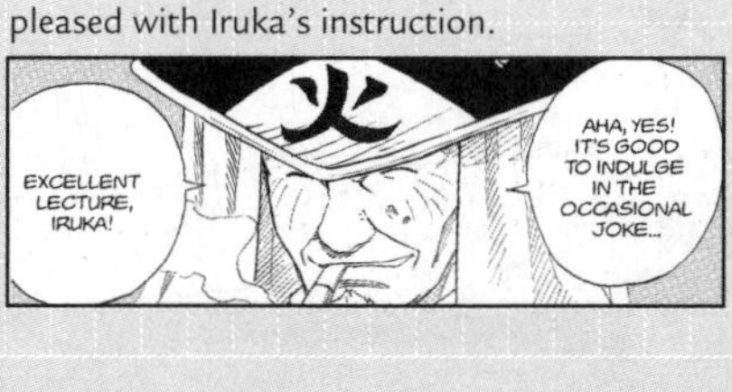
AHA, YES! IT'S GOOD TO INDULGE IN THE OCCASIONAL JOKE...
EXCELLENT LECTURE, IRUKA!

This young chûnin is adored by young and old, male and female!

The students and the Hokage both trust this young Academy teacher. He loves all his students and loves Konoha, and would never harm anyone without cause. On the other hand, he tends to worry too much...

Iruka **Past**

In his youth Iruka hid his sadness, remaining cheerful!

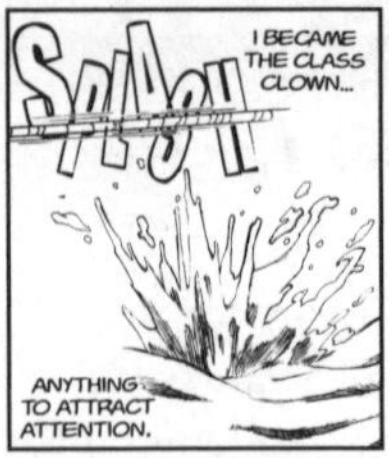
SPLASH
I BECAME THE CLASS CLOWN...
ANYTHING TO ATTRACT ATTENTION.

⬆ To get attention, he often played the clown.

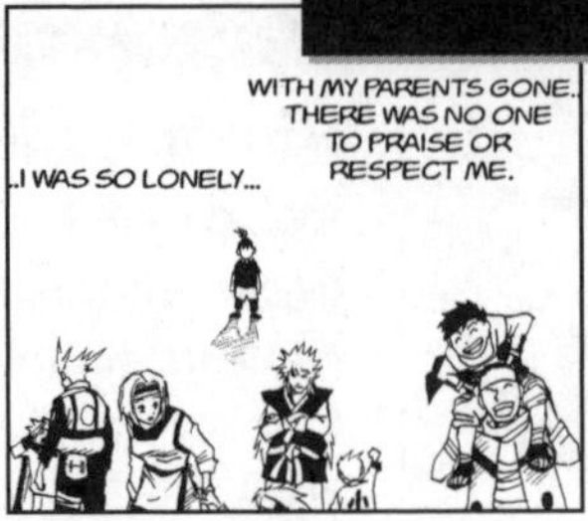
WITH MY PARENTS GONE... THERE WAS NO ONE TO PRAISE OR RESPECT ME.
...I WAS SO LONELY...

⬆ His parents fought bravely against the demon fox.

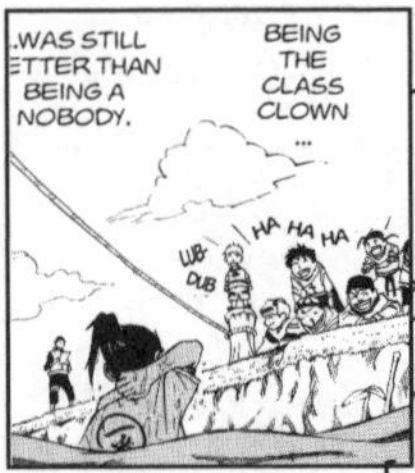
BEING THE CLASS CLOWN...
..WAS STILL ETTER THAN BEING A NOBODY.
HA HA HA
UB- DUB

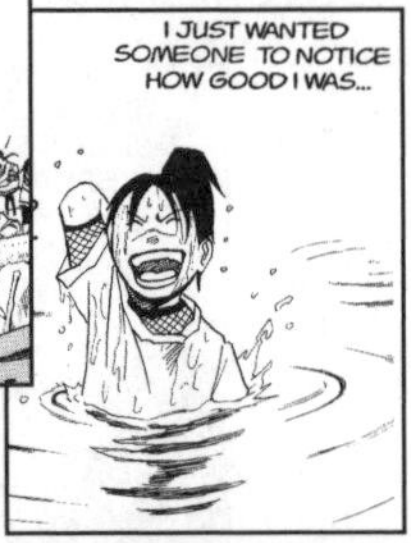
I JUST WANTED SOMEONE TO NOTICE HOW GOOD I WAS...

⬆➡But his actions only isolated him further...

Iruka's heart is clear, broad-minded, and warm. But since he lost his parents at an early age, it is clear that his pain led to an understanding of others...

SPOT LIGHT!

Iruka isn't always gentle!

Top 5 Furious Faces!!

Everyone has their limits!! Here we collect Iruka's most terrifying expressions! If you're a fan of Iruka, and even if you aren't, you may enjoy these rare glimpses!

Number 1

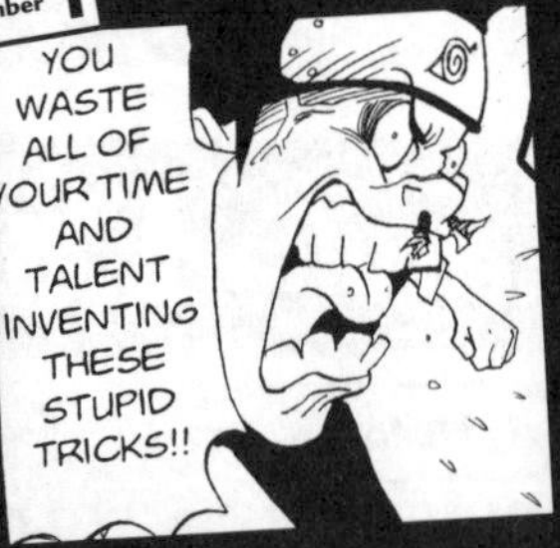
YOU WASTE ALL OF YOUR TIME AND TALENT INVENTING THESE STUPID TRICKS!!

Anger Level: 120%

Naruto's prank caused a nosebleed which knocked him out. His anger was so great his head actually increased in size.

Number 2

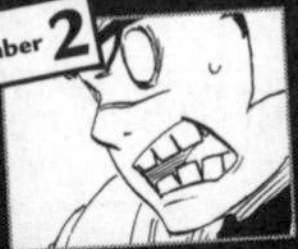

Anger Level: 80%

What could have made him so angry his eyes turned white?!

Number 3

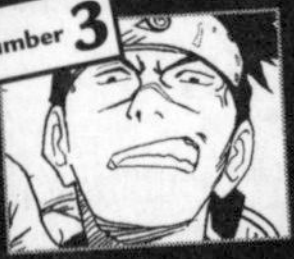

Anger Level: 52%

Standard expression when angry with Naruto. Pretty dang angry.

Number 4

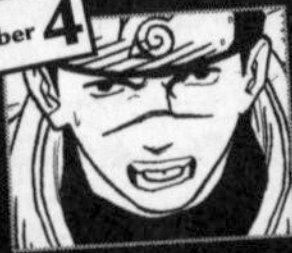

Anger Level: 23%

Iruka protests Kakashi's methods, on behalf of his students.

Number 5

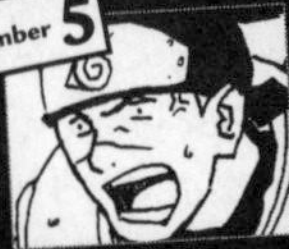

Anger Level: 10%

Naruto's selfishness has him leaning forward.

Iruka Present

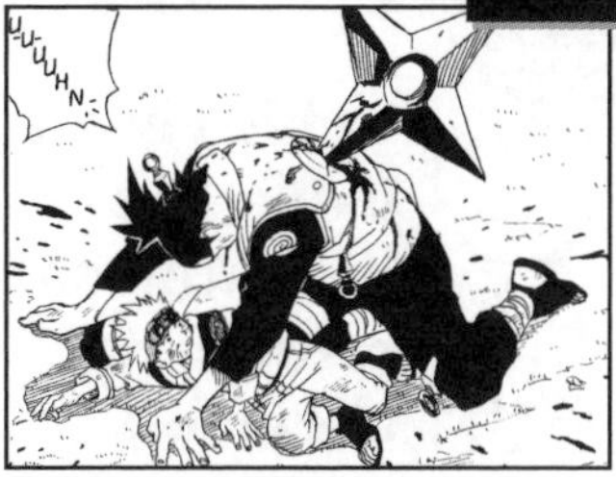
U-U-UUHN...

⬆ Iruka placed himself between Naruto and danger.

Risking his life for his students.

Iruka stands tall, working for his students' futures. Iruka values his time with them more than anything else...which is why he never hesitates to put himself in harm's way to protect them.

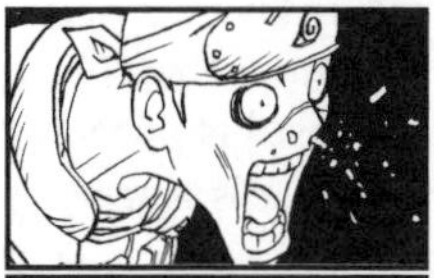

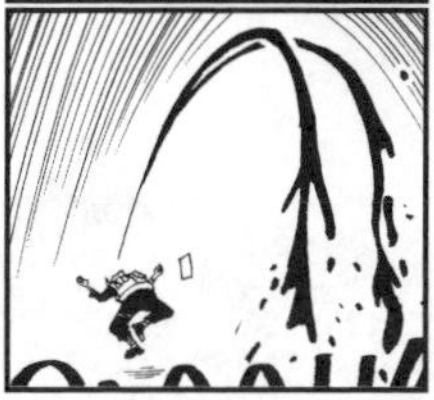

➡ Worried about Naruto, Iruka volunteers to help with the Chûnin Selection Exams.

⬅ Naruto's prank went too far, and gave him a nosebleed!

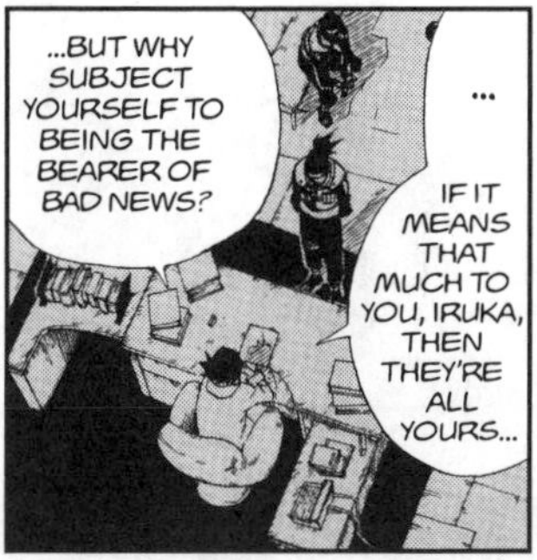
...
...BUT WHY SUBJECT YOURSELF TO BEING THE BEARER OF BAD NEWS?
IF IT MEANS THAT MUCH TO YOU, IRUKA, THEN THEY'RE ALL YOURS...

Iruka Future

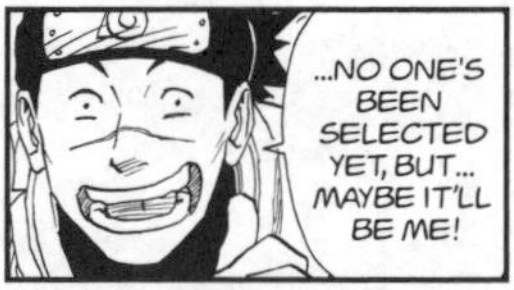
...NO ONE'S BEEN SELECTED YET, BUT... MAYBE IT'LL BE ME!

⬆ He himself has suggested it! The future Fifth Hokage?!

1. Hokage

As far as love for the village goes, he has no rival.

2. Same as now

Iruka values his students more than anything. Perhaps he would prefer to remain a teacher?!

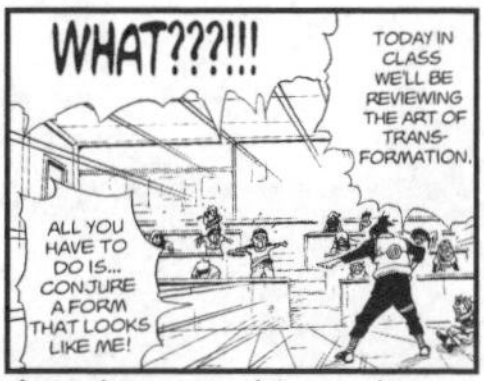
TODAY IN CLASS WE'LL BE REVIEWING THE ART OF TRANS-FORMATION.
WHAT???!!!
ALL YOU HAVE TO DO IS... CONJURE A FORM THAT LOOKS LIKE ME!

⬆ Iruka treats his students like family.

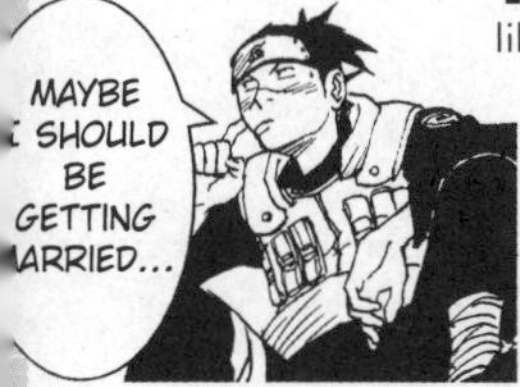
MAYBE SHOULD BE GETTING ARRIED...

3. Or perhaps...

Given Iruka's passion, might he meet that certain someone and suddenly get married?

Following the path of the shinobi? Or...?!

The village people trust him, and he has hidden talents—he could easily have jônin or Anbu in his future. But what will he choose? There are several possibilities...

Iruka Close-up!

Hair

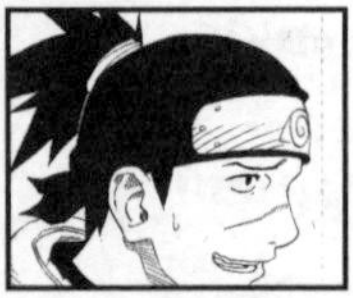

Pulled back quickly for a manly look. What would he look like with it down? Iruka's greatest mystery!

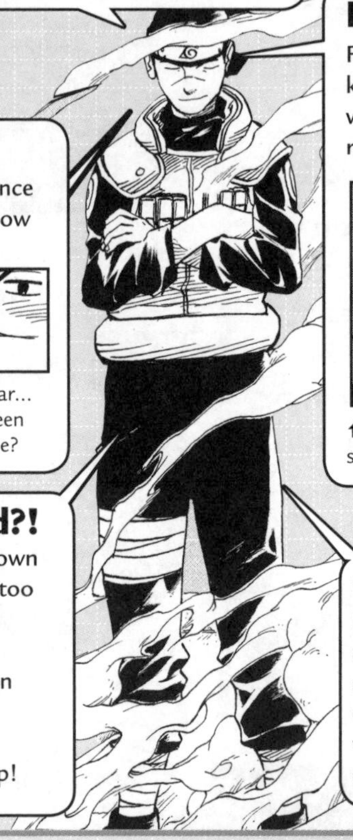

Eyes

Filled with love and kindness. Every student who has left his care remembers him fondly.

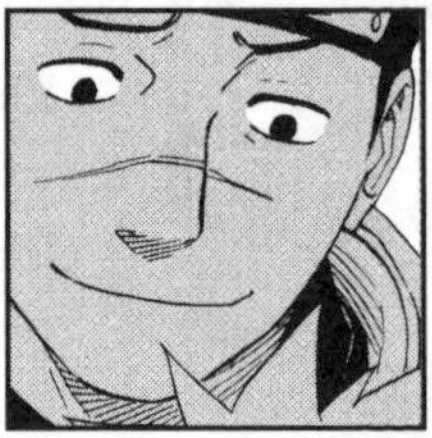

⬆ Those eyes seem to speak right to the heart.

Scar

He's had it since childhood. How did he get it?

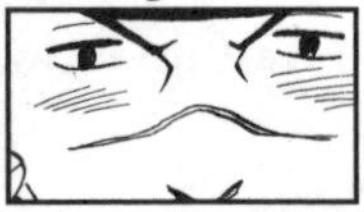

⬆ A straight scar... could it have been made by a blade?

Worried?!

He is well known for worrying too much. When Naruto was on his mission to the Land of Waves, he couldn't sleep!

Costume

Iruka is very serious, and naturally wears the standard Konoha ninja outfit. The vest can be worn by anyone chûnin or higher.

SPOTLIGHT!

A trip to the hot spring refreshes your body and mind!

Since you want to know more about Iruka, we asked him about his favorite thing: hot springs. Do you feel closer to him?

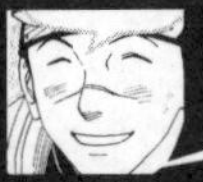

Q: What kind of hot spring do you like?

SULFUR BATHS ARE GOOD FOR WOUNDS AND PAINS, SO I OFTEN USE THEM WHEN I'M HURT.

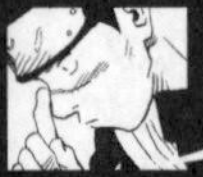

Q: How long do you stay in the water?

WHEN I GET CAUGHT UP IN PLANNING MY NEXT CLASS...TWO HOURS!!

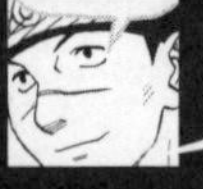

Q: Who would you like to bathe with?

ALL MY STUDENTS! THAT WOULD BE A BLAST!

Iruka Special

Shinobi Question Box

Iruka has fans of all ages, and they all had questions for him!

How did you get that scar on your nose?

<埼玉県> 古屋かずきさん

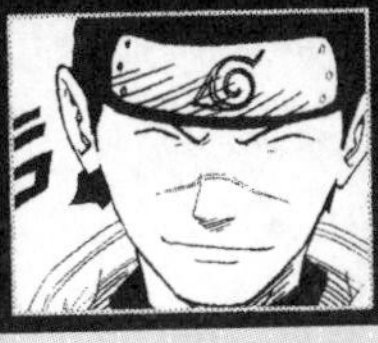

Oh...this? I was on an S rank mission, surrounded by ten enemy jônin...mm? How did you know I was lying?

Do you always buy your students ramen after you yell at them?

<熊本県> 恭さん

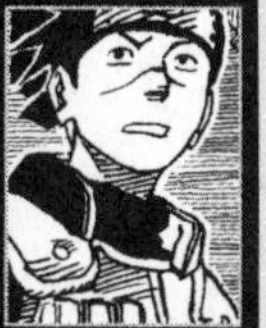

How much do you think I get paid? But when I see them look so dejected... well...

Don't you want to be jônin or Anbu?

<千葉県> もちざわゆみさん

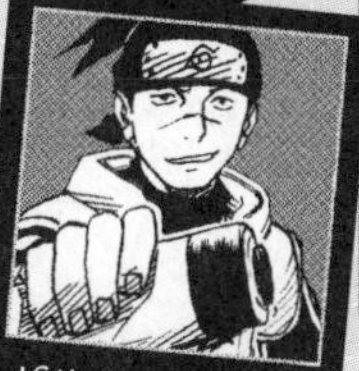

If I'm ordered to be, but I think I can contribute more working as a teacher.

Please marry me, Iruka-sensei!!

<奈良県> 北中千恵さん

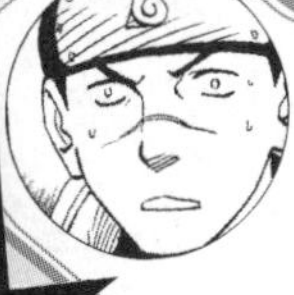

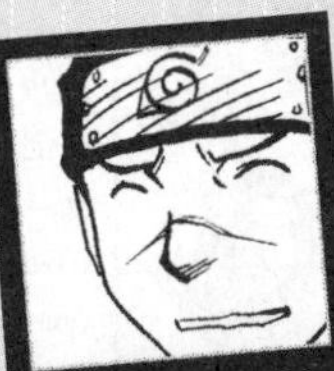

Eh...? Um, so suddenly, I...I mean... aw, now I'm embarrassed!

Why did you want to be a teacher?

<東京都> タカさん

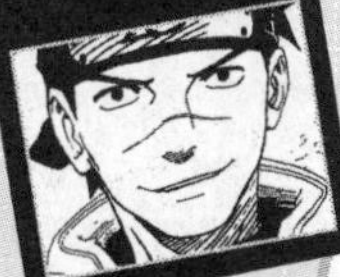

I love my pupils' pure, innocent eyes. They teach me too!

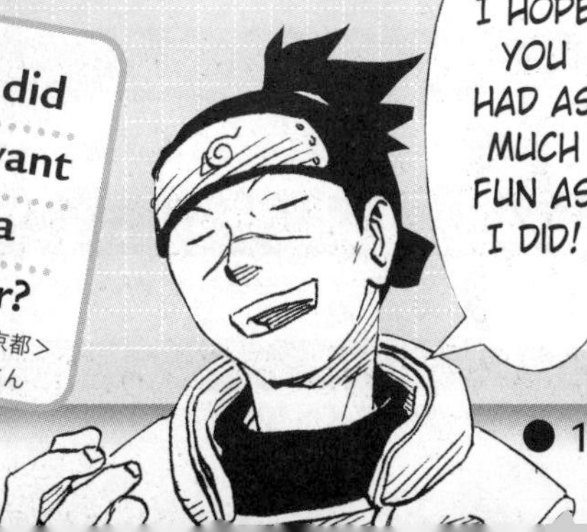
I HOPE YOU HAD AS MUCH FUN AS I DID!

FANTASTIC FAN ART

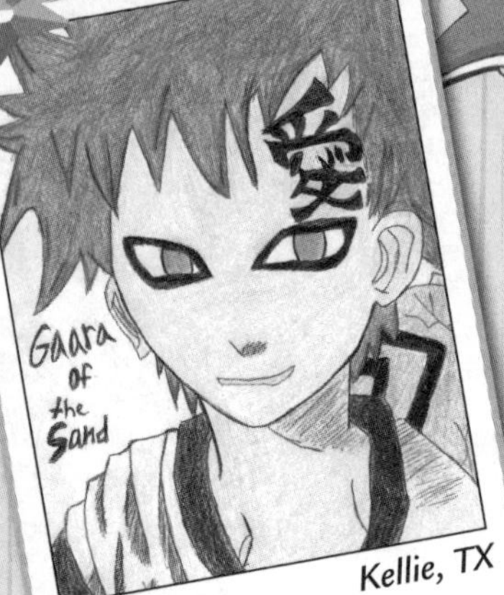
Gaara
of
the
Sand

Kellie, TX

⬆ Gaara is looking at you!

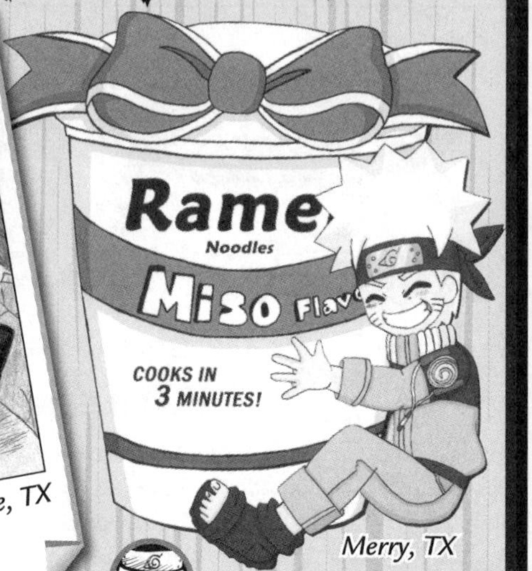
Rame
Noodles
Miso Flav
COOKS IN
3 MINUTES!

Merry, TX

⬆ Naruto loves his ramen.

NARUTO 16 Fan

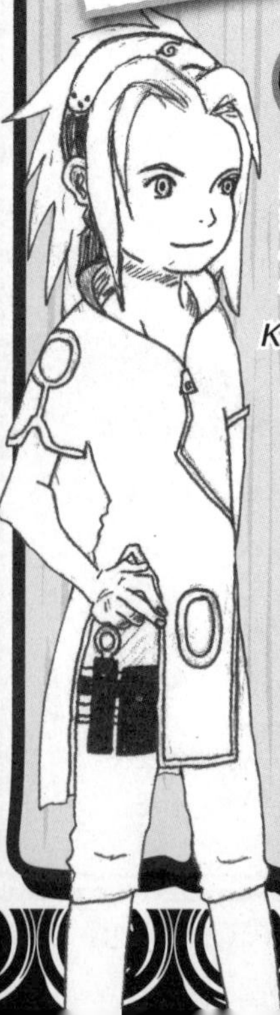

⬅ Don't be fooled by that disarming smile.

Kelly, CA

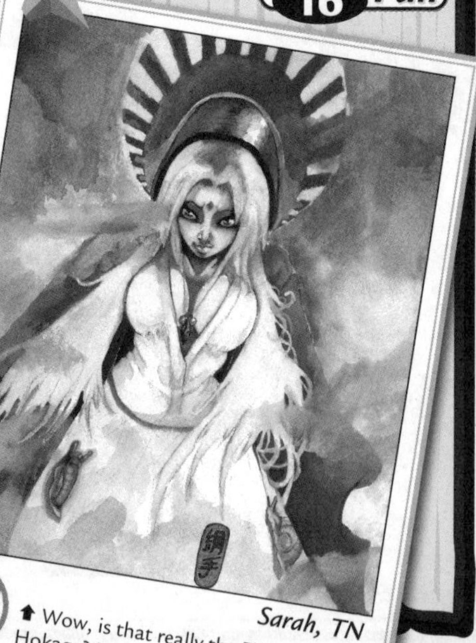

Sarah, TN

⬆ Wow, is that really the Fifth Hokage? Not bad!

Hidden Leaf Village Novel News

The Make-Out Series

Vol. 001

This month's line-up:

- ⊙Paradise news
- ⊙Special feature
- ⊙Interview with Jiraiya

Paradise ① ② ③

Jiraiya

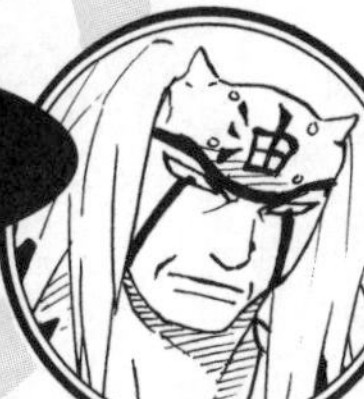

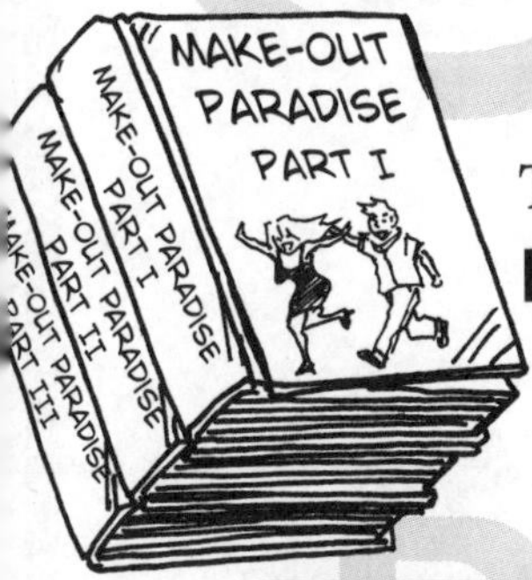
MAKE-OUT PARADISE PART I
MAKE-OUT PARADISE PART I
MAKE-OUT PARADISE PART II
MAKE-OUT PARADISE PART III

120 ryo each

This month's big push! **Paradise Series!!**

The main character and heroine, both new to love, begin dating, and their eyes gradually open to grown-up love. For all men who have known love, and all men who would know love...

Multimedia on the way?!

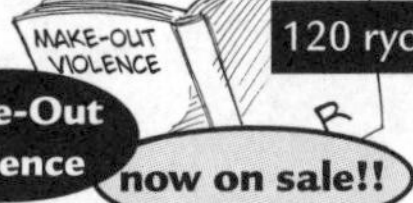
MAKE-OUT VIOLENCE
R

120 ryo each

Make-Out Violence **now on sale!!**

With the movie coming out, the series is getting even more popular! Many licensed products and games are being developed, but the price and sale dates are not yet known.

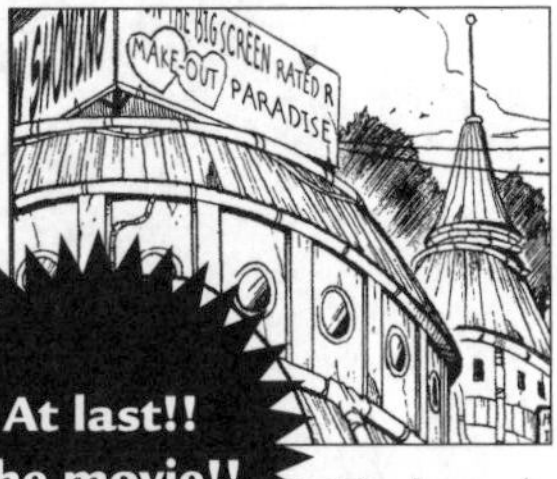
ON THE BIG SCREEN RATED R
MAKE-OUT PARADISE

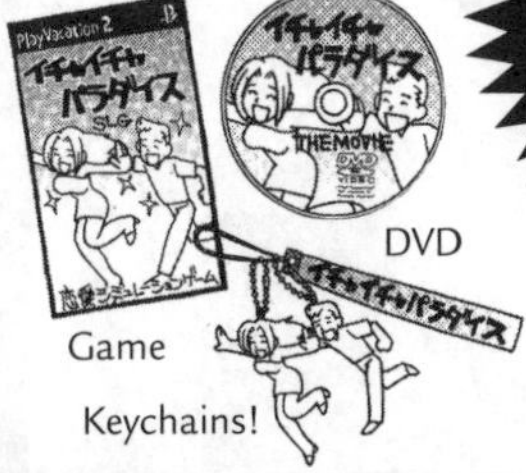
PlayVacation 2
THE MOVIE

DVD

Game

Keychains!

At last!! The movie!!

One admission:

180 ryo each

The first volume of the ***Paradise*** series is now a movie! That wonderful story — those shocking images — they will capture your heart! A must see!!

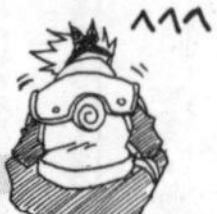

Make-Out

Special feature

The readers respond to the two books!

Make-Out Violence

Out of 100 people surveyed:

- ⊙I wanted to make out ..88
- ⊙I learned the difference between love and romance 6
- ⊙I missed being close to someone 3
- ⊙Love is so fragile 2
- ⊙Other 1

Make-Out Paradise

Out of 100 people surveyed:

- ⊙I wanted to make out ..84
- ⊙It taught me to believe in love 9
- ⊙I learned how different men and women are 3
- ⊙I wanted to fall in love ...2
- ⊙Love is a wonderful thing 1
- ⊙Other 1

I have never seen the bonds between a man and a woman painted so stirringly. ***Make-Out Paradise*** was impressive enough, but this book was even better! I was blown away!

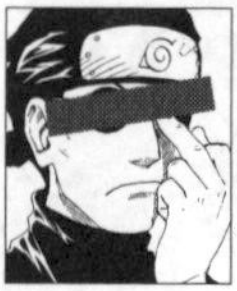

➡ Does not look like he's into smut, but secretly quite the fan? Closet perv Mr. E!

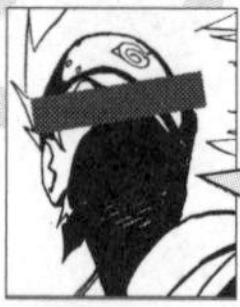

⬆ Mr. K.H. gave a particularly passionate answer.

Love, romance, heartbreak...all the important things I had forgotten as I grew up came flooding back. The main characters' passionate embraces made me blush, but I read it over and over again.

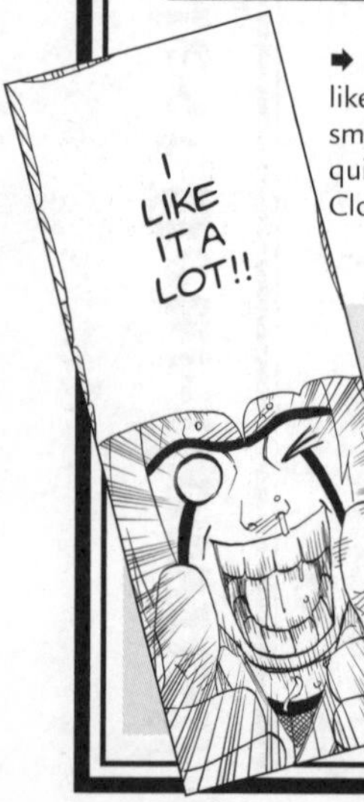
I LIKE IT A LOT!!

Interview with Jiraiya-sensei!

Will there be another?!

Jiraiya: I am currently gathering ideas...when I have enough, I shall begin writing!

Editor: What kind of story?

Jiraiya: I'm still doing research, so I can't tell you...but the theme will be pure love, and the title will be ***Innocence!!***

Mitarashi Anko Special Lecture

Hidden Leaf Village's 12 Funniest Beat-downs!!

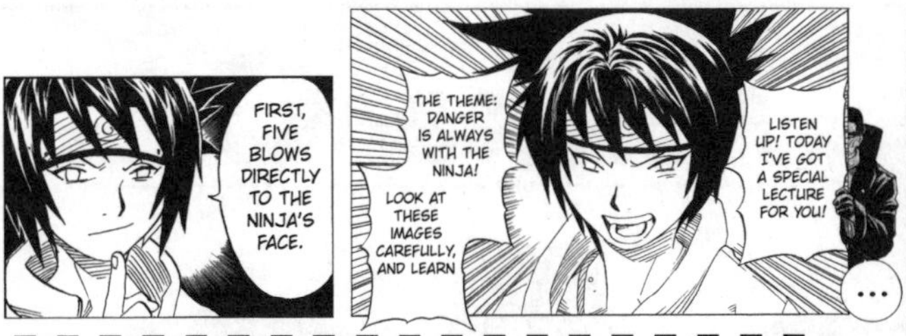

LISTEN UP! TODAY I'VE GOT A SPECIAL LECTURE FOR YOU!
...
THE THEME: DANGER IS ALWAYS WITH THE NINJA!
LOOK AT THESE IMAGES CAREFULLY, AND LEARN
FIRST, FIVE BLOWS DIRECTLY TO THE NINJA'S FACE.

THE DAILY LIFE OF THE NINJA IS A STORM OF SEETHING ANGER AND HILARIOUS VIOLENCE!

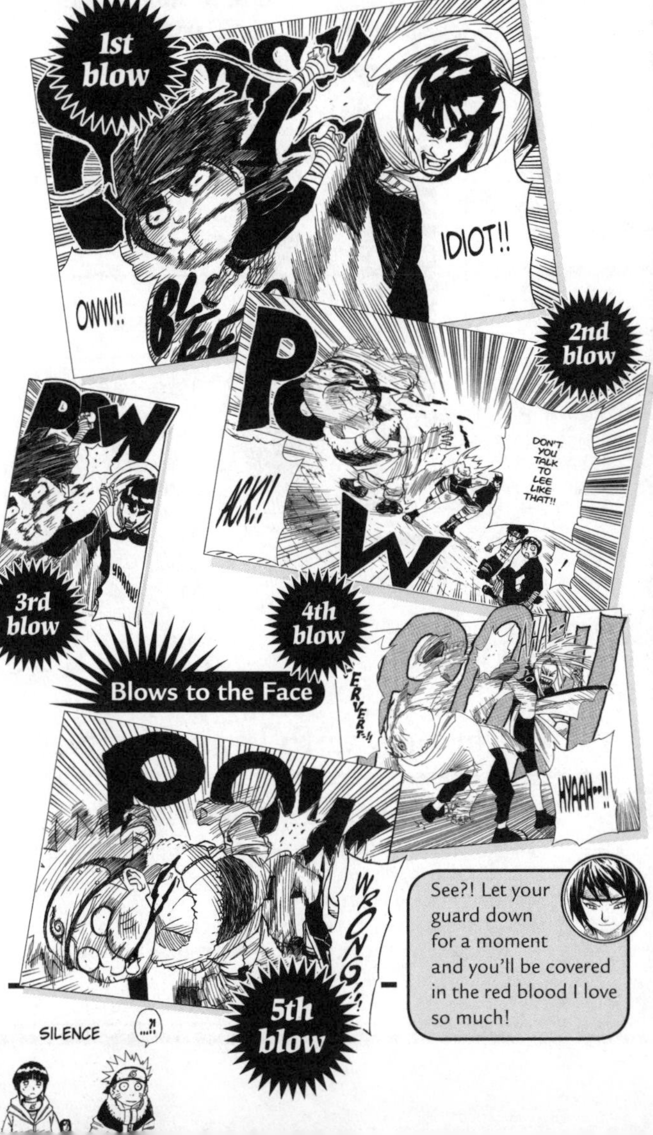

1st blow
IDIOT!!
OWW!!
2nd blow
DON'T YOU TALK TO LEE LIKE THAT!!
ACK!!
!
3rd blow
4th blow
HYAAAH!!
Blows to the Face
5th blow
WRONG!!
SILENCE
...?!

See?! Let your guard down for a moment and you'll be covered in the red blood I love so much!

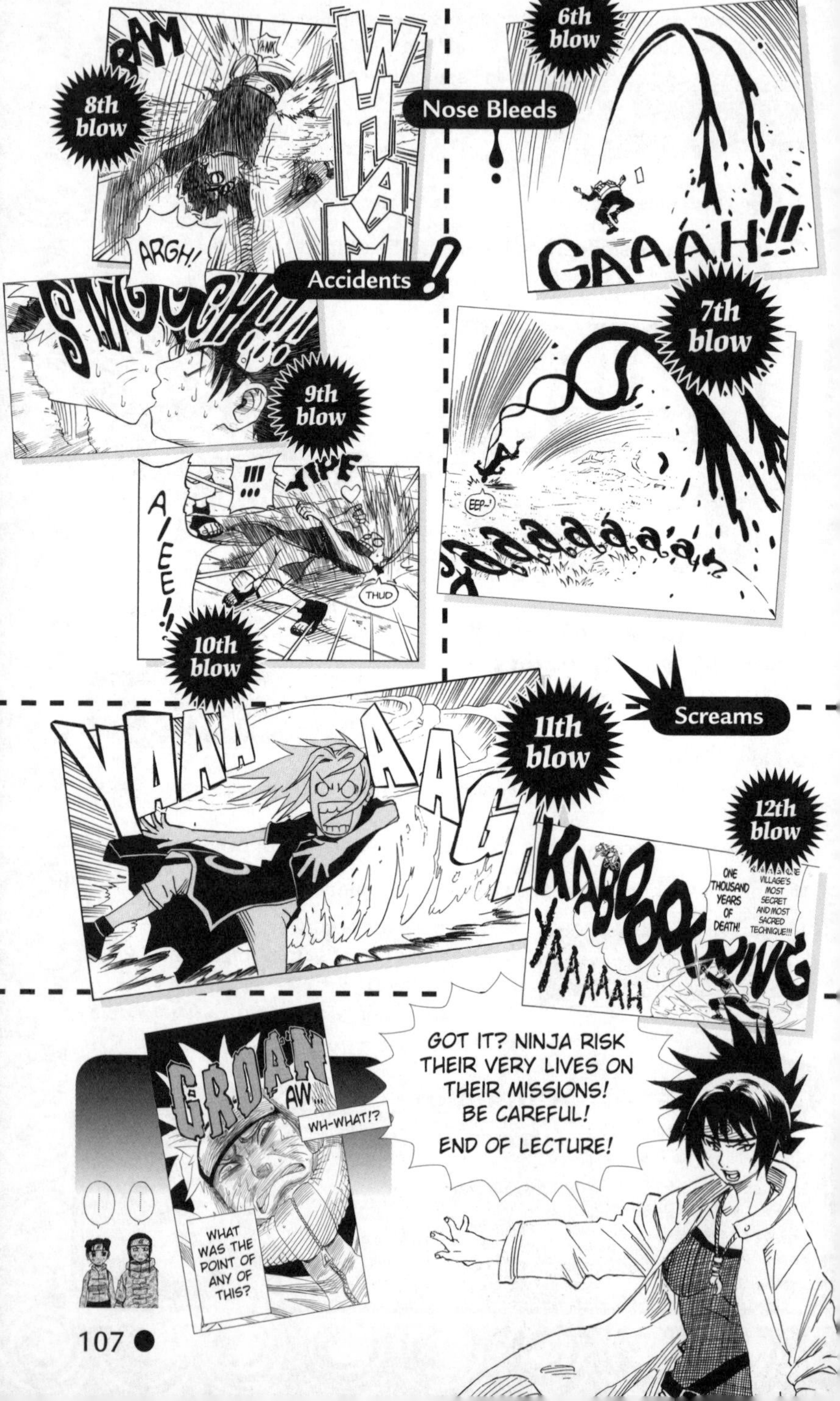
6th blow
GAAAH!!
7th blow
EEP--!
Nose Bleeds
8th blow
BAM
YANK
WHAM
ARGH!
Accidents
SMOOCH
9th blow
YIPE
!!!
...
AIEE!!
THUD
10th blow
Screams
11th blow
YAAAAAAG
12th blow
VILLAGE'S MOST SECRET AND MOST SACRED TECHNIQUE!!!
ONE THOUSAND YEARS OF DEATH!
KABOOOOMING
YAAAAAH
GOT IT? NINJA RISK THEIR VERY LIVES ON THEIR MISSIONS! BE CAREFUL!
END OF LECTURE!
GROAN
AW...
WH-WHAT!?
WHAT WAS THE POINT OF ANY OF THIS?

● He always gets in trouble, and gets everyone else around him in trouble too, but he's the most alive!! <神奈川県> ジャンク屋秀さん

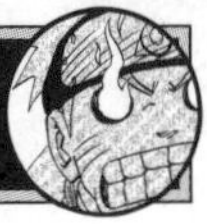

Hey! That's not a compliment!

● He seems like a diamond in the rough. <神奈川県> 田中ゆりさん

● When he used the Ninja Centerfold and turned into a beautiful girl...I fell in love!! <岡山県> 黄金樹さん

● I love his smile when he's happy. It always makes me happy too! <北海道> 楠田暁さん

● That invincible smile when he tied his headband back on after Zabuza stepped on it. <東京都> フチュー舞踏会さん

NARUTO V.S. NARUTO 17 Fan

Naruto side

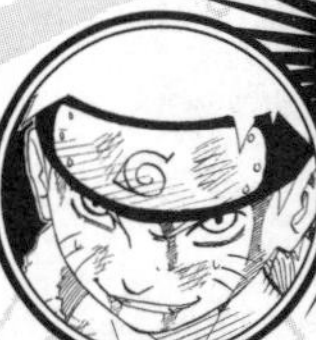

Each group lays out their favorite's strong points... which do you prefer?

● Naruto's smile is the best in the world!! <東京都> 恵理さん

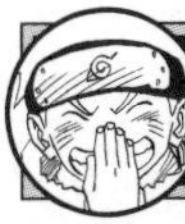

My smile is that good?! Grin ♥

● I love his hair!! <福岡県> 純さん

● He keeps getting stronger *because* he isn't perfect! That's what makes him cool. <山口県> 再不斬願望さん

● The way he works so hard to earn the recognition of others is cool!! <大阪府> 村上真伊さん

● One vote for his unbelievable power in a pinch!! <群馬県> ヨウ.N.さん

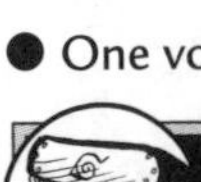

I'll work even harder!

● There's a lot of power in him when he's fighting to protect something. That always steals my heart! <千葉県> 横山まいさん

● Naruto cheers everyone up!! <静岡県> 諒さん

● Naruto has a pure heart. <愛媛県> 瑠さん

Iruka consensus

Iruka-sensei's warm feelings for his students made quite an impact! He's always nice, always strong, and very cool! Everyone wants a teacher like him!

A flood of support from Iruka fans!

● I love his warm aura!! <愛媛県> 衣瑠香さん

● His eyes are beautiful. <青森県> 前田美奈さん

● He gets really angry and he really worries. <千葉県> 矢部瞳さん

◎ Titans ◎

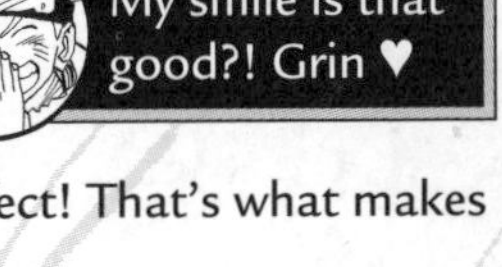
WE WEREN'T ASKING FOR THEM, BUT YOU SENT THEM ANYWAY!

● Sasuke's usually cool and a little snotty, but every now and then he smiles...the contrast is incredible!! <大阪府> 山本葉苗さん

● His entrances are always awesome!! <東京都> 桃香さん

Hmph, ninja have no use for looks.

● Sasuke's the most beautiful boy in Konoha! <神奈川県> 内葉希美さん

● Never wavers in his beliefs, always moving forward — even more than Naruto. Sasuke may be out for revenge, but he has my support! <山口県> 究極龍さん

● Admitting his weakness, but working to overcome it...impossible without true inner strength! <福島県> 憐さん

● Hunk pheromones at his age?! <宮崎県> 黒漆さん

● Cool + strong = popular <東京都> モモミさん

Debate: SASUKE

Sasuke side

Do you like Naruto? Or Sasuke?

Revenge...? I have only one path open to me.

● He always seems serious, but occasionally he does something nice and shows that he values his companions. <滋賀県> 桃花さん

● Inner passion hidden behind a cool exterior. Double cool!! <群馬県> 香月さん

● Unwavering ambition, extreme competitiveness, always ready for a challenge — no one better! <鳥取県> 雷鳴ノ花さん

● Mastering Chidori with the Sharingan and incredible talent... Kakashi's not the only one in love with his talent!! <茨城県> 万鳥子さん

● Knowledge, courage, strength!! I hope he carries my future as well as the village's!! <新潟県> 朽葉さん

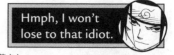

Hmph, I won't lose to that idiot.

Cool attitude, a fighter's spirit. But more than anything, Sasuke's appearance has grabbed the hearts of female readers! If this were limited to only girls, Sasuke would have won by a landslide!

Sasuke consensus
Naruto consensus

Naruto grabbed everyone's hearts with his bright, positive personality. They take great pleasure in watching his growth, his eyes set on his dream...but not many people said he was cool.

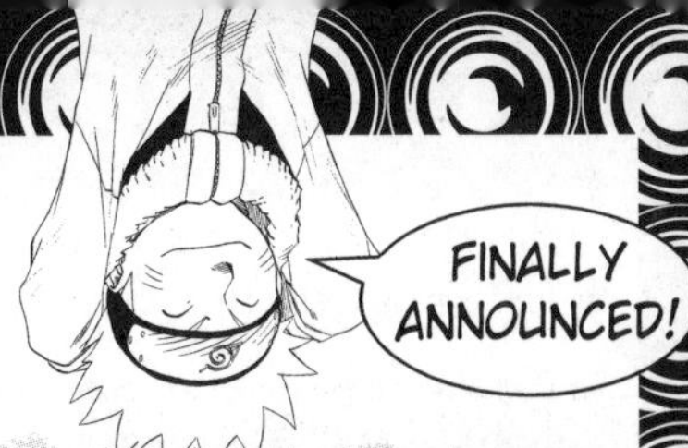
FINALLY ANNOUNCED!

Dream Match Ranking! RESULTS!

What incredible ninja matches do people want to see?
We asked *Naruto* fans to send in the matches they most wanted to see — here are the most popular choices!

No. 1

Hatake Kakashi vs. Guy

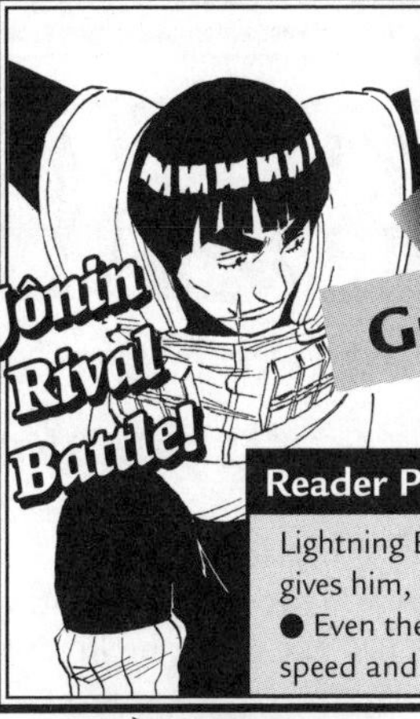

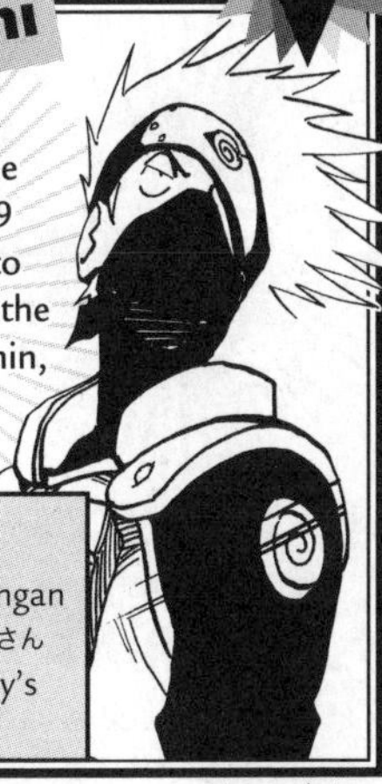

Jônin Rival Battle!

While Guy claims the record is 50 wins, 49 losses, we have yet to see them face off in the manga. Both are jônin, but somehow there isn't much tension!

Reader Predictions

● Between the Lightning Blade and all the moves the Sharingan gives him, Kakashi will win! ＜山梨県＞ アオコさん

● Even the Sharingan can't see through Guy's speed and power! ＜東京都＞ 大阪ザムライさん

No. 2

Uzumaki Naruto vs. Uchiha Sasuke

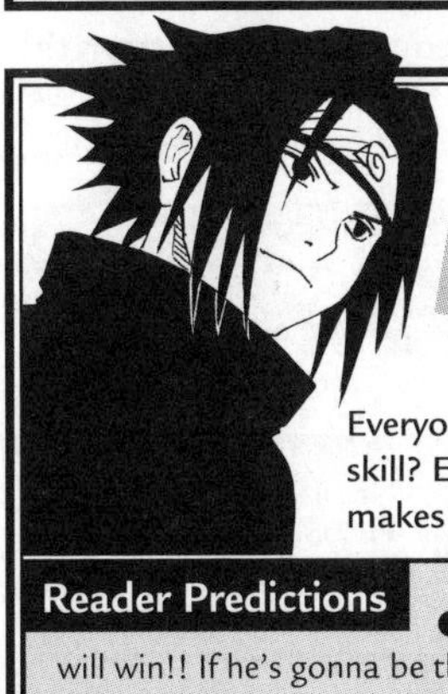

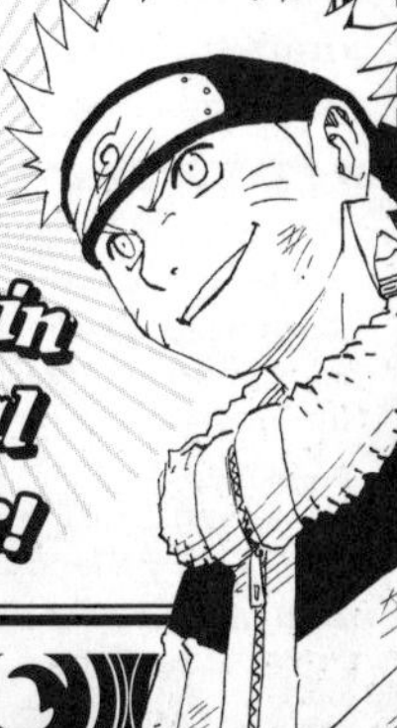

Genin Rival Battle!

Everyone wants to see this! Guts vs. skill? Either one could win, which makes the idea so fascinating!

Reader Predictions

● Of course Naruto will win!! If he's gonna be the Hokage, he can't let anyone beat him! ＜栃木県＞ 紅夜叉さん

● Once he's warmed up, no one can beat Sasuke. ＜京都府＞ 多島幸平さん

No. 3

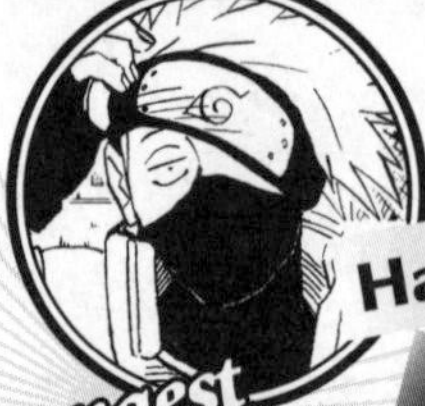

Hatake Kakashi vs. Iruka

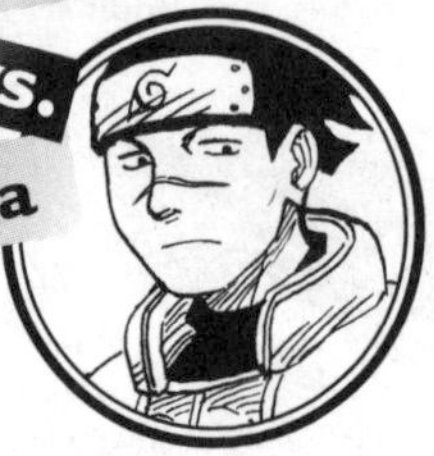

Strongest Teacher Battle!

Both are Naruto's teachers... chûnin vs. jônin – this could be incredible!

Reader Predictions

- No matter how poorly things are going, Iruka will never give up! He'll pull through in the end!!
  ＜埼玉県＞ シンのすけさん
- Once he's warmed up, no one can beat Kakashi.
  ＜群馬県＞ 安田朋子さん

No. 4

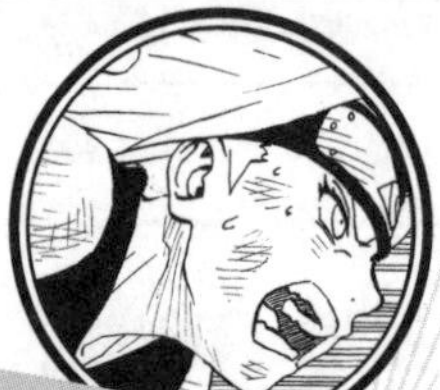

Haruno Sakura vs. Yamanaka Ino

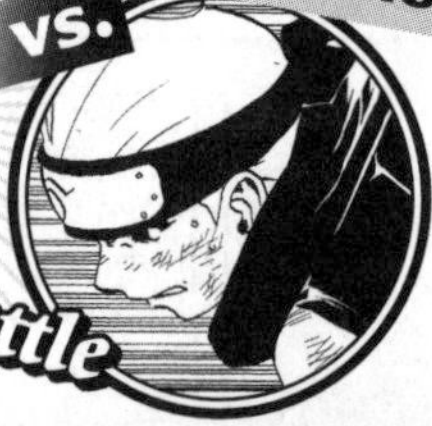

Eternal Friendship Battle

This actually did happen during the Chûnin Exam. Winning and losing may not be the point with these two...

Reader Predictions

- I have faith that Sakura will win if they face off again!
  ＜埼玉県＞サクラん坊さん
- I don't think the same tricks will work on Ino twice. She'll win next time.
  ＜長野県＞ Wild Catさん

No. 5

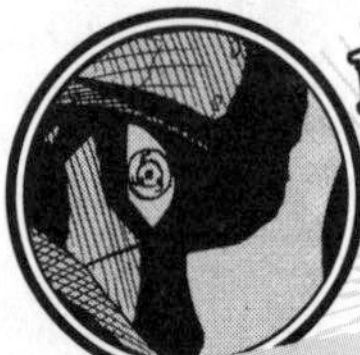

Uchiha Itachi vs. Uchiha Sasuke

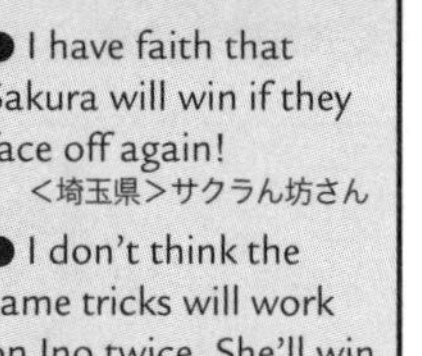

Brothers of Destiny!

Reader Predictions

- Now that Sasuke has the Chidori, he can use his anger as power and win.
  ＜東京都＞ カモメンジャーさん
- We don't know much about Itachi yet, but I don't think anyone can win against someone so terrifying...＜北海道＞ Pすけさん

Sasuke must fight this battle someday. We can't hope for much fair play...

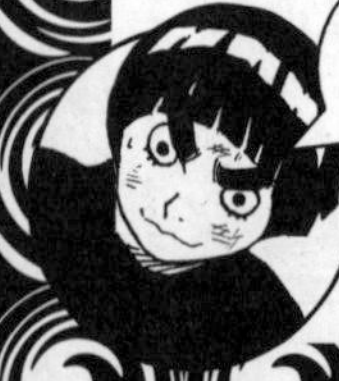
I WANT TO FIGHT UCHIHA!

Match-ups 6–10 are on the next page!!

Match-ups

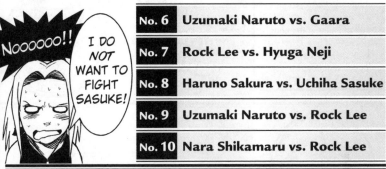

No. 6 – No. 10 !

Lots of Rock Lee battles after sixth place. No matter who Rock Lee fights, the battle is sure to be incredible! But a battle between Sakura and Sasuke is surprisingly popular!

Nooooooo!!

I DO NOT WANT TO FIGHT SASUKE!

No. 6	Uzumaki Naruto vs. Gaara
No. 7	Rock Lee vs. Hyuga Neji
No. 8	Haruno Sakura vs. Uchiha Sasuke
No. 9	Uzumaki Naruto vs. Rock Lee
No. 10	Nara Shikamaru vs. Rock Lee

Other ideas!! Particularly rare ones...

This would be a key battle to determine the heir to the Hyuga can. Most people think Hanabi is stronger, but Hinata may have hidden strengths. <富山県> フーさん ほか

Hyuga Hinata

vs

Hyuga Hanabi

Both are young geniuses. Very different types, but they have difficult childhoods in common. <高知県> 虎川流藻さん ほか

Haku

vs

Gaara

The most dramatic battle in Konoha history?! It would shake the heavens!! <愛媛県> ベイスターズさん ほか

First Hokage + Fourth Hokage tag team

vs

Second Hokage + Third Hokage tag team

Another battle of geniuses. Both carry their clan's reputation. Which is Konoha's greatest clan? <神奈川県> 矢野未奈実さん ほか

Hyuga Neji

vs

Uchiha Sasuke

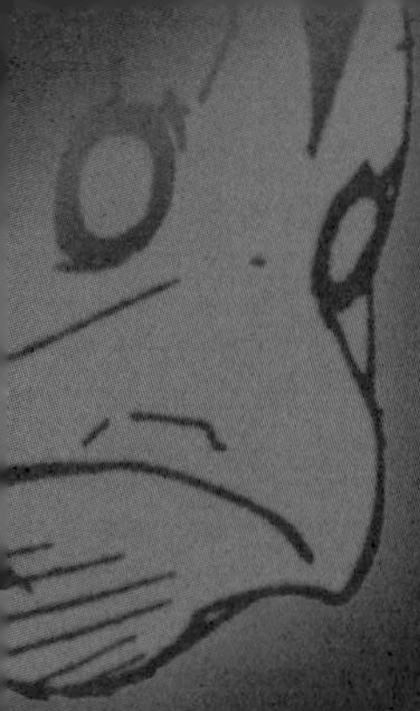
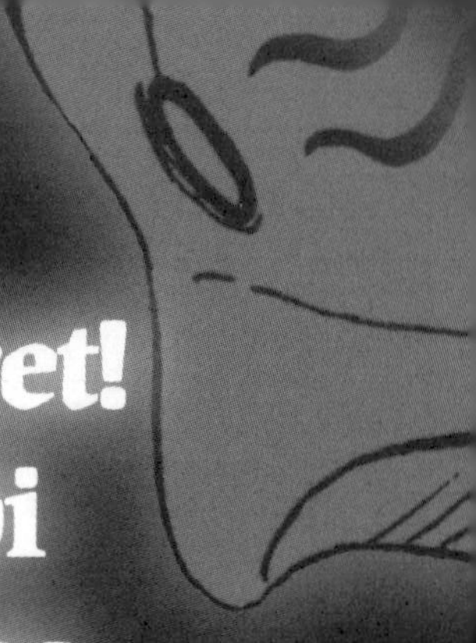

Top Secret! Shinobi Missions

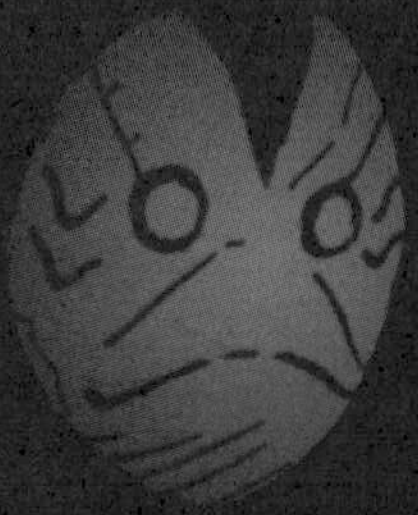

Exclusive to the Fanbook!

Konoha Team 7
Mission Reports

For the village, and their daily bread...secret records of shinobi missions

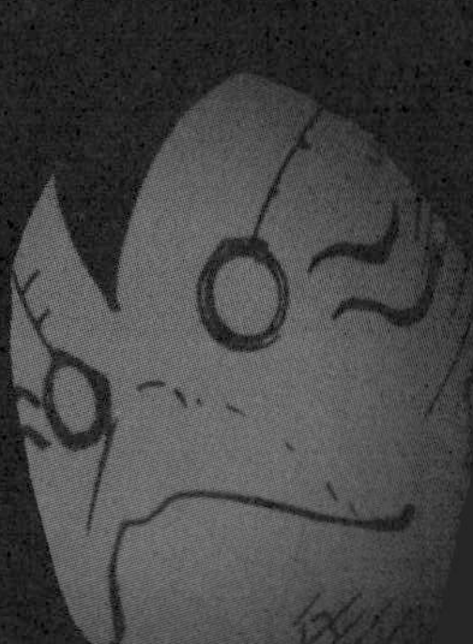

From Babysitting to Assassination
Mission Ranks and Fees

The rank and mission details are decided by the village leaders...

Every day requests flood into the village, and the Hokage and other village leaders classify them with one of five ranks, handing each of them out to appropriate teams. Below is the basic nature of each rank and the normal fees.

WE TAKE THAT TREMENDOUS VARIETY...
...AND SORT THEM INTO CATEGORIES FROM A TO D, BASED ON THE DEGREE OF SKILL THEY REQUIRE.

⬆⬇ Missions beyond the abilities of the team assigned could damage Konoha's military capability.

S
A
B
C
D
Jônin
Chûnin
Genin

IF THE NINJA IN QUESTION COMPLETES THOSE DUTIES SUCCESSFULLY...
DO A GOOD JOB
LINE STA
NEW AS
...THEN THE GRATEFUL PERSON HE HAS HELPED PAYS HIM A FEE...

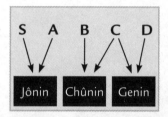

⬆ The fee varies depending on the nature of the mission.

Rank	Classification Basis	Specific mission examples	Fees
S	Mission relates to national secrets.	Request from other countries to join war. VIP assassination or transport of secret documents, etc.	More than one million ryo
A	Mission relates to village and country interests.	Request from other countries to join war. VIP guard duty, subdue ninja squad, etc.	150,000 - 1,000,000 ryo
B	Mission expected to involve battle with other ninja.	Request from other countries to join war. Bodyguard for private individual, spy work, assassination of ninja, etc.	80,000 - 200,000 ryo
C	Mission expected to injure ninja involved.	Request from other countries to join war. Guard private individual, behavior investigation, capture/kill wild animals, etc.	30,000 - 100, 000 ryo
D	Mission involves no direct battle or risk of death.	Request from other countries to join war. Search for missing pets, help harvest potatoes, babysitting, etc.	5000 - 50,000 ryo

Flawless Execution

Mission Performance and Team Organization

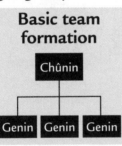

Teams of four carry out missions.

Generally speaking, missions are carried out by a team of four shinobi. Because of this, after passing their certification test, all registered genin are placed into teams. From that point on, team members perform all missions assigned to them.

Team Organization Rules

Chûnin or higher must lead teams.

At least one member of the team must be chûnin or higher. One of the remaining three can be placed as second in command, ready to take over in the event of the leader's death.

Why four-man teams?

1 - To Ensure Mobility

Four is the upper limit for staying coordinated and moving swiftly with no loss of discipline.

2 - To Heighten Security

Groups of larger than four are easier for the enemy to detect and actually more at risk.

I SUSPECT THERE IS ALREADY A LARGE NUMBER OF SAND AND SOUND NINJA INSIDE OUR VILLAGE.
MOVEMENT BY MORE THAN A BASIC TROOP UNIT OF FOUR WILL DESTROY ANY ADVANTAGE OF SWIFTNESS AND MAKES IT HARDER TO HIDE FROM THE ENEMY...
THEY TAUGHT THAT DURING THE PATROL DRILLS AT THE ACADEMY, DIDN'T THEY?

⬆ The necessity of the four-man team is a key topic taught at the Academy.

Team Organization Basics

1. Equalize fighting ability

Teams are selected carefully to avoid putting too much strength into one team.

Basic team formation
Chûnin
Genin
Genin
Genin

2. Specialization toward mission types

Occasionally teams may be assembled from members best suited to carrying out a particular mission.

......OF THE TWENTY-SEVEN OF YOU, SASUKE HAS THE BEST GRADES, NARUTO.
YOU WOULD BE THE BOTTOM OF THE CLASS
THE IDEA IS TO BALANCE YOUR DIFFERENT STRENGTHS... THAT'S WHY YOU ENDED UP TOGETHER!

⬆ The concept of equalizing abilities is fairly new.

Hidden Leaf Village

Team 7 Mission Report

Uzumaki Naruto, with the Nine-Tailed Fox Spirit sealed within him, and Uchiha Sasuke, sole survivor of his clan's tragedy – the 7th is not an easily managed group. We collect all reports filed since the team's formation by the man responsible for keeping the team under control, Hatake Kakashi!

◎ Month
△ Day
Report concerning the certification of Uchiha Sasuke, Uzumaki Naruto, and Haruno Sakura

Conducted genin certification test as usual. Specifically, to steal a bell from me, the true purpose being to see if they were capable of trusting each other. In violation of my instructions, they helped each other, and I submit that they are acceptable as genin.

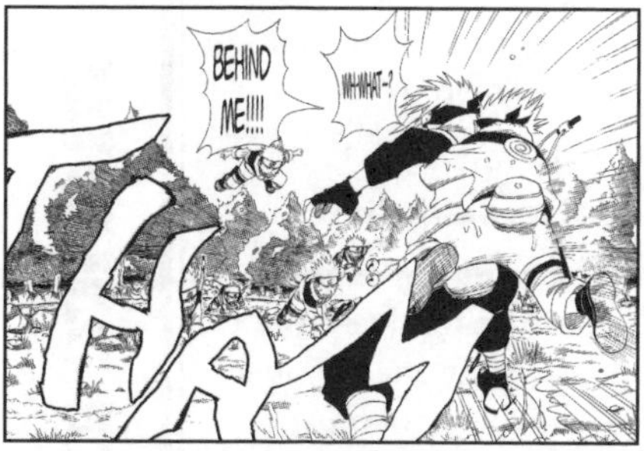
WH-WHAT--?
BEHIND ME!!!!

⬆ Naruto combined ninjutsu and some good ideas and managed to attack me from behind.

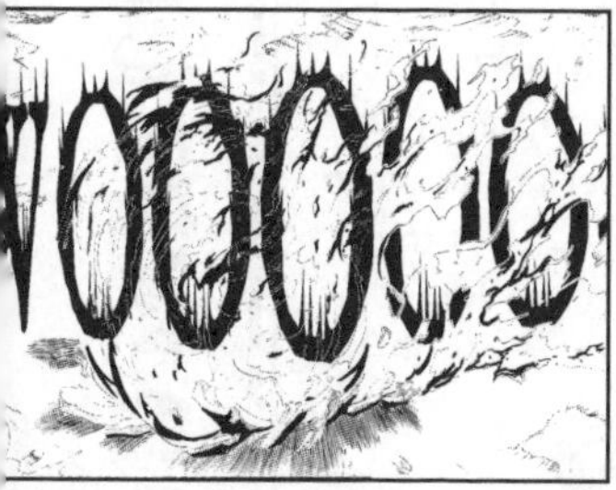

⬅ Sasuke uses Fire Style: Fireball Technique. His abilities are far beyond those of a genin.

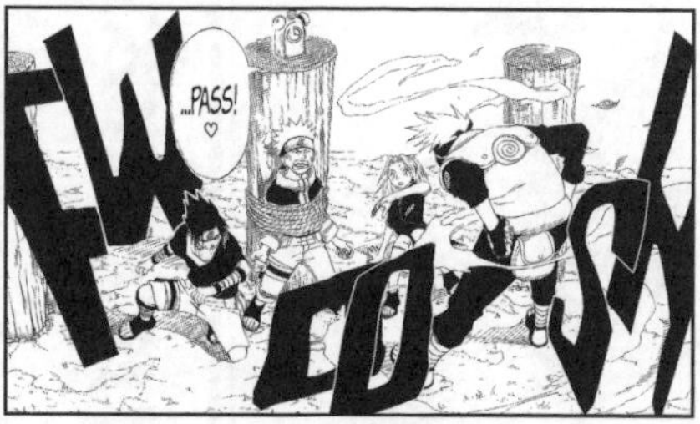
...PASS! ♡

⬆ Recognizing their feelings, I inform them they have passed.

Team Seven Members:

Uchiha Sasuke
Uzumaki Naruto
Haruno Sakura

Jônin in charge:
Hatake Kakashi

○ Month
× Day

Report concerning guarding the Land of Waves bridge builder Tazuna, and the battle with rogue shinobi Zabuza

Report One

Falsehoods in client's request

Tazuna's request began as protection from bandits. But it became clear a man named Gato was after him, trying to retain control of sea trade. The mission was beyond our abilities, but we decided we could not simply abandon it and continued.

THAT'S THE ONE. ON THE SURFACE HE LOOKS LIKE A LEGITIMATE BUSINESSMAN. THE TRUTH IS HE'S A RUTHLESS MURDERING CRIMINAL WHO EMPLOYS GANGS AND TEAMS OF SHINOBI, AND TRAFFICS IN DRUGS AND CONTRABAND.
HE STARTS OUT TAKING OVER COMPANIES... AND ENDS UP RUNNING ENTIRE COUNTRIES.
HE LIVES BY EVERY LOW AND VICIOUS TRADE KNOWN TO MAN.

⬆ Gato, officially the operator of a shipping company.

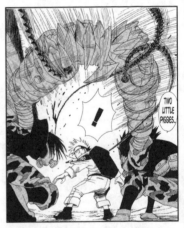

TWO LITTLE PIGGIES...
!

⬆ The chûnin hired by Gato ambushed us while were on the way.

Report Two

Battle with Zabuza

The assassin Gato sent was Momochi Zabuza, a rogue ninja from the Hidden Mist Village. His ninjutsu and taijutsu made the battle quite difficult, but Naruto and the others pulled off some brilliant teamwork, and Zabuza was forced to retreat. At this point another shinobi appeared and we were unable to finish him.

⬆ Naruto's imagination turns the tide.

⬇ Zabuza's ally, disguised as a hunter ninja.

HEH HEH.. YOUR PREDICTION CAME TRUE. ♥
SHFF

Client: **Tazuna**
Bridge builder from the Land of Waves. Currently constructing a large bridge to connect the Land of Waves with other countries.

Duties: **Protection**
Guard him from thieves and the like on the road to the Land of Waves, until construction is completed.

Mission Rank: C

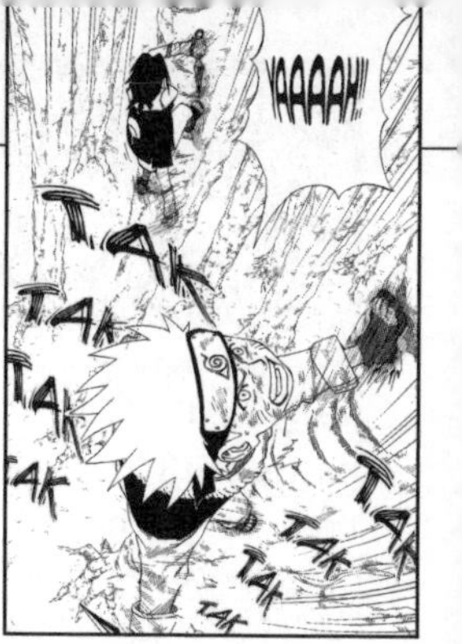
YAAAAH!!
TAK
TAK
TAK
TAK
TAK
TAK
TAK
TAK

⬆ Competition between Naruto and Sasuke leads to rapid progress.

Report Three

Naruto, Sasuke and Sakura train, progress

Aware that Zabuza would attack again, I placed the three genin in intensive training. To improve chakra control, I had them climb trees. This proved effective, and all three improved rapidly.

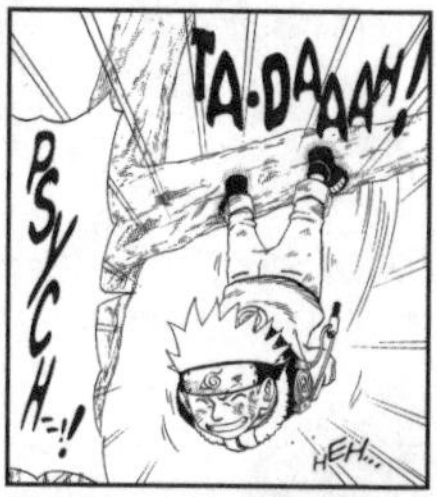
TA-DAAAH!
PSYCH--!
HEH...

⬆ Now able to hang upside-down from a branch.

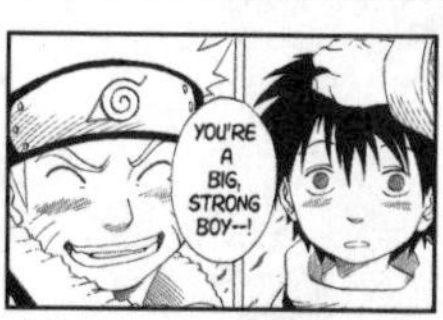
YOU'RE A BIG, STRONG BOY--!

⬆ Naruto encouraged others, improving socially as well.

Report Four

Zabuza reappears, battle with Haku

As expected, Zabuza and the rogue ninja boy Haku appeared before us again. Sasuke and Naruto took on Haku, while I took on Zabuza, but the battle was stopped when Zabuza's employer, Gato, betrayed him. During the battle Sasuke's Sharingan ability appears to have awakened.

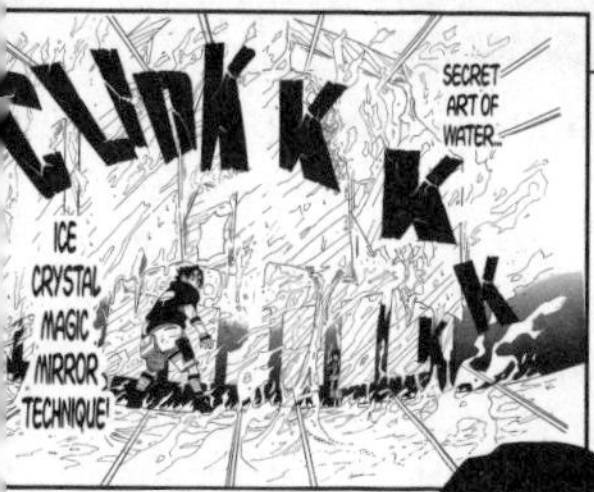
SECRET ART OF WATER...
ICE CRYSTAL MAGIC MIRROR TECHNIQUE!

⬆ Haku used his Kekkei Genkai to make mirrors of ice.

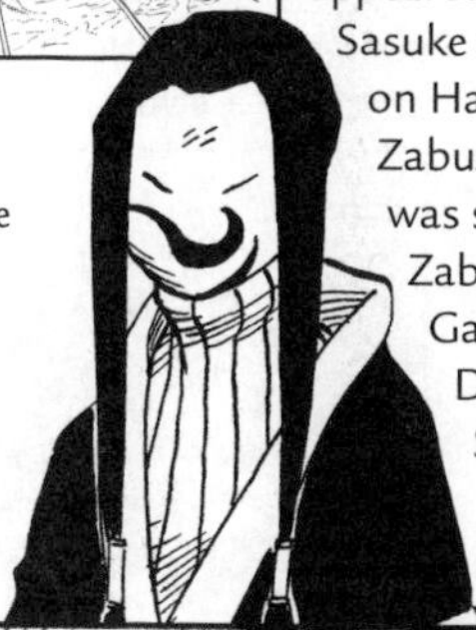

⬇ Anger weakened Naruto's seal.

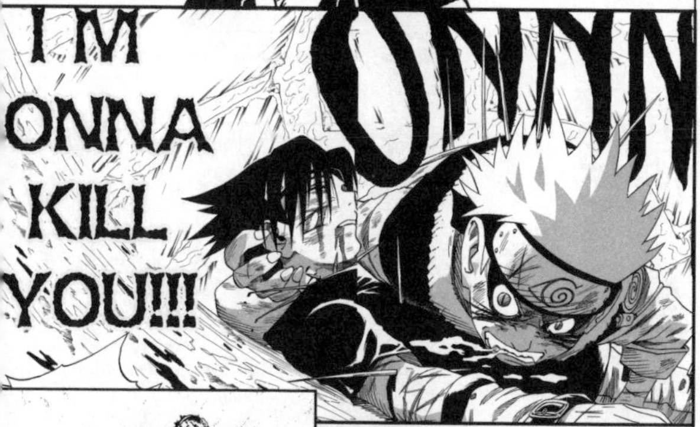
I'M GONNA KILL YOU!!!

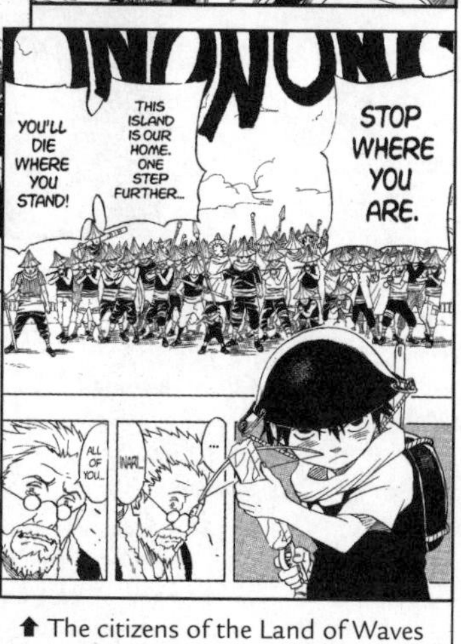
STOP WHERE YOU ARE.
THIS ISLAND IS OUR HOME. ONE STEP FURTHER...
YOU'LL DIE WHERE YOU STAND!
...
INARI...
ALL OF YOU...

⬆ The citizens of the Land of Waves rallied and saved their country.

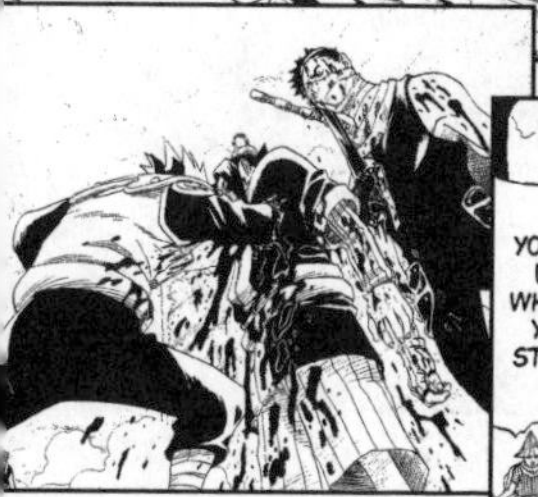

⬆ Haku died saving Zabuza from my Lightning Blade.

Key points to remember:

Strong emotions might open Naruto's seal. We may need to take precautions.

△Month □ Day Report on Team 7 in the Chûnin Selection Exams

Report Two

First exam

Torture expert Morino Ibiki conducted a written test, testing information-gathering capabilities and strength of will. None of Team 7's members buckled under Ibiki's sadistic threats, and all were able to pass.

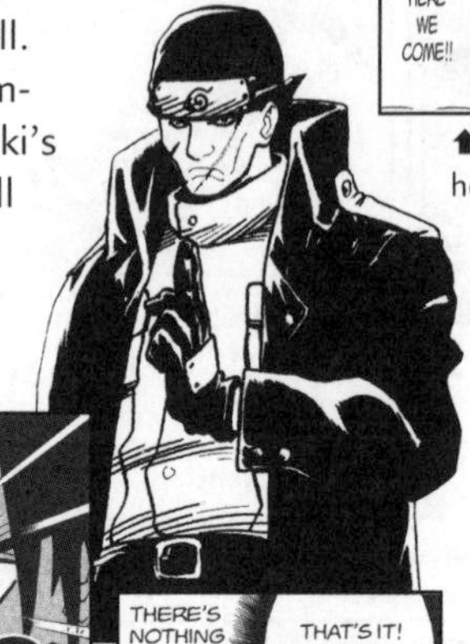

⬇ Sasuke used his Sharingan to gather answers.

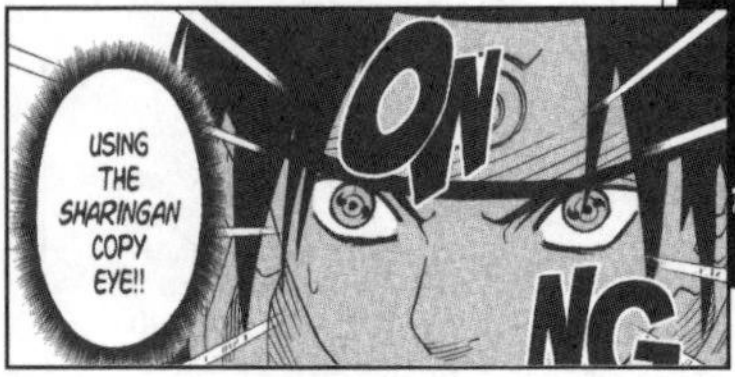
USING THE SHARINGAN COPY EYE!!

➡ Sakura answered all the problems on her own.

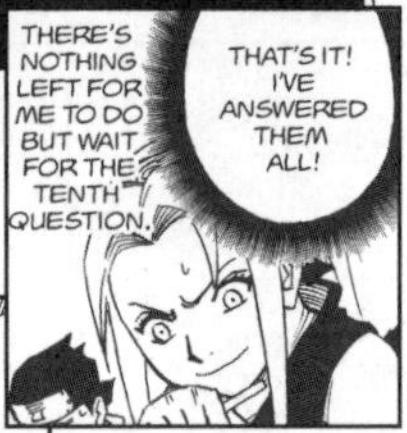
THAT'S IT! I'VE ANSWERED THEM ALL!
THERE'S NOTHING LEFT FOR ME TO DO BUT WAIT FOR THE TENTH QUESTION.

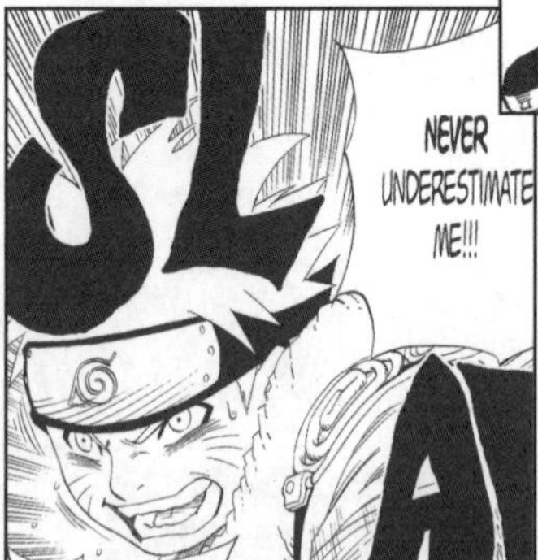
NEVER UNDERESTIMATE ME!!!
I DON'T QUIT, AND I WON'T RUN!!

⬆ Not understanding the point of the test at all, Naruto passed on sheer nerve.

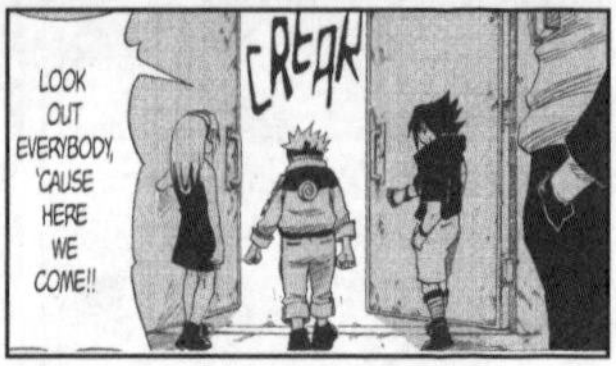
CREAK
LOOK OUT EVERYBODY, 'CAUSE HERE WE COME!!

⬆ All in agreement, they headed off together.

Report One

Pre-exam

Regardless of actual success, I decided the experience gained by taking the test would be beneficial. I did not inform them that they were required to take the test together, but all three made up their minds and asked to take the test.

⬇ No matter what the situation, Naruto remains optimistic.

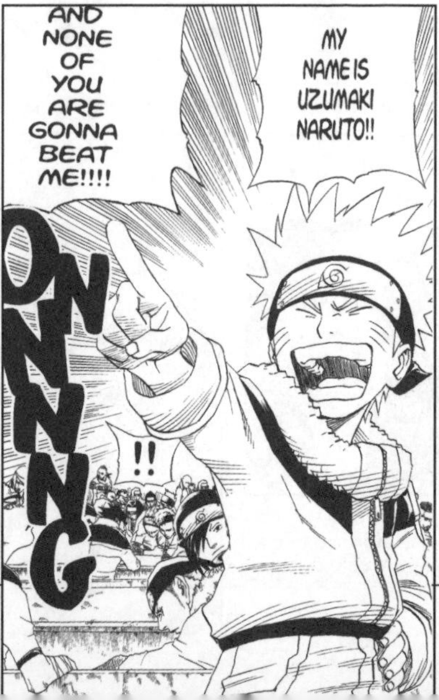
MY NAME IS UZUMAKI NARUTO!!
AND NONE OF YOU ARE GONNA BEAT ME!!!!
!!

Report Three

Second Exam

The second exam involved fighting over scrolls in the Forest of Death, and all three of them showed marked improvement in their fighting abilities. Sasuke ended up with a curse mark, but their teamwork blossomed and they passed the test.

Battle with Hidden Rain shinobi

⬆ They faced off against a group from the Hidden Rain Village.

NOW WHO'S THE TRAPPED RAT?
NICE WORK, NARUTO!
?!

⬆ Using Naruto's Shadow Doppelgangers and some clever team play, they turned the tables.

Battle with three Sound ninja

AS OF NOW, YOU'RE OFF DUTY. JUST WAKE SASUKE FOR US.
THE THREE OF US WANT TO TAKE HIM ON.

⬆ Shinobi from the Hidden Sound Village were after Sasuke's life rather than the scroll.

ICE

⬆ Sakura cut her own hair off, throwing herself into battle.

SIZZ
SAKURA

⬆ Having received a curse seal from Orochimaru, Sasuke momentarily showed terrifying strength.

THUNK

➡ She attacked without fear of kunai, sacrificing herself.

Special Report

Orochimaru's Appearance

One of the Three Great Shinobi, now a rogue ninja, Orochimaru was seen in the Hidden Leaf Village during the exam. It seems his main target was Sasuke, but why is still a mystery. Investigation proceeds with extreme caution.

⬇ Placed a curse mark on Sasuke's neck.

CLENCH

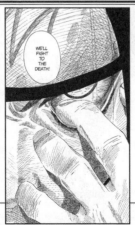

WE'LL FIGHT TO THE DEATH!

➡ Appears to have transformed himself into a Grass ninja.

Report Four

Third Exam Preliminary Round

Far more survivors emerged than expected, so there was a quick preliminary round. Sasuke and Naruto won their one-on-one battles. Sakura had a fierce battle with the best genin kunoichi, Ino, but it ended in a tie and both were eliminated.

Sasuke vs. Yoroi

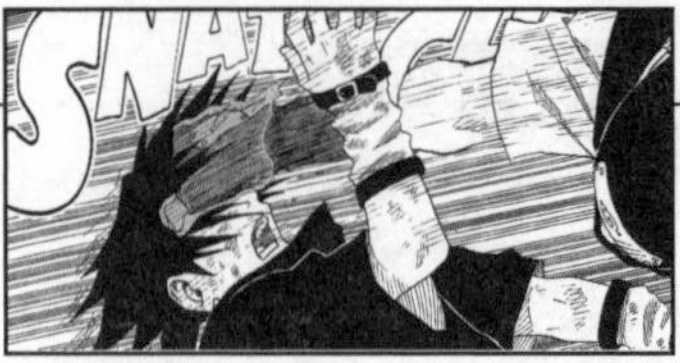

⬆ Sasuke had trouble with Yoroi's chakra draining abilities.

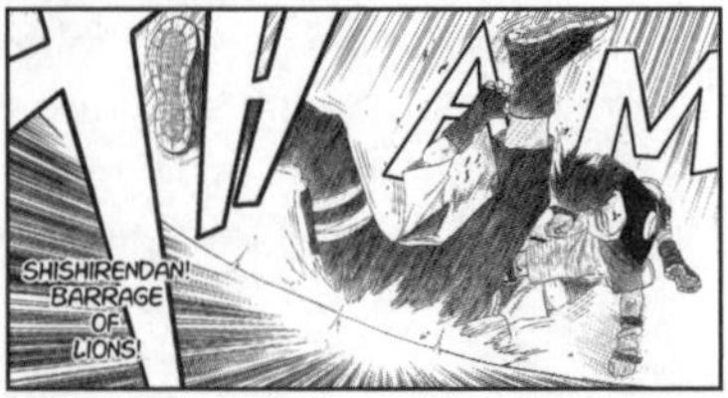
THAM
SHISHIRENDAN! BARRAGE OF LIONS!

⬆ Launched high-speed Barrage of Lions from a Shadow of the Dancing Leaf, finishing him.

Naruto vs. Kiba

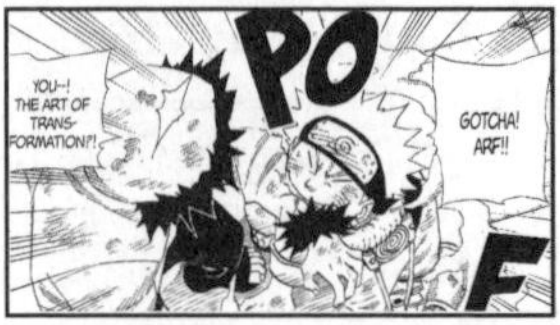
GOTCHA! ARF!!
YOU--! THE ART OF TRANS-FORMATION!?

⬆ Naruto made clever use of the Henge no Jutsu: the Art of Transformation.

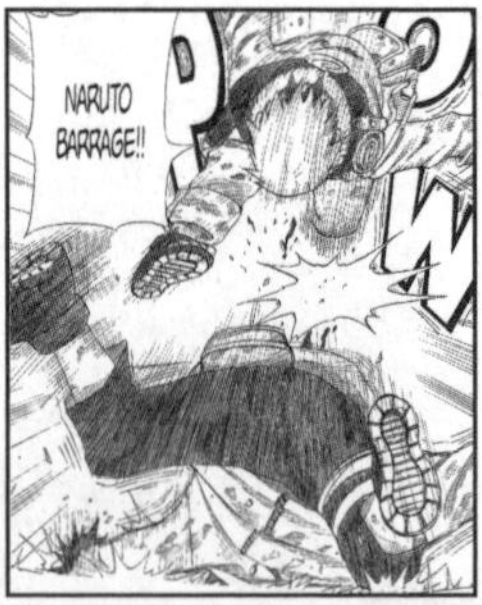
NARUTO BARRAGE!!

⬅ Took Kiba out with a brilliant combination of ninjutsu and taijutsu.

Sakura vs. Ino

⬇ Sakura's mental strength defeated Ino's Mind Transfer Technique.

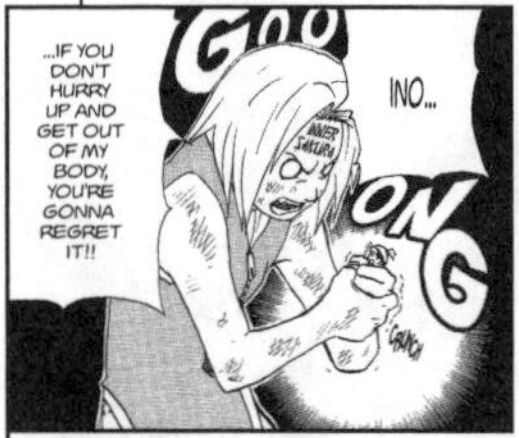
INO...
...IF YOU DON'T HURRY UP AND GET OUT OF MY BODY, YOU'RE GONNA REGRET IT!!

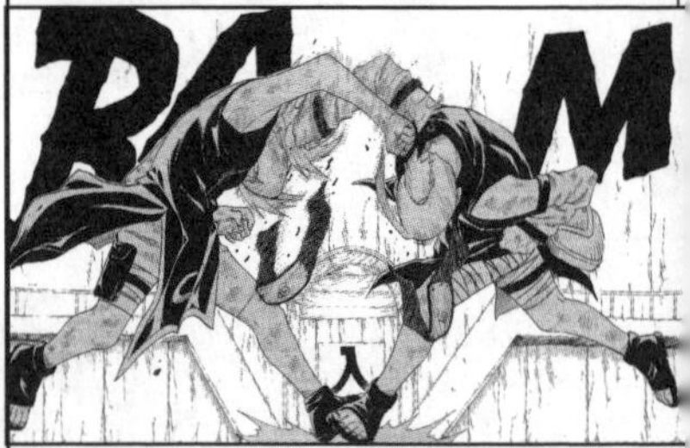
BAM

⬆ Drained of chakra, they knocked each other out.

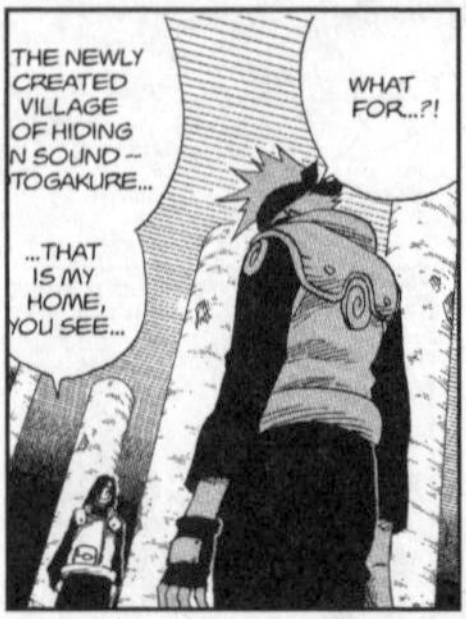
WHAT FOR...?!
THE NEWLY CREATED VILLAGE OF HIDING N SOUND -- TOGAKURE...
...THAT IS MY HOME, YOU SEE...

⬆ Orochimaru enters the village in person. He clearly has further plans.

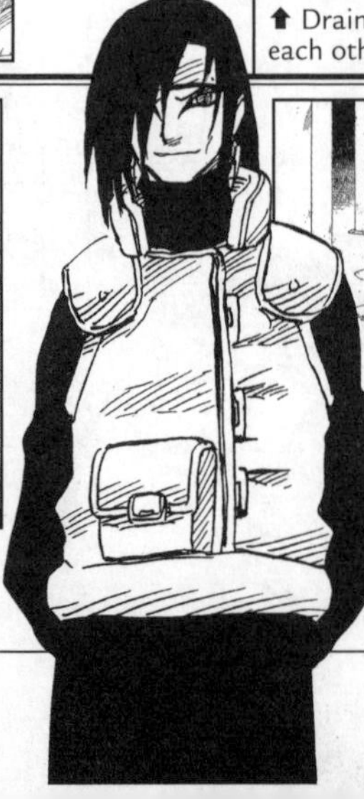

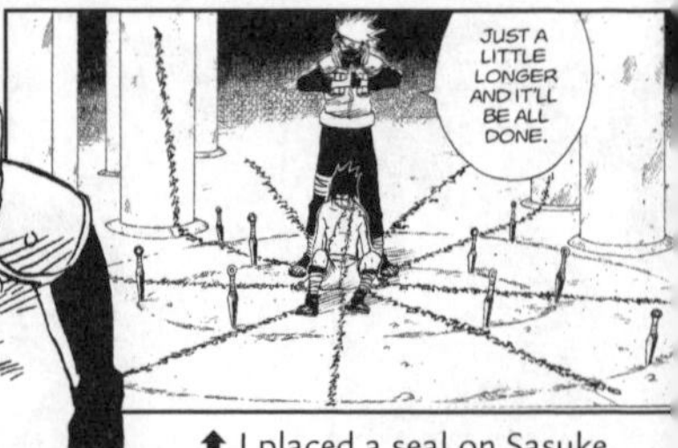
JUST A LITTLE LONGER AND IT'LL BE ALL DONE.

⬆ I placed a seal on Sasuke, restraining the curse mark.

Report Five

Chûnin Selection Exams continue – Naruto and Sasuke train

The results of the preliminary round meant the third test would proceed following a tournament structure, as shown below. For the month until the final round, Naruto was entrusted to Ebisu, while I focused my efforts on Sasuke.

Main Tournament Chart

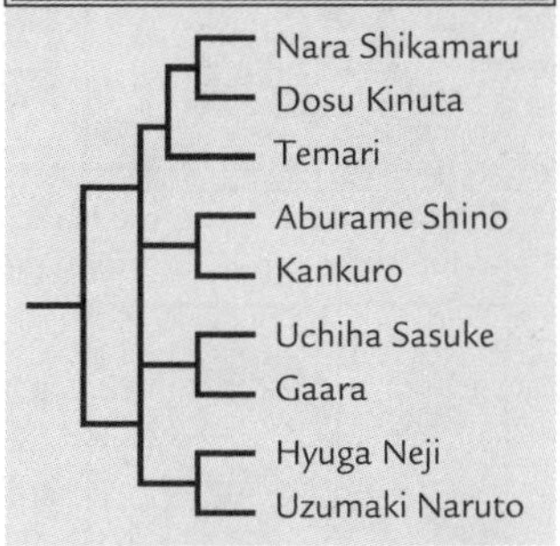
Nara Shikamaru
Dosu Kinuta
Temari
Aburame Shino
Kankuro
Uchiha Sasuke
Gaara
Hyuga Neji
Uzumaki Naruto

⬇ It was Jiraiya who actually instructed Naruto.

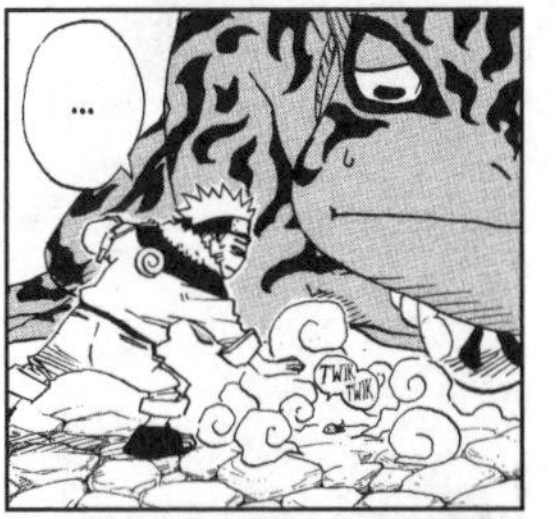
...
TWIK TWIK

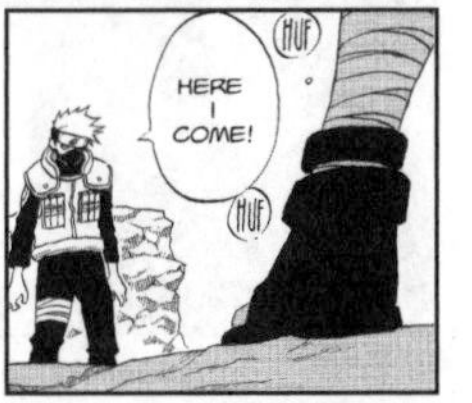
HUF
HERE I COME!
HUF

⬆ As a result of training, Sasuke acquired Chidori.

Report Six

Main Event: Naruto vs. Hyuga Neji

The 8 Trigrams 64 Palms jutsu, using the Byakugan, sealed off Naruto's chakra, but he managed to pull out the demon fox's chakra and use his Shadow Doppelgangers to take down Neji, said to be the strongest genin.

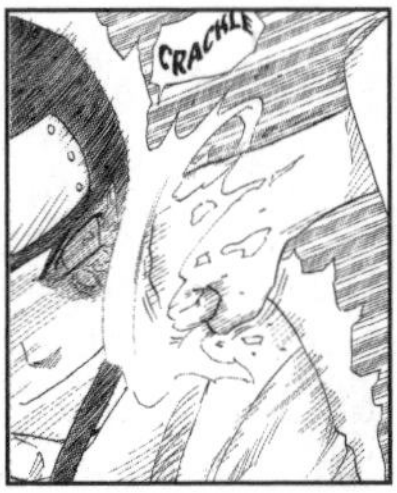
CRACKLE

⬆ Neji's rotation techniques seem like a flawless defense, but...

⬇ Naruto seems to be able to control the Fox Spirit's chakra now.

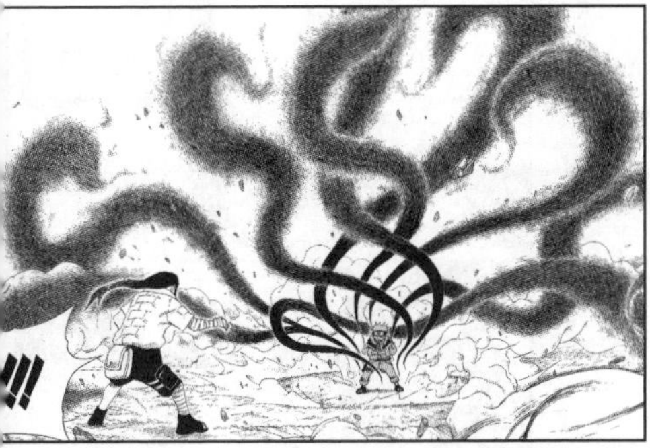

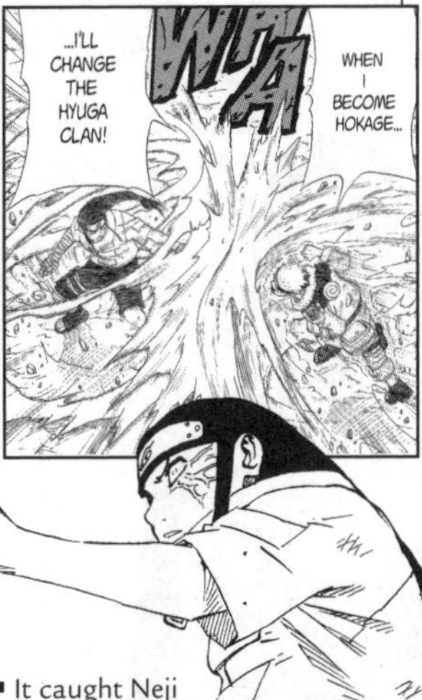
WHEN I BECOME HOKAGE...
WHA
...I'LL CHANGE THE HYUGA CLAN!

➡ When Naruto's quick attacks hit Neji's rotations, it created shock waves.

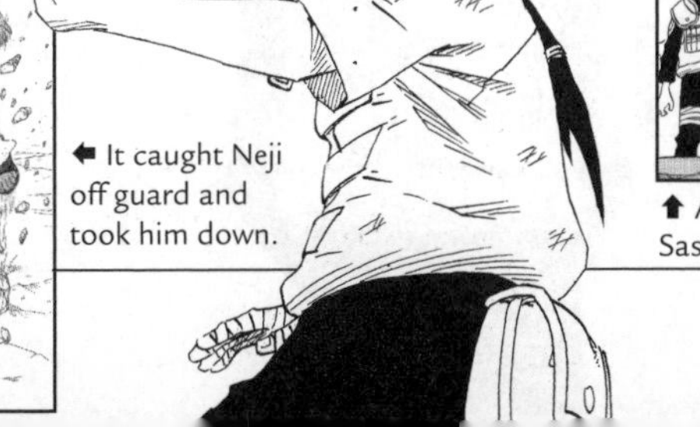

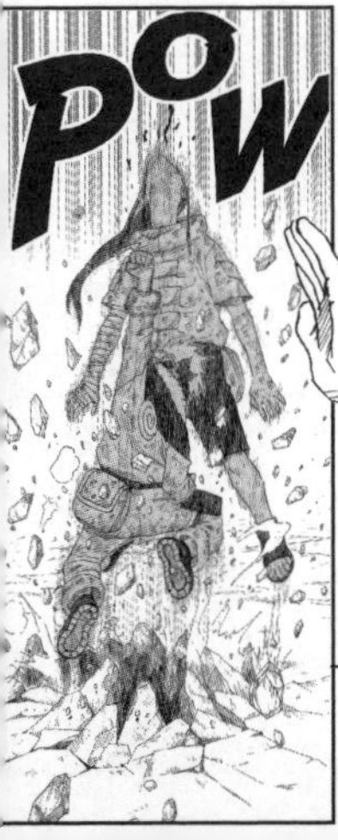
POW

⬅ It caught Neji off guard and took him down.

Special Report

Chûnin Selection Exams Suspended

While Sasuke and Gaara were fighting, the Sound and Sand ninja abruptly revolted. As we feared – Orochimaru's attack on Konoha had begun. Naturally, the Chûnin Exams were abandoned.

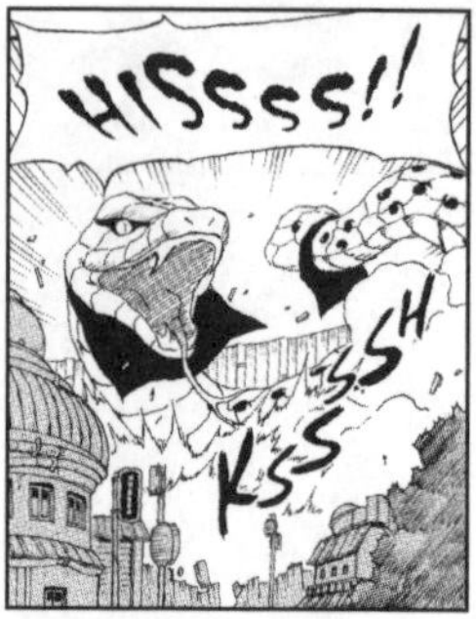
HISSSS!!
SSSH
KSS

⬆ A giant snake appeared and attacked Konoha from outside!

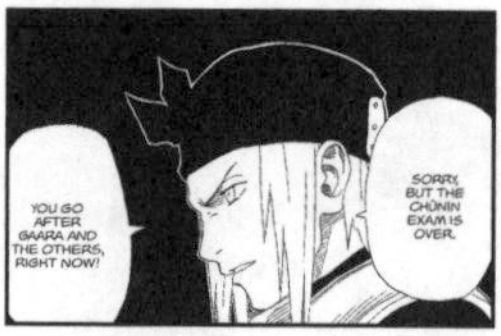
SORRY, BUT THE CHÛNIN EXAM IS OVER.
YOU GO AFTER GAARA AND THE OTHERS, RIGHT NOW!

⬆ The test referee ordered Sasuke to pursue Gaara.

Key points to remember:

We must first ensure the safety of the Hokage and the village. We need to grasp the big picture and improve communication.

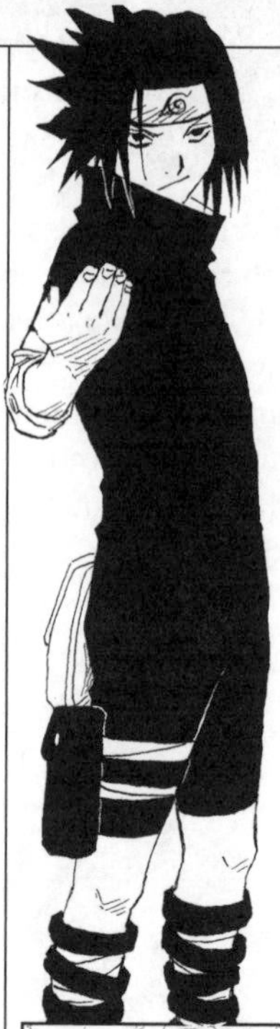

Report Seven

Main Event: Sasuke vs. Gaara

Thanks to training, Sasuke's speed was significantly faster, and he was able to outpace Gaara's Sand Shield. The battle went according to plan – Gaara hid himself inside a shell of sand, but the Chidori managed to pierce it.

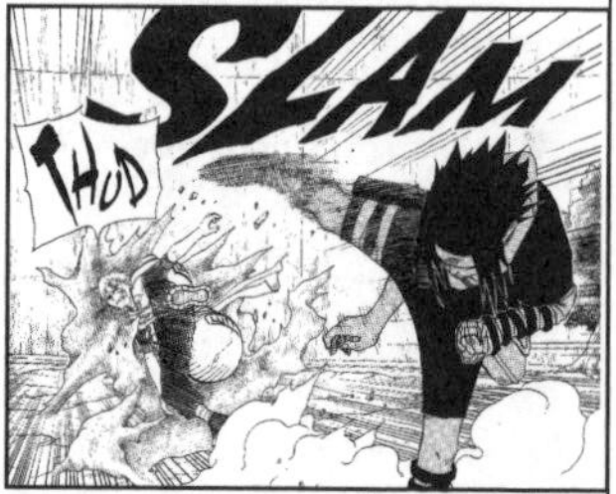
SLAM
THUD

⬆ The Sand Shield was unable to keep up with Sasuke's speed.

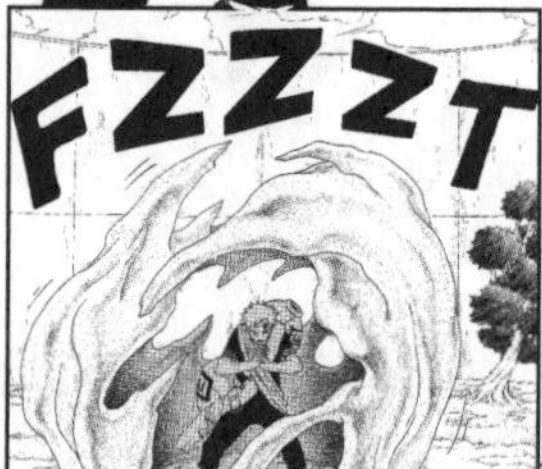
FZZZT

⬆ Gaara made a strong shell of sand, and began forming seals inside it, but...

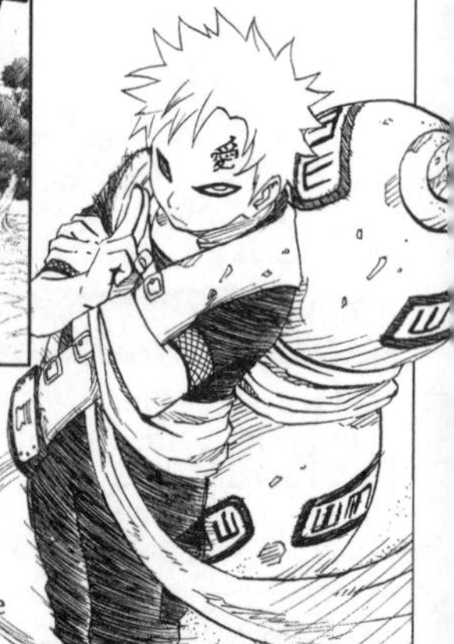

⬇ The Chidori pierced the shell and injured Gaara.

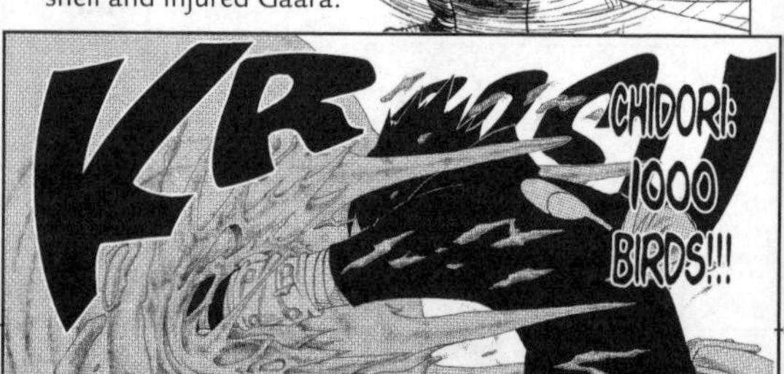
KRSSH
CHIDORI: 1000 BIRDS!!!

□ Month
● Day

Report on pursuit of Sasuke and Gaara and resulting battles

Report One

Pursuit and battle

Sasuke was hot on Gaara's heels, but I determined that a clash between these two would likely result in both their deaths, so I sent Naruto, Sakura, and Shikamaru after Sasuke. The Sound ninja interfered along the way, but Shikamaru took control of the situation and kept them busy while Naruto and Sakura continued after Sasuke.

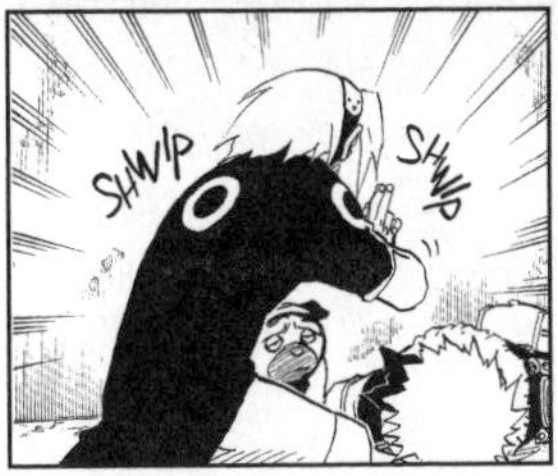
SHWIP
SHWIP

⬆ Sakura used Genjutsu Reflection to free herself and Naruto from the spell.

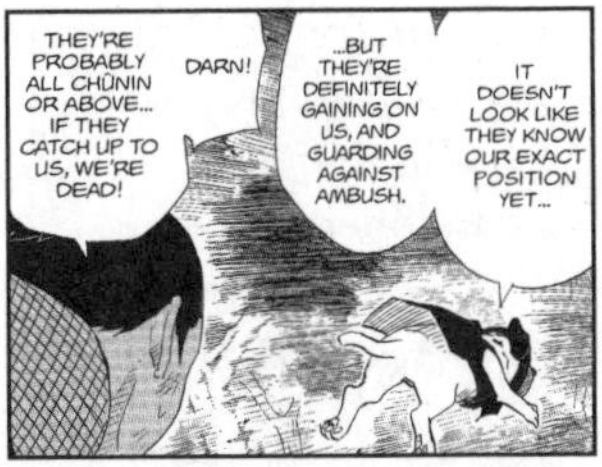
IT DOESN'T LOOK LIKE THEY KNOW OUR EXACT POSITION YET...
...BUT THEY'RE DEFINITELY GAINING ON US, AND GUARDING AGAINST AMBUSH.
DARN!
THEY'RE PROBABLY ALL CHŪNIN OR ABOVE... IF THEY CATCH UP TO US, WE'RE DEAD!

➡ Pakkun followed Sasuke's scent, guiding the other three.

⬇ Shikamaru stopped the Sound ninja with his Shadow Possession technique.

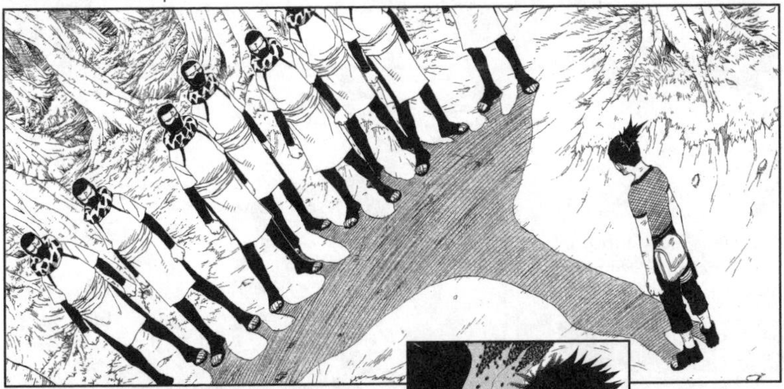

Special Report

Gaara

During his battle with Sasuke, Gaara occasionally showed incredible amounts of chakra. We believe he may yet have powers unknown to us.

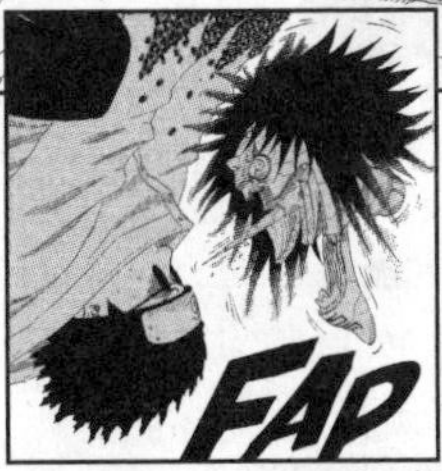
FAP

⬅ Shino fought Kankuro, assisting Sasuke.

Client:
Hatake Kakashi
Faced with an emergency situation, I, Kakashi, personally assigned this mission.

Duties:
Pursuit (possibly battle)
Priority was securing target of pursuit, but battle was a strong possibility.

Mission Rank: **A**

⬇ His body occasionally shows mysterious reactions.

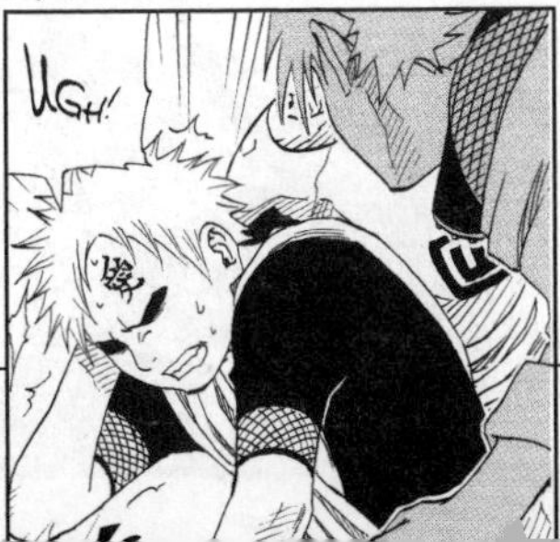
UGH!

Report Three

Hokage battles Orochimaru

Inside the barrier the Sound ninja created within Konoha, the Hokage battled to the death with Orochimaru. Once master and pupil...both knew each others' techniques well, both were extremely powerful ninja, and their battle lasted nearly an hour.

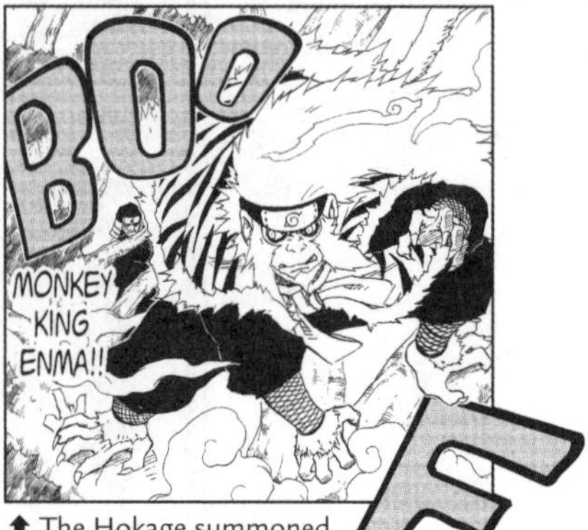
BOOF
MONKEY KING ENMA!!

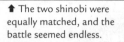

⬆ The Hokage summoned Enma, and they fought together...

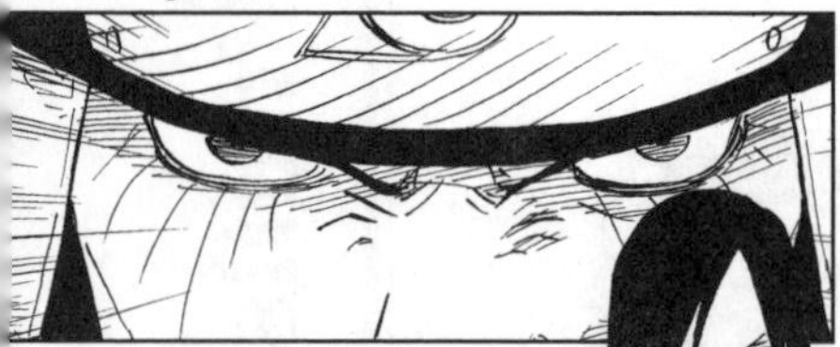

⬆ The two shinobi were equally matched, and the battle seemed endless.

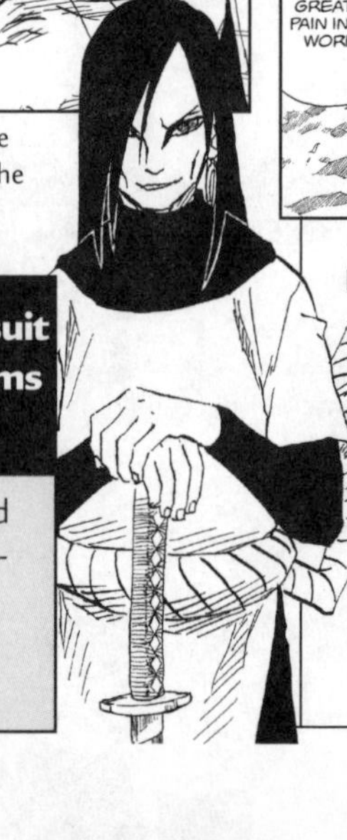

Results of the Pursuit of Gaara – Problems for the Future:

All three genin showed great progress psychologically and should continue to grow impressively.

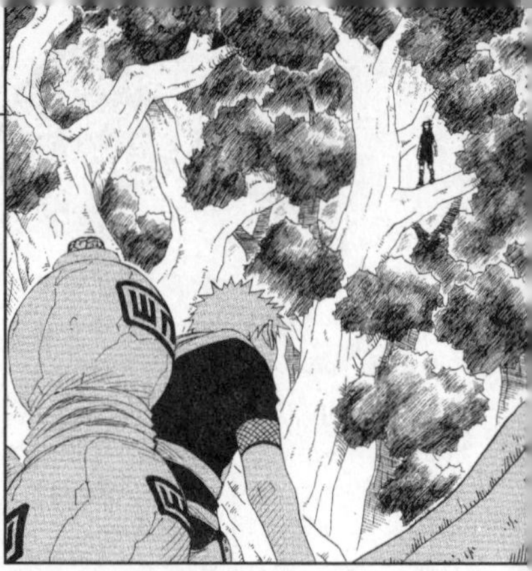

⬆ Gaara chose to wait for Sasuke and face him.

Report Two

Sasuke faces Gaara

Before Naruto and Sakura managed to catch up with Sasuke, he caught up with Gaara...preferably, I had hoped to avoid direct battle between these two, since both seemed likely to get emotional and cause serious damage to themselves and each other. But Naruto arrived in time to save Sasuke and avoid the worst result.

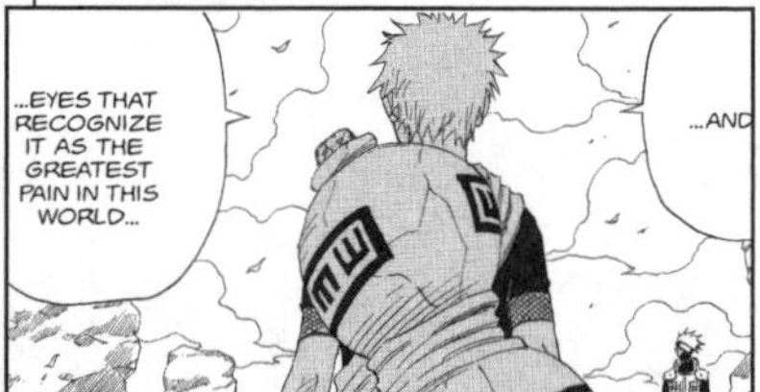
...AND
...EYES THAT RECOGNIZE IT AS THE GREATEST PAIN IN THIS WORLD...

⬆ Claiming a similar understanding, Gaara had previously shown interest in Sasuke.

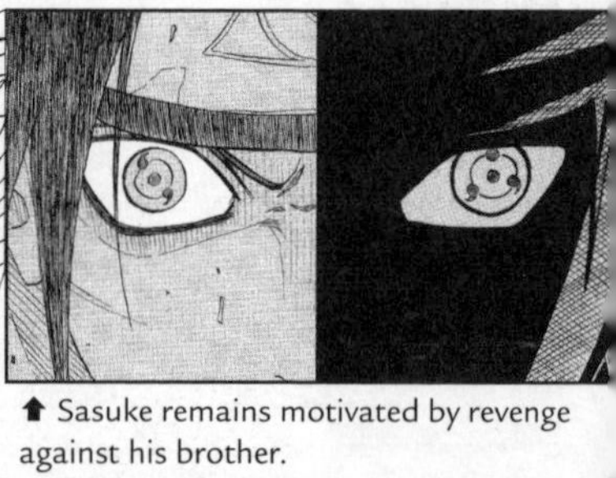

⬆ Sasuke remains motivated by revenge against his brother.

Bonds Stronger Than Blood
History's Best Masters & Pupils

The heart of Konoha, flowing downstream!

Just as trees scatter seeds and those seeds give rise to new life, so is the nindo followed by Konoha ninja passed down from master to pupil. Sixty years of these lessons are charted here.

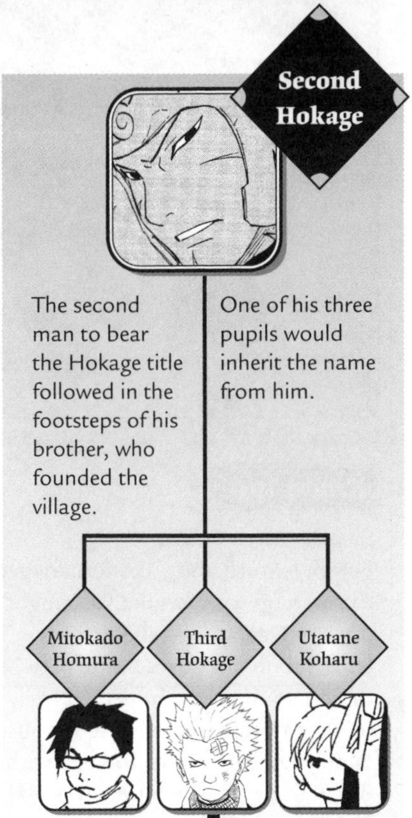

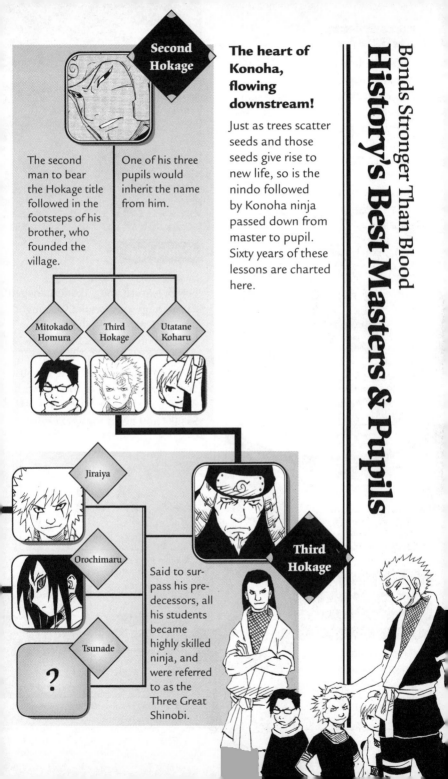

Second Hokage
The second man to bear the Hokage title followed in the footsteps of his brother, who founded the village.
One of his three pupils would inherit the name from him.
Mitokado Homura
Third Hokage
Utatane Koharu

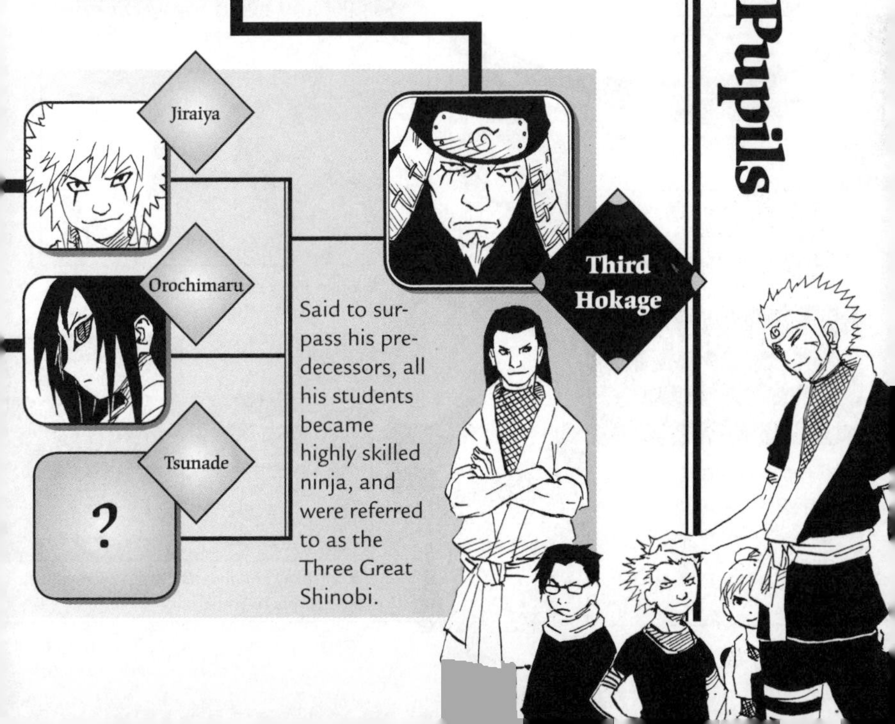

Jiraiya
Orochimaru
Tsunade
?
Third Hokage
Said to surpass his predecessors, all his students became highly skilled ninja, and were referred to as the Three Great Shinobi.

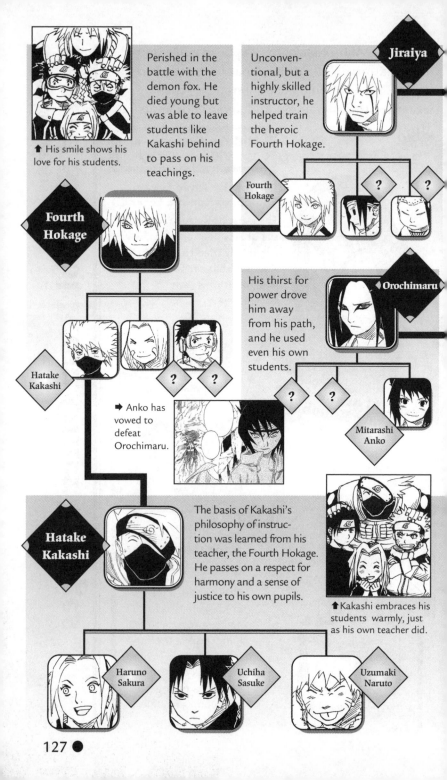

⬆ His smile shows his love for his students.

Perished in the battle with the demon fox. He died young but was able to leave students like Kakashi behind to pass on his teachings.

Jiraiya

Unconventional, but a highly skilled instructor, he helped train the heroic Fourth Hokage.

Fourth Hokage

?

?

Fourth Hokage

Hatake Kakashi

?

?

Orochimaru

His thirst for power drove him away from his path, and he used even his own students.

?

?

Mitarashi Anko

➡ Anko has vowed to defeat Orochimaru.

Hatake Kakashi

The basis of Kakashi's philosophy of instruction was learned from his teacher, the Fourth Hokage. He passes on a respect for harmony and a sense of justice to his own pupils.

⬆Kakashi embraces his students warmly, just as his own teacher did.

Haruno Sakura

Uchiha Sasuke

Uzumaki Naruto

Most Dangerous Feared Shinobi From Other Villages

Konoha's Anbu Black Ops has been collecting information on all enemies that have attacked the village. If you should encounter any of them, exercise utmost caution, and know your limits!

No. 1 Orochimaru

Hidden Sound Village ♪

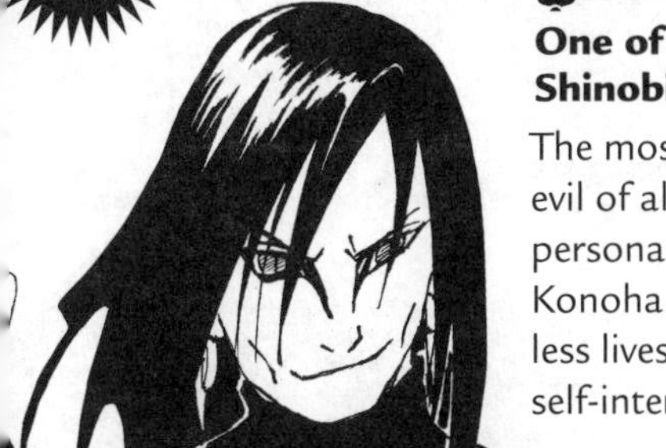

Master of death! Aims to conquer Konoha!

One of the Three Great Shinobi of Konoha Legend!!

The most powerful and most evil of all village enemies, who personally tried to overthrow Konoha...has sacrificed countless lives for his own self-interest.

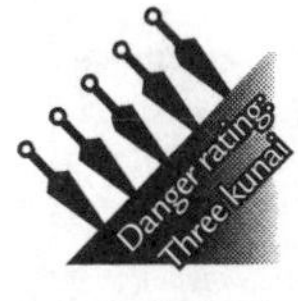
Danger rating: Three kunai

⬇ His diabolical smile shows his inner self.

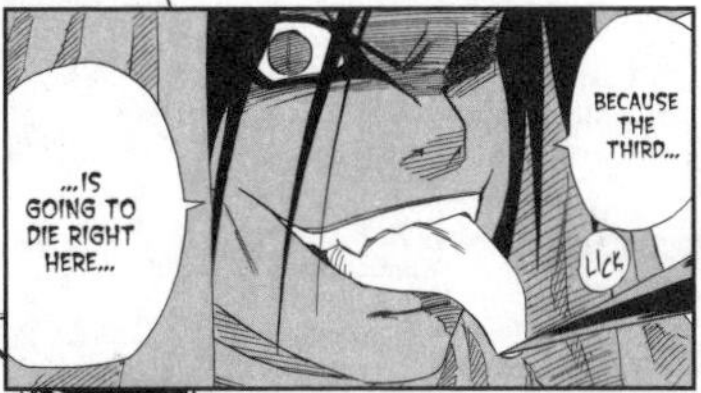
BECAUSE THE THIRD...
LICK
...IS GOING TO DIE RIGHT HERE...

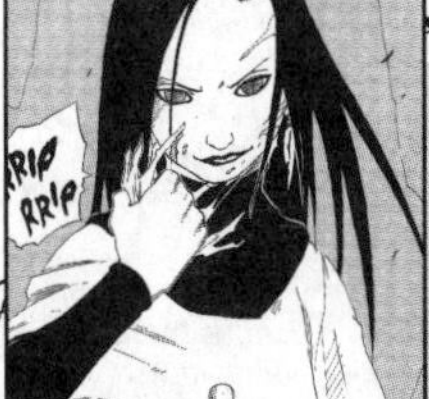
RRIP RRIP

⬅ Showing his true nature, he attacked his former master, The Third Hokage!

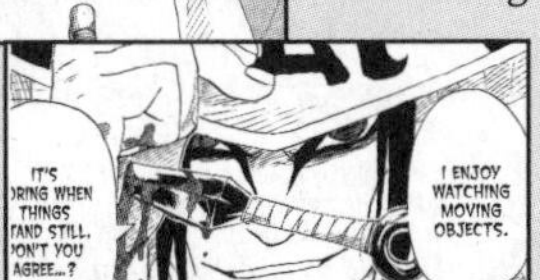
I ENJOY WATCHING MOVING OBJECTS.

⬆ He talks big, but what was his true purpose?!

Attacking Konoha with no mercy!

Orochimaru's unpredictability is the greatest reason to fear him. Despite the carefully laid plans behind his attack on Konoha, there was no logical reason for any of it.

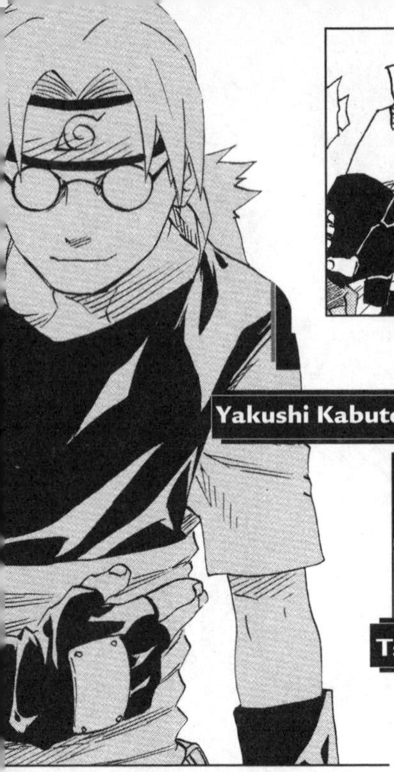

Yakushi Kabuto

No. 2 Shinobi Team 1

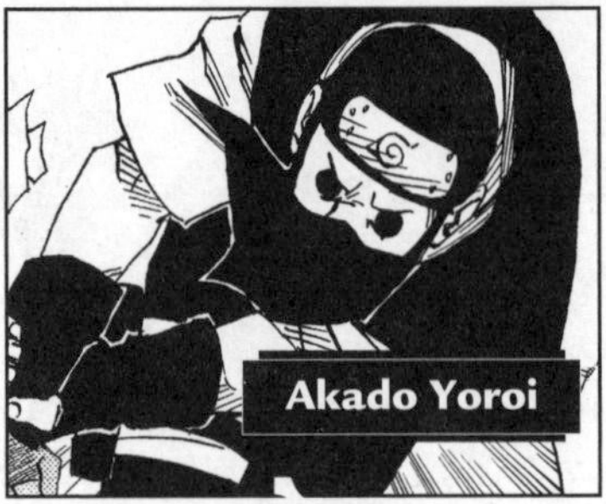

Akado Yoroi

Danger rating: Three kunai

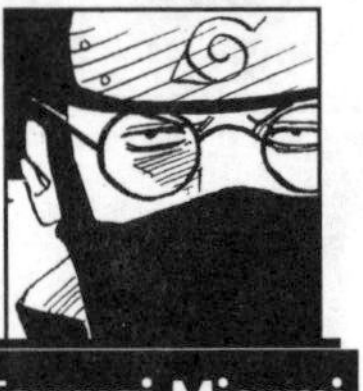

Tsurugi Misumi

The spy group led by Kabuto

Disguised as Konoha ninja, they entered the village and sent information back to Orochimaru. Kabuto in particular appears to be Orochimaru's right-hand man.

No. 3 Shinobi Team 2

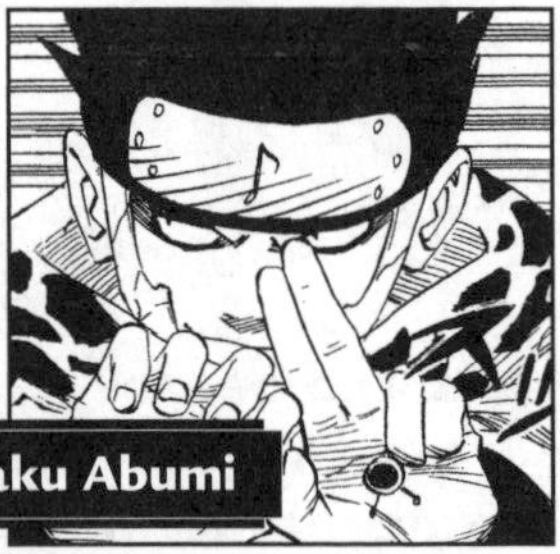

Zaku Abumi

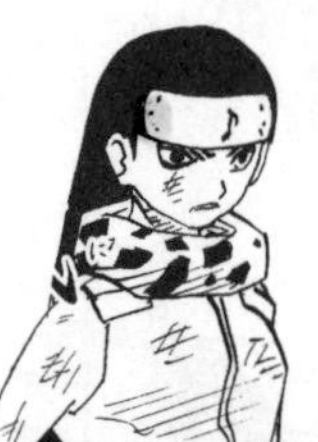

Kin Tsuchi

Fighting ability not to be ignored

These are Orochimaru's assassins. Their selection from the ranks of the Sound ninja is a sign of their ability.

Danger Rating: Two Kunai

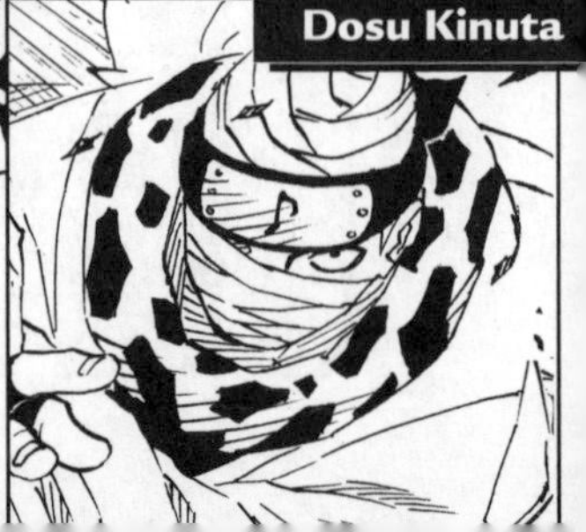

Dosu Kinuta

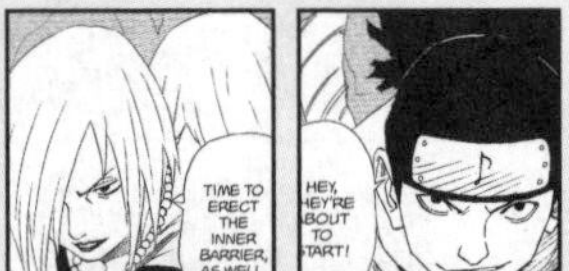
HEY,
TIME TO ERECT THE INNER BARRIER, AS WELL.

Column 1 Oh yeah...

You're evil too...

The Sound Ninja Four

Ordered by Orochimaru to assist in his attack on Konoha, they disguised themselves as the Kazekage's bodyguards. Then they created a barrier so strong even the Third Hokage could not easily break it.

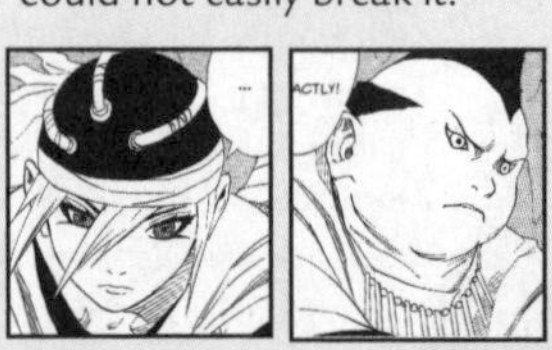
...

No. 4 Momochi Zabuza

!!!
BLINK
I AM NOT THAT EASY TO FOOL!

⬆His silent killing technique was extremely high-level.

Once led a coup d'état

Rogue ninja from the Hidden Mist Village. Once known as the Kijin, he led a coup d'état but died in battle with Kakashi.

Heartless silent killer

Danger Rating: Four kunai

Hidden Mist Village

This boy shared Zabuza's destiny

Life and death are in the hands of fate...

No. 5 Haku

A brilliant ninja who was always at Zabuza's side. Had a Kekkei Genkai, and a harrowing past because of it. He also died in battle with Kakashi.

Danger Rating: Two Kunai

➡His clear smile was a sign of his pure heart.

HEH...
WELL, I'M ONLY A CHILD.

Column 2

Oh yeah...

You're evil too...

Gatô

➡ Officially president of a trading company, but secretly an underworld boss.

IT WAS JUST ON YEAR AGO... THAT H SET HI SIGHTS ON THE LAND OF THE WAVES.
HE CAME UNDER THE GUISE OF A USINESS VENTURE. HEN THE VIOLENCE BEGAN, AND IN NO TIME AT ALL, HE'D TAKE OVER OUR ENTIRE MARINE RANSPORTATION ND SHIPPING INDUSTRY, ND WE WERE ALL NDER HIS THUMB!

Monopolized trade with the Land of Waves and willing to kill for profit. Also engaged in smuggling. Ultimately killed by his own man, Zabuza, drawing the curtains on his life of darkness.

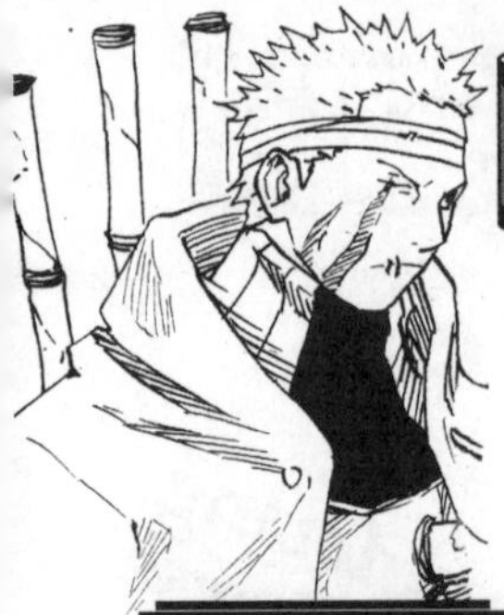

Shigure

Hidden Rain Village

They fear nothing and challenge anyone!

These three came to Konoha for the Chûnin Selection Exams. They went up against Gaara from the Hidden Sand village, but that ended in failure...

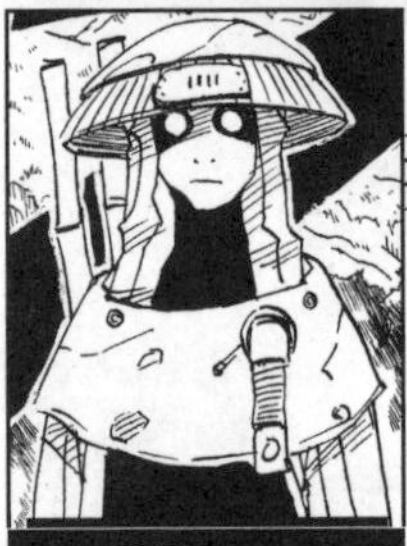

Midare

Danger Rating: Three kunai

No. 7 Ninja Group 1

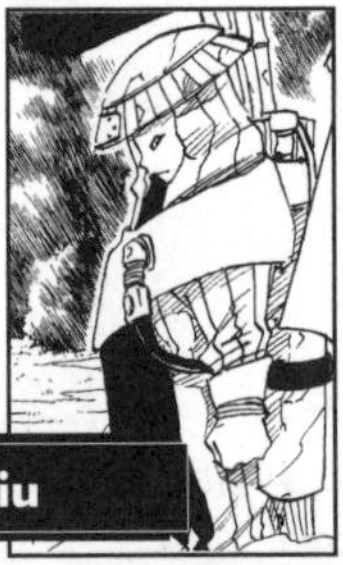

Baiu

No. 8 Ninja Group 2

Creepy Guerrilla Unit

Masters of genjutsu, they confuse their enemies and attack from their blind spot. Their moves support each other, covering all counterattacks.

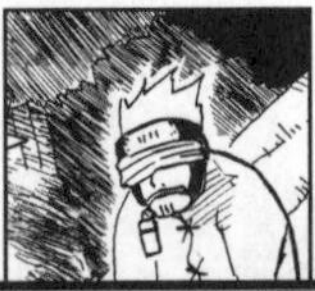

Kagari

Danger Rating: Two kunai

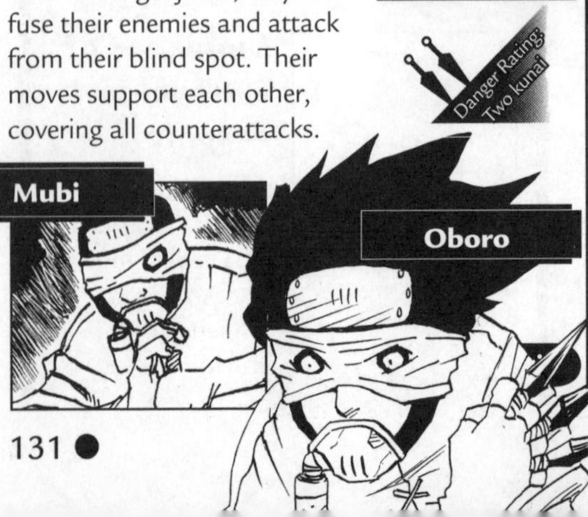

Mubi

Oboro

Danger Rating: Three kunai

No. 6 Oni Brothers

Experienced Killer Combo

Two brother ninja from Hidden Mist, they use unusual chain-like weapons in combination to kill their enemies. The older is cold-hearted while the younger is extremely violent.

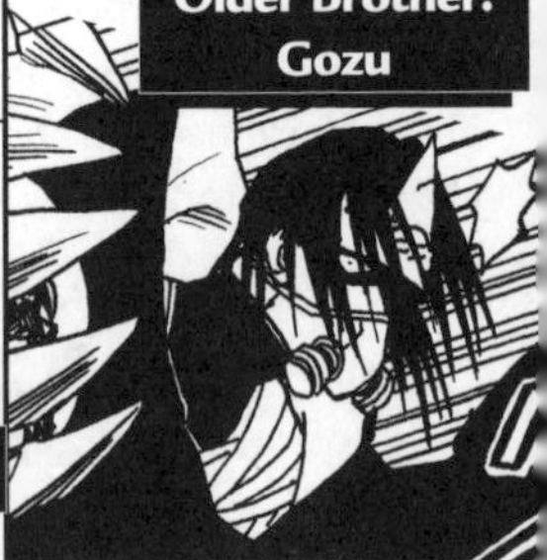

Older Brother: Gozu

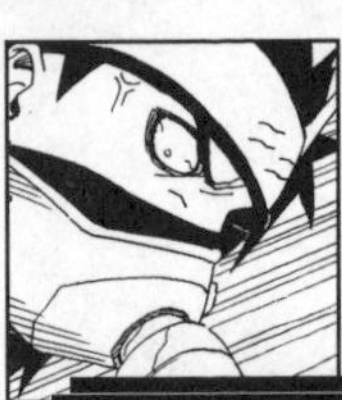

Younger Brother: Meizu

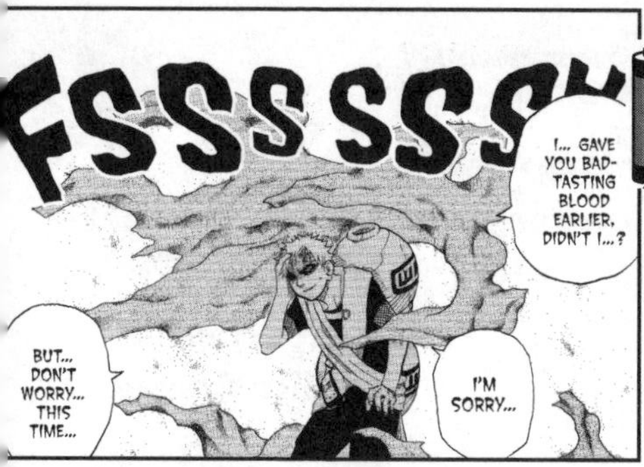
FSSSSSSH
I... GAVE YOU BAD-TASTING BLOOD EARLIER, DIDN'T I...?
I'M SORRY...
BUT... DON'T WORRY... THIS TIME...

Hidden Sand Village

No. 9 **Gaara**

Shouldering great sadness

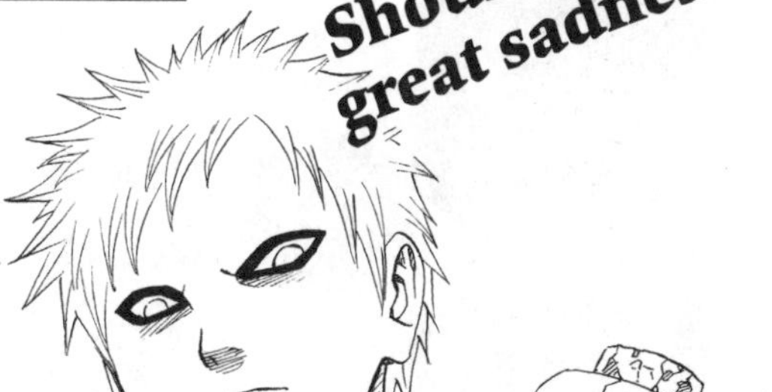

⬆ The sand in his gourd can be both a weapon and a shield.

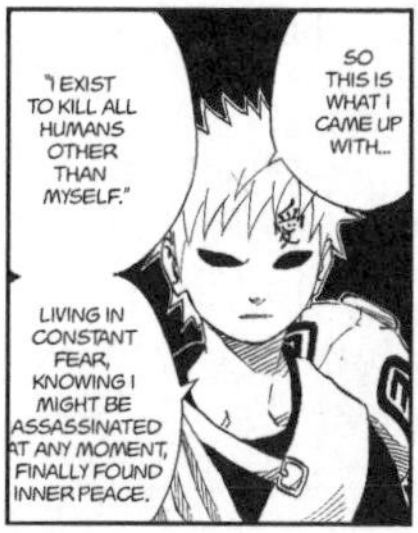
SO THIS IS WHAT I CAME UP WITH...
"I EXIST TO KILL ALL HUMANS OTHER THAN MYSELF."
LIVING IN CONSTANT FEAR, KNOWING I MIGHT BE ASSASSINATED AT ANY MOMENT, FINALLY FOUND INNER PEACE.

⬅ Says scary things without batting an eye.

Loves only himself! Life is battle!

Created as a weapon, Gaara hates the world and lives only to kill. His abilities are beyond those of most chûnin and jônin — he is extremely dangerous.

Danger rating: Four kunai

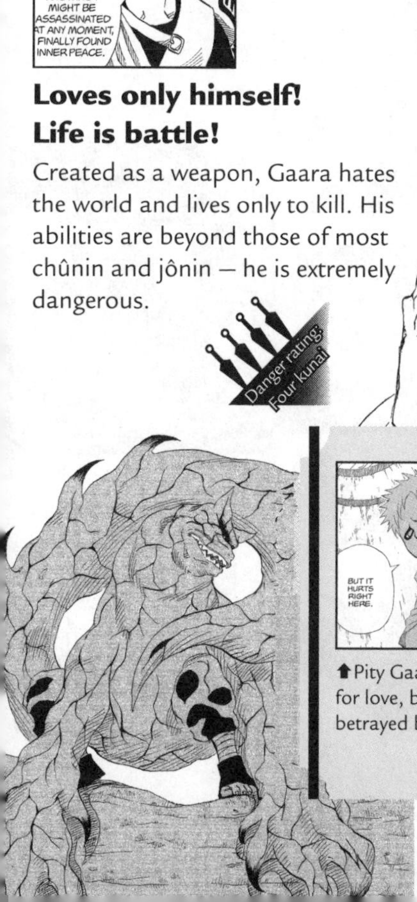

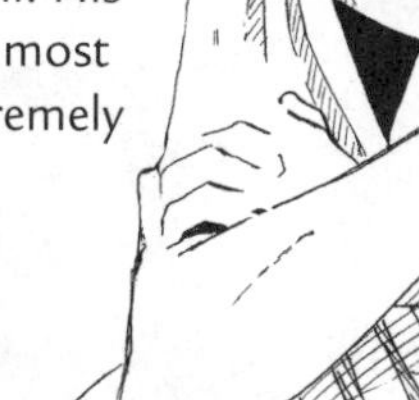
IT DOESN'T BLEED.
BUT IT HURTS RIGHT HERE.
SKRCH

⬆ Pity Gaara! He longs for love, but is always betrayed by it...

Childhood of betrayal and despair

As a child, Gaara's own father tried to assassinate him. That trauma influenced his own cruelty...

No. 10 Kankuro

Danger Rating: Two kunai

Watch out for his Puppet, The Crow!

Gaara's older brother, sent with him from the Hidden Sand Village. He uses his puppet, the Crow, for some very unusual attacks, which have caused problems for many ninja.

Danger Rating: Two kunai

No. 11 Temari

An emotionless girl!

Gaara and Kankuro's older sister. Kicks aside unconscious foes, waves good-bye to dying enemies – extremely heartless personality.

A MAJORITY OF THE SHINOBI RULERS AND LORDS HERE, INCLUDING MYSELF...
...CAME HERE ALMOST SOLELY TO OBSERVE THAT MATCH.

Column 3 **You're evil too...** Oh yeah...

Kazekage

Toying with life, he created Gaara, and then attempted to kill him for his own reasons. But the Kazekage who arrived in Konoha was Orochimaru in disguise, and the real one has yet to show himself.

No. 12 Baki

Leader of the Hidden Sand party

One of the strongest jônin in the Hidden Sand Village, he worked as a pipeline coordinating the movements of his own people and Orochimaru's Hidden Sound Village. Also responsible for keeping an eye on Gaara.

Danger rating: Four kunai

A Special Message From Ebisu!

The Most Elite Teacher in all Konoha!

EXTRA

Anko, sweet red bean paste, has how many calories?!

BAD IDEA!!!

On the ingestion of calories

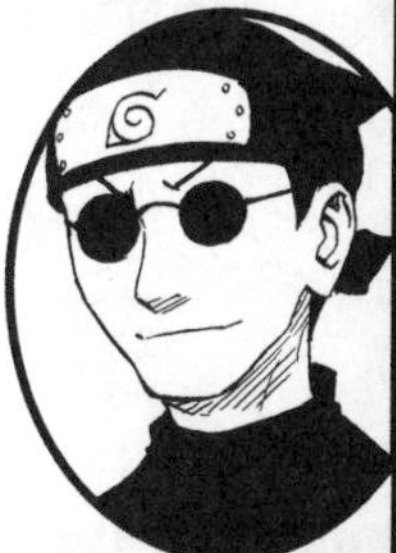

I, Ebisu, will now teach you about the intake of calories. Ninja exercise far more than the average person, and naturally must take in a lot more calories, but they must not take in too many! Let us look at the eating of anko, and learn how not to do this.

THE SCENE IN QUESTION: VOLUME 6, PAGE 69!

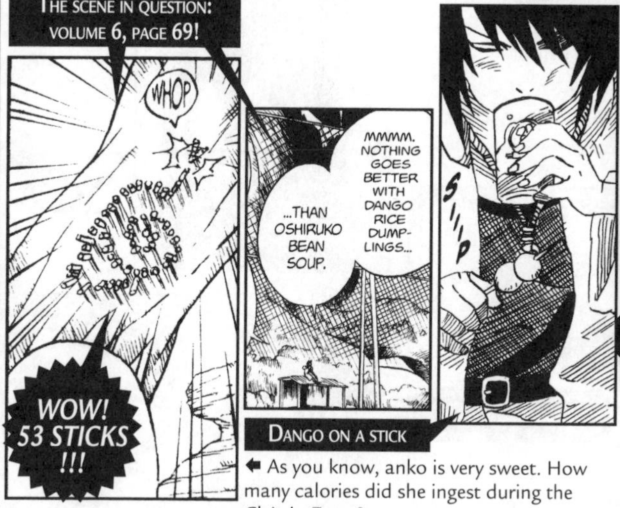

SLIP
MMMM. NOTHING GOES BETTER WITH DANGO RICE DUMPLINGS...
...THAN OSHIRUKO BEAN SOUP.
WHOP
WOW! 53 STICKS !!!

DANGO ON A STICK

⬅ As you know, anko is very sweet. How many calories did she ingest during the Chûnin Exam?

CALORIES IN ONE STICK OF DANGO ➡ ABOUT 120 KCAL
53 STICKS ➡ 6360 KCAL ✚
CALORIES IN ONE CUP OF OSHIRUKO ➡ ABOUT 370 KCAL
= A TOTAL OF 6730 KCAL
(THE CALORIES AN ADULT WOMEN NEEDS IN ABOUT FOUR DAYS.)

18 HOURS OF JOGGING TO BURN ALL THOSE CALORIES OFF!

The figures above show how many calories Anko ingested during one break from the Chûnin Exam! How horrible! Even for a ninja, this is simply too many! All of you must be careful when you eat sweet things!

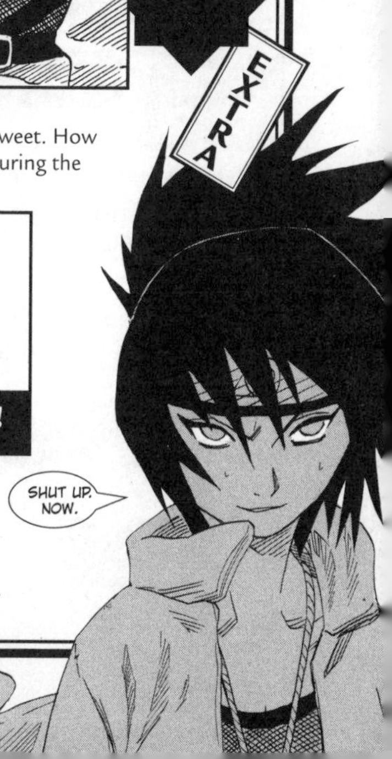

SHUT UP. NOW.

New Ninja Cells!

Think creating a roster for Konoha ninja cells is easy? Balancing skills and experience among team members, and tailoring the unit for each mission takes a lot of thought!

Tornado Trio

⬇ A combo attack any shinobi can be proud of!

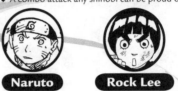

Shikamaru **Naruto** **Rock Lee**

Shikamaru, Naruto, and Rock Lee would make a good team. This is because when facing a strong opponent, Shikamaru can freeze him in his tracks, Rock Lee can use his leaf hurricane to send them in the air, and Naruto jumps in the air and hits him with the Rasengan.

Victor, NY

Shadow Killers

⬇ Wouldn't Orochimaru take over?!

Orochimaru **Zabuza** **Kurenai**

Orochimaru, who possesses extensive knowledge of forbidden jutsu. Momochi Zabuza, a taijutsu specialist and an expert at Silent Killing. Yuhi Kurenai, who would act as powerful support for the rest of the team.

Perry, PA

Super Jutsu Squad

⬇ Does Akamaru get to join too?

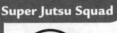

Kankuro **Neji** **Kiba**

Why are they a great team? Because their jutsus are amazing and I believe no one can beat them.

Heather, NY

NARUTO
19 Fan

LOOKS LIKE SOME PRETTY GOOD TEAMS THIS YEAR!

Guy and Lee

Master and Student Life Advice!!

Guy and Rock Lee are ready to help with your troubles...?
An unprecedented whirlwind of advice begins now!!

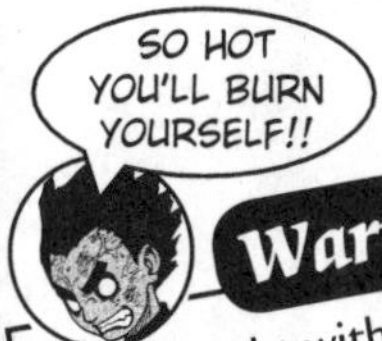
SO HOT YOU'LL BURN YOURSELF!!

Hot-blooded!!

Friendship

We all have problems with friends sometimes.

Warmth

I had a fight with a friend, and the next day at school he apologized... even though it was my fault! I felt so stupid!

<埼玉県> ともともさん

⬆ Ahhhhhhh!! Both of you are such good friends!!!!!

Heat

My brother is two years younger than me and doesn't respect me at all. Please help!

<千葉県> ガンクさん

➡ Your brother is just trying to be friends with you! Really!!

Very spicy

I have a friend who always copies my homework. I want to point out that if he keeps doing this, we'll both be in trouble, but...

<東京都> 仲居学さん

⬆ You should view homework as training for the mind, and do it yourself!

Sweat

Is it possible to be friends with the opposite sex? It seems like love gets in the way of friendship...

<青森県> 青りんごさん

⬆ It's possible. It may become love, but that does not cancel out the friendship!

Spicy

When we play badminton doubles, I always miss and cause problems for the others. Please give me your advice!!

<愛知県> BUNさん

⬅ Deepen your friendship with your partner, and let that friendship synchronize your play!!

Tears

When my friend is working the lunch line, he always gives me extra! Such a good friend, it makes me tear up!

<香川県> 斎藤正志さん

➡ You can tell he wants you to grow up to be big and strong. What a great friend!!

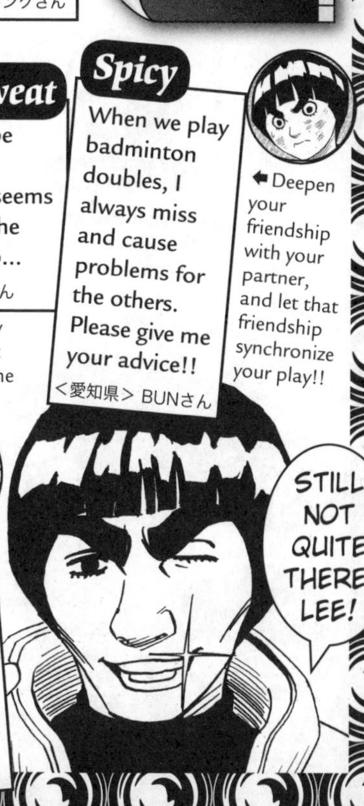
STILL NOT QUITE THERE, LEE!

NARUTO Fan 20

Hot-blooded!!

Love

Always nice Guy can solve all your embarrassing love troubles!! Let your love blossom!!

Depth

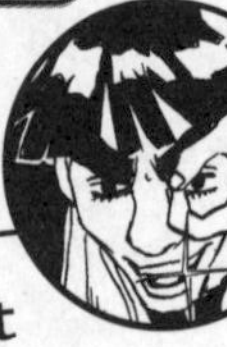

My first heartbreak... I can barely eat. What can I do? Guy, Lee, please help!

<群馬県> なんでやねんさん

⬇ Make sure to eat! Don't diet too much!!

Manly

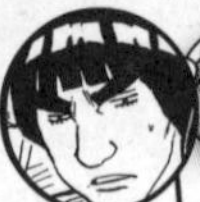

Whenever I'm around the person I most admire, I start acting hostile. How can I change my personality?

<大分県> 愛私羅さん

⬆ The flames of love are smoldering! Tell her how you feel, and let them roar!!

Anger

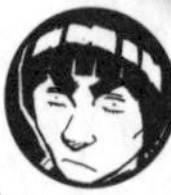

I'm in love with someone... I want to ask him out, but I'm afraid he'll say no. What should I do, Guy?

<千葉県> ろろこさん

➡ Don't be afraid of heartbreak! If one love is lost, you can find another.

Stern

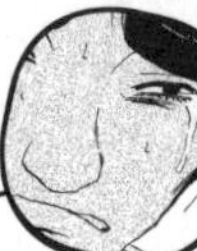

I've had my heart broken so many times, but now I'm in love again. Should I really risk it?

<長崎県> 愛娘。さん

⬇ Yes! Go ahead! You must enjoy your youth!!

Waves

Grown-ups often say that love and romance are different, but how are they different? Do they taste different? Please tell me...

<熊本県> 藤代弥生さん

⬆ Romance is sweet, but love is bittersweet! See?!

Anger

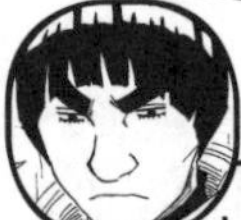

I can't figure out how to love you, Guy-sensei! Please tell me!

<東京都> ひねりっこさん

➡ You already love me enough!!

Heat

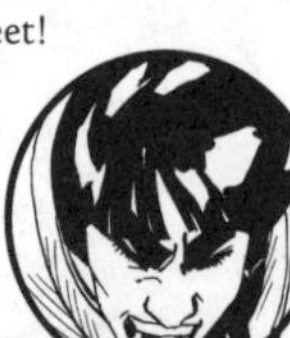

I'm in love with two people — Guy-sensei and Lee! How can I choose between you?!

<愛媛県> りりーさん

⬇ Love us both! Love has no limits!!

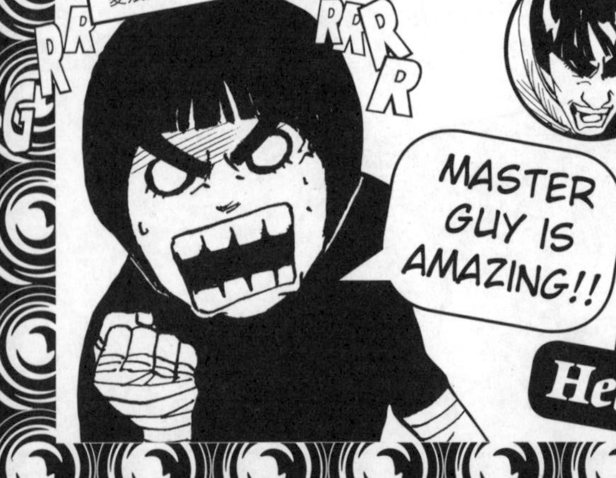
GRR
RRRR
MASTER GUY IS AMAZING!!

Hot-blooded!!

Man tears

Close your eyes, grit your teeth!

Anger

I'm not good at hard work...I'm bad at studying and sports. Help motivate me.

<沖縄県> でいごさん

⬆ If you don't believe in yourself, your efforts are pointless!

Cry

I drink milk every day so I can get taller, but I'm not growing at all!! Why?

<大阪府> 花音ゆずきさん

⬆ Don't worry about your height! Work harder at broadening your heart!!

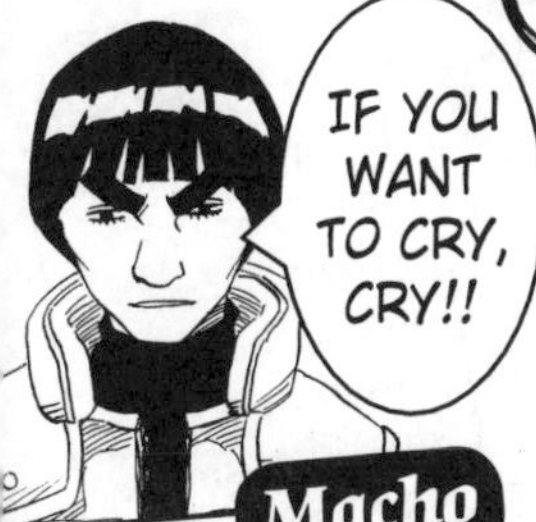
IF YOU WANT TO CRY, CRY!!

Silence

My eyebrows are as thick as Lee's. Should I shave them?

<福岡県> スコンブさん

➡ Why would you do that? Thick eyebrows prove you're a real man!!

Tears

I'm on a diet, but I'm not getting any thinner! Help motivate me!

<北海道> トモエさん

⬆ Don't wish you were thin – believe you *are* thin!!

Macho

How can I become a hot-blooded, powerful man like Guy-sensei and Lee?

<福岡県> 信夫さん

⬆ Count your grains of rice! Eat 100,000 every day! That never fails!

Endurance

I do 60 sit-ups and 70 push-ups every day so I can be a ninja. Will that do the trick?

<福岡県> タマさん

⬇ Absolutely! Let's work out together! Guy will cheer us on!!

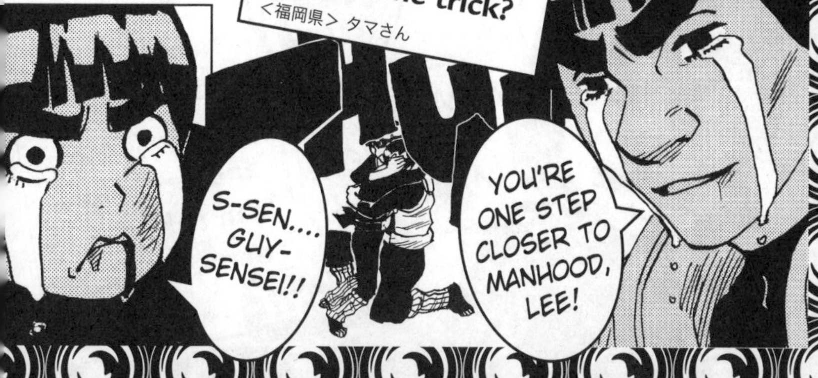
YOU'RE ONE STEP CLOSER TO MANHOOD, LEE!
S-SEN.... GUY-SENSEI!!

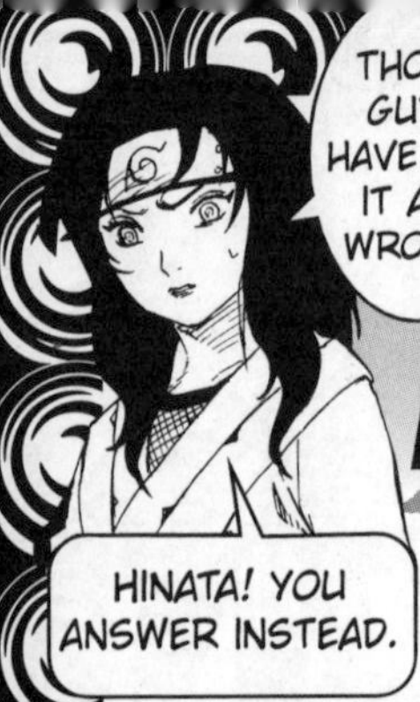
THOSE GUYS HAVE GOT IT ALL WRONG.
HINATA! YOU ANSWER INSTEAD.

Life Advice Emergency Replacement

Hinata's Life Lessons!!

With Guy and Lee washed away by a flood of youthful exuberance, Hinata takes their place! She understands the pain in people's hearts so she might...probably...

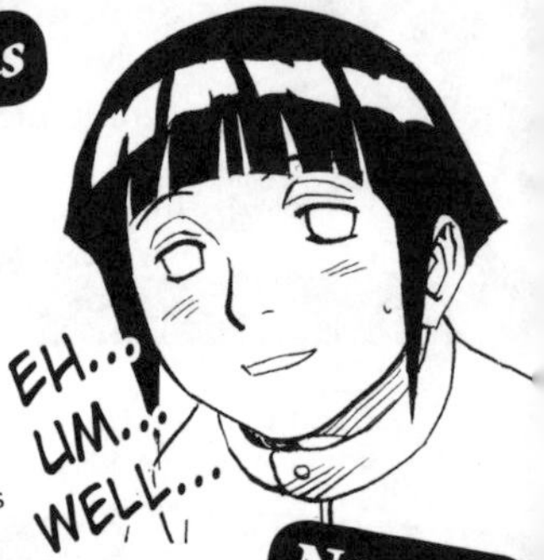
EH... UM... WELL...

Nervous

I'm scared of beetles. How can I learn to like them?

<鹿児島県> 氷麿助さん

⬆ If you pretend they're rhinoceros beetles you...might like them more...

Nervous

I'm training hard to be a ninja. But my mother says I can never be one...

<徳島県> ニンニンさん

⬆ First, you should talk things over with your mother...I think...

Nervous

How can I get eyebrows like Guy-sensei and Lee?

<富山県> ちくさんさん

⬆ Umm... Guy-sensei and Lee are very... special...so...

Nervous

My problem...is zits. They won't go away, and I wonder what people think of me...

<京都府> 佐々山郁さん

⬆ Don't worry. You are still you...

Nervous

My mother always tells me I'm not a child anymore, but when she's angry she says I'm just a child...

<福岡県> ライムさん

➡ Try to understand your mother's feelings...

Embarrassed

The boy I like came to talk to me, but I was too embarrassed to answer...how can I relax?

<埼玉県> 岸谷美紀さん

➡ If it was me... hahh...um... um...I don't know..............

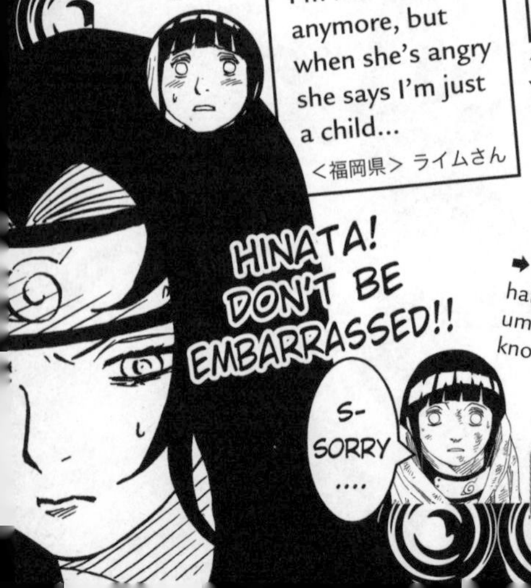
HINATA! DON'T BE EMBARRASSED!!
S-SORRY ....

Original Ninja Gallery

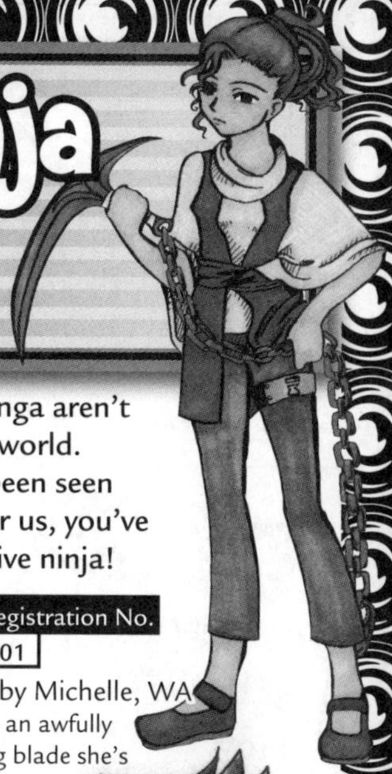

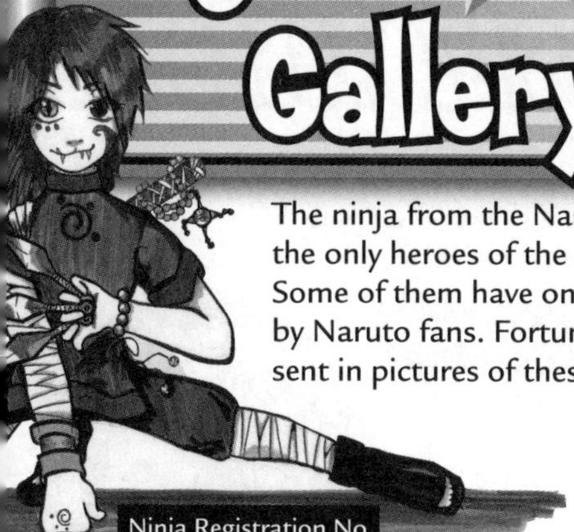

The ninja from the Naruto manga aren't the only heroes of the shinobi world. Some of them have only ever been seen by Naruto fans. Fortunately for us, you've sent in pictures of these secretive ninja!

Ninja Registration No.
FAN-0001

Kaneru, by Michelle, WA
➡ That's an awfully menacing blade she's got there...

Ninja Registration No.
FAN-0002

Risa, by Gabbi, CA
⬆ A new enemy for Naruto?!

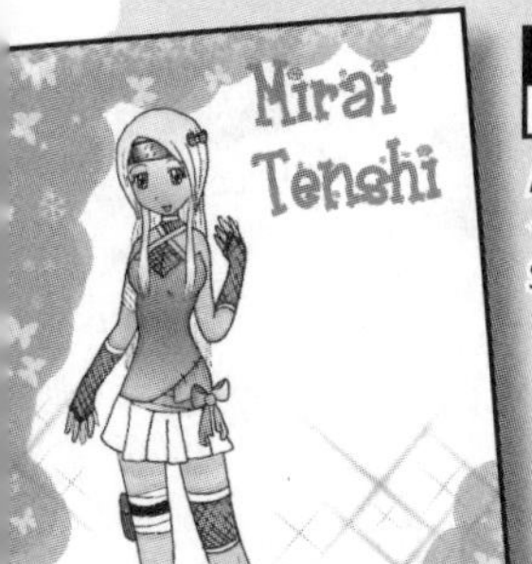
Mirai Tenshi

Ninja Registration No.
FAN-0003

Mirai Tenshi, by Alaina, OR
⬅ Sakura better watch out! She's got another rival here!

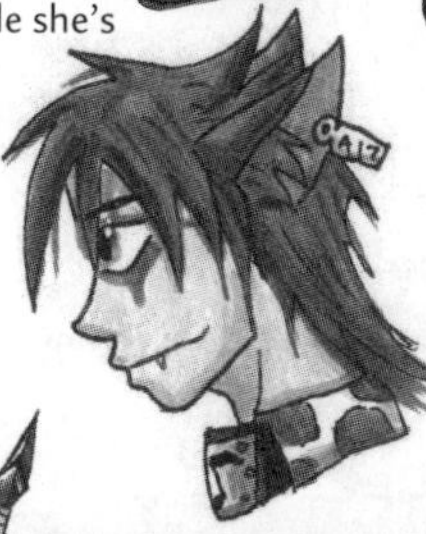

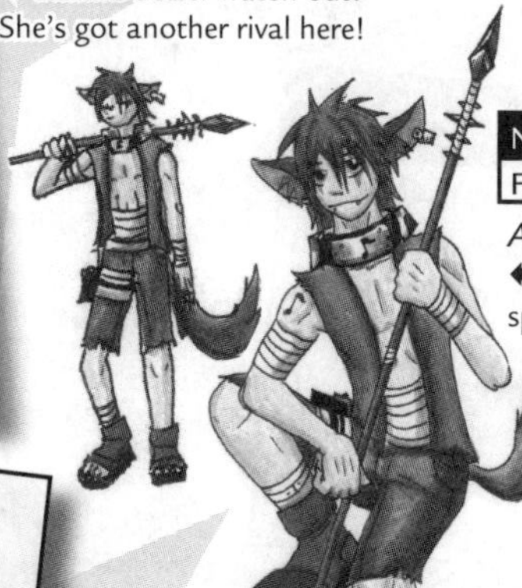

Ninja Registration No.
FAN-0004

Akela, by Sam, OR
⬅ Does he have a wolf spirit inside him?

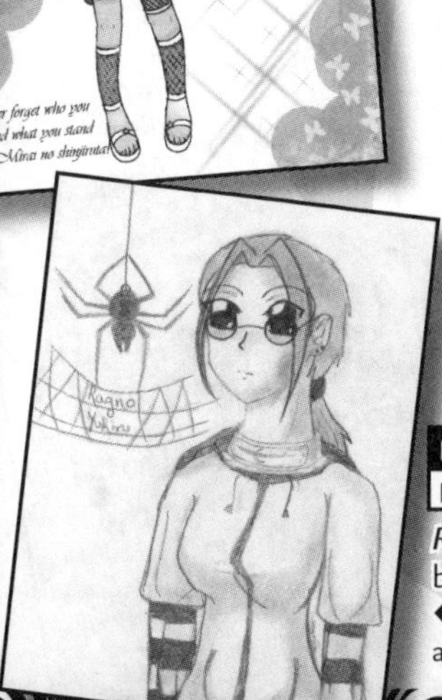
Ragno
Yukiru

Ninja Registration No.
FAN-0005

Ragno Yukiru, by Tonia, VA
⬅ Black widows are very dangerous.

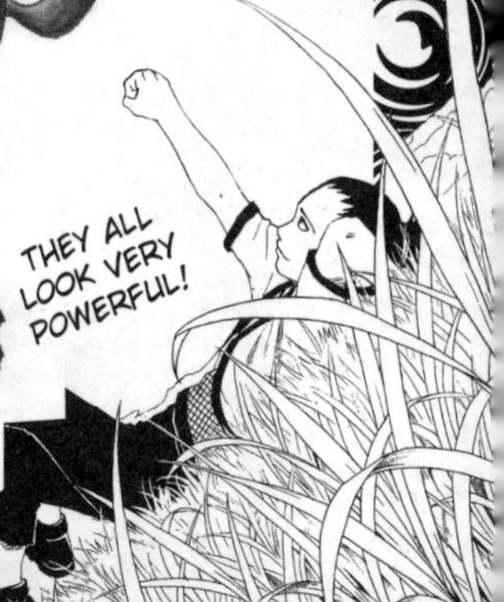
THEY ALL LOOK VERY POWERFUL!

NARUTO Fan 22

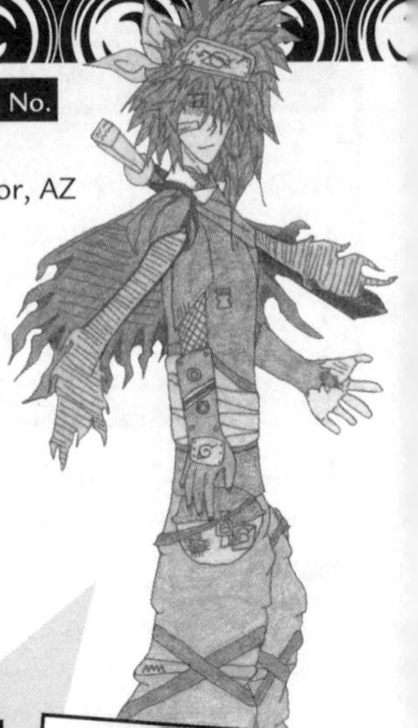

Ninja Registration No.
FAN-0006

Reikuya, by Connor, AZ
➡ The rogue ninja.

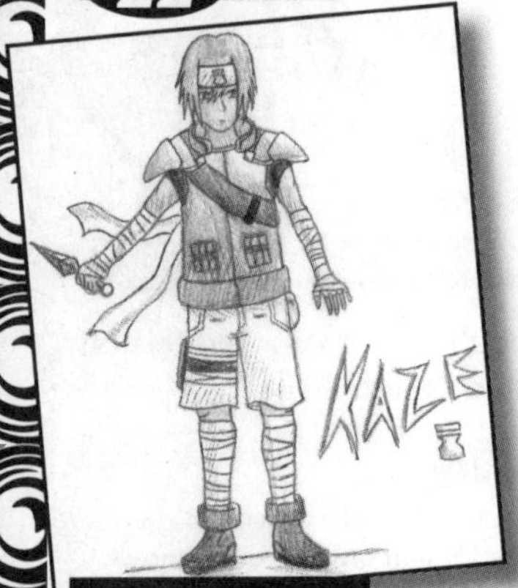
KAZE

Ninja Registration No.
FAN-0007

Kaze, by Gene, NY
⬆ Whose side is he on?

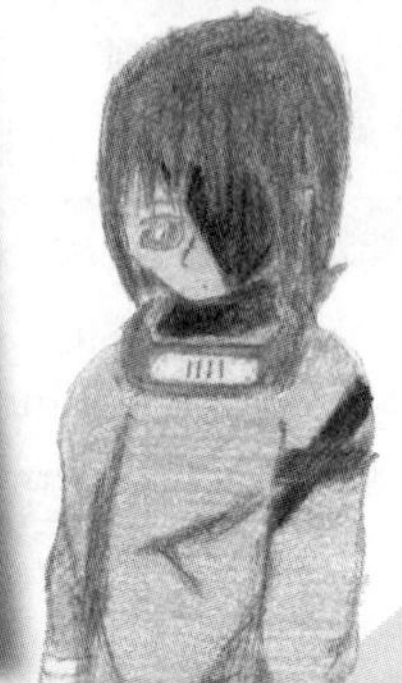

Ninja Registration No.
FAN-0008

Jinmaru, by Dale, NV
⬆ What's he hiding? Sharingan?

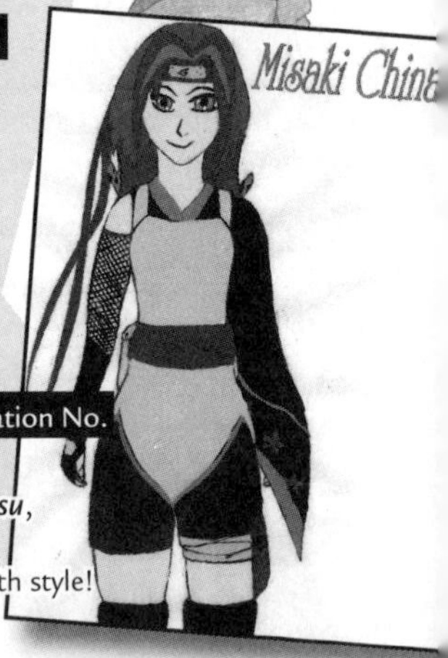

Ninja Registration No.
FAN-0009

Misaki Chinatsu, by Betsy, NC
➡ Kunoichi with style!

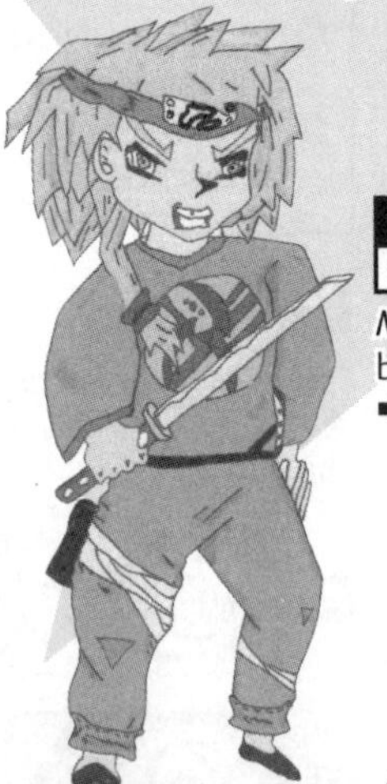

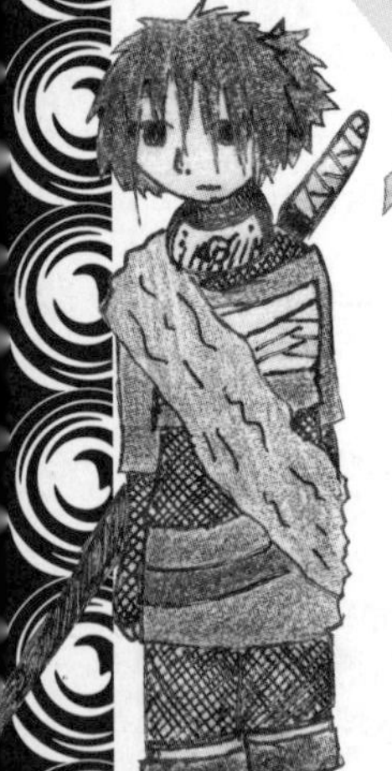

Ninja Registration No.
FAN-0010

Nyoba Ogama, by Jonathan, NC
⬅ He must be a taijutsu expert.

Ninja Registration No.
FAN-0011

Jochen, by Ethan, KS
⬆ Naruto's evil twin?

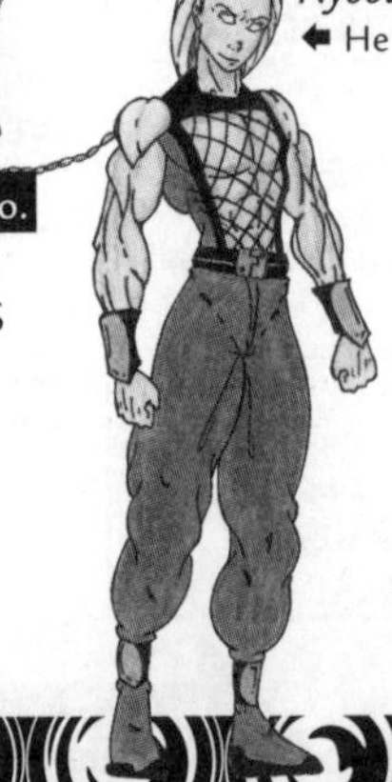

Ninja Registration No.
FAN-0012

Amaya, Night Rain, by Tally, FL
⬆ I think she might be more dangerous than she looks!

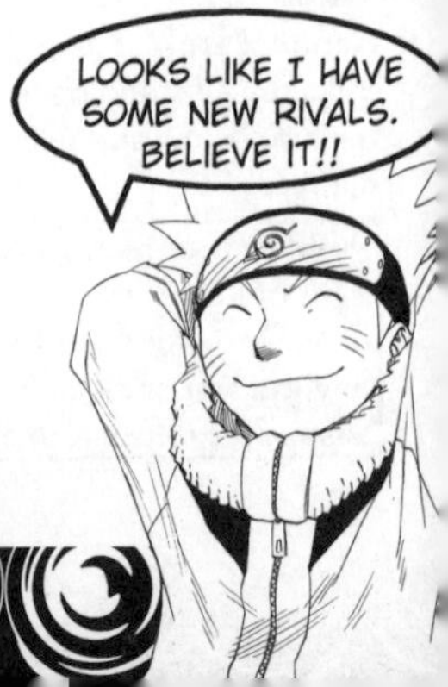
LOOKS LIKE I HAVE SOME NEW RIVALS. BELIEVE IT!!

Unless you can discover the truth, all the gates will not open!

3rd GATE

Are You a Match for Nara Shikamaru's IQ?

SHINOBI IQ Test

DO I HAVE TO?

REALLY?

Ah, please. Why do I have to test your IQ? Right, I just knocked this off, so hurry up and finish. You've got ten minutes. Don't cheat.

Problem 1

Naruto got in a dumpling eating contest with Anko. Anko eats one every seven seconds but Naruto eats one every three seconds. Naruto gave up after 16, but Anko continued eating for another 1 minute and 32 seconds. How many dumplings did Anko eat?

Problem 2

Choose the correct Tetragram Seal from the pictures below.

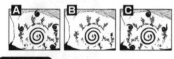

Problem 3

Which picture was the piece to the right taken from?

Problem 4

Naruto, Sasuke, Sakura, Kakashi, and Iruka are all standing in a row. Read the hint below and tell me who is in the middle.

Problem four hint: Naruto is to the right of Kakashi. There are two people between Sakura and Iruka. Naruto and Iruka are next to each other. Sasuke is to the left of Sakura.

Problem 5

Choose the correct meaning of the Konoha Chûnin motto, "Gain knowledge from the heavens and ready thyself for opportunity," from the list below.

> **A** Don't forget to practice every day.
> **B** Prepare for missions by learning many skills.
> **C** React swiftly and intelligently in emergencies.

Problem 6

From the three illustrations below, choose the correct drawing of Sasuke's Sharingan.

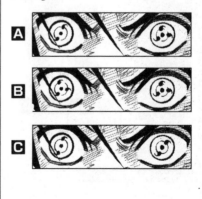

GATE FOUR IS ON PAGE 174!!

Full Investigation: Ninja Academy

Many young shinobi pass through its gates to polish and hone their talents!

The central pillar of the Hidden Leaf Village!! All details revealed!!

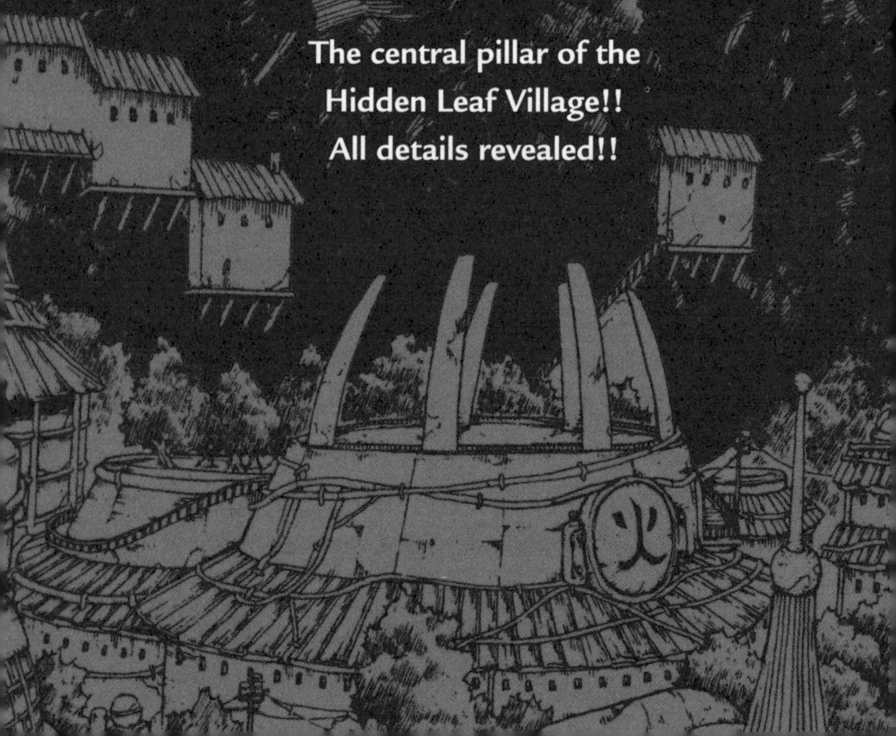

These Minds Will Be the Future
Shinobi Training Grounds

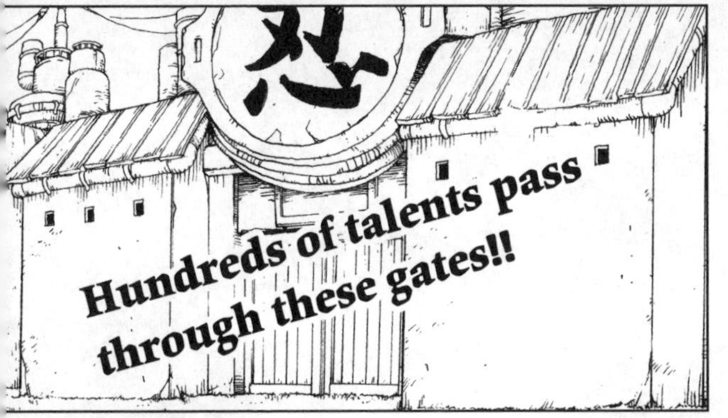
Hundreds of talents pass through these gates!!

Second Hokage

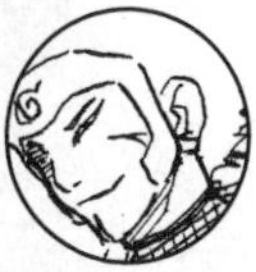

Academy founder. In a time of war, he faced an urgent need for a steady, effective source of fresh warriors.

Third Hokage

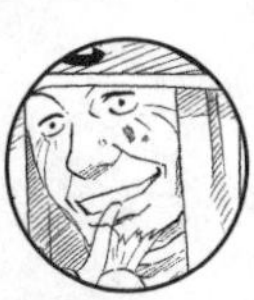

When the Third Hokage took over, he concentrated on improving the educational side of things, developing the Academy as a whole.

Konoha Academy History

50 years ago	Founding	First term: 36 graduates
0		Name officially changed to Academy First Teacher Selection Exam given
40		First Expansion Kunoichi Classes Start
30		Second Expansion
20		First shared practice with Sand Village Half the buildings destroyed in Nine-Tailed Fox attack, rebuilt one year later
10 Present		Third Expansion

Ninja education facilities founded in a time of upheaval

Fifty years ago, the Second Hokage, who needed more military might, founded a ninja training camp at the base of the cliff. At first it was purely educational, but it quickly merged with military and domestic facilities and began calling itself the Academy. After the Second Hokage's death, the Third Hokage perfected the educational systems, and education and training are now carried out under strict standards.

Acceptance Requirements

1. You must love the village and hope to help preserve peace and prosperity.
2. You must have a mind that will not yield, able to endure hard training and work.
3. Be healthy in mind and body.

If the above conditions are met, your admission to the Academy will be granted.

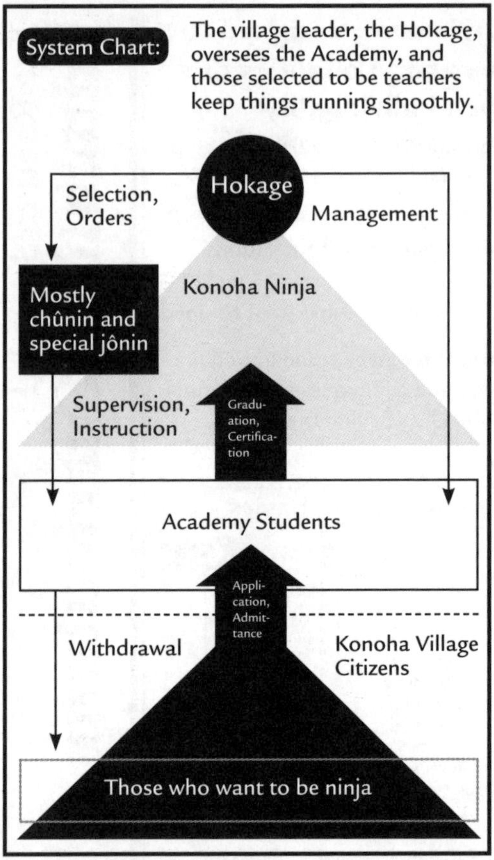
System Chart:
The village leader, the Hokage, oversees the Academy, and those selected to be teachers keep things running smoothly.
Hokage
Selection, Orders
Management
Konoha Ninja
Mostly chûnin and special jônin
Supervision, Instruction
Graduation, Certification
Academy Students
Application, Admittance
Withdrawal
Konoha Village Citizens
Those who want to be ninja

Knowledge for the brilliant, honing body and mind

The motto of Konoha Academy teachers has remained the same since the institute's founding, namely, "Development as shinobi with respect to individuality." In a free, open-minded environment students are allowed to strengthen their bodies and minds, discovering their own ninja paths. When they have found their way, they are guided by the belief that fills them. Konoha's pulse beats on...

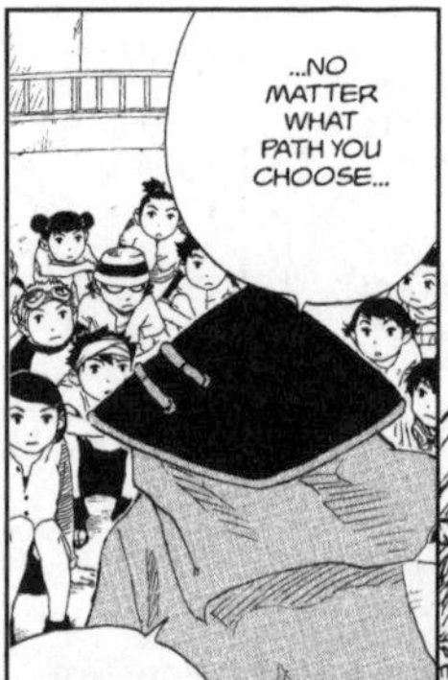
...NO MATTER WHAT PATH YOU CHOOSE...
...NEVER FORGET TO PROTECT THOSE WHO ARE PRECIOUS TO YOU!

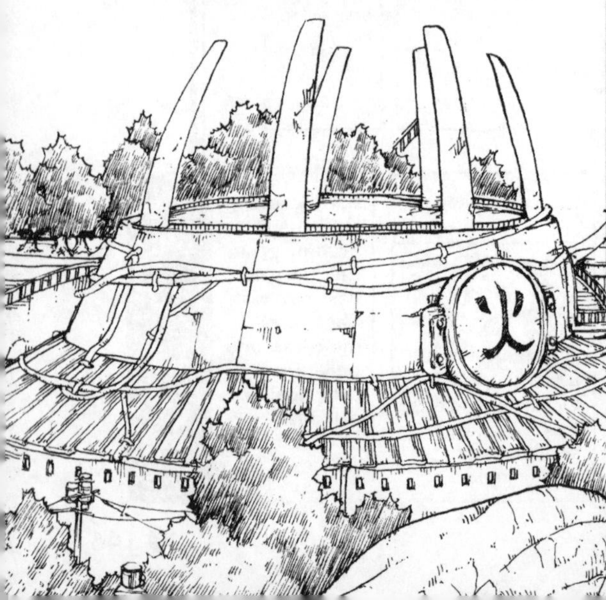

The Road to Shinobi!

Education Curriculum

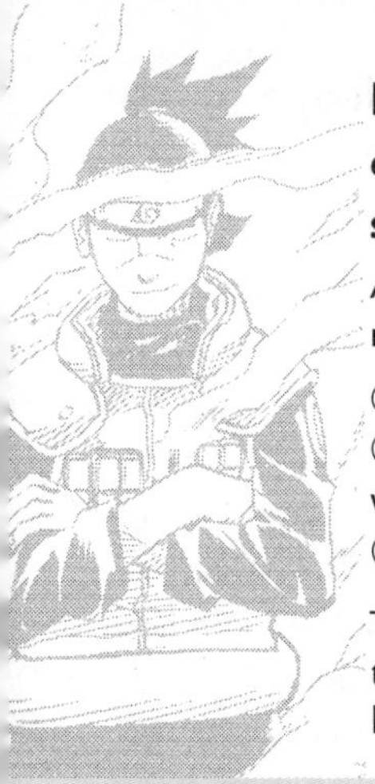

Ninja curriculum, designed to enhance natural qualities and strengthen individuality

Academy education follows a basic developmental pattern (shown in the chart below).

① Basics: Creating the foundations
② Maneuvers: Filling those foundations with skills
③ Application: Allowing those skills to ripen

Through these three steps students acquire the knowledge and techniques every shinobi knows and the ideas behind them.

Genin	Application	Maneuvers	Basics
← Graduation			← Entrance
New genin are put in three-man cells, given an instructor, and sent out on missions. During harsh real battles they discover their true selves!	When students are deemed to have mastered the basics and maneuvers they are moved to the application stage, where they are taught techniques designed for their personality and skills. Private lessons or special seminars help enhance their inherent qualities.	Practical classes quickly have the students using ninja tools, ninjutsu, and physical attacks. Many classes practice team play and simulated battle.	Immediately after entrance, students are given basic training and education. Without sturdy bodies and this fundamental knowledge, they will never be shinobi.

The narrow gate to genin status: Graduation Test

For Academy students to become genin, they need to pass two tests. These are merciless, and only those truly qualified can pass.

Academy Graduation Test

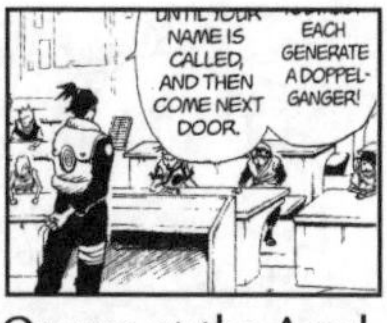
EACH GENERATE A DOPPEL-GANGER!
UNTIL YOUR NAME IS CALLED, AND THEN COME NEXT DOOR.

Occurs at the Academy – a random selection from the basic ninjutsu.

Genin Certification Test

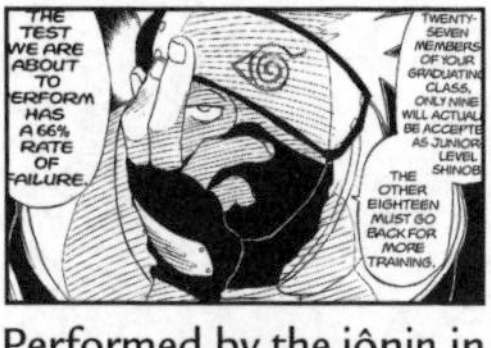
TWENTY-SEVEN MEMBERS OF YOUR GRADUATING CLASS, ONLY NINE WILL ACTUAL BE ACCEPTE AS JUNIOR LEVEL SHINOB
THE OTHER EIGHTEEN MUST GO BACK FOR MORE TRAINING.
THE TEST WE ARE ABOUT TO ERFORM HAS A 66% RATE OF AILURE.

Performed by the jônin in charge after formation of a three man cell. Contents vary.

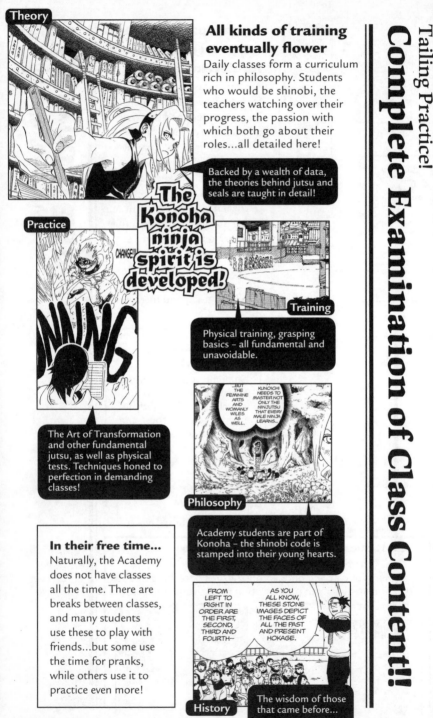

Tailing Practice!

Complete Examination of Class Content!!

All kinds of training eventually flower

Daily classes form a curriculum rich in philosophy. Students who would be shinobi, the teachers watching over their progress, the passion with which both go about their roles...all detailed here!

Theory

Backed by a wealth of data, the theories behind jutsu and seals are taught in detail!

The Konoha ninja spirit is developed!

Practice

CHANGE!!!

The Art of Transformation and other fundamental jutsu, as well as physical tests. Techniques honed to perfection in demanding classes!

Training

Physical training, grasping basics – all fundamental and unavoidable.

KUNOICHI NEEDS TO MASTER NOT ONLY THE NINJUTSU THAT EVERY MALE NINJA LEARNS...
...BUT THE FEMININE ARTS AND WOMANLY WILES AS WELL.

Philosophy

Academy students are part of Konoha – the shinobi code is stamped into their young hearts.

AS YOU ALL KNOW, THESE STONE IMAGES DEPICT THE FACES OF ALL THE PAST AND PRESENT HOKAGE.
FROM LEFT TO RIGHT IN ORDER ARE THE FIRST, SECOND, THIRD AND FOURTH--

History

The wisdom of those that came before...

In their free time...

Naturally, the Academy does not have classes all the time. There are breaks between classes, and many students use these to play with friends...but some use the time for pranks, while others use it to practice even more!

Completely Recreated!! Classroom Layout!!

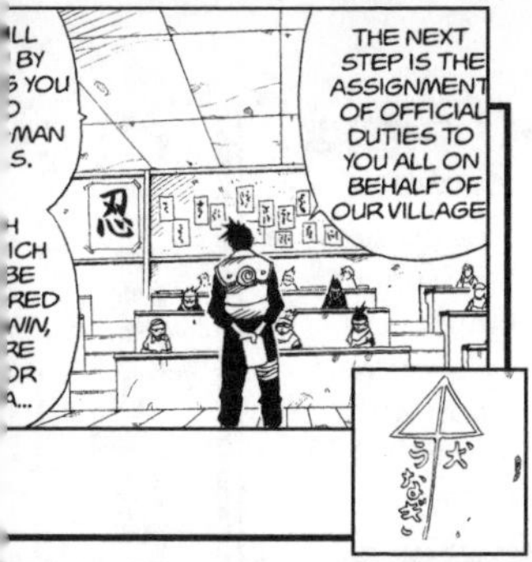
THE NEXT STEP IS THE ASSIGNMENT OF OFFICIAL DUTIES TO YOU ALL ON BEHALF OF OUR VILLAGE

Large, spacious rooms – a good environment for developing talent!!

Academy classrooms are fairly large with high ceilings. They were designed this way on the theory that expansive classrooms lead to expansive education, and they are carefully laid out to avoid causing the students stress. The picture to the left is a recreation of one of the many classrooms. While there are minor differences between the rooms, the basic layout remains the same. There are also larger classrooms for major tests, and meeting rooms.

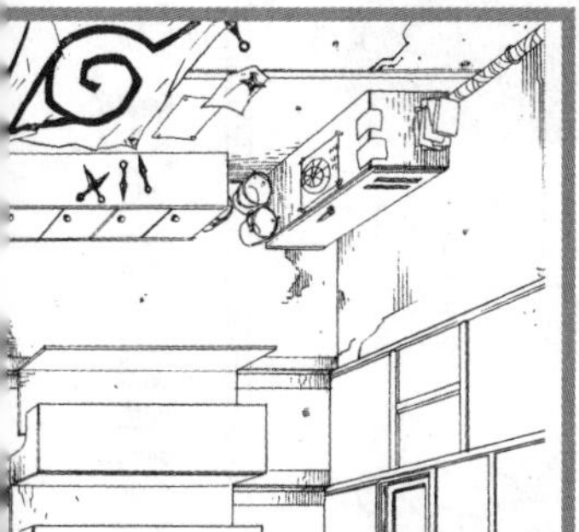

Big windows with a great view!

Sunlight pours in through these windows, keeping the classroom brightly lit. In emergencies, these can also be used as exits.

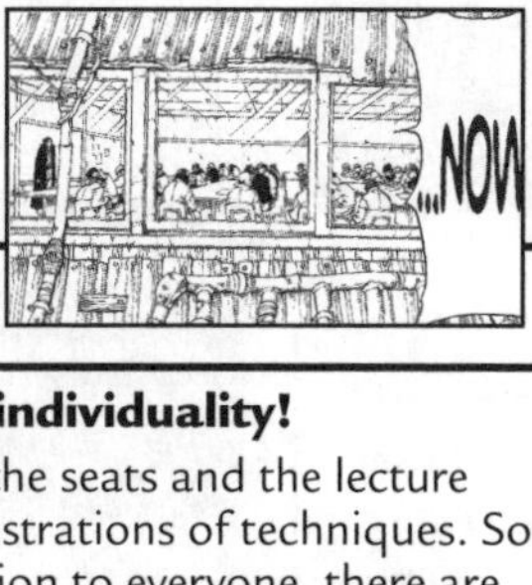
...NOW

Elite educators encourage individuality!

There is a large space between the seats and the lecture podium for carrying out demonstrations of techniques. So that one teacher can pay attention to everyone, there are only a few seats in each room.

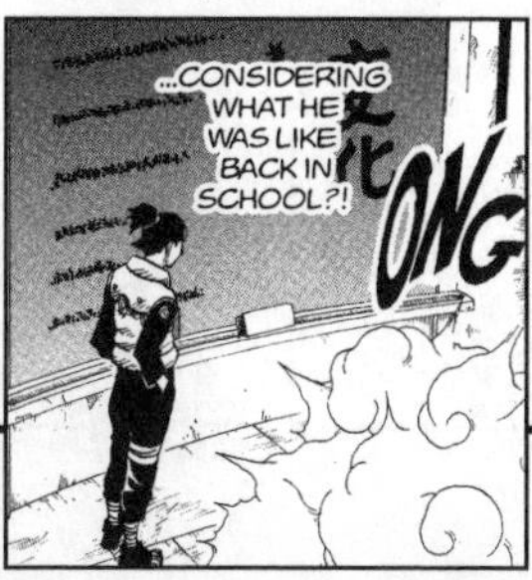
...CONSIDERING WHAT HE WAS LIKE BACK IN SCHOOL?!
ONG

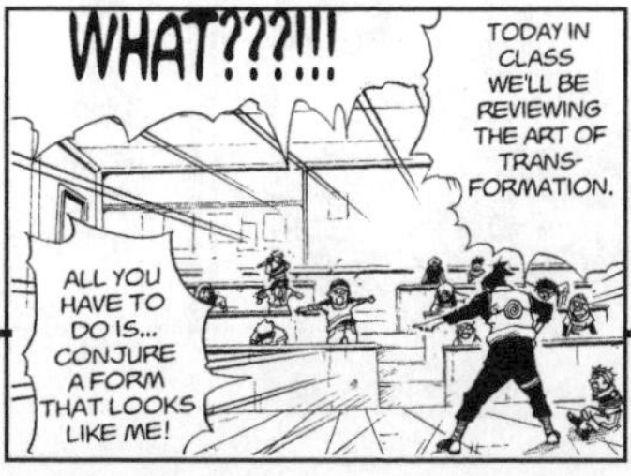
TODAY IN CLASS WE'LL BE REVIEWING THE ART OF TRANS-FORMATION.
WHAT???!!!
ALL YOU HAVE TO DO IS... CONJURE A FORM THAT LOOKS LIKE ME!

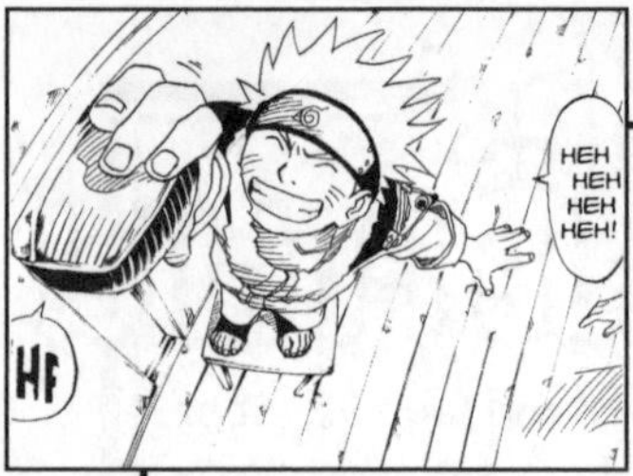
HEH HEH HEH HEH!
HF

Entrance perfect for booby traps!
The entrance is an ordinary door, but if a mischievous student applies himself, it could have other uses!

Instructions and schedules posted here!
This wall can have anything from messages from the Hokage to pieces made by students. But no graffiti!

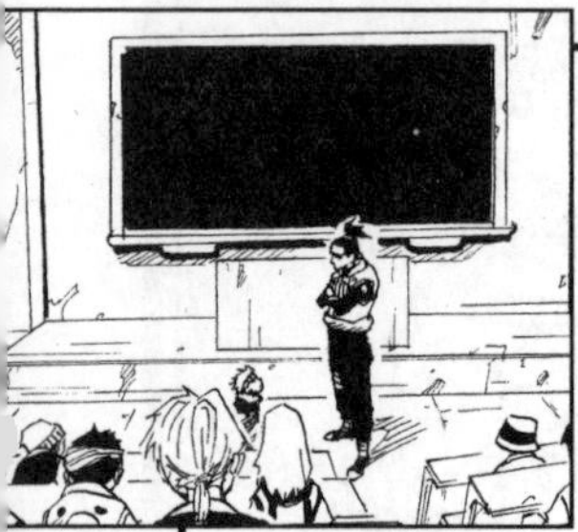

The blackboard that displays the teacher's passion!
Matching the size of the classes, the blackboard is unusually large as well. The teacher's passion displayed on this board seeps into the minds of the students...

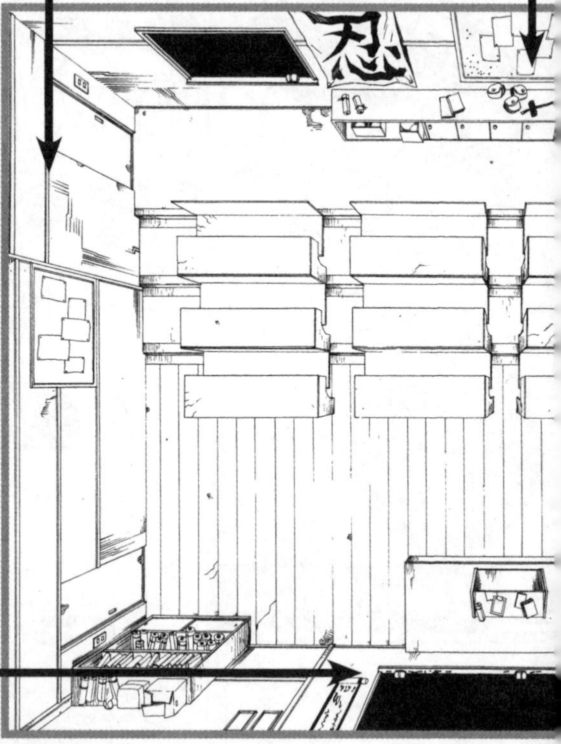

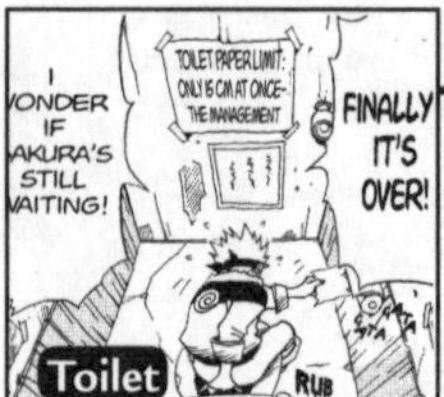
Toilet
TOILET PAPER LIMIT: ONLY 15 CM AT ONCE- THE MANAGEMENT
FINALLY IT'S OVER!
RUB

⬆ Even the stalls are huge! But the toilet paper rolls are of limited length...

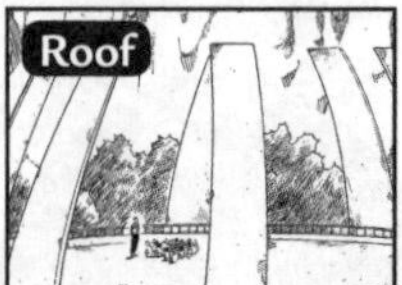
Roof

⬆ Directly below Hokage Rock – excellent for history lectures.

⬇ For large weapons and ninja tools – usually dark.

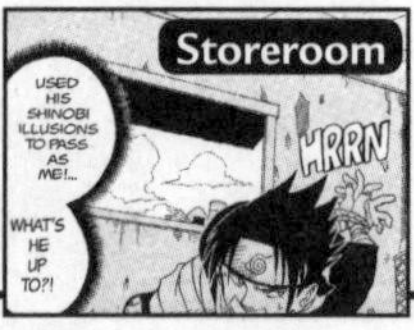
Storeroom
HRRN
USED HIS SHINOBI ILLUSIONS TO PASS AS ME!...
WHAT'S HE UP TO?!

The Academy grounds are fairly large, and there are all sorts of places around the campus. These beautiful grounds help raise unique and skilled students!

Naruto's Classmates' Report Cards! Made Public!

Naruto daringly snuck into the Hokage's house and found eight of his classmates' report cards! Below you can see their evaluations (+1) from their time in the Academy!!

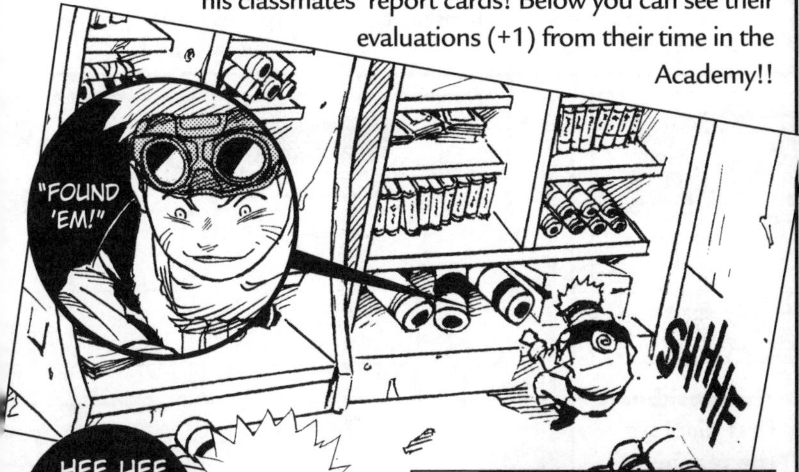

"FOUND 'EM!"
SHHHF

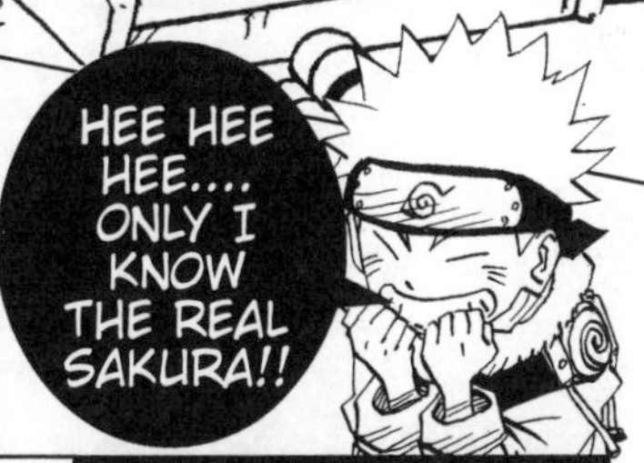

HEE HEE HEE.... ONLY I KNOW THE REAL SAKURA!!

Uchiha Sasuke

Ninjutsu	A	Cooperation	F
Taijutsu	A	Positivity	C
Genjutsu	A	Classroom Attitude	B

Comments

Has an incredible sense for ninjutsu, taijutsu, and genjutsu, and has maintained top grades. Frequently strikes out on his own during cooperative exercises – needs to work on teamwork and cooperation.

Haruno Sakura

Ninjutsu	B	Cooperation	B
Taijutsu	C	Positivity	B
Genjutsu	B	Classroom Attitude	A

Comments

Worth watching, both for her range of knowledge and control of chakra, but doesn't seem to enjoy taijutsu. Occasionally prone to emotional outbursts, but if she channels that energy she should be able to improve on all her skills.

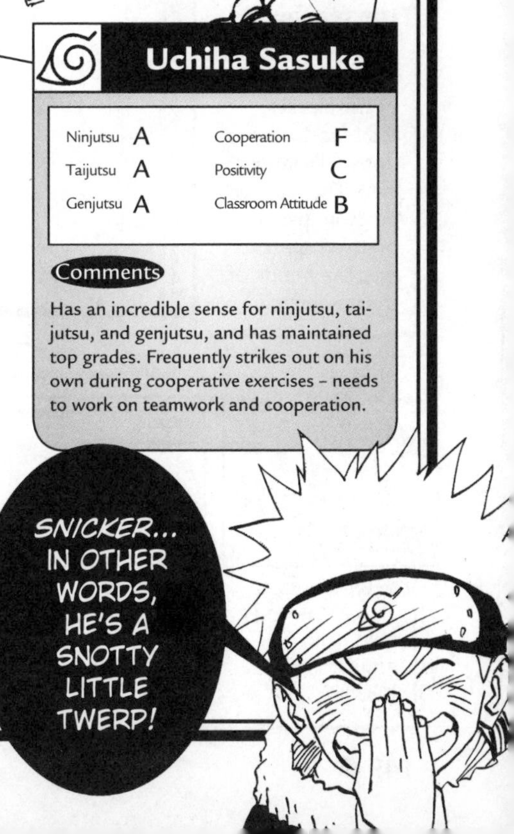

SNICKER... IN OTHER WORDS, HE'S A SNOTTY LITTLE TWERP!

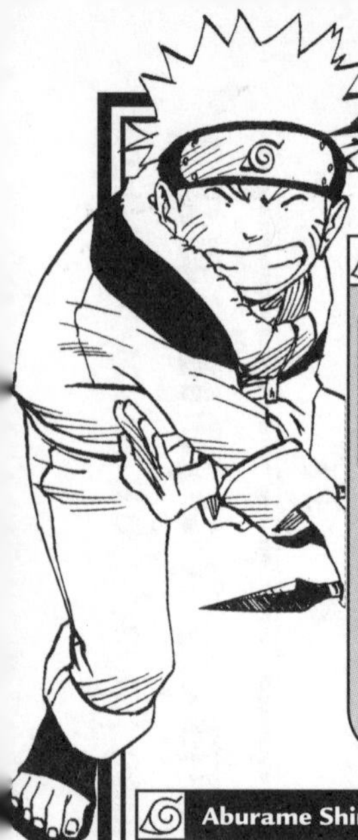
COCKY IDIOT, SLEEPY IDIOT, AND EATING IDIOT -- THE IDIOT TRIO!

Akimichi Choji

Ninjutsu	B	Cooperation	B
Taijutsu	B	Positivity	B
Genjutsu	C	Classroom Attitude	C

Comments

No one rivals his knowledge and interest in food. I once yelled at him for eating too early and he went berserk.

Nara Shikamaru

Ninjutsu	B	Cooperation	B
Taijutsu	C	Positivity	C
Genjutsu	C	Classroom Attitude	F

Comments

Absolutely not motivated. Sleeps all the time – it's amazing that he hasn't flunked out.

Yamanaka Ino

Ninjutsu	A	Cooperation	B
Taijutsu	B	Positivity	A
Genjutsu	B	Classroom Attitude	B

Comments

Outstanding grades, and gets others to follow her lead. Occasionally lets that go to her head...

Aburame Shino

Ninjutsu	A	Cooperation	B
Taijutsu	B	Positivity	C
Genjutsu	B	Classroom Attitude	B

Comments

Extremely mature for an Academy student. I'd like to see him play occasionally, to develop his emotions.

Hyuga Hinata

Ninjutsu	B	Cooperation	A
Taijutsu	A	Positivity	F
Genjutsu	B	Classroom Attitude	A

Comments

Very retiring and pessimistic. I can't tell her to follow the problem students' lead, but she needs to put herself forward.

Inuzuka Kiba

Ninjutsu	B	Cooperation	C
Taijutsu	A	Positivity	A
Genjutsu	C	Classroom Attitude	C

Comments

Very violent. Takes good care of his dog, but needs to pay more attention to those around him.

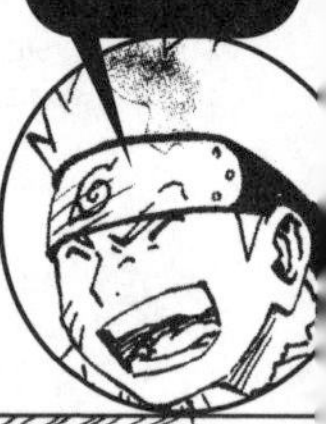
KIBA WAS ALWAYS TOO LOUD! I BARELY REMEMBER THE OTHER TWO...

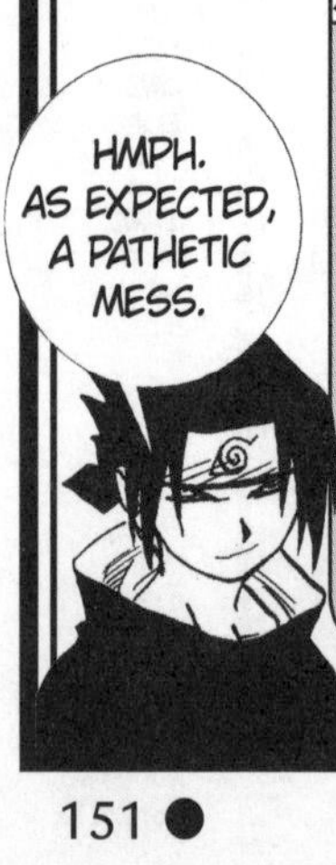
HMPH. AS EXPECTED, A PATHETIC MESS.

Uzumaki Naruto

Ninjutsu	F	Cooperation	F
Taijutsu	B	Positivity	A
Genjutsu	F	Classroom Attitude	F

Comments

Stands out both for his poor grades and his poor behavior. Has guts and motivation, but never studies!!

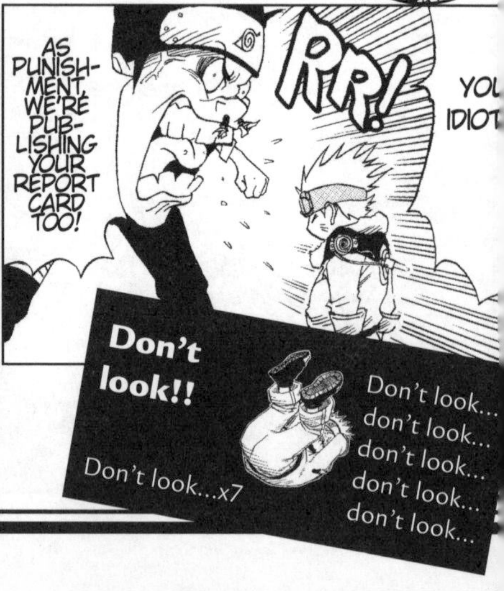
RR!
AS PUNISHMENT, WE'RE PUBLISHING YOUR REPORT CARD TOO!
Don't look!!
Don't look...x7
Don't look... don't look... don't look... don't look... don't look...

Konoha Academy Special Lecture

Complete Guide to Shinobi Signs!

Place your hands together and will the jutsu to begin!!

丑申卯
子亥酉丑
午酉子寅
戌寅巳丑未
巳亥未子
壬申酉辰
酉丑午未
寅巳子申
卯亥辰未
子丑申酉
壬子亥

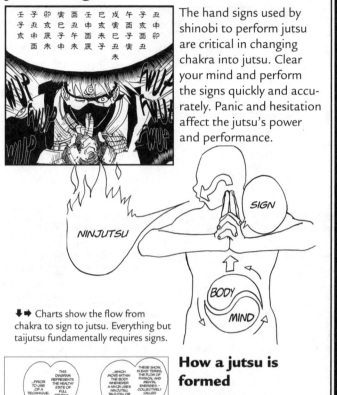

The hand signs used by shinobi to perform jutsu are critical in changing chakra into jutsu. Clear your mind and perform the signs quickly and accurately. Panic and hesitation affect the jutsu's power and performance.

SIGN
NINJUTSU
BODY
MIND

⬇➡ Charts show the flow from chakra to sign to jutsu. Everything but taijutsu fundamentally requires signs.

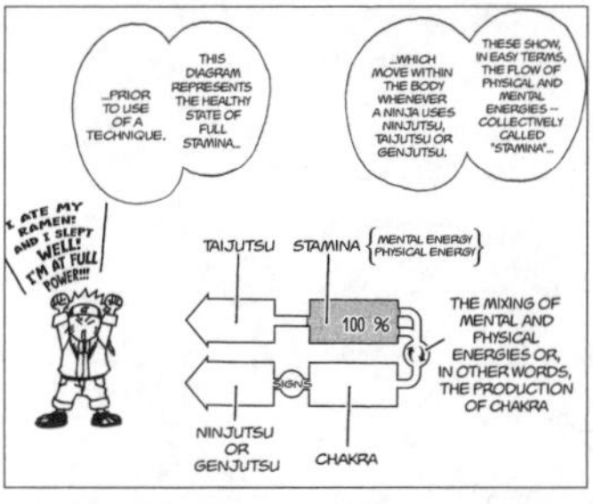

THESE SHOW, IN EASY TERMS, THE FLOW OF PHYSICAL AND MENTAL ENERGIES -- COLLECTIVELY CALLED "STAMINA"...
...WHICH MOVE WITHIN THE BODY WHENEVER A NINJA USES NINJUTSU, TAIJUTSU OR GENJUTSU.
THIS DIAGRAM REPRESENTS THE HEALTHY STATE OF FULL STAMINA...
...PRIOR TO USE OF A TECHNIQUE.
I ATE MY RAMEN! AND I SLEPT WELL! I'M AT FULL POWER!!!
TAIJUTSU
STAMINA
MENTAL ENERGY
PHYSICAL ENERGY
100 %
THE MIXING OF MENTAL AND PHYSICAL ENERGIES OR, IN OTHER WORDS, THE PRODUCTION OF CHAKRA
SIGNS
NINJUTSU OR GENJUTSU
CHAKRA

How a jutsu is formed

To perform a shinobi jutsu, first summon chakra, then transform it into a jutsu using a hand sign. In an actual fight, you will have to form these signs while evading enemy attacks, so staying calm and being able to make the signs quickly and accurately is critical.

FWUP
FWUP
FWUP

Complete Secret Scroll!

The Twelve Basic Signs!!

The twelve fundamental signs needed to create most shinobi jutsu, passed to you in secrecy! The trick to remembering them is to shout the name while forming the sign with your hands. Practice this until your fingers can move reflectively!

Saru/ Monkey

⬆ Thumbs lie flat on pinkies.

Tatsu/ Dragon

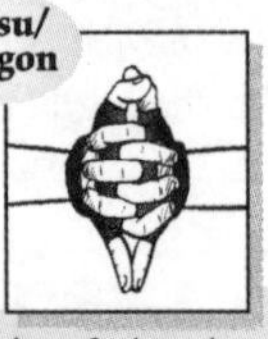

⬆ Left thumb on top.

Ne/Rat

⬆ Left thumb on the outside.

Tori/Bird

⬆ Be careful with the angle of the thumbs and the location of the fingertips.

Mi/Snake

⬆ Left thumb on the outside.

Ushi/Ox

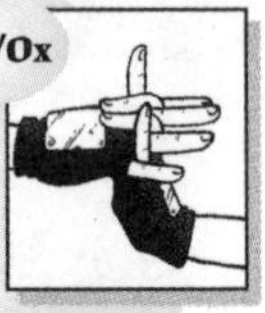

⬆ Right hand horizontal, left hand vertical.

Inu/Dog

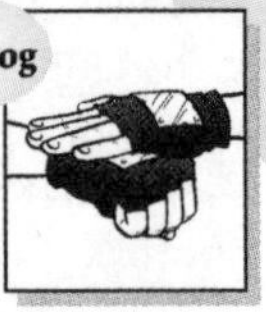

⬆ Left hand flat on right fist.

Uma/ Horse

⬆ Both elbows out, index fingers form a triangle.

Tora/Tiger

⬆ Both thumbs straight up.

I/Boar

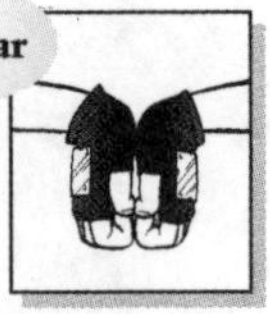

⬆ Wrists need great flexibility.

Hitsuji/ Ram

⬆ Left thumb on top, hands together vertically.

U/Hare

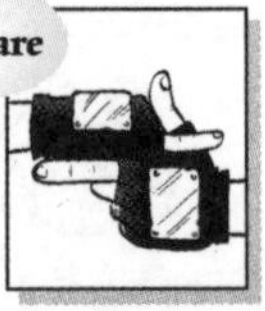

⬆ Aside from pinky, right fingers gently curled.

Advanced Signs

Some jutsu require unique signs beyond these twelve, especially forbidden jutsu and secret techniques – jutsu that produce unusual effects or unparalleled power.

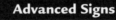

FWUP
I THINK THE ODDS ARE 100% I'M GONNA HIT MY TARGET, DON'T YOU THINK?

⬆ Shintenshin no Jutsu. This unique sign seems to suggest the heart.

➡ This sign is used in the Multiple Shadow Doppelgangers jutsu. It forms a cross with the index and middle fingers of each hand.

IF WE WERE TO DISSIPATE ALL OF THE ILLUSIONS SIMULTANEOUSLY, WHOEVER'S CASTING THEM...
...WOULDN'T BE ABLE TO JUST HURL KNIVES AT US WITHOUT US SEEING WHERE THEY'RE HIDING!

Smooth Signs for Fire Style Technique!!

Once you've memorized the twelve signs, time to put them into practice!! Let's start with the Fire Style Technique, and try to make the sign series flow!

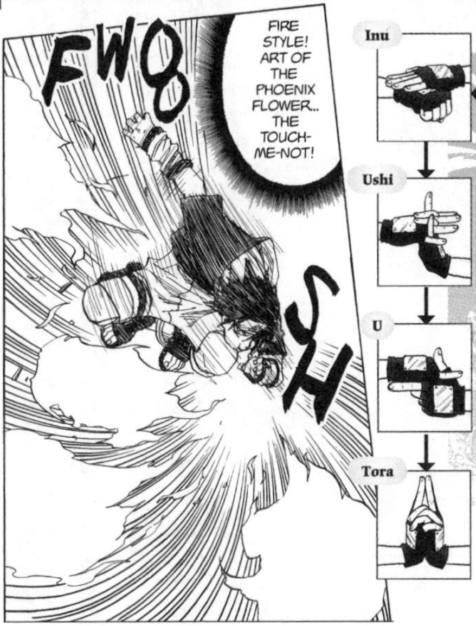
FIRE STYLE! ART OF THE PHOENIX FLOWER.. THE TOUCH-ME-NOT!
Ushi
U
Tora

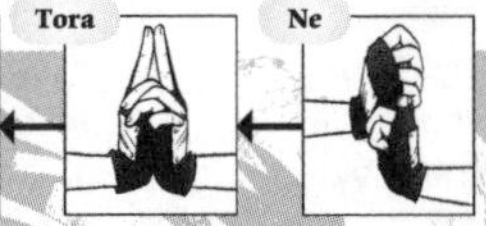
Ne
Tora
Inu

Fire Style: Art of the Phoenix Flower!

Sprouting fire like a phoenix flower seed, a wave of fire hits the enemy with the force of a shotgun. The trick to these signs is making the transition from Ushi to U smoothly.

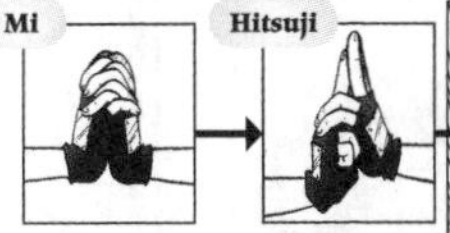
Mi
Hitsuji

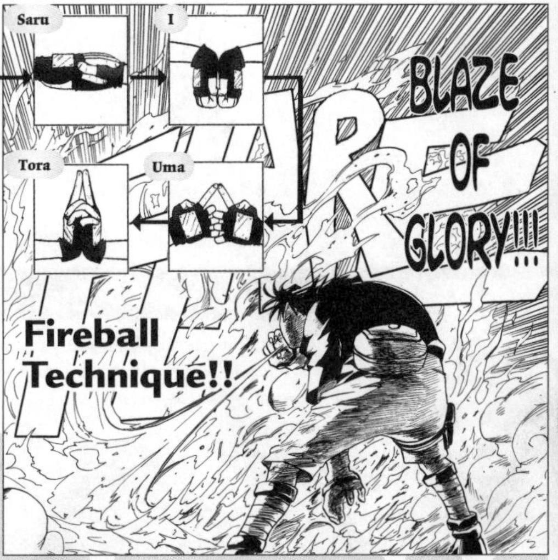
Saru
I
Uma
Tora
BLAZE OF GLORY!!!
Fireball Technique!!

Fire Style: Fireball Technique!!

The chakra inside the caster changes into fire, which pours out of him into a giant fireball, blanketing everything in sight. The difficulty is the same as the Phoenix Flower, but there are more signs used. The hitsuji-saru-i section is particularly hard.

Quick Sign Formation!!

Time to put your knowledge into practice! The main point with signs is to make them quickly and precisely. Practice over and over until you can make them all in the time allotted!

Start with something easy.
Beginners

Bunshin no Jutsu: Art of the Shadow Doppelganger

Bunshin no Jutsu is a basic ninjutsu, with few signs and an easy flow. First practice making the signs slowly, and then gradually increase your speed.

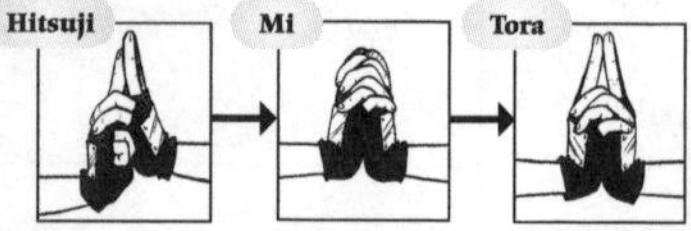
Hitsuji
Mi
Tora

Goal time:
5 seconds

Key: Before you start making signs spread your fingers and calm your nerves. This is basic!

A little more complicated?
Intermediate

Kuchiyose no Jutsu: The Art of Summoning

I→ Inu→Tori→ Saru→Hitsuji

Bunshin no Jutsu is a basic ninjutsu, with few signs and an easy flow. First practice making the signs slowly, and then gradually increase your speed.

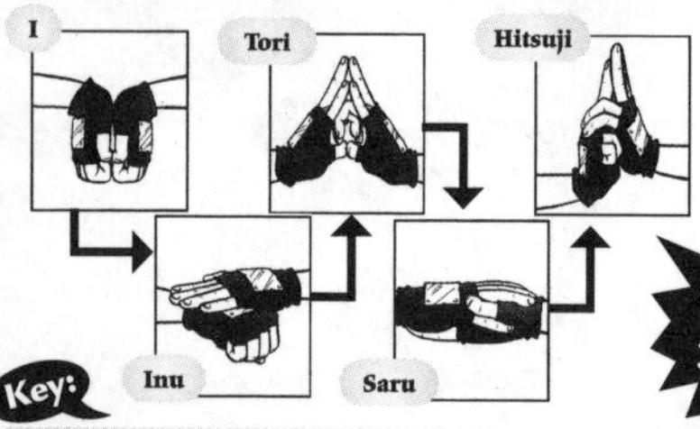
I
Tori
Hitsuji
Inu
Saru

Goal time:
3 seconds

Key: If you can get past the tricky Inu→Tori→Saru bit, the final Hitsuji is easy!

Extremely Hard!
Advanced

Shuriken Shadow Doppelganger Technique

Ushi→Inu→Tatsu→Ne→Inu→I→Mi→Tora

Key: Set your tempo around the Inu sign, which occurs twice, and keep rhythmical!

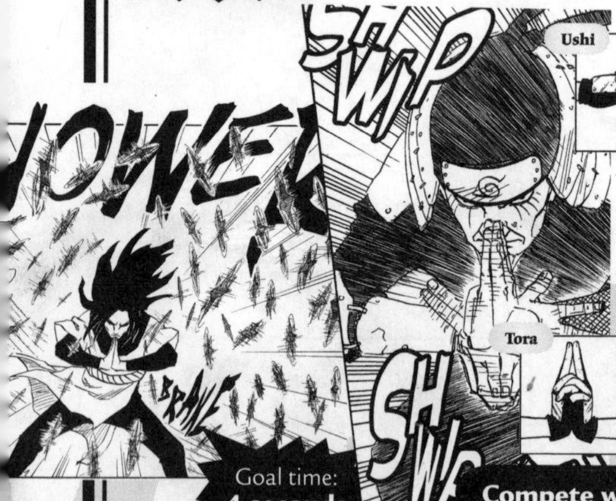

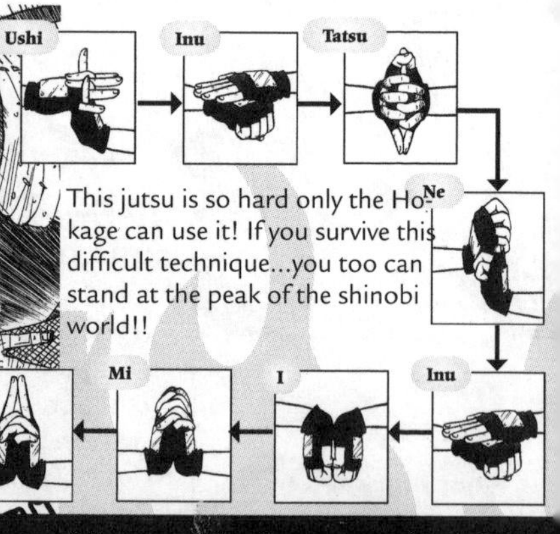
Ushi
Inu
Tatsu
Ne
Inu
I
Mi
Tora

This jutsu is so hard only the Hokage can use it! If you survive this difficult technique...you too can stand at the peak of the shinobi world!!

Goal time:
4 seconds

Compete with your friends to see who's faster

Uzumaki Naruto's Legendary Pranks!

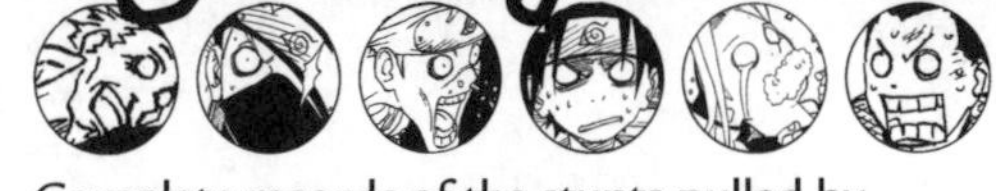

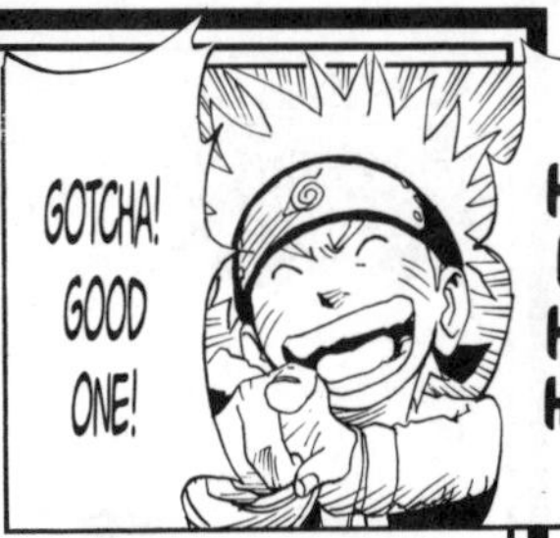
HA HA HA HA!!
GOTCHA! GOOD ONE!

Complete records of the stunts pulled by Konoha's resident master prankster, Naruto! Also, his victims' comments.

Most Spectacular!! Attention Getter #1!!

Impact ✦✦✦✦✦
Creativity ✦✦✦
Annoyance ✦✦✦✦

Hokage Rock Graffiti!

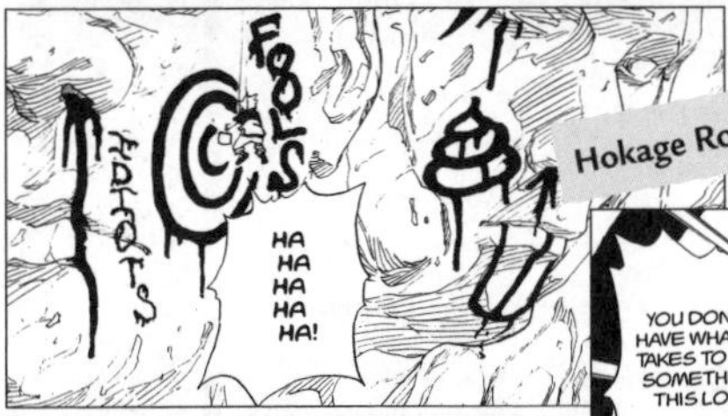
HA HA HA HA HA!

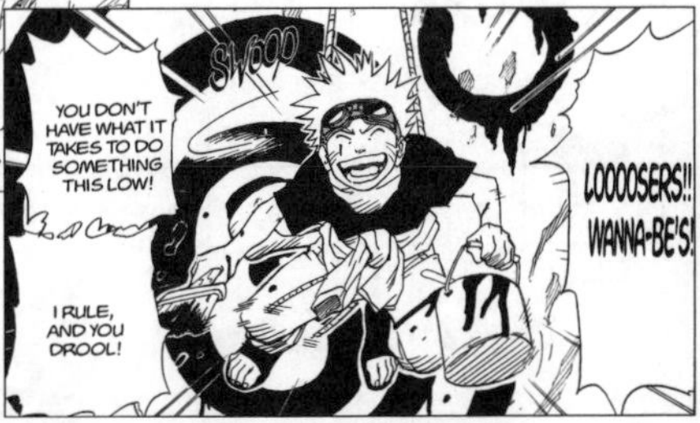
SWOOP
LOOOOSERS!! WANNA-BE'S!
YOU DON'T HAVE WHAT IT TAKES TO DO SOMETHING THIS LOW!
I RULE, AND YOU DROOL!

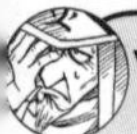

Victim's comment:
Agile and spectacular...I'd respect him more if he hadn't drawn on my face!

Heart Beat #1!!

Transformation Jutsu

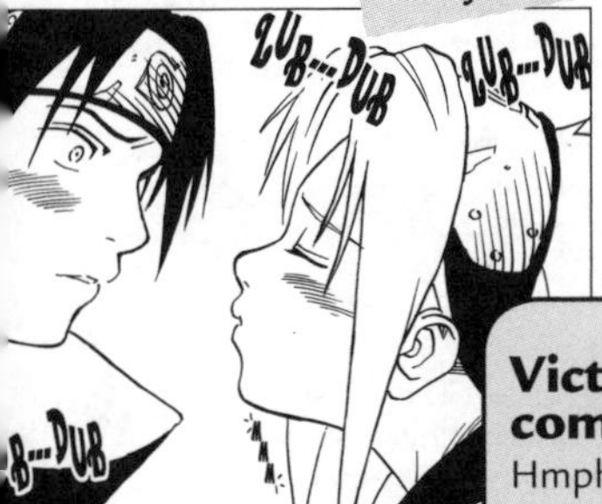
LUB...DUB
LUB...DUB
B...DUB

Impact ✦✦
Creativity ✦
Annoyance ✦✦✦✦

Victim's comment:
Hmph, just like that idiot. Actually, the fact that he even managed to look like me is impressive...

Most Spectacular!! Attention Getter #1!!

Ninja Centerfold

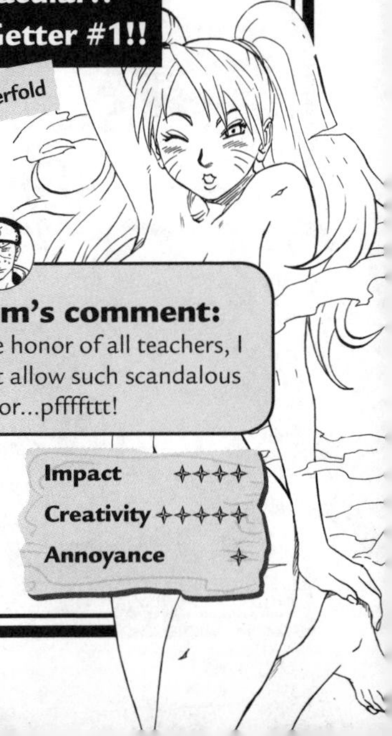

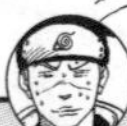

Victim's comment:
For the honor of all teachers, I cannot allow such scandalous behavior...pfffftttt!

Impact ✦✦✦✦
Creativity ✦✦✦✦✦
Annoyance ✦

Interest Level #1!!

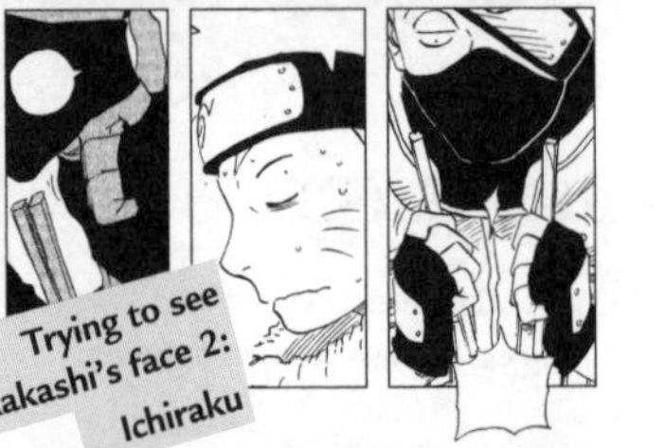

Trying to see Kakashi's face 2: Ichiraku

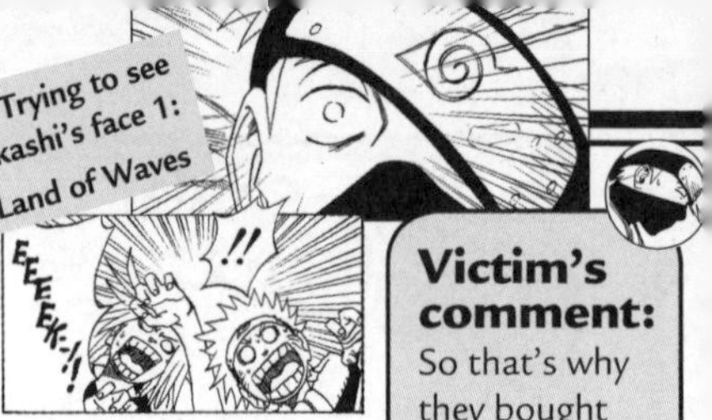
!!
EEEEK-!!

Trying to see Kakashi's face 1: Land of Waves

Impact	✦✦
Creativity	✦
Annoyance	✦✦✦

Victim's comment:
So that's why they bought me ramen? I'd show them my face any time!!

Surprise #1!!

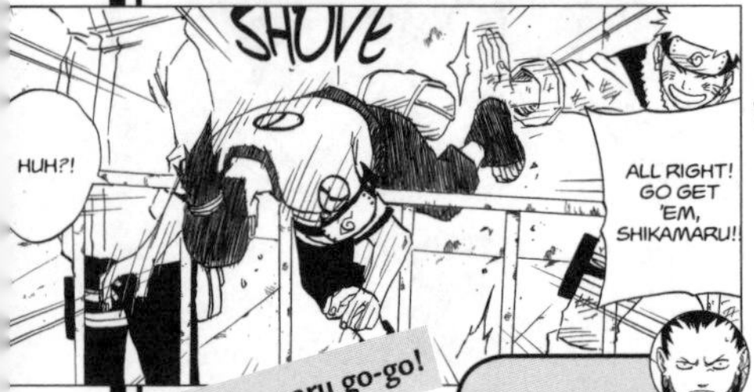
SHOVE
ALL RIGHT! GO GET 'EM, SHIKAMARU!!
HUH?!

Shikamaru go-go!

Impact	✦✦✦
Creativity	✦
Annoyance	✦✦✦

Victim's comment:
I so didn't want to fight... all his fault!

Performance #1!!

Pretending to fall out of tree!

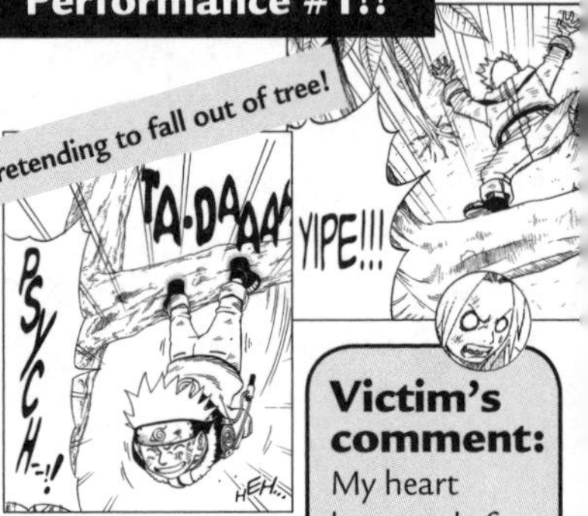
YIPE!!!
TA-DAAA
PSYCH-!!
HEH...

Impact	✦✦✦
Creativity	✦✦
Annoyance	✦✦

Victim's comment:
My heart beats only for Sasuke! I'll kill you!!

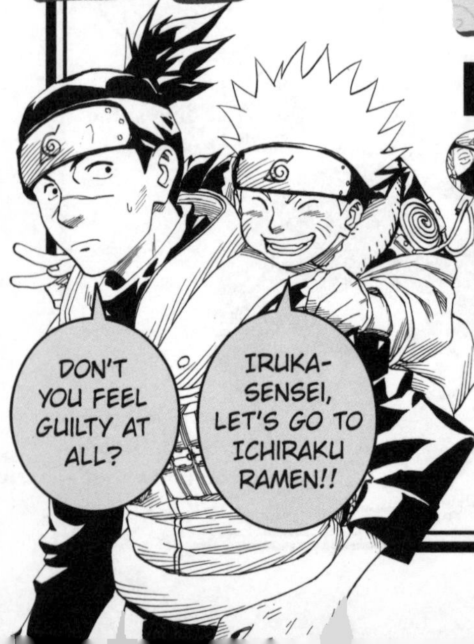
IRUKA-SENSEI, LET'S GO TO ICHIRAKU RAMEN!!
DON'T YOU FEEL GUILTY AT ALL?

Obviousness #1!!

Victim's comment:
Mm? I'm a jônin? I was making them put their guard down, observing their reactions.

Impact	✦
Creativity	✦
Annoyance	✦✦✦

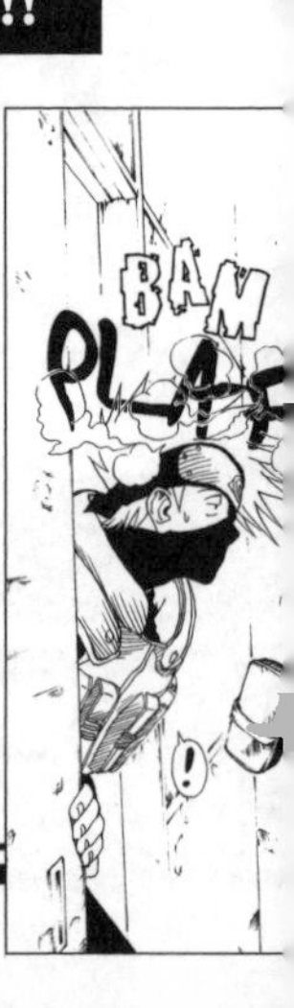
BAM
PLAF
!

Draw Rock Lee

Copy with your almighty eyes!!

We proudly — and for the first time (!) — present the secret power of Kekkei Genkai: Sharingan, the amazing ability to copy everything with just a glimpse!

1 There was once a bowl with cracks...

2 Fill it up with a lot of rice...

3 Gimme two pieces of nori, cause I love...

4 Gimme a couple of quail eggs...

5 Put in a plum and pour on some soy sauce...

6 Finish by adding some seaweed!

THIS IS THE SO-CALLED **REFLECTION** TECHNIQUE.
DON'T YOU LIE TO ME...

And if you turn it around, before you know it, it's Rock Lee!

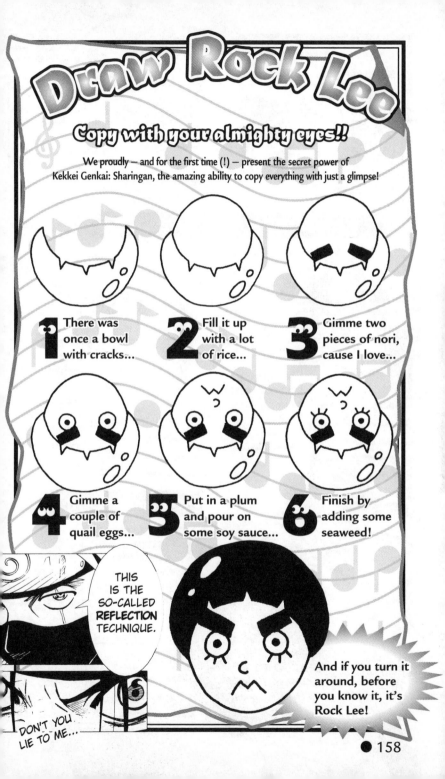

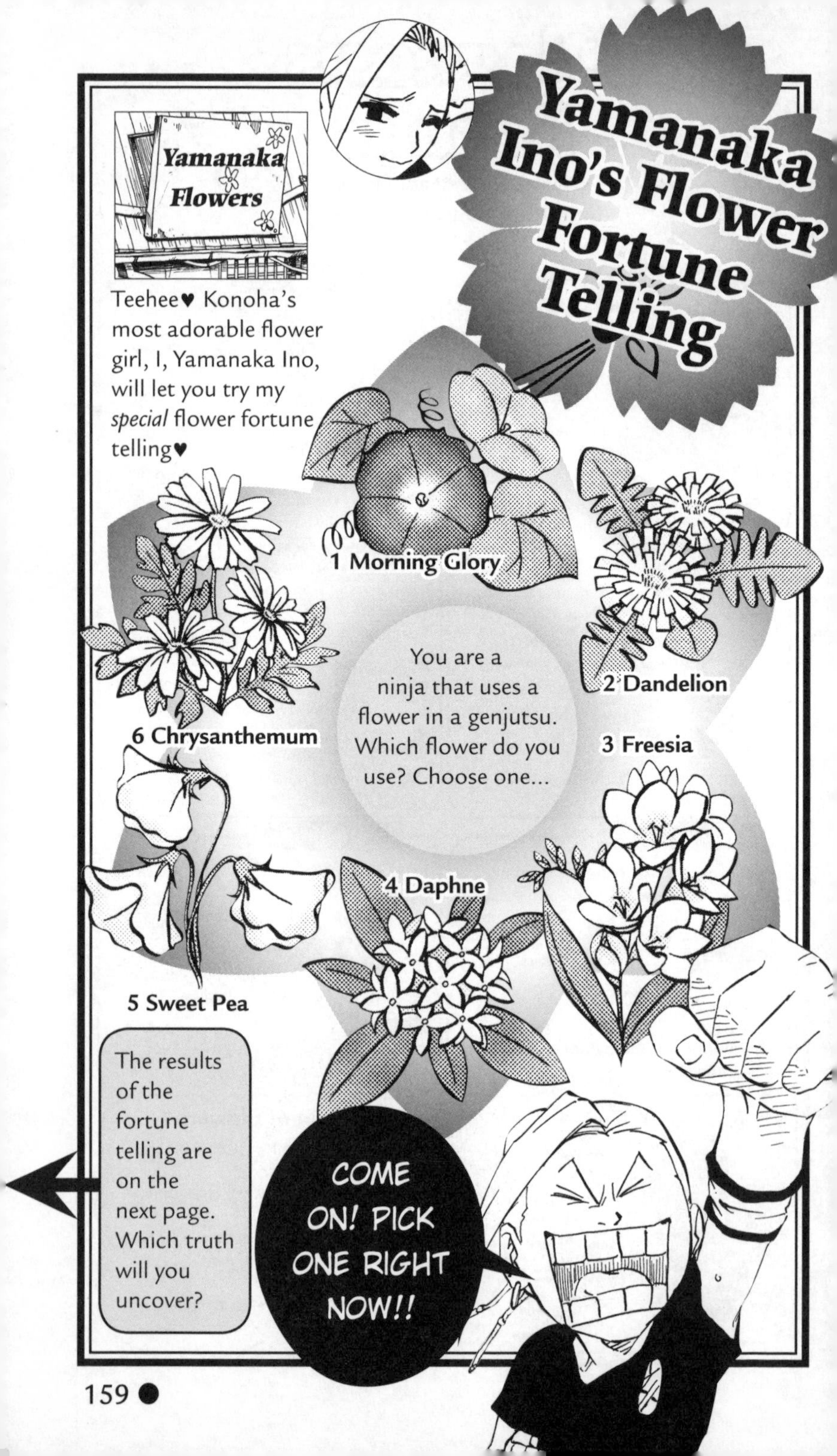
Yamanaka Ino's Flower Fortune Telling
Yamanaka Flowers
Teehee♥ Konoha's most adorable flower girl, I, Yamanaka Ino, will let you try my *special* flower fortune telling♥
You are a ninja that uses a flower in a genjutsu. Which flower do you use? Choose one...
1 Morning Glory
2 Dandelion
3 Freesia
4 Daphne
5 Sweet Pea
6 Chrysanthemum
The results of the fortune telling are on the next page. Which truth will you uncover?
COME ON! PICK ONE RIGHT NOW!!

Yamanaka Ino's Flower Fortune Telling

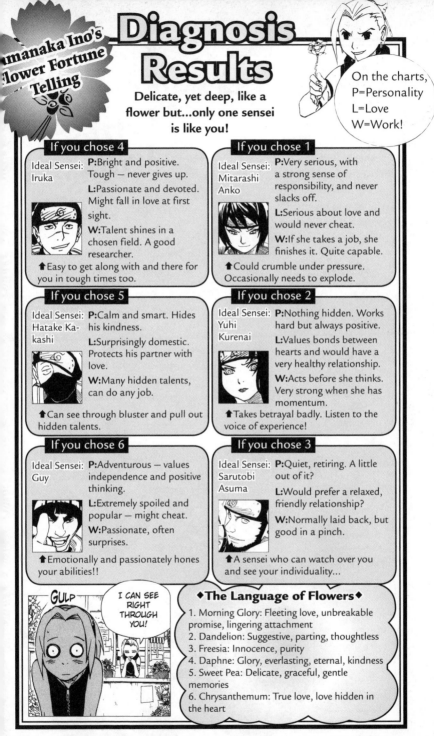

Diagnosis Results

Delicate, yet deep, like a flower but...only one sensei is like you!

On the charts,
P=Personality
L=Love
W=Work!

If you chose 1

Ideal Sensei: Mitarashi Anko

P:Very serious, with a strong sense of responsibility, and never slacks off.

L:Serious about love and would never cheat.

W:If she takes a job, she finishes it. Quite capable.

⬆Could crumble under pressure. Occasionally needs to explode.

If you chose 2

Ideal Sensei: Yuhi Kurenai

P:Nothing hidden. Works hard but always positive.

L:Values bonds between hearts and would have a very healthy relationship.

W:Acts before she thinks. Very strong when she has momentum.

⬆Takes betrayal badly. Listen to the voice of experience!

If you chose 3

Ideal Sensei: Sarutobi Asuma

P:Quiet, retiring. A little out of it?

L:Would prefer a relaxed, friendly relationship?

W:Normally laid back, but good in a pinch.

⬆A sensei who can watch over you and see your individuality...

If you chose 4

Ideal Sensei: Iruka

P:Bright and positive. Tough — never gives up.

L:Passionate and devoted. Might fall in love at first sight.

W:Talent shines in a chosen field. A good researcher.

⬆Easy to get along with and there for you in tough times too.

If you chose 5

Ideal Sensei: Hatake Kakashi

P:Calm and smart. Hides his kindness.

L:Surprisingly domestic. Protects his partner with love.

W:Many hidden talents, can do any job.

⬆Can see through bluster and pull out hidden talents.

If you chose 6

Ideal Sensei: Guy

P:Adventurous — values independence and positive thinking.

L:Extremely spoiled and popular — might cheat.

W:Passionate, often surprises.

⬆Emotionally and passionately hones your abilities!!

I CAN SEE RIGHT THROUGH YOU!
GULP

◆The Language of Flowers◆

1. Morning Glory: Fleeting love, unbreakable promise, lingering attachment
2. Dandelion: Suggestive, parting, thoughtless
3. Freesia: Innocence, purity
4. Daphne: Glory, everlasting, eternal, kindness
5. Sweet Pea: Delicate, graceful, gentle memories
6. Chrysanthemum: True love, love hidden in the heart

Naruto Design Academy Gallery

Naruto and his friends can always use new clothes, gadgets, and other essential ninja accessories. Your ideas help make the world of Naruto even more interesting!

1 Naruto Gear

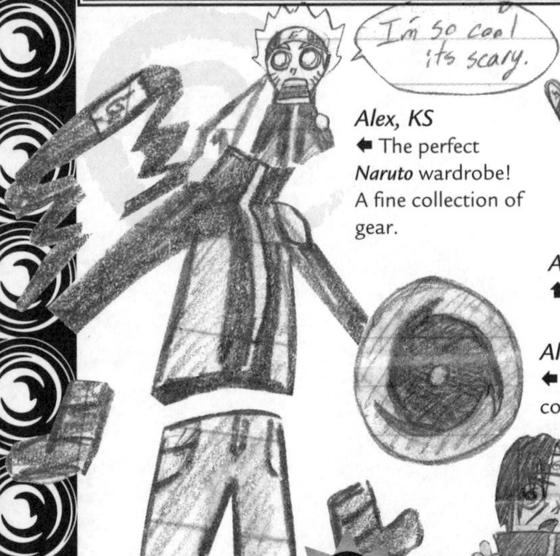
I'm so cool its scary.

Alex, KS
⬅ The perfect *Naruto* wardrobe! A fine collection of gear.

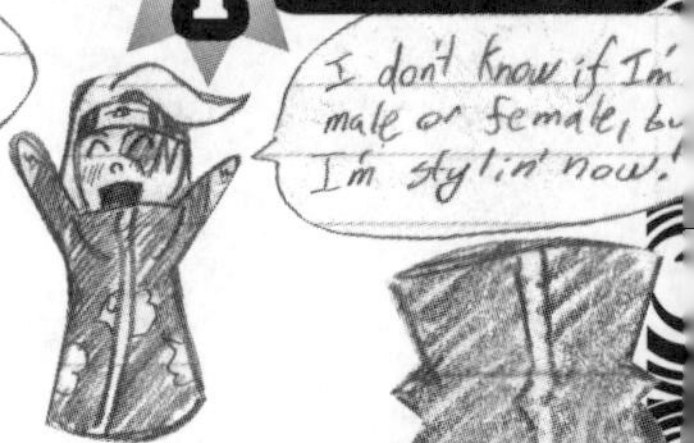
I don't know if I'm male or female, bu I'm stylin' now!

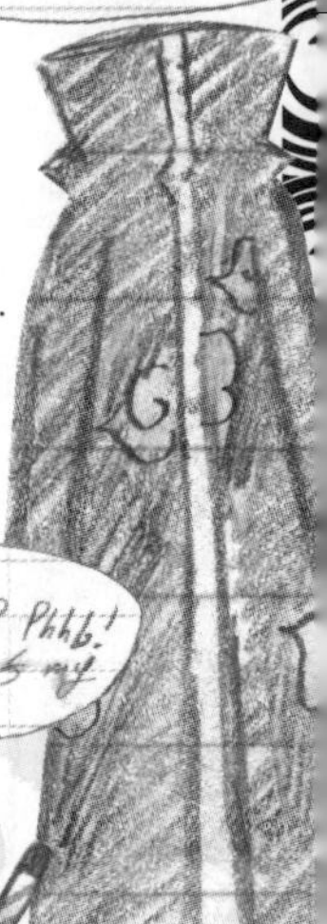

Alex, KS
⬆➡ Akatsuki robes.

Alex, KS
⬅ Mangekyo contact lenses

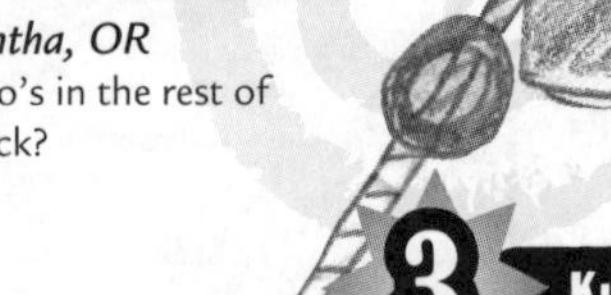
String Theory? Phhb! Get a load of my Mangekyo!

2 Naruto Playing Cards

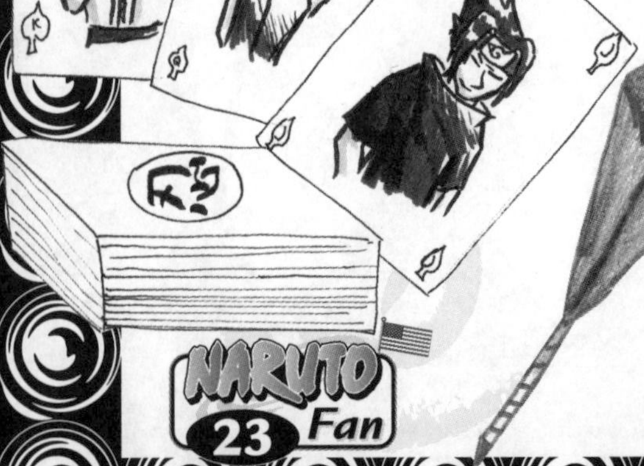

Samantha, OR
⬅ Who's in the rest of the deck?

3 Kunai Pen

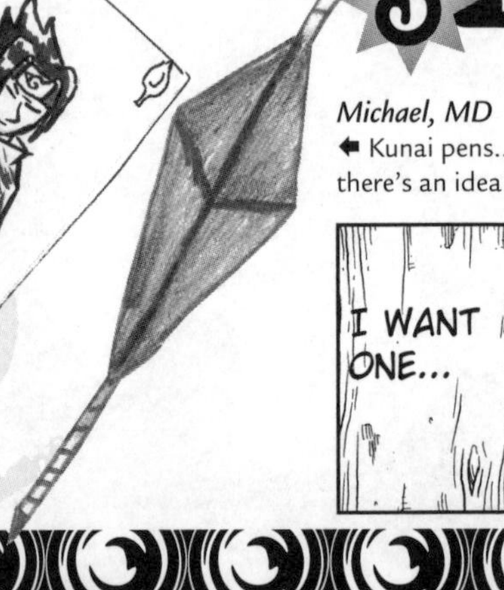

Michael, MD
⬅ Kunai pens...now there's an idea!

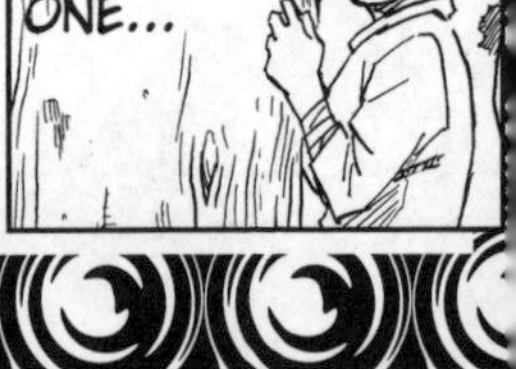
I WANT ONE...

Fan Costume Play Gallery

We know Naruto fans like to dress up as their favorite characters from the manga, and we love to see the awesome costumes you've put together! It's even more fun to show everyone all the hard work and skill you've put into your creations. Let's see what you've done!

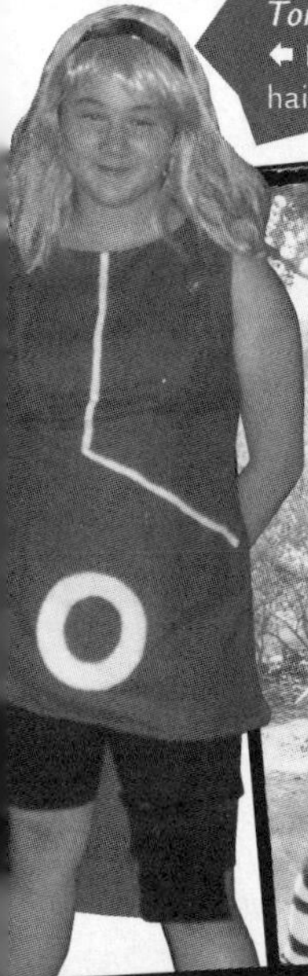

Toni, CA
⬅ Love your hair, Sakura!

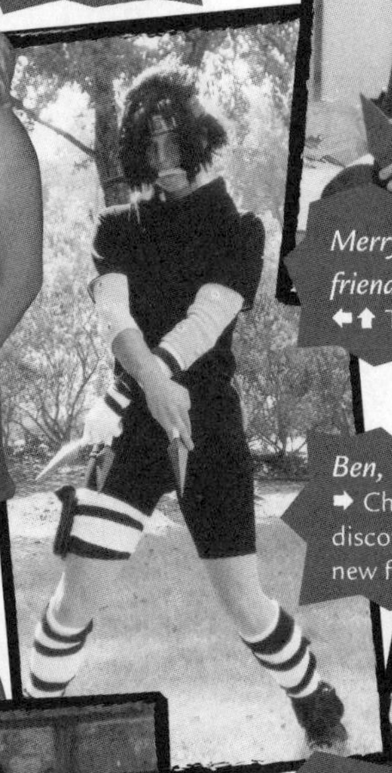

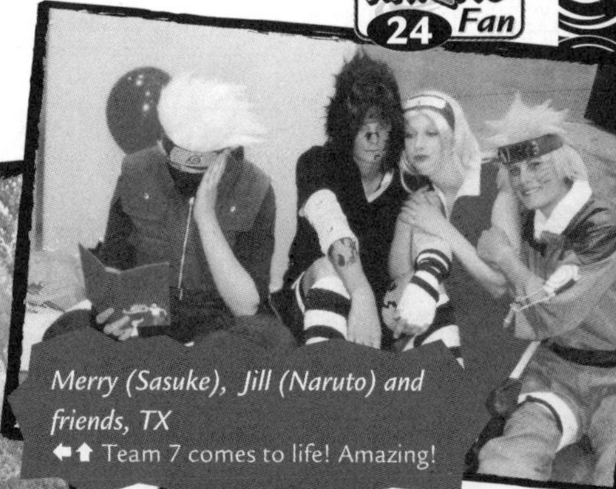

Merry (Sasuke), Jill (Naruto) and friends, TX
⬅⬆ Team 7 comes to life! Amazing!

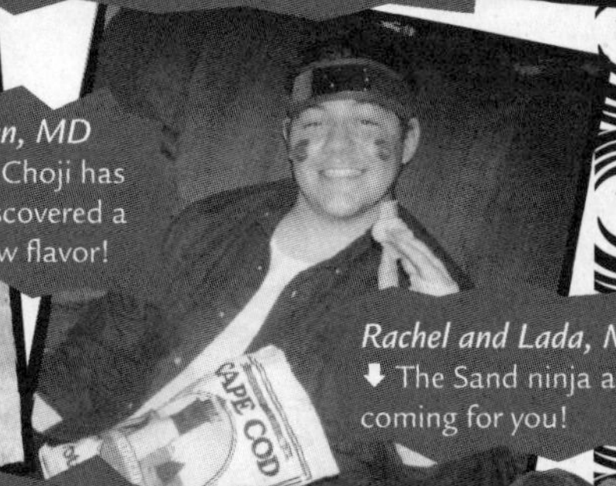
CAPE COD

Ben, MD
➡ Choji has discovered a new flavor!

Rachel and Lada, MT
⬇ The Sand ninja are coming for you!

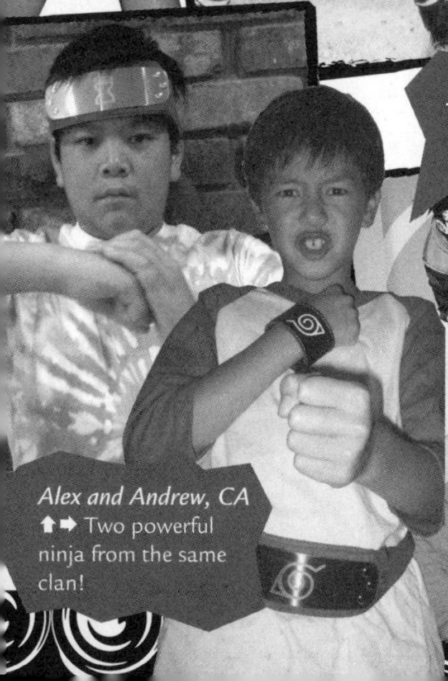

Alex and Andrew, CA
⬆➡ Two powerful ninja from the same clan!

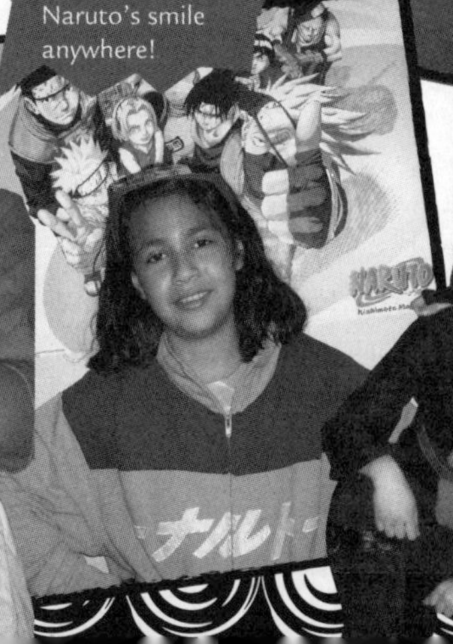
NARUTO
ナルト

Jaquelyn, IL
⬇ We'd recognize Naruto's smile anywhere!

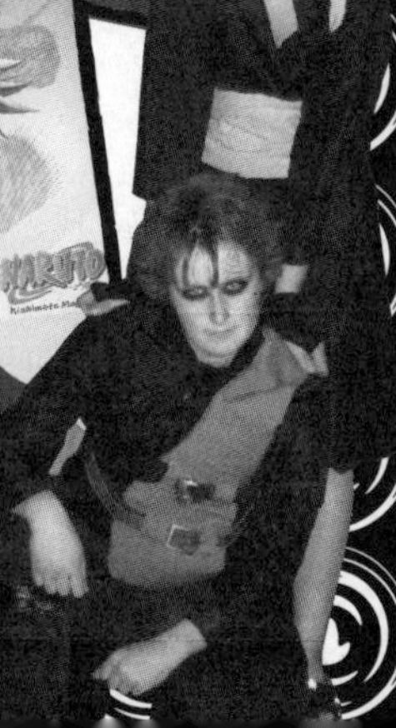

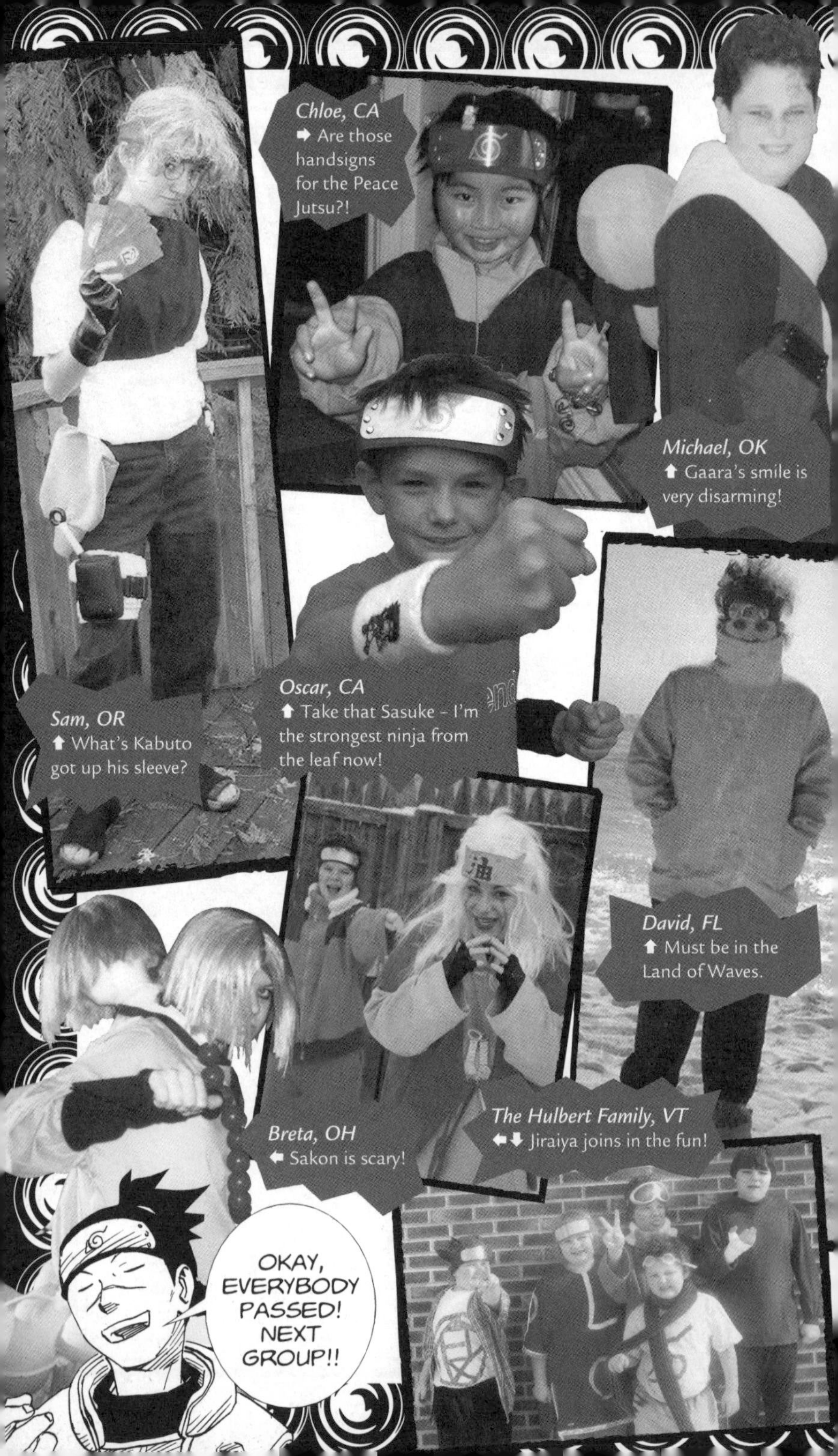
Chloe, CA
➡ Are those handsigns for the Peace Jutsu?!
Michael, OK
⬆ Gaara's smile is very disarming!
Sam, OR
⬆ What's Kabuto got up his sleeve?
Oscar, CA
⬆ Take that Sasuke – I'm the strongest ninja from the leaf now!
David, FL
⬆ Must be in the Land of Waves.
Breta, OH
⬅ Sakon is scary!
The Hulbert Family, VT
⬅⬇ Jiraiya joins in the fun!
OKAY, EVERYBODY PASSED! NEXT GROUP!!

Do it at Home!

You can look like Rock!

THE ROCK LEE CUT!!

Time for a change? Here's your ticket! Get ahead of the trend and knock-em dead now!

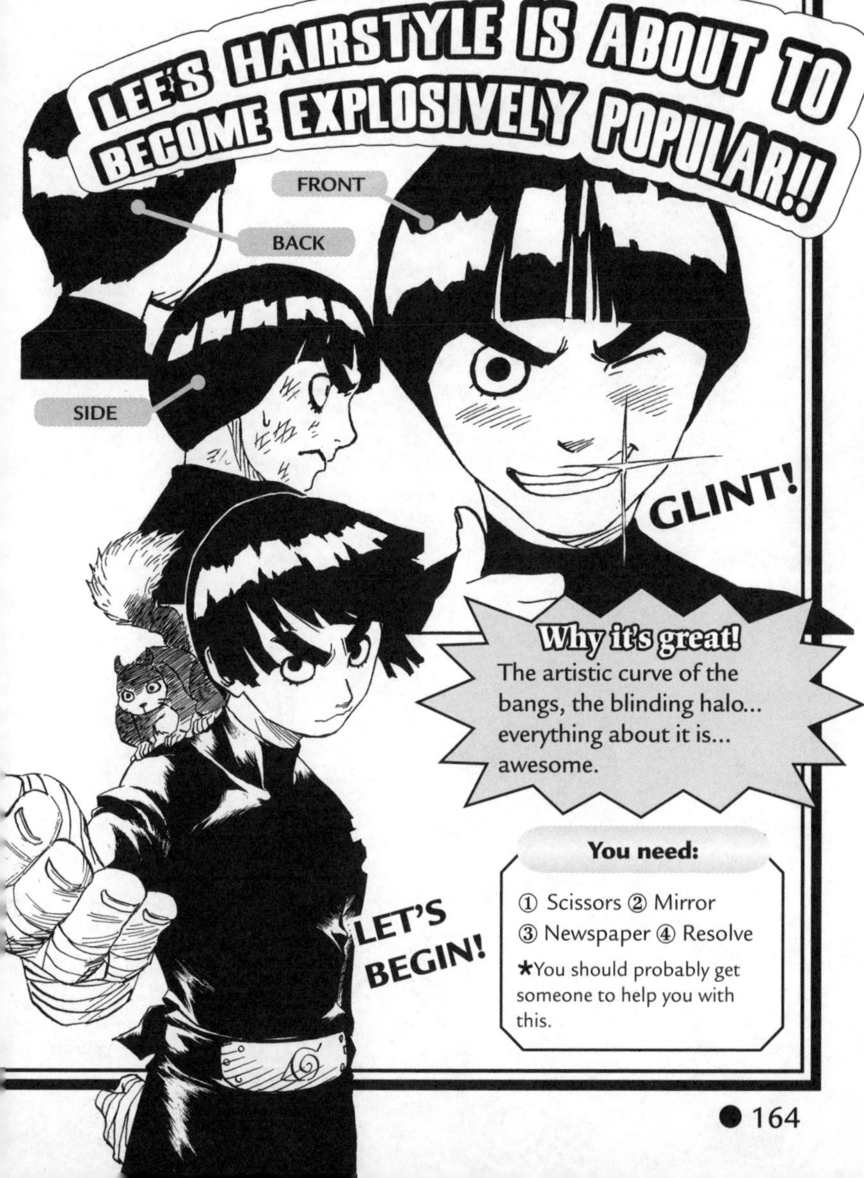

LEE'S HAIRSTYLE IS ABOUT TO BECOME EXPLOSIVELY POPULAR!!
FRONT
BACK
SIDE
GLINT!
LET'S BEGIN!

Why it's great!
The artistic curve of the bangs, the blinding halo... everything about it is... awesome.

You need:

① Scissors ② Mirror
③ Newspaper ④ Resolve

*You should probably get someone to help you with this.

The Rock Lee Cut! Forbidden Technique...open!

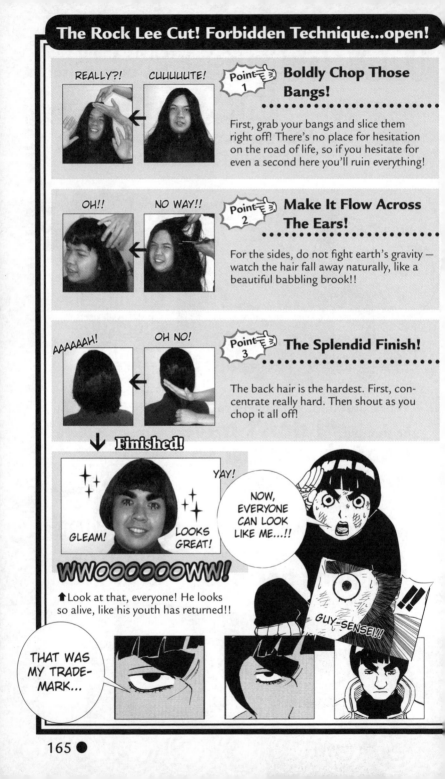

REALLY?!
CUUUUUTE!

Point 1 Boldly Chop Those Bangs!

First, grab your bangs and slice them right off! There's no place for hesitation on the road of life, so if you hesitate for even a second here you'll ruin everything!

OH!!
NO WAY!!

Point 2 Make It Flow Across The Ears!

For the sides, do not fight earth's gravity—watch the hair fall away naturally, like a beautiful babbling brook!!

AAAAAAH!
OH NO!

Point 3 The Splendid Finish!

The back hair is the hardest. First, concentrate really hard. Then shout as you chop it all off!

Finished!

YAY!
GLEAM!
LOOKS GREAT!
WWOOOOOOOWW!

⬆Look at that, everyone! He looks so alive, like his youth has returned!!

NOW, EVERYONE CAN LOOK LIKE ME...!!
!!
GUY-SENSEI!!!

THAT WAS MY TRADE-MARK...

The Rock Lee in My Class...

Tell us about the Lee in your life!

NARUTO Fan 25

From all across the country, tales of bittersweet youth!!

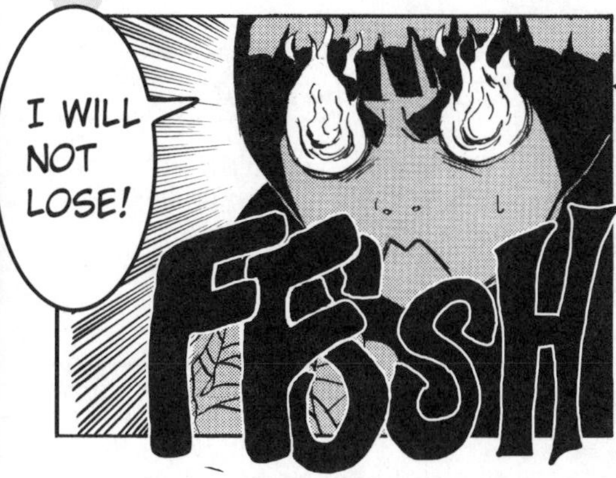
I WILL NOT LOSE!
FSSH

The Hothead Prize!

My friend from the judo club tried to break a board with his fist but broke his fist on the board. He is Rock Lee.

<福岡県> ゆるがし番傘さん

⬆ What a painful way to learn you lack calcium! The shame...

When my buddy got tired of running, he shouted, **"I don't have enough chakra to run!"** *He is Rock Lee!*

<長野県> フーポンさん

My friend had a fight with the teacher, and shouted very seriously, **"I'm going home!!!"**

<鳥取県> UCHIWAさん

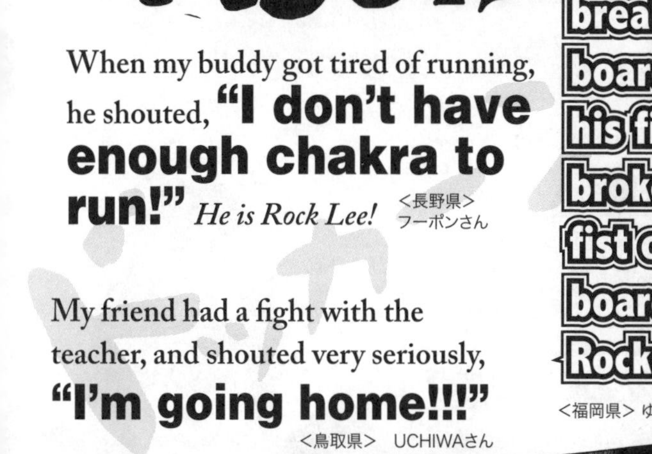
HA....SUCH POWERFUL CRIES!

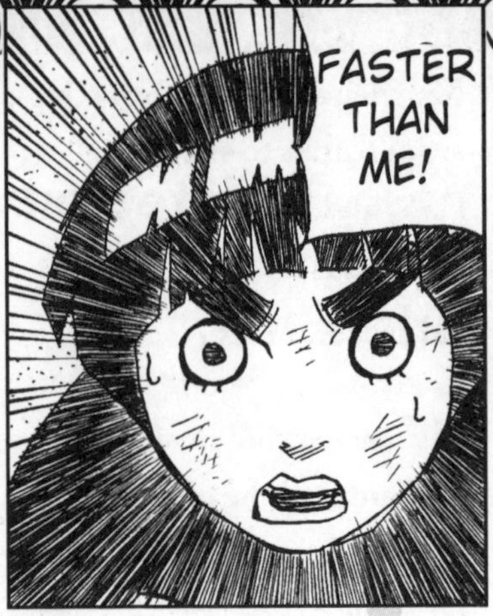
FASTER THAN ME!

My friend says you should eat instant ramen three minutes after you put the hot water in!
He is Rock Lee! <鹿児島県> 横井直哉さん

My friend, talking in his sleep, whispered sweetly, **"I won't let you sleep tonight."**
He is Rock Lee! <新潟県> マロさん

While he was running, My friend **dislocated his shoulder**.
He is Rock Lee!! <山梨県> 高橋浩さん

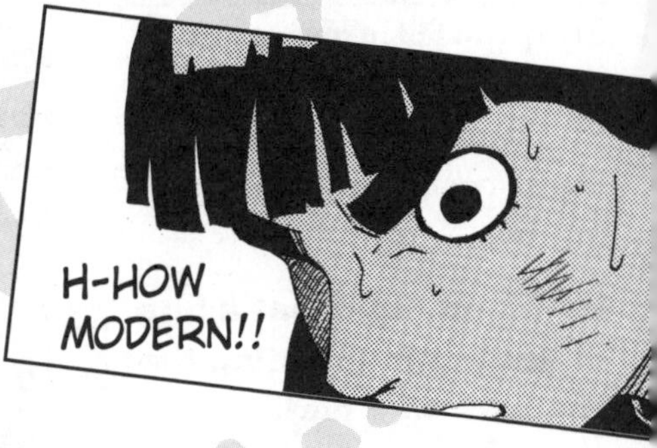
H-HOW MODERN!!

So we could all have fun on our field trip, my bud brought a game console.
He is Rock Lee! <岡山県> 鈴木了さん

I know a kid who spent the whole class sitting on an **invisible chair**.
He is Rock Lee! <鳥取県> 池田大輔さん

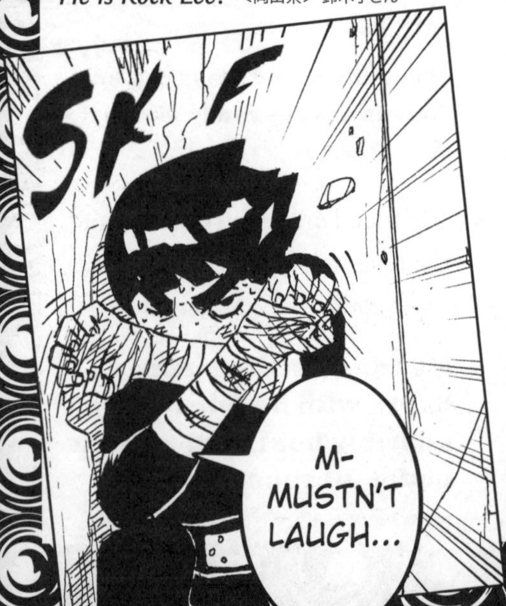
SKF
M-MUSTN'T LAUGH...

This one kid was in a milk drinking contest with the rest of the class...but he was the only one using a straw!
He is Rock Lee! <長野県> 七七・リーさん

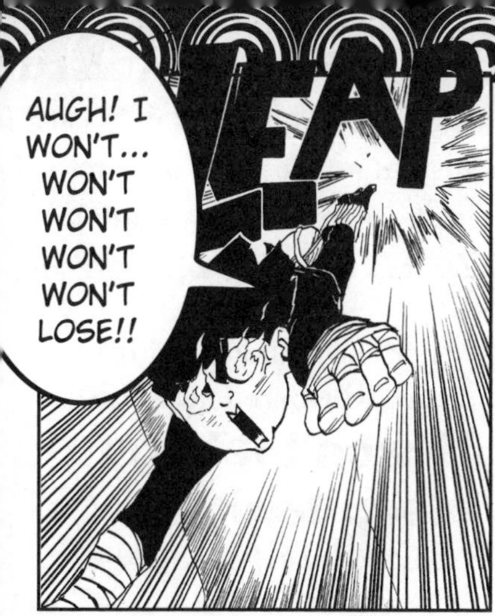
AUGH! I WON'T... WON'T WON'T WON'T WON'T LOSE!!
LEAP

My friend forgot to bring his swim trunks to swimming class, and **insisted on swimming in his briefs.** *He is Rock Lee!*
＜大阪府＞ 横ヤマンさん

My teacher told my friend to try harder, so he concentrated very hard...and farted.
He is Rock Lee! ＜広島県＞ 平本泰理さん

My friend fell in love at first sight...with the poster of Vivaldi on the music room wall.
She is Rock Lee!! ＜京都府＞ たまさん

My little sister got absolutely furious with a character in a novel.
She is Rock Lee! ＜石川県＞ 桜月津花さん

My friend didn't eat a bite of her lunch, insisting that she was on a diet.
She is Rock Lee! ＜静岡県＞ 西川彩子さん

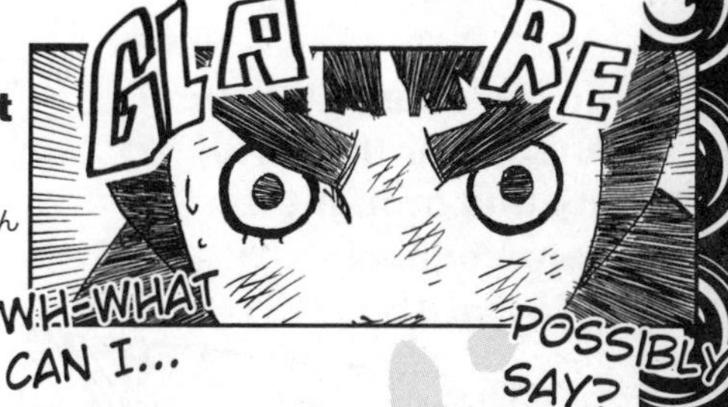
GLARE
WH-WHAT CAN I...
POSSIBLY SAY?

My friend played baseball while she had a 100 degree fever, and they won!
She is Rock Lee!
＜愛知県＞ なっピ～さん

When my friend plays tag her face is always really serious.
She is Rock Lee!! ＜福岡県＞ まきウズ・けいさん

My friend only eats spaghetti and the doctor got really mad at her.
She is Rock Lee! ＜徳島県＞ 流咲さん

My friend always starts fights with people he can't possibly beat, and loses in under 30 seconds!
He is Rock Lee! ＜沖縄県＞ 仲松大志さん

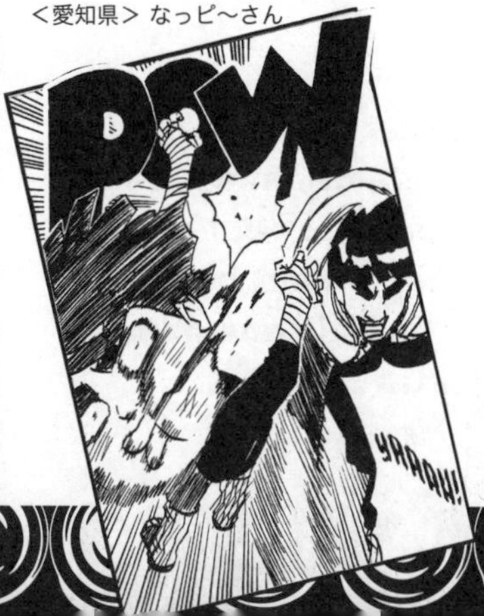
POW
YAAAAH!

FANTASTIC FAN ART

NARUTO 26 Fan

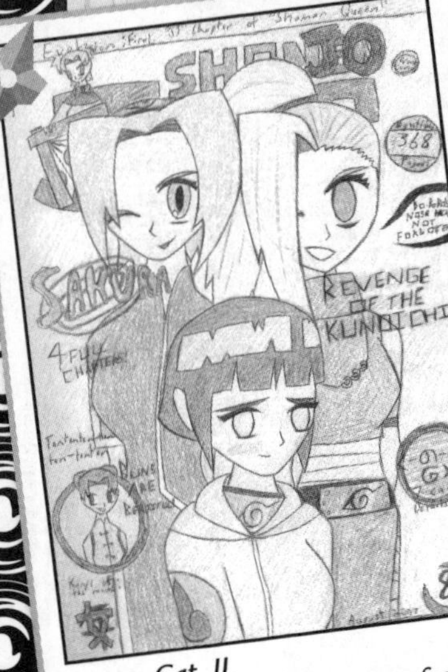
REVENGE OF THE KUNOICHI

Cat, IL
⬆ This magazine cover features powerful Kunoichi!

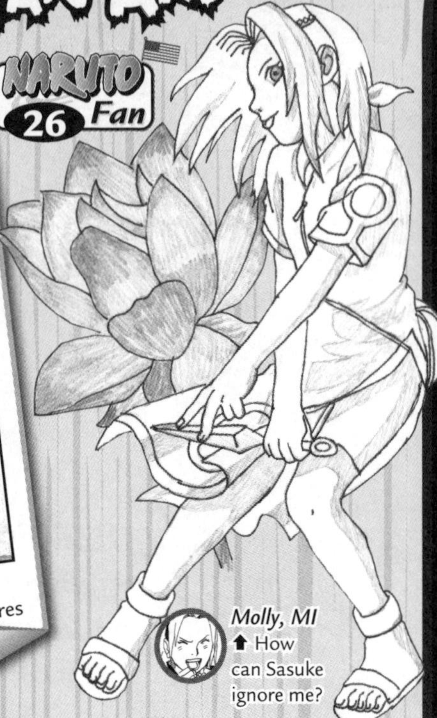

Molly, MI
⬆ How can Sasuke ignore me?

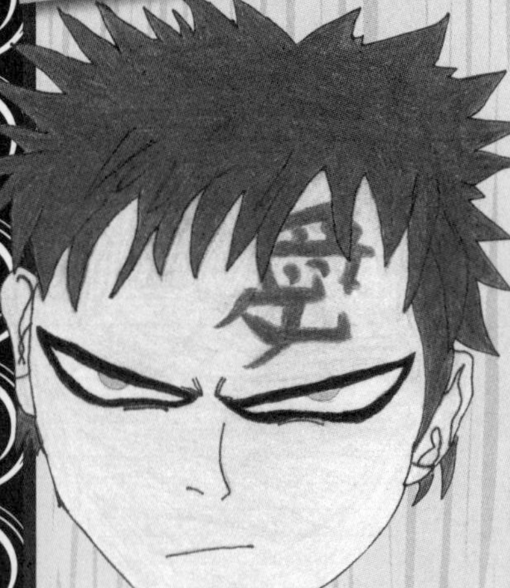
GAARA

Daniel, VA
⬆ Now that's a serious frown even for Gaara!

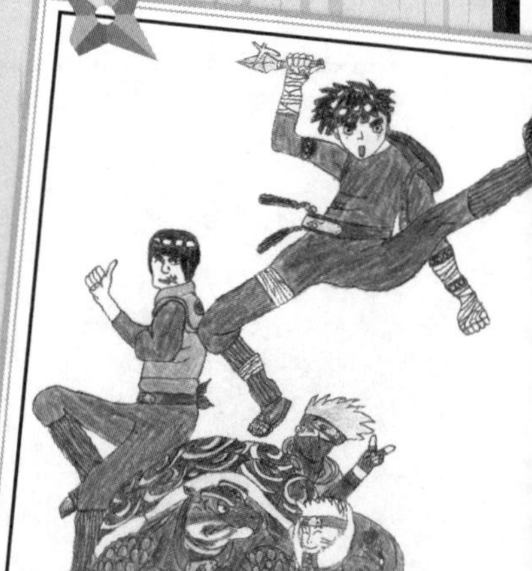

Anna-Marie, SK, Canada
⬆ We make a great team!

Naruto Around the World!!

Naruto's popularity spreads across the entire world!!

Foreign editions of Naruto!

French Edition

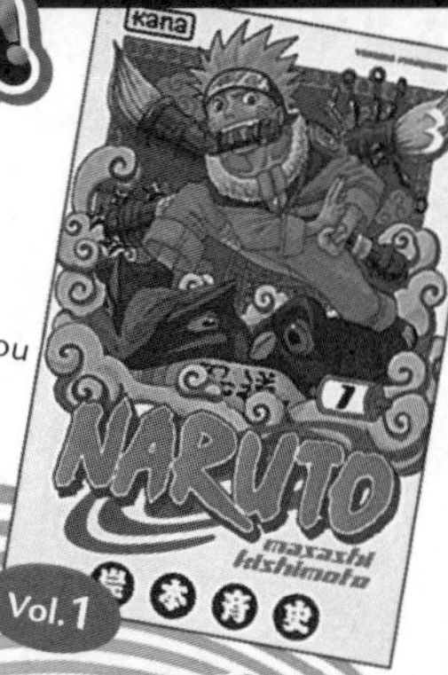
kana
NARUTO
masashi kishimoto
岸本斉史

Vol. 1

➡ Can you spot the difference from the Japanese edition?

Publisher: Dargaud

Language: French

Thai Edition

Vol. 8

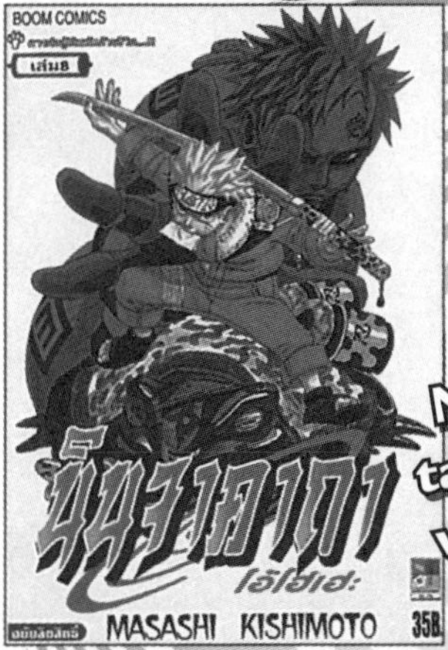
BOOM COMICS
MASASHI KISHIMOTO
35B.

Publisher: Nation Language: Thai

⬆ The title logo changes dramatically!

Naruto takes the world by storm!

Singapore Edition

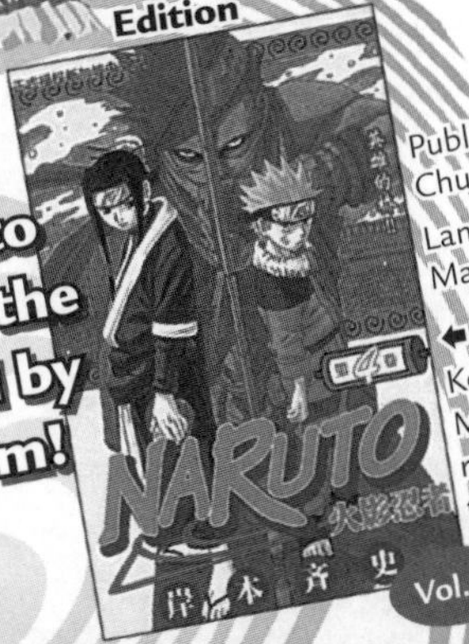
NARUTO
火影忍者
岸本斉史

Vol. 4

Publisher: Chuang Yi

Language: Mandarin

⬅ The Konoha Mark replaces the spiral

Korean Edition

Vol. 10

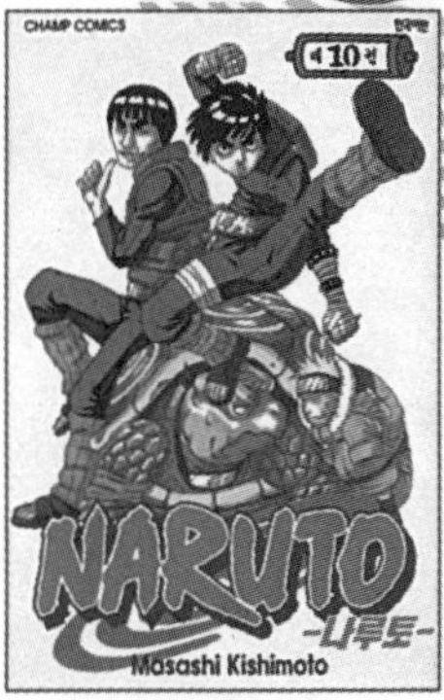
CHAMP COMICS
NARUTO
-나루토-
Masashi Kishimoto

Publisher: Daiwon

Language: Korean

⬆ Japanese manga is very popular in Korea, and it sticks close to the original.

Taiwan Edition

Vol. 2

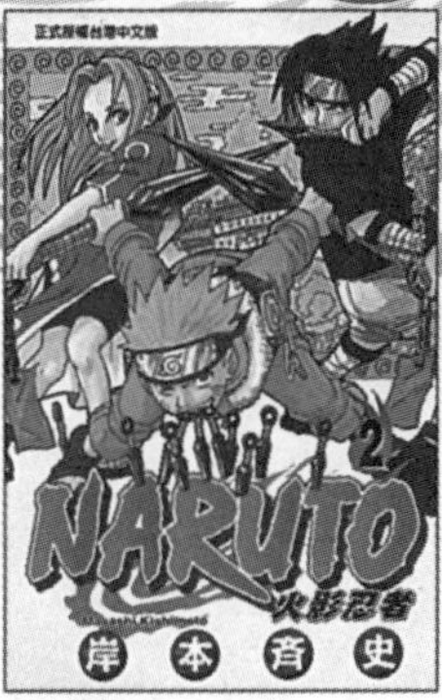
NARUTO
火影忍者
岸本斉史

Publisher: Tongli

Language: Mandarin

⬆ The spiral under the title is inventive!

Hong Kong Edition

Vol. 7

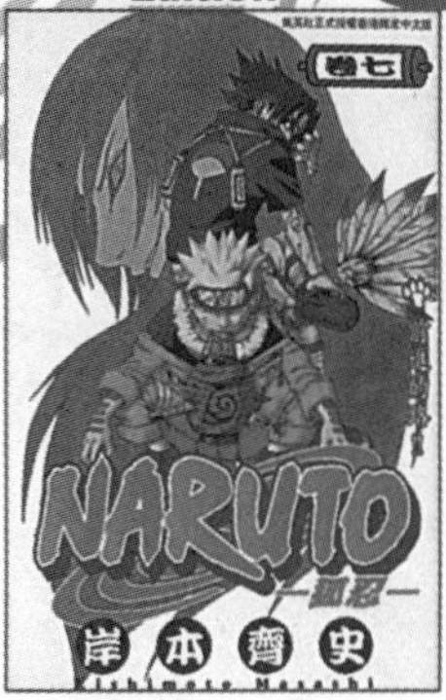
NARUTO
岸本齊史

Publisher: Rightman

Language: Cantonese

⬆ See the characters for "Fox Ninja" under the title?

Naruto Worldwide We compare!!

Art of the Shadow Doppelganger!

Japanese Edition

vol 1, page 54-55

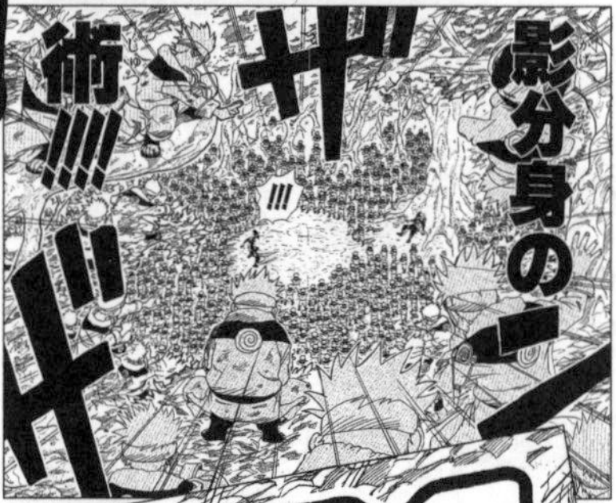
影分身の術!!!!
!!!

French Edition

⬇ Strong impact! The shape of the letters is so powerful! Even though I can't read it...multi... clonage???

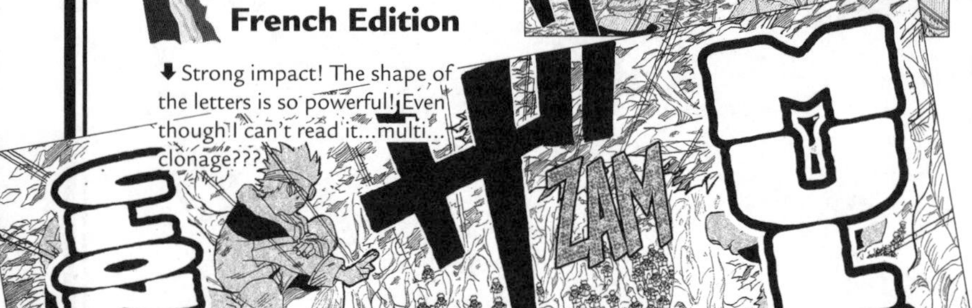
MULTI!!
CLONAGE!!
ZAM
!!!

Thai Edition

➡ The picture is backwards, like looking in a mirror! The letters are powerful as well!

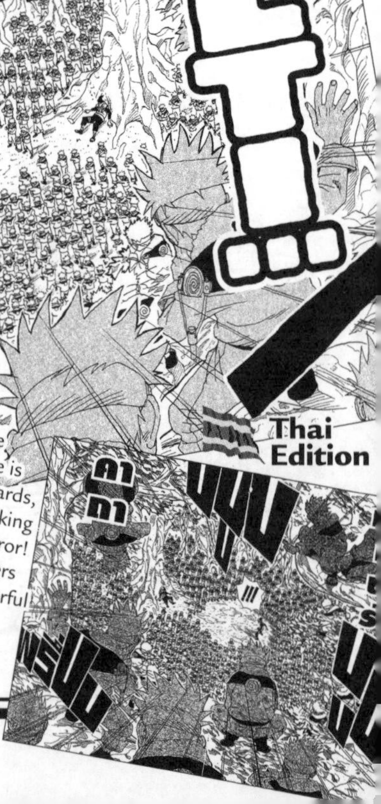

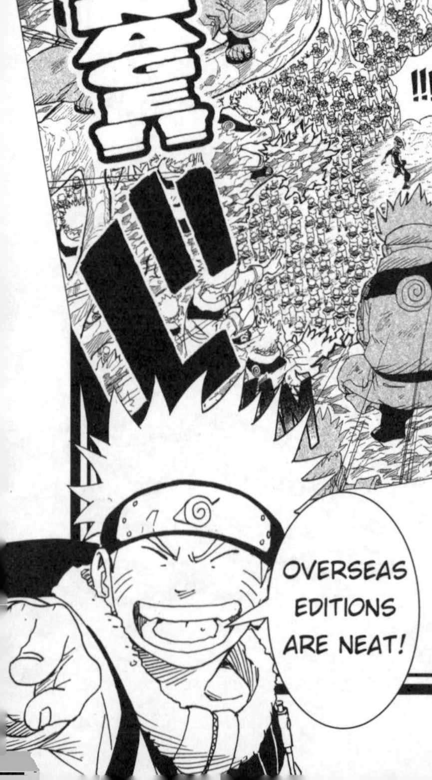
OVERSEAS EDITIONS ARE NEAT!

One Thousand Years of Death!

Hong Kong Edition

⬇ You can almost read it like Japanese. But somehow this version looks more painful…

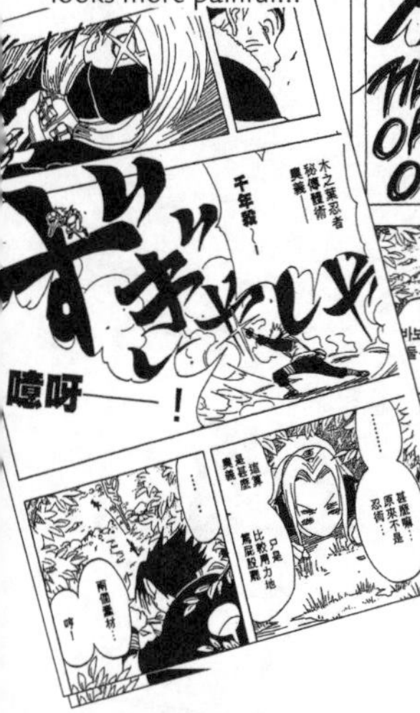
木之葉忍者秘傳體術奧義——
千年殺～
噫呀——!

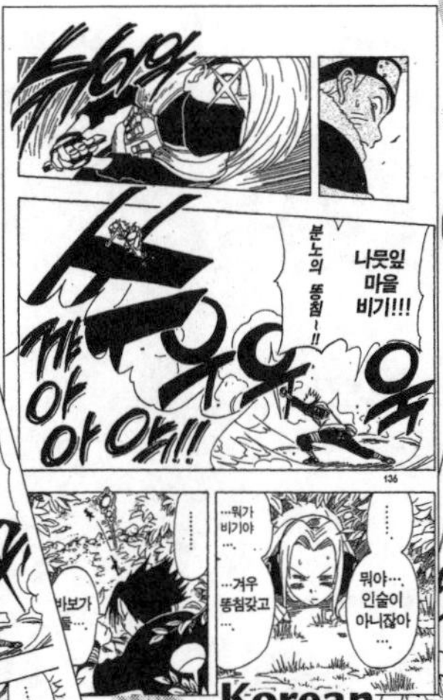
나뭇잎 마을 비기!!!
분노의 똥침~!!
캬아아아악!!
…뭐가 비기야
…겨우 똥침갖고…
뭐야… 인술이 아니잖아…
바보가…

Japanese Edition

vol 1, page 136

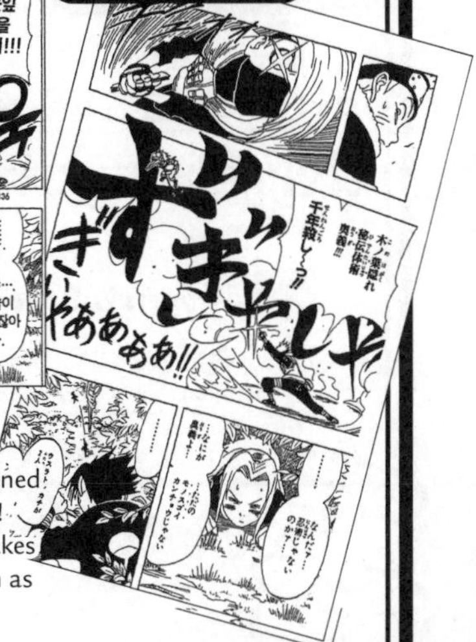
木ノ葉隠れ秘伝体術奥義!!
千年殺し～っ!!
ぎゃあああああ!!

Korean Edition

⬆ Look what happened to the sound effects! Naruto's scream makes quite the impression as well!

Make-Out Paradise!

The feature you've all been waiting for — the foreign versions of *Make-Out*! Enjoy these covers at your leisure!

Thailand

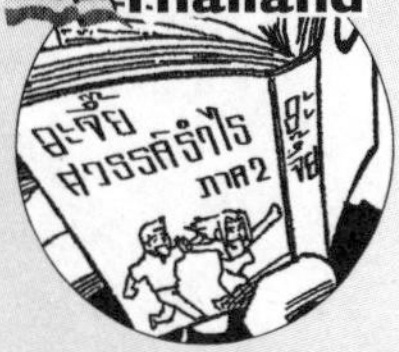

Hong Kong

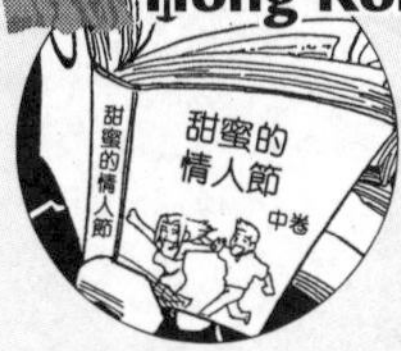
甜蜜的情人節
中卷

France

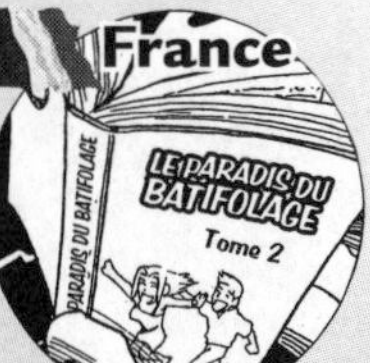
LE PARADIS DU BATIFOLAGE
Tome 2

Korea

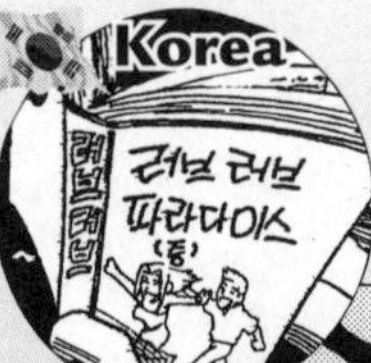
러브 러브 파라다이스

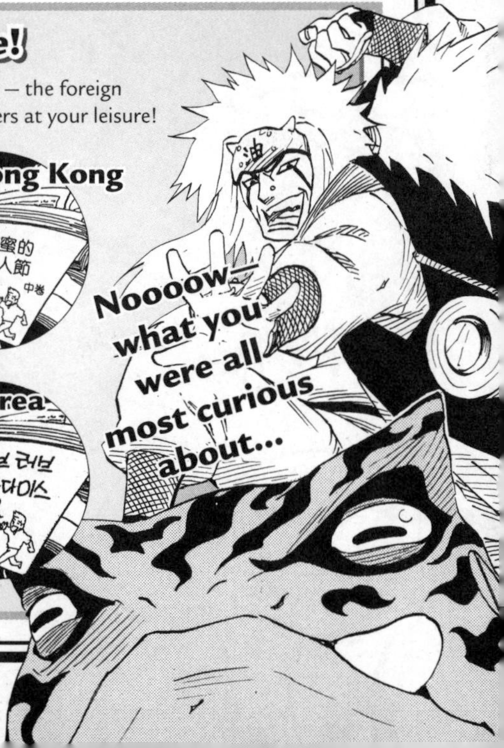
Nooooow— what you were all most curious about…

French Edition

Korean Edition

NA-RU-TO...

나루토

⬆️➡️ By simply changing the letters, the shop becomes a sidewalk café in France, and a BBQ shop in Korea...obviously not.

Inner Sakura

⬇️ Inner Sakura has become a worldwide phenomenon...which country's inner Sakura do you like?

French Edition	Hong Kong Edition	Korean Edition	Thai Edition

YEAH!!

看我的！

Foreign editions of the magazine are also huge!

American Edition

SHONEN JUMP

Taiwanese Edition

FORMOSA YOUTH

➡️ Naruto is the most popular title in the Taiwanese magazine!

⬆️ Naruto is serialized here too! Nothing can stop it!!

TAKE A LOOK IF YOU GET THE CHANCE!

Unless you can discover the truth, all the gates will not open!

4th GATE

Hyuga Neji's Frightening Kekkei Genkai Ability!

BYAKUGAN!! CHAKRA LINE MAZE!!

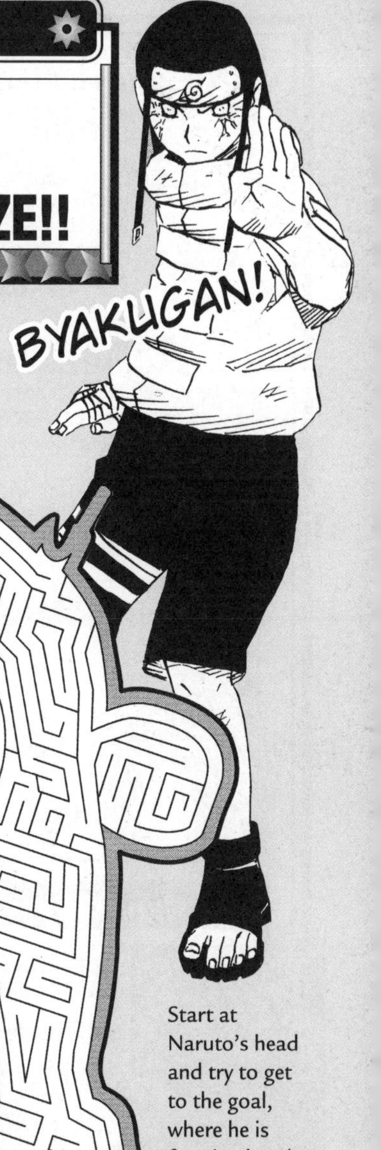
BYAKUGAN!

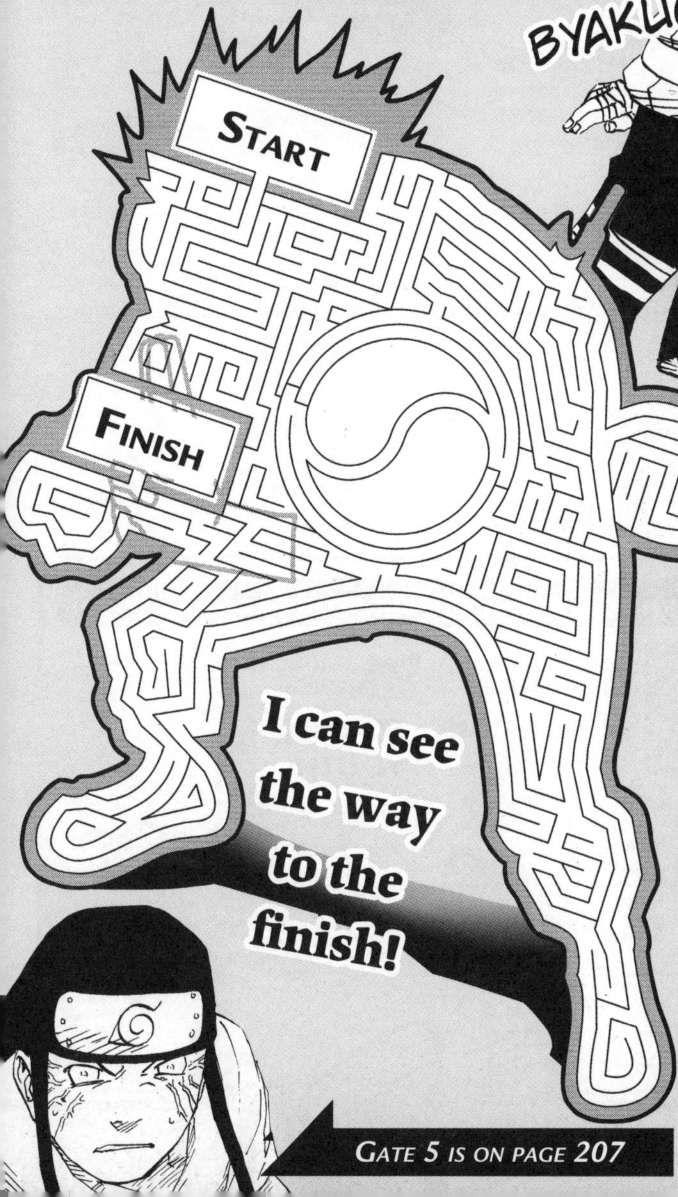
START
FINISH
I can see the way to the finish!

Start at Naruto's head and try to get to the goal, where he is forming hand signs. Use the famous Hyuga Byakugan to pick out the correct lines of chakra flow!

GATE 5 IS ON PAGE 207

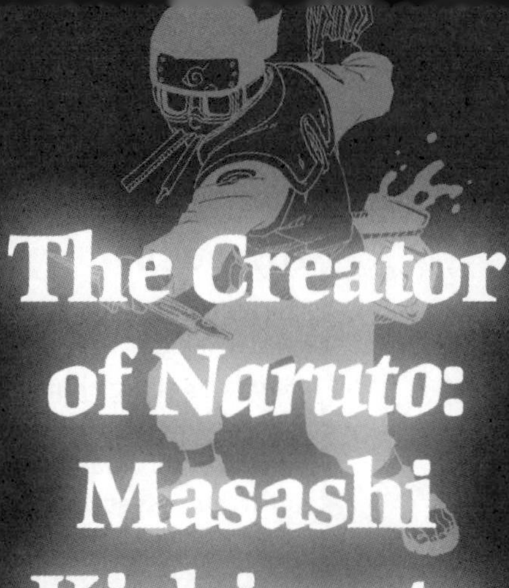

The Creator of *Naruto*: Masashi Kishimoto

The mastermind behind *Naruto*...

Everything you always wanted to know about Kishimoto-sensei – now revealed!

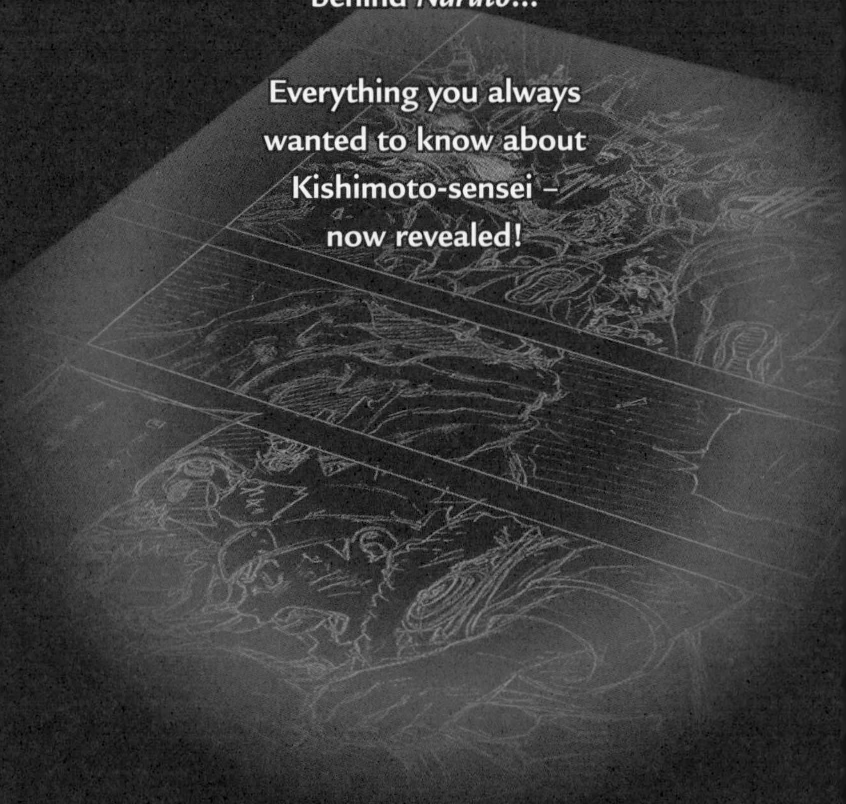

Team 7 Special Mission Report

Infiltration! Masashi Kishimoto's Castle

Searching for the impenetrable fortress!

The lights never go off in Kishimoto-sensei's office, where pages are churned out every day...Naruto's team infiltrates this mansion, unearthing its secrets!!

First Report

The assistants' desks are covered in toys!

From bottle caps to expensive models, the desks are brimming with action figures! Kishimoto-sensei declares, "They come in handy when drawing people."

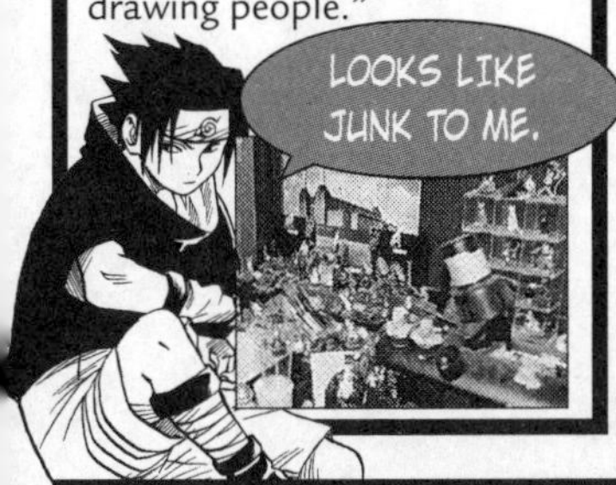
LOOKS LIKE JUNK TO ME.

Second Report

Piles of treasures surround Sensei's desk!

Sensei's desk is surrounded by what he refers to as his "treasures." They all give him power!

Presents from fans

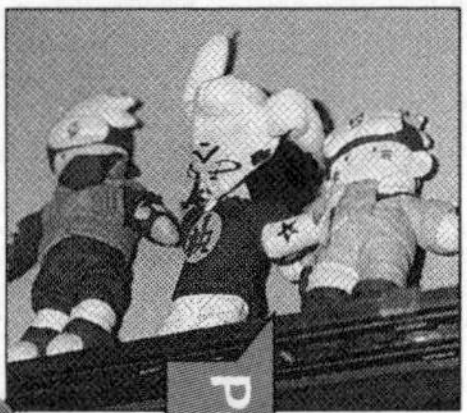

➡ Stuffed dolls made from felt. So cute!

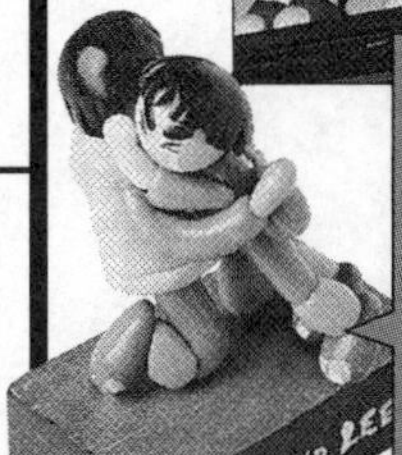
GAI AND LEE

⬅ Guy and Lee, made from papier-mâché! Amazing!

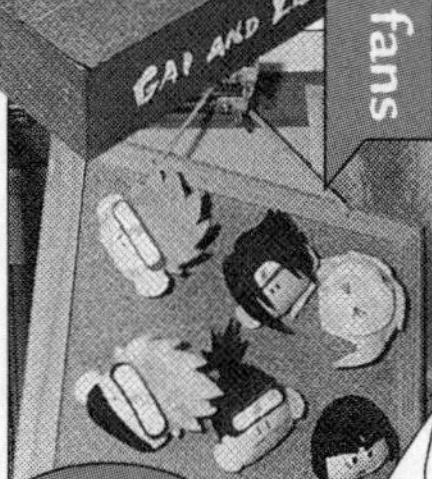

⬅ Stuffed faces: perfectly capturing the essence of each character!!

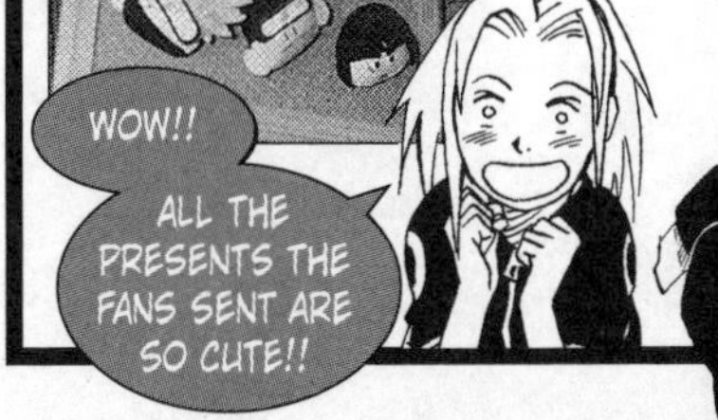
WOW!!
ALL THE PRESENTS THE FANS SENT ARE SO CUTE!!

Naruto design sheets drawn by Sensei's favorite animators

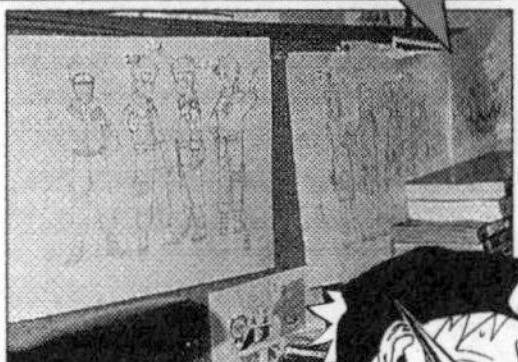

⬆ Drawn by the anime character designer, Tetsuya Nishio.

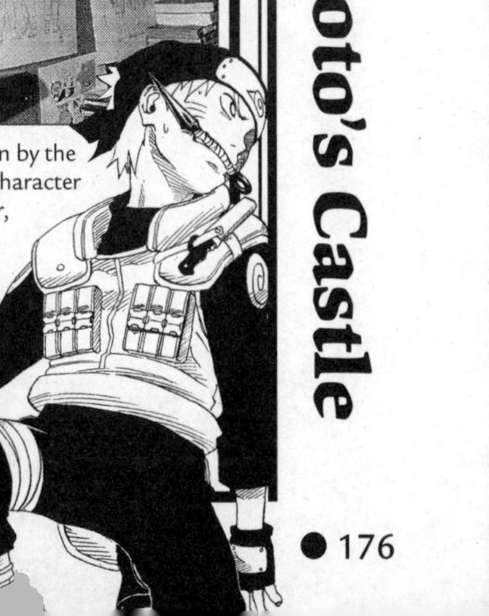

Third Report

Aiiee!! Ukki was supposed to be dead!

Sensei let it wither away... is it a ghost? No! A fan sent him a replacement!

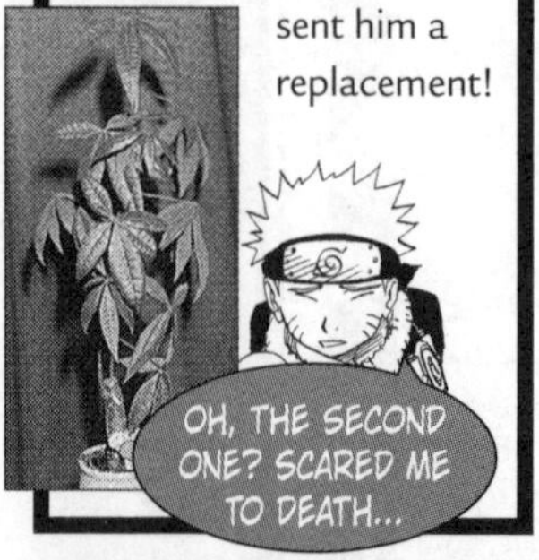
OH, THE SECOND ONE? SCARED ME TO DEATH...

Map of Kishimoto-sensei's work rooms

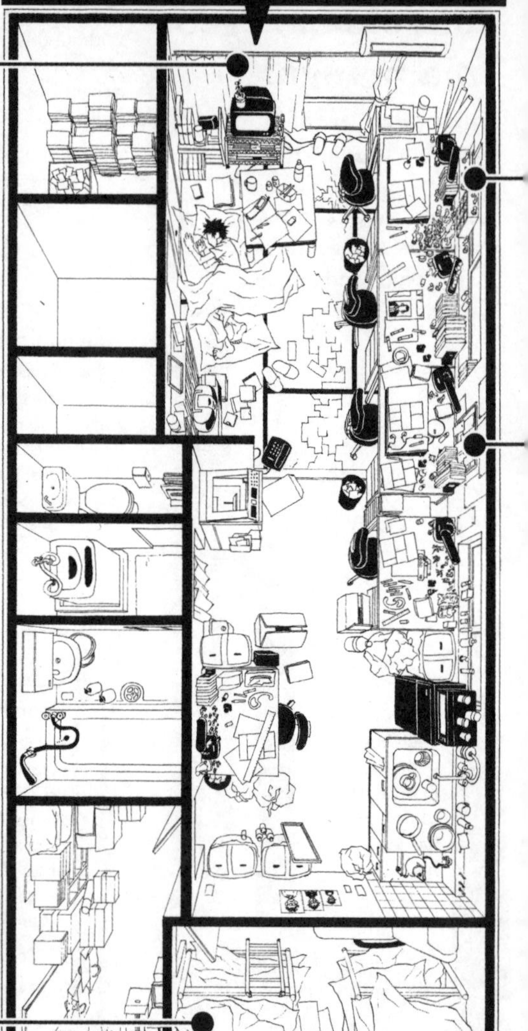

Fourth Report

The assistants' nap room is Naruto's world!?

This room is for assistants who need to sleep over...and is filled with items Kakashi-sensei would love!!

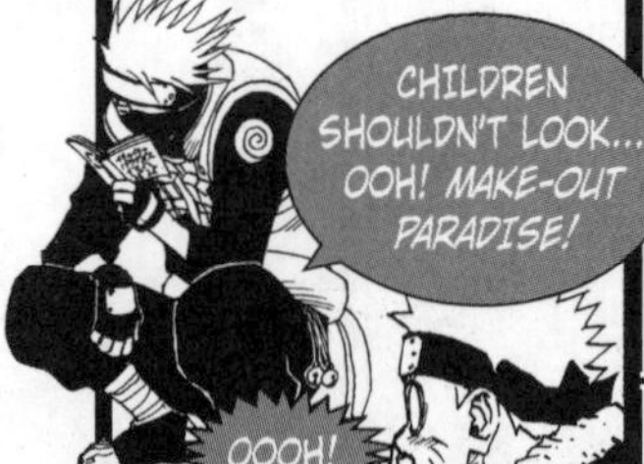
CHILDREN SHOULDN'T LOOK... OOH! MAKE-OUT PARADISE!
OOOH!

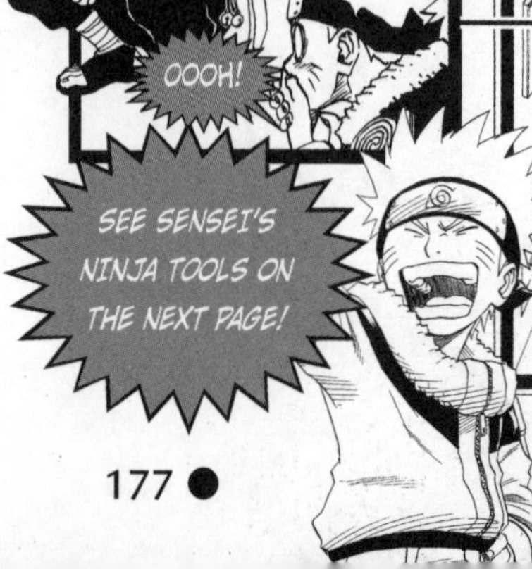
SEE SENSEI'S NINJA TOOLS ON THE NEXT PAGE!

Kishimoto-sensei's Soul!

Special Display: Beloved Tools

All the tools used to create his gem of a manga!

These tools have all suffered with him through rain, wind, and thunder! Stained with Sensei's sweat and tears, they have all become a part of him and are all on display here!

First Tool

Manuscript Paper

Without this, nothing can be drawn! He uses a slightly heavier paper called IC 135g.

Second Tool

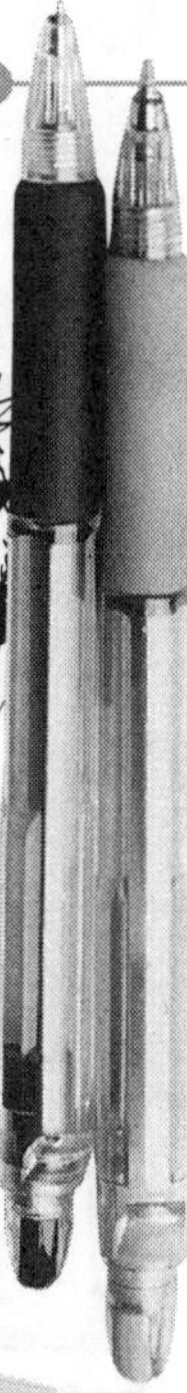

Mechanical Pencil

When sketching in the rough versions of the page, nothing is better! They're just ordinary mechanical pencils, sold anywhere! Sensei uses both B and HB lead.

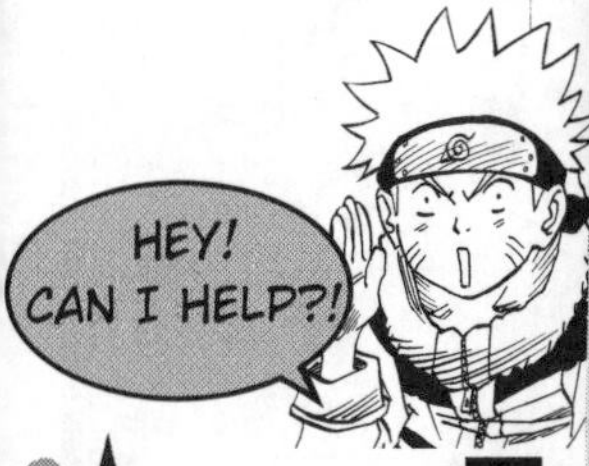
HEY!
CAN I HELP?!

Third Tool

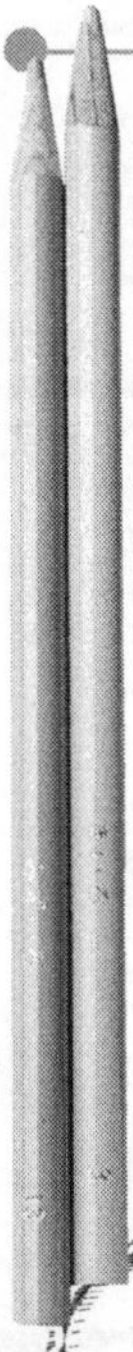

Colored Pencils

For writing instructions to his assistants after the roughs are done. Color helps draw attention to the differences between figures and backgrounds!

Fourth Tool

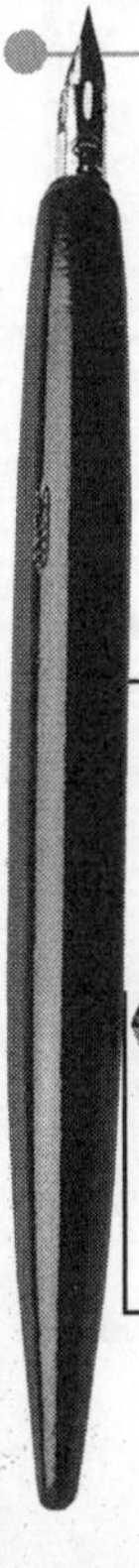

G pen

Draws all the main lines — the life of the manga! The same pen Sensei has used since his debut.

Related item

⬇ The G pen is used so often, he goes through one nib a page.

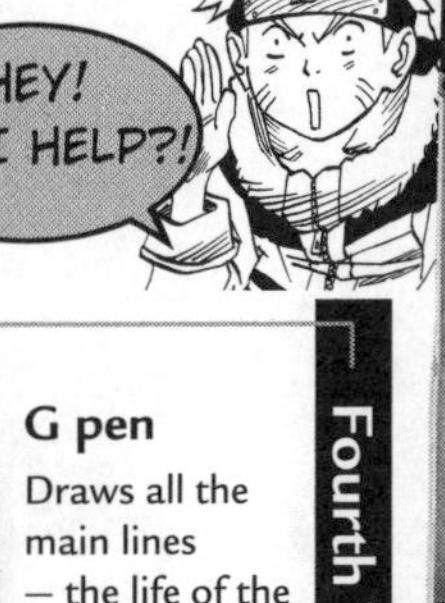

Nibs

➡ Touch this to the nib, and the ink flows smoothly.

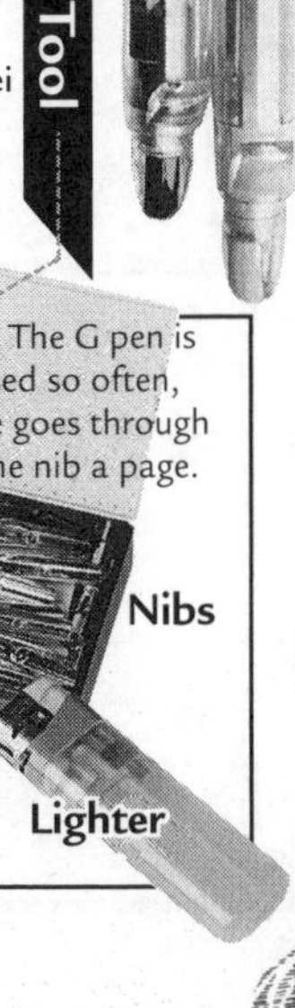

Lighter

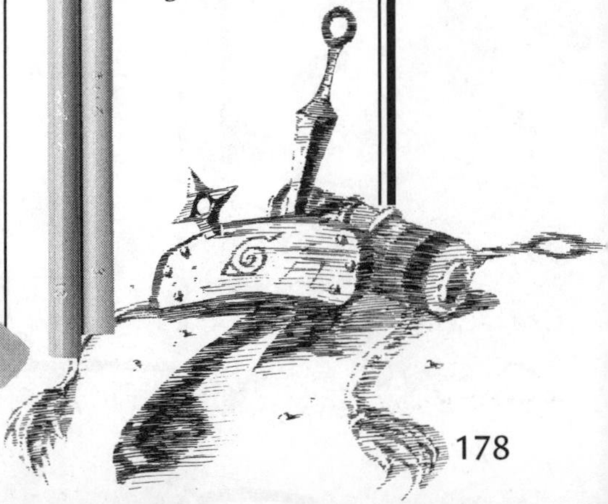

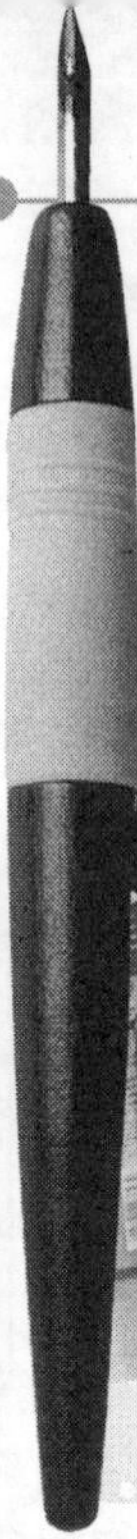

Round Pen

Produces a slightly finer line than the G pen; often used for drawing characters in the background, or detail work.

Fifth Tool

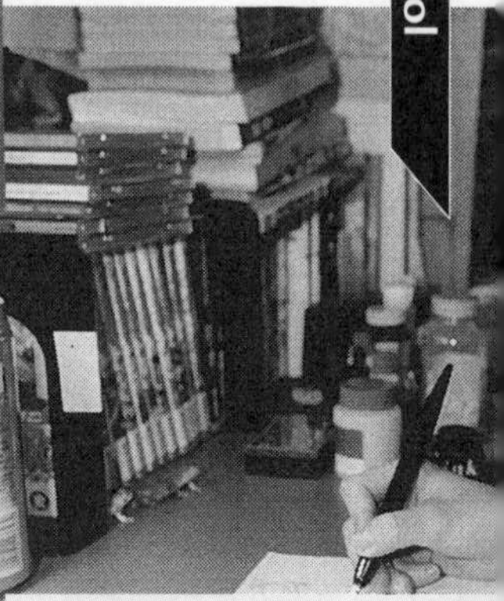

Sensei hard at wo
using his beloved
ninja tools!

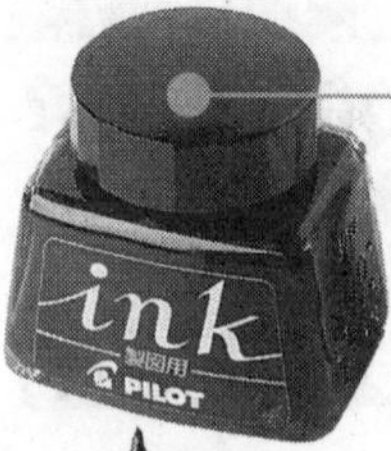
ink
PILOT

Ink (Pilot Drafting)

Required for use with the G pen and round pen! Sensei has used the same kind of ink for years.

Sixth Tool

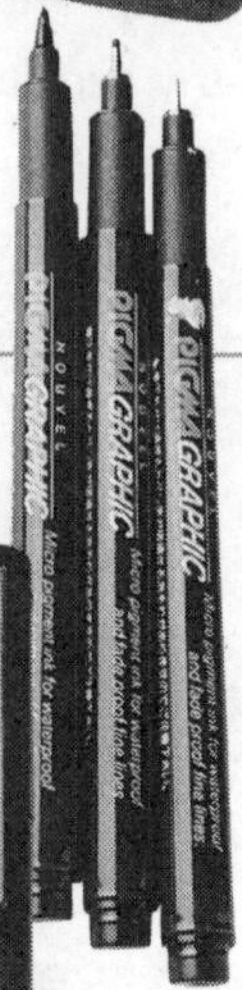
PIGMA GRAPHIC
PIGMA GRAPHIC
PIGMA GRAPHIC

Milli pen

(.05mm/.1mm/.8mm)

Produces very, very fine lines, used for the finishing touches. Three types and sizes, each with their own uses.

Seventh Tool

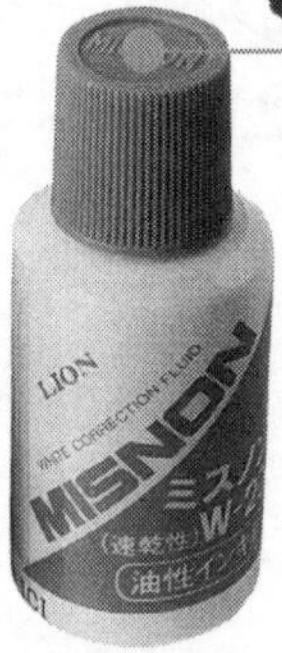
LION
MISNON

Correction fluid (Misnon, for oil-based inks)

Used to erase stray lines. Very delicate work, so he uses a brush instead of a correction pen!

Eighth Tool

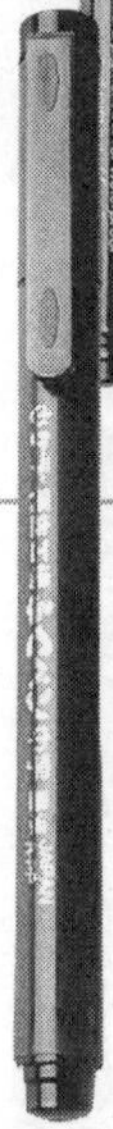

Brush

Used to fill in large areas. These days, this type of work is almost entirely done by his assistants, so he doesn't use it often.

Ninth Tool

Utility Knife

Used to trim screentone into the correct shape.

Tenth Tool

Refillable Marker

Used for color pages — 288 different colors, and he's used them all!

Eleventh Tool

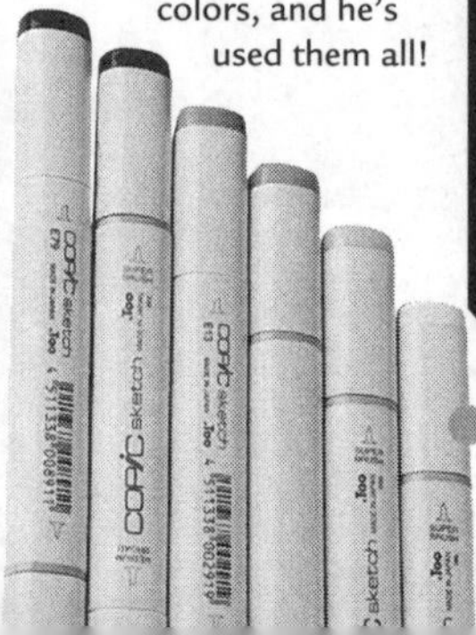
COPIC sketch
COPIC sketch

Vitamins and Eyedrops!!

The best friend of any artist?! Sensei takes his vitamins daily and uses eyedrops when he gets sleepy!!

Twelfth Tool

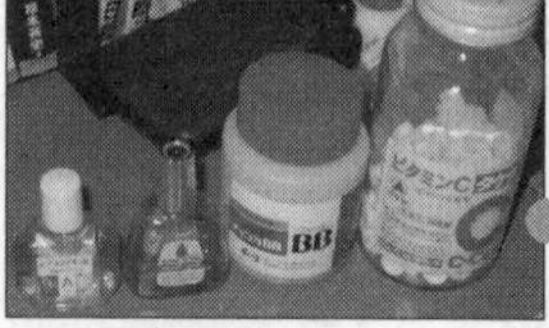

Q&A with Kishimoto-sensei!

Opinions? Questions? Anything goes!

Questions and opinions from many readers, answered by the sensei himself!

Opinion Box !

I really hope Rock Lee recovers!!

＜福岡県＞ モンチャックさん

Lee has not yet achieved his goal. I'm sure he won't give up yet.

Can you at least give us a hint what the remaining member of the Three Great Shinobi is like!?

＜大分県＞ 加藤雄基さん

By the time this book comes out, she may have shown up already. Hint? She's a woman!

I want to know more about the Uchiha tragedy, and about Itachi. Please tell us someday!

＜千葉県＞ くないヒサトさん

This may also have happened by the time this fanbook is published. Either way, I promise to tell the whole story! Look forward to it!

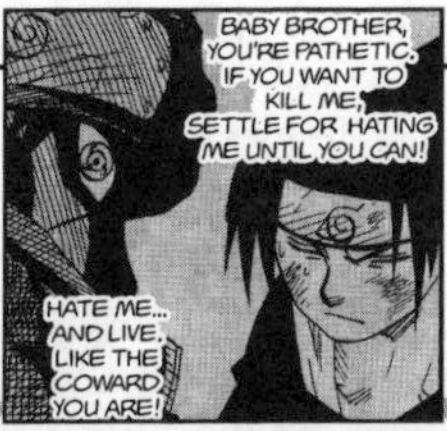
BABY BROTHER, YOU'RE PATHETIC. IF YOU WANT TO KILL ME, SETTLE FOR HATING ME UNTIL YOU CAN!
HATE ME... AND LIVE... LIKE THE COWARD YOU ARE!

⬅ The blood-stained tale of the Uchiha Clan will soon be told.

I'm a senior in high school. My grades are terrible – 41st out of the 43 people in my class...just like someone else I know. Please help!

＜千葉県＞ 田舎上等♥さん

I understand...I know just how you feel. But do not lose hope! Keep fighting!

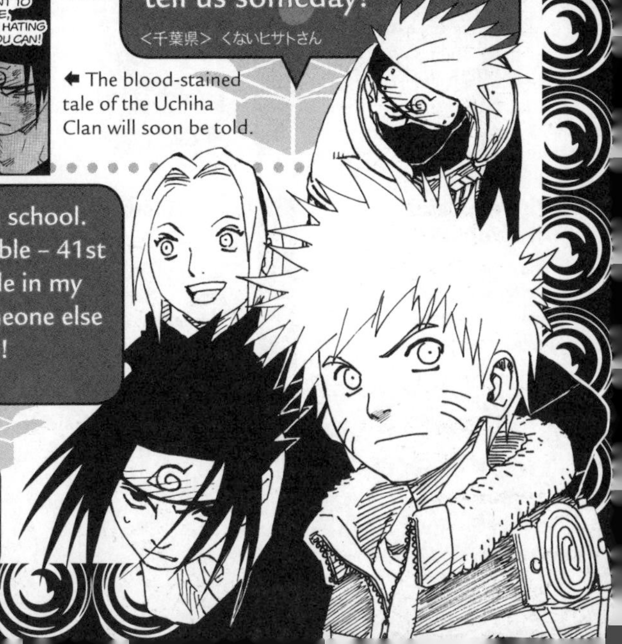

Question Box ?

When you take a week off to collect reference material, where do you go?

<東京都> 葉蕾煌さん

Mountains, temples, towns. The look of Naruto is collected from all over.

The idea of protecting people important to you shows up in *Naruto* a lot, but who is important to you?

<神奈川県> 村田歩さん

Everyone around me. Including the fans who support me!

Why do animals let themselves be summoned by Kuchiyose?

<大坂府> 亀谷良介さん

That's a tough one. Maybe they just crave human contact (even at the risk of their lives?) Or do they get fed? I wish I knew.

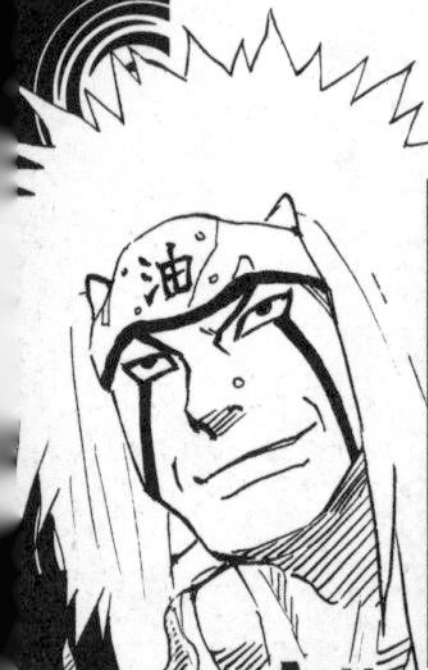
油

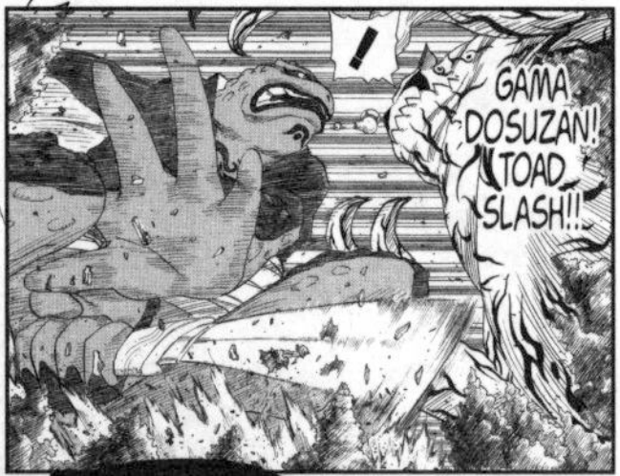
!
GAMA DOSUZAN! TOAD SLASH!!

⬇ The mysteries of the Kuchiyose animals — even Kishimoto does not know. We leave it to your imaginations!

Now that the Chûnin Selection Exams are finished, will the supporting cast stop showing up?

<茨城県> 國田恵美さん

I like all the characters and plan to keep using them!!

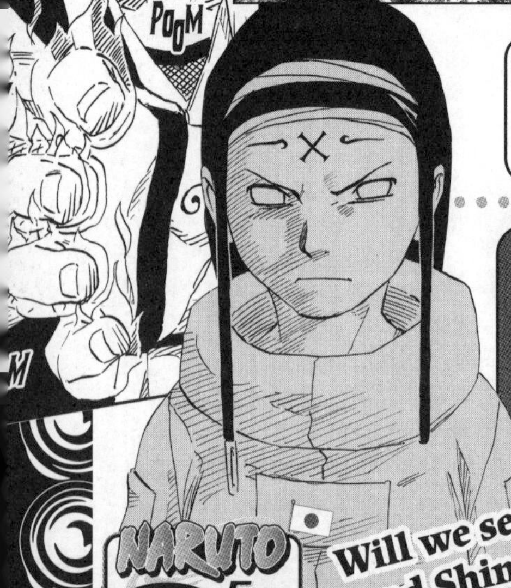
POOM

Will we see Neji and Shino and Gaara again?!

Get assigned to the right missions for you!
Now you can take the top secret exam!

Personality profiles help missions succeed!

Ninja Psychology Test!

Problems

1 Preparation

You are a Konoha ninja. Your mission: to retrieve secret documents stolen by the daimyo of another country. What do you take with you?

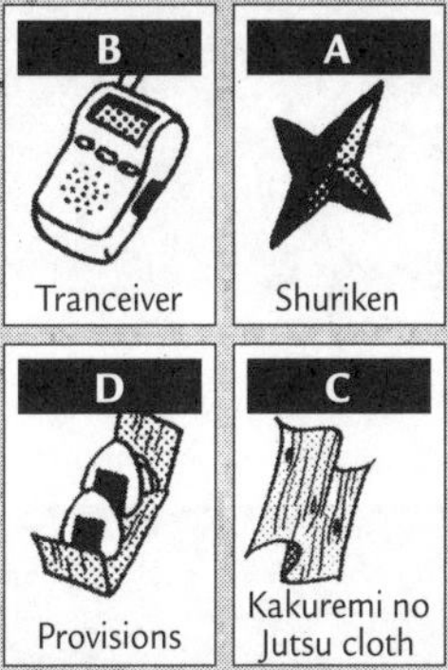

A Shuriken
B Tranceiver
C Kakuremi no Jutsu cloth
D Provisions

2 Confirmation

You reach the daimyo's mansion and see his face through binoculars... Draw this sinister man's eyes!

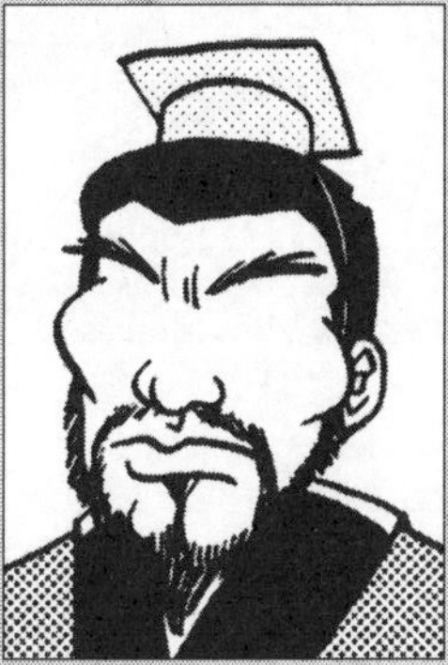

3 Action

You sneak into the storeroom in the corner of the daimyo's mansion and find three big boxes. The secret documents are in one of these. Which one is it?

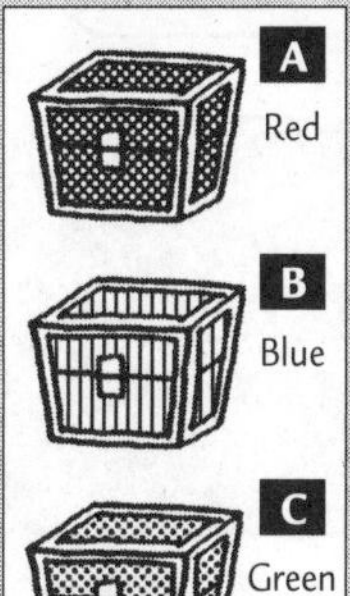

A Red
B Blue
C Green

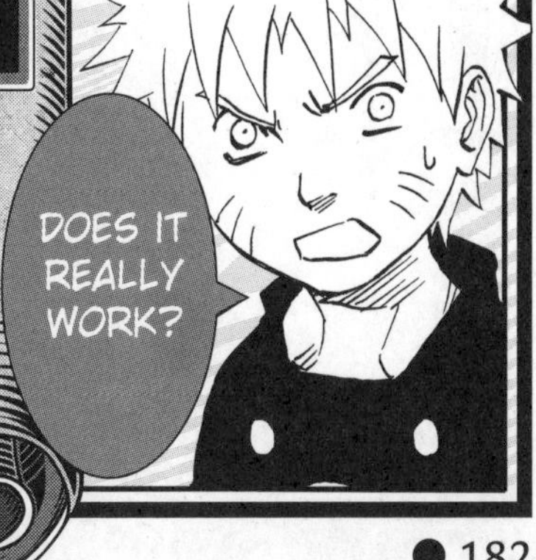

DOES IT REALLY WORK?

Problem Creation Assistance: Yoshie Watanabe

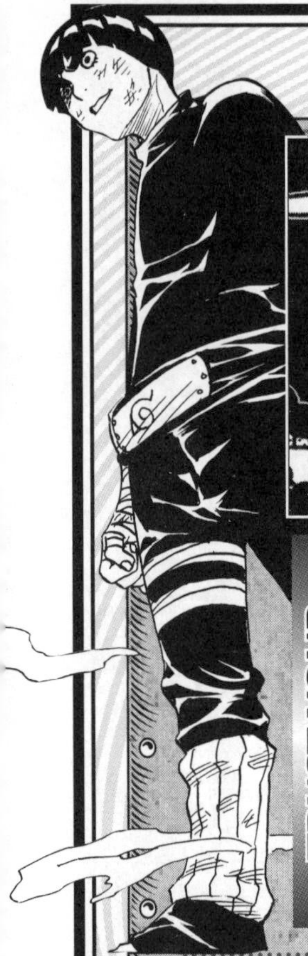

4 Danger

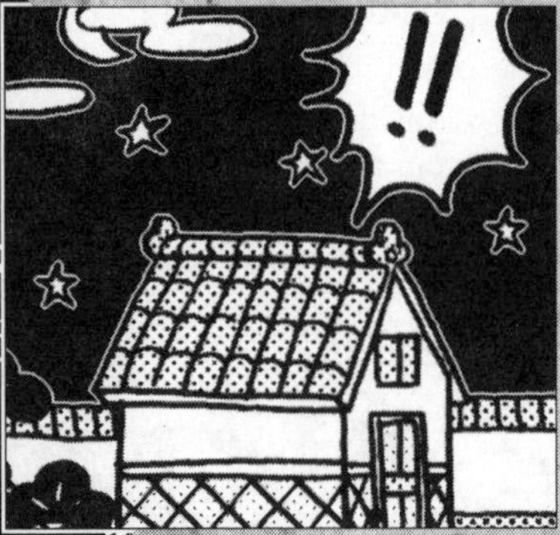
!!

When you try to leave the storeroom with the documents in hand, ninja suddenly appear in the doorway. The daimyo's agents! How many are there?

5 Battle

TRUST YOUR INSTINCTS WHEN YOU ANSWER!

The ninja attack! What do you do?

- **A** "They started it...I finish it!" — Fight!
- **B** "I have to get the documents home!" — Run.
- **C** "If I die here, what will happen to those I leave behind?" — Return the documents and apologize.

6 Henge

After you shake off the ninja and return home to the village, you receive a vacation as a reward. You enjoy your free time thoroughly. Wouldn't it be fun to use Henge no Jutsu to take the form of an animal for the entire day? Which animal would you choose?

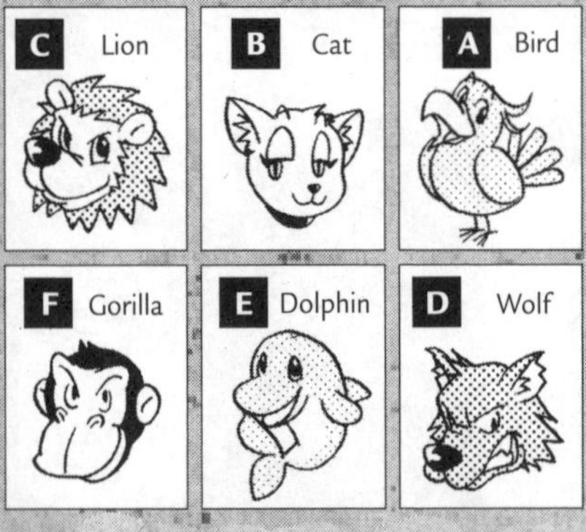
A Bird
B Cat
C Lion
D Wolf
E Dolphin
F Gorilla

All the answers on the next page! Kishimoto-sensei takes the test as well!

Ninja Psychology Test
Kishimoto-sensei's Answers

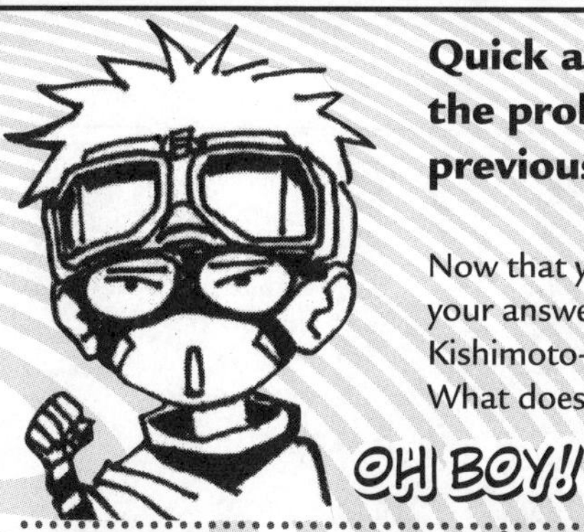
OH BOY!

Quick answers to the problems on the previous pages!

Now that you've all chosen your answers, we had Kishimoto-sensei take the test. What does it tell us about him?

1 **C** **Kakuremi no Jutsu cloth**

Reason

If I have this, I could probably steal the other three...

2

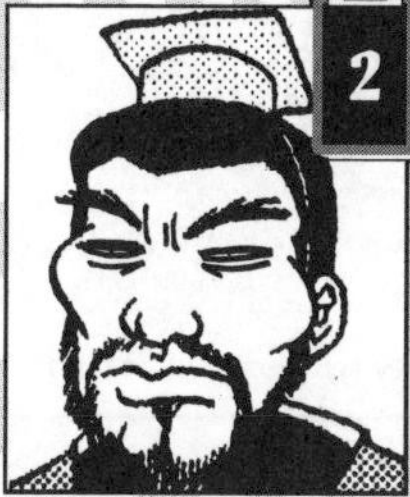

Reason

He's a bad guy, so I made the eyes as evil as possible.

3 **B** **Blue**

Reason

Just a guess. A hunch. Red seemed dangerous.

4 **Five**

Reason

Another hunch, or a mental image... when I imagined the situation, it seemed like five would show up.

5 **C**

"If I die here, what will happen to those I leave behind?" — Return the documents and apologize.

Reason

See, if I apologize, they let their guard down, and I have a better chance...

6 **A** **Bird**

Reason

I always dreamed of flying through the clouds! Sounds like fun!

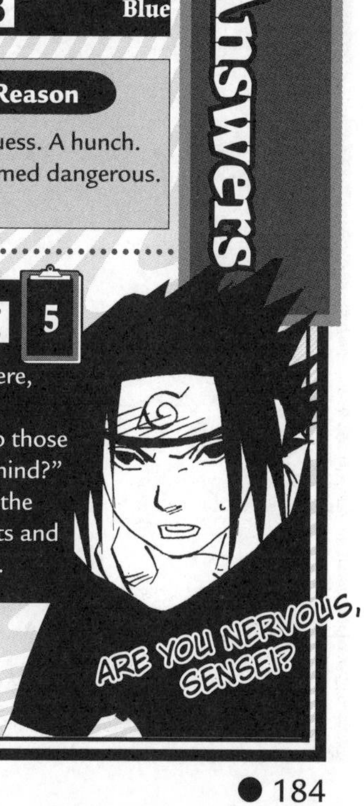
ARE YOU NERVOUS, SENSEI?

So, what are the test results? I'm sure you can't guess...see next page!

Ninja Psychology Test Answers

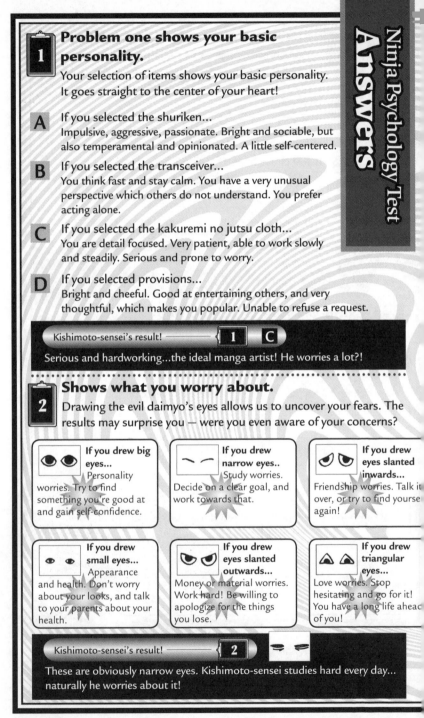

1 Problem one shows your basic personality.

Your selection of items shows your basic personality. It goes straight to the center of your heart!

A If you selected the shuriken...
Impulsive, aggressive, passionate. Bright and sociable, but also temperamental and opinionated. A little self-centered.

B If you selected the transceiver...
You think fast and stay calm. You have a very unusual perspective which others do not understand. You prefer acting alone.

C If you selected the kakuremi no jutsu cloth...
You are detail focused. Very patient, able to work slowly and steadily. Serious and prone to worry.

D If you selected provisions...
Bright and cheeful. Good at entertaining others, and very thoughtful, which makes you popular. Unable to refuse a request.

Kishimoto-sensei's result! —— 1 C

Serious and hardworking...the ideal manga artist! He worries a lot?!

2 Shows what you worry about.

Drawing the evil daimyo's eyes allows us to uncover your fears. The results may surprise you — were you even aware of your concerns?

If you drew big eyes... Personality worries. Try to find something you're good at and gain self-confidence.

If you drew narrow eyes.. Study worries. Decide on a clear goal, and work towards that.

If you drew eyes slanted inwards... Friendship worries. Talk it over, or try to find yourse again!

If you drew small eyes... Appearance and health. Don't worry about your looks, and talk to your parents about your health.

If you drew eyes slanted outwards... Money or material worries. Work hard! Be willing to apologize for the things you lose.

If you drew triangular eyes... Love worries. Stop hesitating and go for it! You have a long life aheac of you!

Kishimoto-sensei's result! —— 2

These are obviously narrow eyes. Kishimoto-sensei studies hard every day... naturally he worries about it!

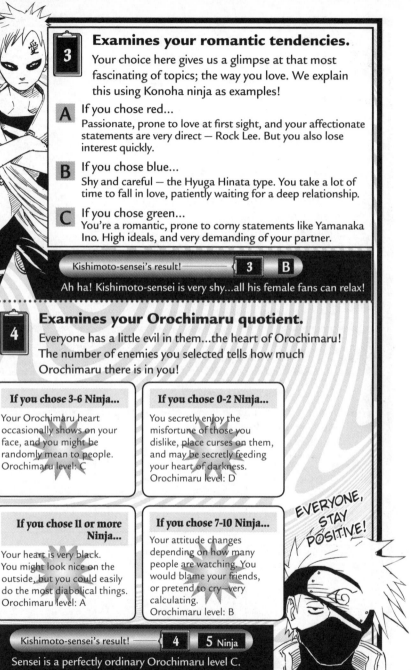

Examines your romantic tendencies.

3

Your choice here gives us a glimpse at that most fascinating of topics; the way you love. We explain this using Konoha ninja as examples!

A If you chose red...
Passionate, prone to love at first sight, and your affectionate statements are very direct — Rock Lee. But you also lose interest quickly.

B If you chose blue...
Shy and careful — the Hyuga Hinata type. You take a lot of time to fall in love, patiently waiting for a deep relationship.

C If you chose green...
You're a romantic, prone to corny statements like Yamanaka Ino. High ideals, and very demanding of your partner.

Kishimoto-sensei's result! ——— **3** **B**

Ah ha! Kishimoto-sensei is very shy...all his female fans can relax!

Examines your Orochimaru quotient.

4

Everyone has a little evil in them...the heart of Orochimaru! The number of enemies you selected tells how much Orochimaru there is in you!

If you chose 3-6 Ninja...
Your Orochimaru heart occasionally shows on your face, and you might be randomly mean to people. Orochimaru level: C

If you chose 0-2 Ninja...
You secretly enjoy the misfortune of those you dislike, place curses on them, and may be secretly feeding your heart of darkness. Orochimaru level: D

If you chose 11 or more Ninja...
Your heart is very black. You might look nice on the outside, but you could easily do the most diabolical things. Orochimaru level: A

If you chose 7-10 Ninja...
Your attitude changes depending on how many people are watching. You would blame your friends, or pretend to cry—very calculating. Orochimaru level: B

EVERYONE, STAY POSITIVE!

Kishimoto-sensei's result! ——— **4** **5 Ninja**

Sensei is a perfectly ordinary Orochimaru level C. A little evil makes people more interesting. And makes it easier to write villains!

5 Examines your friendships.

The way you behave in front of enemies demonstrates how you behave with friends. Your friends are your greatest treasure. Treat them well.

A If you chose "They started it...I finish it!"— Fight...
You are outgoing and make friends easily. You express emotions directly...so you might also have many enemies.

B If you chose "I have to get the documents home!" — Run...
You are serious and smart, and your friends admire you. You don't talk about yourself much, so people may feel you are distant.

C If you chose "If I die here, what will happen to those I leave behind?" — Return the documents and apologize...

Everyone thinks you're funny. They invite you over often, but it's difficult to make close friendships?

Kishimoto-sensei's result! — 5 C

Readers do appreciate his humor! Possibly accurate? But he seems to have lots of good friends...

6 Shows the job you are best suited for.

The final problem shows your ideal profession based on the animal you selected. May help with your plans for the future!

A If you chose Bird:
You take a different route from most people. You are very skilled, and would be good at many jobs. Adventurer, reporter, pilot, translator.

B If you chose Cat:
You would choose a flashy job that draws attention and makes people jealous. Model, singer, actor.

C If you chose Lion:
You know how to succeed and are very charismatic, and are good at delegating. Politician, management, movie director, sports coach.

D If you chose Wolf:
Intelligent, capable of living under your own power. Successful in a highly specialized field. Doctor, lawyer, programmer.

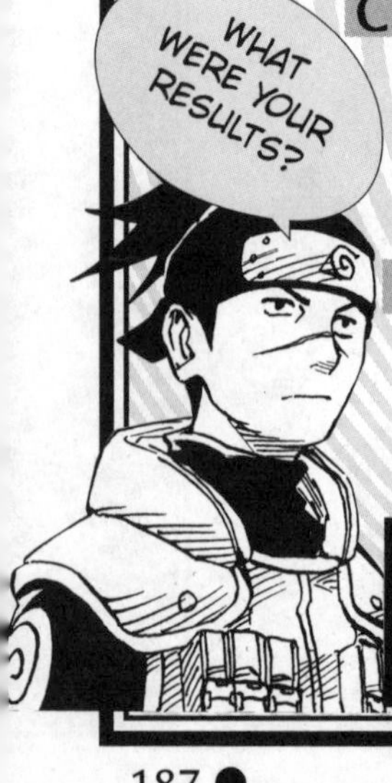
WHAT WERE YOUR RESULTS?

E If you chose Dolphin:
You will live a happy life surrounded by many friends. Jobs that require teamwork: athlete, policeman, teacher.

F If you chose Gorilla:
Delicate, emotional. Suited for a literary or artistic profession. Manga artist, designer, painter.

Kishimoto-sensei's result! — 6 A

Surprisingly, he did not chose gorilla. But "very skilled, and would be good at many jobs" sounds right...

Masashi Kishimoto

Manga Artist

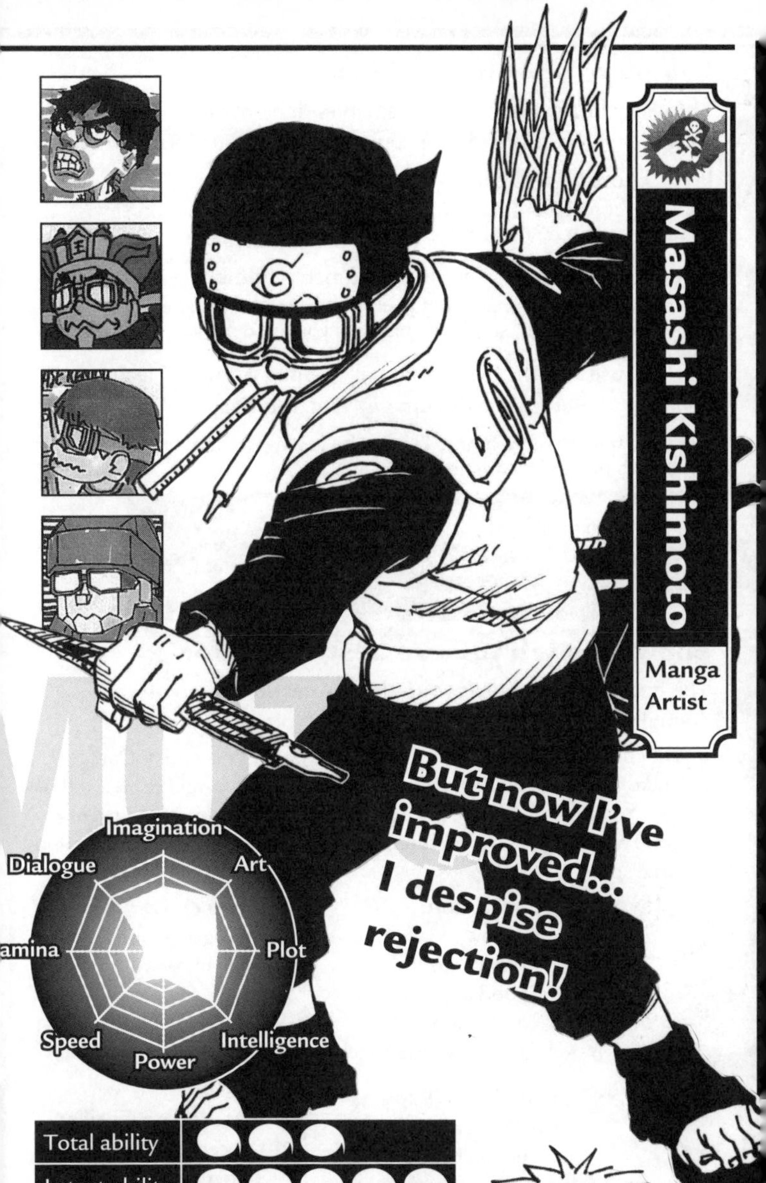

But now I've improved... I despise rejection!
Imagination
Art
Plot
Intelligence
Power
Speed
amina
Dialogue

Total ability	●●●
Latent ability	●●●●●
Luck	●●●●

* All parameters as determined by his Japanese editors.

The high rating for latent ability shows his true talent. His low stamina is a little worrying...

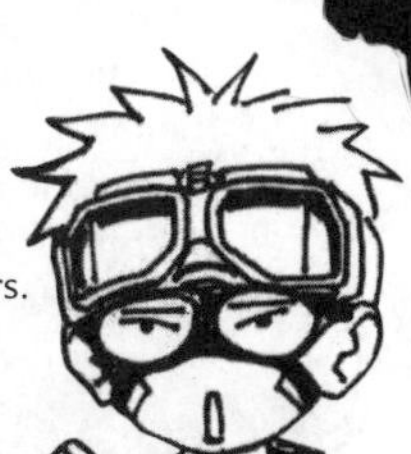

STORIES POUR OUT OF HIM — ART LIKE NO OTHER! A GREAT MANGA HOPE POISED TO OPEN A NEW AGE!

Since a very young age Masashi Kishimoto loved nothing more than drawing, and sacrificed everything to improve his art. As he grew older, he naturally began to dream about being a manga artist someday. When he drew or wrote stories, his main goal was originality. He did not want to copy anyone but to create something uniquely his own. The ultimate result of this effort was *Naruto*. But he is still not satisfied. Never forgetting his childhood thirst to improve, he continues to hone his skills daily.

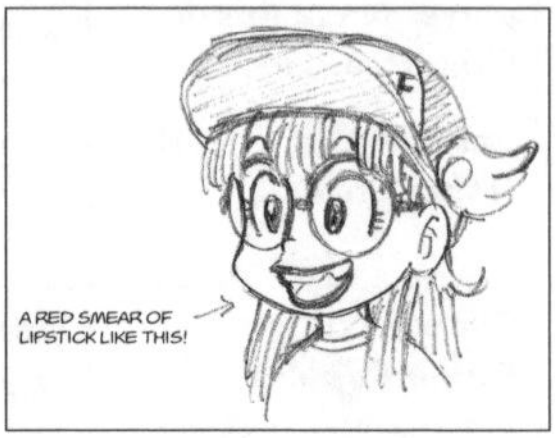
A RED SMEAR OF LIPSTICK LIKE THIS!

⬆ His mother drew in lipstick on one of his pictures, infuriating him.

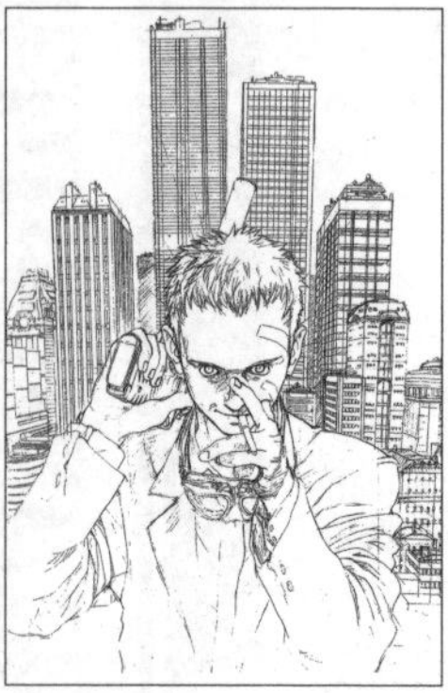

⬅ He is already making plans for his next series! Here's a picture...

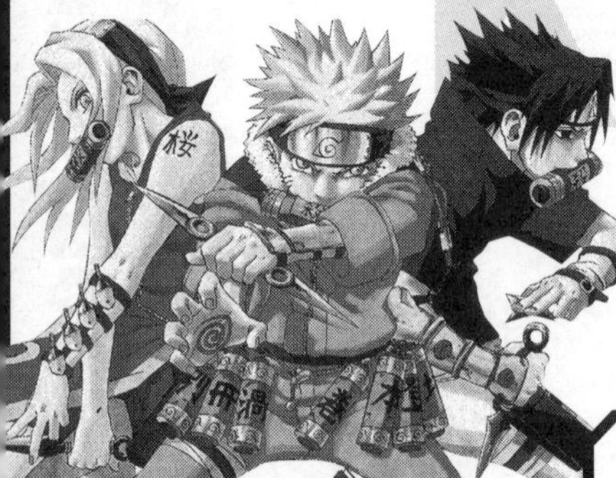

⬅ Unique characters and powerful art are the source of his appeal!

Hop★Step Award Age: 21
Naruto serialization begins: 24
Mission experience:
Akamaru Jump short stories: 2
Weekly Jump short stories: 1
Weekly Jump serialized issues: 140
(As of October 4th, 2002)

DOB: November 8th, 1974 (27, Scorpio)
H: 170 cm (5'6"), W: 57 kg (125.5 lbs),
Blood Type: O
Personality: Laid-back
Favorite Food: Ramen Tonkotsu (Pork Bone Soup)
Least Favorite Food: Liver
Favorite manga artists: Akira Toriyama, Katsuhiro Otomo
Favorite phrase: So so
Hobby: Watching movies

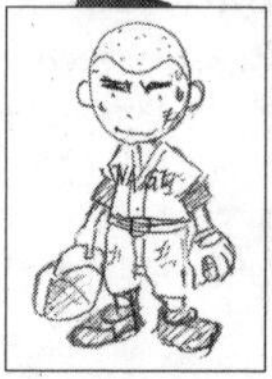

As you can tell from his hobby — watching movies — he enjoys anything involving the arts. But in the past, he was on the baseball team?

Footsteps on the Path of Life
Masashi Kishimoto Timeline

Any number of experiences and encounters created the man who exists today...let us look back upon them together!

Year	What happened in the world	What happened to Masashi Kishimoto
1974	**The legendary Japanese baseball player Nagashima Shigeo retires.** **Sato Eisaku wins the Nobel prize.**	**Masashi Kishimoto's Birth!** He and his twin brother were born in Okayama Prefecture, in Katsuta ward! They were born prematurely and quickly placed in an incubator. He was already drawing before he could walk and talk?!
1979	**Space Invaders Video Game Popular** Video games become popular across Japan.	**Enters Kindergarten** At this stage, he was fascinated by anything that moved — insects, rivers, television, etc. The extreme concentration demonstrated at this age helped to develop his powers of observation.
1981	**"Ruby no Yubiwa," The Ruby Ring, the fifth single by Terao Akira, a Japanese singer, is a big hit!** **Nameneko Boom begins.** For some reason, these cats dressed like delinquents are hugely popular! **Dragon Quest series hits big!!** The video game, a collaboration work between Yuji Horii and Akira Toriyama, sells unprecedented numbers!! 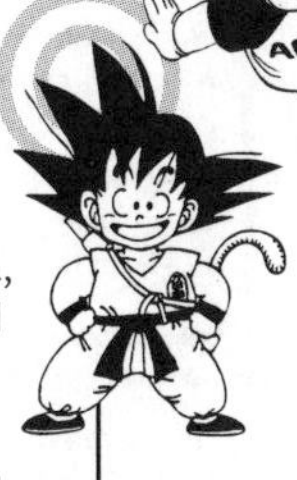 ➡ Goku, short version — when Sensei was most obsessed.	**Early Childhood** **Enters Elementary School** Already obsessed with drawing, he would even draw during games of hide and seek. Became a fan of *Dr. Slump*. 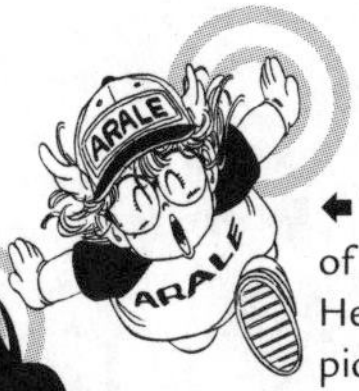 ⬅ The main character of *Dr. Slump,* Arale. He drew many pictures of her. **Teenage Years** As he got older, his passion for drawing only increased. *Dragon Ball* in particular made a profound impact on him, and he drew *Dragon Ball* characters on a daily basis!
1987	**The Japan National Railroad (JNR) goes public, and becomes Japan Railway Company (JR).** **Dr. Tonegawa receives Nobel Prize.**	**Begins Junior High** Just after starting junior high, he decides to join the baseball team and plays passionately. During this time in his life, he faces his greatest danger - being attacked by a gang of monkeys!

What happened in the world	What happened to Masashi Kishimoto	Year
Seoul Olympics - Suzuki Daichi earns a Gold Medal	**Encounters *Akira*** Being on the baseball team was pulling him away from his love of drawing. What sparked his passion once again was the poster for the movie *Akira*!	1988
Germany unites	**Enters High School** Around this time, his plans for the future began to solidify around "manga artist." Bought all the equipment, but then realized manga required a story as well as art!!	1990
Gulf War begins; Soviet Union collapses. Wakata Boom (Wakanohana and Takanohana, two popular sumo wrestlers) **splits the nation**.	**Draws first manga** A 31-page manga he planned to submit to *Jump's* contest! But when his family read it...he decided to reject it himself and put it in a drawer.	1991
J League Soccer begins. Crown Prince marries.	**Enters Art School** Chose to major in art because he wanted to draw better, to draw manga. As his art improved rapidly, he drew manga daily.	1993
Kobe Earthquake. Hideo Nomo wins Rookie of the Year in the major leagues!! Nomo's first year in the majors earns him the highest prize! He was the first of a wave of Japanese players headed overseas. 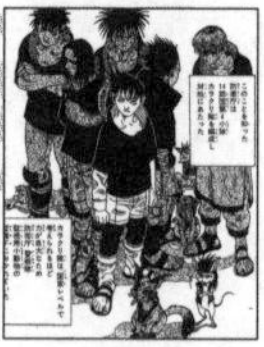 ➡ The main character, an enhanced human created to defeat a powerful evil! 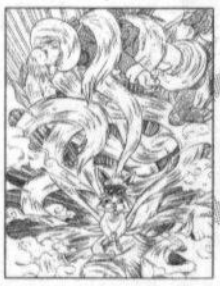 ⬅ Naruto was not a ninja, but a nine-tailed demon fox disguised as a human!!	**His manga *Karakuri* wins the Hop★Step Prize!!** In his freshmen year, he drew a manga called *Karakuri* and submitted it to the *Jump* Hop★Step contest. He won an award (he didn't win the contest), taking his first big step toward success!	1995
	Graduates art school. That summer, the short story *Naruto* runs in *Akamaru Jump*. After graduation, retreated to his hometown where he began working on ideas for a serial. That year, the short story that would later give birth to his current series ran in *Akamaru Jump* and was very popular!	1997
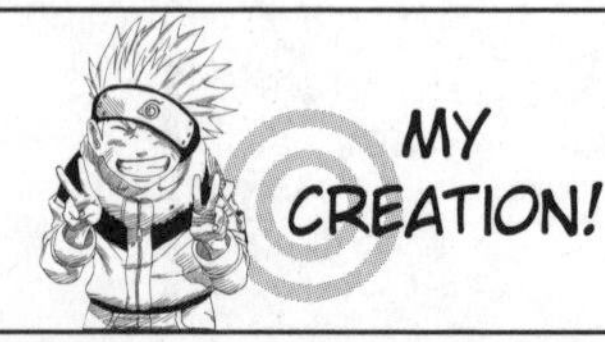 MY CREATION!	***Naruto* serialization begins in *Weekly Shonen Jump*!!** *Naruto* serialization begins two years after the short story version, with the character as unique as ever!	1999

Interview

Masashi Kishimoto Reveals

Past, Present & Future

Kishimoto-sensei may be young, but there are few manga artists more successful. His work entertains readers around the world. But he had no easy path to success. He told us about how he got there, his passion for manga, and his plans for the future.

Q: First, could you tell us about where you were born, and your childhood?

Kishimoto: I was born in Okayama Prefecture, in a place called Katsuta. They have a lot of unusual customs there. [*laughs*] (*1)

"I loved to draw. I was a professional scribbler." [*laughs*]

Q: Did you already dream of becoming a manga artist?

Kishimoto: Yeah...all because of *Dragon Ball*.

Q: What games did you play when you were little?

Kishimoto: Obviously, I loved to draw. I was a professional scribbler. [*laughs*] And in elementary school there was the Nintendo, and remote controlled cars... but my parents didn't buy us a lot of things. My remote controlled car was a Bargello (*2) but then I found a Grasshopper remodeling set, and forced it on top of the Bargello, leaving the body off-balance. This made it look so awful that I stopped playing with it. [laughs]

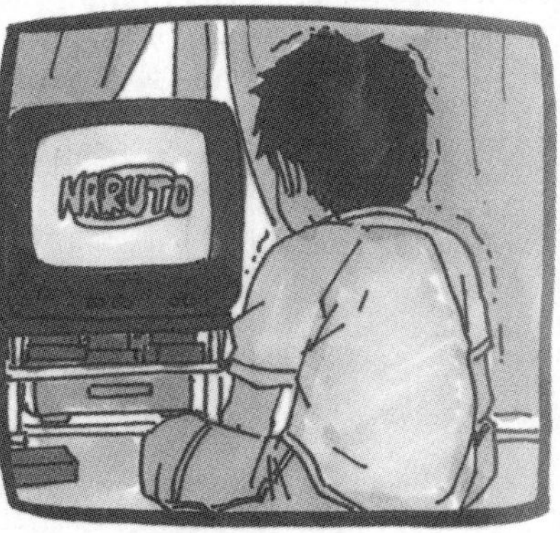
NARUTO

*1 Strange customs — For example, hefting mochi on your back and crawling around, digging a hole in front of your neighbor's home with a giant rock, etc. Illustration: Heh heh heh heh!

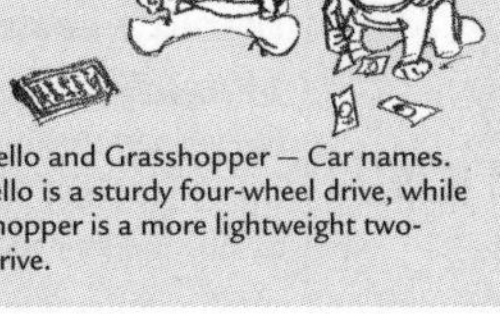

*2 Bargello and Grasshopper — Car names. A Bargello is a sturdy four-wheel drive, while a grasshopper is a more lightweight two-wheel drive.

*3 Toriyama Akira-sensei — Creator of *Dr. Slump* and *Dragon Ball*, character designer for *Dragon Quest*.

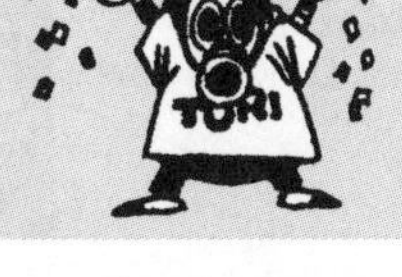
TORI

"I sat on my bike for about an hour staring at the poster."

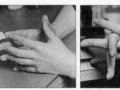

threw the ball so close it almost hit me, but I managed to tap it between my hands, and the squeeze was successful. I will never forget that.

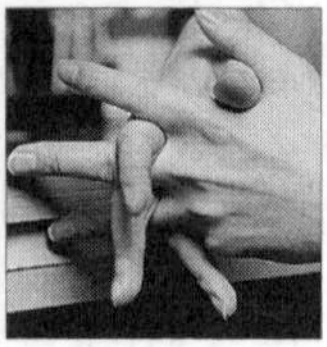

Q: So baseball was more important than drawing in junior high?

Kishimoto: Yeah...in elementary school, people often told me how good my art was, but in junior high, nobody cares if you can draw. Besides, the girls weren't impressed. [*laughs*] So I thought I was better off playing sports. I began to think I could never be a manga artist.

Then, one day, I saw a poster for the movie *Akira* (*7) hanging outside the tobacco shop, and it blew me away! I'd been out riding, so I sat on my bike for about an hour staring at the poster. I thought it was seriously cool.

What impressed me most was the bird's-eye view (*8) of the main character on his bike, and the perspective was unbelievable. Even the bike was in perspective, (*9) and I could tell it had been drawn by a genius. That picture is what made me get serious about becoming a manga artist.

Q: What attracted you to *Dragon Ball*?

Kishimoto: The art and story – everything, but most of all... Toriyama-sensei (*3) can really draw. He never needed more than one line. His sense is just so cool. Even as a child, I understood this. Toriyama-sensei is like a god to me.

Q: So in junior high, it was all about art?

Kishimoto: No... after I read *Touch* (*4) I joined the baseball team, and my life revolved around that for a while.

Q: Can you tell us what position you played and where you were in the line-up?

Kishimoto: I batted second and played second base. (*5) I was small, so I couldn't hit at all. I spent all my time practicing bunting, trying to be good at something. So I was the best bunter on the team.

When I was in my second year, some older kids had me pinch hit for a squeeze, (*6) since I was good at bunting. Then the pitcher

*8 Bird's-eye view — A picture drawn from above, looking down, or a design from a similar point of view. This is considered to be the most difficult point of view to draw.

*9 Perspective — Objects closer at hand are drawn larger, and objects farther away are drawn smaller, giving a sense of depth.

*6 Squeeze — A play designed to bring a runner home from third with a sacrifice bunt. Unless the bat hits the ball, the play will fail.

*7 Akira — A famous sci-fi action manga set in a post-apocalyptic future. Drawn by Ootomo Katsuhiru.

*4 Touch — Inspired by his twin brother's death, the older twin becomes a successful baseball player. Kishimoto-sensei himself has a younger twin brother.

*5 Second base — A position in baseball. Often called the key to the infield, usually given to a great defensive player.

I filled an entire notebook with hands. [*laughs*]

I was also trying to develop my own art style. I would copy any artist's work I liked, trying to capture what I liked and make it my own.

About halfway through high school I started to realize there was no point in keeping up with my classes. I wanted to work as an artist, so I assumed I had to go to art school.

I was in a very strict college prep class in high school, and once, in my senior year, in the middle of class, I asked the teacher if I could go do a design for a plaster model. He said no. I realized the world made no sense. [*laughs*] I ended up staying after school that day to work on the design...

Q: So in high school, it was all about art?

Kishimoto: Yeah. I was drawing every second I could spare, even during class. One time, I drew this amazing picture on the back of a test answer sheet, but the teacher got mad at me, and I was forced to erase it. I cried my eyes out. [*laughs*]

I could tell my art wasn't as good as the professionals, so I was trying to figure out how to make it better.

Q: What did you do, specifically?

Kishimoto: I would draw the same thing from all kinds of angles. I spent weeks drawing nothing but hands. Hands are really hard, but they can be so expressive. A tightly clenched fist looks completely different from a lightly clenched one. I think

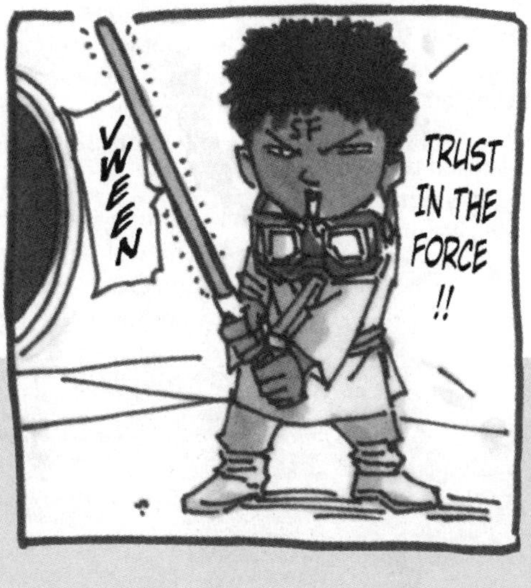
TRUST IN THE FORCE !!
VWEEN
SF

Q: So how did you actually become a manga artist?

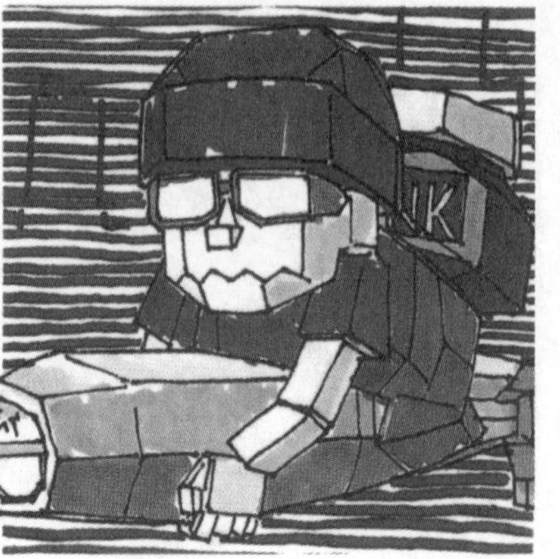

K

Kishimoto: In my sophomore year, I drew a manga called *Karakuri* and submitted it to the Hop ☆ Step Award. (*12) But I never heard back from the publisher. I thought, "Oh well. I wonder who did win?" and went to the convenience store to see. I flipped through the pages of *Jump*...and I was one of the winners. They never contacted me, so I found out by reading the magazine! [*laughs*]

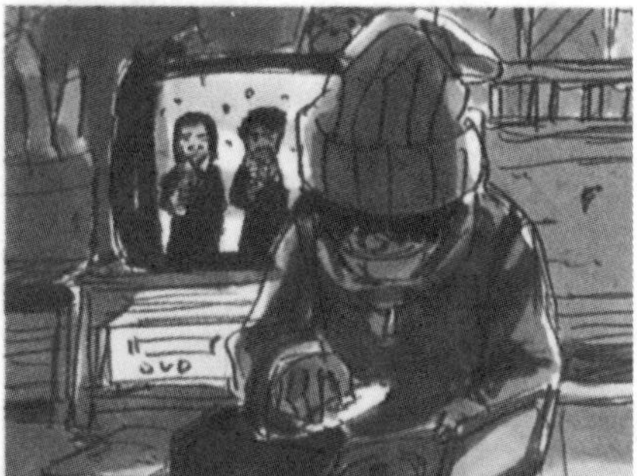

DVD

Q: So you eventually went to art school?

Kishimoto: Yes, in Kyushu. I stayed in the dorm. It had two desks and two beds in a very small room. I spent a year there drawing pictures and manga.

Q: What kind of manga?

Kishimoto: Samurai manga. I thought it was the thing to do – Western fantasy was really big at the time, but I thought, "This is Japan." But when the book was coming together, *Rurouni Kenshin* (*10) started. And then *Blade of the Immortal*. (*11) Both of those were so much better than mine that I gave up.

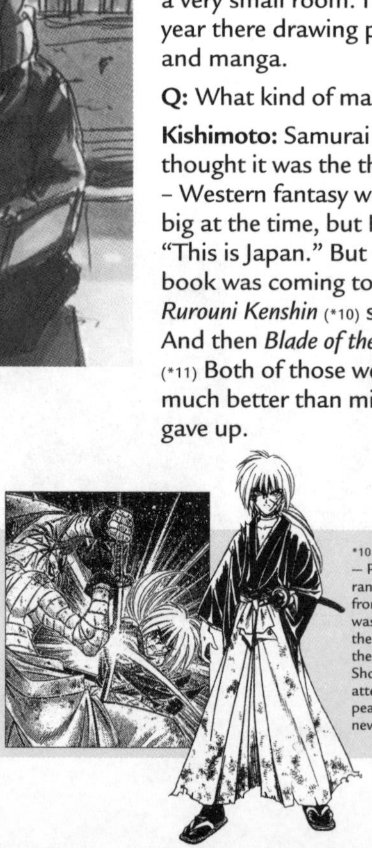

*11 *Blade of the Immortal — Mugen no Junin —* runs in *Afternoon*. A girl out for revenge on her parents' killers travels with an immortal samurai. Drawn by Samura Hiroaki.

*12 The Hop ☆ Step Award is given out once a month — currently called the Tenkaichi Manga award. It has discovered manga famous manga artists, including *One Piece's* Oda Eiichiro.

*10 *Rurouni Kenshin* — Popular manga, ran in *Weekly Jump* from '94. Kenshin was a member of the Ishinshishi in the last days of the Shogunate, but is attempting to live peacefully in the new Meiji era.

Q: You must have been thrilled.

Kishimoto: Absolutely! It was the happiest moment of my life. But when people are so happy, they can't say anything, right? They just make strange noises and quiver. So I bought that copy of *Jump*, but I was so happy that the moment I was out of the store, I threw it across the street!! Yeehah! [*laughs very hard*]

So I thought, I've got to calm down before I get run over. So I crossed the street – at the crosswalk – picked up the magazine... [*laughs*] and went home, but I still couldn't believe it. I feel like an idiot now, but I sat around the house pinching myself. [*laughs*] Then I got a call from my tantou (editor), Yahagi-san (*13), and I was so nervous I accidentally hung up on him! "Oh noooooo!" [*laughs*]

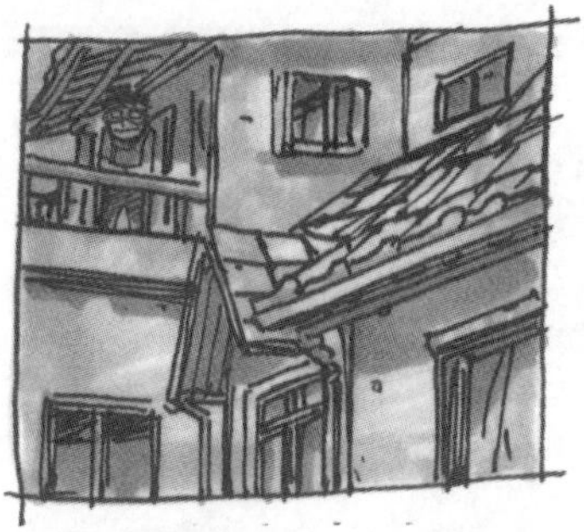

He called back immediately, but still. [*laughs*] Then he asked me if I was ready to try this professionally, and I said yes right away. So he said he would be my tantou! I had a *Jump* tantou! I was thrilled. I knew I had reached the starting line for becoming a manga artist.

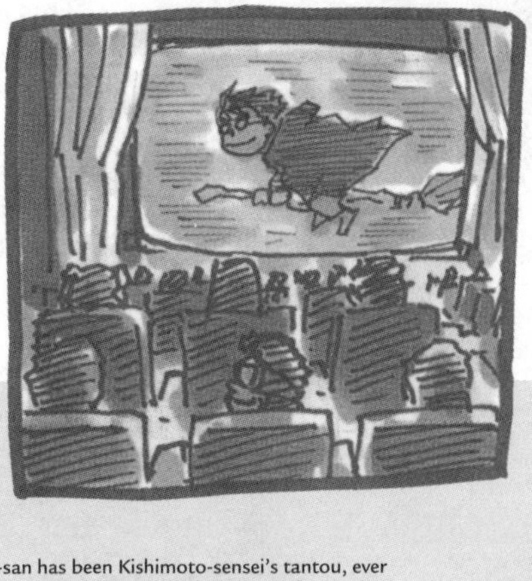

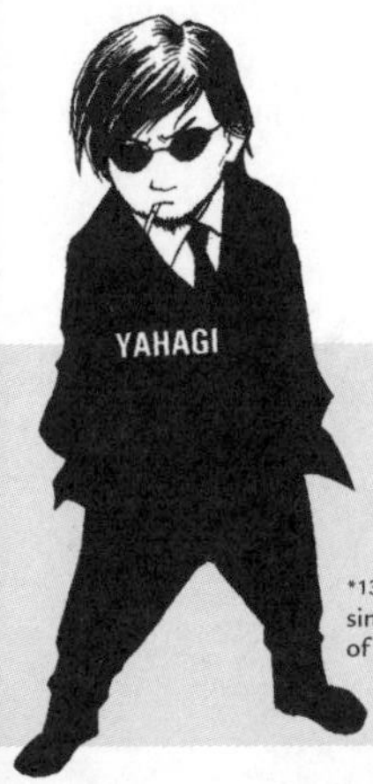
YAHAGI

*13 Yahagi-san has been Kishimoto-sensei's tantou, ever since the Hop ☆ Step Award, to the present day. He is one of *Weekly Shonen Jump*'s editors.

"There were times when I was sure I'd never pull it off."

Q: Did everything go smoothly after that?

Kishimoto: Oh, no. I really didn't have any idea how to go about drawing a manga. I wrote all kinds of things, but they all got rejected. There were times when I was sure I'd never pull it off. So I decided I should just draw what I like. I love ramen, so I decided to do a book about ramen. The first version was all about the secret ingredients in the soup, but it went through a few [*laughs*] modifications and ended up as *Naruto*. The story ran in *Akamaru Jump**, and was very popular.

But after that there was another long period where nothing I drew worked...Even my baseball manga (*14) was rejected. So I decided this was it, and I pulled everything they had liked about the rejected books, and the characters from the *Naruto* story (*15) that appeared in *Akamaru Jump* and put them in a Name or Storyboard. "If this is rejected, I'm trying a different magazine," I thought.

But this time it made it through the editor's meeting. (*16) But this was also incredibly lucky – usually, when they decide which pieces should run as a series, they start immediately, but with *Naruto*, they decided it would start in three months time. So I had about eight issues planned by the time it started. If that hadn't happened, I might never have made it! So in that sense, *Naruto* has been a very fortunate manga.

* *Akamaru Jump* comes out three times a year, while *Weekly Jump* is on vacation, and features short stories by up and coming artists.

** *Name* – rough draft of the manga, with all the dialogue but only rough pencil sketches of the eventual art.

*16 Editor's meeting — held once a month, with all *Jump* editors in attendance. This is where they decide which series to run.

*15 Akamaru Naruto — appearance and personality are very much the same, but the setting is almost completely different. This version can be found on page 209.

*14 Rejected baseball manga — entitled simply "Baseball Team," it drew on his own experiences in junior high. But he knew a little too much about baseball, and it ended up being very grim.

About Naruto

acceptance. Then I needed someone who would accept him, and that person became Iruka. As the setting came together, I decided the village needed a leader, and created the Hokage. And I needed a teacher for Naruto, so I created Kakashi.

Q: Was Konohagakure inspired by an actual place?

Kishimoto: Yeah, my home town. I'd lived there most of my life. It was close to a Self-Defense Force base, and there were lots of training grounds around town. That was the kind of place I grew up in, so the special forces, the organization, and the three-man cell were all influenced by this, and this gave shape to the worldview of the series.

Q: Now let's talk about your current work on *Naruto*. Why did you choose to do a ninja manga?

Kishimoto: I just like Japanese things. Even Americans know all about samurai and ninja too, don't they? Like Sho Kosugi. (*17) So I thought I'd give it a try.

Q: In what order did you create the characters?

Kishimoto: Naruto came first, and with him came the theme of the search for

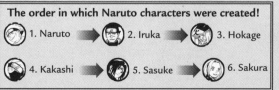

The order in which Naruto characters were created!

1. Naruto ➤ 2. Iruka ➤ 3. Hokage

4. Kakashi ➤ 5. Sasuke ➤ 6. Sakura

*17 Sho Kosugi — Japanese action actor, star of many Hollywood ninja films. His son, Kane Kosugi, is also an actor.

Old Man Monet

to write the story. *Slam Dunk* (*20) was also terrific because of the rivalry between the main characters.

Q: One last question: Can you tell us anything about future plot developments?

Kishimoto: Let's see... All the foreshadowing I've laid down so far will begin to pay off. We'll see Itachi and some other characters that have been mentioned only by name. I'm going to try to make the manga even more interesting and fun!

> **"We'll see Itachi and some other characters that have been mentioned only by name."**

Q: Did Sasuke and Sakura come after that?

Kishimoto: Yes. I started drawing the manga without Sasuke, but the story didn't go anywhere. I thought, if I don't do something the manga will be over in ten weeks! [*laughs*] When I talked to my editor, he suggested giving Naruto a rival. That person became Sasuke. Then I decided I needed a heroine, and created Sakura. Suddenly, it became a lot easier to figure out what should happen next! Pit the main character and his rival against each other, and both of them start to develop. Like Goku (*18) and Kuririn (*19) do in *Dragon Ball*. I wanted the main character to be human, like Kuririn, because character flaws make it easier

*20 *Slam Dunk* — *Jump* basketball manga. The main character, Sakuragi, has a rival named Rukawa, who is a naturally skilled player.

*18 Goku — main character of *Dragon Ball*. Very skilled fighter, becomes rapidly stronger as he trains.

*19 Kuririn — another *Dragon Ball* character. Studies under the same teacher as Goku — at first they are rivals, but Goku quickly out paces him.

The Story's Themes Made Clear
Naruto Liner Notes

Each episode's theme analyzed by the Sensei himself!

"When I write a story, I always have a theme in mind," Kishimoto says. So we asked him to explain the themes of Naruto to us! What was the true theme underlying each episode...?

Story beginning ~ Genin Certification

Theme: Recognition

Who will recognize you, and who will you recognize...this was the original theme. While I was writing stories and getting rejected I was constantly hoping someone would recognize my abilities. So it was easy for me to get behind!

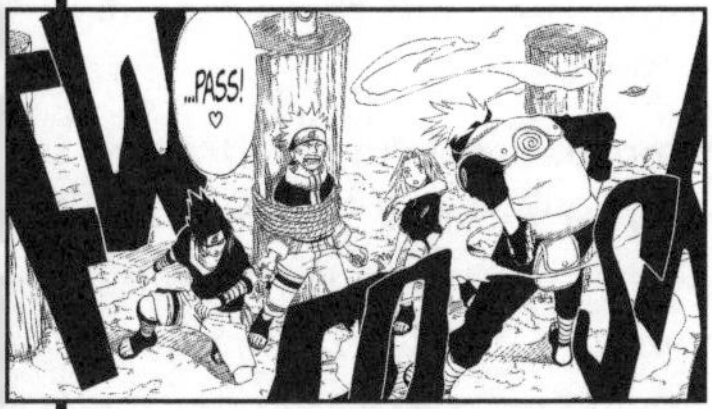
...PASS! ♡

⬆ Kakashi also understood Naruto.

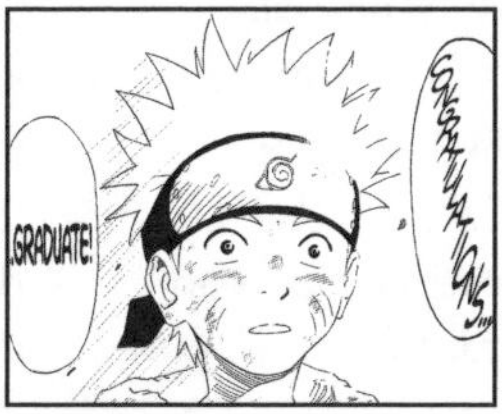
CONGRATULATIONS...
GRADUATE!

⬆ The first person to recognize Naruto...was Iruka.

Battle with Zabuza and Haku

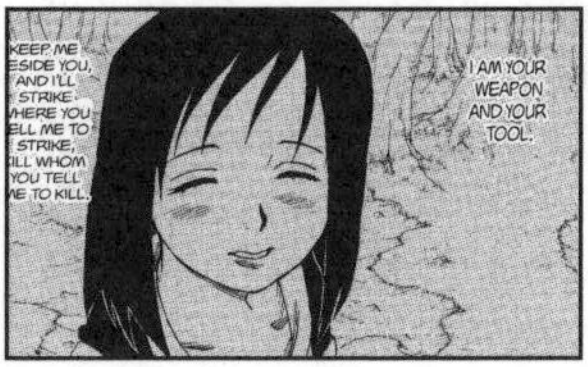
I AM YOUR WEAPON AND YOUR TOOL.

⬆ Haku swore to be Zabuza's weapon...

Theme: Can you live without emotions?

If I was going to write about ninja, I knew I had to look at this theme. Can people kill their emotions and live as objects...in the end, neither Zabuza or Haku were capable of it.

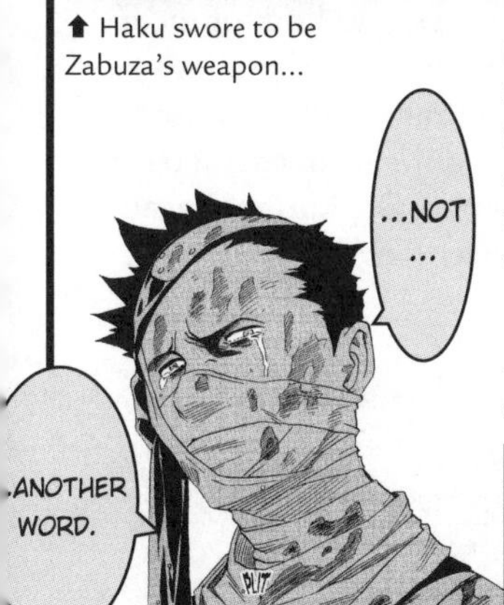
...NOT ...
ANOTHER WORD.
PLIT

⬇ The shinobi law — to have no emotions — is much too difficult.

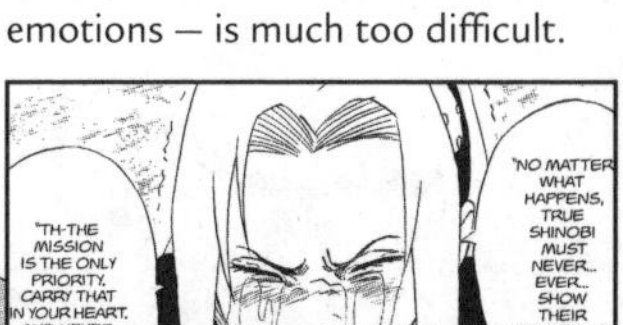
"NO MATTER WHAT HAPPENS, TRUE SHINOBI MUST NEVER... EVER... SHOW THEIR EMOTIONS!
"TH-THE MISSION IS THE ONLY PRIORITY. CARRY THAT IN YOUR HEART. AND NEVER, NEVER, SH-SHED A TEAR."

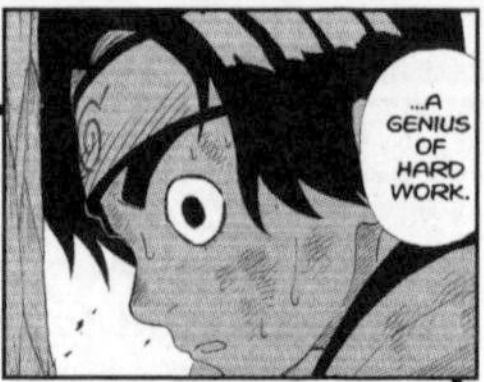
...A GENIUS OF HARD WORK.

⬆ Lee was unable to use ninjutsu but became a ninja through sheer effort!

Chûnin Selection Exams

With the Chûnin Selection Exams I ended up creating a different theme for each character. Especially with Lee, Hinata and Neji, these themes link together.

Theme 1: Effort

Lee's theme is effort. There's been a tendency to view hard work as uncool recently, but I disagree, so I wanted to show that effort always pays off.

Theme 2: Have Confidence in Yourself

People are discriminated against by circumstances of birth and their own abilities, but I'd like to believe that people can change, and I wanted to show that. Hinata's theme is essentially that having confidence in yourself allows you to become someone you want to be.

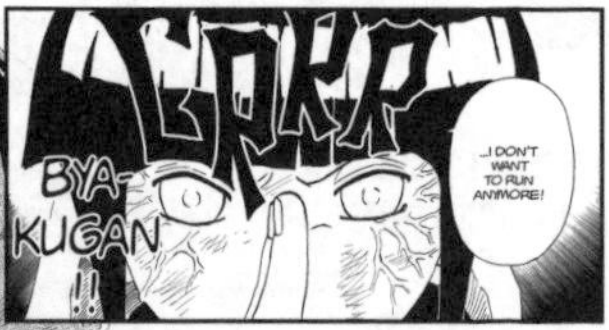
...I DON'T WANT TO RUN ANYMORE!
BYA-KUGAN!!

⬆ Hinata fought till the bitter end, casting aside her old weak self!

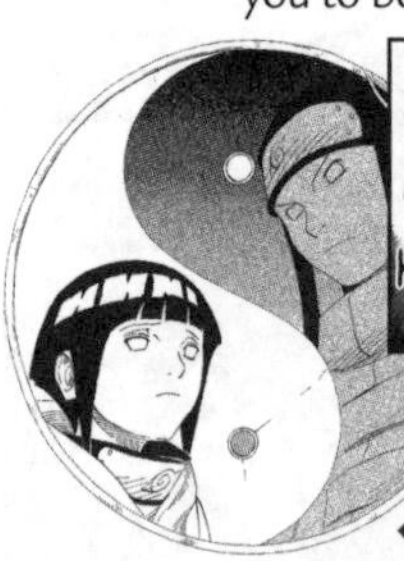

⬅ Both were at the mercy of fate, but their feelings are changing steadily.

Theme 3: What is Fate?

Fate is the main theme of Naruto and Neji's fight. Neji believes destiny cannot be altered and suffers because of it, but in opposition to that Naruto actively tries to change it.

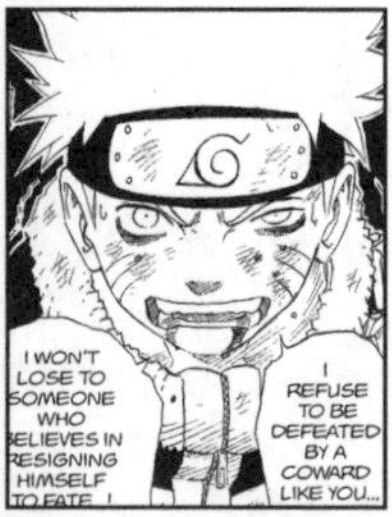
I REFUSE TO BE DEFEATED BY A COWARD LIKE YOU...
I WON'T LOSE TO SOMEONE WHO BELIEVES IN RESIGNING HIMSELF TO FATE!

⬆ Changing fate with his own hands...Naruto's conviction melted Neji's heart.

Gaara and Naruto

Theme: The strength of a fighter

Gaara's theme was also created in opposition to Naruto. He has a family, but is unable to trust anyone, while Naruto had no family, but was recognized and is able to trust people. Which one is true strength?

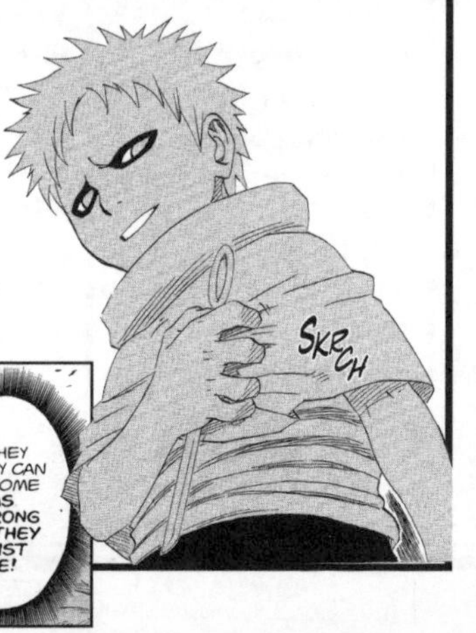
SKRCH

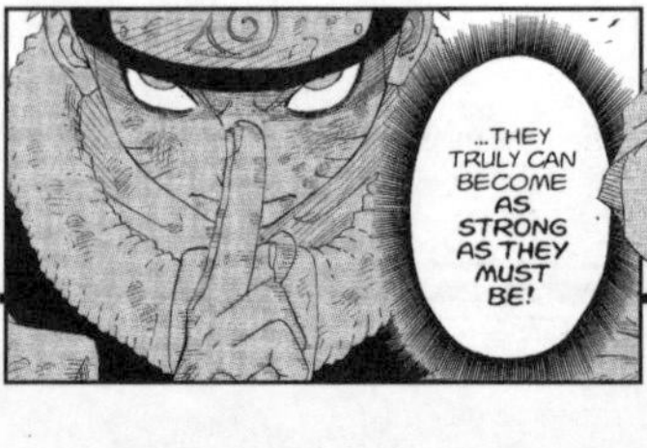
...THEY TRULY CAN BECOME AS STRONG AS THEY MUST BE!

➡ Naruto realized the true meaning of strength while fighting Gaara.

We made him take the survey!

Hidden Leaf Village Citizen Poll!

Kishimoto-sensei took the poll like a citizen...what did he honestly think?

The following survey ran in *Weekly Shonen Jump* as part of the Naruto Fan Participation Corner, and Sensei took the poll as one reader! What were his answers?

Which sensei do you want to teach you ninjutsu?

Iruka
He's the ideal teacher. I don't really want Guy to teach me...he's too absurd.

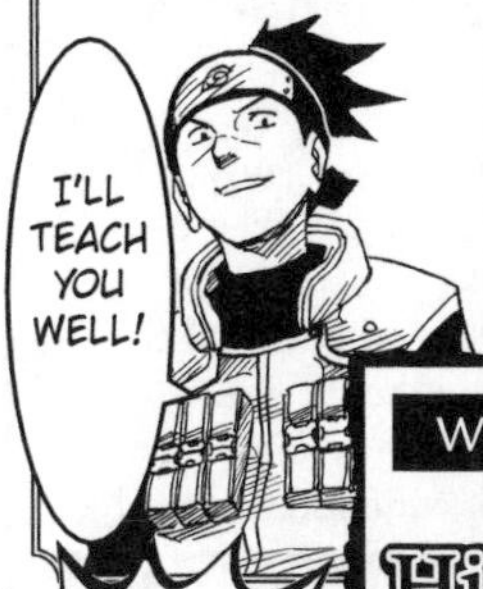
I'LL TEACH YOU WELL!

Who should be the Fifth Hokage?

Hatake Kakashi
Yeah, Kakashi...he's certainly qualified. But truthfully, I want it to be Naruto!

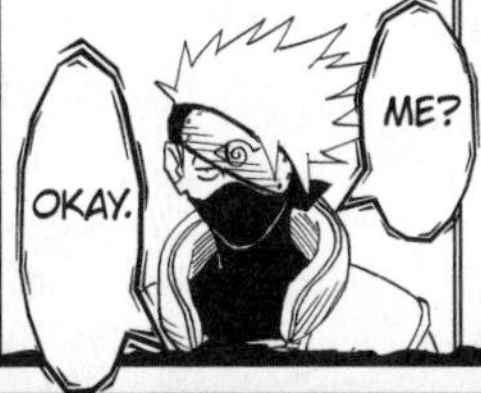
ME?
OKAY.

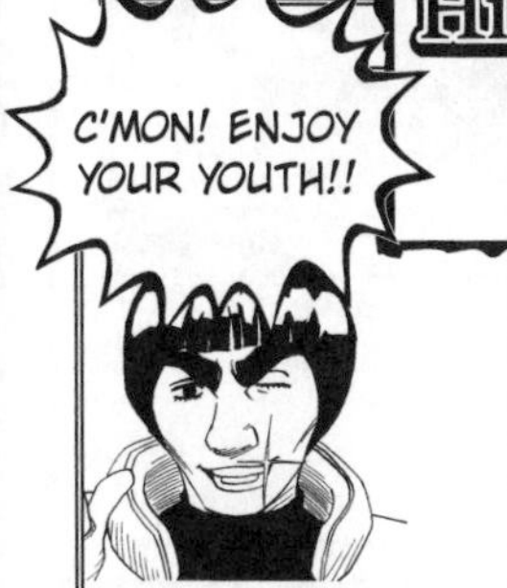
C'MON! ENJOY YOUR YOUTH!!

Who is the most cheerful character in Konohagakure?

Guy
Guy is the only answer I could give! His cheer is light years beyond Naruto's!

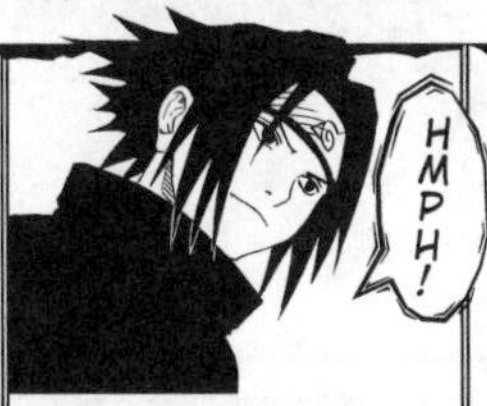
HMPH!

Who would you like as a rival?

Uchiha Sasuke
Rival? Sasuke. Gets attention, and would provide motivation just by being there!

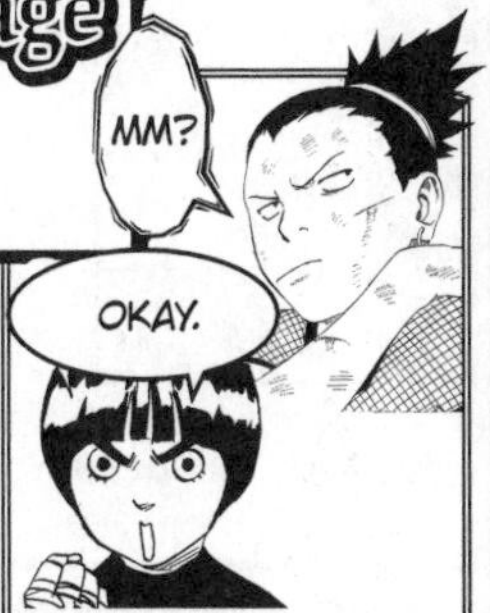
MM?
OKAY.

Who would you like to team up with?

Shikamaru and Lee
Shikamaru is very smart and can be relied on. Lee is a good guy and would make a great friend!

Kishimoto-sensei's Lifestyle

Everyone wants to know! Sensei daily and weekly schedule!!

Weekly Routine

Sunday	Watching movies and videos, cleaning — recharging!
Monday	Based on the storyboard drawn at the end of last week, penciling starts!! (Storyboard: a rough plan of the manga, with all layouts and dialogue.)
Tuesday	Pencils finished, and inking begins in the evening.
Wednesday	Wednesday the pages are due! Inking finishes, final touches, and done!
Thursday	With no time to relax, meeting with the editor to decide the next part of the story!
Friday	The day is spent figuring out the details of the story, layouts, and framing!!
Saturday	Starts in on the storyboard. Generally finished during the day, or early the next morning!!

Back to top

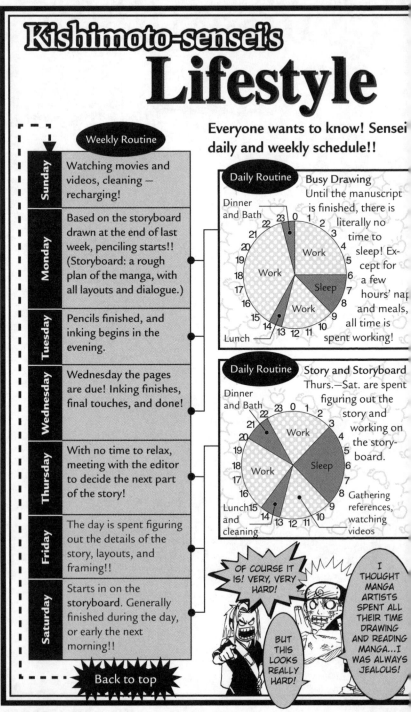

Daily Routine

Busy Drawing

Dinner and Bath
23 0 1 2 3 4 5 6 7 8 9 10 11 12 13 14 15 16 17 18 19 20 21 22
Work
Work
Sleep
Work
Lunch

Until the manuscript is finished, there is literally no time to sleep! Except for a few hours' nap and meals, all time is spent working!

Daily Routine

Story and Storyboard

Dinner and Bath
23 0 1 2 3 4 5 6 7 8 9 10 11 12 13 14 15 16 17 18 19 20 21 22
Work
Sleep
Work
Lunch and cleaning
Gathering references, watching videos

Thurs.—Sat. are spent figuring out the story and working on the storyboard.

I THOUGHT MANGA ARTISTS SPENT ALL THEIR TIME DRAWING AND READING MANGA...I WAS ALWAYS JEALOUS!
BUT THIS LOOKS REALLY HARD!
OF COURSE IT IS! VERY, VERY HARD!

FANTASTIC FAN ART

NARUTO 28 Fan

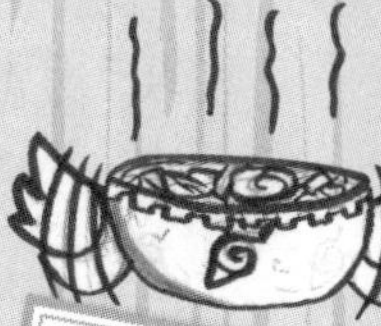

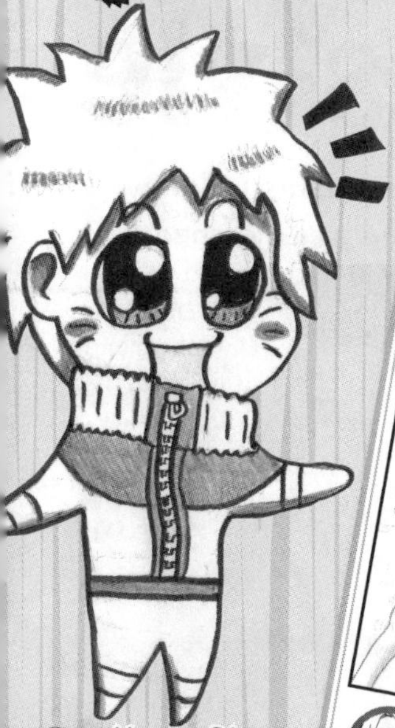

Nancee, CA
⬆ Ha Ha! I didn't know ramen could fly!

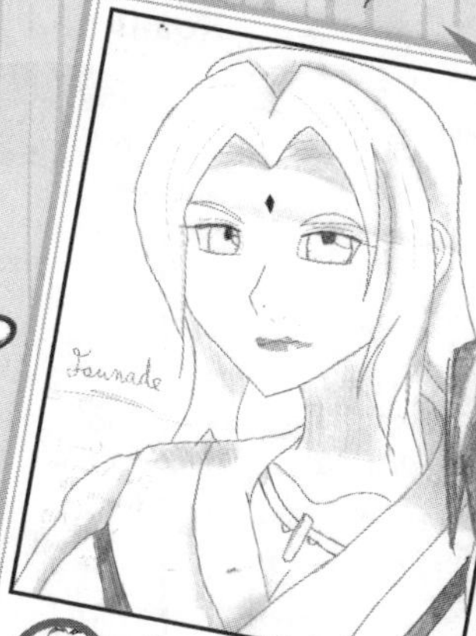
Tsunade

Courtney, TN
⬆ Tsunade is just so beautiful, isn't she?

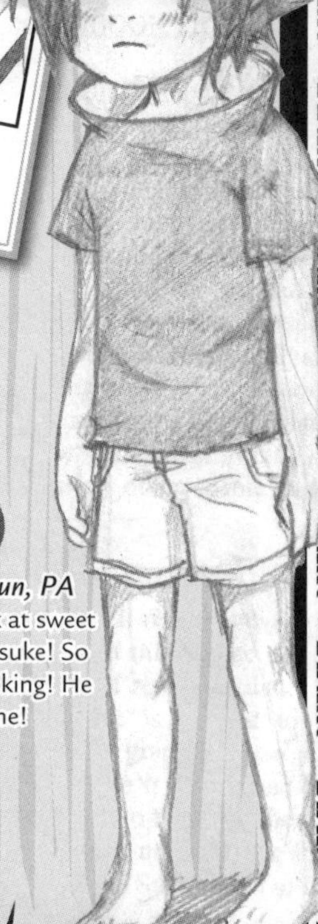

Soo Hyun, PA
➡ Look at sweet little Sasuke! So lost-looking! He needs me!

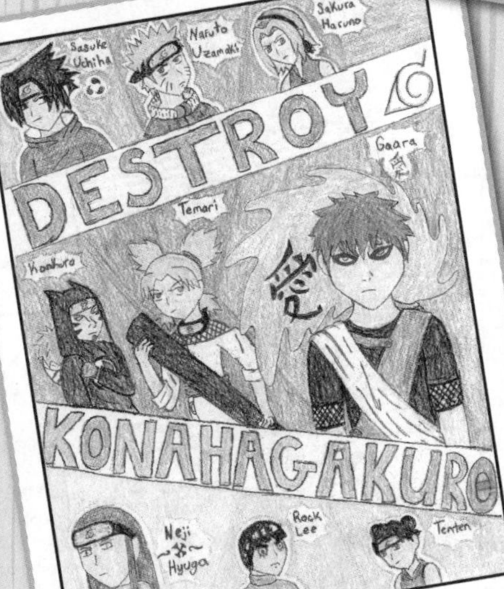
Sasuke Uchiha
Naruto Uzamaki
Sakura Haruno
DESTROY
Gaara
Temari
Kankuro
KONAHAGAKURO
Neji Hyuga
Rock Lee
Tenten

Ashleigh, PA
⬆ Ashleigh really captured the essence of each ninja in this drawing.

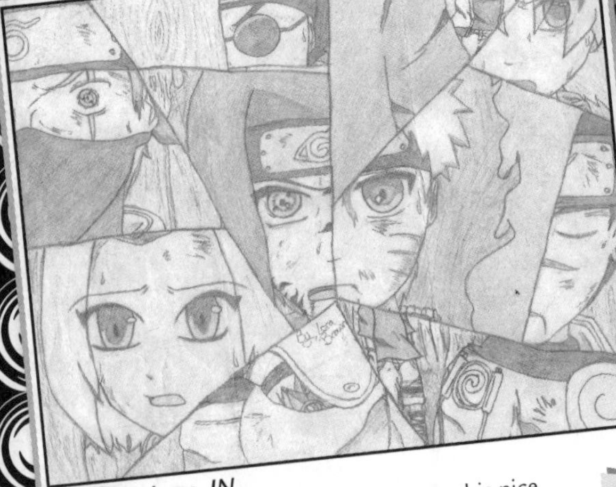

Lora, IN

⬆ I wish I could create layouts this nice. It's so unique.

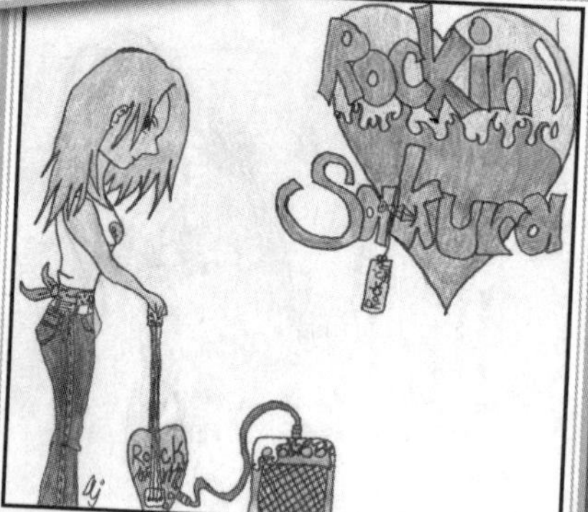
Rockin
Sakura

AJ, OR

⬆ I wonder what her music sounds like?

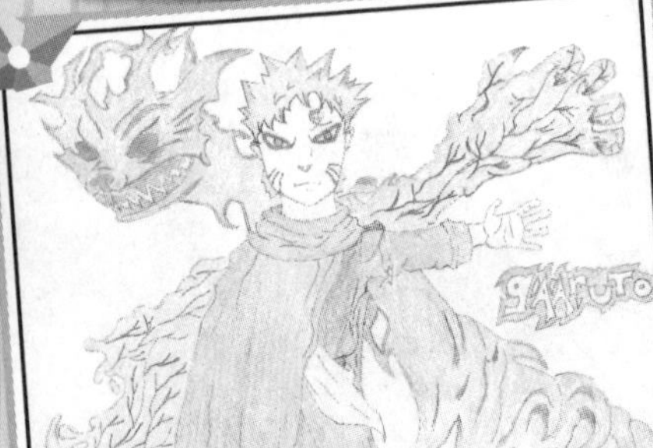

Dalmain, NY

⬆ Is that a new combo jutsu that only a Jinchûriki Host can do?

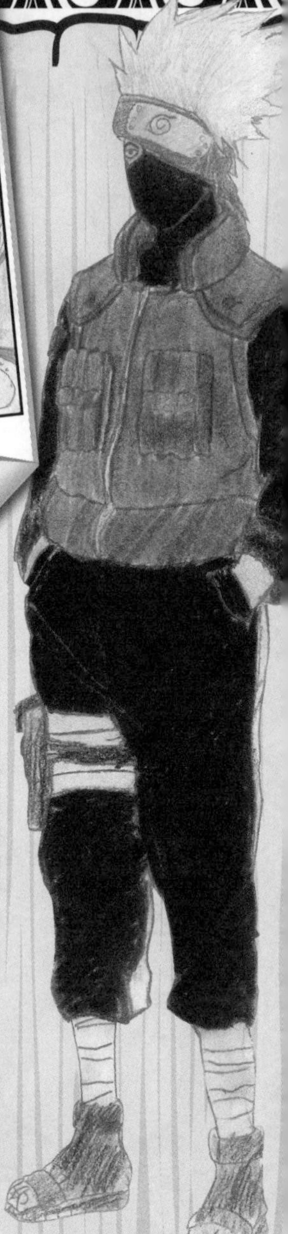

Cat, VT

⬆ Kakashi: calm and collect on the outside, but inside...

FANTASTIC FAN ART

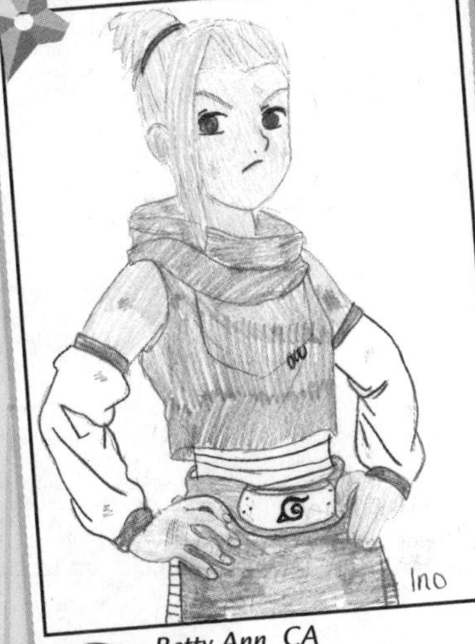

Ino

Betty Ann, CA
⬆ Hmph, now this one is a very good likeness, don't you think?

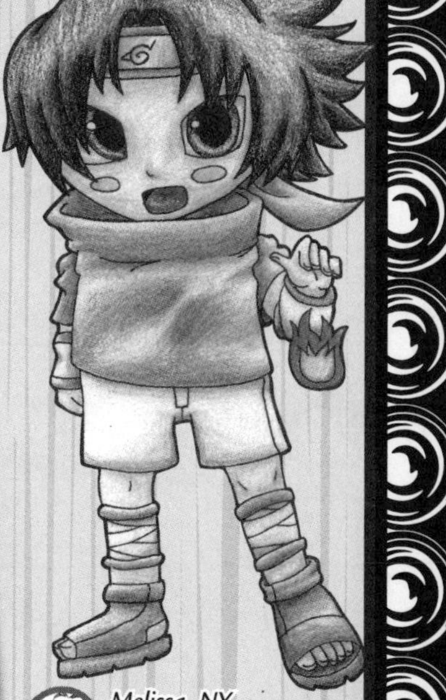

Melissa, NY
⬆ This is just such a cute drawing of Sasuke!

Cyndyl, GA
⬅ Don't be fooled by the cuteness. It's still Orochimaru!

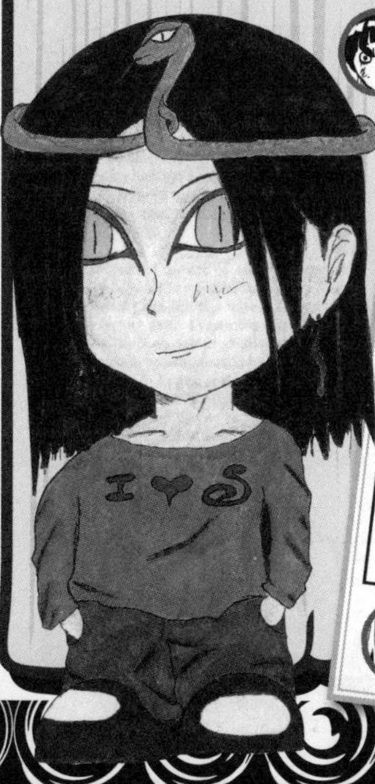

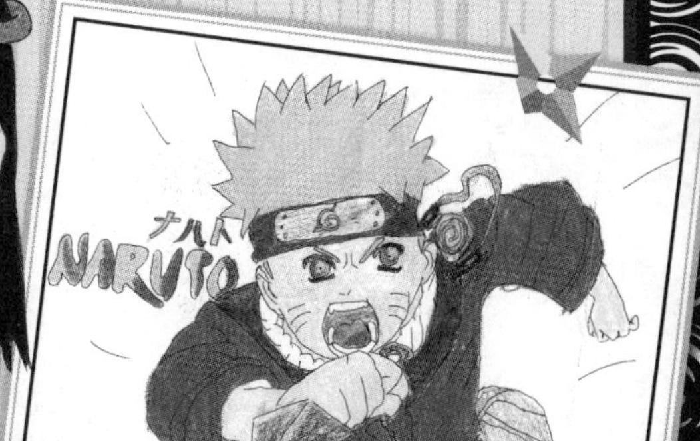

ナルト
NARUTO

Lisa, CA
⬆ Naruto charges into battle!

Unless you can discover the truth, all the gates will not open!

5th GATE

Haruno Sakura Tests Your Naruto Knowledge!

NARUTO CULT QUIZ

IF YOU'VE BEEN STUDYING CAREFULLY, THIS IS EASY!

The final gate tests how much you know about us! If you're a true *Naruto* fan, you should be able to answer all of these. Let's begin!

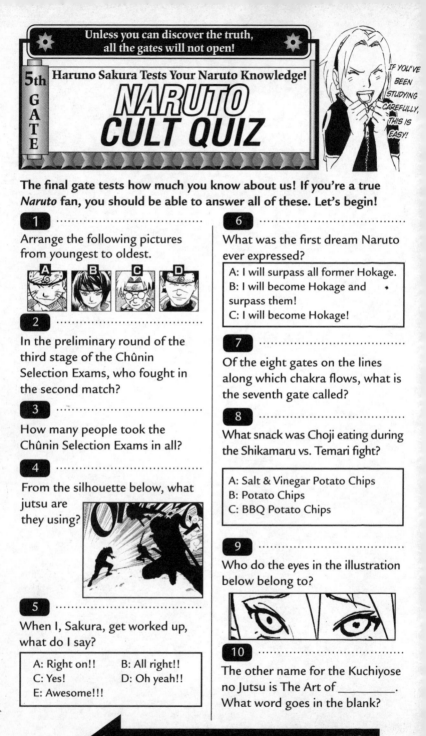

1

Arrange the following pictures from youngest to oldest.

A
B
C
D

2

In the preliminary round of the third stage of the Chûnin Selection Exams, who fought in the second match?

3

How many people took the Chûnin Selection Exams in all?

4

From the silhouette below, what jutsu are they using?

5

When I, Sakura, get worked up, what do I say?

A: Right on!! B: All right!!
C: Yes! D: Oh yeah!!
E: Awesome!!!

6

What was the first dream Naruto ever expressed?

A: I will surpass all former Hokage.
B: I will become Hokage and surpass them!
C: I will become Hokage!

7

Of the eight gates on the lines along which chakra flows, what is the seventh gate called?

8

What snack was Choji eating during the Shikamaru vs. Temari fight?

A: Salt & Vinegar Potato Chips
B: Potato Chips
C: BBQ Potato Chips

9

Who do the eyes in the illustration below belong to?

10

The other name for the Kuchiyose no Jutsu is The Art of ________. What word goes in the blank?

ANSWERS TO ALL FIVE GATES BEGIN ON PAGE 256!!

Naruto's First Appearance!

This short story was published in August 1997 in *Weekly Shonen Jump's* spin-off magazine, *Akamaru Jump*. It's a different Naruto than you know now, but you can still see the promise that led to serialization. This is where Masashi Kishimoto and Naruto's legends began!

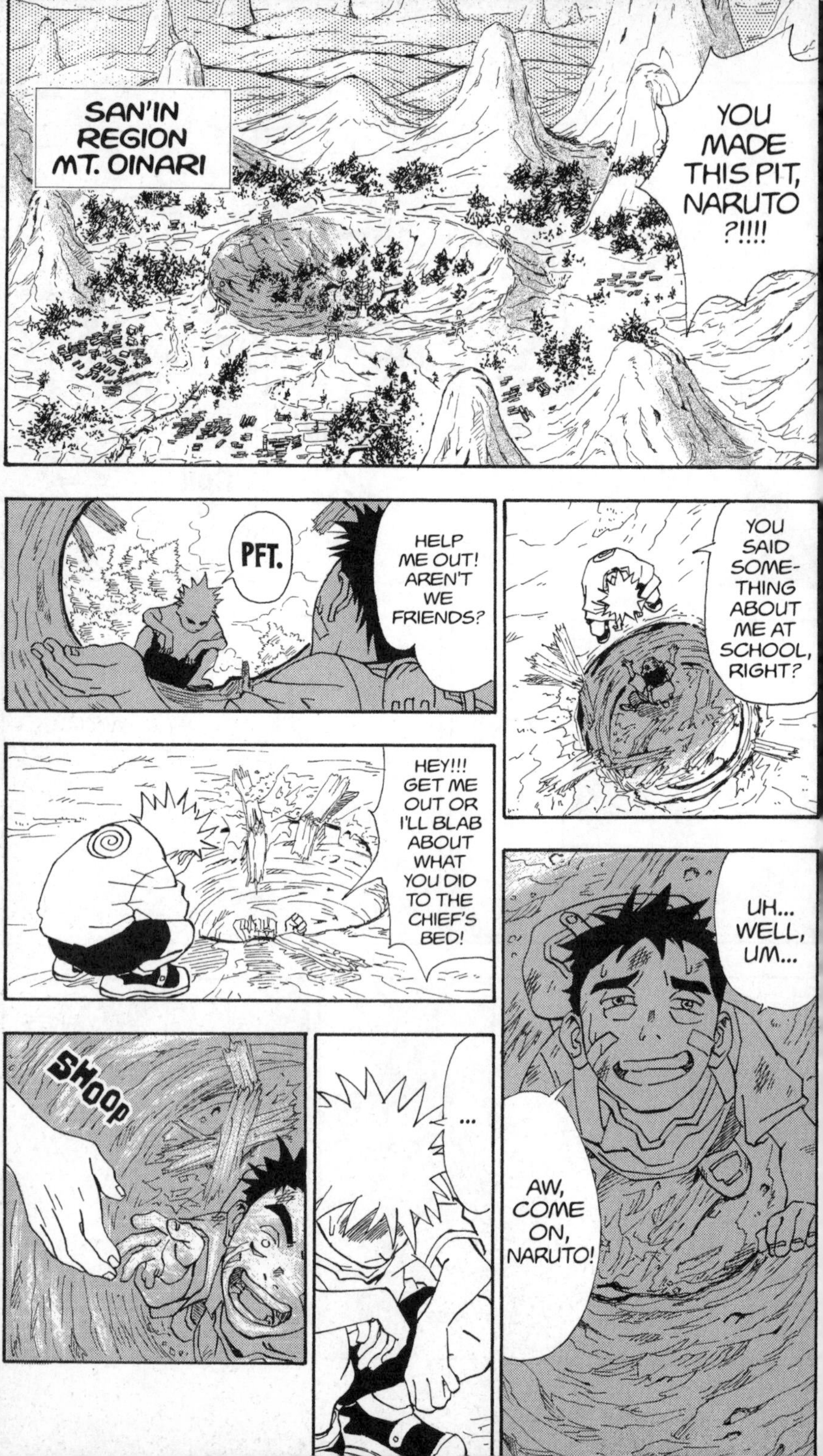
SAN'IN REGION MT. OINARI
YOU MADE THIS PIT, NARUTO?!!!!
YOU SAID SOME-THING ABOUT ME AT SCHOOL, RIGHT?
HELP ME OUT! AREN'T WE FRIENDS?
PFT.
HEY!!! GET ME OUT OR I'LL BLAB ABOUT WHAT YOU DID TO THE CHIEF'S BED!
UH... WELL, UM...
AW, COME ON, NARUTO!
...
SHOOP

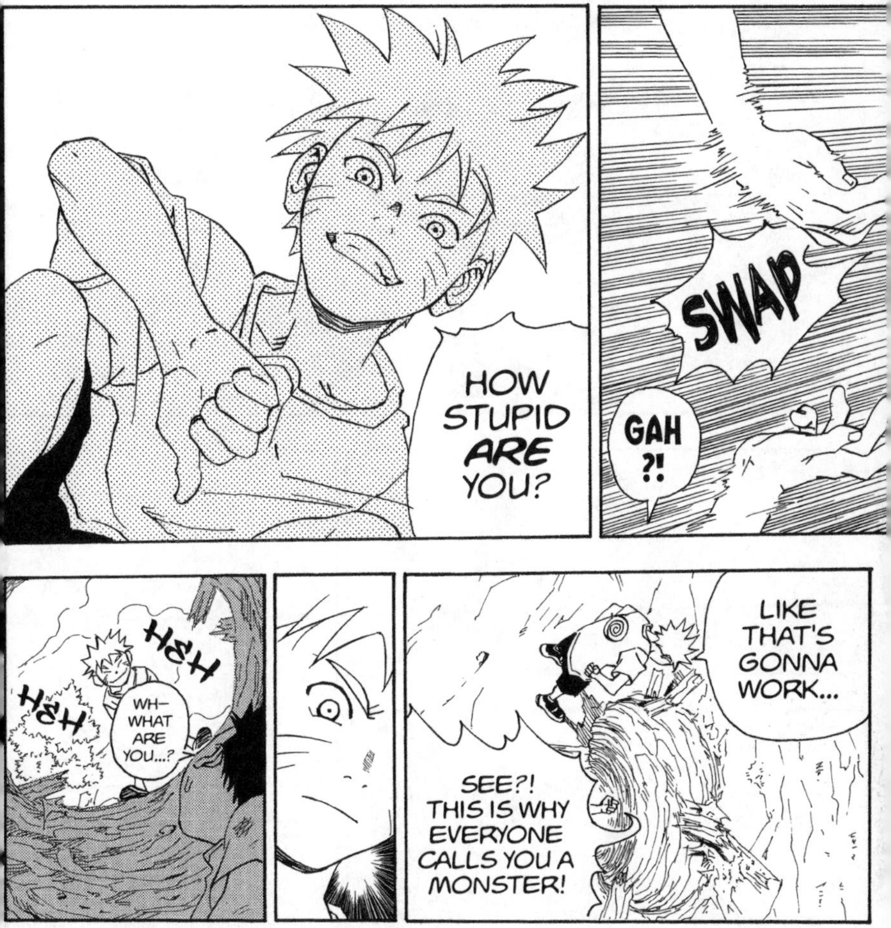
SWAP
GAH ?!
HOW STUPID ARE YOU?
LIKE THAT'S GONNA WORK...
SEE?! THIS IS WHY EVERYONE CALLS YOU A MONSTER!
HEH
HEH
WH- WHAT ARE YOU...?
TAKES TEN DAYS TO GET MY SCENT OUT. ♡
DON'T ...
PLEASE ...
HERE IT COMES!
AUGGGHHH!!!

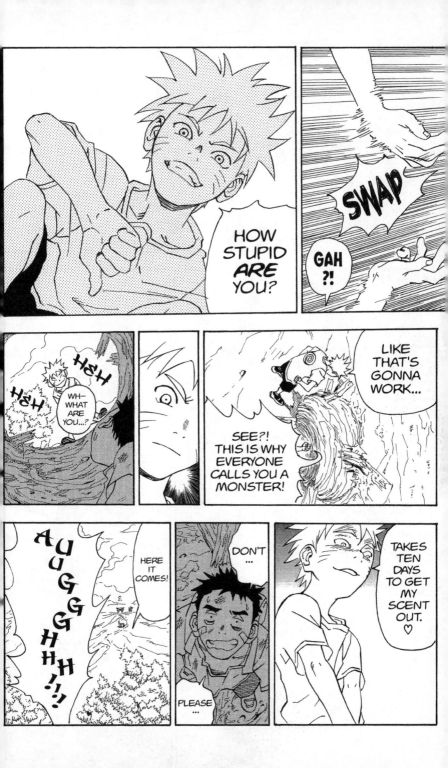

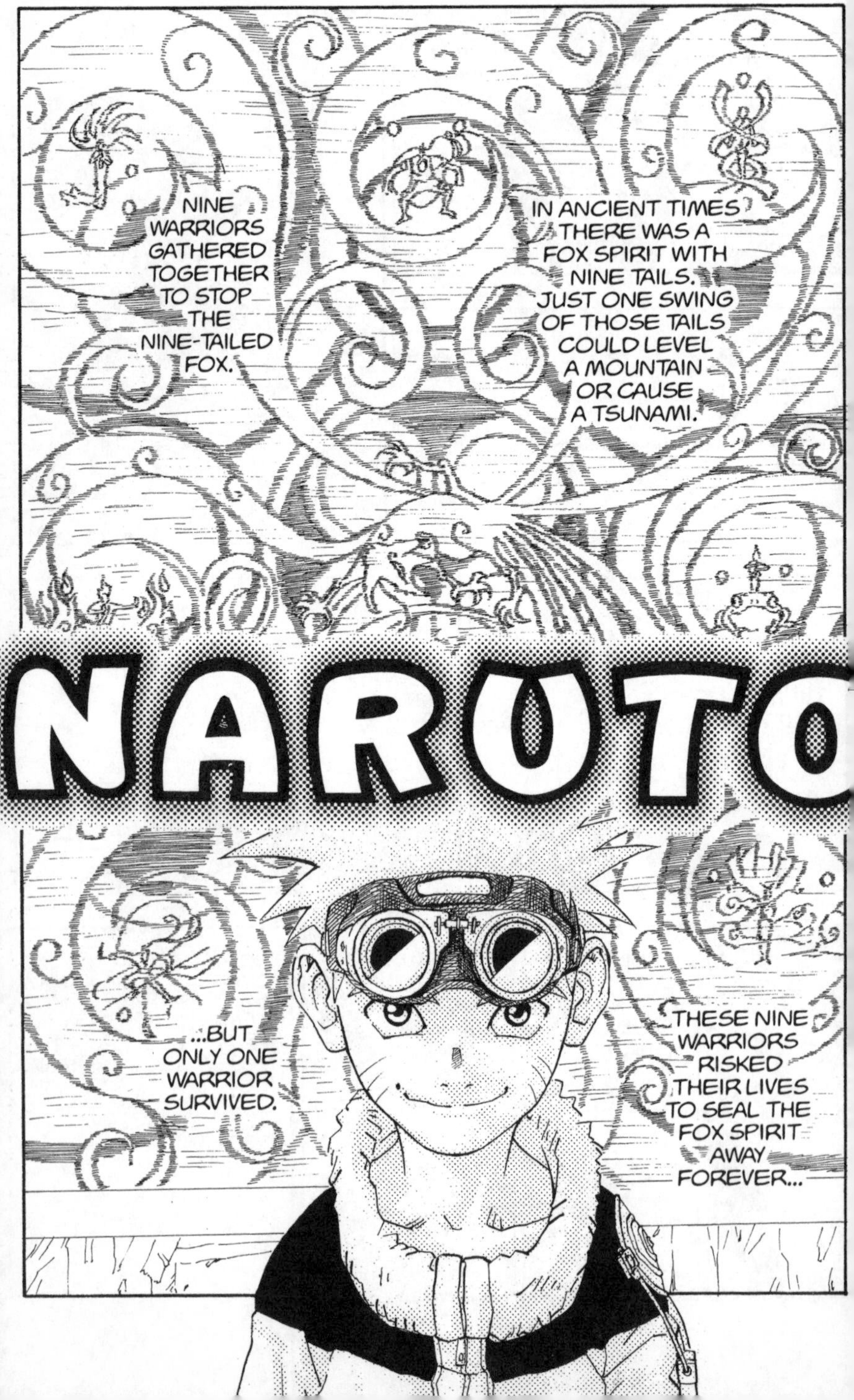
IN ANCIENT TIMES THERE WAS A FOX SPIRIT WITH NINE TAILS. JUST ONE SWING OF THOSE TAILS COULD LEVEL A MOUNTAIN OR CAUSE A TSUNAMI.
NINE WARRIORS GATHERED TOGETHER TO STOP THE NINE-TAILED FOX.
NARUTO
THESE NINE WARRIORS RISKED THEIR LIVES TO SEAL THE FOX SPIRIT AWAY FOREVER...
...BUT ONLY ONE WARRIOR SURVIVED.

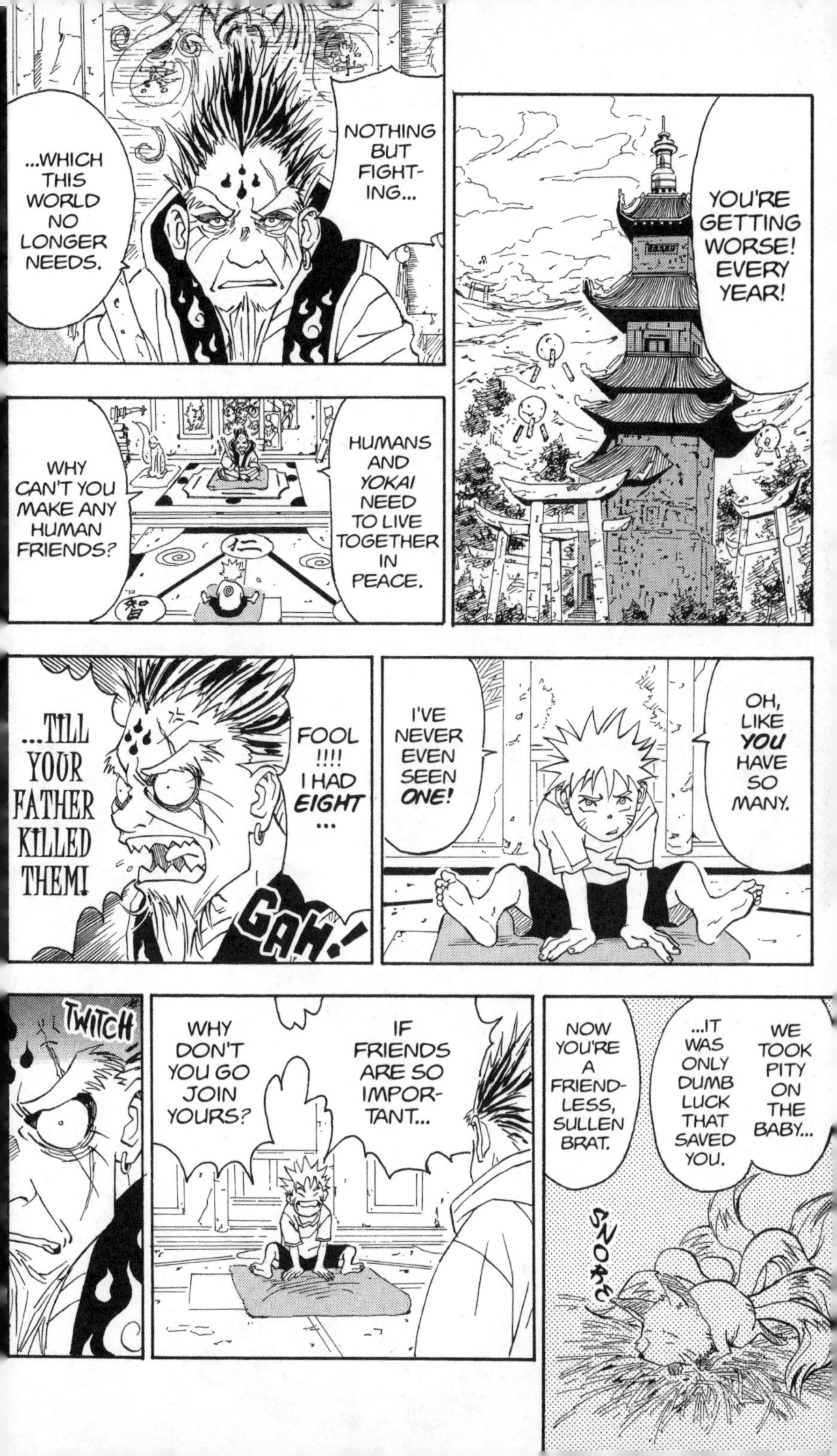
YOU'RE GETTING WORSE! EVERY YEAR!
NOTHING BUT FIGHTING...
...WHICH THIS WORLD NO LONGER NEEDS.
HUMANS AND YOKAI NEED TO LIVE TOGETHER IN PEACE.
WHY CAN'T YOU MAKE ANY HUMAN FRIENDS?
OH, LIKE YOU HAVE SO MANY.
I'VE NEVER EVEN SEEN ONE!
FOOL!!!! I HAD EIGHT...
...TILL YOUR FATHER KILLED THEM!
GAH!
WE TOOK PITY ON THE BABY...
...IT WAS ONLY DUMB LUCK THAT SAVED YOU.
NOW YOU'RE A FRIENDLESS, SULLEN BRAT.
SNORE
IF FRIENDS ARE SO IMPORTANT...
WHY DON'T YOU GO JOIN YOURS?
TWITCH

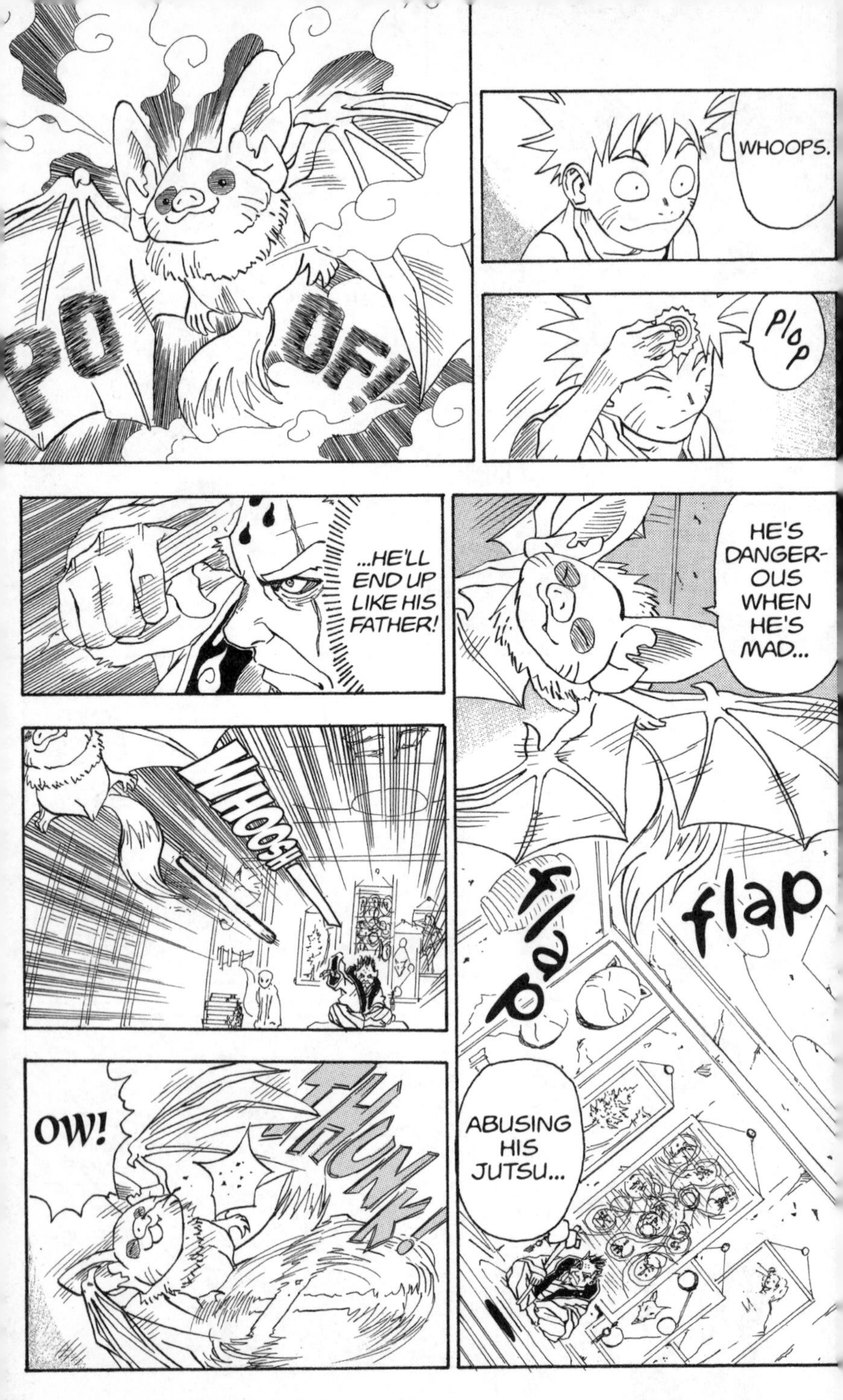
WHOOPS.
Plop
POOF!
HE'S DANGER-OUS WHEN HE'S MAD...
flap
flap
ABUSING HIS JUTSU...
...HE'LL END UP LIKE HIS FATHER!
WHOOSH
THUNK!
OW!

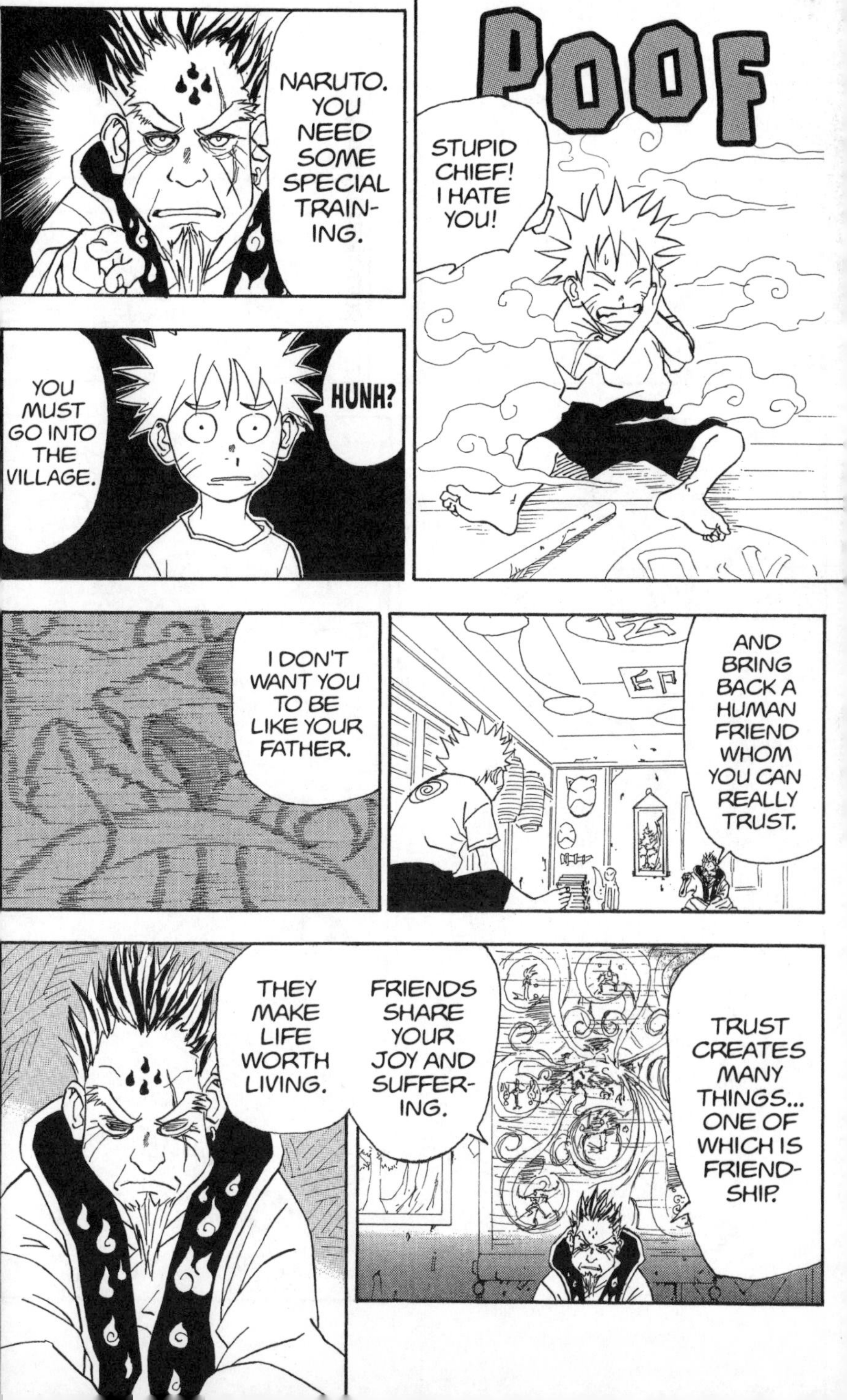
POOF
STUPID CHIEF! I HATE YOU!
NARUTO. YOU NEED SOME SPECIAL TRAIN-ING.
HUNH?
YOU MUST GO INTO THE VILLAGE.
AND BRING BACK A HUMAN FRIEND WHOM YOU CAN REALLY TRUST.
I DON'T WANT YOU TO BE LIKE YOUR FATHER.
TRUST CREATES MANY THINGS... ONE OF WHICH IS FRIEND-SHIP.
FRIENDS SHARE YOUR JOY AND SUFFER-ING.
THEY MAKE LIFE WORTH LIVING.

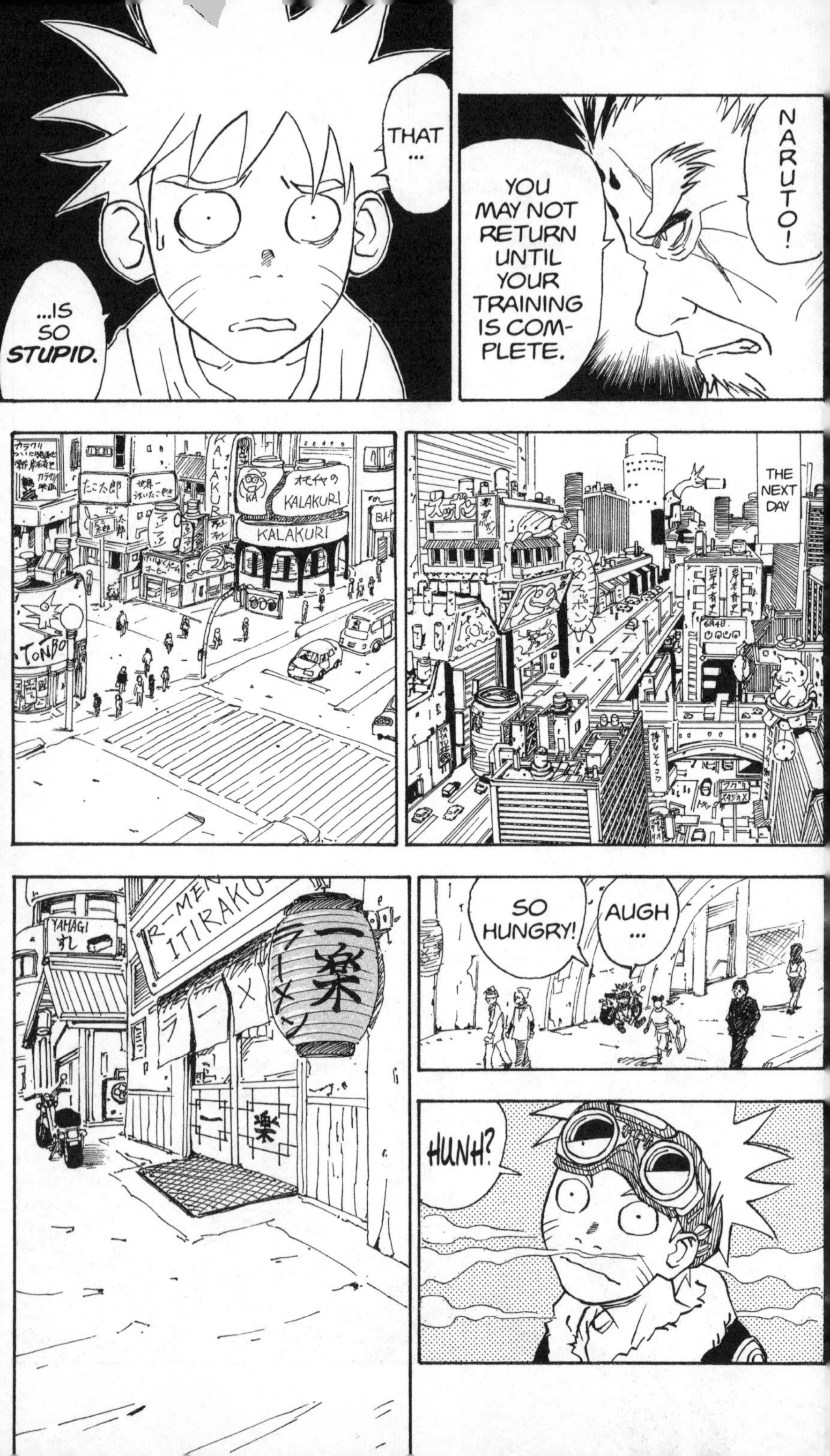
NARUTO!
YOU MAY NOT RETURN UNTIL YOUR TRAINING IS COMPLETE.
THAT...
...IS SO STUPID.
THE NEXT DAY
KALAKURI
オモチャの KALAKURI
KALAKURI
TONBO
AUGH...
SO HUNGRY!
HUNH?
R-MEN ITIRAKU
一楽 ラーメン
YAMAGI すし

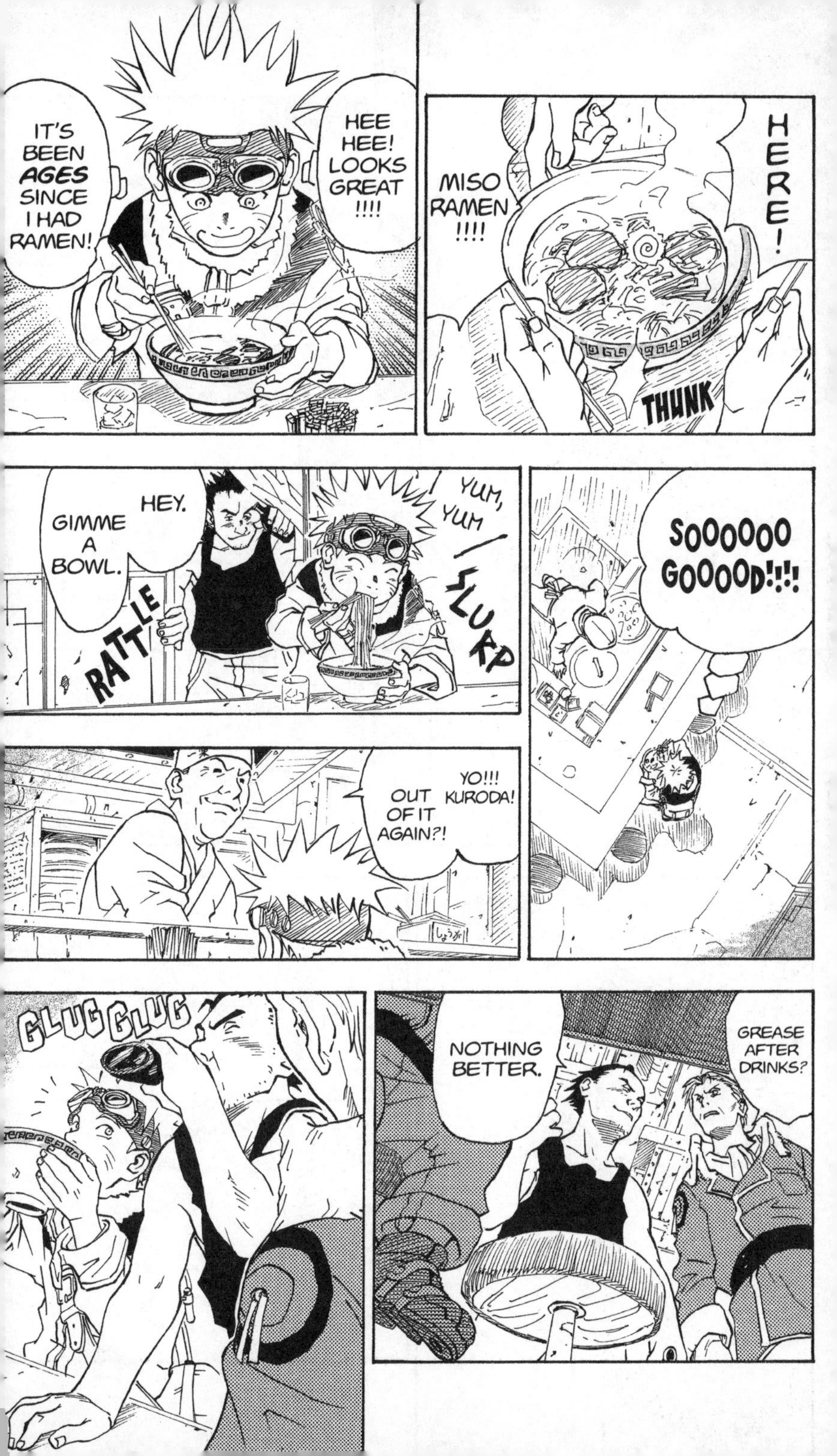
HERE!
MISO RAMEN!!!!
THUNK
HEE HEE! LOOKS GREAT!!!!
IT'S BEEN AGES SINCE I HAD RAMEN!
SOOOOOO GOOOOD!!!
YUM, YUM
SLURP
HEY. GIMME A BOWL.
RATTLE
YO!!! KURODA! OUT OF IT AGAIN?!
GREASE AFTER DRINKS?
NOTHING BETTER.
GLUG GLUG

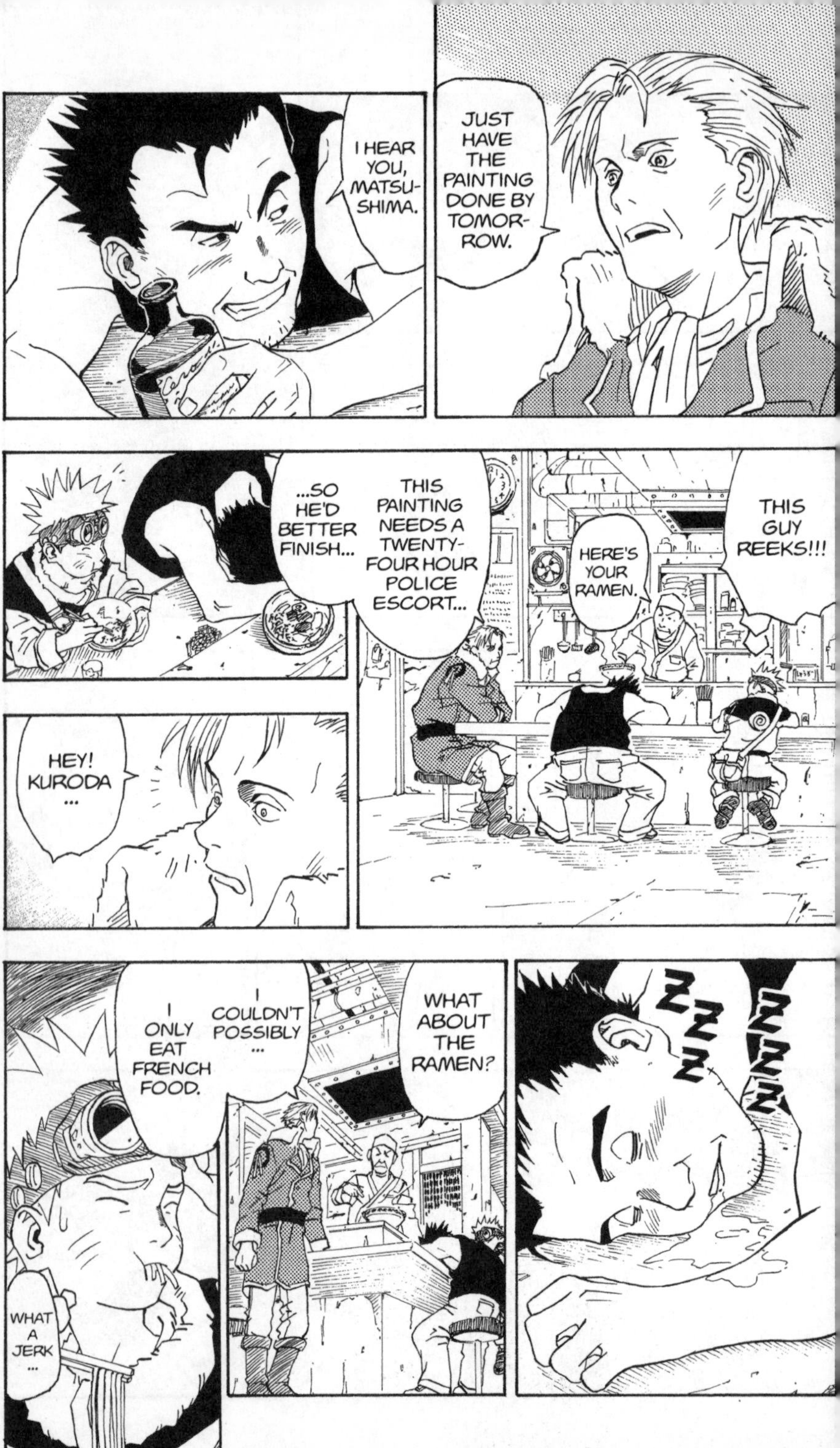
JUST HAVE THE PAINTING DONE BY TOMORROW.
I HEAR YOU, MATSUSHIMA.
THIS GUY REEKS!!!
HERE'S YOUR RAMEN.
THIS PAINTING NEEDS A TWENTY-FOUR HOUR POLICE ESCORT...
...SO HE'D BETTER FINISH...
HEY! KURODA ...
ZZZ
ZZZZ
WHAT ABOUT THE RAMEN?
I COULDN'T POSSIBLY ...
I ONLY EAT FRENCH FOOD.
WHAT A JERK ...

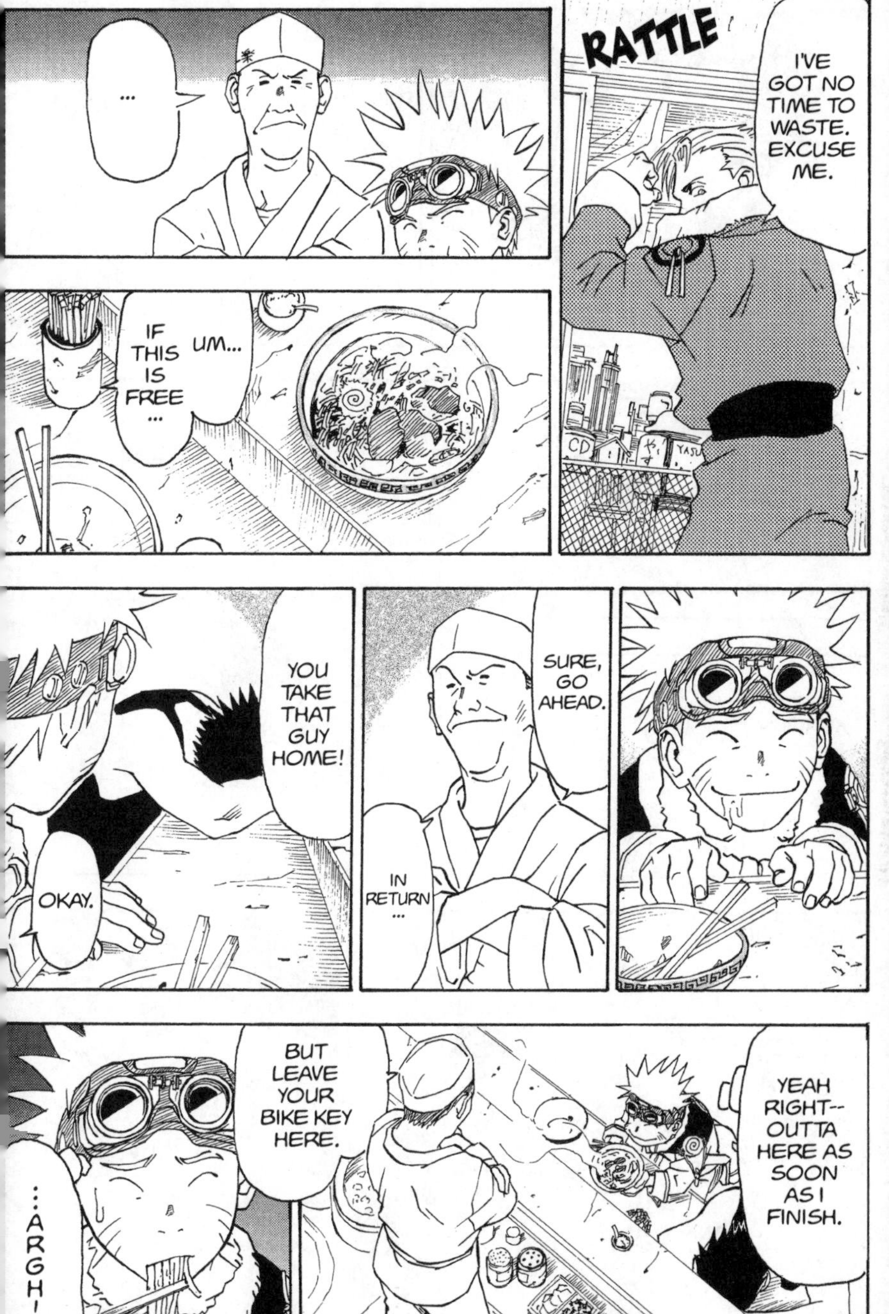
RATTLE
I'VE GOT NO TIME TO WASTE. EXCUSE ME.
CD
YASU
...
UM... IF THIS IS FREE ...
SURE, GO AHEAD.
IN RETURN ...
YOU TAKE THAT GUY HOME!
OKAY.
YEAH RIGHT-- OUTTA HERE AS SOON AS I FINISH.
BUT LEAVE YOUR BIKE KEY HERE.
...ARGH!

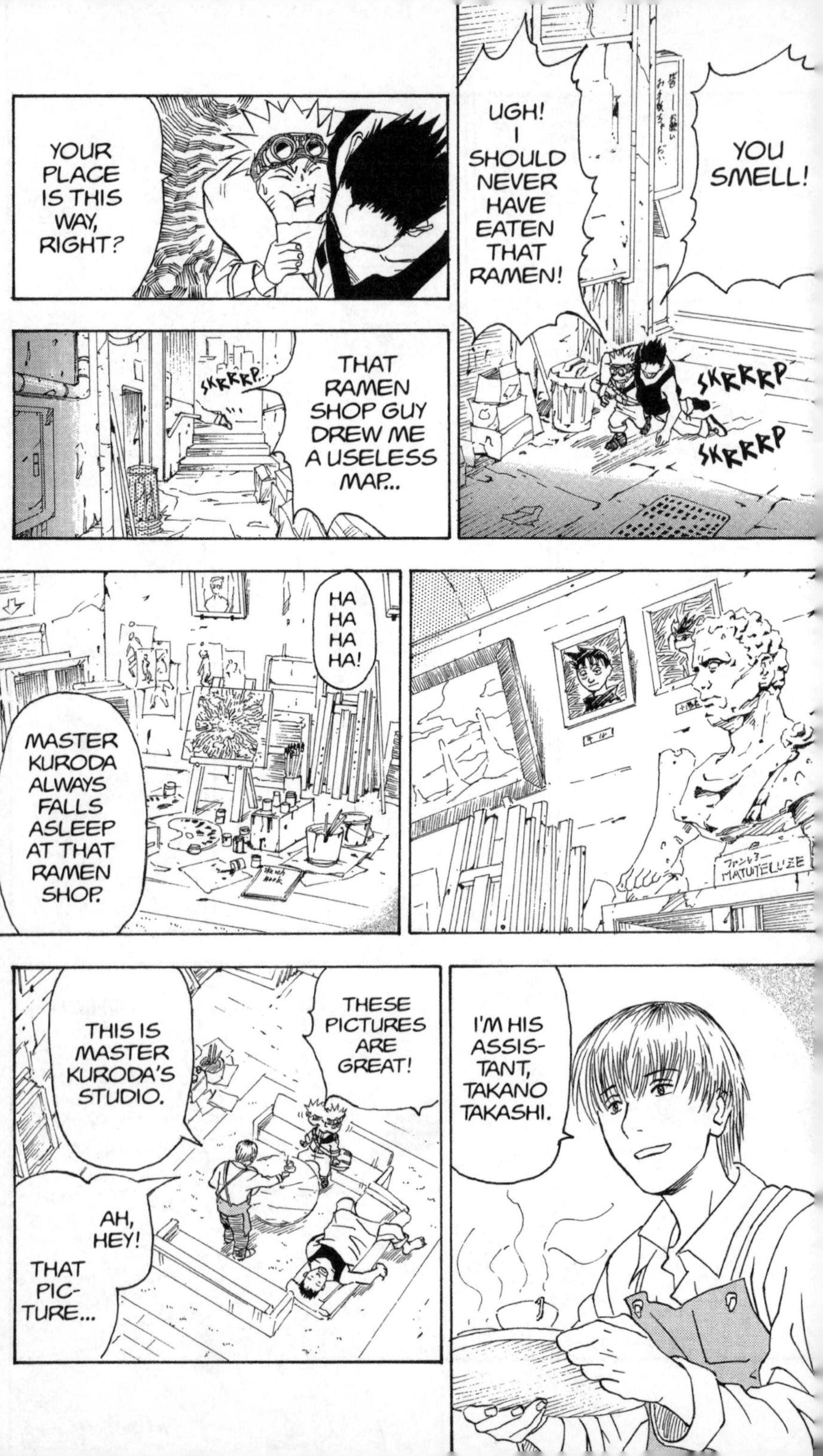
YOU SMELL!
UGH! I SHOULD NEVER HAVE EATEN THAT RAMEN!
SKRRRP
SKRRRP
YOUR PLACE IS THIS WAY, RIGHT?
SKRRRP...
THAT RAMEN SHOP GUY DREW ME A USELESS MAP...
HA HA HA HA!
MASTER KURODA ALWAYS FALLS ASLEEP AT THAT RAMEN SHOP.
I'M HIS ASSISTANT, TAKANO TAKASHI.
THESE PICTURES ARE GREAT!
THIS IS MASTER KURODA'S STUDIO.
AH, HEY!
THAT PICTURE...

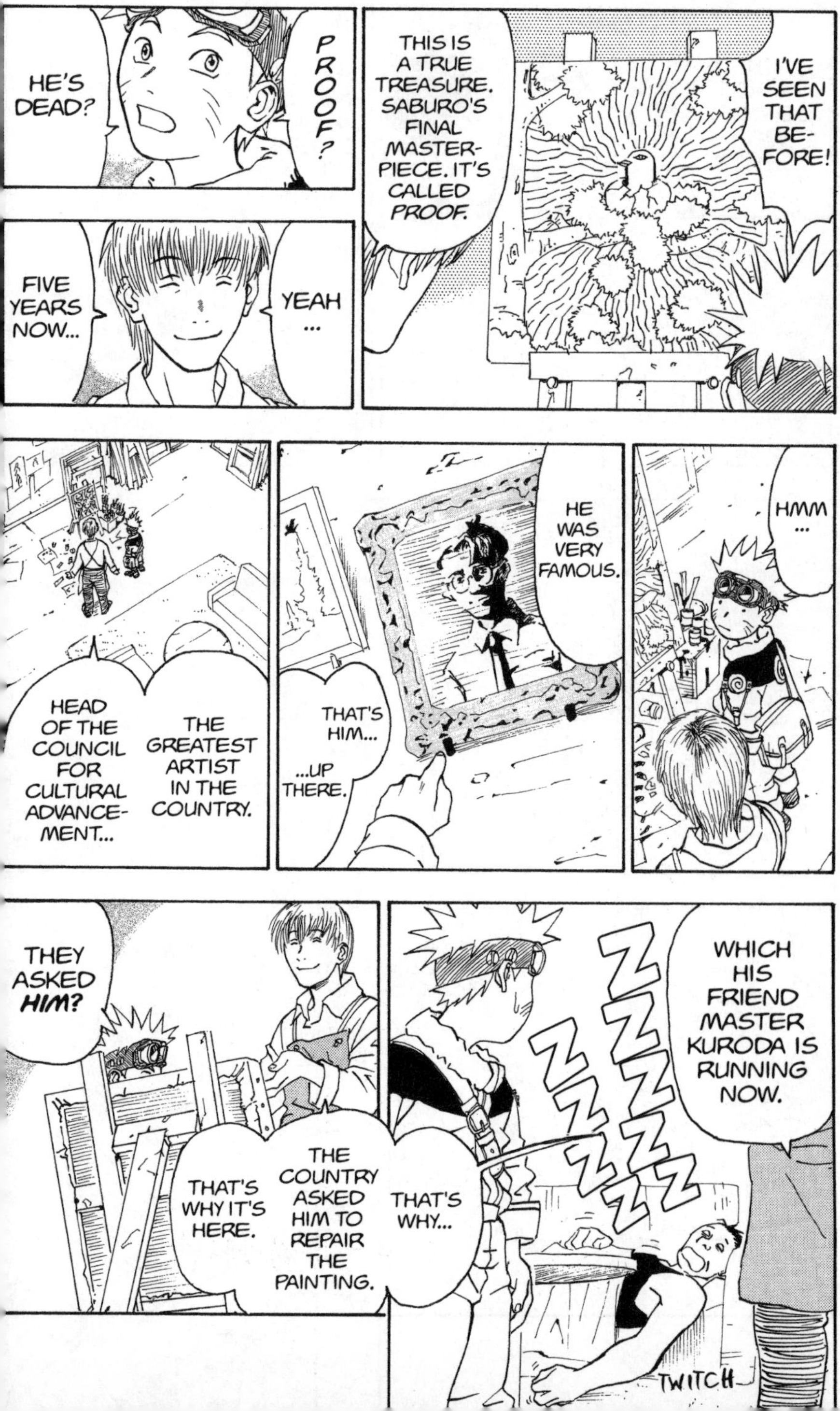
THIS IS A TRUE TREASURE. SABURO'S FINAL MASTERPIECE. IT'S CALLED *PROOF.*
I'VE SEEN THAT BEFORE!
PROOF?
HE'S DEAD?
YEAH...
FIVE YEARS NOW...
HMM...
HE WAS VERY FAMOUS.
THAT'S HIM...
...UP THERE.
THE GREATEST ARTIST IN THE COUNTRY.
HEAD OF THE COUNCIL FOR CULTURAL ADVANCEMENT...
WHICH HIS FRIEND MASTER KURODA IS RUNNING NOW.
ZZZZZZZ
TWITCH
THEY ASKED ***HIM?***
THAT'S WHY...
THE COUNTRY ASKED HIM TO REPAIR THE PAINTING.
THAT'S WHY IT'S HERE.

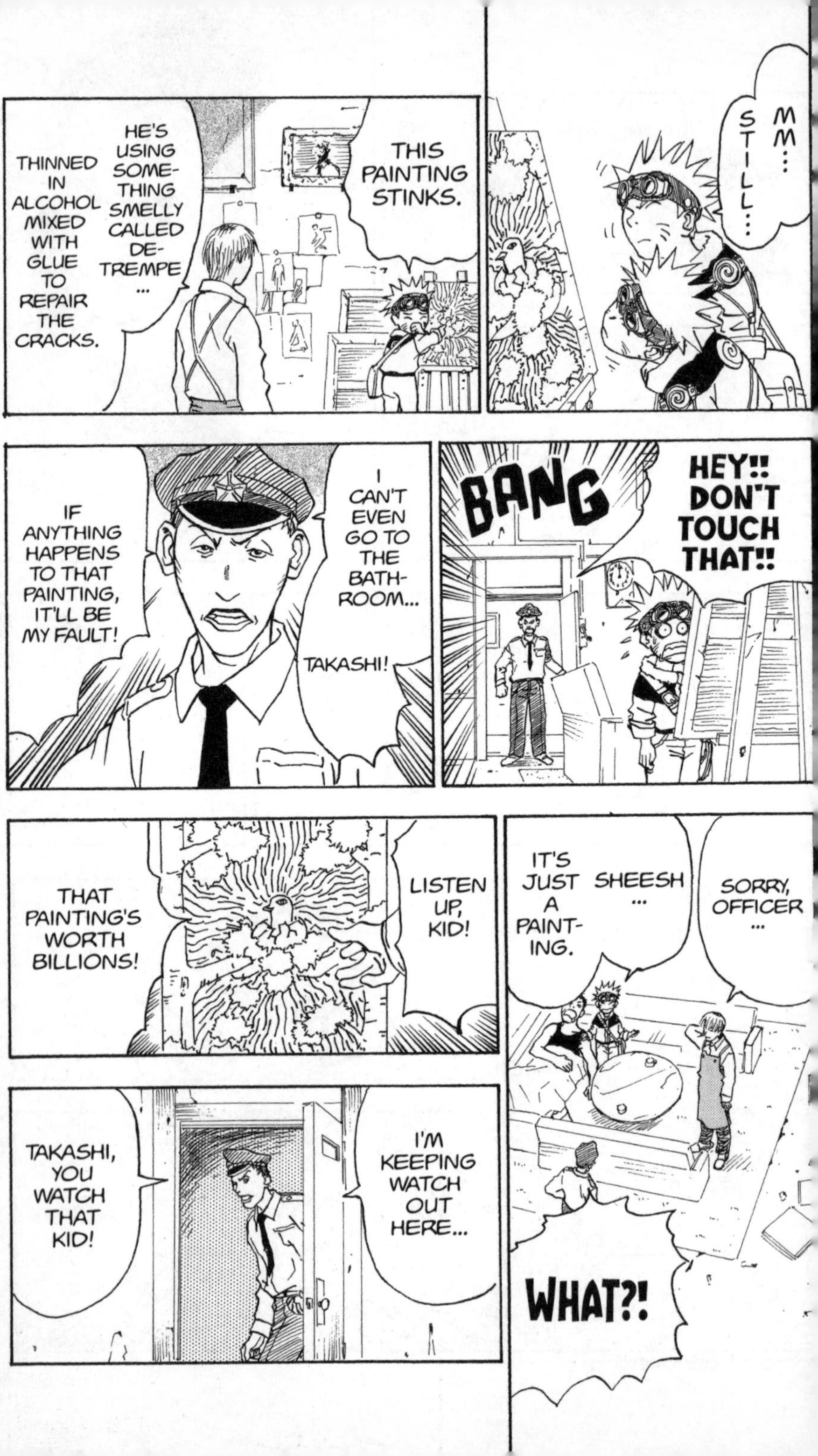
MM... STILL...
THIS PAINTING STINKS.
HE'S USING SOMETHING SMELLY CALLED DETREMPE...
THINNED IN ALCOHOL MIXED WITH GLUE TO REPAIR THE CRACKS.
BANG
HEY!! DON'T TOUCH THAT!!
I CAN'T EVEN GO TO THE BATHROOM...
TAKASHI!
IF ANYTHING HAPPENS TO THAT PAINTING, IT'LL BE MY FAULT!
SORRY, OFFICER...
SHEESH...
IT'S JUST A PAINTING.
WHAT?!
LISTEN UP, KID!
THAT PAINTING'S WORTH BILLIONS!
I'M KEEPING WATCH OUT HERE...
TAKASHI, YOU WATCH THAT KID!

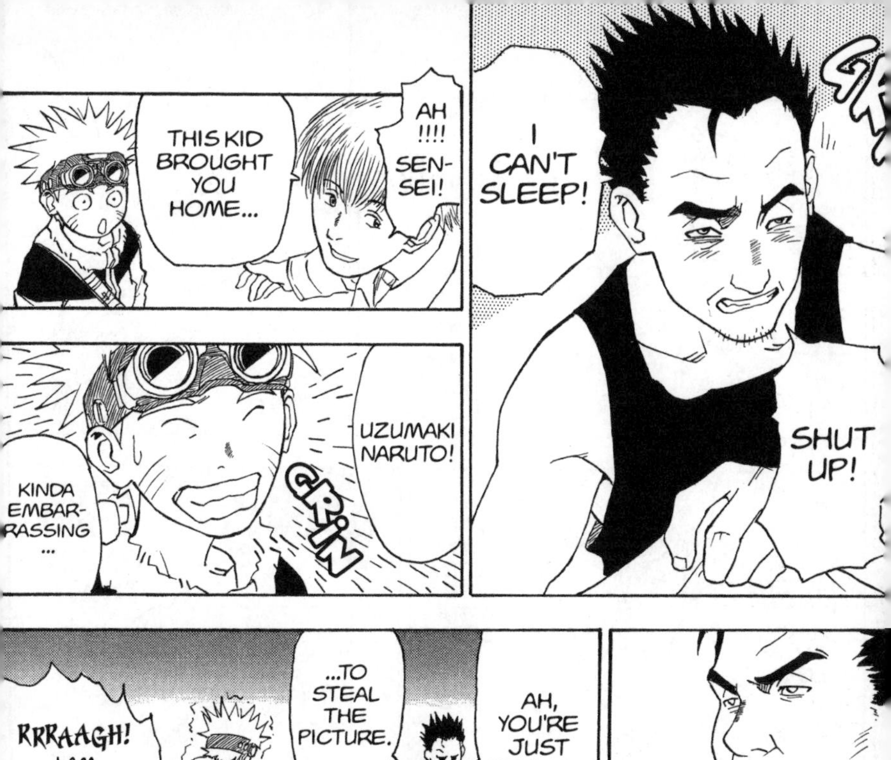
GR
I CAN'T SLEEP!
SHUT UP!
AH !!!! SEN-SEI!
THIS KID BROUGHT YOU HOME...
UZUMAKI NARUTO!
GRIN
KINDA EMBARRASSING ...
AH, YOU'RE JUST TRYING...
...TO STEAL THE PICTURE.
RRRAAGH! I AM SO NOT MAKING FRIENDS WITH HIM!!!
BUT AS THANKS ...
DRINK WITH ME.
ARE YOU NUTS?
I CAN'T DRINK!
SWISH

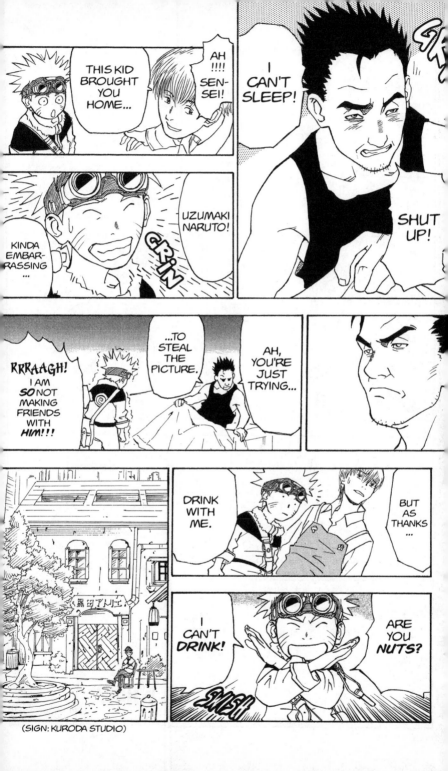

(SIGN: KURODA STUDIO)

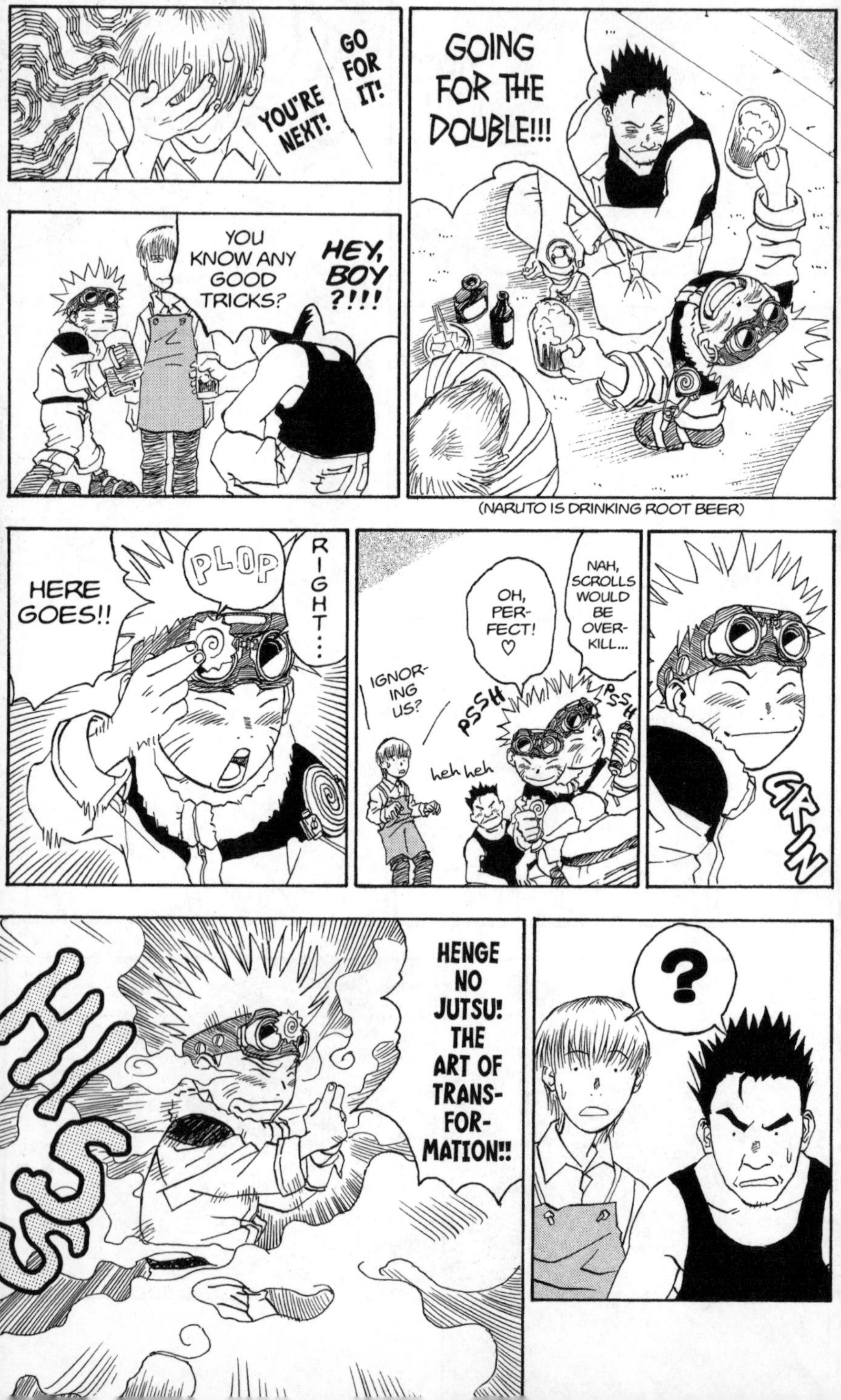
GOING FOR THE DOUBLE!!!
GO FOR IT!
YOU'RE NEXT!
HEY, BOY?!!!
YOU KNOW ANY GOOD TRICKS?
(NARUTO IS DRINKING ROOT BEER)
GRIN
NAH, SCROLLS WOULD BE OVER-KILL...
OH, PER-FECT! ♡
PSSH
PSSH
IGNOR-ING US?
heh heh
RIGHT...
PLOP
HERE GOES!!
?
HENGE NO JUTSU! THE ART OF TRANS-FOR-MATION!!
HISS

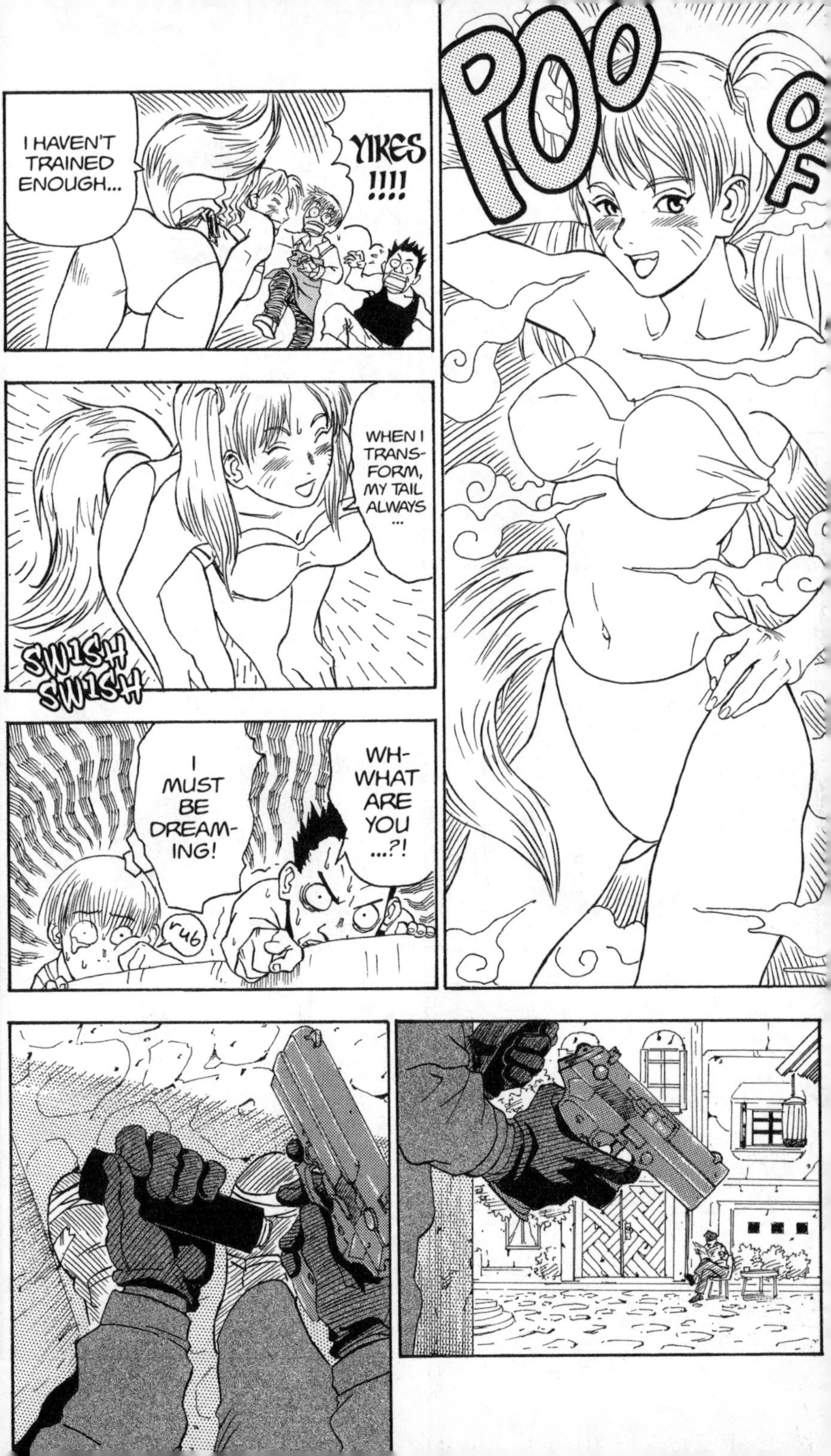
POOF
YIKES!!!!
I HAVEN'T TRAINED ENOUGH...
WHEN I TRANSFORM, MY TAIL ALWAYS...
SWISH SWISH
WH-WHAT ARE YOU...?!
I MUST BE DREAMING!
rub

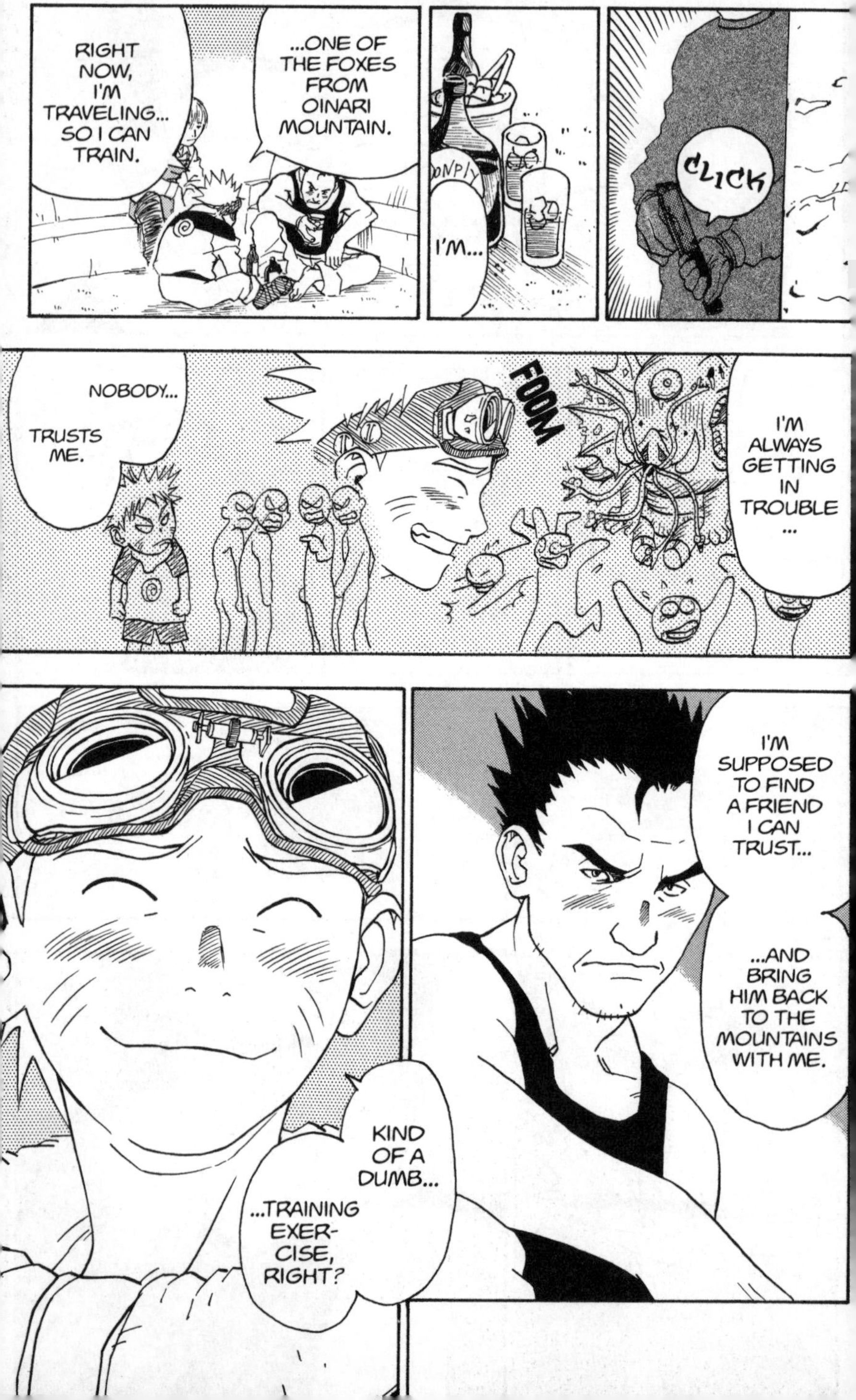
CLICK
I'M...
...ONE OF THE FOXES FROM OINARI MOUNTAIN.
RIGHT NOW, I'M TRAVELING... SO I CAN TRAIN.
I'M ALWAYS GETTING IN TROUBLE...
FOOM
NOBODY...
TRUSTS ME.
I'M SUPPOSED TO FIND A FRIEND I CAN TRUST...
...AND BRING HIM BACK TO THE MOUNTAINS WITH ME.
KIND OF A DUMB...
...TRAINING EXER-CISE, RIGHT?

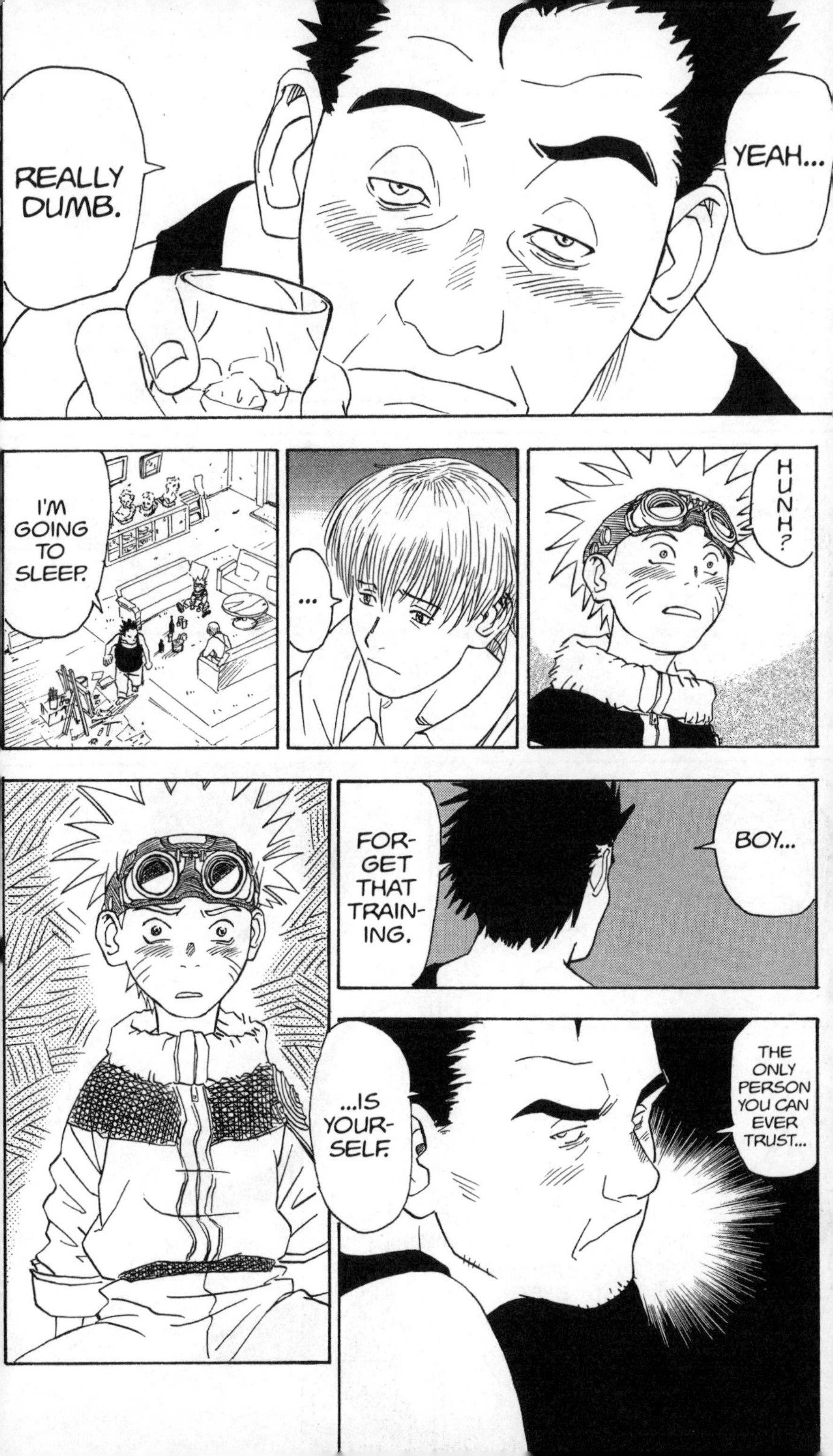
YEAH...
REALLY DUMB.
HUNH?
...
I'M GOING TO SLEEP.
BOY...
FOR-GET THAT TRAIN-ING.
THE ONLY PERSON YOU CAN EVER TRUST...
...IS YOUR-SELF.

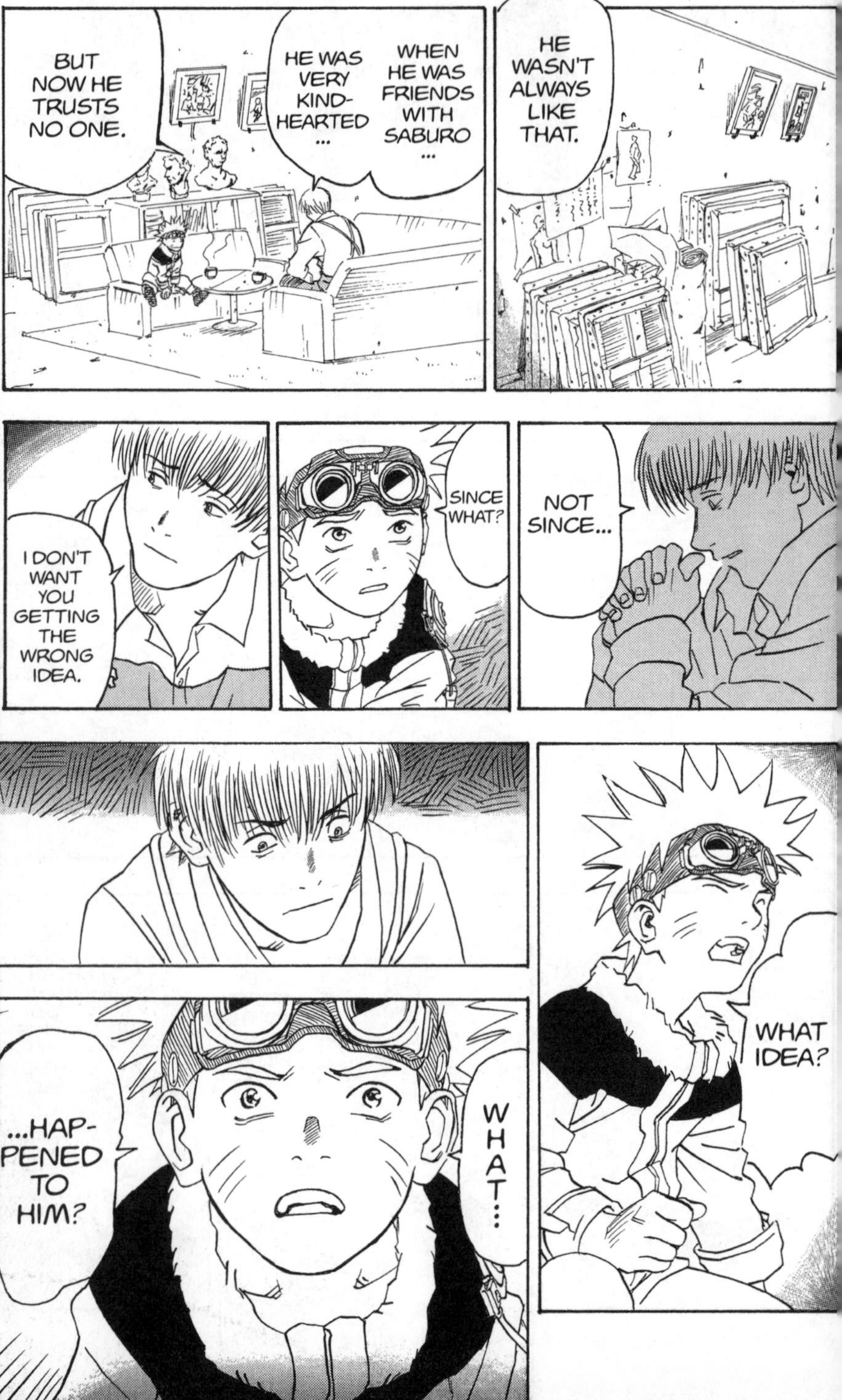
HE WASN'T ALWAYS LIKE THAT.
WHEN HE WAS FRIENDS WITH SABURO ...
HE WAS VERY KIND-HEARTED ...
BUT NOW HE TRUSTS NO ONE.
NOT SINCE...
SINCE WHAT?
I DON'T WANT YOU GETTING THE WRONG IDEA.
WHAT IDEA?
WHAT...
...HAP-PENED TO HIM?

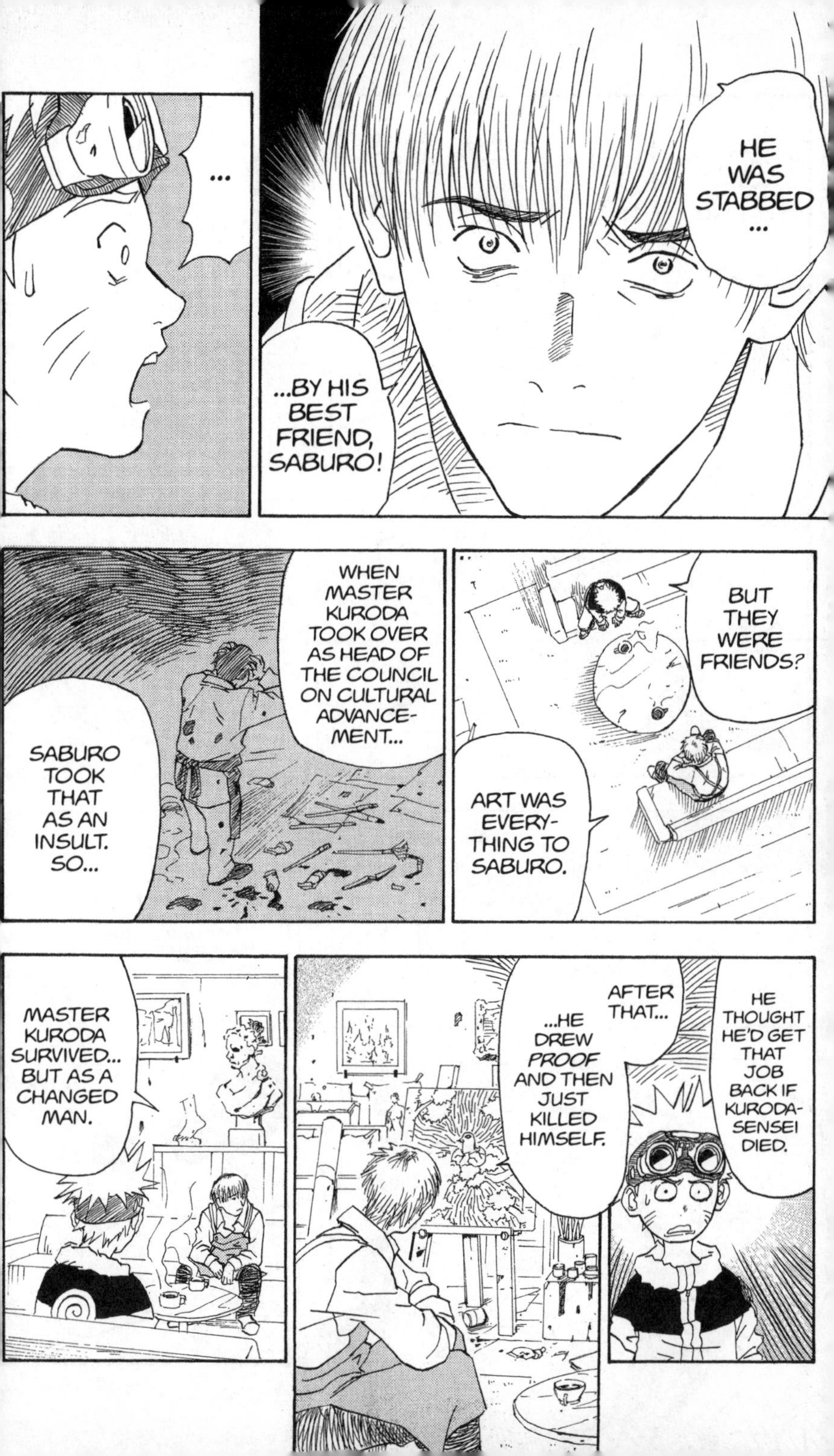
HE WAS STABBED...
...BY HIS BEST FRIEND, SABURO!
...
BUT THEY WERE FRIENDS?
ART WAS EVERY-THING TO SABURO.
WHEN MASTER KURODA TOOK OVER AS HEAD OF THE COUNCIL ON CULTURAL ADVANCE-MENT...
SABURO TOOK THAT AS AN INSULT. SO...
HE THOUGHT HE'D GET THAT JOB BACK IF KURODA-SENSEI DIED.
AFTER THAT...
...HE DREW *PROOF* AND THEN JUST KILLED HIMSELF.
MASTER KURODA SURVIVED... BUT AS A CHANGED MAN.

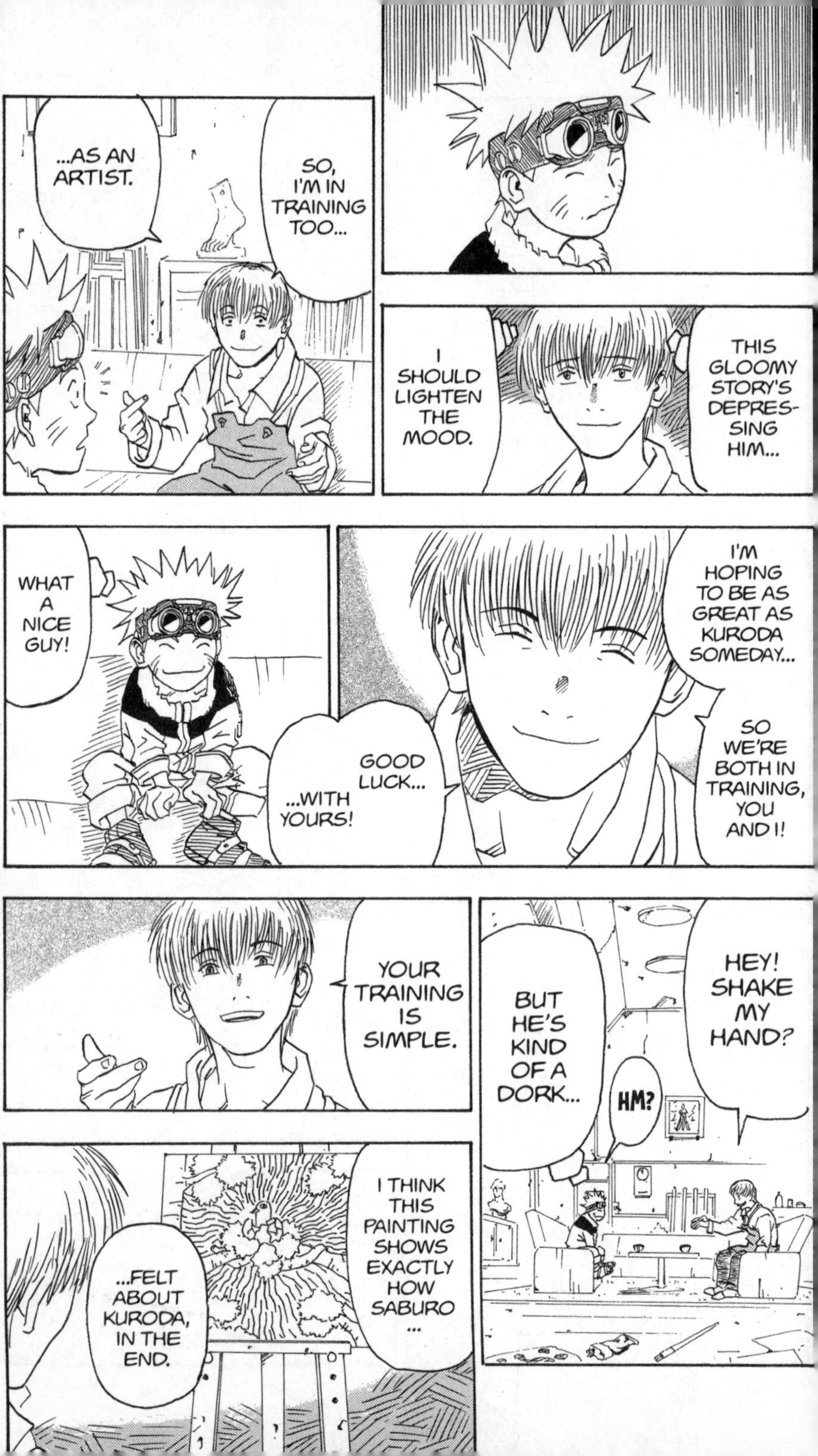
SO, I'M IN TRAINING TOO...
...AS AN ARTIST.
THIS GLOOMY STORY'S DEPRES-SING HIM...
I SHOULD LIGHTEN THE MOOD.
I'M HOPING TO BE AS GREAT AS KURODA SOMEDAY...
SO WE'RE BOTH IN TRAINING, YOU AND I!
GOOD LUCK...
...WITH YOURS!
WHAT A NICE GUY!
HEY! SHAKE MY HAND?
BUT HE'S KIND OF A DORK...
HM?
YOUR TRAINING IS SIMPLE.
I THINK THIS PAINTING SHOWS EXACTLY HOW SABURO ...
...FELT ABOUT KURODA, IN THE END.

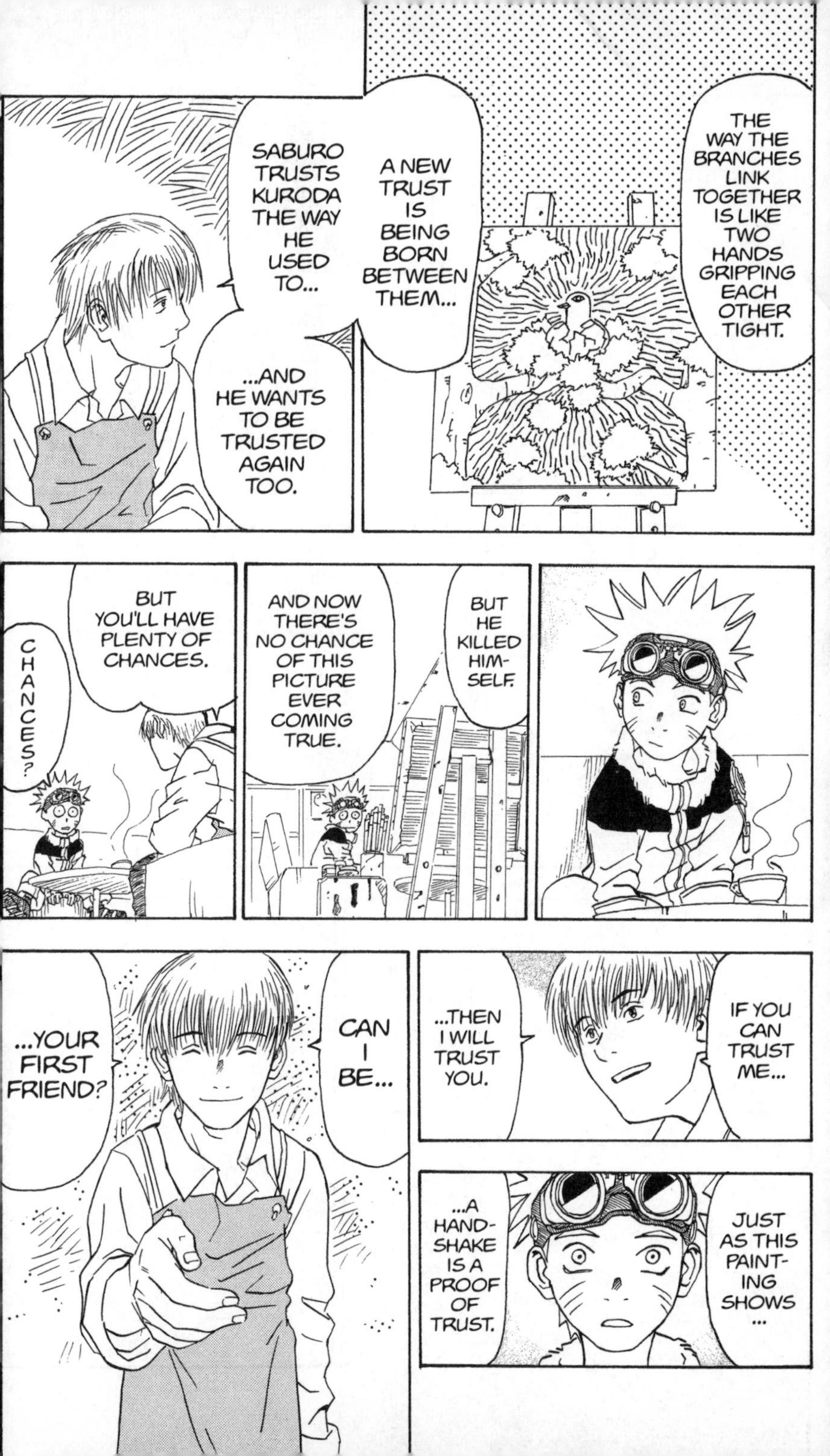
THE WAY THE BRANCHES LINK TOGETHER IS LIKE TWO HANDS GRIPPING EACH OTHER TIGHT.
A NEW TRUST IS BEING BORN BETWEEN THEM...
SABURO TRUSTS KURODA THE WAY HE USED TO...
...AND HE WANTS TO BE TRUSTED AGAIN TOO.
BUT HE KILLED HIM-SELF.
AND NOW THERE'S NO CHANCE OF THIS PICTURE EVER COMING TRUE.
BUT YOU'LL HAVE PLENTY OF CHANCES.
CHANCES?
IF YOU CAN TRUST ME...
...THEN I WILL TRUST YOU.
JUST AS THIS PAINT-ING SHOWS...
...A HAND-SHAKE IS A PROOF OF TRUST.
CAN I BE...
...YOUR FIRST FRIEND?

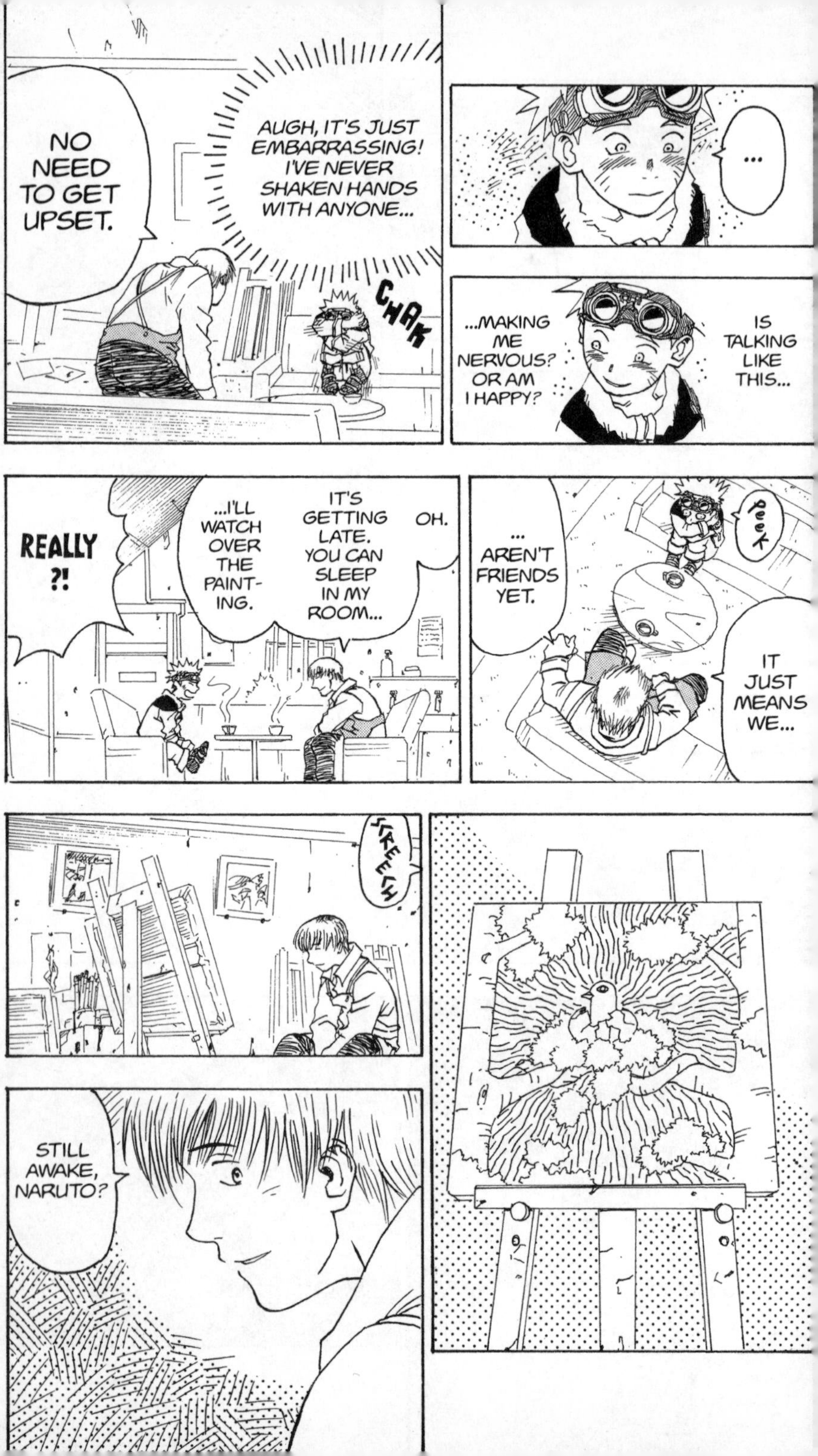
...
IS TALKING LIKE THIS...
...MAKING ME NERVOUS? OR AM I HAPPY?
AUGH, IT'S JUST EMBARRASSING! I'VE NEVER SHAKEN HANDS WITH ANYONE...
CHAK
NO NEED TO GET UPSET.
PEEK
IT JUST MEANS WE...
... AREN'T FRIENDS YET.
OH.
IT'S GETTING LATE. YOU CAN SLEEP IN MY ROOM...
...I'LL WATCH OVER THE PAINT-ING.
REALLY ?!
SKREECH
STILL AWAKE, NARUTO?

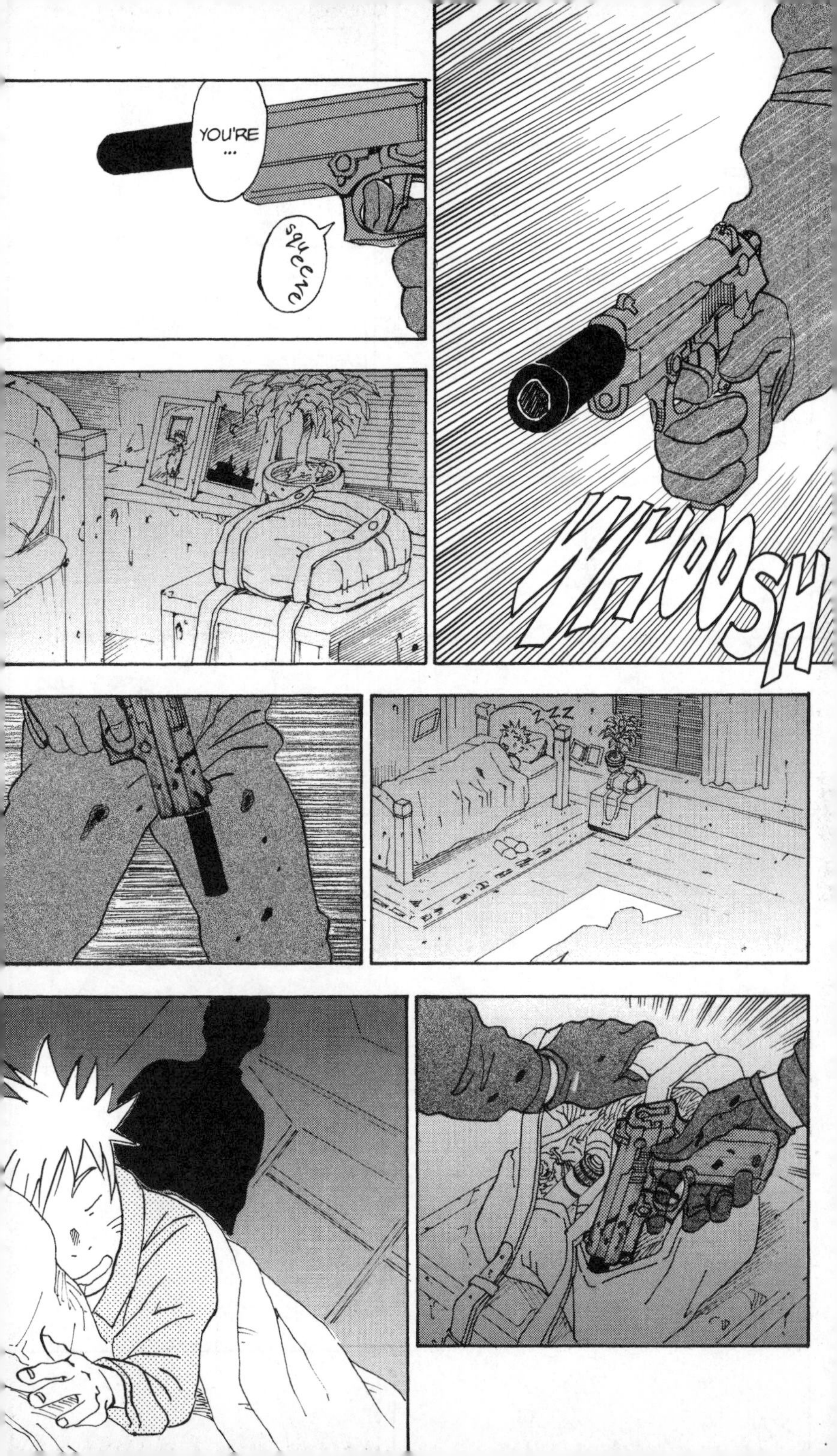
WHOOSH
YOU'RE ...
squeeze
ZZZ

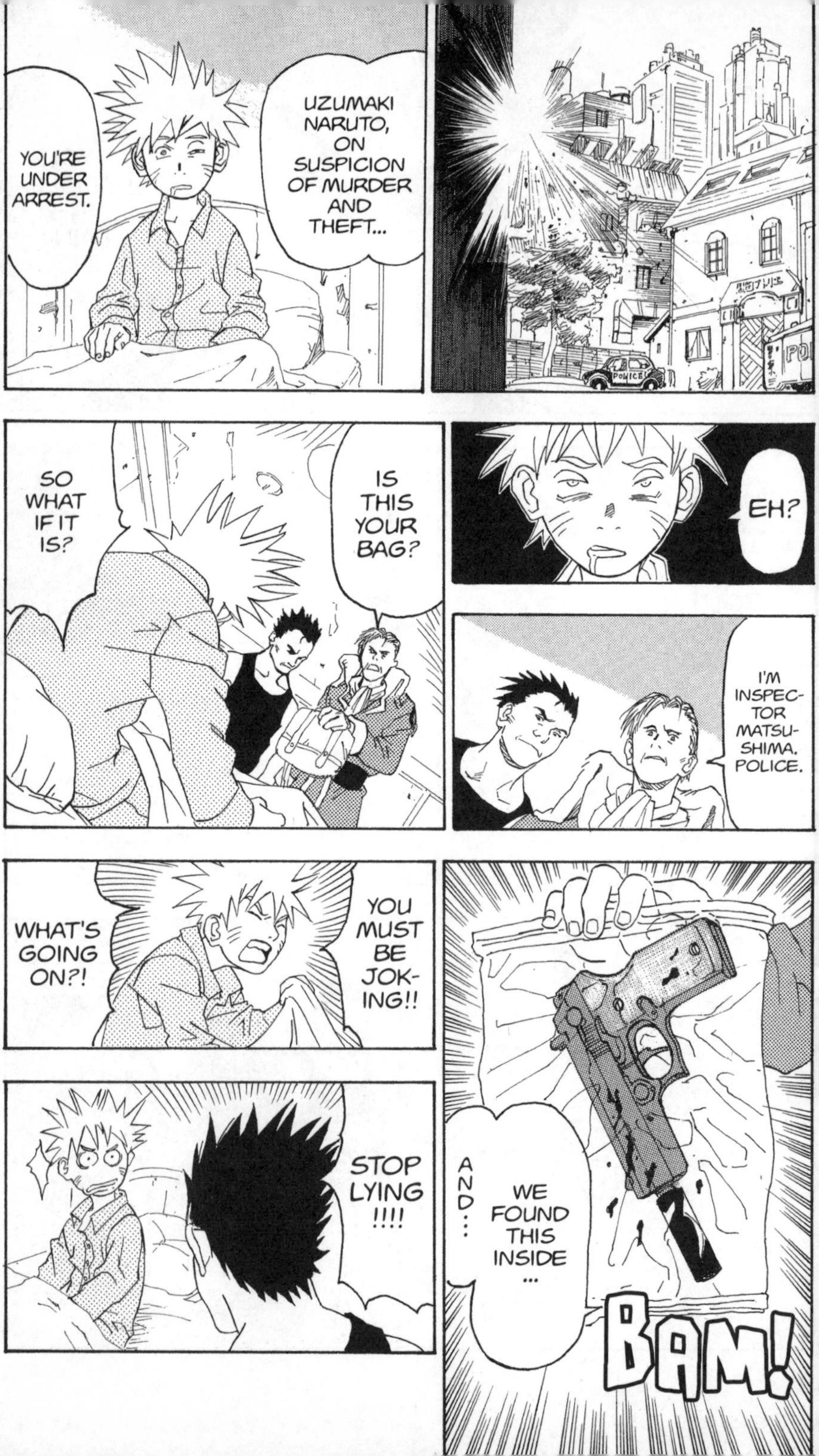
UZUMAKI NARUTO, ON SUSPICION OF MURDER AND THEFT...
YOU'RE UNDER ARREST.
EH?
I'M INSPECTOR MATSUSHIMA. POLICE.
IS THIS YOUR BAG?
SO WHAT IF IT IS?
WE FOUND THIS INSIDE ...
AND...
BAM!
YOU MUST BE JOKING!!
WHAT'S GOING ON?!
STOP LYING!!!!

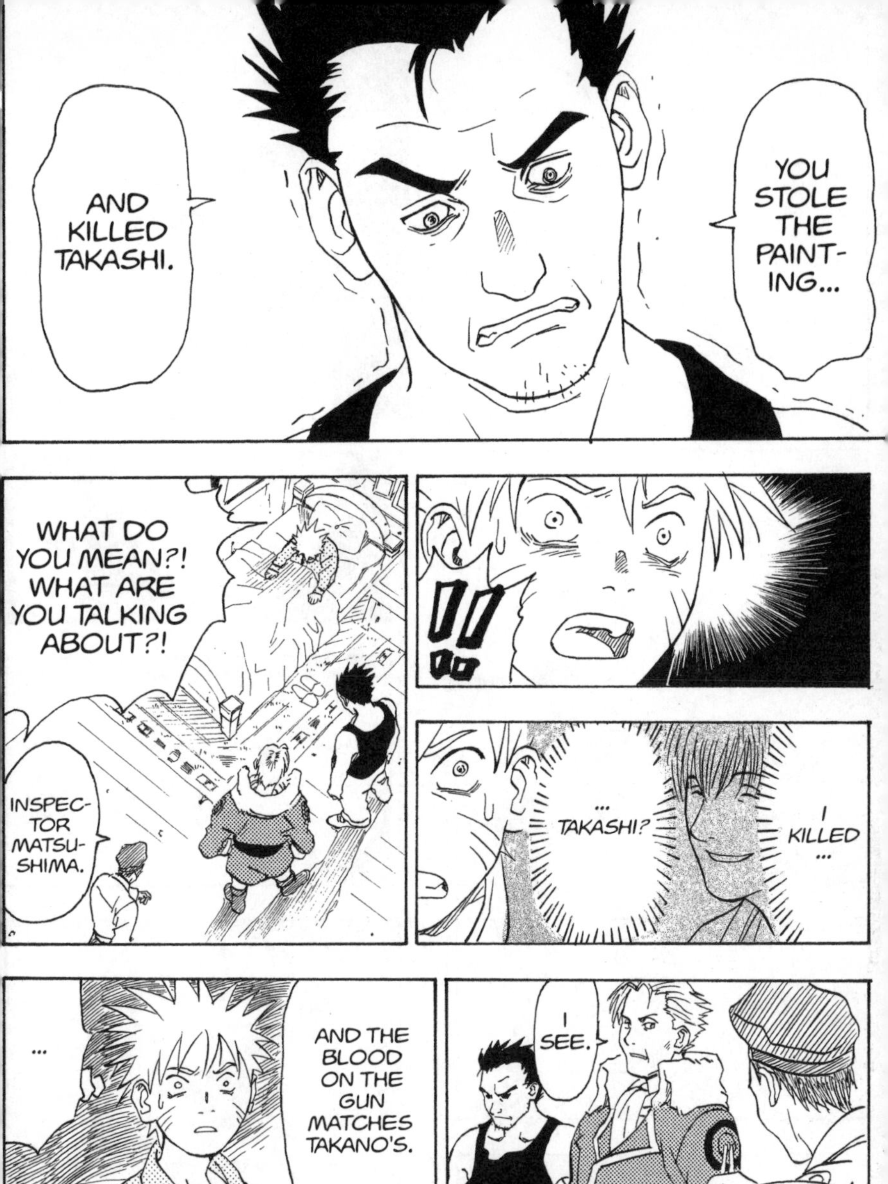
YOU STOLE THE PAINTING...
AND KILLED TAKASHI.
I KILLED ...
... TAKASHI?
WHAT DO YOU MEAN?! WHAT ARE YOU TALKING ABOUT?!
INSPECTOR MATSUSHIMA.
I SEE.
WE CAN'T FIND PROOF.
AND THE BLOOD ON THE GUN MATCHES TAKANO'S.
...

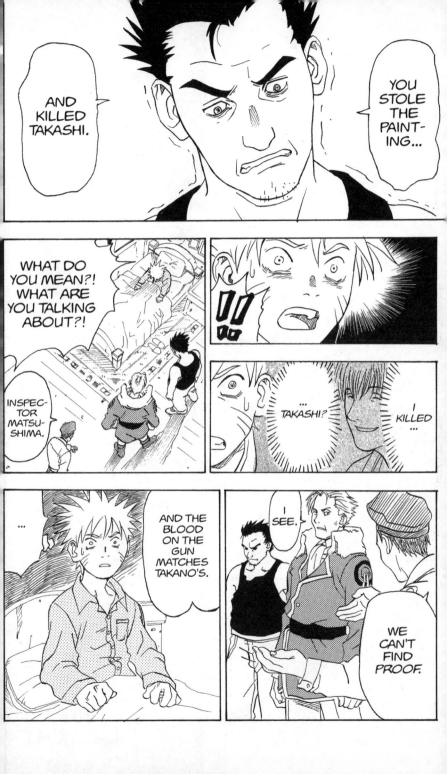

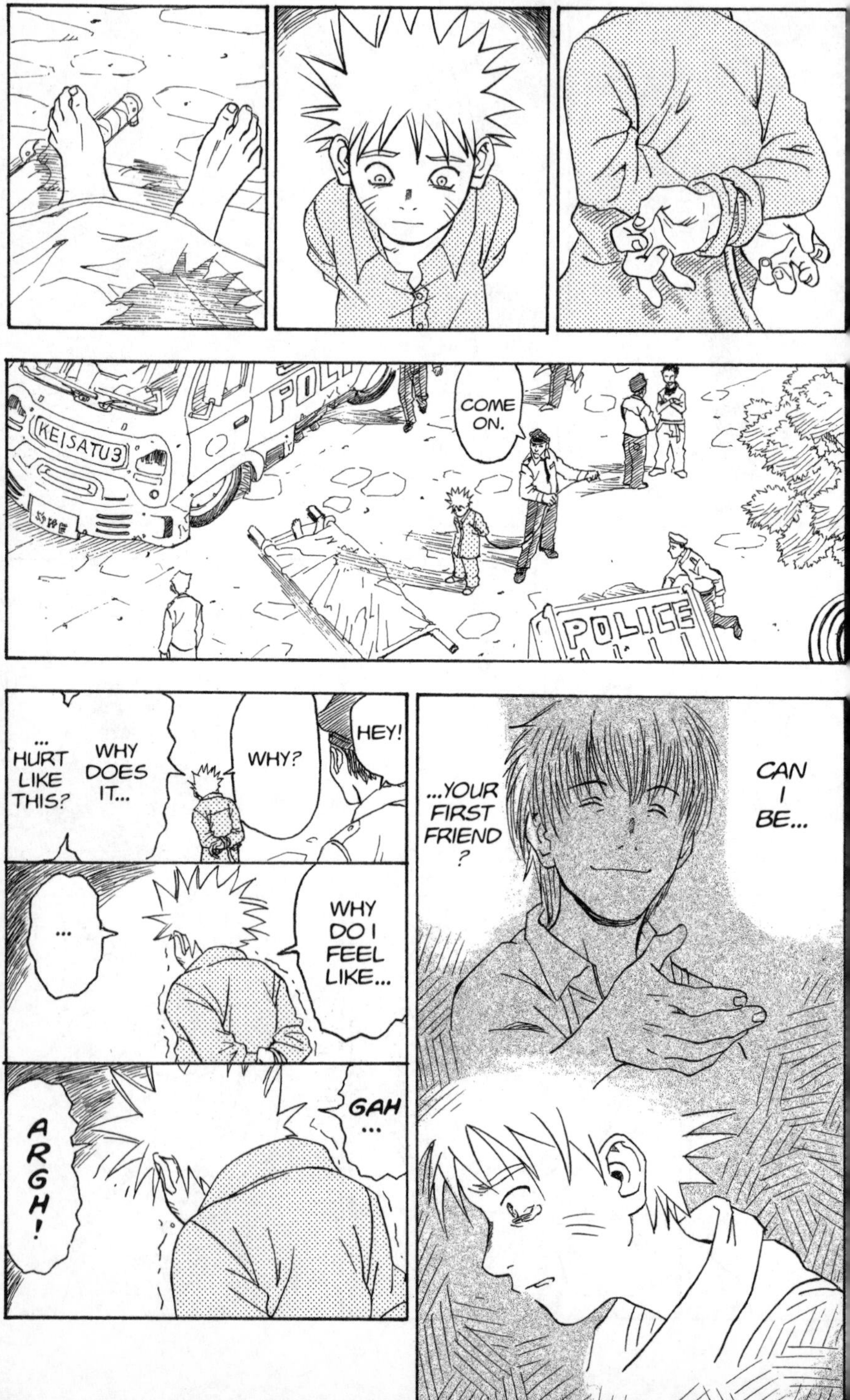
COME ON.
KEISATU3
POLICE
CAN I BE...
...YOUR FIRST FRIEND?
HEY!
WHY?
WHY DOES IT...
...HURT LIKE THIS?
WHY DO I FEEL LIKE...
...
GAH...
ARGH!

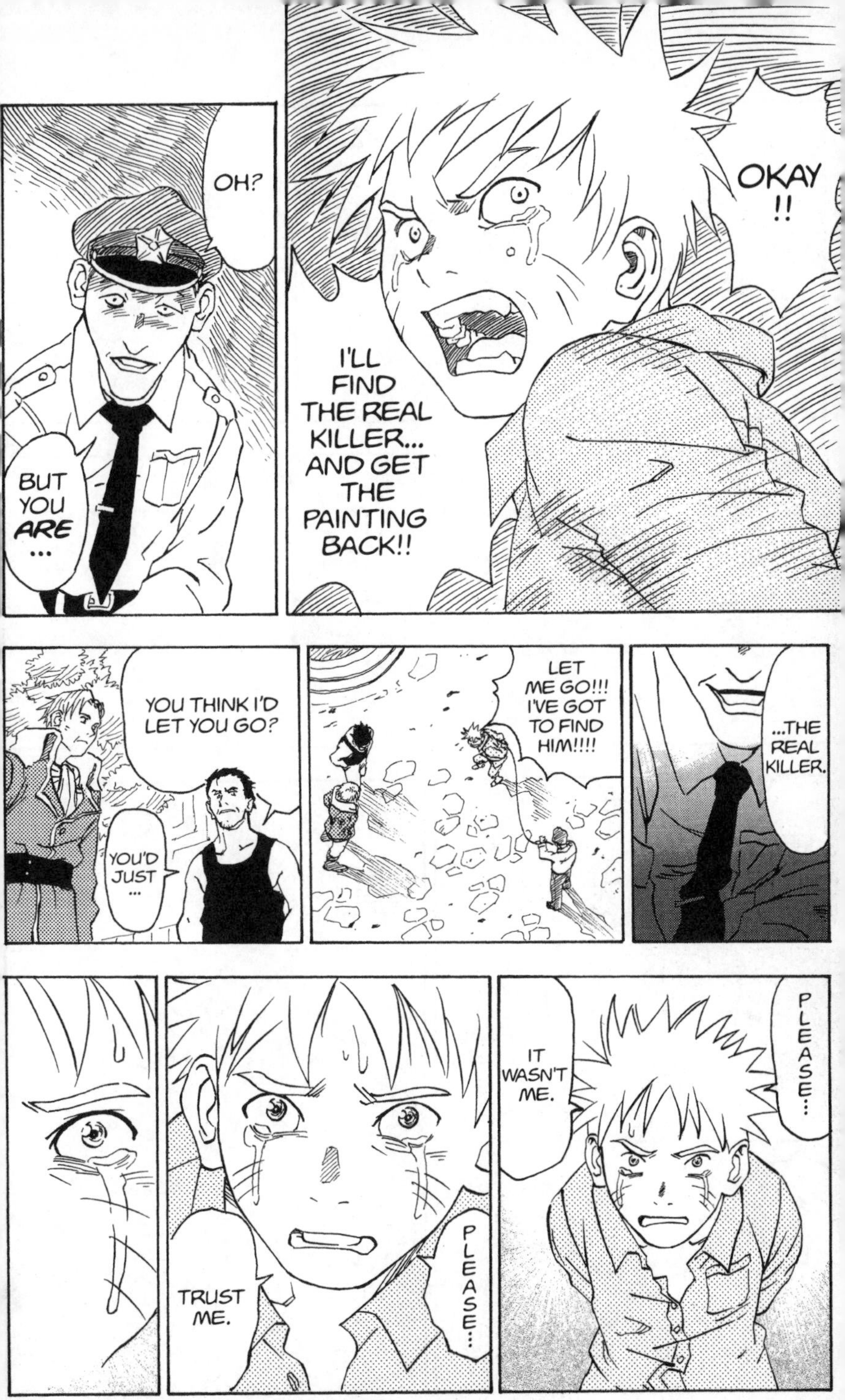
OKAY !!
I'LL FIND THE REAL KILLER... AND GET THE PAINTING BACK!!
OH?
BUT YOU ARE ...
...THE REAL KILLER.
LET ME GO!!! I'VE GOT TO FIND HIM!!!!
YOU THINK I'D LET YOU GO?
YOU'D JUST ...
PLEASE...
IT WASN'T ME.
PLEASE...
TRUST ME.

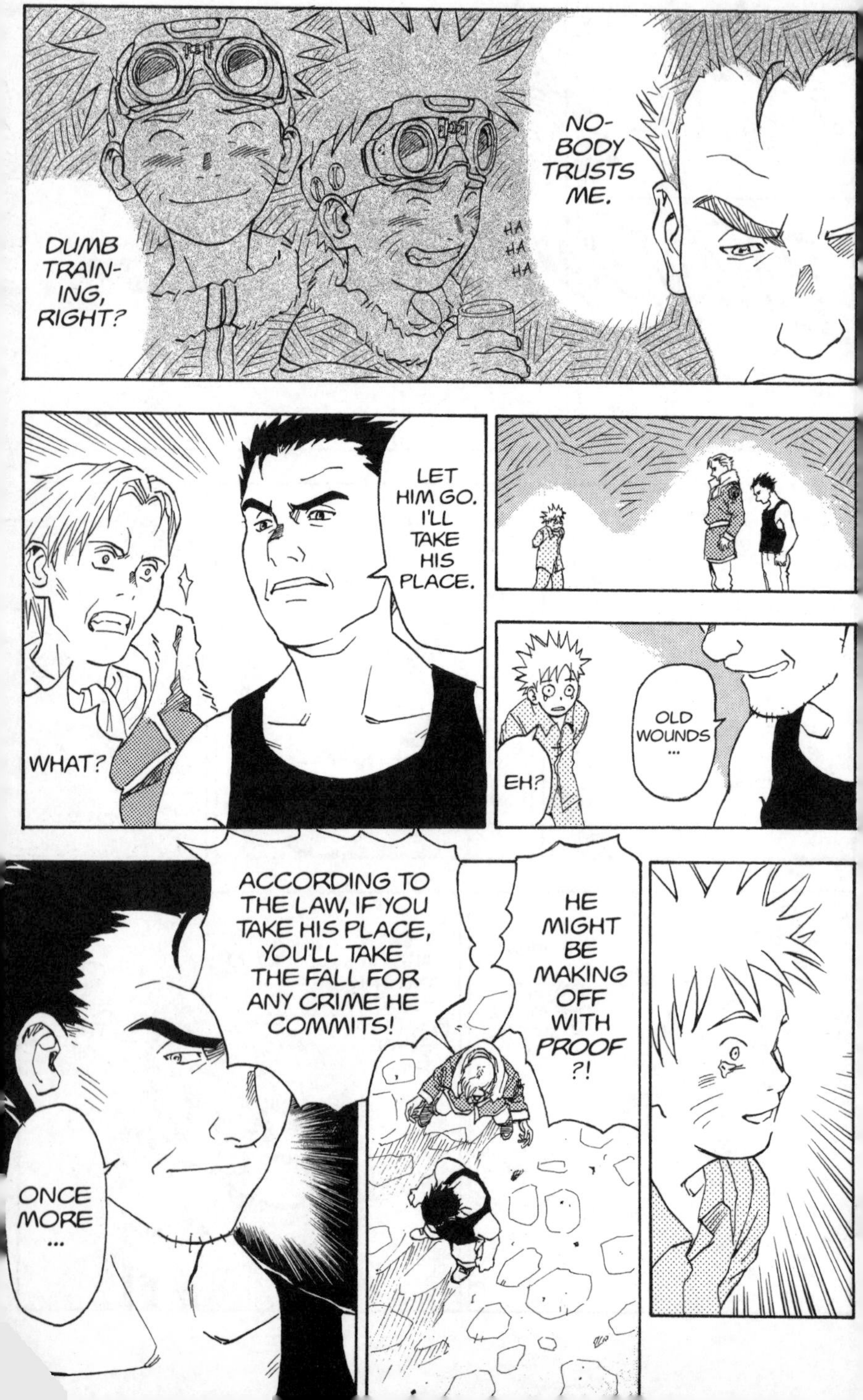
NO-BODY TRUSTS ME.
HA HA HA
DUMB TRAIN-ING, RIGHT?
OLD WOUNDS...
EH?
LET HIM GO. I'LL TAKE HIS PLACE.
WHAT?
HE MIGHT BE MAKING OFF WITH *PROOF*?!
ACCORDING TO THE LAW, IF YOU TAKE HIS PLACE, YOU'LL TAKE THE FALL FOR ANY CRIME HE COMMITS!
ONCE MORE...

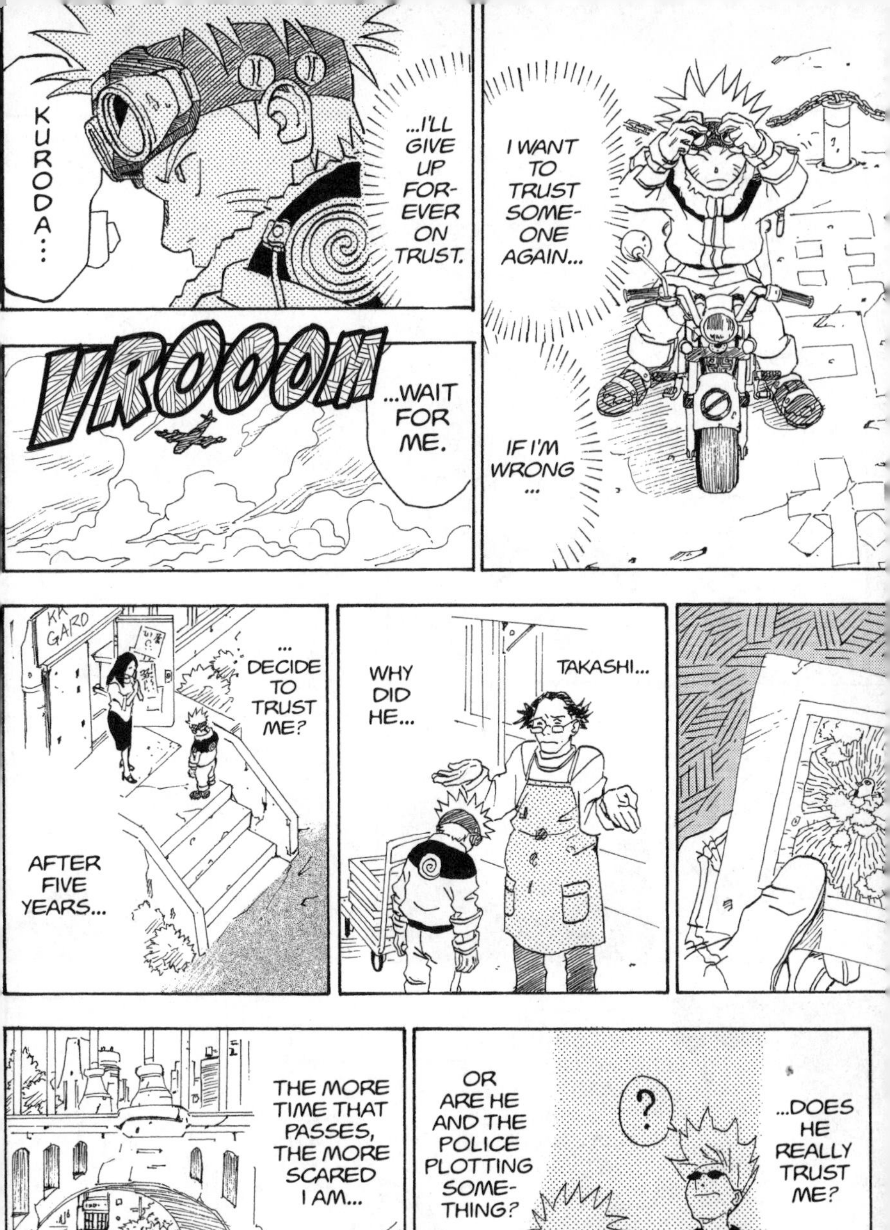
I WANT TO TRUST SOMEONE AGAIN...
IF I'M WRONG...
...I'LL GIVE UP FOREVER ON TRUST.
KURODA...
...WAIT FOR ME.
VROOOM
TAKASHI...
WHY DID HE...
...DECIDE TO TRUST ME?
AFTER FIVE YEARS...
...DOES HE REALLY TRUST ME?
?
OR ARE HE AND THE POLICE PLOTTING SOME-THING?
THE MORE TIME THAT PASSES, THE MORE SCARED I AM...

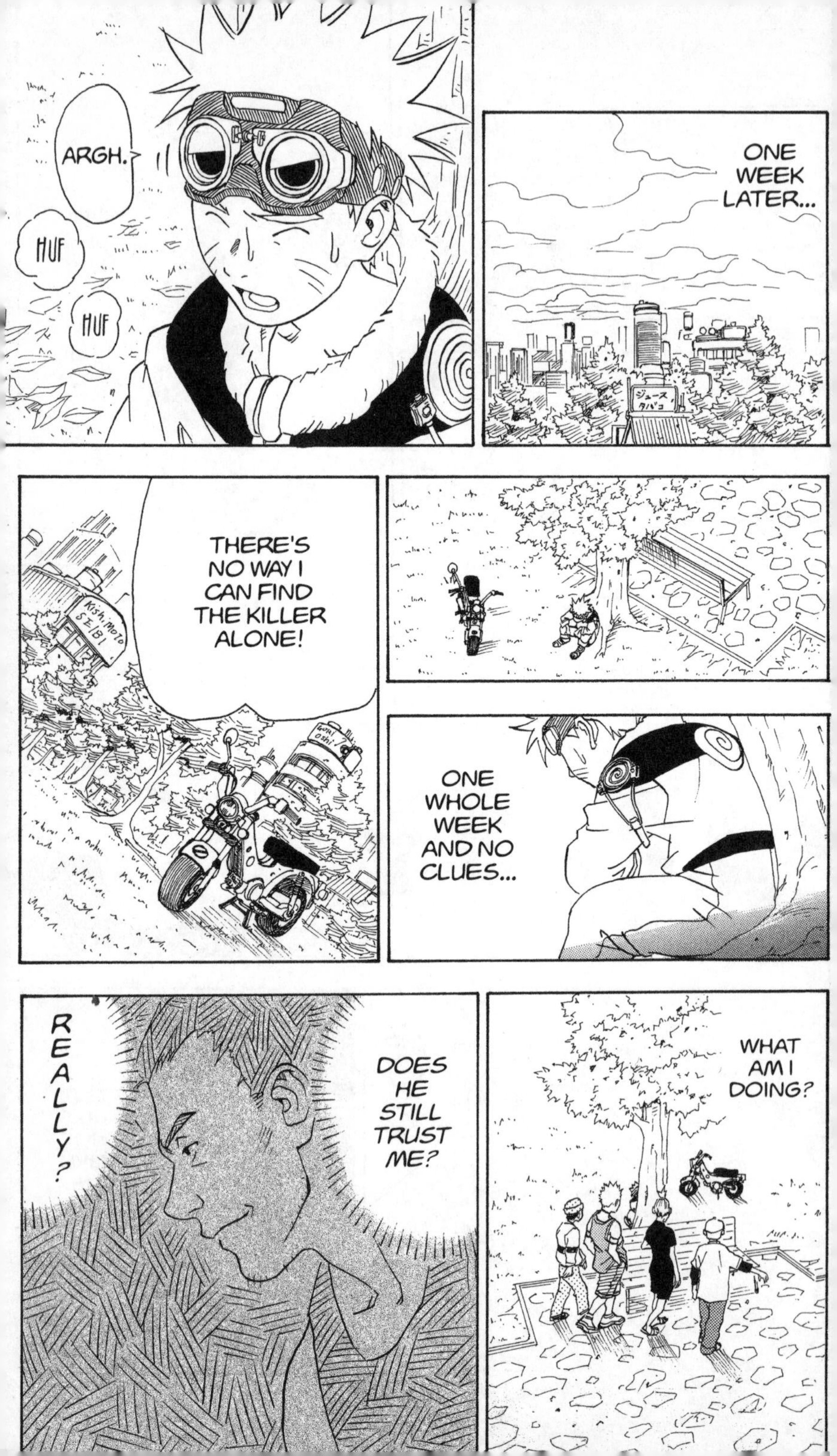
ONE WEEK LATER...
ジュース
タバコ
ARGH.
HUF
HUF
ONE WHOLE WEEK AND NO CLUES...
THERE'S NO WAY I CAN FIND THE KILLER ALONE!
WHAT AM I DOING?
DOES HE STILL TRUST ME?
REALLY?

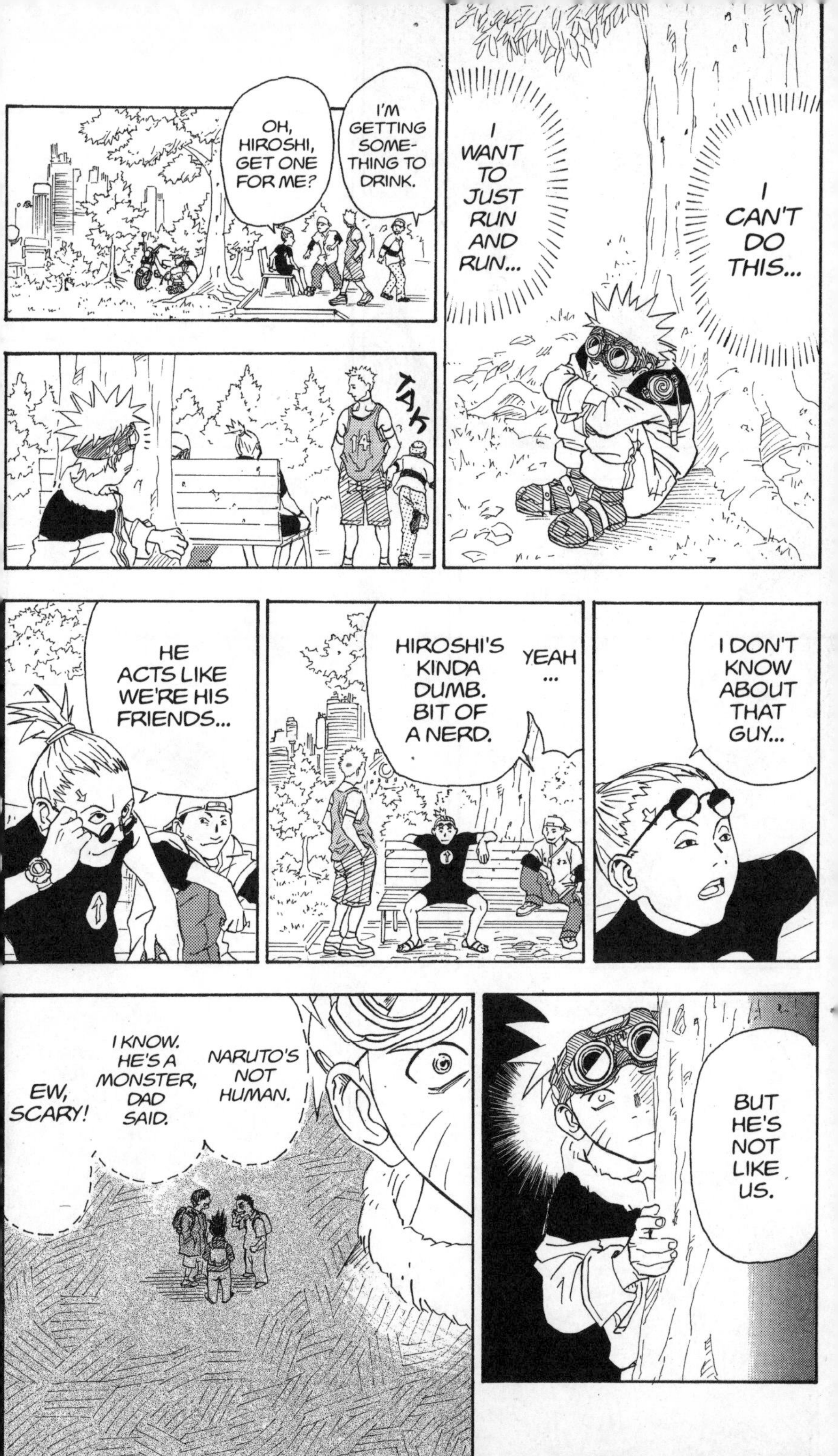
I CAN'T DO THIS...
I WANT TO JUST RUN AND RUN...
I'M GETTING SOME-THING TO DRINK.
OH, HIROSHI, GET ONE FOR ME?
TAK
I DON'T KNOW ABOUT THAT GUY...
YEAH ...
HIROSHI'S KINDA DUMB. BIT OF A NERD.
HE ACTS LIKE WE'RE HIS FRIENDS...
BUT HE'S NOT LIKE US.
NARUTO'S NOT HUMAN.
I KNOW. HE'S A MONSTER, DAD SAID.
EW, SCARY!

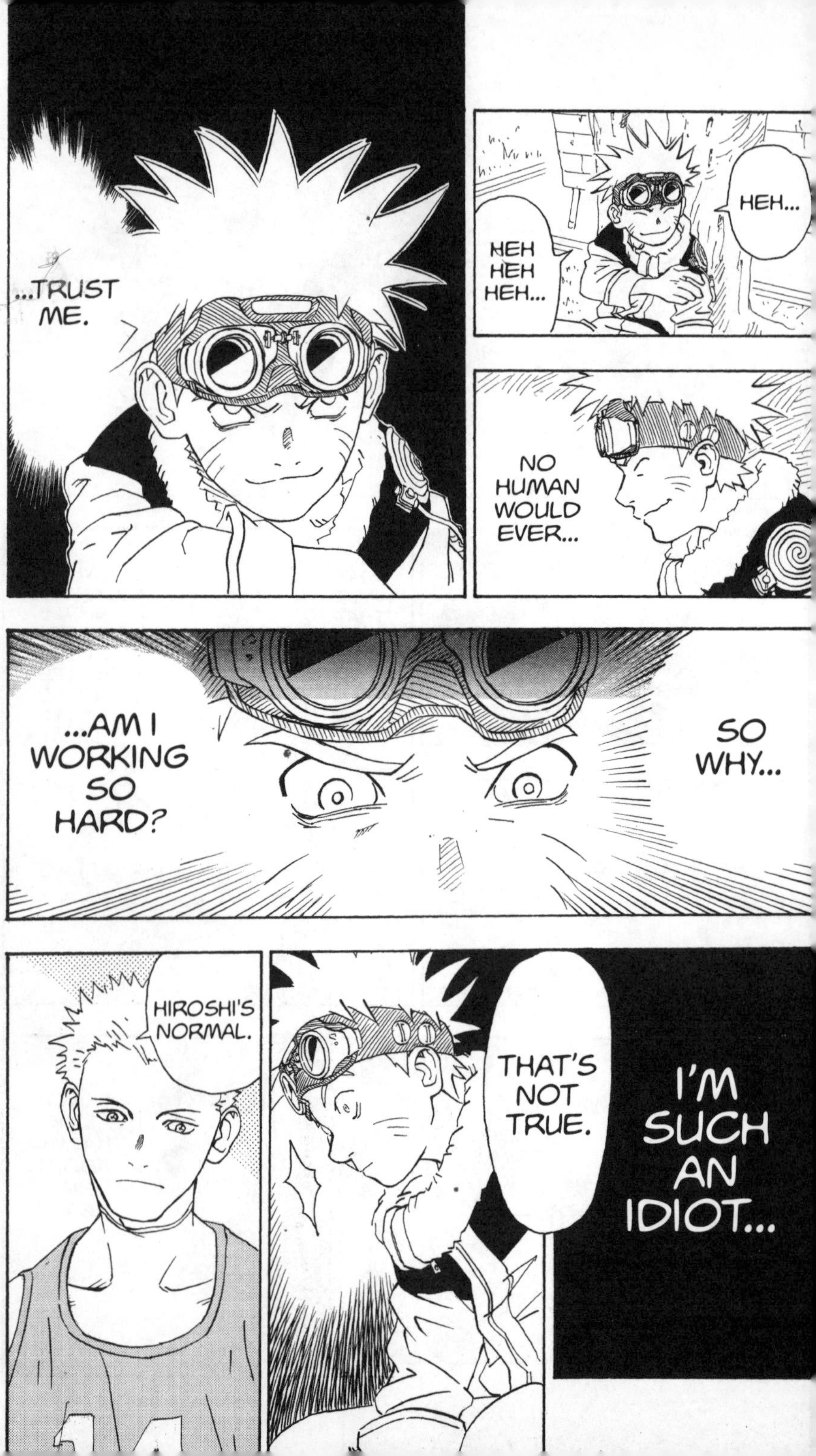
HEH...
HEH HEH HEH...
NO HUMAN WOULD EVER...
...TRUST ME.
SO WHY...
...AM I WORKING SO HARD?
I'M SUCH AN IDIOT...
THAT'S NOT TRUE.
HIROSHI'S NORMAL.

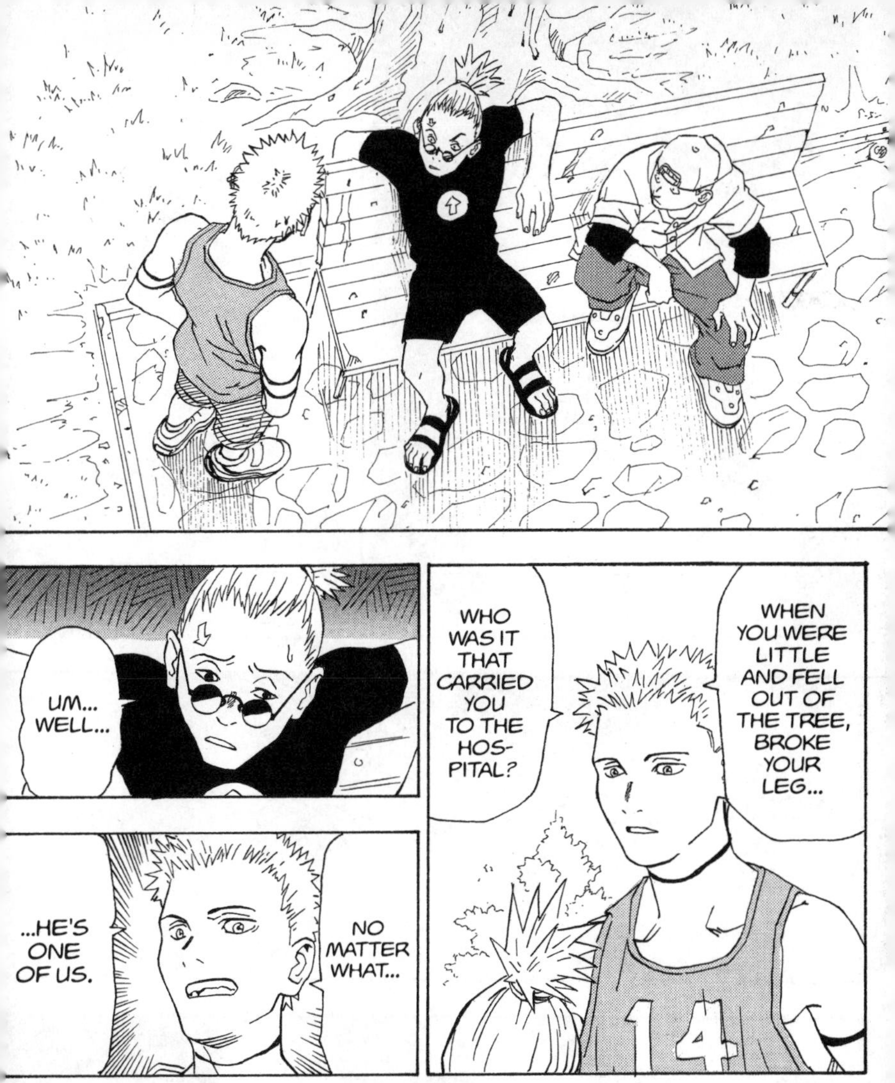
WHEN YOU WERE LITTLE AND FELL OUT OF THE TREE, BROKE YOUR LEG...
WHO WAS IT THAT CARRIED YOU TO THE HOS-PITAL?
UM... WELL...
NO MATTER WHAT...
...HE'S ONE OF US.
NEVER TALK THAT WAY ABOUT HIM AGAIN!
SORRY.
AH, HIRO-SHI!
HUF HUF GOT THOSE DRINKS ...
MM?
WHY'S EVERY-ONE SO GLUM?

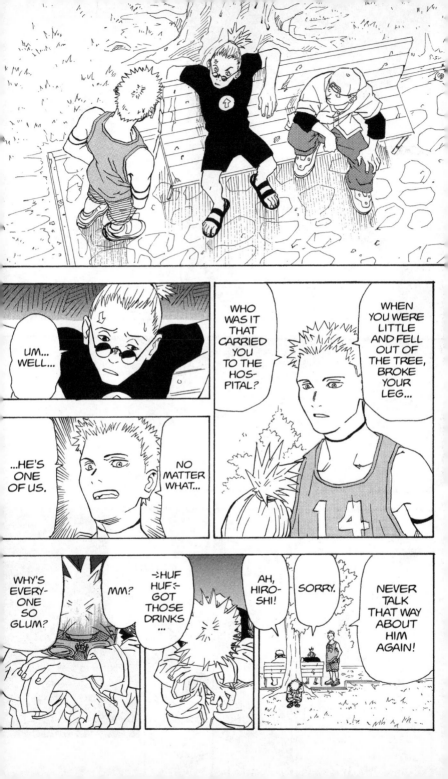

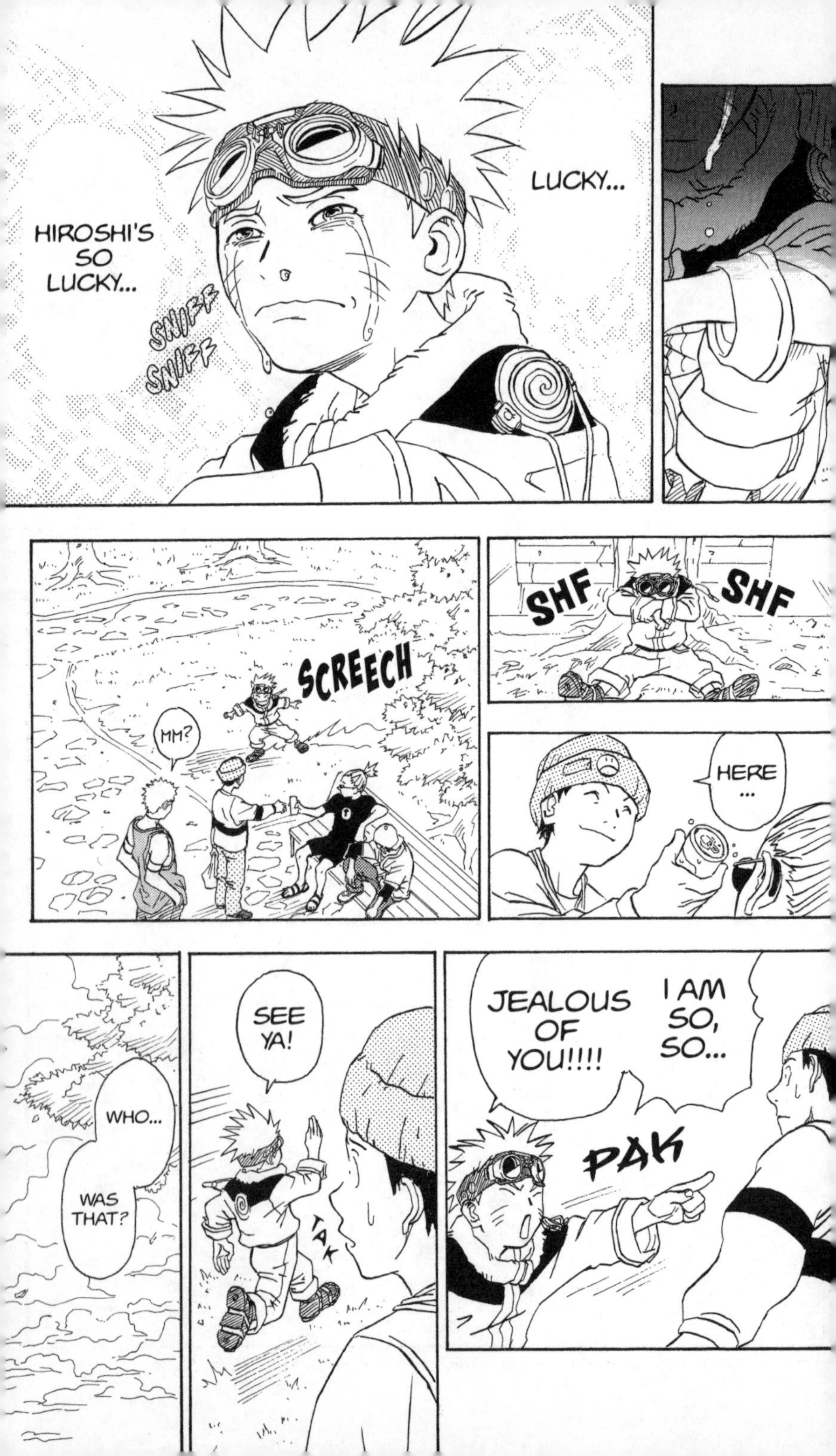
LUCKY...
HIROSHI'S SO LUCKY...
SNIFF SNIFF
SHF SHF
HERE ...
SCREECH
MM?
I AM SO, SO...
JEALOUS OF YOU!!!!!
PAK
SEE YA!
TAK
WHO...
WAS THAT?

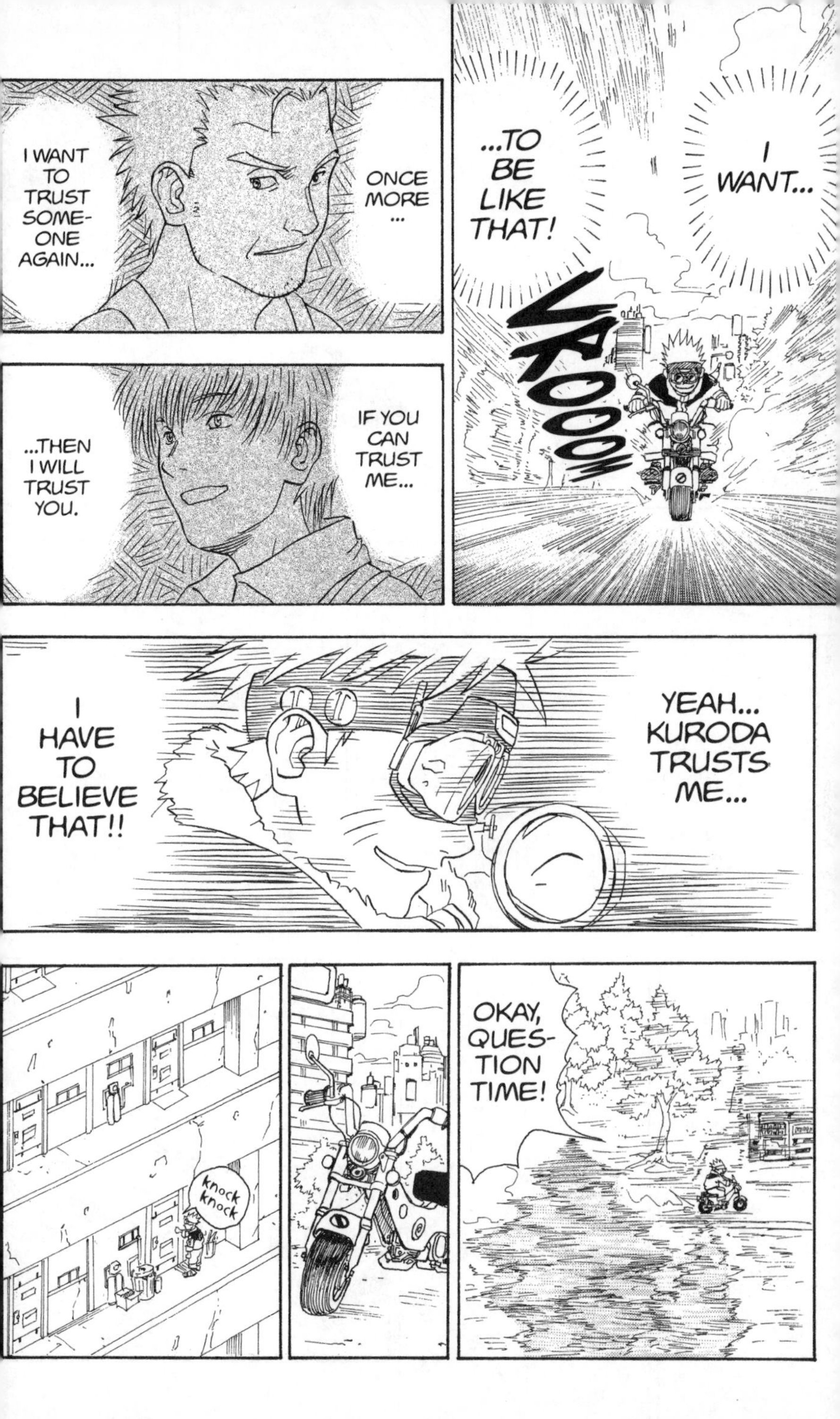
I WANT...
...TO BE LIKE THAT!
VROOOM
ONCE MORE...
I WANT TO TRUST SOMEONE AGAIN...
IF YOU CAN TRUST ME...
...THEN I WILL TRUST YOU.
YEAH... KURODA TRUSTS ME...
I HAVE TO BELIEVE THAT!!
OKAY, QUESTION TIME!
knock knock

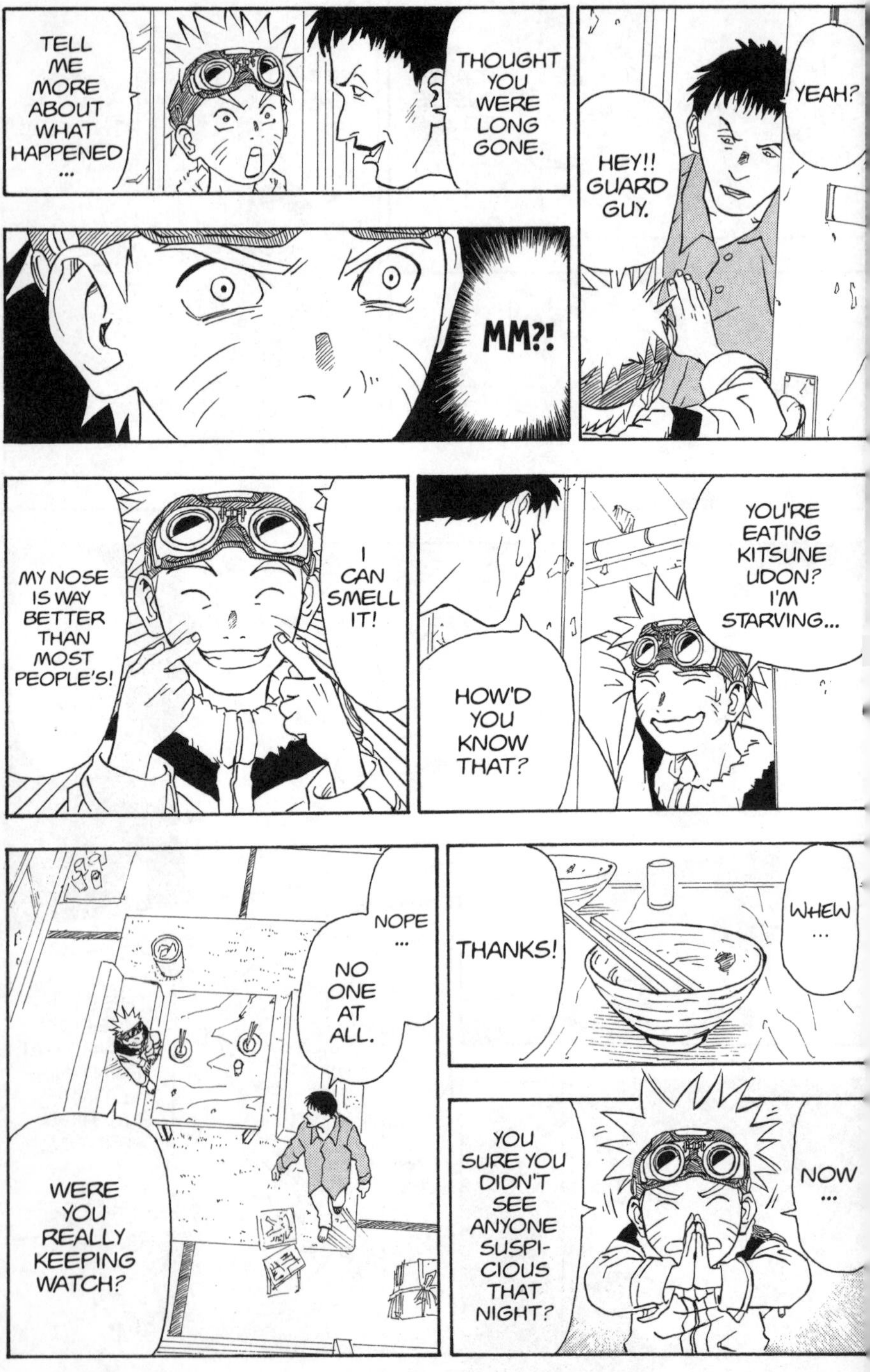
HEY!! GUARD GUY.
YEAH?
THOUGHT YOU WERE LONG GONE.
TELL ME MORE ABOUT WHAT HAPPENED ...
MM?!
YOU'RE EATING KITSUNE UDON? I'M STARVING...
HOW'D YOU KNOW THAT?
I CAN SMELL IT!
MY NOSE IS WAY BETTER THAN MOST PEOPLE'S!
WHEW ...
THANKS!
NOW ...
YOU SURE YOU DIDN'T SEE ANYONE SUSPI-CIOUS THAT NIGHT?
NOPE ...
NO ONE AT ALL.
WERE YOU REALLY KEEPING WATCH?

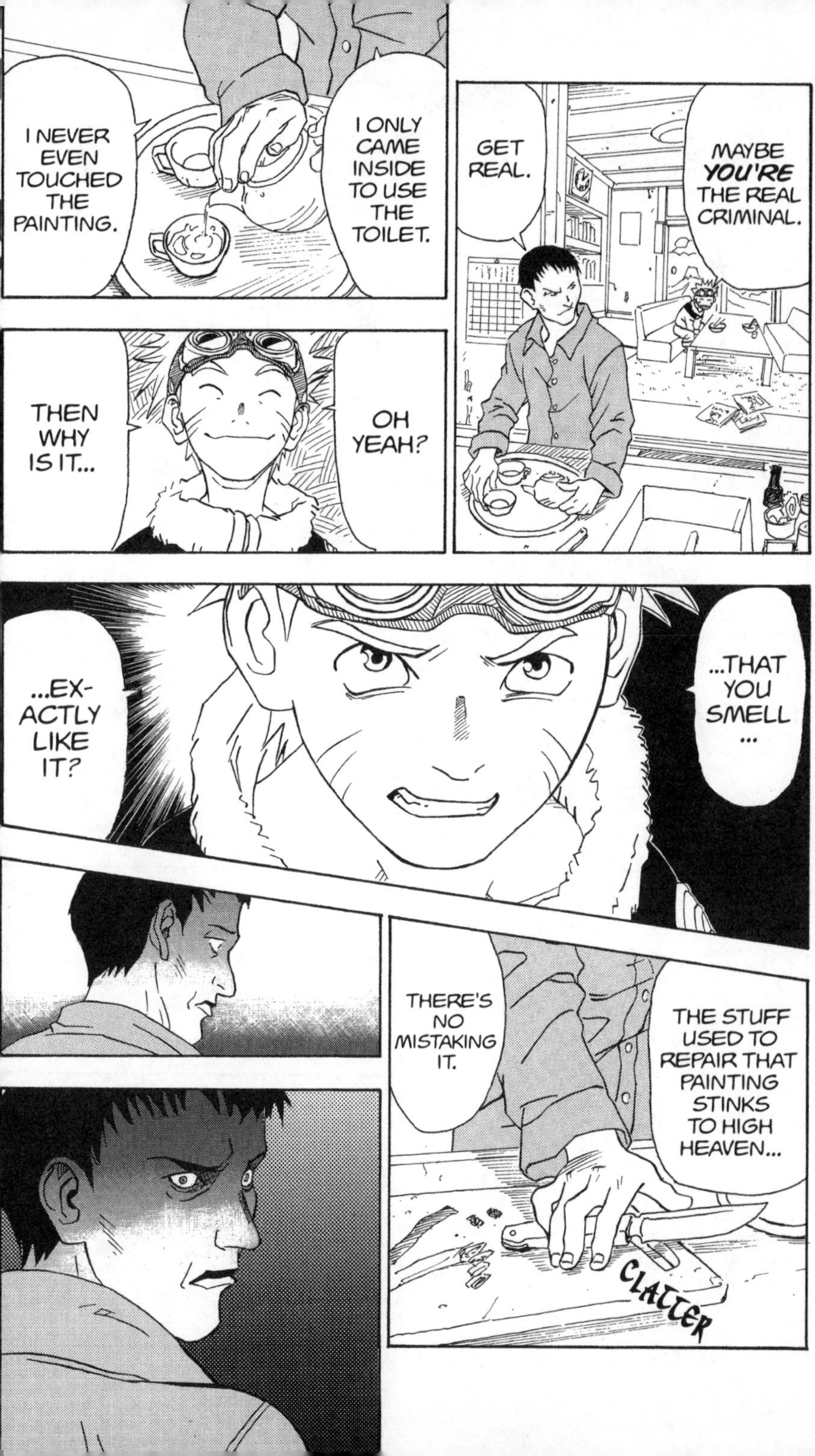
MAYBE **YOU'RE** THE REAL CRIMINAL.
GET REAL.
I ONLY CAME INSIDE TO USE THE TOILET.
I NEVER EVEN TOUCHED THE PAINTING.
OH YEAH?
THEN WHY IS IT...
...THAT YOU SMELL ...
...EX-ACTLY LIKE IT?
THE STUFF USED TO REPAIR THAT PAINTING STINKS TO HIGH HEAVEN...
THERE'S NO MISTAKING IT.
CLATTER

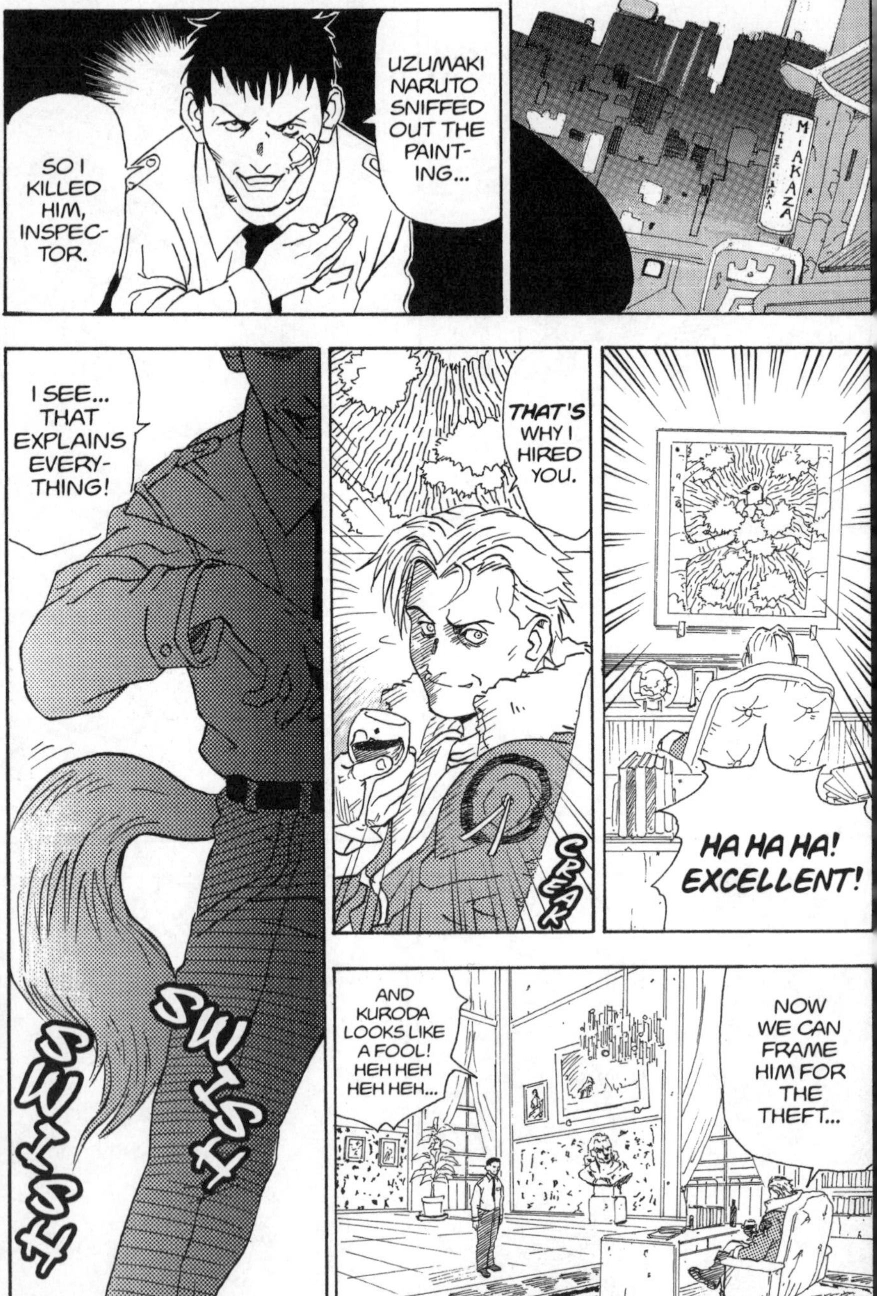
MIAKAZA
UZUMAKI NARUTO SNIFFED OUT THE PAINTING...
SO I KILLED HIM, INSPECTOR.
HA HA HA! EXCELLENT!
THAT'S WHY I HIRED YOU.
CREAK
NOW WE CAN FRAME HIM FOR THE THEFT...
AND KURODA LOOKS LIKE A FOOL! HEH HEH HEH HEH...
I SEE... THAT EXPLAINS EVERYTHING!
SWISH
SWISH

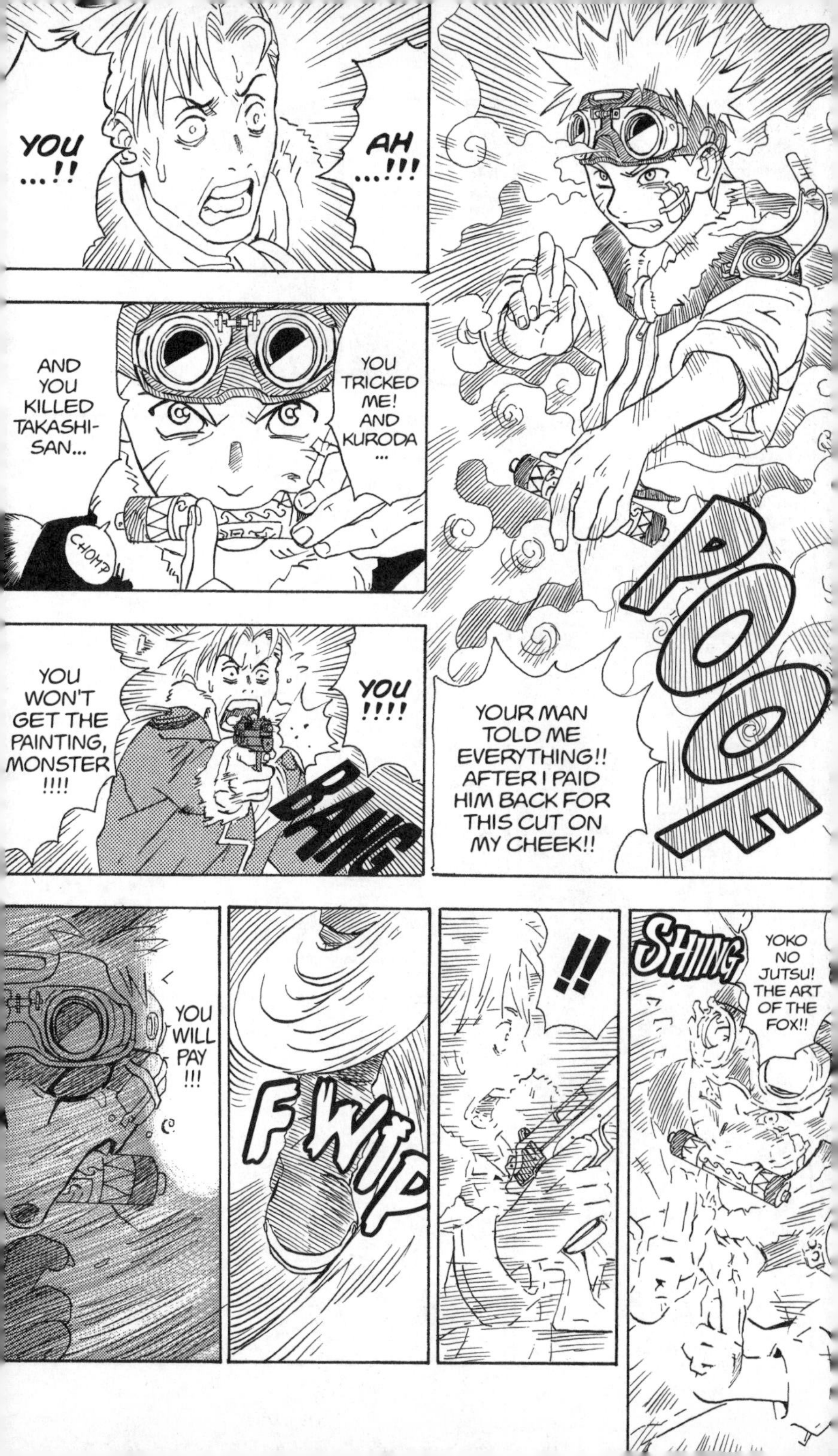
POOF
YOUR MAN TOLD ME EVERYTHING!! AFTER I PAID HIM BACK FOR THIS CUT ON MY CHEEK!!
AH ...!!!
YOU ...!!
YOU TRICKED ME! AND KURODA ...
AND YOU KILLED TAKASHI-SAN...
CHOMP
YOU !!!!
YOU WON'T GET THE PAINTING, MONSTER !!!!
BANG
SHIING
YOKO NO JUTSU! THE ART OF THE FOX!!
!!
FWIP
YOU WILL PAY !!!

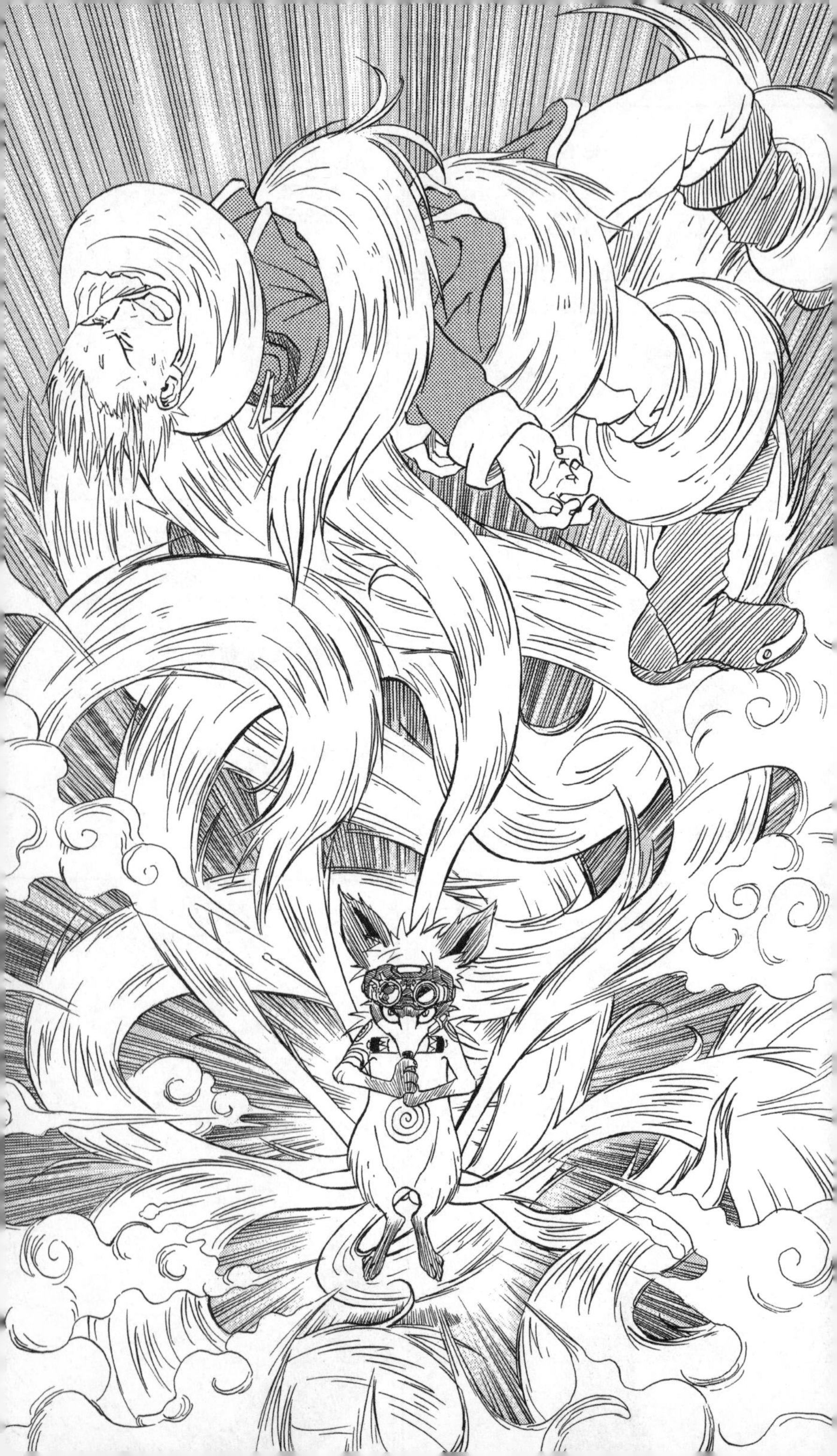

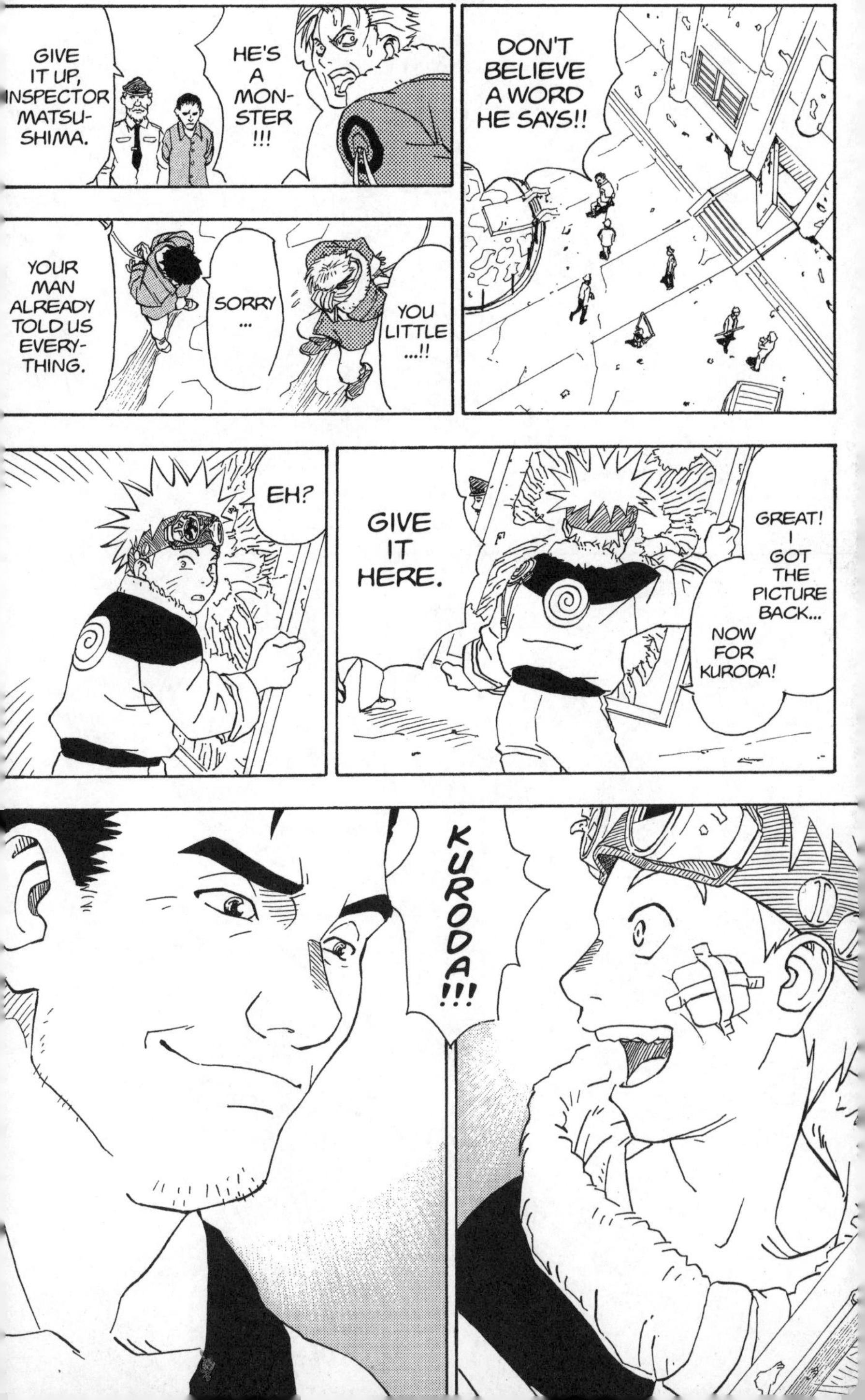
DON'T BELIEVE A WORD HE SAYS!!
HE'S A MON-STER!!!
GIVE IT UP, INSPECTOR MATSU-SHIMA.
YOU LITTLE ...!!
SORRY ...
YOUR MAN ALREADY TOLD US EVERY-THING.
GREAT! I GOT THE PICTURE BACK...
NOW FOR KURODA!
GIVE IT HERE.
EH?
KURODA!!!

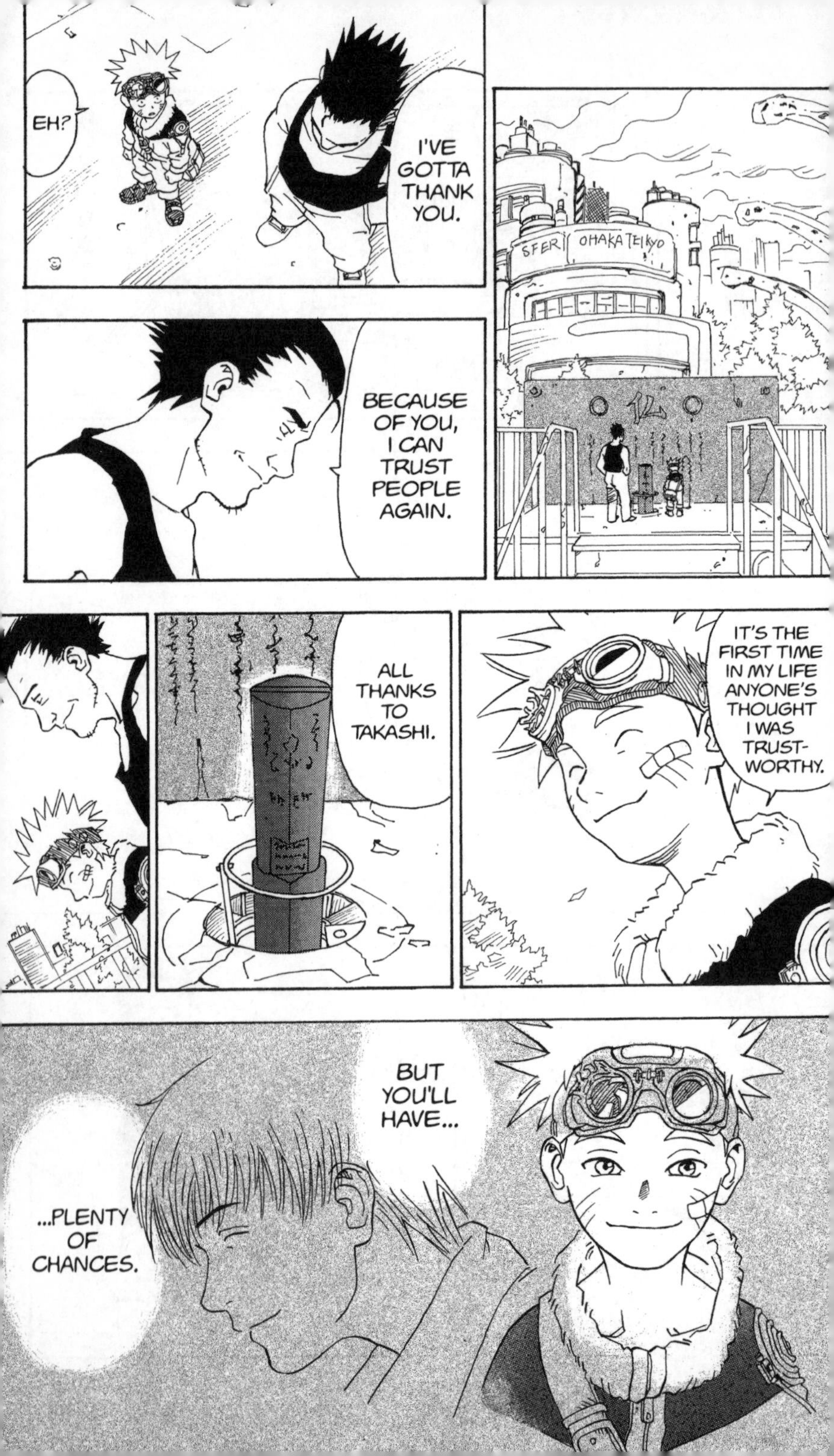
EH?
I'VE GOTTA THANK YOU.
BECAUSE OF YOU, I CAN TRUST PEOPLE AGAIN.
SFERI OHAKA TEIKYO
ALL THANKS TO TAKASHI.
IT'S THE FIRST TIME IN MY LIFE ANYONE'S THOUGHT I WAS TRUST-WORTHY.
BUT YOU'LL HAVE...
...PLENTY OF CHANCES.

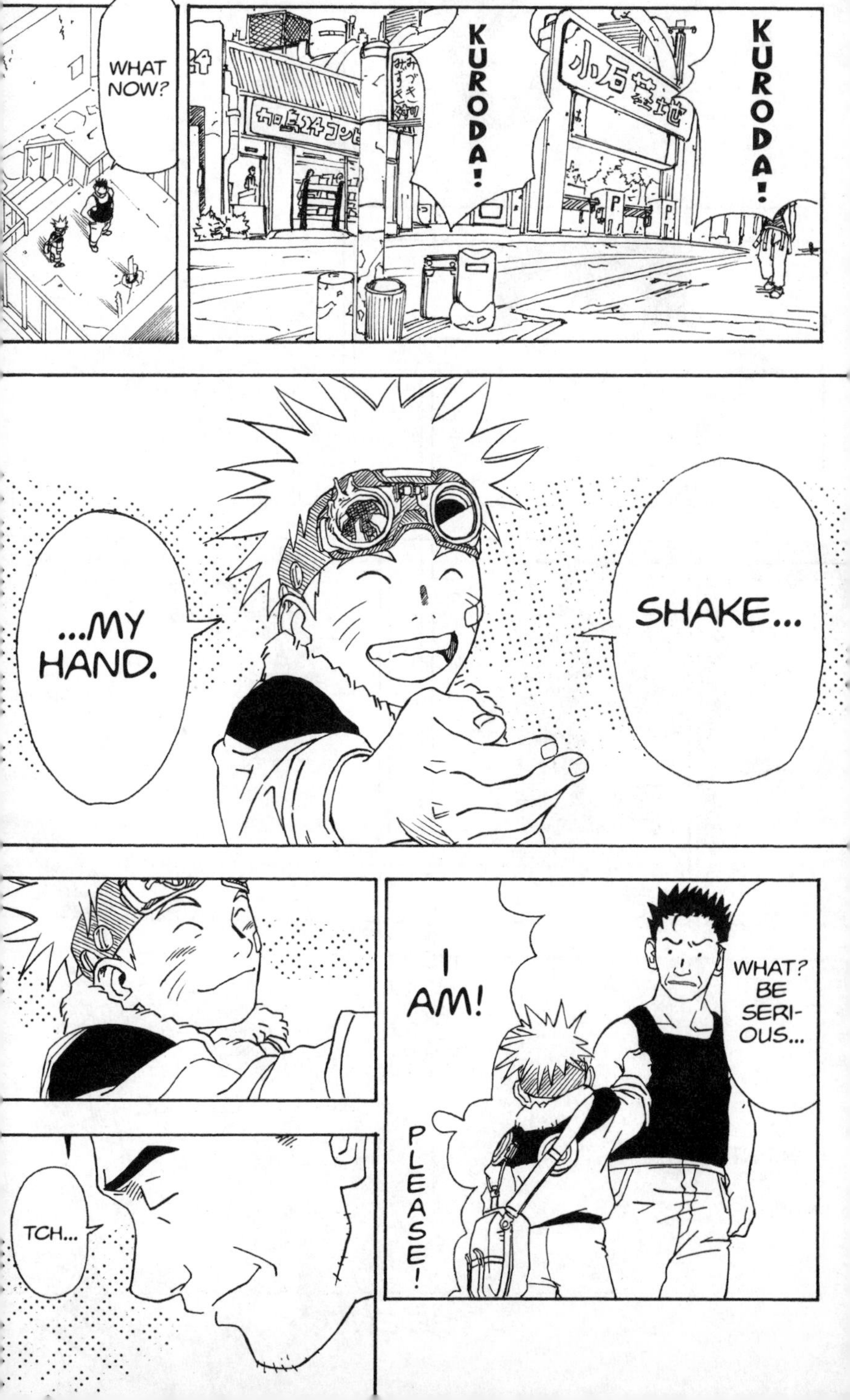
KURODA!
KURODA!
WHAT NOW?
SHAKE...
...MY HAND.
WHAT? BE SERI-OUS...
I AM!
PLEASE!
TCH...

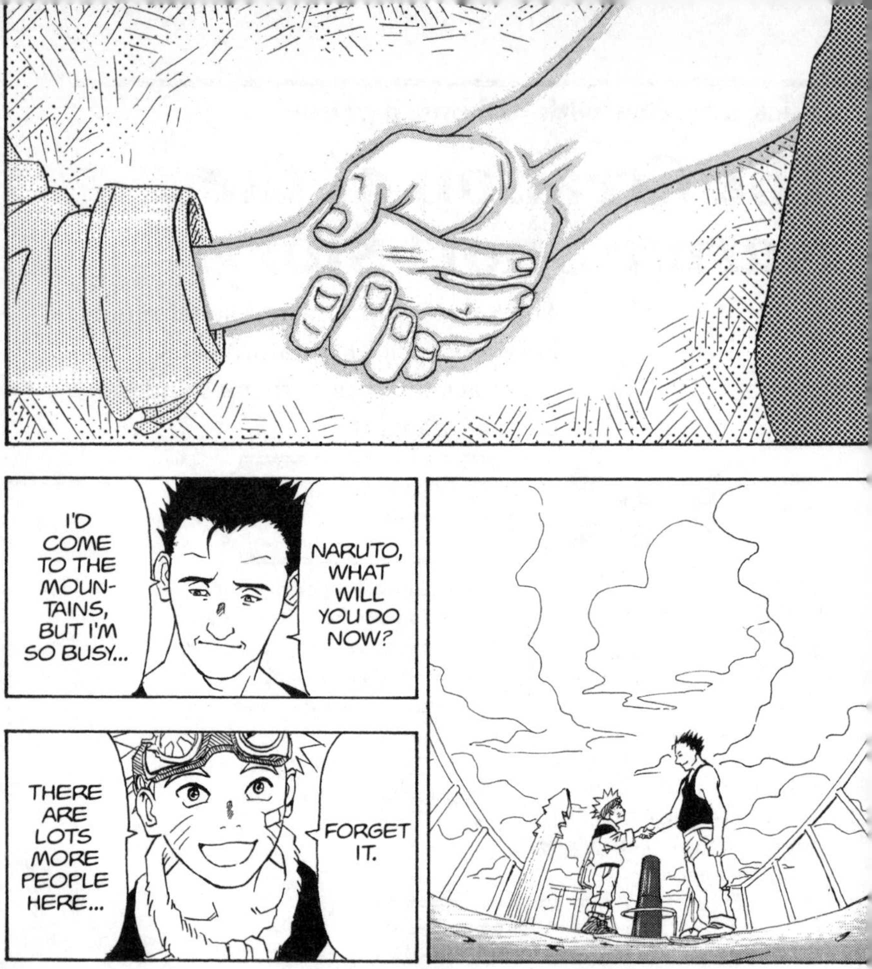
NARUTO, WHAT WILL YOU DO NOW?
I'D COME TO THE MOUNTAINS, BUT I'M SO BUSY...
FORGET IT.
THERE ARE LOTS MORE PEOPLE HERE...
OKAY...
BUY YOU A DRINK ON THE WAY HOME?
NO! ABSOLUTELY NOT! HOW ABOUT RAMEN INSTEAD?
CHIEF WASN'T LYING...
...FRIENDS ARE WORTH MAKING.

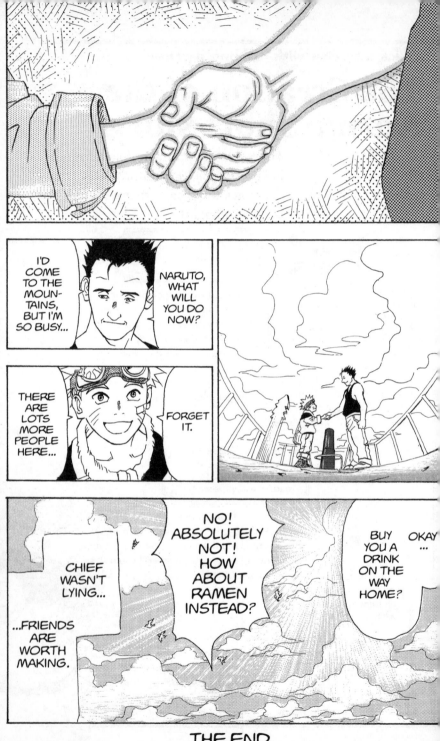

THE END

Quick Interview with Kishimoto-sensei!!

The Creation of the *Naruto* Short Story!

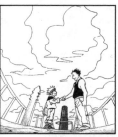

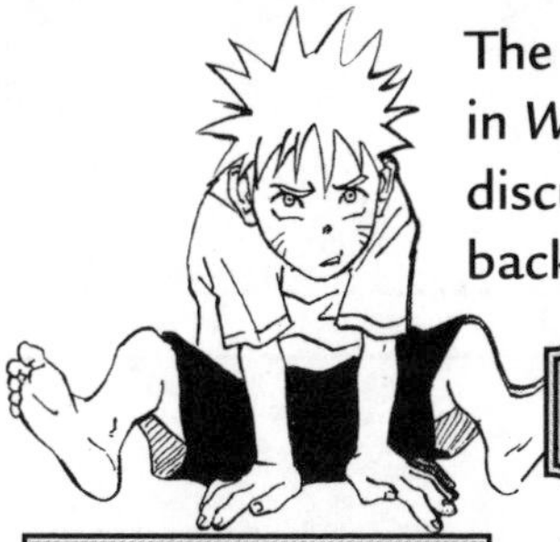

The first big step toward serialization in *Weekly Jump*! Kishimoto-sensei discusses the story's themes and looks back at it again!!

Q. What made you want to draw this story?

A. I'd been working on my story *Karakuri* (an all-out action story), which won the Hop Skip prize, while trying to get it ready to run in *Akamaru*, but the rough drafts weren't good enough. So I decided to do a story that was mostly drama, and ended up with *Naruto*.

Q. Tell us what the short story version of Naruto's character has in common with the one in the main series.

A. It's a type of character I find easy to relate to, and I'd been using it in a lot of stories, so there shouldn't be many differences.

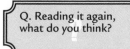

Q. What message were you trying to give to your readers with this story?

A. The theme of this story is trusting other people. At the beginning of the story, nobody trusts Naruto, and Kuroda doesn't trust anyone. But by putting these two together, I could show how important trust is.

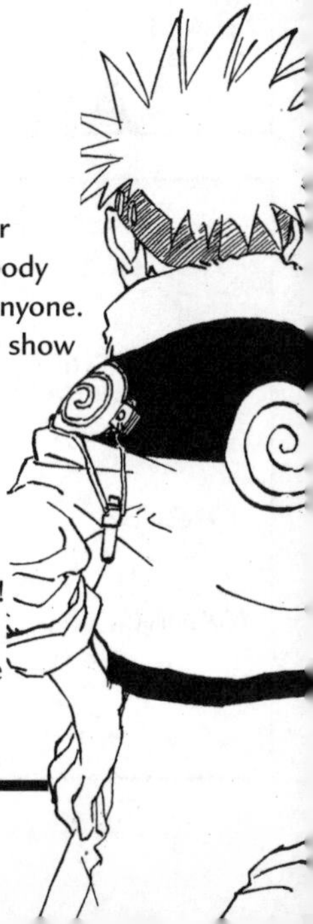

Q. Reading it again, what do you think?

A. It's pretty embarrassing. My art sucks! And the story's a mess! This character Hiroshi in the middle...he just shows up out of nowhere. I could go on all day. I remember I was having trouble doing my art in the shonen style. But the poll results were very good, and I was really happy. So I'll always remember it fondly.

Unless you can discover the truth, all the gates will not open!

ANSWERS

THE TRUTH BEHIND ALL FIVE GATES

KAIMON SCROLL

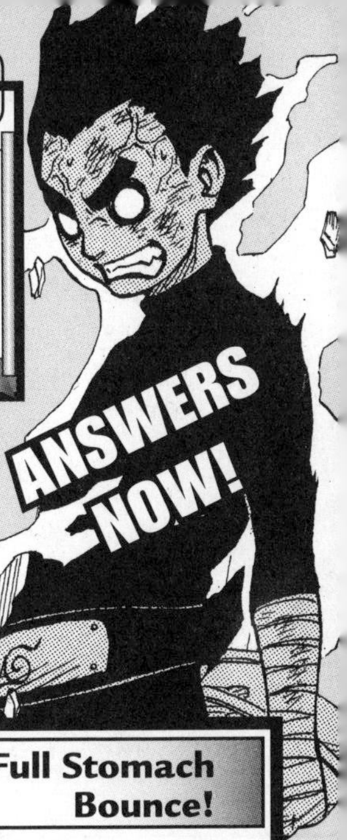
ANSWERS NOW!

You put all your knowledge and skills to the test on these five gates!! And now...you can compare your answers!! When that final Kaimon opens...you will know the truth!!

1st GATE Multiple Shadow Doppelganger

Open your eyes wide! As round as Lee's.

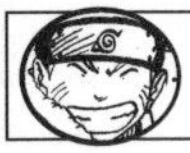

"Uzumaki Naruto makes no mistakes!" → (G)

You made tons!

A = Eyes round like Rock Lee's!
B = The Kunai is bent all weird!
C = Not wearing shoes...barefoot!
D = Those pants...belong to the Kirigakure Demon!
E = Are those cheeks a little lonely?
F = These cheeks have four lines!
H = Check the bottoms of the pants... where are the stitches?
I = The Konoha mark on the headband is way too big!!

2nd GATE Full Stomach Bounce!

Following your appetite is surprisingly successful?

Tomato Juice	Lemon Tea	Katsudon	Milk	Start! Hyorogan
Lemonade	Yakisoba	Sushi	Mac & Cheese	Coffee
Takoyaki	Ramen	Mineral Water	Cafe au Lait	Pudding
Orange Juice	Hamburger	Fruit Punch	Yogurt Drink	Herb Tea
Beef Stew	Fried Chicken	Spaghetti	Cocoa	Dumplings
	Yakiniku! Goal!	Aojiru	Fried Rice	Oolong Tea
	Cola	Meat Dumplings	Genmai Tea	Apple Juice
	Fried Egg	Green Tea	Curried Rice	Mapo Tofu

In all, 27 items consumed!

(Combined calories= 10,000/The average calories needed by a 12-year-old boy every day is about 1200.)

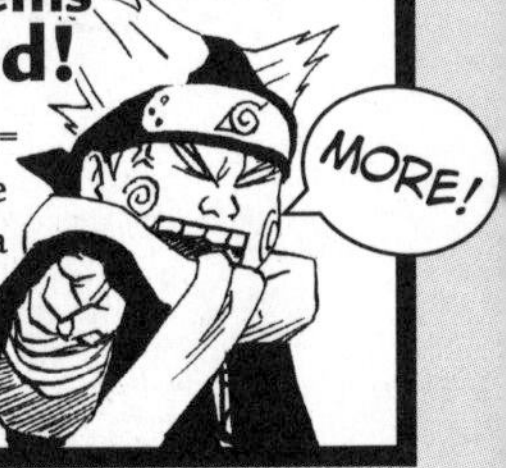
MORE!

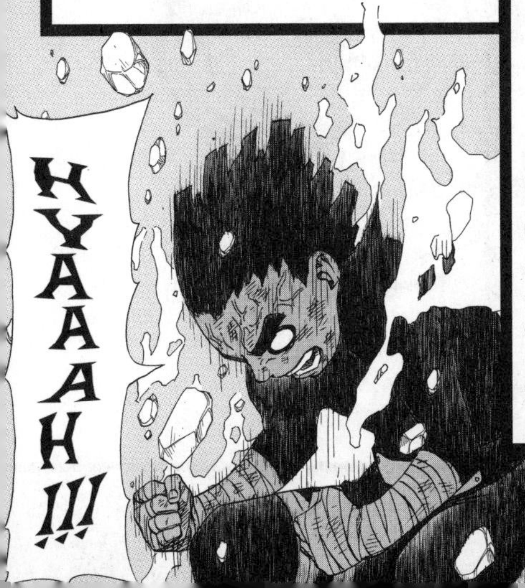
HYAAAAH!!!

3rd GATE Shinobi IQ

If you get them all right, you qualify as genin...

1: 20
2: B
3: B
4: Kakashi
5: B
6: C

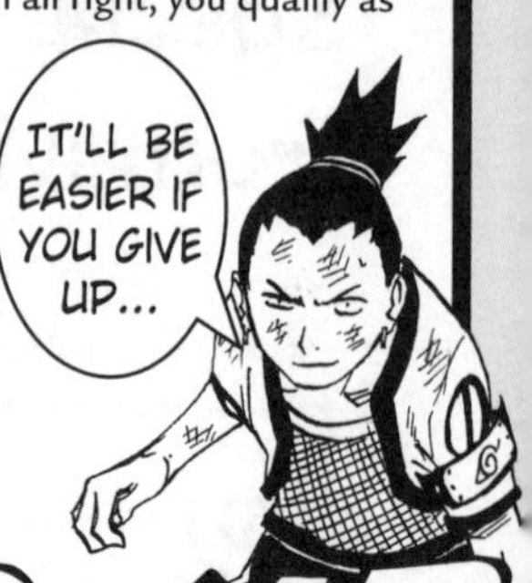
IT'LL BE EASIER IF YOU GIVE UP...

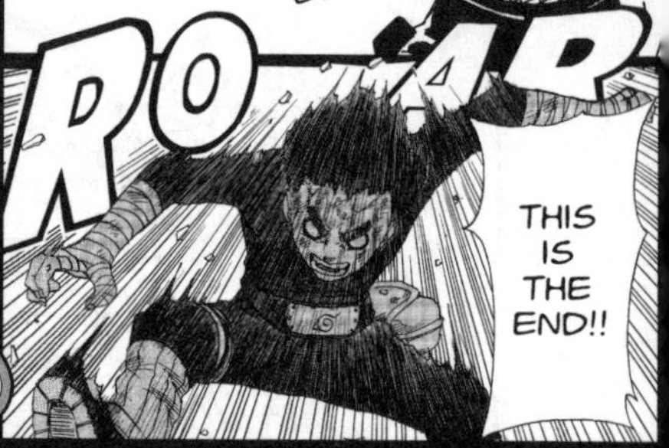
ROAR
THIS IS THE END!!

4th GATE Byakugan!! Chakra Line Maze!!

Calm your heart like a mirrored lake surface, and you will find the path.

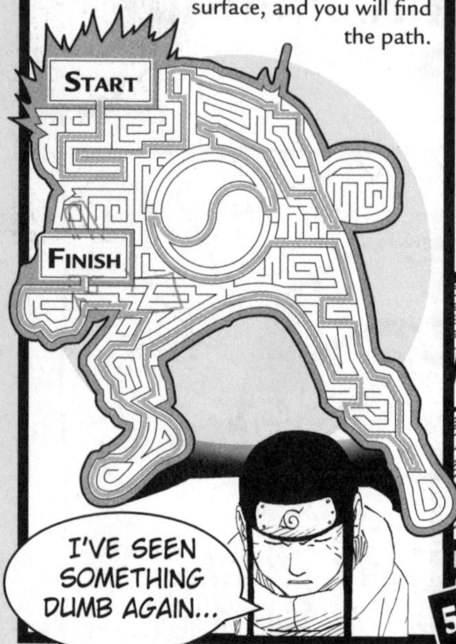
START
FINISH
I'VE SEEN SOMETHING DUMB AGAIN...

5th GATE Naruto Cult Quiz

If you hesitated for even a moment, read the manga and this fanbook again!

1: A→C→B→D
(Naruto is 12, Kabuto 19, Anko 24, Iruka 25)
2: Aburame Shino vs. Zaku Abumi
3: 153
4: Mikazuki no Mai: Crescent Moon Dance
5: A through E are all correct
6: A
7: Kyomon
8: C
9: Uzumaki Naruto (while using the Ninja Centerfold)

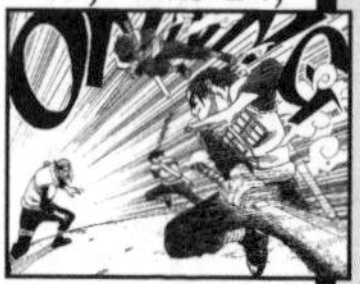

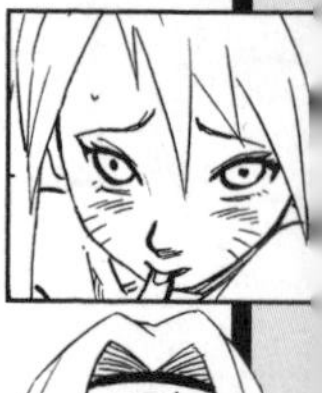

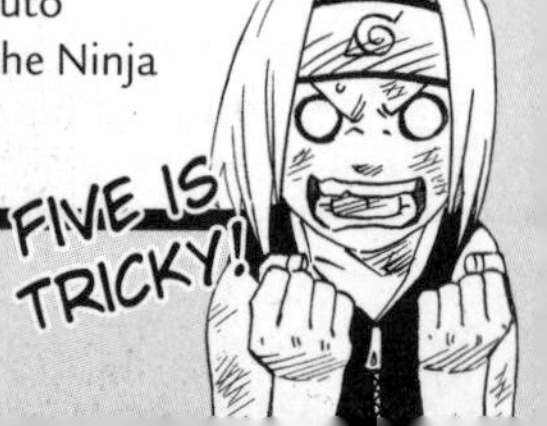
FIVE IS TRICKY!

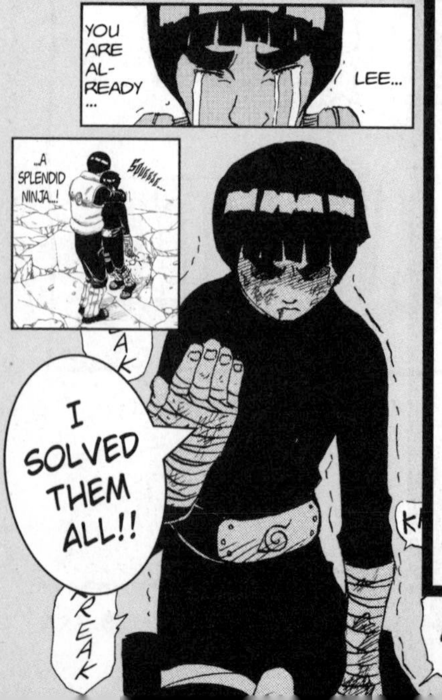
LEE...
YOU ARE AL-READY ...
...A SPLENDID NINJA...!
I SOLVED THEM ALL!!
POP

Special Message from Masashi Kishimoto

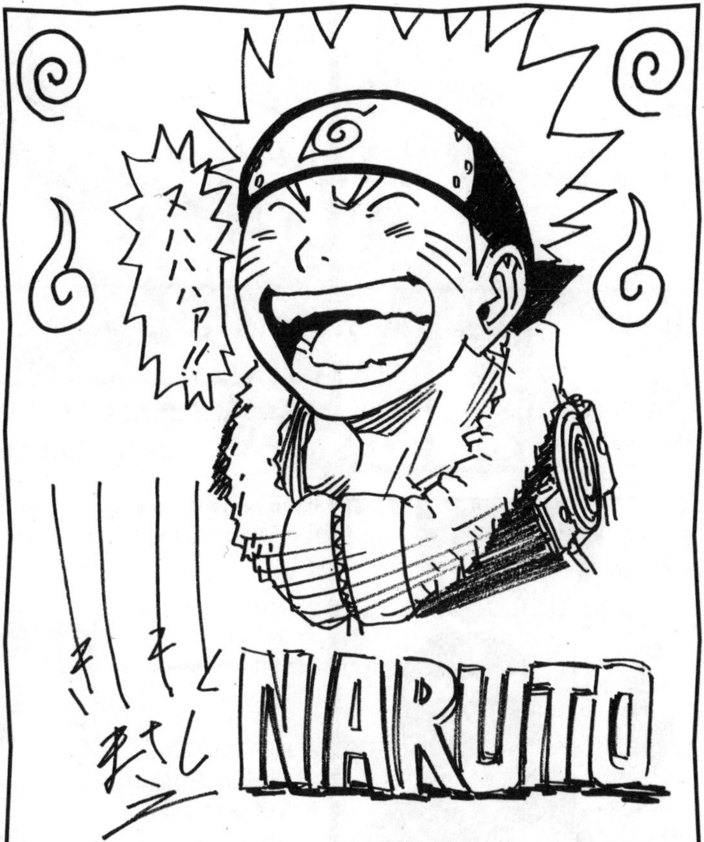

ヌハハハアー!!
まさし
NARUTO

Naruto: Nu ha ha haa!!
Kishimoto Masashi

Secret Files: The End

この本の制作に関わって
下さった皆さん、
この本を手にとって下さった皆さんに
心から感謝します！😄

これからも
「NARUTO－ナルト－」を
応援してください！！

2002.10.4
P.S. 昨日 (10/3) から始まったアニメもヨロシクね！！

THANK YOU TO EVERYONE INVOLVED IN THE
PRODUCTION OF THIS BOOK AND EVERYONE WHO
PICKED UP A COPY!

PLEASE KEEP SUPPORTING NARUTO!
2002.10.4

PS: THE ANIME STARTED YESTERDAY...WATCH
THAT TOO!

Read where the ninja action began in the manga

Fiction based on your favorite characters' adventures

JOURNEY INTO THE WORLD OF NARUTO BOOKS!

Hardcover art book with full-color images, a Masashi Kishimoto interview and a double-sided poster

NARUTO © 1999 by Masashi Kishimoto/SHUEISHA Inc.
NARUTO -SHIRO NO DOUJI, KEPPU NO KIJIN-© 2002 by Masashi Kishimoto, Masatoshi
.usakabe/SHUEISHA Inc.
ZUMAKI -NARUTO ILLUSTRATION BOOK- © 2004 by Masashi Kishimoto/SHUEISHA Inc.

RATED
T
FOR
TEEN
ratings.viz.com

viz
media
www.viz.com

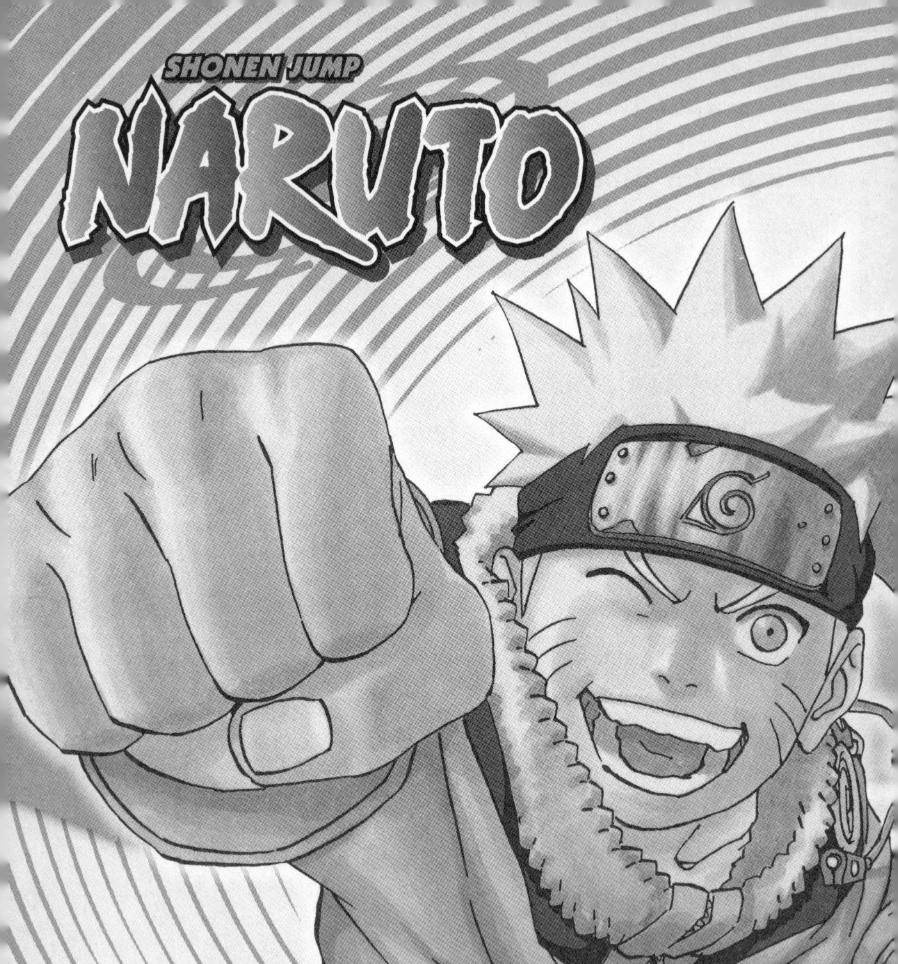
SHONEN JUMP
NARUTO

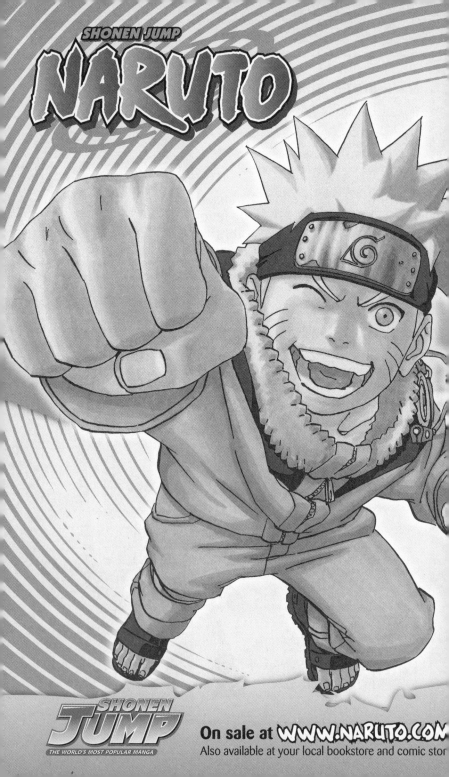

P9-DMV-536

Naruto: The Official Fanbook

Translation/Andrew Cunningham (Translation by Design)
Cover Design/Sean Lee
Touch-Up Art & Manga Lettering/Sabrina Heep
Design Manager, Product/Carolina Ugalde
Lead Designer/Izumi Hirayama
Graphic Design/Nozomi Akashi, Hudson Yards,
Caleena Lee, Melanie Lewis
Consultant/Naomi Kokubo
Copy Chief/Rebecca Downer
Editorial Director/Masumi Washington
Supervising Editor/Joel Enos
Editor/Mike Montesa

Editor in Chief, Books/Alvin Lu
Editor in Chief, Magazines/Marc Weidenbaum
VP, Publishing Licensing/Rika Inouye
VP, Sales & Product Marketing/Gonzalo Ferreyra
VP, Creative/Linda Espinosa
Publisher/Hyoe Narita

NARUTO [HIDEN · HYO-NO SHO] © 2002 by Masashi
Kishimoto
All rights reserved.
First published in Japan in 2002 by SHUEISHA Inc., Tokyo.
English translation rights arranged by SHUEISHA Inc.
The stories, characters and incidents mentioned in this
publication are entirely fictional.

This volume contains some material that was originally
published in English in **SHONEN JUMP** #50, 51, 53 & 56.
Artwork in the magazine may have been slightly altered
from that presented here.

No portion of this book may be reproduced or transmitted
in any form or by any means without written permission
from the copyright holders.

Printed in China

Published by VIZ Media, LLC
295 Bay Street
San Francisco, CA 94133

SHONEN JUMP Profiles Edition
10 9 8 7 6 5 4 3
First printing, February 2008
Third printing, July 2008

www.viz.com

Naruto volumes
1–27 on sale now!

The New *Naruto*
starts in Vol. 28!

Catch all the fun and
excitement of *Naruto* in
SHONEN JUMP magazine
monthly and in manga
editions bi-monthly!